*Language Learning
and
Concept Acquisition:
Foundational Issues*

THEORETICAL ISSUES IN
COGNITIVE SCIENCE

ZENON W. PYLYSHYN

University of Western Ontario
Series Editor

Language Learning and Concept Acquisition: Foundational Issues, William Demopoulos & Ausonio Marras, Editors (1986)

From Models to Modules: Studies in Cognitive Sciences from the McGill Workshops, Irwin Gopnik & Myrna Gopnik, Editors (1986)

Meaning and Cognitive Structure: Issues in the Computational Theory of Mind, Edited by Zenon W. Pylyshyn & William Demopoulos (1986)

The Robot's Dilemma: The Frame Problem in Artificial Intelligence, edited by Zenon W. Pylyshyn (1986)

LANGUAGE LEARNING
AND
CONCEPT ACQUISITION:
Foundational Issues

Edited by

William Demopoulos

Ausonio Marras

University of Western Ontario
London, Canada

ABLEX PUBLISHING CORPORATION
NORWOOD, NEW JERSEY

Printed in the United States of America

Library of Congress Cataloging-in-Publication Data
Main entry under title:

Language learning and concept acquisition.

(Theoretical issues in cognitive science)
Bibliography: p.
Includes indexes.
1. Language acquisition. 2. Concepts.
I. Demopoulos, William. II. Marras, Ausonio.
P118.L365 1985   401'.9   85-13455.
ISBN 0-89391-316-2

Ablex Publishing Corporation
355 Chestnut Street
Norwood, New Jersey 07648

Contents

LIST OF CONTRIBUTORS

JANET W. ASTINGTON, Department of Applied Psychology, Ontario Institute for Studies in Education, Toronto, Ontario, Canada

JOHN CASE, Department of Computer Science, State University of New York, Buffalo, New York

SUSAN CAREY, Department of Psychology, Massachusetts Institute of Technology, Cambridge, Massachusetts

LILA R. GLEITMAN, Department of Psychology, University of Pennsylvania, Philadelphia, Pennsylvania

FRANK C. KEIL, Department of Psychology, Cornell University, Ithaca, New York

MICHAEL H. KELLY, Department of Psychology, Cornell University, Ithaca, New York

DAVID R. OLSON, Department of Applied Psychology, Ontario Institute for Studies in Education, Toronto, Ontario, Canada

DANIEL N. OSHERSON, Center for Cognitive Science, Massachusetts Institute of Technology, Cambridge, Massachusetts

MASSIMO PIATTELLI-PALMARINI, Florence Center for the History and Philosophy of Science, Florence, Italy, and Center for Cognitive Science, Massachusetts Institute of Technology, Cambridge, Massachusetts

STEVEN PINKER, Department of Psychology and Center for Cognitive Science, Massachusetts Institute of Technology, Cambridge, Massachusetts

MARK S. SEIDENBERG, Department of Psychology, McGill University, Montreal, Quebec, Canada

MICHAEL STOB, Department of Mathematics, Calvin College, Grand Rapids, Michigan

SCOTT WEINSTEIN, Department of Philosophy, University of Pennsylvania, Philadelphia, Pennsylvania

Preface

Most of the papers in this volume grew out of a conference on learning sponsored by the philosophy and psychology departments and the Centre for Cognitive Science at The University of Western Ontario in the spring of 1983, and funded in part by a grant* from the Social Sciences and Humanities Research Council of Canada. Other papers were contributed by participants after the conference and by invitees who were unable to attend. Only one of the papers (by Susan Carey) has previously been published, and another (by Lila Gleitman) is being published concomitantly in another volume. For the sake of maximizing thematic unity and keeping the size of the volume within manageable proportions, some of the papers presented at the conference had to be omitted.

The aim of this volume, like that of the conference, was to bring together some of the recent work on learning by researchers in various disciplines who share an interest in the systematic study of cognition and, particularly, in the study of the formal and semantic aspects of language acquisition. A recurring theme in this work is that language learning involves the acquisition of certain competences and the formation of a system of beliefs which are significantly underdetermined by the linguistic and nonlinguistic inputs available to the learner. Theories of language learning must thus confront the epistemological problem of how it is possible to induce and fixate a belief-system on the basis of exposure to limited data. A typical strategy in dealing with this problem has been to specify various types of formal and empirical constraints on linguistic and conceptual development in terms of specific hypotheses about the character of what is learned and about the kinds of resources and strategies available to the learner. Most of the papers in this volume are concerned with the specification and evaluation of such constraints. In particular, some of the papers focus on the hypothesis that language learning has a significant biological basis, that it is species specific and task specific, and that it involves "selective," rather than merely "instructive," learning strategies. The relevance of these papers to the ongoing debate in cognitive and developmental psychology and psycholinguistics on the biological versus environmental conditions on learning should be obvious; so too should be their relevance to the long-standing rationalist/empiricist controversy in philosophy on the idea of innate knowledge and on the nature and status of inductive inference. We trust this volume will be useful to students and researchers both in the cognitive sciences and in philosophy.

---

*SSHRC 443-83-0022. In preparing the volume, one of us (W.D.) was assisted by the Social Sciences and Humanities Research Council of Canada (#410-84-0442). Both grants are gratefully acknowledged.

Part I
Empirical Aspects
of
First Language Acquisition

Chapter 1
Biological Dispositions to Learn Language*

Lila R. Gleitman
University of Pennsylvania

Language learning clearly is an outcome of specific exposure conditions, but just as clearly requires specific biological adaptations. There is no controversy about this claim as stated, for it is obvious to to point of banality. To believe that special biological adaptations are a requirement, it is enough to notice that all the children but none of the dogs and cats in the house acquire language. To believe that language is nevertheless learned, it is sufficient to note the massive correlation between living in France and learning French, and living in Germany and learning German. Controversy does arise, however, on the issue of whether language knowledge is based on a specific and segregated mental faculty, or instead utilizes the same machinery in the head that is implicated in the acquisition of all complex cognitive functions. Many linguistic theories postulate not only a distinct mental representation or faculty of language (a "language organ," in Chomsky's wording, functioning as autonomously as, say, the liver), but a highly modularized system internal to language itself (Chomsky, 1981). Proponents of such positions expect that language learning will be largely maturationally de- termined, that the maturation functions may be quite separate from those in other cognitive domains, and that different modules within the language system may mature quasi-independently. In clear contrast, most developmental psycholin- guists hold that language acquisition is best described by a global learning procedure that is responsible for the acquisition of, say, knitting, arithmetic, and ancient history as well as, say, English (e.g., Slobin, 1973; Bever, 1982). They

* This paper summarizes work I have done over a period of years with many collaborators, who are cited in the text. Many—indeed most—of the theoretical and experimental ideas described are attributable to these collaborators. Particularly, the paper is organized around a position that postulates a bottom-up learning process mediated by the child's distinctive encoding of open and closed class members of the morphological stock; these ideas were developed in their present form in collaboration with Eric Wanner (see Gleitman & Wanner, 1984). Another presentation of the ideas expressed herein, in a closely related format, appears in Friedman and Klivington (in press). I thank Henry Gleitman for significant help in reading earlier drafts of this paper, and offering many detailed suggestions for improvement. I also thank the National Foundation for the March of Dimes, which supported much of the research described as well as the writing of this paper.

expect that the unfolding of language will be jointly dependent on specific opportunities to receive relevant data and on cognitive development.

Rudimentary current evidence about learning is insufficient to adjudicate these distinct claims about how biology and experience interact to produce language knowledge. Exacerbating these difficulties, there are at present many contending descriptions of grammar—of what is finally learned. Given disagreements on *what* is learned, it is hard to devise an adequate description of *how* it is learned (see Wexler & Culicover, 1980, and Pinker, 1982, for quite disparate formal models of a learning procedure based on correspondingly disparate conjectures about the grammar that is attained). But in my view, the presently available evidence tips the balance of plausibility toward a biologically preprogrammed learning procedure specific to language.

In the present discussion, I first present a schematic description of the language learning task, followed by a sketch of the kinds of argument often put forward in favor of significant and relatively autonomous biological preprogramming supporting that learning. Thereafter, I summarize the kinds of investigation that are being carried out by our own group of investigators.

1 Analysis of the language learning problem

Chomsky (1965) and other investigators (Pinker, 1979; Wexler & Culicover, 1980) have provided a schematic analysis of language learning; roughly, it looks like this:

1.   The learner receives some sample utterances from the language.
2.   The learner simultaneously observes situations: objects, scenes, and events in the world.
3.   These utterance/situation pairs constitute the input to language learning.
4.   The learner's job is to project from these sample utterance/situation pairs a system, or grammar, that encompasses all sentence/meaning pairs in the language. This job includes, of course, learning the meanings and forms of words, for these affect the meanings of sentences. But it also includes learning the syntactic structures, for these affect the meaning of sentences even when the component words are held constant (i.e., *Caesar killed Brutus* and *Brutus killed Caesar* mean different things).
5.   For learning to proceed, the learner must have some means for representing the utterances and the situations to himself in a linguistically relevant way. For example, though the learner receives utterances in the form of continuously varying sound waves, he must be disposed to represent these as sequences of discrete formatives such as phone, syllable, word, phrase, and sentence. And though he receives impressions of some single object, he must be disposed to represent it in various ways, such as 'Fido,' 'dog,'

'mammal,' 'physical object,' and not in other ways, such as 'undetached dog-parts.'

6. The learner must also have some strategies for manipulating these data in the interest of extracting the regularities that bind them.

7. The learner must have some perspective on the kinds of descriptive devices, or rule systems, that he is willing to countenance as statements of the regularities. To put this another way, different language learning "machines" (particular representational systems, with particular computational procedures) will construct different grammars, based on the same data.

8. Finally, the learner must have some criterion that will lead him to stabilize on a particular conjecture about the grammar, to decide once and for all that his learning job is completed.

As presented, this analysis is neutral about many issues. For example, it is possible that tutors are required for some of these steps to be taken successfully. Perhaps the learner requires the caretakers to say only very simple sentences, or sentences of restricted kinds, early in the learning period; and perhaps the learner requires reinforcement for correct performances and correction of errors he makes along the way. Depending on whether these additional conditions are met, quite different kinds of machines will be able to learn a human language. Therefore it is of some interest to examine the real input circumstances of children and the early generalizations they draw from these inputs. This may help to disentangle the kinds of internal and external resources learners recruit to crack the language code.

2 A Significant Innate Basis for Language Learning

Three main kinds of argument favor the supposition that language and its learning are biologically preprogrammed. The first two derive from empirical study of learning: (1) language learning proceeds in uniform ways within and across linguistic communities, despite extensive variability of the input provided to individuals; and (2) the character of what is learned is not simply related to the input sample. A third argument is logical: (3) the child acquires many linguistic generalizations which experience could not have made available.

2.1 Uniform Learning

Inquiry into language learning is constrained by one main principle. The right theory has to cope with the fact that everybody does it, by specifying a learning device guaranteed to converge on the grammar of any language to which it is exposed, in finite time, and in fair indifference to particulars of the sample data received (Wexler, 1982). This principle is based on the real facts of the matter.

Under widely varying environmental circumstances, learning different languages under different conditions of culture and child rearing, and with different motivations and talents, all nonpathological children acquire their native tongue at a high level of proficiency within a narrow developmental time frame. (This does not mean there are no differences in final attainment, but these differences pale into insignificance when compared with the samenesses.)

Moreover, there are very interesting similarities in the course this learning takes. Isolated words appear at about age 1, followed by two-word utterances at about age 2. Thereafter, sometime during the third year of life, there is a sudden spurt of vocabulary growth accompanied, coincidentally or not, by elaboration of the sentence structures. By about 4 years of age the speaker sounds essentially adult, though his sentences tend to be quite short because the use of embeddings is limited, and though some item-specific information continues to come in about through age 8 or 9. (By item-specific information, I have reference particularly to some features of derivational morphology, and significant growth of vocabulary.)

Summarizing, similarities in the pattern of learning are observed across individuals and across linguistic communities. Lenneberg (1967) was perhaps the first to argue that these uniformities in course of learning, despite differences in experience, are a beginning indicant that language learning has a significant biological basis. He provided some normative evidence that the achievement of basic milestones in language learning is predictable from the child's age and seems to be intercalated quite closely to developments that are known on other grounds to be maturationally dependent (e.g., sitting, standing, walking, and jumping). Other findings were used by Lenneberg to argue that there is a sensitive (or critical) period for language learning. For example, foreign accents are typical in adult learners but not child learners of second languages even when time of exposure and use are equated. Downs Syndrome individuals that he studied seemed to acquire language in the same way as normals, only slower; and their learning seemed to stop at about puberty whatever their current competence with the language. Finally, Lenneberg maintained that recovery from brain injury that implicates language is likely in children but rare in adults. On such evidence, he conjectured that the capacity for language learning tends to whither away as the brain matures.

Not all of Lenneberg's findings have withstood subsequent review too well, however. For example, in later discussion I'll present a rather different picture of learning in Downs Syndrome individuals. Moreover, the results about the course of learning (from Lenneberg and others) are so fragmentary as to be consistent with quite distinct conjectures about the processes that underlie this learning: though there are gross similarities among children whose age is the same, there may be detailed distinctions among them consequent on distinctions in their exposure conditions. Certainly that is true for specific vocabulary learning, and who is to say, and on what grounds, that this detail is "unimportant"?

Symmetrically, the differences in environment may have been overestimated. Indeed, no two mothers will say exactly the same sentences to their offspring. But still the set of input utterances may be constrained in various ways (they may be especially "simple" sentences) and they may be presented under special conditions (e.g., accompanied by corrections or relevant didactic comments, said only in the presence of "easily interpretable events," etc.). Under these improved conditions, perhaps any open-minded all-purpose inductive device would generate the same uniformities in the course of learning as are observed for young children acquiring their native tongue. However, as I'll now try to show, closer inspection of patterns of development gives more weight to the view that special dispositions in the learner are guiding language acquisition.

2.2 Character of Learning; Disparities Between Input and Output

The character of language knowledge at various developmental moments is hard to reconcile with the superficial properties of the input data. To be sure, the child learns from what he hears. But he does not directly copy these heard sentences, but makes systematic errors. These errors can be understood, but only by claiming the learner filters the input data through an emerging system of rules of grammar, rules to which he is never directly exposed. (No one explains the language rules to the children. One reason is that the mothers don't explicitly know the rules. The other reason is that the children wouldn't understand the explanations.)

2.2.1 Noncanonical sentences in; canonical sentences out. Some convincing examples were developed by Bellugi (1967). One of her cases concerned interrogative structures. In simple sentences of English, auxiliary verbs appear after the subject noun-phrase but before the verb (e.g., *I can eat pizza*). But in yes/no questions, the auxiliary precedes the subject (e.g., *Can I eat pizza?*). And in so-called wh-questions, this subject/auxiliary inversion appears again (e.g., *What can I eat?*), this time without the object noun-phrase (*pizza*) and with an initial "wh-word" (e.g., *what* or *when* or *who*) instead. The learner of English is exposed by his caretakers to many such wh-questions (about 10% of all the utterances he hears, according to the estimate of Newport, 1977). Nevertheless, young learners generally do not reproduce these forms that they hear so often. Instead they produce a form that is virtually never spoken by adults, namely, *What I can eat?* or sometimes even *What can I can eat?* A related finding, also from Bellugi (1967), is that, while over 90% of maternal auxiliaries in declaratives are contracted (e.g., *We'll go out now*), the child uses only the uncontracted forms early in the learning period (*We will go out now*). In light of such findings, the sense in which the child is learning the language from the presented environment of utterances is evidently quite abstract.

There is a generalization that predicts these errors, as Bellugi pointed out: The child is biased toward "canonical" surface structure formats for his utterances (see also Gleitman & Wanner, 1982; Slobin & Bever, 1982). In the canonical declarative sentence of English, the subject does precede the whole verb-phrase, including its auxiliary. An abstract movement transformation reorders these elements in questions.[1] If it is supposed that the child acquires formation rules that underlie the declarative first and countenances movement rules only later, this particular error is predictable. Similarly, it is possible to suppose that only the full canonical forms (*will*) of words like *'ll* are entered into the learner's mental lexicon. Contraction is achieved by a rule that operates on these abstract lexical representations under restricted circumstances. (For further discussion, see section 2.3 below.) In sum, it is certainly possible to explain why the young child does not behave exactly like his models, who contract and invert. To explain this, one can invoke a bias toward canonical forms in the language being learned. But this, in turn, implies that the young learner has an ability to reconstruct the canonical forms for questions and for words like *'ll*. These canonical forms are related to the utterances he actually hears, but only by covert rules. Considering the tender age of the language learning humans who apparently can perform the complex data manipulations required to recover these rules—quite effortlessly and unconsciously—it is likely that significant biological dispositions are guiding their analyses.

2.2.2 *Open class/closed class.* An even more general disparity between input and output, as Brown (1973), Gleitman and Wanner (1982), and many others have discussed, has to do with the differential pattern of acquisition of the so-called open class and closed class stock of morphological items (usually called

---

[1] Certain linguistic characterizations (see, e.g., Chomsky, 1965, for an early description) assume that interrogative sentences are at some level represented in a format whose phrase organization is just like that of declarative sentences, with the subject noun-phrase preceding the auxiliary and the object noun-phrase following the verb. A rule obligatorily applies to such structures, inverting the order of the subject and the auxiliary. But for those interrogatives beginning with a so-called "wh-word," there is an additional complication: the object noun-phrase is a question morpheme (*wh-*) joined with a pronoun (e.g., *-at* or *-en*, as in *what* or *when*), i.e., *I can eat what* or, following the inversion, *Can I eat what*. A further obligatory rule applies to such structures. The wh-word is moved to the left, yielding *What can I eat?* One virtue of such an analysis is that it conforms transparently to the semantics of questions: *What can I eat* seems to be the way of querying ("wh?") that unknown thing (*-at*), labelled by a noun-phrase, that can be eaten. Another virtue is that it materially simplifies the description of sentence form. For example, a reasonable generalization about many verbs (e.g., *rely on*) is that they must be followed by a noun-phrase: *John relied on* sounds strange because it does not have such a following noun-phrase. But this generalization seems to be defeated in wh-questions where, indeed, *rely on* does occur without a following noun-phrase: *What did John rely on?* The solution is that, at some stage of derivation, this sentence did have the noun-phrase, namely *wh-thing* or *what*, but that noun-phrase was subsequently "moved." As I am now arguing, the facts about the speech of 2- and 3-year-olds lend independent plausibility to such conjectures about the mental representation of sentences. Thus, I believe, they bear on the psychological relevance of grammatical descriptions that do or do not countenance movement rules (compare, e.g., Wexler & Culicover, 1980 and Pinker, 1982).

content and *functor* words by psychologists). The distinction between these two classes is not easy to state formally (and in fact is partly controversial; see Kean, 1979, for the clearest explication). But technicalities aside, it is fairly clear. It has been known for some time that there are lexical categories that admit new members freely: new verbs, nouns, and adjectives are being created by language users every day (hence "open class"). Other lexical categories change their membership only very slowly over historical time (hence "closed class"). The closed class includes the "little" words and affixes, the conjunctions, prepositions, inflectional and derivational suffixes, relativizers, and verbal auxiliaries. These examples given, it is obvious that the closed class and open class morphemes are different in many ways. The closed class items are restricted in semantic content (nobody's name is a preposition) and in syntactic function (as follows from the fact, stated above, that they belong to only certain lexical classes). They differ phonologically as well: closed class morphemes are in most usages unstressed, some are subsyllabic, and many more become subsyllabic by contraction (e.g., *will* contracts to *'ll*).

Perhaps the most striking fact about early speech and the context in which it is learned is that open class and closed class materials are made available to the learner simultaneously, but these subcomponents of the morphological stock are incorporated into the child's speech at different developmental moments. The mother's speech consists of simple sentences like "The book is on the table," including the closed class items *the, is,* and *on.* But there is a well-known stage of language learning, the so-called two-word or telegraphic stage, at which the output is "Book table," with all the closed class items omitted. Thus the most primitive learners seem to have certain devices that allow them to filter out the closed class.

It is not obvious how to explain these developing speech patterns without begging the questions of language learning. For example, even if it were possible to say that the omitted items were the meaningless ones, which it emphatically is not, one wouldn't want to claim that the child examines the semantics of closed class words and, on the basis of this, decides to omit them all. This would beg the question at issue: how the semantics of such items are arrived at in the first place. Ditto for a claim based on the syntactic functioning of closed class items. Gleitman and Wanner (1982, 1984) conjectured that it is the special phonology of the closed class items that renders them opaque to youngest learners—they are subsyllabic items or unstressed syllables. Differential attention to the unit *stressed syllable* in the incoming speech wave represents, we believe, one of the significant biases of young learners.[2] Because of the child's selective

---

[2] The specific acoustic correlates of primary stress in English include longer duration, higher fundamental frequency, and intensity. For the arguments that follow to hold, it would be necessary to show that related acoustic properties are available and exploited to mark phrase boundaries in the nonstress-accent languages, and that these are the properties to which infants are sensitive and which they reproduce in their first utterances (see Fernald, 1984, for review of supportive evidence).

attention to stressed syllables, the pattern of acquisition does not mirror the environment directly, but mirrors the environment only as it is mediated by these preexisting biases as to how to represent the sound wave. (See Fernald, 1984, for a full discussion of acoustic-perceptual dispositions in infants, and the position that the filtering effect of these predispositions plays a role in language learning.)

It is very interesting to notice that the distinction between the open class and closed class morphological components is an organizing factor in language use even after learning is complete. For example, in adults, speech errors differ for the two classes and almost never involve an exchange between an open class and a closed class item (Garrett, 1975); the patterns of long-term language forgetting differ for the two classes (Dorian, 1978); judgmental performance differs for the two classes (Gleitman & Gleitman, 1970, 1979) as do properties of reading acquisition (Gleitman & Rozin, 1977; Rozin & Gleitman, 1977); finally, the very definition of the distinction between Broca's and Wernicke's aphasia involves a differential dissolution of these two subcomponents of speech performance (Bradley, Garrett, & Zurif, 1979; Marin, Saffran, & Schwartz, 1976; but see also Linebarger, Schwartz, & Saffran, 1983, for evidence that the language faculty itself may be intact in Broca's aphasics).

2.2.3 Lexical selections and argument roles. So far I've noted learning biases of the child in the syntactic and morphophonological domains that act to predict a difference between what goes into the child's ear and what first comes out of his mouth. The case for lexical category acquisition is just as clear. Evidently, a learner hears verbs and adjectives as well as nouns early in life. But the child's earliest words are overwhelmingly nouns that encode simple concrete objects; verbs that encode activities tend to appear later, and verbs that encode mental states later still; finally, adjectives that encode properties of things are later than all these others (e.g., Nelson, 1973; Gentner, 1982; Feldman, Goldin-Meadow, & Gleitman, 1978). Similarly, certain syntactically rather than lexically encoded semantic-relational categories (e.g., "agent of the action," for example, *John* in *John eats peas*) uniformly appear early and others (e.g., "instrument of the action," for example, *knife* in *John eats peas with a knife*) are uniformaly found later, again though instances of all of them appear in the child's database—his mother's speech—from the beginning (Bloom, Lightbown, & Hood, 1975).

In sum, the child is clearly learning from what he hears (English from English, French from French), but the detailed properties of the development are hard to describe as arising very simply or directly from the environment of heard utterances. Likely, global aspects of cognitive development will account for many of these learning patterns: the fact that there is attention to concrete objects and physical activities before mental states and properties is unlikely to have specifically linguistic sources. But the morphophonemic and syntactic choices of novice language learners are less likely to be explained as deriving from general properties of cognitive development.

2.3 Language Knowledge that Experience Could not Provide

Another kind of argument for innate language learning capacities comes from logical analyses by Chomsky (1975). This has to do with the learning of certain language properties that experience could hardly have made available. Taking one of his examples, a distinction between higher and lower clause in a phrase structure configuration determines certain properties of movement transformations and of the reference of pronouns. (The characterization of the linguistic facts are perforce rough in this discussion, but will have to do for a sketch.) Specifically, consider again the movement of certain material in English yes/no questions. In the sentence *Is the man a fool?*, the *is* has moved to the left from its canonical position in declarative sentences, *The man is a fool*. But can any *is* in a declarative sentence be moved to form a yes/no question? It is impossible to judge from one-clause sentences alone. The issue is resolved by looking at more complex sentences, that contain more than one clause: It is the *is* in the higher clause, never the *is* in the lower clause, that moves to form yes/no questions from structures underlying, e.g., *The man who is a fool is amusing* and *The man is a fool who is amusing*. This generalization explains the acceptability of yes/no questions such as *Is the man who is a fool amusing?* and *Is the man a fool who is amusing?* but the absence of *Is the man who a fool is amusing?* and *Is the man is a fool who amusing?* Whether *is* moves depends on its structural position in the sentence.

Notice that an alternative analysis, namely serial position of the two *is*'s in the string of words, as opposed to structural position of the two *is*'s in a clause hierarchy, could not explain the facts about English structure: in the examples just given, the moving *is* was once the first *is* in the sentence, but once the second. Learners apparently know that movement rules are structure-dependent, not simply serial-order-dependent. To my knowledge, no child ever makes the mistake of saying "Is the man is a fool who amusing?" The important point here is that it's hard to conceive how the environment literally gives the required information to the learner. Surely only the correct sentences, not the incorrect ones, appear in the input data. But the generalization required for producing new correct sentences is not directly presented, for no hierarchy of clauses appears in real utterances—only a string of words is directly observable to the listener. And certainly there is no instruction about clauses. Even if mothers knew something explicit about these matters, which they don't, it wouldn't do much good for them to tell the aspiring learners that: "It's the *is* in the higher clause that moves."

Many generalizations about sentence form turn on the same or related configural distinctions (though again the characterization being used here is rough and underestimates the complexity of the descriptive facts). To give one more example, co-reference is possible when the pronoun precedes its antecedent but only if the pronoun is in a lower clause than the antecedent. For example, the man mentioned in the second clause could be the one who arrived in the sentence *When he arrived, the man danced* but not in the sentence *He arrived when the man danced*. Even in these hard cases where the pronoun precedes its potential antecedent, learners come to interpret co-reference correctly, without special tutoring, and without an opportunity directly to experience the hierarchical structures.

As a final example, to explain what is finally learned, it has been necessary for Chomsky (and indeed, all syntacticians, to my knowledge) to postulate certain ghostly null elements in the representation of sentences. For example, a sentence I took up earlier was *What can I eat?* Many linguists will transcribe this sentence as *What can I eat Ø*, as though some "trace" of its canonical phrase structure, with object noun-phrase following the verb, were somehow still there in the question form. Many descriptive facts about English speech can be explained only by postulating such soundless, tasteless, odorless entities in the mental representation of sentences. As one example, note that the item *is*, which can contract in many positions in English sentences (e.g., *What's your name?*), in other positions cannot contract: one can say *I wonder who he is* but not *I wonder who he's*. Suppose that a "trace" of the moved noun-phrase constituent appears in the underlying structure of this sentence (*I wonder who he is Ø*). It can now be postulated that contraction is prohibited preceding the deletion site. This claim is useful if and only if a large number of superficially distinct restrictions on contraction can be subsumed under the same generalization, and indeed this turns out to be the case.

To give one more example, the same principle explains why one can use the *wanna* contraction of *want to* in *This is the rabbit who I wanna banish* but not in **This is the rabbit who I wanna vanish*. Under an analysis similar to that given in the preceding section, there is a missing noun-phrase in each of these sentences: in each case a rabbit has disappeared. But that noun-phrase is missing from different places in the underlying representations of these sentences, a consequence of the fact that *vanish* is an intransitive verb (whose subject is missing) while *banish* is a transitive verb (whose object is missing). That is, the mental structure of these sentences is plausibly transcribed as *This is the rabbit who I want to banish Ø* and *This is the rabbit who I want Ø to vanish*. In each case, the trace, Ø, appears where once there was a rabbit. But only in the second case does the trace intervene between *want* and *to*. If it is contiguous *want* and *to* that contract to *wanna*, the real facts about restrictions on contraction are explained. As a further demonstration of the power of this analysis, notice that *This is the rabbit who I want to visit* is ambiguous (between *I want to visit the rabbit* and *I want the rabbit to visit*) while *This is the rabbit who I wanna visit* is not: only the transitive reading of the verb *visit* remains under the contraction, for the same reasons as stated above. Young children honor these very abstractly described restrictions on contraction and have never been observed to err during the learning period. This implies that mentally they are in possession of a descriptive device that involves something like these null elements though they never "heard" them.

Summarizing, it is hard to imagine how the environment instructs the learner that not serial order simply, but the hierarchical arrangement of clauses, determines properties of sentences and their interpretations, or that spirit-like null elements determine whether contraction is possible and, given the contraction, what the meaning must be of potentially ambiguous sentences. Yet errors on these properties are so rare that no one, to my knowledge, has so far succeeded in observing one made by a child. In short, errorless learning of structural properties of the language not transparently offered to experience—the poverty of the stimulus information—forms still another sort of argument that learning biases, this time biases in the formation and interpretation of configural structures underlying sentences, are required as explanations of how language organization is achieved by the child.

3 The Deprivation Paradigm

During the last several years, my associates and I have looked at some natural cases where some of the components of the language learning situation are varied. We have operated by taking to heart the view that utterance/situation pairs are required input to language learning, as described in the schema for learning with which I began. Therefore we have looked at situations where this information is changed. Certain populations of learners allow us to see what happens if there is less or different information about the utterances; other populations allow us to see what happens if there is less or different information about the world. Symmetrically, certain populations are exposed to normal input data but differ from the normal in their current or final mental state. In these latter cases, we are asking what happens when different learning devices are exposed to the same data.

3.1 Varying the Language Samples

There seems to be quite general agreement that a learner exposed to random samples of the sentences of a language would be unable to converge on the grammar. The main difficulty is the richness of the incoming data, which would seem to support so bewildering a variety of generalizations, including wrong and irrelevant ones, that we would expect learners to vary extremely in the time at which they hit on the grammar of their language. It is usually assumed, following findings from Brown and Hanlon (1970), that negative feedback, or correction, from the environment cannot be relied on to solve this problem. This is not so much that feedback for ungrammaticalness is never given, though Brown and Hanlon have shown it is rare. The main problem is that for a variety of structures and contents—such as those described in the preceding section—the child never errs in the first place so no opportunity to correct him, or to describe his learning as a consequence of such correction, arises. Another problem, as Brown and Hanlon showed, is that correction is given very often for matters other than grammaticalness of the child's utterances, for example their truth or moral propriety. Should the child construe all corrections, then, as grammatical corrections, he might falsely conclude that *ink-on-the-wall* is an outlawed phrase, rather than an outlawed act. In light of these difficulties, most investigators assume that language learning is on positive examples only. Formally speaking, it is a lot easier to develop a mechanical procedure for learning from presented sample utterances if it is assumed that that procedure receives negative feedback when it makes a false generalization, i.e., if it is told that some new sentence it tries out is not a correct sentence of the language being learned (for that demonstration, see Gold, 1967). Hence some proposals have considered whether restrictions or simplifications of sentences presented to novices can substitute for overt corrections.

3.1.1 Effects of maternal simplification: The Motherese Hypothesis. The paradox so far is that language learning is hard to describe given positive data only (a sample of the correct sentences) and yet all the real learners seem to do very well even though they receive only, or almost only, such positive data. A very popular response to this problem among developmental psycholinguists has been to suppose the environment provides detailed support for learning by ordering the input utterances (see the collection of articles edited by Snow & Ferguson, 1977, for many papers adopting this position). We have called this "the Motherese Hypothesis." It holds that caretakers present linguistic information in a set sequence, essentially smallest sentences to littlest ears. And in fact there is no doubt that adults speak quite differently to children than to adults, so the utterances heard by the children are not random selections from the adult language. The utterances to youngest learners are very short, slow in rate, and the like. Some investigators propose that this natural simplification from caretakers (whatever its source of motivation) plays a causal role in learning. Evidence favoring this hypothesis comes from Fernald (1982, 1984) who has shown that infants prefer to listen to the prosodically exaggerated forms of Motherese, which is used in every known culture: apparently, as Fernald states, Motherese is "sweet music to the species." Gleitman and Wanner have proposed that these exaggerated prosodic cues can help an appropriately preprogrammed learner to reconstruct a global parse of the input sentences, a reconstruction that materially simplifies subsequent steps in the language learning task.

But evidently there are limits on the work that Motherese can do for the learner. Particularly it is hard to maintain the view that the preselection of syntactic types by caretakers can bear materially on the acquisition of grammar. Though restricting the sentence types may exclude certain hypotheses from being considered early, it may also make available hypotheses that would be insupportable given the full range of the language structures. As I described in the preceding section, the child would be unable to distinguish the "string movement" hypothesis from the "structure movement" hypothesis if all the input sentences were uniclausal (for discussion see Chomsky, 1975, and Wexler & Culicover, 1980); if more complex sentences are offered, the string movement hypothesis fails on data. However, there is at least some surface plausibility to the idea that the mother first teaches the child some easy structures. After he learns these, she moves on to the next lesson. To help this idea go through, we would have to grant the caretaker some implicit metric of syntactic/semantic complexity so that in principle she could choose judiciously the sentences that might be good to say to learners. Here too there are some initial supportive findings: caretakers' speech changes to some degree, in correspondence with the learner's age (Newport, 1977).

In our studies of the Motherese hypothesis (Newport, Gleitman, & Gleitman, 1977), we first collected extensive samples of maternal speech to young learners (age range 15 to 27 months). Rather to our surprise, the properties of this speech did not seem promising as aids to learning syntactic forms. The mothers' speech forms were only rarely (less than 10% of the time) canonical sentences, and they were neither uniform syntactically, nor more explicit in how they mapped onto the meanings, than the sentences used among adults. They *were* short and clear, but this hardly suggests anything very specific about how they reveal the syntax of the language. But it is still possible that some less obvious properties of maternal speech are especially useful to learners. To study this, we revisited the original mother/child pairs 6 months after the first measurement. Analyzing the child's speech at these two times, we were in a position to compute growth scores for each child on many linguistic dimensions. The question was which properties of the mother's speech at time one had predicted the child's rate of growth on each measure, explaining his status at time two. (The correlational analysis used a partialling procedure that removed baseline differences among the learners.)

One interesting outcome of these studies was that a number of dimensions of learning rate were utterly indifferent to large differences in the speech pattern of the mothers. For example, the child's increasing tendency to express predicates (as verbs) and their obligatory arguments (as nouns) was not predictable from the particular speech forms presented. In contrast, in the age range studied, the child's progress with the closed class morphology was a rather strict function of maternal speech style. For example, almost all the variance in rate of learning the English auxiliary verbs is predicted by the preponderance of yes/no questions in maternal speech (for a replication of this finding, see Furrow, Nelson, & Benedict, 1979). The effect of these is to place the closed class items in first serial position, with stress and without contraction (e.g., *Will you pass the salt?* rather than *You will pass the salt, You'll pass the salt,* or *'Ll you pass the salt?*). Thus either, or both, positional biases or biases toward stressed syllables (as conjectured by Gleitman & Wanner) can be postulated for the child; and mothers whose usage gets through these child filters have children who learn the closed class materials the faster.

Recall from the earlier discussion, however, that these environmental factors do not say much about *what* is learned. For one thing, as just stated, no known special properties of Motherese explain the learning patterns for open class materials or their organization in the child's sentences. Further, the evidence is clear that children first learn to say declaratives with auxiliaries in *medial unstressed* position even though the environment favoring learning how to do so is hearing those auxiliaries in *initial stressed* position.

In sum, certain universal properties of natural languages (e.g., expressing the predicates and arguments of propositions) seem to emerge in the child at maturationally fixed moments, and are insensitive to the naturally occurring variation among mothers. But elements and functions of the closed class, for children in this age range, seem to be closely affected by specifiable facts about the input. Even here, however, the environment exerts its influence only as the information it provides is filtered through the child's learning biases. For example the serial position, but not the frequency, of maternal auxiliary use affected the learning rate (for a general discussion of the Motherese hypothesis and its limitations, see Gleitman, Newport, & Gleitman, 1984).

Unfortunately, while these studies preclude certain strong forms of the Motherese hypothesis, they leave almost everything unresolved. First, the limited effects of environment on language learning that we found may be attributable to threshold effects of various sorts, to the attenuated sample, or to the measures or analyses used. These complaints are fair even though they lose some force given the positive findings for the closed class component. Nonetheless, there was clear impetus for looking at cases in which the child's environment was more radically altered.

3.1.2 The creation of language: Isolated Deaf children. We therefore next studied a population grossly deprived of formal linguistic stimulation (Feldman, Goldin-Meadow, and Gleitman, 1978). These were six deaf children of hearing parents who had decided to educate their children orally, by having them taught to vocalize and lip read. Accordingly, in advance of the planned training period, the parents made no attempt to teach a manual language. More important, these parents did not *know* a manual language, so they were not in a position to present the easiest sentences first, the harder ones later. It has been observed that children in these circumstances develop an informal system of communicative gestures, called "home sign." It was the genesis of this system that we wished to study. Though many questions arise about how precisely we could analyze this exotic communication system, it is fair to say that the interpretive puzzles we faced are not materially different from those confounding the study of 2- and 3-year old English speakers by adult English-speaking psycholinguists. In each case, one has to try to interpret the child's messages relying heavily on their real-world context of use (cf., Bloom, 1970). In doing so, one encounters the same perils and pitfalls as the language learner himself. We settled for using the methods traditionally employed in studying normal language learning. And we achieved about the same results, for early stages.

These linguistic isolates began to make single gestures (invented by themselves) at the same developmental moment that hearing learners of English speak one word at a time. Two- and three-sign sequences, encoding the same semantic/relational roles, appeared at the same age as hearing learners speak in two- and three-word sentences. To the (rough) extent that the words in these primitive sentences are serially ordered by young hearing learners according to these semantic roles, similar serial ordering of the same categories described the self-generated gesture system. It seems then that even if the environment provides no sample sentences, the child has the internal wherewithal to invent forms himself, to render the same meanings.

These results become more interesting when compared to the findings mentioned earlier, concerning the hearing learners. To the degree that the propositional forms and meanings appeared in indifference to variations in maternal input, these same properties appeared at the same time in the deaf learners, exposed to no formal language input. The closed class subcomponent, responsive at this stage to variations in maternal input, did not appear at all in the signing of the isolated youngsters. The first suggestion here is that the closed class is laid down later, and in a different developmental pattern than other properties of the language system, an argument I made earlier based on quite different observational evidence (see section 2 above). The second suggestion is that the one subcomponent of the language system is more environmentally dependent than the other, and may not appear in some exposure conditions.

3.1.3 The creation of language: Creoles from Pidgins. A fascinating line of research (Sankoff & LaBerge, 1973; Bickerton, 1975) concerns the process of language formation among linguistically heterogeneous populations: pidgins, and their creolization. This work shows that there are very interesting overlaps between the rudimentary first attempts of young children learning an elaborated natural language, and the devices that appear early in the history of a new language. For example, at the first stages of both, the sentences are uniclausal, have rigid canonical phrase orders, etc. (for an admirable discussion that makes these connections to language acquisition research, see Slobin, 1977).

Most interesting of all in the present context, this work suggests that the final (phonological) steps in creating a closed class morphology may be carried out by 5- to 8-year-old youngsters exposed to a pidgin as their first language. The pidgin itself characteristically contains only impoverished closed class resources, again a property shared with the speech forms of very young learners. The learners who hear a pidgin refine, grammaticize, and expand upon its open class resources in late stages of their learning. In a final step, these new resources are phonologically reduced by the learners, reproducing the destressed (and often contracted) closed class morphology that is characteristic of fully elaborated languages (see Zwicky, 1976, for discussion of closed class items, and their distribution in languages of the world).

A very similar development has been observed by Newport (1982) and Newport and Supalla (1980). They study adults who learned formal sign language (ASL) in early childhood from their deaf parents, and have shown that this learning is virtually identical to learning of spoken languages. But they also study mature deaf individuals who were isolated from ASL (and spoken language) during early childhood, the normal language learning period, either because of the oralist beliefs of their caretakers or because they acquired deafness later in life. That is, these investigators studied subjects like those of Feldman et al. (1978) when they grew up. I've already noted that these isolated individuals develop a pidginized form of language, one that lacks complex embedding devices, closed class items, and the like. Newport and Supalla have shown that, when these individuals are finally exposed to formal ASL, if at ages later than 6 or 7 years, they again learn a form of that language that is highly deficient in the ASL equivalents of closed class morphology. They drop their own home sign pidgin, but they create a pidgin from the elaborated language to which they are now exposed. This is common in adult learners of any language.

Now the most fascinating result from these investigators is for deaf children of such first-generation deaf individuals. Keep in mind that these deaf signers who acquired the language relatively late are the ones who use a rather pidginized form of ASL. Their sentences, of course, form the basis for the second-generation deaf child's induction of ASL. Now (unlike the younger deaf isolates) these learners at approximately 4 and 5 years of age refine, expand, and grammaticize certain open class resources, and create a closed class morphology in the course of their learning. In a nutshell, for both the spoken pidgin of Sankoff and LaBerge and the gestural pidgin of Newport and Supalla, the first-language learning situation, carried out at the correct maturational moment, creates new resources out of the air, resources that are abstract and are the very hallmarks of fully elaborated natural languages.

3.1.4 Summary comments. The evidence reviewed suggests that certain syntactic properties, though not all (those which involve the closed class being the exception), appear in the learner in the same way even though the utterance samples vary. The studies of the deaf isolates suggest that there is no requirement for an experienced tutor who presents the easy sentences first to secure the first principles of natural language syntax. On the contrary, should the environment for first-language learning be deficient in the sample utterances, the learner will improve the language in the course of learning it.

3.2 Varying the interpretive information

There is more to the child's input than a sample of utterances—presumably it would be impossible to learn language just from listening to the radio. Specifically, in the logic sketched earlier, it was asserted—in agreement with most investigators, whatever their theoretical persuasions—that the child requires a real world context that accompanies the speech events: some situation that he can interpret. In fact, many investigators assert that there is little mystery left in the language learning feat once it has been acknowledged that the child can interpret the extralinguistic world meaningfully (e.g., Bates & MacWhinney, 1982). However, it is not so easy to state just how "relying on meaning" *succeeds* in helping a child learn language.

One difficulty is that every object in the world can be described by many different kinds of words, a fact I alluded to earlier: the same object out there can be called *Felix*, a *cat*, a *mammal*, etc. On seeing the object then, the child still has a problem in determining the intended meaning of a word used to refer to it (the analysis of "basic level categories," e.g., Rosch, Mervis, Gray, Johnson, & Boyes-Braem, 1976, is sure to be of use in approaching such problems but the fact is that children finally acquire superordinate and subordinate terms as well as basic terms). Similarly, any given scene or event in the world can be described by many different sentences. For instance, scenes suitable to *The cat is on the mat* are just as suitable to *The mat is under the cat* and *Get that damn cat off the new mat*. Thus there is a considerable distance between meaningfully interpreting a scene and catching just how a heard sentence relates to it. To maintain the position that the scene helps the child learn, it will be necessary to provide the natural (perceptual and/or cognitive) analysis of the world that biases the learner to see cats-on-mats, not mats-under-cats, plus a conspiratorial agreement between mother and child such that the mother refer to scenes only in ways that match these biases, whatever they will turn out to be (for very useful discussions of the relations between language and perception, see Miller & Johnson-Laird, 1976, and Jackendoff, 1984). In addition, there will have to be a further conspiracy for marking specially any other intents for, after all, the grammar that is ultimately learned has to allow for the saying and comprehension of *mat-under-cat*.

A related problem has to do with how the utterance is to be analyzed, even assuming that the co-conspirators have figured out how to be united on the interpretation. For example, suppose the mother says "Rabbit jumps" when the learner can see a rabbit jumping. And suppose, with Pinker (1982), that the child believes things are to be the nouns, actions are to be the verbs. Even in these very favorable circumstances there seem to be at least two choices the learner can make. He can suppose English is a noun or subject-first language, in which case *rabbit* is the required noun; or he can suppose English is a verb or predicate-first language, in which case *rabbit* is the required verb.[3] Given all this, it's hard to know how the child gets started.

Summarizing once again, all parties agree that language is learned in partial dependence on the real scenes that are there to be interpreted in the world. However, to my knowledge, nobody has succeeded in providing the required cognitive-perceptual analysis of how scenes are to be interpreted against heard utterances.

Our approach (Landau, 1982; Landau and Gleitman, 1985) to these problems has been to look once more at differing environments in which language is learned. In the studies I've mentioned, the learner was in some ways deprived of information about language forms. What happens if the child is deprived of some opportunities to interpret heard utterances against the world of objects and events? Surely, a blind learner suffers some such deprivations. Though he can hear, and touch objects, so can a sighted learner. A claim in the literature (Bruner, 1974/75) is that a child learns which words refer to what—and hence their meanings—because, as he listens, he follows his mother's gaze and pointing gestures. Even supposing (falsely) that the mother of a blind child names objects only when the child is holding them, in what sense could this be equivalent to gazing and pointing, in directing reference making?

In the light of these limitations on the blind learners' opportunities to discern the referents of many heard words and sentences, we have been surprised to discover that blindness hardly delays language onset; moreover, after the first few words are said, the pattern of linguistic development is virtually identical for sighted children and for neurologically intact blind children. This includes both the development of a lexicon, used appropriately to map onto the world, and the development of syntactic structure and the semantic/relational categories this describes. Apparently, receiving different, and less, interpretive information has no dramatic effect on overall acquisition rate or the character of that learning.

Some details of the blind child's learning are quite interesting. We expected to find the largest differences between blind and sighted children in acquiring the visual vocabulary, words like *look* and *see*, for here the information base is maximally different from the normal. However, blind children seem to use these words as early as do sighted children. In the education literature, such uses are

---

[3] A comeback to this supposed difficulty, of course, is that, over many utterances that dissociate *rabbit* and *jumping*, a distributional analyzer can make the choice. But the semantic bootstrap notion has been put forward as a crucial step that precedes and renders possible subsequent distributional analysis; moreover, its very purpose is to relieve the learner of the burdensome tasks of storing and manipulating large quantities of data so as to dissociate, over the corpus as a whole, rabbits from jumping situations and jumping activities from rabbit objects.

called *verbalism*, often said to be detrimental to the child, who should be discouraged from use of the sighted vocabulary lest he fall victim to "loose thinking." But, on the contrary, the meanings a blind child comes up with seem quite appropriate, though of course they map onto a different sensory world. A sighted child told to "Look up" will tilt his head and orient his eyes upward—even if he is blindfolded during the testing. But our blind subject raises her hands, keeping the head immobile. It is not that the blind child simply conflates *look* and *touch*. For one thing, she responds to "Touch the doll, but don't look at it" by a tap or scratch on the doll, and then to "Now you can look at it" by exploring it manually. And in response to "Touch behind you" she touches her back, but in response to "Look behind you" she searches the space behind her with her hands (again, without turning the head).

On this and much related evidence, we think the blind English-speaking child has developed a distinction as made in French, between *toucher* and *tâter*, between manual contact and apprehension by manual exploration. The question is whether the maternal contexts of use of the sighted terms is special, providing a basis on which the child could develop her special construals. Our finding is that no very superficial description of the contexts explains the learning. For one thing, the caretakers use *look* and *see* to their blind offspring in a surprising way: just as they do to their sighted offspring: to mean 'perceive' on some occasions (e.g., "Look at this boot"), to mean 'consider an event or state of affairs' on other occasions (e.g., "Let's see if granny's home," said while dialing the telephone) and to mean 'resemble' on others (e.g., "Oh, you look like a kangaroo in those overalls"). As these examples begin to show, it is not even possible to say that the mother of a blind child reserves the use of *look* and *see* to occasions when the listener has a relevant object in hand or close to hand—a generalization that potentially could explain how she settled on the interpretation 'explore or apprehend manually.'

To be sure, there is a correlational effect here: usually the mother speaks of *looking* when her blind child is near some target object. But the trouble is that this situational factor is not very informative. This is because the mother says a goodly variety of simple verbs (e.g., *have, play, give, put, hold, say, be*) under the same circumstances: since the child is blind, the mother most often talks of things nearby. But this means that many verbs cannot be discriminated from each other in terms of the nearbyness of things talked about. Rather, our conclusion in the investigations of the blind is that these children recruit several sources of information that jointly can be informative about which verb has which meaning. A contribution is made by the situational factors (e.g., *look* but not *get* or *come* is usually used when a target object is near by). But a separate contribution is made by examining the constraints on the syntactic forms in which the different verbs participate. Space forbids reproducing a full description here. But as an example, notice that *give* is a verb that takes three noun-phrases, the first of which expresses the agent of the action (e.g., *John gives Mary the* *ball*). But *look*, an inalienable perceptual activity, can express no agent (i.e., it is semantically incoherent and syntactically anomalous to say **John looks Mary the ball*). We take the position that a child disposed by nature to analyze these syntactic formats can extract and differentiate the verb meanings, while a learner dependent on observation of linguistic circumstances alone has an insufficient basis for making these inductions. Considering the intricacy of the syntactic analyses required even of blind toddlers, we take their success as another argument for significant biological support of language learning.

3.3 Varying the Endowment of the Learner

The literature just sketched is consistent with a maturationally driven acquisition process, heavily dependent on specific linguistic and perceptual representations, with progress relatively independent of exposure time or type. If this position is correct, then organisms differently endowed should not be able to learn under anything like the same exposure conditions. For cats and dogs, however, there are many arguments much weaker than their lack of a "language faculty" that will serve to explain why they don't learn English. The case has been made more interestingly for primates by Premack and Premack (1983), for they have shown that chimpanzees have certain general conceptual wherewithal in common with humans: but that still does not allow them to function with syntactic categories like those of a human language. My colleagues and I have begun to look at special human populations to pursue this kind of issue.

3.3.1 Language learning in Downs Syndrome (DS) retardates. Fowler (1981) first examined the linguistic functioning of a small group of Downs Syndrome adolescents who for 3 years had shown no further linguistic development (had arrived at some steady final state). They were selected for homogeneity on several measures of cognitive function (e.g., mental age, about 6 years) and an anchor measure of language function (mean length of utterance, MLU, 3.0 to 3.5). This is the level usually achieved by normals between ages 2 and 3. It is important to note that these individuals differ extensively from one another in other aspects of cognitive functioning, for example, some of them were vastly better than others at primitive arithmetic, but this did not predict differences among them in language skill. Not only their gross language level as assessed by MLU, but also the internal properties of their language knowledge, as assessed by a variety of standard instruments used by developmental psycholinguists, were found to be the same as that of 2½-year-old normal controls. This similarity in the course and character of early language learning between normal and DS children has also been found by many others (e.g., Lenneberg, 1967; Lackner, 1976). Hence it looks as if DS individuals may be a diminished case of the normal endowment. (In contrast, non-DS retardates we have studied differ both from the DS individuals and from each other in linguistic developmental patterning, making them a less likely group to study for the present questions.)

The important issue to Fowler, Gelman, and Gleitman had to do with the course of language development in the DS population, and so we instituted a longitudinal study of individuals whose IQ was about the same as the original adolescent group. This study is still underway, and the number of subjects is very small, but a few generalizations are already apparent, particularly from the detailed case history of an individual, "Jenny," whose learning has so far been studied for about 3 years. These individuals began to speak very late, at about 5 years of age. But once language was manifest at all in Jenny, her rate of growth was normal for some succeeding time. Correcting for the onset-time difference, she traversed Roger Brown's (1973) first four stages of language learning in the same absolute period of time required by normals. The internal structure of the knowledge at each interim measurement was virtually identical to that of much younger normals traversing the same stages. However, at this point (MLU about 3.5) Jenny's learning came to a halt. Perhaps the halt is permanent: it has extended 14 months so far, but we have to wait to see if learning starts up once more. The same halt in progress, extending for more than a year subsequent to observed growth—and at chronological ages as young as 7 or 8 years—has been observed for other subjects being studied, but it remains to be shown whether these apparent halt points will turn out to be coherent—as they seem to be for Jenny—with specifiable stages in the normal growth of language. The adolescent population mentioned above suggests, however, that at least some DS individuals at this IQ level reach just the ceiling of attainment that characterizes Jenny's steady state (equivalent to that of 2-year-old normals) and then learn no more.

Summarizing, the interest of the longitudinal findings has to do with two main points: (1) learning is not slow, but at normal pace, until some ceiling is achieved, often at a point very early in life; and (2) the character of knowledge is the same as for normals at the same stage of language development. The progress of the DS individuals, limited as it is, suggests to us that a very low-level, automatic process is at work to determine the rockbottom aspects of linguistic function.

3.3.2 Other populations. So far the findings I have discussed suggest that language learning survives intact despite many differences in the exposure conditions: exposure to a pidgin or an elaborated language, to speech which varies among individual mothers, to speech with diminished opportunity to observe the world (the blind case), or to no speech at all (the isolated deaf children). In contrast, a change in endowment has dramatic consequences for language learning. For the retardates, there is a very low ceiling on accomplishment. This motivates a search for yet other populations that would allow us to disentangle effects of biological status and effects of exposure.

One such population we are studying is children who differ in gestational age at birth (Gleitman & Landau, in preparation). This work is still underway, and it has many technical problems of which the worst is that prematurity is often accompanied by neurological defects that may be relevant to language attainment. We have attempted to control such variables by choosing only individuals whose birthweight was normal for their gestational age and who had no observable neurological abnormalities, but one should still be wary about the generalizations that can be drawn. Acknowledging this, our current findings do suggest that there is a stable effect of prematurity on language onset: onset time is better predicted by time since conception (neurological status) than time since birth (exposure time).

Another potential source of evidence for the contribution of biology to language learning is the character of the learning process in those who are exposed late to a new language, for example, child second-language learners. If biological status bears a significant burden of explanation for the character of language knowledge, independent of exposure, we might expect both the rate and the patterns of learning to differ for second-language learners. This would help explain a very striking phenomenon. A 4-year-old foreign child, transported to America, requires only 1 year's exposure to speak English like a native 5-year-old who has had 5 years of exposure and practice. Of course another interpretation has to do with the fact that the emigré has priorly learned some other language. But a related, and again very large and striking phenomenon that escapes this defect has to do with native bilingualism. Many children are brought up in homes where two or three languages are spoken. Anecdotal evidence—but rather voluminous anecdotal evidence—suggests that the two or three languages are learned as fast as one; namely, at the level of peers learning a single one of the two or three languages. This is a pretty queer kind of learning, it seems. It can handle twice as much data without apparent strain—and handle the additional problem of disentangling two data bases which, if confused, would yield an incoherent system. A theory in which induction from information provided in the environment is not the limiting factor on rate of acquisition could handle these facts (if they are real facts) rather easily: it would be the present expressive power of the learning machinery that is the limiting factor in language growth.

Experimental evidence on this topic is thin. Though there is an enormous literature on child bilingualism and second-language learning, generally it has not focussed on the kinds of issue I have considered in this chapter. There is only one study I know of that seems to attack them directly in the way that is required. That is Newport and Supalla's ongoing studies, mentioned earlier, of deaf individuals learning ASL at different ages. Because of oralist teaching methods and because deafness is often acquired late, there are cases of deaf individuals learning a *first* language at ages ranging from infancy to the late 40s! They are left without a formal language until put in a situation where ASL is used. Newport and Supalla's preliminary findings are that the character of final knowledge of the manual language is predictable from the age of the learner at first exposure, independent of the number of years the individual subsequently used it: as stated in an earlier section of this chapter, late learners fail to acquire the closed class ASL morphology even after decades of exposure and everyday use. Such findings strengthen the case that the neurological status of the learner is dramatically implicated in what he can learn. In this case, evidence was provided supporting the lay impression that young children are better language learners than adults. Whether that evidence is strong enough to support Lenneberg's claim for a "critical period" roughly equivalent to that involved in duck imprinting or bird song learning remains for further investigation to determine.

4 Conclusions

I have tried to describe some of the complex facts about language learning that I suppose are at least within calling distance of an explanation just in case there are task-specific, biologically given predispositions in humans to support them. I know of no extant learning theory specific enough in its claims about the human representational system and learning strategies to explain these same facts, and to subsume as well learning and knowledge of other human cognitive systems. Possibly, such a global learning theory can be developed and can be successful. Until or unless such a theory is developed, such language-specific learning devices as proposed, for example, by Wexler and Culicover (1980), are the closest thing we have to an account of how language is acquired. I myself therefore do not take Chomsky's postulation of an autonomous "language faculty" with principles of learning all its own as an approach that makes extravagant claims on fragmentary evidence. On the contrary. I take that claim as representing appropriate scientific modesty given the state of the art in describing *either* language or its learning. At their best, schematic models offered by linguists and learnability theorists go some small way toward describing the awesomely complex facts about the learning of human language. They go no distance whatsoever in describing "all learning" or "all human knowledge." Therefore, at present, they are best interpreted as interim descriptions of language, and nothing else. It will be a victory for psychology, but one I scarcely anticipate in the near future (say, within a millenium) if that task-specific view turns out to be too modest after all.

References

Bates, E., & MacWhinney, B. (1982). Functionalist approaches to grammar. In E. Wanner & L. R. Gleitman (Eds.), *Language acquisition: State of the art*. Cambridge, MA: Cambridge University Press.

Bellugi, U. (1967). *The acquisition of negation.* Unpublished doctoral dissertation. Cambridge, MA: Harvard University.

Bever, T. G. (1982). Some implications of the nonspecific bases of language. In E. Wanner & L. R. Gleitman (Eds.), *Language acquisition: State of the art.* Cambridge, MA: Cambridge University Press.

Bickerton, D. (1975). *Dynamics of a creole system.* New York: Cambridge University Press.

Bloom, L. (1970). *Language development: Form and function in emerging grammars.* Cambridge, MA: MIT Press.

Bloom, L., Lightbown, P., & Hood, L. (1975). Structure and variation in child language. *Monographs of the Society for Research in Child Development, 40* (Serial No. 160).

Bradley, D. C., Garrett, M. F., & Zurif, E. G. (1979). Syntactic deficits in Broca's aphasia. In D. Caplan (Ed.), *Biological studies of mental processes.* Cambridge, MA: MIT Press.

Brown, R. (1973). *A first language: The early stages.* Cambridge, MA: Harvard University Press.

Brown, R., & Hanlon, C. (1970). Derivational complexity and order of acquisition in child speech. In J. Hayes (Ed.), *Cognition and the development of language.* New York: Wiley.

Bruner, J. S. (1974/75). From communication to language: A psychological perspective. *Cognition, 3,* 255–287.

Chomsky, N. (1965). *Aspects of the theory of syntax.* Cambridge, MA: MIT Press.

Chomsky, N. (1975). *Reflections on language.* New York: Random House.

Chomsky, N. (1981). *Lectures on government and binding.* Dordrecht: Foris.

Dorian, N. (1978). The fate of morphological complexity in language death. *Language, 54,* 590–609.

Feldman, H., Goldin-Meadow, S., & Gleitman, L. (1978). Beyond Herodotus: The creation of language by linguistically deprived deaf children. In A. Lock (Ed.), *Action, symbol, and gesture: The emergence of language.* New York: Academic.

Fernald, A. (1982). *Acoustic determinants of infant preference for "motherese."* Unpublished Ph.D. dissertation. Eugene: University of Oregon.

Fernald, A. (1984). The perceptual and affective salience of mothers' speech to infants. In L. Feagans, C. Garvey, & R. Golinkoff (Eds.), *The origins and growth of communication.* Norwood, NJ: Ablex.

Fowler, A. (1981). *Language learning in Downs Syndrome children.* Unpublished manuscript. Philadelphia: University of Pennsylvania.

Furrow, D., Nelson, K., & Benedict, H. (1979). Mothers' speech to children and syntactic development: Some simple relationships. *Journal of Child Language, 6,* 423–442.

Garrett, M. F. (1975). The analysis of sentence production. In G. H. Bower (Ed.), *The psychology of learning and motivation,* Vol. 9. New York: Academic.

Gentner, D. (1982). Why nouns are learned before verbs: Linguistic relativity vs. natural partitioning. In S. Kuczaj (Ed.), *Language development: Language, culture, and cognition.* Hillsdale, NJ: Erlbaum.

Gleitman, H., & Gleitman, L. R. (1979). Language use and language judgment. In C. J. Fillmore, D. Kempler, & W. S-Y. Wang (Eds.), *Individual differences in language ability and language behavior.* New York: Academic.

Gleitman, L. R., & Gleitman, H. (1970). *Phrase and paraphrase.* New York: Norton.

Gleitman, L. R., & Landau, B. (in preparation). Effects of gestational age on language onset and development.

Gleitman, L. R., Newport, E. L., & Gleitman, H. (in press). The current status of the Motherese hypothesis. *Journal of child language.*

Gleitman, L. R., & Rozin, P. (1977). The structure and acquisition of reading I: Relations between orthographies and the structure of language. In A. Reber & D. Scarborough (Eds.), *Toward a psychology of reading.* Hillsdale, NJ: Erlbaum.

Gleitman, L. R., & Wanner, E. (1982). Language acquisition: The state of the state of the art. In

E. Wanner & L. R. Gleitman (Eds.), *Language acquisition: The state of the art*. New York: Cambridge University Press.

Gleitman, L. R., & Wanner, E. (1984). Current issues in language learning. In M. Bornstein & M. E. Lamb (Eds.). *Developmental psychology*. Hillsdale, NJ: Erlbaum.

Gleitman, L. R., & Wanner, E. (1984). Richly specified input to language learning. In O. Selfridge, E. L. Rissland, & M. Arbib (Eds.), *Adaptive control of ill-defined systems*. New York: Plenum.

Gold, E. M. (1967). Language identification in the limit. *Information and Control, 10*, 447–474.

Jackendoff, R. (1984). *Semantics and cognition*. Cambridge, MA: MIT Press.

Kean, M. L. (1979). Agrammatism: A phonological deficit? *Cognition, 7*, 69–84.

Lackner, J. R. (1976). A developmental study of language behavior in retarded children. In D. M. Morehead & A. E. Morehead (Eds.), *Normal and deficient child language*. Baltimore: University Park Press.

Landau, B. (1982). *Language learning in blind children*. Unpublished Ph.D. dissertation. Philadelphia: University of Pennsylvania.

Landau, B., & Gleitman, L. R. (1985). *Language and experience*. Cambridge, MA: Harvard University Press.

Lenneberg, E. (1967). *Biological foundations of language*. New York: Wiley.

Linebarger, M. C., Schwartz, M. F., & Saffran, E. M. (1983). Sensitivity to grammatical structure in so-called agrammatic aphasics. *Cognition, 13*, 361–392.

Marin, O., Saffran, E., & Schwartz, M. (1976). Dissociations of language in aphasia: Implications for normal function. *Annals of the New York Academy of Sciences, 280*, 868–884.

Miller, G. A., & Johnson-Laird, P. N. (1976). *Language and perception*. Cambridge, MA: Harvard University Press.

Nelson, K. (1973). Structure and strategy in learning to talk. *Monographs of the Society for Research in Child Development, 38*(1–2, Serial No. 149).

Newport, E. L. (1977). Motherese: The speech of mothers to young children. In N. J. Castellan, D. B. Pisoni, & G. Potts (Eds.), *Cognitive theory*, Vol. 2. Hillsdale, NJ: Erlbaum.

Newport, E. L. (1982). Task specificity in language learning? Evidence from speech perception and American Sign Language. In E. Wanner & L. R. Gleitman (Eds.), *Language acquisition: The state of the art*. New York: Cambridge University Press.

Newport, E. L., Gleitman, H., & Gleitman, L. R. (1977). Mother, I'd rather do it myself: Some effects and noneffects of maternal speech style. In C. E. Snow & C. A. Ferguson (Eds.), *Talking to children: Language input and acquisition*. Cambridge, MA: Cambridge University Press.

Newport, E. L., & Supalla, T. (1980). The structuring of language: Clues from the acquisition of signed and spoken language. In U. Bellugi & M. Studdert-Kennedy (Eds.), *Signed and spoken language: Biological constraints on linguistic form*. Dahlem Konferenzen. Weinheim/Deerfield Beach, Fl./Basil: Verlag Chemie.

Pinker, S. (1979). Formal models of language learning. *Cognition, 7*, 217–283.

Pinker, S. (1982). A theory of the acquisition of lexical interpretive grammars. In J. Bresnan (Ed.), *The mental representation of grammatical relations*. Cambridge, MA: MIT Press.

Premack, D., & Premack, A. J. (1983). *The mind of an ape*. New York: Norton.

Rosch, E., Mervis, C. B., Gray, W. D., Johnson, D. M., & Boyes-Braem, P. (1977). Basic objects in natural categories. *Cognitive Psychology, 8*, 382–439.

Rozin, P., & Gleitman, L. R. (1977). The acquisition and structure of reading II: The reading process and the acquisition of the alphabetic principle. In A. Reber & D. Scarborough (Eds.), *Toward a psychology of reading*. Hillsdale, NJ: Erlbaum.

Sankoff, G., & Laberge, S. (1973). On the acquisition of native speakers by a language. *Kivung, 6*, 32–47.

Slobin, D. I. (1973). Cognitive prerequisites for the development of grammar. In C. A. Ferguson & D. I. Slobin (Eds.), *Studies of child language development.* New York: Holt, Rinehart and Winston.

Slobin, D. I. (1977). Language change in childhood and in history. In J. Macnamara (Ed.), *Language learning and thought.* New York: Academic.

Slobin, D. I., & Bever, T. G. (1982). Children use canonical sentence schemas: A crosslinguistic study of word order and inflections. *Cognition,* 12 (229–266).

Snow, C. E., & Ferguson, C. A. (Eds.) (1977). *Talking to children: Language input and acquisition.* New York: Cambridge University Press.

Wexler, K. (1982). A principle theory for language acquisition. In E. Wanner & L. R. Gleitman (Eds.), *Language acquisition: State of the Art.* Cambridge, MA: Cambridge University Press.

Wexler, K., & Culicover, P. (1980). *Formal principles of language acquisition.* Cambridge, MA: MIT Press.

Zwicky, A. M. (1976). *On clitics.* Paper read at the Third International Phonologie-Tagung at the University of Vienna, Sept. 2, 1976.

Chapter 2

Evidence from Great Apes Concerning the Biological Bases of Language*

Mark S. Seidenberg

McGill University, Montreal, Canada

Until recently it was generally assumed that studies such as Gardner and Gardner (1971) and Patterson (1978) had demonstrated that great apes possess the capacity to acquire rudimentary linguistic skills. There is now little agreement about their behavior as a consequence of subsequent studies (e.g., Terrace, Petitto, Sanders, & Bever, 1979) and critical analyses of the earlier ape language research (e.g., Seidenberg & Petitto, 1979). History suggests that when an issue is polemicized, as this one has been, it is often simply set aside. However, I think that it would be unfortunate if some important implications of this research were obscured in the haze of conflicting claims. Taken with related research on the non-linguistic cognitive capacities of lower primates, and with some innovative research on language acquisition in children, the ape language studies provide important evidence bearing on a basic question in the cognitive sciences.

The question concerns the relationship between language and other cognitive capacities. Stated simply, is language the expression of a domain-specific capacity (or faculty), or is it merely one of many expressions of a general capacity to engage in intelligent behavior? The domain-specificity claim is familiar from the work of Chomsky (e.g., 1978) and has recently been incorporated by Fodor (1983) into a general theory of the organization of intelligence. The notion that language is derived from non-specific cognitive capacities to think and learn is familiar from the work of Piaget (1955, 1980), and has been elaborated by Bates and MacWhinney (1982), Bruner (1975), Anderson (1983), and others. In this chapter, I will argue that the only way to accommodate the data from recent studies of ape intelligence is in terms of the domain-specificity claim. That is, when the research on both the linguistic and non-linguistic capacities of apes is considered, it strongly supports the idea that language results from a biologically given, species-specific, autonomous faculty. Only this hypothesis provides a

* I would like to thank Laura Petitto for discussing these issues with me and commenting on an earlier draft of the paper. I am also grateful to her for permission to extensively cite her unpublished thesis.

principled explanation of the behavior that has been observed. This is a positive, non-trivial result, although not necessarily one the ape language researchers would themselves promote.

The Logic of Ape Language Research

At first glance, studies of ape language seem to be premised on denial of the obvious. Humans acquire and use natural languages, and lower primates do not. This irrefutable fact would seem to constrain a priori what might be learned by training apes to perform "linguistically." It might be useful to consider, then, how it was thought that these projects could be informative.

One reason to study lower primates is simply because it would be valuable to understand the behavior of other intelligent species. While no doubt the motivation for much traditional primatological research, this will not account for the notoriety of recent ape language research. Much of the interest in these studies derives from the possibility that they might bear on other issues, such as the evolutionary differentiation of humans from other primates, the origins and evolution of language, and the relationship between linguistic and non-linguistic intelligence.

The ape language research has often been placed in the context of evolutionary questions (e.g., Fouts, 1974, 1975; Parker & Gibson, 1979; Walker, 1983). The theory of evolution, together with the fact that humans, gorillas, and chimpanzees evolved from a common ancestor, leads to a general expectation that these species might exhibit similar behaviors, which could be revealed through comparative studies. As Wasserman (1981, p. 246) has stated, "The hypothesis that man and animal share cognitive capacities is simply the single most important idea of comparative psychology." Whether such commonalities exist among primates is an empirical question, and the facts about evolution suggest that it might be an interesting one.

Note, however, that evolution provides no basis on which to anticipate particular behavioral similarities, in terms of language or otherwise. Evolution is a theory of speciation, not of behavioral continuity. From the fact that various primates shared a common ancestor and the fact that species evolve, no specific behavioral commonalities necessarily follow. Particular homologies (or analogies) are a consequence of actual events, largely unknown, that are incidental in terms of the theory of the evolutionary process. As a consequence, comparisons of behavior need to be interpreted in the context of a theory of behavioral similarity, not merely in terms of evolution.

This point has not been sufficiently appreciated in the ape language literature. The problem is that general evolutionary facts are sometimes used in order to *establish* behavioral similarities (see, e.g., Fouts, 1974). The apes exhibit complex behaviors that are ambiguous at best. The interpretation of these behaviors is assisted by appeals to evolution, leading to the conclusion that an ape's behavior corresponds to that of a human *because* apes and humans descended from a common ancestor. However, this reasoning is entirely circular. In the absence of an explicit theory as to how particular behaviors evolved, evolutionary facts such as common ancestry provide no basis on which to mediate comparisons of behavior.

A clear example of this inappropriate appeal to evolution is seen in a book by Gribbin and Cherfas (1982). The authors describe recent research using techniques from molecular biology which have been used to infer the evolutionary history of hominids (e.g., Sarich & Wilson, 1967). This research is controversial because the evolutionary timetable that results from these techniques is inconsistent with that developed from the paleontological record. The degree of genetic overlap among various primates (as measured, e.g., by similarities in blood proteins such as albumin) is used to infer the evolutionary sequence. These studies have yielded the conclusion that humans and chimpanzees share about 99% of their genetic material (King & Wilson, 1975). From the fact that humans and chimpanzees are genetically similar (and therefore close evolutionary relatives), Gribbin and Cherfas imply that we must be behaviorally alike as well. Numerous examples of behavioral similarities are then described. It is as though the new genetic discoveries indicate that we are more similar in behavior than previously thought. However, the molecular biological facts have no bearing on identifying behavioral continuities across species; they are facts about body chemistry, not behavior. Overlap at the level of DNA is consistent with the existence of such continuities, but does not itself validate (or invalidate) them. Nonetheless, these data are widely cited in discussion of ape language as strongly corroborating evidence (e.g., by Rumbaugh & Gill, 1976; Patterson, 1980a; and Tanner & Zihlman, 1976).[1]

Another problematical argument from evolution is seen in attempts to relate ape language to questions concerning the origin of language (see, e.g., many papers in Wescott, 1974; Harnad, Steklis, & Lancaster, 1976; and Reynolds, 1981). Chimpanzees are thought to be less highly evolved than humans; therefore, by studying their natural communicative behavior, and observing their progress in learning one or another aspect of human language, we might gain evidence concerning the structure of proto-languages and the evolution of the linguistic capacity in humans. The problem here is that humans did not evolve from chimpanzees. The two species are collateral descendents from a common ancestor

---

[1] I think this point should be clear. A model of the Brooklyn Bridge, a loom, and a computational device with the power of a Turing machine could be constructed out of identical sets of Tinker Toys. Nothing whatever would follow about their relatedness at higher levels of analysis. The biochemical facts would be compelling only if there were a theory relating them to behavior. Reductionists must also contend with the fact that, as Malmi (1976) noted in an interesting discussion of these issues, the 1% difference involves at least 40 million base-pairs.

which have evolved in parallel (Ploog & Melnechuk, 1969). Nor are chimpanzees "less highly evolved" than humans; they simply evolved in a different manner. Inferences from the behavior of chimpanzees to the behavior of a common ancestor who existed several million years ago can only be acknowledged as speculative at best (see Parker & Gibson, 1979, for a tour de force argument of this kind).

Evaluating the question of behavioral continuities across species has proven to be a hugely complex problem. There is basic disagreement about first principles among comparative psychologists, ethologists, sociobiologists, physical anthropologists, and behavioral ecologists. I think it is fair to say that lack of a clear theory of comparative study has contributed to difficulties in interpreting the behavior of signing apes. The questionable appeals to evolution discussed above are only one manifestation of this problem.[2]

Despite these difficulties with specific applications of the concept, evolution provides a rationale for comparative, behavioral studies of related species. Psychologists have shown special interest in comparative studies of language because it seems to be a uniquely human endeavor. Such studies were thought to have the potential to provide an empirical test of Chomsky's claim that there is a language faculty specific to humans. One strategy might be to determine whether the natural communicative behaviors of lower primates share important properties with human language. This research is being pursued to interesting ends by Seyfarth, Cheney, and Marler (1980; Seyfarth & Cheney, 1980; see also Struhsaker, 1967). Although these behaviors exhibit interesting properties, it is highly unlikely that lower primates will be revealed to possess a natural communicative system closely resembling human language.

A second strategy has been to train apes in particular linguistic skills. What might be learned from such laboratory studies that is not revealed by studying the natural communicative behaviors of apes? These studies have often been motivated by the idea that if the ape were provided with a linguistic model and appropriate learning experiences, neither of which occur in the wild, it could acquire linguistic skills. This view presupposes an empiricist, learning-theoretic view of language acquisition, as Gardner and Gardner (1971, 1974a, b) explicitly acknowledge. Many papers in this area express the sense that these experiments would provide a definitive refutation of Chomsky's critique of Skinner. Given the well-known inadequacies of the learning-theoretic account of human language acquisition (Fodor, Bever, & Garrett, 1974), there seems to be little basis for

---

[2] I don't at all mean to suggest by these remarks that an evolutionary theory of the origins of language is impossible in principle. It is possible, for example, that, given an understanding of the neurological bases of language, and additional information about the evolution of the brain (drawing perhaps upon data such as Holloway's, 1976), such an explanation could be developed (see Deacon, 1979, for an attempt along these lines). My only point is that evolutionary (and biochemical) facts of the sort mentioned in the text are not sufficient, and that they are little help in drawing behavioral comparisons.

expecting that an ape, trained in this manner, would come to exhibit elaborate linguistic behavior. Construed in this manner, the ape language experiments could only provide a test of how much linguistic behavior could be acquired through application of the precepts of *Verbal Behavior*. This places ape language research in a very different context from studies of child language (as other papers in this volume confirm). The very limited accomplishments of the apes trained in this manner seem to provide mostly negative evidence concerning the power of this approach.

A more interesting basis for these studies might be provided by the hypothesis that the capacities of the primate brain are not fully realized under natural conditions (Harlow, 1958). Specifically, it could be assumed first, that apes possess a capacity to produce or comprehend at least some aspects of language that is unexpressed in their natural environment, and second, that the laboratory conditions of these experiments provide a means for realizing this capacity. However, the validity of these assumptions is unclear. The traditional answer as to why the apes' putative linguistic capacity isn't manifested in their natural behavior (dating from Yerkes, 1925) is that apes lack the capacity to physically produce speech signals, as Lieberman (1968) later substantiated. With a little effort (e.g., the motor theory of speech perception), this might also explain their failure to comprehend language. Given an alternate means of expression, the ape could capitalize on its latent capacities. The manual gestures of sign languages were thought to provide this alternative. These studies have relied upon a "molding" technique (i.e., physically shaping the ape's hands into signs) rather than conditioning of specific responses; "molding" would be sufficient if in fact the ape merely needed to be given a means for expressing an inchoate linguistic ability.

This logic is inconsistent, however. Apes lack part of the neuro- and motor-physiology that supports speech. The sign language researchers proposed to overcome this limitation by exploiting the apes' natural ability to gesture. This effort would only succeed if they were capable of using the alternate modality. But if apes possess this capacity, the explanation for the fact that they fail to naturally express their linguistic capacity is wholly lost. It is interesting to note in this regard that the natural communication of lower primates is not primarily gestural. On their own, they seem to make little of their opportunity to use their hands for communication.[3]

There have been other attempts to explain why apes might have an unrealized linguistic capacity (e.g., language lacks adaptational significance for apes; they lack the motivation to use it; they actually have a language but humans are

---

[3] This logic also ignores the fact that having an intact vocal system is not a necessary prerequisite for human language. Evidence from the sign languages of the deaf suggests that humans have evolved a modality-free capacity for language, rather than a capacity for speech (Bellugi & Seidenberg, in preparation).

incapable of perceiving it, etc.). I do not find these persuasive, but perhaps a better explanation could be developed. Here I only want to make explicit the fact that in teaching sign language to apes, it is often presupposed that (a) they possess a latent, unexpressed capacity to use language; (b) they possess a physical means for realizing this capacity; and (c) there is a principled reason why this capacity is not naturally realized. However, (c) cannot be explained in terms of the absence of (b), leaving (a) in doubt.

I have suggested that it is unclear why sign language training should result in the production of communicative behaviors qualitatively different from those observed among untrained apes. Nonetheless, there is enough ambiguity in our understanding of the evolution of language and its biological bases to suggest that these studies might have been revealing in unexpected ways. With this in mind, we turn to the evidence. In the discussion that follows, I emphasize the studies in which apes were trained to use sign language, because these provide most of the data on which various linguistic attributions have been based. Although both Premack (1976) and Rumbaugh (1977) initially placed their research, which does not involve signing, in the context of language acquisition, they now view it as bearing primarily on other issues, to which I return later in the paper.

Results of the Sign Language Projects

Although this research has been controversial, a careful reading of the literature suggests that the behaviors of signing apes exhibited no important similarities to human language. Many claims have been made on behalf of these animals (e.g., that they could name objects and answer questions, that they used a rudimentary syntax, that they created novel expressions and comprehended their trainers' utterances, etc.), but they cannot be sustained by the available evidence. In general there are two problems: the behavioral evidence that could establish these claims has not been provided, and the evidence that is available is consistent with non-linguistic interpretations.

As Petitto and I have described elsewhere (Seidenberg & Petitto, 1979, 1981), part of the problem is that crucial information about the apes' actual behavior needed in order to establish their linguistic competence is simply unavailable. It is remarkable how little systematic information about the performance of signing apes has been provided in nearly 15 years of research. The primary data are lists of the signs in the animals' vocabularies, supplemented by examples of their usage. However, the vocabulary lists represent *hypotheses* about their performance, not *data*. The question is, what is the basis for concluding that the gesture believed to be *banana* corresponded in any interesting way to the word *banana* in a human's vocabulary? This could only be established by a systematic analysis of how the gesture was actually used, but none has been provided. There have been no analyses, for example, of the events (such as presence of particular objects) correlated with the ape's production of a sign. Gestures are assigned glosses on the basis of the trainers' intentions in teaching the ape, rather than on the basis of their actual performance. In this way, the trainers project their own use of signs onto the apes' use of them. These studies clearly establish what the signs meant to the trainers; how they functioned for the animals is unclear.

Other claims are supported by example. Washoe is said to use contrastive sign order (evidence for syntax) because she signed *baby mine* and not *mine baby* (Gardner & Gardner, 1974a). Koko is said to combine signs creatively because she signed *cookie rock* to describe a stale sweet roll (Patterson, 1978). The problem with these examples is that the conditions under which they occurred are ambiguous, and as a consequence they cannot be interpreted outside the context of a thorough and systematic analysis of a wider range of behaviors. This is the most telling point of Terrace et al.'s (1979) data on Nim. Their data—primarily a listing of nearly 20,000 of the chimpanzee's utterances—are not without important limitations; for example, there is little systematic analysis of the contexts in which the utterances occurred. Nonetheless, their corpus is revealing. Looking at isolated examples, it appears that Nim too produced "novel" combinations such as *cookie rock*. Looking at the entire corpus, however, it is clear that his combinations were heterogeneous. Many are interpretable with a little imagination; most are not. An alternative hypothesis consistent with the data is that Nim had simple principles for combining signs without reference to meaning or context; a number of "creative" utterances fall out of this process, as does a lot of word salad. It doesn't follow that a process of this type necessarily underlay Washoe or Koko's "creative" combinations; it merely demonstrates that provocative examples cannot be interpreted outside a broader context. I think this point should be obvious, but these examples have exerted enormous influence.[4]

Looking again at the Nim data, it is clear that, as with Washoe's *baby mine*, some pairs of signs appeared in preferred orders (e.g., *me Nim* occurred more often than *Nim me*). Isolating these examples from the corpus, it might appear that Nim's utterances exhibited a rudimentary syntactic structure. However, these asymmetries are not consistent across sign classes; they appear to be specific to certain vocabulary items, as might be expected if stereotypic combinations were produced in a rote, mechanized fashion. Nor was there any evidence that sign order was used contrastively; for example, both *me give* and *give me* appear in the corpus, but there is no evidence that their meanings differed in appropriate

---

[4] Dennett (1983) ascribes great importance to the role of "anecdotes" in understanding animal behavior. He has in mind a special sense of "anecdote," however. He notes that "novel" behaviors may be highly revealing and advocates research strategems which "have the virtue of provoking novel but interpretable behavior, of generating anecdotes under controlled (and hence scientifically admissible) conditions" (p. 348). Behaviors observed in this manner would not have the casual character of the *cookie rock* examples.

contexts. Finally, Nim's mean length of utterance (MLU), which provides a rough estimate of the complexity of his utterances, was essentially flat across the course of the experiment.

It is seen, then, that the Nim data contain examples of behaviors which, in the Washoe and Koko studies, are cited as evidence for linguistic abilities in signing apes. These data suggest that Nim's behavior very closely resembled that of other signing apes. However, only the Nim data permit these examples to be evaluated in the context of a broad range of utterances. When this is done, it is seen that the examples are both consistent with and suggestive of much simpler, non-linguistic interpretations. These alternative interpretations could not be evaluated with regard to other signing apes simply because the relevant data were not provided.

In support of their conclusions, Gardner and Gardner (1980; Gardner, 1981), Patterson (1980b), and others (e.g., Van Cantfort & Rimpau, 1982) assert that Nim's behavior was aberrant. They correctly note that it does not necessarily follow from the fact that Nim failed to sign creatively that Washoe and Koko failed as well. Possibly Nim was badly trained or less intelligent; maybe there are individual differences among apes in regard to linguistic skill. However, as these examples suggest, nothing in the available data indicates that Nim's behavior differed remarkably from that of the other signing apes. What differs is the interpretation of behaviors such as *cookie rock* or *baby mine*. When such behaviors are evaluated within the broader context of a corpus of utterances, it is clear that they cannot bear the weight of evidence they have been assigned.

I have suggested, then, that the conclusion that apes such as Washoe or Koko exhibited linguistic skills was based on examples inappropriately isolated from their general behavior. The net effect of this selective reading of their behavior was to make it very difficult to evaluate alternative, non-linguistic interpretations. In this way, the ape language research departed from the normal process of scientific inquiry in a profound way. The ape language researchers employed what I have termed a *consistency criterion* in evaluating their subjects' behavior (Seidenberg, 1983). They merely cite examples that are consistent with a linguistic interpretation. Washoe signing *baby mine* is consistent with the hypothesis that her utterances were structured. Koko signing *cookie rock* is consistent with the hypothesis that she could combine signs creatively. However, these behaviors are also consistent with non-linguistic interpretations whose validity could not be directly assessed because the relevant data were not presented. In other words, the linguistic interpretation of these examples could not be falsified.

The absence of any attempt to systematically address the many non-linguistic interpretations of ape signing is the single most devastating failure of the ape language research. The consistency criterion represents a radical departure from normal scientific inquiry. Contrast this method with one recently proposed by Dennett (1983). Dennett is at pains to develop a method for evaluating complex, ambiguous animal behaviors (such as those involved in communication) which may involve intentional states (such as beliefs and desires). As Dennett notes, the notorious problem in evaluating such behaviors is that they appear to be consistent with a variety of interpretations, ranging from non-intentional, behavioristic, "kill-joy" hypotheses to those involving second- or third-order intentional attributions. Dennett advocates a strategy whereby the range of alternative hypotheses is explicitly stated and evaluated with regard to the behavioral evidence. Clever and devious experiments might be developed so as to obtain data critically bearing upon one or another alternative. This is a cogent articulation of a familiar strategy, although in practice it turns out to be quite difficult to obtain the critical disambiguating data. The problem is that no such strategy is employed in the ape language research. The researchers evaluate the consistency of the data relative to the single hypothesis that the apes' signing is the result of particular linguistic skills; other interpretations are hardly acknowledged, and the data bearing on them are not solicited.

It is interesting to observe that, in entertaining only a single level of analysis, the ape language researchers follow the strategy of radical behaviorists. The behaviorist is committed to a particular level of analysis, one that does not acknowledge higher-level, intentional explanations. The ape language researchers are committed to such higher-order, linguistic analyses of their subjects' behaviors, and fail to evaluate lower level ones. It is this a priori commitment to one or another level which Dennett argues against.

Breadth of Comparisons

A related problem concerns the nature of the comparisons between ape and human behaviors offered in this literature. As I stated above, whatever the merits of evolutionary or biological arguments, behavioral comparisons require an adequate theory of the behaviors in question. With a sufficiently narrow conception of a linguistic skill, it is a simple (if uninteresting) matter to establish "continuity" across species. As Chomsky (1980) has noted, "This is much like the question whether humans can fly, almost as well as chickens though not as well as Canada geese." In the ape language research, linguistic skills are conceptualized in a manner that limits the interest of the resulting comparisons. Consider, for example, naming. It is widely believed (following Terrace et al., 1979) that while apes cannot combine signs into sentences, they can nonetheless use signs to name objects. The validity of this claim rests on the theory of the naming task and the evidence from actual performance bearing on it. It is often asserted in this literature that a barrier to drawing decisive conclusions about the apes' performance is the absence of any general agreement about the "definition" of language or particular linguistic functions such as naming. Evaluating whether the ape could name objects, for example, is difficult because of our limited understanding of the concepts of meaning and referring. It is sometimes suggested that these limitations preclude making theoretically informed comparisons across species (Gardner & Gardner, 1974b). I think that the limitations on our knowledge of linguistic structures and functions have been overstated. Given our understanding of language, revealing comparisons between the ape and human are possible. The general strategy must be to understand the principles governing the ape's use of signs (in naming, for example), and to determine whether these principles could account for analogous behavior in humans. It is important to acknowledge the theoretical lacunae, but these do not preclude detailed comparisons of ape and child. Indeed, I doubt if the technical questions in the theory of meaning or syntax have much bearing on understanding the nature of ape signing.[5]

What, then, of the claim that apes can learn to use names? The first point to note is that, whatever one's theory of naming, the conclusion cannot be sustained on the basis of the evidence currently available. As with other aspects of the apes' actual performance, very little systematic data related to naming has been reported. Terrace et al.'s (1979) large corpus of utterances provides little information about how these were actually used. Nor does Patterson provide documentation of how Koko used the several hundred names for objects in her putative vocabulary. The primary evidence that apes can name objects derives from the Gardners' experiments in which Washoe signed the names of objects (or pictures of objects) presented in a box (Gardner & Gardner, 1971, 1974a). While this task could provide interesting information about the ape's use of signs, it does not provide a good basis for determining whether its ability to name objects was comparable to that of a child. The problem is that the task could be performed successfully if the ape had learned simple associations between signs and objects. Construed as a test of naming, it presumes a behavioral theory of meaning and reference, a theory known to give a poor account of the child's knowledge and use of names (MacNamara, 1983). Thus, the manner in which the task was constructed limits the potential for drawing positive comparisons to children.

It would be important nonetheless to know if the ape could learn to perform this task; if nothing else, it would provide information about its ability to form certain associations. As noted previously (Seidenberg & Petitto, 1979), there are important unanswered questions about Washoe's performance on this task; details concerning the stimuli, scoring procedure, and Washoe's performance have not been provided. Although it appears that she probably learned some such associations, the number of signs used correctly on this task, the reliability of her sign usage and whether her performance generalized to new exemplars without specific training are unclear. There is independent evidence, however, from a

---

[5] This situation is a common one in science. To take an example from a very different domain, our theoretical understanding of the molecular bases of water currently does not provide an explanation for why water boils at 100°C and freezes at 0°C (Franks, 1981). This basic limitation does not preclude distinguishing water from other substances.

study by Savage-Rumbaugh and Rumbaugh (1978) suggesting that it is difficult for apes to form associations between arbitrary symbols and particular referents. They explicitly attempted to teach their apes such assocations (using lexigrams rather than manual signs); the apes had limited success in learning these associations even with intensive training.

Whether the ape's use of names depends greatly upon such associations is as yet unclear. In pursuing this question, however, other interesting issues could be addressed which might provide the bridge to deeper comparisons to children. For example, it appears that apes can learn to identify categories of objects (Premack, 1976), and interesting additional questions could be asked about this behavior. Does the ape categorize objects on the basis of their functions, as Nelson (1974) has suggested of children? Do apes respond to semantic features that determine category membership, as Clark (1974) suggests is true of children? Are they capable of abstracting prototypical members of categories (Rosch, 1973)? While each of these proposals presents difficulties as a characterization of the basis of object naming in children, information concerning the apes' performance would provide a more substantive basis for comparisons to children. At the same time, it might be determined whether the apes' associative and categorial processes differ in any important respect from those observed in other species (e.g., pigeons; Herrnstein, Loveland, & Cable, 1976). At the present time, however, I think it is premature to conclude that the apes could name objects under any interesting conception of this skill. Given a more adequate theory of naming (or referential communication in general), I believe it would be possible to delineate the ways in which the ape's performance differs from that of a child. However, there are many unanswered empirical questions in this regard.

This skeptical view of the ape's ability to name is also prompted by my own experiences with Nim. It was clear to me that, while Nim did consistently associate a very small number of signs with particular objects (or classes of objects), his general strategies for producing signs were quite different. Rather than associating particular signs with particular objects, he associated groups of signs with stereotypic situations. For example, eating contexts (e.g., sitting in the kitchen of his residence) would invariably provoke a cascade of eating-related signs: eat, more, drink, give, etc. Other very general contexts (e.g., a picture book in the classroom) would produce other clusters of signs. Another strategy was simply to imitate signs in the teacher's input. This was a very clever strategy for producing signs the teacher would consider ''contextually appropriate.'' In neither case was sign production mediated by specific associations between signs and objects.

Another example of the manner in which the conceptualization of a task limits the interest of cross-species comparisons is provided by the Gardners' test of Washoe's ability to answer questions (Gardner & Gardner, 1975). Washoe was trained to respond to questions such as *who that* or *where that*, and was tested on 500 trials. Each response was scored as correct if it contained a sign from 1 to 5 pre-designated target categories (in the above examples, a proper noun or a locative, respectively). It is reported that Washoe answered questions correctly on a statistically significant proportion of trials. A response was scored as correct if it anywhere contained an item from the target category; the appropriateness of the signs to the contexts was ignored. Thus, if a banana were held up, and the question were "what that?" the response *you me give ball more* would be scored as correct, because it contains the sign *ball*, a member of the target category noun.

The effect of this procedure is to permit Washoe to perform at the reported levels by means of various non-linguistic strategies. One, for example, would be to generate very long chains of signs, increasing the probability that one of them would be from a target category. Another would be to associate a small number of signs with each target frame. This could be accomplished during the extensive pretraining on the task. It insults the intelligence of the animal to think it would not latch upon these strategies, since they are much simpler than actually being able to comprehend and answer questions. Because of the manner in which the task was constructed, the data provide no basis for interesting comparisons to question-answering in humans. Although the test is promoted as a test of Washoe's ability to understand and answer questions, no specific linguistic knowledge was required in order to perform it.[6]

This study is representative of the literature in several ways. First, a linguistic skill (question-answering) is construed in a manner that bears a remote relation to the human skill. Answering questions is not simply a matter of responding with items from particular syntactic categories. Second, the task was constructed so as to permit simple, non-linguistic responding strategies. Third, the results were interpreted in the richest possible way (as evidence for the ability to understand and answer questions), and other interpretations were not evaluated. Finally, the data were reported in a fragmentary manner; although there were 500 trials on the test, only a few examples of her actual responses were described. This made it difficult to ascertain exactly how Washoe had performed the task.

Given the partial reporting of the results of this experiment, all that could be said was that the data did not provide compelling evidence for a linguistic skill. It remained a possibility, however, that while the task afforded a simple, non-linguistic strategy for performance, Washoe did understand and respond correctly. However, I recently obtained the unpublished list of Washoe's responses to the 500 questions.[7] These confirm that Washoe's strategy was, in general, to associate a small number of signs with each question frame. For example, 71%

---

[6] This experiment is actually messier than this discussion suggests (see Seidenberg & Petitto, 1979). The conditions created a very complex discrimination task for which it is difficult to appropriately assess the chance probabilities of correct responses, even on an associative basis.

[7] I thank Beatrice and Allen Gardner for providing this information.

of the responses to the question "Who that?" contained the signs *Roger, Washoe*, or *you*; 75% of the responses to "Who action?" (e.g., *"Who eat?"*) contained *you* or *me*; and 58% of the responses to "Who trait?" (e.g., *"Who funny?"*) included *you* or *me*. Collapsing across the three types of "who" questions, it is seen that four signs—*Roger, Washoe, you*, and *me*—account for 83% of all correct responses. A similar pattern holds for most of the other questions (e.g., 82% of the responses to "What now?" contained the response *time*, as in *time eat*; 100% of the responses to "Whose that?" contained *yours* or *mine*). The only exceptions to this pattern are the questions "What want" and "What that." For the former, Washoe appeared to use the strategy of responding with a food name. For the latter, she responded by correctly naming 26 different items, consistent with her performance on the box test. These data present a very different picture of her ability to answer questions than in the 1975 report.

I have suggested that there are two related problems in the ape language literature. One is the failure to consider simpler interpretations; the other is the reduction of linguistic skills to non-linguistic tasks. Both derive from attending to examples of the apes' utterances without regard to the *processes* by which they were produced. It is because of these factors that ape sign language appears to be a Clever Hans effect. Hans was the famous nineteenth-century horse who could tap his hoof to indicate the correct answers to simple problems of addition (he could also use the other three types of arithmetic operations, change common fractions into decimals and back again, and give the day of the month; Miller, 1962). Careful investigation by Pfungst (1911) revealed that the horse's responses were unwittingly cued by humans. Sebeok (1980) provides fascinating details of this case and others like it. The "Clever Hans effect" is often taken to refer to cases in which an animal's behavior is cued in a simple manner. Umiker-Sebeok and Sebeok (1980) believe that much of ape signing is cued in this manner. I don't believe that any simple notion of cuing will account for the apes' behaviors; as I have suggested, they use more general responding strategies such as "produce signs from a certain cluster in certain contexts." Unlike Hans, their behavior is not dependent upon particular signals from particular people. Much of the discussion of ape signing as a "Clever Hans" effect misses the mark because it only considers the narrow question of experimenter cuing. The Gardners, for example, stress the fact that the double-blind testing conditions of their naming test ensured that Washoe was not cued by the experimenter, while Umiker-Sebeok and Sebeok (1980) believe that unconscious, uncontrollable cuing pervades such experiments. I think it is more important to emphasize the fact that the ape could use sign production strategies that require neither cuing from the trainer nor knowledge of the language.

The correspondence between the Hans case and ape signing runs much deeper than the question of cuing. Hans could be said to add under a sufficiently narrow conceptualization of that skill. Given an inadequate theory of the task—one that focused on a narrow range of behaviors and ignored the processes by which they were produced—it was possible to draw positive comparisons across species. Once Pfungst attended to the processes by which Hans responded, it was obvious how his behavior differed from that of a human. The inadequate conceptualization of a quintessentially human skill, the focus on a narrow range of behaviors without regard to the manner in which they were produced, and the failure to evaluate simpler alternatives, are exactly the problems I have attributed to ape language research.

What did signing apes learn? Most discussions of the signing apes' behaviors have attempted to relate them to human language. However, these behaviors may be better understood by considering the demand characteristics of the sign language experiments. The researchers attempted to create an environment in which the ape would sign communicatively. However, they may only have succeeded in creating a task which could be successfully performed if the ape merely learned the *instrumental function* of signing in the laboratory context. Assume for a moment that the apes knew nothing of the meanings or grammatical functions of individual signs, or even close associations between signs and objects. The ape could perform in a manner consistent with the descriptions in the literature by learning the *consequences* of producing particular sign sequences. The experimenter's task was to create conditions under which signing was elicited. In doing so, the apes learned that signing was highly valued. Producing signs became a means for obtaining desired outcomes (food, attention, playtime, etc.). Under these conditions, the ape's task was to determine which sign (or signs) was required in a particular context. The ape could fulfill the demands of the experimental context in several ways, the "strategies" I have alluded to above. It might associate particular signs with certain objects or general contexts. It could imitate the teacher's input. It might generate long chains of signs, increasing the probability of producing a sign that would satisfy the teacher. In other words, it could develop rituals of varying complexity that produced the desired outcomes.

I believe that this account of ape signing is essentially correct. The apes had little or no knowledge of the specific meanings or grammatical functions of signs; they were not symbolic, iconic, or indexical. None of this knowledge was required given the demand characteristics of these experiments. The ape's task reduced to finding the sign or signs that met the requirements of the teacher, who would then effect desired outcomes. These requirements varied across contexts and experiments. In the Gardners' naming test, Washoe had to produce the particular sign associated with a particular object (or class of objects). This was perhaps the most restrictive context, but only a small proportion of her sign vocabulary was tested in this way (specifically, concrete nouns). In their question test, the requirements were less restricted; here all that was needed was a sign from a set of "correct" answers. In the Nim project, in which there were no specific comprehension tests and the primary goal was simply to record a large corpus of utterances, the demands upon the subject were even more minimal.

The most extreme case is represented by the Koko project, in which nearly any utterance is satisfactory because her trainer interprets even anomalous ones as Koko being funny, or lying, or expressing a special insight.

The Nim data are again revealing in this regard. The most striking aspect of the data is that seven signs—*me, you, Nim, more, eat, drink, give*—account for a very high proportion of his output. The distribution of Nim's signs by frequency is highly skewed. A small number of signs (principally the above seven) occur very frequently; the remaining signs occur very infrequently. For example, these seven signs account for 84% of the tokens in his 25 most frequent two-sign utterances, and 83% of the tokens in the 25 most frequent three-sign utterances. The occurrence of these particular signs with numbing regularity is easily explained. The experimenters created a context in which "contextually appropriate" signing was the basic demand upon the subject. Each of the above signs could be interpreted by the teacher as appropriate. In this context it was difficult to *dissuade* Nim from producing these signs.

There are many other examples of this kind of instrumental use of language. A child may say something it does not understand, knowing only that an adult will find it funny. I know curses in several languages and that they are likely to elicit aggressive responses, but I have no idea what they mean. The apes' behavior is perhaps most closely related to that of at least some autistic children who have been trained to sign (Creedon, 1973; Konstantareas, Oxman, & Webster, 1977). My own experience with such children (those described by Creedon) suggests that they too learned to produce sequences of signs in a ritualistic fashion because it was demanded in the therapeutic context. These children learn the outcomes associated with utterances, not their intensional content. Much closer comparisons between the signing of these children and that of chimpanzees would be useful.

All of these examples fit Skinner's (1957) description of mands. Mands are instrumental utterances likely to evoke responses from the addressee. As such examples suggest, the manding function can be effected even when knowledge of the language is wholly absent. There is no need for linguistic forms to be used at all to perform this function; under the appropriate circumstances, a smile may be sufficient. Seen in this light, the fact that the apes learned to sign is not critical to interpreting their behavior; it would not be qualitatively different had they been taught to use other arbitrary behaviors in this way. If this view is correct, ape signing is more closely analogous to the use of tools than to language. Tools, like the signs in these apes' vocabularies, do not have meanings or grammatical functions. They are the instruments by which certain outcomes can be obtained. As studies dating from Köhler (1927) and Yerkes (1925) have demonstrated, chimpanzees can use tools in solving problems. Thus, the signing behavior of apes represents the adaptation of a native intelligence to the peculiar demands of the signing context. In this way, their behavior is continuous with that of apes who were not language-trained.

This discussion suggests that the apes used signs instrumentally to meet the demands of the laboratory context.[8] It implies that their behavior might change substantially if the eliciting conditions were varied. This represents an interesting empirical question. Savage-Rumbaugh and Rumbaugh (1978) have come closest to designing experiments that would address this issue. They present a series of experiments in which chimpanzees were required to produce lexigram responses under various carefully controlled contingencies. These happen to have been instrumental, but a similar strategy could be employed to evaluate non-instrumental lexigram usage. This study provides crucial information about the cognitive capacities of chimpanzees. They describe the heroic measures needed in order to train the animals so as to use lexigrams in a non-trivial way. Their procedures involved the step-by-step manipulation of various false associations, position biases, and response strategies over a period of several months and tens of thousands of trials. My own feeling is that it will be very difficult to create conditions under which the ape uses signs non-instrumentally. The conditions in the various ape language experiments afforded the subjects many other ways of using signs, and the fact that they use them instrumentally across a wide range of conditions may reflect a powerful generalization about their behavior.

Another way to introduce very different task demands is to study comprehension rather than production. The strategies that will be effective for one task will not work for the other. Although the comprehension abilities of signing apes have only been assessed superficially, there is one careful study of comprehension in a non-human species. That is Herman, Richards, and Wolz's (1983) elegant study of two bottle-nosed dolphins. The dolphins show an impressive ability to comprehend simple syntactic structures, and are able to follow instructions to move objects around their pool. The strategies that work in the sign production studies are irrelevant to this task. Although the behavior of the dolphins is clear (unlike that of the signing apes), the knowledge and processes that mediate their performance are not. These bear further investigation and comparison to the performance of children and the signing apes. Here I only want to note the possibility that, as long as animal language researchers focus on either comprehension *or* production skills, the potential for creating a non-linguistic, problem-solving environment is very great. Perhaps the most powerful strategy would be to use an integrated approach in which both skills are required. The only study of this type to date is Savage-Rumbaugh and colleagues' research with Austin and Sherman concerning chimpanzees' cooperative tool use (Savage-Rumbaugh, Rumbaugh, & Boysen, 1978).

I have suggested, then, that there never was any evidence that signing apes exhibited linguistic skills. Given this radical conclusion, it is necessary to con-

---

[8] The extreme statement of this hypothesis is that the ape's behavior is similar to that of a dog that has been trained to perform one arbitrary sequence of behaviors before being given a bone, and another before being taken for a walk.

sider why it was so widely believed that they had (indeed, why this is still believed in many quarters). One important factor was the existence of movies and television films documenting the behavior of Washoe and Koko.[9] These appear to provide dramatic evidence of the apes' abilities. Personally I find these films unconvincing and misleading. The Washoe and Koko films invite skepticism about the manner in which particular examples were selected and edited. The filmmaker's methodology is fundamentally inconsistent with that of the scientist. The filmmaker's task is to present the most compelling, cinematic examples consistent with a particular point of view, while the scientist's task is to evaluate a range of behaviors without selective editing of the sample, and without a particular a priori commitment to the results. It is ironic that one of the basic problems in the ape language literature is that the researchers essentially followed the filmmaker's method, relying upon isolated examples consistent with their point of view. The filmed examples of novel combinations are not compelling for exactly the same reason as the published examples. Furthermore, the examples are interpreted through the eyes of the narrator. In the Washoe films, for example, much of the interpretation is provided by Beatrice Gardner, who elaborates Washoe's signing by providing stress and intonation that contribute heavily to the impression that Washoe is talking. In the numerous films of Koko, Patterson provides a running commentary that often appears inconsistent with what is on the screen.[10]

The films illustrate in an extreme fashion the fact that the apes' behaviors have been heavily filtered by researchers committed to a particular point of view. This filtering took at least two forms. One was partial presentation of the behavioral data. This is important because of pragmatic constraints on undertaking independent replication studies (it is for this reason that Terrace et al.'s, (1979), study has had enormous impact, despite its imperfections). Second, few people had the knowledge, either of primates or of sign languages, necessary to interpret the ape researchers' claims. So, for example, when it was falsely claimed that Washoe or Koko learned American Sign Language (ASL), few people knew enough about the language to refute the claim (Seidenberg & Petitto, 1979). Similarly, viewing the apes on film, most observers are dependent upon the commentary of the narrator-translator because they don't know the language and aren't familiar with the behavior of chimpanzees or gorillas. Independently evaluating the apes' behavior under these conditions is extremely difficult, and the

---

[9] These include "The first signs of Washoe," from the public television series "Nova"; "Teaching sign language to the chimpanzee Washoe," a film widely used in teaching; and Barbet Schroeder's documentary film "Koko, a talking gorilla."

[10] It is interesting to observe that viewing the ape films and films of Herman et al.'s (1983) dolphins yield very different subjective experiences. Films of the apes leave a strong impression that they are talking in a very human-like way. The dolphin films do not leave the impression that they are comprehending language, even though they have learned a far more complex skill than the apes. (I am grateful to Thomas Bever for discussion of this point.)

willingness of viewers to draw definitive conclusions about the apes' performance based on these films is difficult to comprehend.

Language and Cognition

In light of these observations, it might seem remarkable that it was so widely believed that signing apes could talk. There are other factors, largely extra-scientific, which can account for this belief, especially among the non-specialist, general public, but they are beyond the scope of this chapter. However, there is another factor that is important to consider. It is abundantly clear that apes are extremely intelligent beings. Given their general intelligence, why *shouldn't* they possess some rudimentary linguistic ability? It is the fact that apes are intelligent that generated the language studies in the first place. This question invites consideration of the studies of the apes' non-linguistic cognitive capacities.

These studies have demonstrated that apes are capable of a wide range of intelligent behaviors. The classic studies of Yerkes and Köhler showed chimpanzees to be able to solve complex problems. In the modern research of this type, Premack (1971; 1976; Premack & Premack, 1983; Woodruff & Premack, 1981; Willan, Premack & Woodruff, 1981) reports that apes can perform a number of complex tasks. Among these are making same-different judgments based on physical identity or common properties of objects; completing analogies (such as key:lock::can-opener:can); identifying causal relations between instruments and objects; and conservation of liquid or solid quantity. Savage-Rumbaugh et al. (1978) describe chimpanzees who can cooperate in order to obtain a common goal, using several tools appropriately. Although not wholly free of methodological and conceptual limitations, these studies present convincing evidence of the chimpanzee's ability to perform a wide range of intelligent tasks. The results of these laboratory studies are also consistent with the picture presented by descriptions of ape behavior under more natural conditions (e.g., Menzel, 1974; van Lawick-Goodall, 1970). Chevalier-Skolnikoff (1976) and Parker and Gibson (1979) observe that lower primates exhibit behaviors that are characteristic of Piaget's stage of sensori-motor intelligence.

Although Premack (1971) and Rumbaugh (1977) originally related their research to the question of language in non-human primates, more recently they have presented it as addressing the "preconditions" (Premack) or "cognitive prerequisites" of language (Savage-Rumbaugh and Rumbaugh). It is for this reason that the above discussion of language largely focused on the signing apes. Their current views are consistent with the Piagetian idea that language emerges out of general cognitive capacities, rather than involving a domain-specific type of knowledge. The question which then arises is this: why should an animal so demonstrably intelligent fail so miserably with regard to language? If these studies of synonymy judgments, analogies, cooperative tool use, and the like are in fact concerned with cognitive skills that are the basis for language acquisition, they leave unanswered exactly why the apes do not progress further in using language. If the Piagetian claim that language emerges out of sensorimotor intelligence is correct, and they possess this intelligence, as Chevalier-Skolnikoff suggests, it is unclear why they do not exhibit linguistic skills comparable to that of a young child. The striking dichotomy between the apes' linguistic and cognitive capacities is the most important finding emerging from these studies and it requires an explanation.

One possibility is that while the view that language acquisition is parasitic upon general cognitive capacities is correct, apes don't possess the right ones. Absence of the "right" prerequisites would then account for the absence of language. It is difficult to evaluate this possibility because of vagueness of theories proposing that language evolves from pre-linguistic cognitive capacities. These theories rely heavily upon metaphors such as the "mapping" of linguistic forms onto non-linguistic actions, or the matching of grammatical forms and actions by "analogy," or the "building up" of linguistic forms from a non-linguistic base (Petitto, 1983). However, one relatively explicit proposal concerns the role of pointing. Werner and Kaplan (1963) and others have identified several types of pointing behavior; here I have in mind the advanced form in which the individual uses a pointing gesture to index an object or location. Indexical referencing of this kind typically involves mutual visual regard of the indexed item, and shared eye gaze and attention. This kind of pointing is distinct from (and emerges after) simpler, non-communicative uses of pointing gestures (e.g., to explore physical space). This form of pointing has been analyzed as the basis for the child's early acquisition of several linguistic forms. According to Clark (1978), the child's knowledge of verbal deictic terms such as *here, there, you,* and *me* emerges directly out of indexical pointing gestures in a natural and continuous progression. Clark (1978) also analyzes pointing gestures as nascent markers of definite and indefinite reference (i.e., the precursors of *the* and *a*). Because pointing functions to direct the adult's attention to objects, events, or people, and to convey requests, Bates, Camaioni, and Volterra (1975) analyze these gestures as protodeclaratives and protoimperatives. Once pointing gestures are firmly established, verbal deictic terms are thought to be mapped onto these "prelinguistic placeholders" (Bruner, 1981).

It appears that chimpanzees and gorillas do not use pointing gestures of this kind (see Parker & Gibson, 1979, p. 373, for discussion). Premack and Premack (1983) observed that pointing emerged among some chimpanzees in the course of learning another task. Although it is not clear whether this behavior was isomorphic with indexical pointing (rather than a simpler type of pointing), this is a potentially important finding, and it bears further investigation. It is clear in any case that indexical pointing is a complex skill that is not part of the natural communicative repertoire of lower primates.

The ape's failure to acquire simple deictic and referential terms could then be seen as secondary to the inability to point. This would at the same time seem to provide support for the idea that language production is parasitic upon non-verbal intelligence. The problem is that it isn't clear that this account of language acquisition will succeed. There are strong arguments against it (see Piatelli-Palmarini, 1980; Gleitman & Wanner, 1982). Specific evidence concerning the role of pointing is available from Petitto's (1983) study of the acquisition of American Sign Language as a first language by two deaf children. Her results strongly argue against the idea that names and deictic terms are "mapped onto" pre-linguistic pointing gestures. The study is decisive because indexical pointing is incorporated within the grammar of the language. The shift from pre-linguistic pointing to speech involves a change in modality, while the shift from pre-linguistic pointing to pointing in ASL does not. This provides a powerful means for testing whether pointing plays a crucial role in early language. If certain early linguistic forms were "mapped onto" indexical pointing, there should be no discontinuity between the pre-linguistic and linguistic uses of pointing in the acquisition of ASL. The deaf child might be expected to show facilitation in the acquisition of lexical items (such as *me* and *you*) which have the same form as pre-linguistic points, compared to hearing children learning spoken forms.

Petitto's basic findings are these. Very young deaf children use pointing gestures prior to the acquisition of any lexical signs (at 10 to 12 months). These include points to self (proto-ME) and other (proto-YOU). Acquisition of a sign vocabulary and the emergence of structured sign combinations closely follow the timetable for hearing children acquiring speech. During this early acquisition phase (approximately 1 to 2 years of age), deaf children continue to use para-linguistic deictic pointing (i.e., points that are not within the vocabulary or grammar of ASL), as do hearing children. However, both deaf children in Petitto's study failed to point to self or other during this period. That is, they did not use the signs *me* or *you*, even though their forms are *identical* to those of self–addressee indexical points that had been used earlier. Instead, they used full lexical items (names) to refer to self or addressee. Thus, a selective function of pointing disappeared for an extended period, even though the children's acquisition of the language was in all other respects normal.

For one child, pointing to the addressee returned at age 22 months, but in a remarkable way. She exhibited a consistent reversal error, thinking that the sign *you* referred to herself. Pronoun reversals of this type have been observed in some hearing children acquiring speech (Chiat, 1982). However, the deaf child's error is dramatic because she would point to another person while referring to herself, despite the transparency of the indexical gesture. She treated the *you* gesture as a name for herself despite the fact that its form is indexical. That is, she oversymbolized. She did not use the *me* gesture at this time, presumably because she already had a sign for indicating herself, namely *you*, and she continued to refer to other persons by name. The second child exhibited sporadic pronoun reversal errors, and other errors (e.g., failure to indicate the referents of third person pronouns; substitutions of *me* for *mine* and *you* for *your*). Complete recovery of the *you* and *me* pointing gestures was not accomplished until 25 months in one child, and 27 months in the other. In sum, neither child showed a smooth transition from the prelinguistic use of self–addressee pointing to the use of these same forms as the signs *me* and *you* in ASL.

Two contrasts between the behavior of these children and that of apes should be noted. First, apes do not show the prelinguistic deictic pointing which deaf children use as early as 10 months of age. Second, during the period when the deaf children did not have control over *you* and *me* pointing, their behavior could not be corrected. Sign languages, with their external articulators, allow for physical manipulation in a way that speech does not. There are amusing examples in Petitto's data of the mothers attempting to "mold" the children's hands into *me* or *you* points. These attempts utterly fail. I do not believe that apes will show this resistance; it was not difficult, for example, to fashion a *me* sign for Nim through molding.

These findings are discussed in greater detail in Petitto (1983). The long period of selective avoidance of pointing to self and others, and the errors that initially occurred when pointing returned are difficult to reconcile with the view that linguistic forms are mapped onto prelinguistic pointing. Were this the case, no loss of the pointing function should have occurred. Furthermore, the child's acquisition of the language proceeded normally despite the disruption in the use of pointing. The reversal errors occurred only because the child had acquired meta-linguistic knowledge of the aribtrary, symbolic relationship between most signs and their referents. Unfortunately, this knowledge fails in the case of the genuinely indexical signs *you* and *me*.

Thus, the fact that lower primates do not engage in referential pointing is important, but if, as Petitto's results suggest, pointing does not itself provide the basis for early language, it will not account for their lack of linguistic skill.

Petitto's results suggest that the child's early language is not elaborated out of mechanisms of sensori-motor intelligence such as pointing. It is rare that the performance of children can be related to this question in such a direct fashion. Her performance data complement other empirical and theoretical arguments bearing on this issue (see Piatelli-Palmarini, 1980, for a summary). The research on the cognitive and linguistic capacities of apes can be seen as providing another source of evidence converging on the view that language is the result of a biologically constrained, species-specific, autonomous faculty. A direct explanation of the disparity between the ape's linguistic and non-linguistic abilities is provided by the hypothesis that language is not merely elaborated out of other cognitive capacities. If language is the expression of a domain-specific faculty—Universal Grmmar in Chomsky's theory—the ape, lacking this faculty, would fail to show the ability to use language even though its other cognitive capacities could be quite sophisticated.

I think that this is the important implication of recent ape research. Studies such as Petitto's provide independent evidence for the existence of a language faculty in humans, as does much other work in theoretical linguistics and language acquisition (see other chapters in this volume). The ape research is also consistent with this evidence. Taken only as addressing the question of linguistic abilities in apes, the sign language research and related studies appear to permit only dishearteningly negative conclusions. Taken in the context of studies of the cognitive capacities of apes, and research on child language acquisition, the data provide positive evidence for the independence of a uniquely human language faculty.

This is not to deny that non-linguistic cognitive capacities play any role in language acquisition. A precise characterization of the interactions among different sources of knowledge is a primary goal of current research. It could also be the case that apes lack cognitive capacities that contribute to the achievement of higher linguistic competence. Further studies of apes may be able to provide additional information concerning both their own capacities, and the bases of language in humans.[11]

---

[11] Since this paper went to press, there have been a number of developments in the animal language area. One was a fresh spasm of mass-media coverage of "talking apes," principally Patterson's gorilla Koko. Patterson's credibility is extremely low because she has effectively placed herself outside the constraints of organized science, since Patterson (1978) has not published her findings in the scientific journals, and her research is funded by a private foundation. Her claims are solely promoted in the mass media, which report them uncritically. Under these conditions, it is not possible to independently verify any of these claims. Anyone persuaded by the coverage in the mass media should have the privilege of watching several uninterrupted minutes of film documenting Patterson's interactions with Koko. Having seen such films, I can report that they leave a very different impression than the 10- or 20-second excerpts presented in television news reports. Similarly, at the 1985 meeting of the American Association for the Advancement of Science, Fouts reported on filmed examples of chimpanzees signing to each other. Again, having seen some of this film, it does not provide the basis for a systematic evaluation of the apes' behavior, for reasons noted in the text.

A second recent development is Savage-Rumbaugh's work with a pygmy chimpanzee who appears to acquire signing skills rapidly and without intensive training. This research is as yet unpublished, but it is certainly promising. Since the chimpanzee learns signing skills more rapidly, the study should eventually provide a much stronger basis for evaluating what has been learned.

References

Anderson, J. R. (1983). *The architecture of cognition*. Cambridge, MA: Harvard University Press.
Bates, E., & MacWhinney, B. (1982). Functionalist approaches to grammar. In E. Wanner & L. Gleitman (Eds.), *Language acquisition: The state of the art*. Cambridge: Cambridge University Press.
Bates, E., Camaioni, L., & Volterra, V. (1975). The acquisition of performatives prior to speech. *Merrill-Palmer Quarterly, 21*, 205–226.
Bellugi, U., & Seidenberg, M. S. (in preparation). *Modality and language*.
Bruner, J. S. (1975). The ontogenesis of speech acts. *Journal of Child Language, 2*, 1–19.

Bruner, J. S. (1981). Harvard University lecture.

Chevalier-Skolnikoff, S. (1976). The ontogeny of primate intelligence and its implications for communicative potential: A preliminary report. In S. Harnad, H. Steklis, & J. Lancaster (Eds.), *Origins and evolution of speech and language. Annals of the New York Academy of Sciences, 280.*

Chiat, S. (1982). If I were you and you were me: the analysis of pronouns in a pronoun-reversing child. *Journal of Child Language, 8,* 75–91.

Chomsky, N. (1978). On the biological basis of language capacities. In G. Miller & E. Lenneberg (Eds.), *Psychology and biology of language and thought: Essays in honor of Eric Lenneberg.* New York: Academic.

Chomsky, N. (1980). Human language and other semiotic systems. In T. A. Sebeok & J. Umiker-Sebeok (Eds.), *Speaking of apes: A critical anthology of two-way communication with man.* New York: Plenum.

Clark, E. V. (1974). Some aspects of the conceptual basis for first language acquisition. In R. L. Schiefelbusch & L. L. Lloyd (Eds.), *Language perspectives—Acquisition, retardation and intervention.* Baltimore, MD: University Park Press.

Clark, E. V. (1978). From gesture to word: On the natural history of deixis in language acquisition. In J. S. Bruner & A. Garton (Eds.), *Human growth and development: Wolfson College lectures 1976.* Oxford: Clarendon Press.

Creedon, M. P. (1973). *Language development in nonverbal autistic children using simultaneous communication system.* Paper presented at the Biennial Meeting of the Society for Research in Child Development.

Deacon, T. W. (1979). *Neural substrates of symbol acquisition.* Unpublished manuscript, Harvard University.

Dennett, D. C. (1983). Intentional systems in cognitive ethology: The "Panglossian paradigm" defended. *Behavioral and Brain Sciences, 6,* 343–390.

Fodor, J. A. (1983). *Modularity of mind.* Cambridge, MA: Bradford-MIT Press.

Fodor, J. A., Bever, T. G., & Garrett, M. F. (1974). *The psychology of language.* New York: MacGraw-Hill.

Fouts, R. S. (1974). Language: origin, definitions, and chimpanzees. *Journal of Human Evolution, 3,* 475–482.

Fouts, R. S. (1975). Capacities for language in great apes. In R. H. Tuttle (Ed.), *Socioecology and psychology of primates.* The Hague: Mouton.

Franks, F. (1981). *Polywater.* Cambridge, MA: MIT Press.

Gardner, B. T. (1981). Review of H. S. Terrace, *Nim: The story of a chimpanzee who learned signed language. Contemporary Psychology, 26,* 422.

Gardner, B. T., & Gardner, R. A. (1971). Two-way communication with an infant chimpanzee. In A. Schrier and F. Stollnitz (Eds.), *Behavior of non-human primates,* Vol. 4. New York: Academic.

Gardner, B. T., & Gardner, R. A. (1974a). Comparing the early utterances of child and chimpanzee. In A. Pick (Ed.), *Minnesota symposium on child psychology,* Vol. 8. Minneapolis: University of Minnesota Press.

Gardner, B. T., & Gardner, R. A. (1975). Evidence for sentence constituents in the early utterances of child and chimpanzee. *Journal of Experimental Psychology: General, 104,* 244–267.

Gardner, B. T., & Gardner, R. A. (1980). Two comparative psychologists look at language acquisition. In K. Nelson (Ed.), *Children's language,* Vol. 2. New York: Gardner.

Gardner, R. A., & Gardner, B. T. (1974b). Review of R. Brown, *A first language. American Journal of Psychology, 87,* 729–736.

Gleitman, L. R., & Wanner, E. (1982). Language acquisition: The state of the art. In E. Wanner & L. R. Gleitman (Eds.), *Language acquisition: The state of the art.* Cambridge: Cambridge University Press.

Gribbin, J., & Cherfas, J. (1982). *The monkey puzzle: Are apes descended from man?* London: Triad-Paladin.

Harlow, H. F. (1958). The nature of love. *American Psychologist, 13*, 673–685.

Harnad, S., Steklis, H., & Lancaster, J. (1976). *Origins and evolution of speech and language. Annals of the New York Academy of Sciences, 280.*

Herman, L. M., Richards, D. G., & Wolz, J. P. (1983). *Comprehension of sentences by bottlenosed dolphins.* Paper presented at the annual meeting of the Psychonomic Society.

Herrnstein, R. J., Loveland, D., & Cable, C. (1976). Natural concepts in pigeons. *Journal of Experimental Psychology: Animal Behavior Processes, 2*, 285–311.

Holloway, R. L. (1976). Paleoneurological evidence for language origins. In S. Harnad, H. Steklis, & J. Lancaster (Eds.), *Origins and evolution of speech and language. Annals of the New York Academy of Sciences, 280.*

King, M. C., & Wilson, A. C. (1975). Evolution at two levels in humans and chimpanzees. *Science, 188*, 107–116.

Köhler, W. (1927). *The mentality of apes.* 2d rev. ed. New York: Vintage.

Konstantareas, J., Oxman, J., & Webster, C. D. (1977). Simultaneous communication with autistic and other severely dysfunctional nonverbal children. *Journal of Communication Disorders, 10*, 267–282.

Lieberman, P. (1968). Primate vocalizations and human linguistic ability. *Journal of the Acoustical Society of America, 44*, 1574–1584.

MacNamara, J. (1983). *Names for things.* Cambridge, MA: Bradford Books-MIT Press.

Malmi, W. A. (1976). Chimpanzees and language evolution. In S. Harnad, H. Steklis, & J. Lancaster (Eds.), *Origins and evolution of speech and language. Annals of the New York Academy of Sciences, 280.*

Menzel, E. W. (1974). A group of chimpanzees in a one-acre field. In A. M. Schrier & F. Stollnitz (Eds.), *Behavior of nonhuman primates*, Vol. 5. New York: Academic.

Miller, G. A. (1962). *Psychology: The science of mental life.* New York: Harper & Row.

Nelson, K. (1974). Concept, word and sentence: Interrelations in acquisition and development. *Psychological Review, 81*, 267–285.

Parker, S. T., & Gibson, K. R. (1979). A developmental model of the evolution of language and intelligence in early hominids. *Behavioral and Brain sciences, 2*,313–366.

Patterson, F. G. (1978). The gestures of a gorilla: Language acquisition in another pongid. *Brain and Language, 5*, 72–97.

Patterson, F. G. (1980a). Innovative uses of language by a gorilla: A case study. In K. Nelson (Ed.), *Children's language*, Vol. 2. New York: Gardner.

Patterson, F. G. (1980b). More on Nim Chimpsky. *New York University Education Quarterly, 11*, 33.

Petitto, L. A. (1983). *From gesture to symbol: The relationship between form and meaning in the acquisition of personal pronouns in American Sign Language.* Unpublished Ph.D. dissertation. Cambridge, MA: Harvard University.

Pfungst, O. (1911). *Clever Hans, The Horse of Mr. von Osten.* New York: Holt.

Piaget, J. (1955). *The language and thought of the child.* Cleveland: World Publishing Co.

Piaget, J. (1980). The psychogenesis of knowledge and its epistemological significance. In M. Piattelli-Palmarini (Ed.), *Language and learning: The debate between Jean Piaget and Noam Chomsky.* Cambridge, MA: Harvard University Press.

Piattelli-Palmarini, M. (Ed.). (1980). *Language and learning: The debate between Jean Piaget and Noam Chomsky.* Cambridge, MA: Harvard University Press.

Ploog, D., & Melnechuk, T. (Eds.). (1969). Primate communication. *Neurosciences Research Program Bulletin, 7*, 419–510.

Premack, D. (1971). Language in chimpanzee? *Science, 172*, 808–822.

Premack, D. (1976). *Intelligence in ape and man.* Hillsdale, NJ: Erlbaum.

Premack, D., & Premack, A. J. (1983). *The mind of an ape.* New York: Norton.

Reynolds, P. C. (1981). *On the evolution of human behavior.* Berkeley, CA: University of California Press.

Rosch, E. (1973). On the internal structure of perceptual and semantic categories. In T. E. Moore (Ed.), *Cognitive development and the acquisition of language.* New York: Academic.

Rumbaugh, D. M. (1977). *Language learning by a chimpanzee: The LANA project.* New York: Academic.

Rumbaugh, D. M., & Gill, T. V. (1976). The mastery of language-type skills by the chimpanzee (*Pan*). In S. Harnad, H. Steklis, & J. Lancaster (Eds.), *Origins and evolution of speech and language. Annals of the New York Academy of Sciences, 280.*

Sarich, V., & Wilson, A. (1967). An immunological timescale for hominid evolution. *Science, 158,* 1200–1203.

Savage-Rumbaugh, E. S., & Rumbaugh, D. M. (1978). Symbolization, language and chimpanzees: A theoretical reevaluation based on initial language acquisition processes in four young *Pan Troglodytes. Brain and Language, 6,* 265–300.

Savage-Rumbaugh, E. S., Rumbaugh, D. M., & Boysen, S. (1978). Symbolic communication between two chimpanzees (*Pan Troglodytes*). *Science, 201,* 641–644.

Sebeok, T. A. (1980). Looking in the destination for what should have been sought in the source. In T. A. Sebeok & J. Umiker-Sebeok (Eds.), *Speaking of apes: A critical anthology of two-way communication with man.* New York: Plenum.

Seidenberg, M. S. (1983). Steps toward an ethological science. *Behavioral and Brain Sciences, 6,* 377.

Seidenberg, M. S., & Petitto, L. A. (1979). Signing behavior in apes: A critical review. *Cognition, 7,* 177–215.

Seidenberg, M. S., & Petitto, L. A. (1981). Ape signing: Problems of method and interpretation. *Annals of the New York Academy of Sciences, 364,* 115–130.

Seyfarth, R. M., & Cheney, D. L. (1980). The ontogeny of vervet alarm calling behavior: A preliminary report. *Zeitschrift für Tierpsychologie, 54,* 37–56.

Seyfarth, R. M., Cheney, D. L., & Marler, P. (1980). Vervet monkey alarm calls: Evidence for predator classification and semantic communication. *Science, 210,* 801–803.

Skinner, B. F. (1957). *Verbal behavior.* New York: Appleton-Century-Crofts.

Struhsaker, T. T. (1967). Auditory communication among vervet monkeys (*Cercopithecus aethiops*). In S. A. Altmann (Ed.), *Social communication among primates.* Chicago: University of Chicago Press.

Tanner, N., & Zihlman, A. (1976). The evolution of human communications: What can primates tell us? In S. Harnad, H. Steklis, & J. Lancaster (Eds.), *Origins and evolution of speech and language. Annals of the New York Academy of Sciences, 280.*

Terrace, H. S., Petitto, L. A., Sanders, R. J., & Bever, T. G. (1979). Can an ape create a sentence? *Science, 206,* 891–902.

Umiker-Sebeok, J., & Sebeok, T. A. (1980). Questioning apes. In T. A. Sebeok & J. Umiker-Sebeok (Eds.), *Speaking of apes: A critical anthology of two-way communication with man.* New York: Plenum.

Van Cantfort, T. E., & Rimpau, J. B. (1982). Sign language studies with children and chimpanzees. *Sign Language Studies, 34,* 15–72.

van Lawick-Goodall, J. (1970). Tool-using in primates and other vertebrates. In D. S. Lehrman, R. A. Hinde, & E. Shaw (Eds.), *Advances in the study of behavior,* Vol. 3. New York: Academic.

Walker, S. (1983). *Animal thought.* London: Routledge & Kegan Paul.

Wasserman, E. A. (1981). Comparative psychology returns: A review of Hulse, Fowler and Honig's *Cognitive processes in animal behavior. Journal of the Experimental Analysis of Behavior, 35,* 243–257.

Werner, H., & Kaplan, B. (1963). *Symbol formation.* New York: Wiley.

Wescott, R. W. (1974). *Language origins.* Silver Spring, MD: Linstok Press.

Willan, D. J., Premack, D., & Woodruff, G. (1981). Reasoning in the chimpanzee: I. Analogical reasoning. *Journal of Experimental Psychology: Animal Behavior Processes, 7,* 1–17.

Woodruff, G., & Premack, D. (1981). Primitive mathematical concepts in the chimpanzee: Proportionality and numerosity. *Nature, 293,* 568–570.

Yerkes, R. M. (1925). *Almost human.* New York: Century.

Chapter 3
Productivity and Conservatism in Language Acquisition*

Steven Pinker
Massachusetts Institute of Technology

When a child learns a language, the task he or she faces is to generalize beyond the finite sample of input sentences to the correct infinite set that defines the adult language. That task is especially difficult because the child has no access to information about which strings of words are *not* sentences in the language. Certainly no one deliberately presents children with ungrammatical strings labelled as such. And as far as we know, (a) parents do not systematically correct their children when the children speak ungrammatically; (b) parents are no more likely to misunderstand their children when they speak ungrammatically; (c) when parents do correct their children, the corrections are contingent on the truth value of the child's utterance rather than its well-formedness; and (d) on those rare occasions when children *are* corrected for speaking ungrammatically, they do not take the corrections to heart (Brown & Hanlon, 1970; Braine, 1971). The reason that this lack of "negative evidence" makes the language acquisition task difficult is the following. Imagine that the child is a rational hypothesis tester in that he or she never rejects the current hypothesis if that hypothesis is consistent with all the data heard. In that case any hypothesis that generates all the sentences in the language plus some sentences not in the language will never be rejected by the child. That is because the input data, lacking direct information about which strings are ungrammatical, cannot disconfirm such hypotheses (Gold, 1967; Osherson, Stob, & Weinstein, in press; see Pinker, 1979, for review and discussion). Figure 1(a) uses Venn diagrams to illustrate the child's problem; "H" refers to the set of sentences generated by the child's hypothesis grammar; "T" refers to the set of sentences in the target (adult) language. Figure 1(b–d) illustrate other situations in which this problem does *not* arise: when a hypothesis language is less inclusive than the correct language; when the two languages

---

* Preparation of this paper was supported by NSF grants BNS 82-16546 and BNS 82-19450 and by NIH grant 1 R01 HD 18381, and by a grant from the Sloan Foundation to the MIT Center for Cognitive Science. I thank my former collaborator, David Lebeaux, for his help in formulating some of the positions described here, and Susan Carey and Dan Osherson for helpful comments.

partially intersect; or when they are disjoint. In all three cases the child can be made aware of his or her mistakes by positive data alone.

The Conservatism Hypothesis

Many theorists have attempted to explain the child's success at language acquisition despite this daunting logical problem by proposing that the child obeys a "monotonicity condition" on the hypotheses he or she entertains. Specifically, it has been claimed that in many domains of grammar there are series of hypotheses available to the child such that each grammar generates all the sentences that are generated by the previous grammar in the series plus some sentences not generated by the previous grammar. None of these grammars generates any ungrammatical sentences. It is claimed that the child hypothesizes the earliest grammar (i.e., smallest language) that is consistent with the input data, and then abandons that grammar when some input sentence is encountered that the grammar cannot generate. In this way, the child does not have to worry about abandoning overgenerating grammars in the absence of negative evidence; he or she never entertains an overgenerating grammar to begin with. Language development would thus consist of a process of progressing from the most restrictive and conservative hypothesis about the target language to increasingly inclusive and nonrestrictive hypotheses, without ever considering an overly inclusive hypothesis.

Naturally, not all hypotheses can be arranged in an inclusiveness hierarchy, because many languages neither properly contain nor are properly contained by other languages. The child is conservative with regard to his or her selection of hypotheses from classes of hypotheses that do generate nested sets. In terms of Figure 2, in which hypotheses are arranged in a multi-rooted tree in which a hypothesis at a mother node is a proper subset of its daughter nodes and sister nodes are disjoint or partially intersecting, the conservatism conjecture would restrict the child to exploring the tree of hypotheses from the roots down.

Versions of this hypothesis can be found in many discussions of language

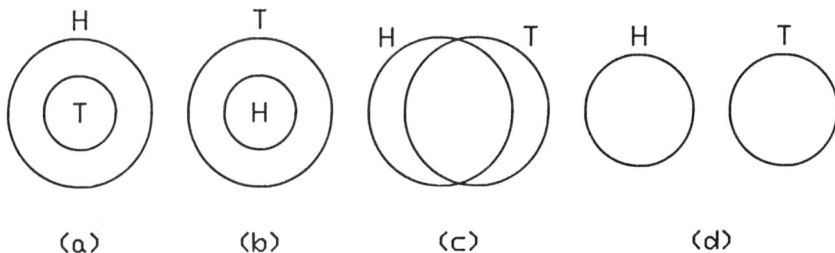

Figure 1.

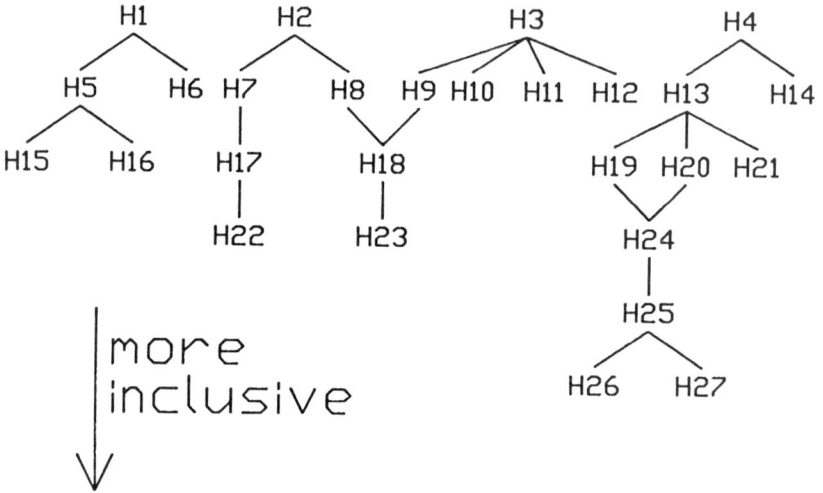

Figure 2.

acquisition. Probably the most widely discussed was suggested by Baker (1979; see also Maratsos, 1978, and Bresnan, 1978). Baker considered how the child might exploit certain regularities in the language to generalize beyond the information given. For example, the child might observe pairs of sentences such as (1a) and (1b) below and coin a general dativization rule that transforms structures like (1a) into structures like (1b). That would subsequently allow him or her to hear a sentence such as (1c) and generalize that (1d) is also in the language, without ever having heard (1d) in the input. The problem, Baker pointed out, is that these generalizations are seldom exceptionless, as is shown in (1e) and (1f). A child applying a productive dative rule to (1e) would mistakenly generate (1f), and no evidence in the input would ever show him or her the error. Hence Baker suggested that perhaps children enter certain verb subcategorization frames into their grammars as those frames are exemplified by input sentences, and only use the verbs in sentences corresponding to those frames. That is, the child would *not* apply productive rules such as dativization; he or she would simply learn the subcategorization frames exemplified in (1a–e) when they are heard in the input; (1f) would never be hypothesized because it is never heard.[1]

---

[1] Baker originally argued that this account also favored a characterization of the dative alternation as lexical rather than transformational. However, the issues concerning productivity and conservatism are largely independent of the debate over the best characterization of the productive rule in question (see Pinker, 1982, 1984; and Wasow, 1981).

(1a) John gave the ball to Mary.
(1b) John gave Mary the ball.
(1c) John told the story to Mary.
(1d) John told Mary the story.
(1e) John announced the news to Mary.
(1f) *John announced Mary the news.

There are many other proposals that also have the child hypothesize rules in this conservative fashion. Wexler (1979; Wexler & Culicover, 1980) raises the possibility that children are born with the full set of surface filters possible in any language (see Chomsky & Lasnik, 1977), and then discard them one by one as sentences violating each one are heard. Similar proposals have been made concerning the set of possible "bounding nodes" that define domains of subjacency in long-distance binding constructions in different ways for different languages: the child would at first assume that all the universally possible bounding nodes are indeed bounding nodes in the language, and would strike individual bounding nodes off the list as he or she encountered input sentences with filler-gap dependencies spanning those nodes. Baker (1981) and Pinker (1984) have proposed that children extend inflectional and positional privileges to individual auxiliaries when a given auxiliary is heard in the input as possessing a given privilege, and only then. Lapointe (1981) and Pinker (1984) argue that children assume that the target language is configurational and has a fixed constituent order unless they witness sentences violating phrasal coherence or sets of sentences exemplifying word order freedom. Jakubowicz (1983) argues that children at first require pronouns, like anaphors, to be bound locally, and loosen that restriction when they hear pronouns that are locally free. Dell (1981) suggests that children adopt a more restrictive setting for a certain parameterized phonological rule as the default assumption. In fact, both he and Berwick and Weinberg (1983) have elevated the narrowest-first property to a general principle of language acquisition, which Berwick and Weinberg call the "subset principle."[2] In sum, versions of the conservatism hypothesis are widespread in contemporary debates on language acquisition, and it behooves us to examine their viability.

---

[2] Note that most of these proposals concern sets of rules in a given grammatical domain or component, rather than sets of whole grammars. Thus within a component, a given rule can be said to be more restrictive than another if it generates a subset of the sentences that the other rule generates, holding the rest of the grammar constant. Usually it is assumed that the grammar as a whole consists of components that interact minimally with one another. To the extent that these interactions are truly minimal, rules that can be ordered in terms of restrictiveness when they are considered as part of one grammar will be ordered in the same way when they are considered as part of some other grammar. That is why it is possible to talk of the relative restrictiveness of indidivual rules in the same breath as one talks of the relative restrictiveness of individual grammars.

The Conservatism Hypothesis and the Facts of Language Development

The conservatism hypothesis makes a strong prediction about the course of acquisition in children: children should never possess a rule capable of generating a superset of the sentences generable by the adult rule. Under the strongest version of the hypothesis, it predicts that children should never make grammatical mistakes (excluding cases of speech errors, processing limitations, etc.) at a point in development in which they are also producing a correct alternative to the mistake. Thus one can evaluate the conservatism hypothesis empirically by verifying whether children make the relevant sorts of errors.

Developmental Evidence Consistent with the Conservatism Hypothesis

Cases where the child could easily make some overinclusive error, given the seductiveness of the generalization opportunity presented by the data, but does not, are prima facie support for the conservatism hypothesis. Unfortunately, despite the vast number of facts noted about children's language development, we do not have anything like the degree of documentation on children's possible but nonoccurring errors that we would need to evaluate the hypothesis fully. The reason is obvious: unlike errors, which leap out of transcripts of children's speech and can be cited by any parent, possible but nonoccurring errors can only be documented when one actively looks for some type of error and fails to find it. And there are still few theories of language acquisition that are precise enough to generate developmental predictions about which sorts of errors should never occur. Nonetheless, there are at least a fair number of cases in which one can say with some confidence that acquisition of a rule proceeds from the specific to the general, with no overgenerating rules in the intermediate stages. Maratsos (1978, in press; Maratsos & Chalkley, 1981) was the first developmental psycholinguist to call attention to children's errorless acquisition of many rules, and in Pinker (1984) I attempt to list other such cases. Here are some striking examples:

- Children learning fixed constituent order languages do not go through a stage in which they act as if their language had free constituent order. However, children learning languages with some constituent order freedom have been known to pass through stages in which they utter only a subset of the permissible orders (Braine, 1976; Brown, 1973; Pinker, 1984).
- Children learning a configurational language do not go through a stage in which they act as if their language was nonconfigurational. That is, they do not utter sentences with words dislocated from their phrases (e.g. an adjective separated from the head noun it modifies by intervening words belonging to a verb phrase; Pinker, 1984).

- Children never invert main verbs in questions; they do not invert auxiliaries and quasi-auxiliaries that are uninvertible or rarely inverted in adult speech (e.g. *better, might*); they never directly negate nonauxiliaries (e.g. **I ate not; *I aten't*). Furthermore, they often refuse to invert auxiliaries that are invertable in the adult language (Major, 1974; Kuczaj & Maratsos, 1979; Wells, 1979; Pinker, 1984).
- Children make few errors whereby they simultaneously assign a word to its correct syntactic category plus some incorrect syntactic category (Maratsos & Chalkley, 1981; Maratsos, in press; Macnamara, 1982).
- Children do not inflect auxiliaries, nor utter them in ungrammatical sequences (Baker, 1981; Major, 1974; Pinker, 1984).
- When young children use complement-taking verbs such as *want* or *tell*, they do not allow the understood complement subject to corefer with the matrix subject if there is a matrix object present, nor with some argument not listed in the sentence (Bloom, Lightbown, & Hood, 1975; Pinker, 1984).
- It is difficult to find cases in which children seem to adopt faulty rules of agreement that force elements to agree with other elements that they do not govern (Pinker, 1984).

Developmental Evidence That May not Be Consistent with the Conservatism Hypothesis

Recently it has been pointed out that cases such as those summarized above, where the child fails to make tempting overgeneralizations, may be the rule rather than the exception in language development (e.g. Maratsos, 1983; Maratsos & Chalkley, 1981; Pinker, 1982). If so, it would certainly be consistent with the conservatism hypothesis. However, it would be preposterous to maintain that children *never* make systematic errors; any parent can recite cases of obvious errors during language development, and the literature is full of more carefully documented reports. Here is a haphazard sample of error patterns that have been recorded:

- Children the world over pass through stages in which they fail to respect distinctions made in the morphology of their language. For example, they use a single inflection for both genders, or use the wrong case for one of the verb's arguments, or fail to differentiate complementizers for the finiteness or polarity of their complements (Slobin, 1973, 1984).
- Children often overgeneralize productive rules of inflection to exceptional stems (Ervin, 1964; Slobin, 1984).
- Children at first fail to use a variety of obligatory closed-class morphemes in their speech (Brown, 1973). In the case of obligatory complementizers like *to*, children often omit them for some matrix verbs (e.g., as in *I want go*) while including them for others (Bloom, Tackeff, & Lahey, 1984). Since

English contains some matrix verbs that allow complementizers and others that do not, the omissions in these cases could be the result of an actively formulated faulty hypothesis, rather than an across-the-board obliviousness to a particular morpheme (Pinker, 1984).

- Children often fail to invert subject and auxiliary in English wh-questions (Brown, 1968), and they often invert subject and auxiliary for the quasi-wh-word how come which does not permit inversion (Kuczaj & Brannick, 1979).

Of course, childhood errors are only counterexamples to the conservatism hypothesis if the child generates both them and their correct alternatives. In many of the cases cited above, the child does pass through a stage in which he or she uses both the correct and incorrect forms in free variation and hence is most likely not entertaining strictly nested hypothesis languages. This has been documented clearly in the case of extending regular inflectional morphology to irregular stems (Brown, 1973; Ervin, 1964; Kuczaj, 1981) and in underdifferentiating inflectional morphology (Slobin, 1973), and in the acquisition of obligatory closed-class morphemes, which are often used sometimes and omitted sometimes over an extended period of time (Brown, 1973). In many of these cases, however, simultaneous use of both correct and incorrect forms follows a stage of near-exclusive use of the one of the two forms, and such cases could represent the temporary survival of a to-be-expunged rule during a transitional period from one hypothesis to another, rather than a stable interim hypothesis. If so, conservatism would not be violated. But in the case of inversion in wh-questions, the child appears to have a truly optional rule right from the start (Erreich, 1984; Pinker, 1984): children invert some of the time, and fail to invert some of the time, both in wh-questions and in yes-no questions. Thus there seems to be at least one case in which children entertain an overly inclusive grammar; and the long duration of some of the "transitional" periods in the acquisition of morphology suggests that overly inclusive hypotheses might be held there as well. If so, a strong conservatism hypothesis would be empirically false.

Evidence for Productivity in the Acquisition of Verb Subcategorizations

Some of the most dramatic cases of productivity, including productivity that leads to overinclusiveness, can be found for the case that inspired the clearest and most widely discussed conservative learning mechanism, that for verb subcategorizations. There is good evidence both from records of spontaneous speech and from controlled experiments that children often produce verbs in argument frames that they never heard exemplified in the input. In each case the child's error is not random, but there is some pattern in English as a whole that seduces the child into making a generalization that can be overapplied; that is, the child applies the regularity to legitimate and illegitimate cases alike, thereby generating too large a language. The regularities in the input to the child, and the name of the associated rules, are listed in (2); some of the nonexperimental evidence for nonconservatism or productivity, originally summarized in Pinker (1984), is listed in (3).

(2a) Passive:
> John liked Mary
> Mary was liked by John

(2b) Dative:
> John gave a book to Mary
> John gave Mary a book

(2c) Causative:
> The door opened
> John opened the door

(2d) "Figure/Ground Reversal":
> I loaded hay onto the wagon
> I loaded the wagon with hay

(2e) Denominalization:
> I formatted the file using Nroff
> I Nroffed the file

(3a) I don't like being falled down on! (Wasow, 1981)
> He's gonna die you, David. The tiger will come and eat David and then he will be died and I won't have a brother any more (Bowerman, 1982a)
> I think it's not fulled up to the top (Slobin, 1985)
> I don't want to get waded (Tom Roeper, personal communication)
> I don't want to get waved over (Tom Roeper, personal communication)
> Is it all needled? (Clark, 1982)
> How was it shoelaced? (Clark, 1982)
> It was bandaided (Clark, 1982)
> But I need it watered and soaped [talking about a rag for washing a car] (Clark, 1982)
> I don't want to be dogeared today [asking for her hair not to be arranged in "dogears"] (Clark, 1982)

(3b) I'll brush him his hair (Mazurkewich & White, 1984)
> Mummy, open Hadwen the door (Mazurkewich & White, 1984)
> You please write me lady (Pinker, 1984; unpublished data from Roger Brown)
> I go write you something (Pinker, 1984; unpublished data from Roger Brown)
> When Fraser come back he goin' write me another snowman (Pinker, 1984; unpublished data from Roger Brown)
> I said her no (Bowerman, 1983)
> Don't say me that or you'll make me cry (Bowerman, 1983)
> Button me the rest [of the snaps on her pajamas] (Bowerman, 1983)
> Put Eva the yukky one first [of two types of medicine] (Bowerman, 1983)

(3c) Mommy, can you stay this open? (Bowerman, 1982a)
      Who deaded my kitty cat? (Bowerman, 1982a)
      I come it closer so it won't fall. (Bowerman, 1982a)
      Will you climb me up there and hold me. (Bowerman, 1982a)
      Are you gonna nice yourself? (Bowerman, 1982a)

(3d) Feel your hand to that. (Bowerman, 1982b)
      Can I fill some salt into the bear? (Bowerman, 1982b)
      I'm going to cover a screen over me. (Bowerman, 1982b)
      I poured you . . . with water. (Bowerman, 1982b; my ellipses)
      I don't want it because I spilled it of orange juice (Bowerman, 1982b)

(3e) Don't broom my mess (Clark, 1982)
      I'm crackering my soup (Clark, 1982)
      That truck is cementing (Clark, 1982)
      The buzzer is buzzering (Clark, 1982)
      It's snowflaking so hard that you can't see this person (Clark, 1982)

Experimental Evidence for Productivity in the Acquisition of Passive and Dative Forms

There is also experimental evidence for potentially error-producing productivity in children. In collaboration with Jess Gropen, David Lebeaux, Annie Zaenen, Ronald Wilson, and Loren Ann Frost, I have conducted a set of studies in which we taught children novel verbs by performing an action (using small toys) for which there was no English verb, and narrating the action using the novel verb in a single grammatical context. For example, we taught children the verb *to flose*, which could mean, depending on the condition, to leapfrog over (action predicates), to hear with the help of an ear trumpet (perception predicates), or to suspend (spatial predicates). These predicates were embedded either exclusively in active sentences, or exclusively in passive sentences (depending on the condition and child); after the child seemed to have learned the predicate, we tested his or her ability to comprehend it, both in the voice taught and the voice not taught. We tested comprehension in the standard way, by uttering active or passive sentences containing the verb and having the child act them out with toys. We also tried to induce the child to produce active and passive sentences with each predicate, by acting out a scenario and asking the child to describe what was happening, focusing on the agent or the patient when asking the question (i.e., "Look at the x [x = agent or patient]. Can you tell me what's happening with the x?"). The production task was administered before the comprehension task (since the latter involved presenting the child with the form that we wanted to see him or her produce); all actions were reversible with the toys we used; and word form, pairing of words with actions, pairing of actions with voice taught, and order of training of voices were all counterbalanced, as were the most important combinations of these factors. Some of the results (expressed

as percent correct) from the children between 4 and 5½ years of age are reproduced below in (4). Means representing productive performance are shown in
italics.

(4)

ACTION VERBS (Lebeaux & Pinker, 1981)

PRODUCTION:

	Voice Taught	
Voice Tested	active	passive
active	.94	.84
passive	..59	.62

COMPREHENSION:

	Voice Taught	
Voice tested	active	passive
active		
passive	(all > .97)	

PERCEPTION VERBS (Lebeaux & Pinker, 1981)

PRODUCTION:

	Voice Taught	
Voice Tested	active	passive
active	.97	.88
passive	.69	.94

COMPREHENSION:

	Voice Taught	
Voice Tested	active	passive
active		
passive	(all > .97)	

SPATIAL VERBS (Pinker & Frost, 1983)

PRODUCTION:

	Voice Taught	
Voice Tested	active	passive
active	.88	.63
passive	.25	.63

COMPREHENSION:

	Voice Taught	
Voice Tested	active	passive
active	.81	1.00
passive	.88	.50

It is quite clear from these data that preschool children have a productive rule of passivization that they can use to generate a passive sentence with a given verb even if the input data up to that point had only included active sentences with that verb, and vice-versa.[3] As such, the child is taking the risk of generating a form that, for all he or she knows, may be ungrammatical in adult English. Though virtually all actional verbs have passive participial counterparts in adult English, there are many nonactional verbs that do not, such as *cost, weigh, contain, resemble, have*, and the nonactional senses of *touch, elude*, and *escape*. Even generalizations in the reverse direction, from passive to active, are at least in principle hazardous, since (according to some analyses) *rumor* (as in *it is rumored that Kennedy will run*) is a verb that exists only in the passive form.

We have also discovered that children can create dative subcategorization frames of the form *V—Direct Object—to—Indirect Object* having heard a predicate only in the context *V—Indirect Object—Direct Object*, and, more rarely, vice-versa (Wilson, Pinker, Zaenen, & Lebeaux, 1981). This time the novel verbs denoted an act of transfer using a special instrument (e.g. a type of lazy-Susan, with which one animal could send a second animal to a third). We used one or the other version of the dative alternation exclusively to describe the action during the training phases, and, in the production test, we fished for *to* dative and double-object dative forms from the child by focusing on the recipient or the patient, respectively, when we asked him or her to describe an event we acted out. (This manipulation, like the one we used for the experiments on passivization, was intended to exploit the felicity conditions attached to the alternative grammatical forms so as to induce children to produce them on cue if their grammar permitted the forms at all.) The results were clouded by the fact that preschool children have a great deal of difficulty in using or comprehending double-object forms with lexical, animate patients.[4] Thus performance was rotten with all double-object forms, including *give* which we included as a control, and the productivity that we did observe (in the condition where the double-object form was taught, and the *to* form produced) could not have been the result of applying a productive rule generalizing from one subcategorization frame to another.[5] But it is productivity all the same, and potentially risky productivity, since some verbs in adult English such as *envy, begrudge, bet, and*

---

[3] Whether this rule is best characterized as a transformational rule, a lexical rule, or a pair of rules, one lexical, one transformational, was not addressed in those studies; see Footnote 1.

[4] In experiments currently in progress, Jess Gropen and I have been trying to improve children's baseline performance with the double-object form in general, using existing verbs such as *show*. Following such practice children do use productive double-object forms of verbs heard only in the *to* object form.

[5] That is because the children had not mastered the double-object form that would have to serve as the input to the productive rule. Instead, I argue in Pinker (1984) that the productive mechanism is one that maps from thematic roles to grammatical relations, rather than from one lexical form to another. See Williams (1981) for further arguments for a mechanism of this sort.

cost exist only in the double-object form. The data are reproduced below in (5); as before, means representing productive performance are reproduced in italics.[6]

(5)

TRANSFER VERBS

PRODUCTION:

		Form Taught	
Form Tested		to	double object
to		.87	.75
double object		.03	.06

COMPREHENSION:

		Form Taught	
Form Tested		to	double object
to		1.00	1.00
double object		.03	.06

Why Children Can't Always Be Conservative

It should come as no surprise that children have been found to overgenerate in some of these cases, because one can often show that an acquisition strategy that never overgenerated would be psychologically implausible. Consider what the child must do to acquire inflectional morphology. Languages can force elements to be inflected for a variety of features, such as case, gender, number, person, animacy, humanness, shape, definiteness, social status, tense, aspect, modality, mood, polarity, and so on. Individual languages draw on some subset of these features to encode their morphology, so the child has no a priori way of knowing what an inflected element is inflected for. Certainly the child cannot tell by examining a word or sentence from the input in isolation. Furthermore, even if one assumes that the input to the child consists not only of parental sentences but also of some encoding of the intended meaning of the sentences extracted from their nonlinguistic contexts, it is still hard to show how the child induces his or her language's morphology-relevant features. The problem is that inflections are usually *obligatory*; hence the child cannot infer the features encoded in an inflection by attending to the pragmatically salient parts of the

---

[6] Children were also productive in a way not shown in these tables. When they failed to use the double-object form in production despite the pragmatic bias we attempted to set up, they used the *to* object form most of the time even if they had been exposed only to the double-object form. When they erred in acting out the double-object form in the comprehension test, most of the time they acted out the sentence as if it had a *to* inserted between the two postverbal noun phrases. Thus children's performance in the conditions corresponding to the lower right hand cells in each matrix can also be considered to be productive if we take the nature of the errors as further evidence that the children had concocted *to* object forms having heard only their double-object counterparts.

parent's intended message. For example, when a parent says *the dog wants his supper*, there is nothing in the perceptual or communicative context that signals to the child that the suffix on *want* encodes present tense, imperfective aspect, and third person singular subject—the parent encodes these features because the language forces him or her to do so, not because he or she necessarily wishes for the child to know about their current values.

How then, should the child proceed if he or she must avoid making errors? The only choice is for him or her is to assume as a default that an unknown affix encodes *all* the potentially grammatically relevant feature values that are true of the current sentence in context. That is, for the child to be able to hypothesize right away that *wants* is sensitive to present tense, imperfective aspect, and third person singular subject (which he or she must do to avoid saying *I wants supper* and the like), it is hard to see how he or she could avoid also assuming that it is sensitive to nonhuman animate definite subject, indicative mood, affirmative polarity, declarative sentence modality, third person singular indefinite nonhuman inanimate mass object, and so on. That way he or she would avoid overgenerating (since he or she would simply avoid using the word in any context whose feature values conflicted with the ones that were true of the sentence in which the item was originally learned), and can eliminate all the spurious features (e.g., the one specifying an inanimate object) when they are counterexemplified in future input sentences (such as when *wants* occurs with an animate definite count noun as its object). The child would gradually expand his or her usage of the inflected word until it coincided with adult usage, without ever overgenerating or requiring negative evidence.

Clearly, this model is a nonstarter. Even if one believes that there are severe constraints on the set of morphologically encodable features (e.g., Slobin, 1985; Talmy, 1978), and on the possible governing configurations that sanction the agreement of one element with the features of some other element (e.g. Bresnan, 1982; Chomsky, 1981), the set of possible features that the child must entertain at one time under this "exhaustive hypothesization" model is still large enough to strain credulity. For example, I have calculated that for some extremely simple inputs the child would have to keep in mind at one time as many as 120 feature constraints (Pinker, 1984). Furthermore, the empirical evidence is fatal to such a model, and not only because of the fact that children often nonconservatively use closed-class morphemes in inappropriate contexts. The exhaustive model predicts that affixes encoding more information should be mastered earlier than affixes encoding less information, because in the former case fewer of the incorrect features that had been hypothesized from early inputs would have to be expunged by later inputs. Brown (1973) has shown that the opposite happens: the more complex an affix, the later children supply it in obligatory contexts.

Obviously, in the case of the acquisition of inflectional morphology and other closed class morphemes, the child does not adopt a strategy that prevents him or her from ever overgenerating. This strategy would have to be psychologically implausible, because the less inclusive hypotheses are far more demanding of memory space and processing resources than more inclusive hypotheses. In principle that does leave him or her vulnerable to permanent overgeneration in the absence of negative evidence—for example, nothing in the input strictly contradicts a simple but overgenerating hypothesis that *want* and *wants* alternate in free variation. And so it is with all the other cases of overgeneration cited in the previous section. We know that children do not invariably adhere to a conservative learning strategy, but that leaves us without a solution to the original problem.

Two Nonconservative Mechanisms that Recover from Overgeneration

In attempting to formulate a theory that accounts for the acquisition of grammars in a manner consistent with the facts of human language development, I have proposed two mechanisms that allow the child to recover from errors and acquire less inclusive languages without adopting a least-inclusive-first strategy. The first mechanism can acquire rules that are more conservative than ones the child already has; the second in effect changes the class of learnable languages so that nested subclasses of languages are excluded.[7]

---

[7] There is a type of nonconservative mechanism that children conceivably might use to recover from overgeneration that I will not discuss here. It is occasionally conjectured that children could be sensitive to the nonoccurrence of particular forms in the input, and could conclude that if such forms do not occur within some maximum temporal interval, they must be ungrammatical (e.g., Chomsky, 1981). It is hard to evaluate this "indirect negative evidence" conjecture, since no one has proposed a precise formulation of it. Any such formulation must deal with the following problem: language use is highly creative, and so the forms that a child will hear in any reasonable interval will be only a sample of the forms permitted in the language. A form may not have occurred in parental speech because it is ungrammatical *or* because one's parents may not have had the occasion to use the form yet. Any viable "indirect negative evidence" hypothesis must specify for which forms the child monitors the frequency of occurrence, and what criterion the child uses to decide when to declare a nonoccurring form to be ungrammatical. See Wexler (1981), Mazurkewich and White (1983), and Pinker (1984) for further discussion.

The child could use the presence of form A in the input as evidence that the absence in the input of a related form B is due to B being ungrammatical (i.e., the presence of A could indicate that opportunities to utter B are not vanishingly rare, e.g., for different versions of the dative). That might appear to be a version of indirect negative evidence in that the absence of B in the input leads the child to a hypothesis that excludes B from his or her language. This, however, would broaden the meaning of "indirect negative evidence" to encompass virtually any strategy that uses positive evidence to expand the hypothesis language—in the absence of that bit of positive evidence, the hypothesized language would have been smaller. For example, conservatism strategies would all be construed as using indirect negative evidence. It would appear to be more useful to restrict the term to cases where some piece of collateral evidence, such as frequency of a related form or elapsed time, rather than the mere presence of an alternative form, is the crucial event causing the child to rule out forms that have not yet occurred.

Constraint Sampling

In the case of inflectional morphology discussed above (and, for that matter, in the case of the acquisition of closed-class morphemes in general), we were faced with the absurdity of a model that first hypothesized the largest possible set of constraints for an affix and then whittled the set down as each constraint was counterexemplified in subsequent inputs. But it is not necessary to have the child hypothesize an exhaustive set of constraints in order to show how he or she can discover features that are not signaled pragmatically, semantically, phonologically, etc. Imagine that the child had a mechanism of the following sort. Every time an inflectable element in the input is processed, the child adds a *single* feature constraint to the lexical entry for that element. That constraint is randomly assembled within the following boundary conditions: (a) all constraints must be admissible according to Universal Grammar; (b) all the features and government relations that potentially can be encoded in a constraint have a nonzero probability of being included in the constraint hypothesized on a given occasion; (c) every constraint must be consistent with the current input sentence-plus-context; (d) constraints that were hypothesized previously but disconfirmed by subsequent inputs are not hypothesized a second time (or at least have a successively lower probability of being hypothesized every time they are disconfirmed). For example, on one occasion a child might hypothesize that *wants* is sensitive to object animacy, and this constraint is retained until it is disconfirmed. On another occasion he or she might hypothesize that it is sensitive to subject number, and that hypothesis will be retained indefinitely, since no subsequent input will ever disconfirm it. Eventually all the correct feature constraints for a word or affix will be hypothesized, and none will be disconfirmed, whereas any incorrect feature constraint will at one point or another run up against a disconfirming input. In the limit the correct set of constraints will be attained, but the course of development will be from simple hypotheses to complex hypotheses, in accord with Brown's data and with noncontroversial assumptions about the child's processing capacity. It will also be from general to specific, in accord with Slobin's data (but, of course, contradicting the conservatism hypothesis when two morphemes that differ along one feature in the adult grammar both lack that feature in an early stage in development and hence are used in free variation). Note that as in the conservatism hypothesis, the child is involuntarily forced to entertain as a hypothesis the least inclusive natural language that is consistent with the data; the difference is that he or she is not forced to do so from the outset but in the limit.

Note that this process may be applied to many cases other than the hypothesization of features for inflections. In Pinker (1984) I discuss a variety of cases of rule acquisition in which an error pattern and its subsequent disappearance can be accounted for by a process whereby the child at first lacks some feature constraining a given rule, and then probabilistically samples from some space of possible feature constraints relevant to that rule type, achieving the more restrictive adult state when the correct constraint is finally hypothesized. For example, some of the overly productive lexicosyntactic rules that led to the errors in (3) could result from the child's not yet having hypothesized the necessary constraints on the rule (e.g., dativization generally applies when the lexical item is monosyllabic and the oblique object is a prospective possessor of the direct object, Mazurkewich & White, 1983; causativization generally applies when the causal relation is direct and stereotypic, Gergely & Bever, in press; Denominal verb formation generally applies when the source noun plays certain semantic roles, e.g., instrument, agent, manner, Clark & Clark, 1979). Overtensing errors (e.g., *does it rolls?*; see Erreich, Valian, & Winzemer, 1980) are unlearned when it occurs to the child that the finiteness of a complement verb is a feature that an auxiliary or other complement-taking verb may constrain. Failure to invert in *wh*-questions may disappear when the child first entertains the possibility that the presence or absence of an inversion feature is dictated by the embeddedness of a clause and the presence of particular *wh*-words. These accounts, of course, are all contingent on particular theories of the adult rule (i.e., they may only be put forward if the error is blocked in the adult grammar by a particular feature appended to a rule, and if there is some universal principle defining a relatively constrained space of possible features for the child to have to sample from). See Pinker (1984) for developmental and linguistic evidence for these accounts.

This learning algorithm is not fancy; it does not have any features that surprise most people; and it is not terribly original (in fact, it incorporates some simple assumptions that lay at the heart of many of the mathematical models of learning examined in the 1950s; e.g., Bush & Estes, 1959). Yet in this domain it solves part of the oft-discussed learnability problem posed by the absence of negative evidence, without making incorrect developmental predictions. How does it accomplish this? It does so by abandoning the assumption that the child is a completely rational inductive hypothesis tester, one who never abandons a hypothesis unless it is contradicted by some input datum. For example, imagine a child who has hypothesized that *wants* is to be used for third person subjects, but who has not yet realized that it can only be used for singular third person subjects. Such a child will utter sentences such as *they leaves*, and in the absence of negative evidence there is no input, strictly speaking, that proves the child wrong (*they leave* and *they leaves* could be free variants, as far as the child is concerned, and the rarity of *they leaves* could be due to sampling error in the parental input corpus). Under the constraint sampling model sketched above, it would eventually occur to the child to add the hypothesis that *want* is sensitive to subject number, but not because the input forces that move. The child just can't help it; he or she is a born constraint-hypothesizer. Weinstein (1979) has given such nonconservative, seemingly nonrational strategies the technical label "Kafkaesque" (after Gregor Samsa, who awoke one morning metamorphosed into a cockroach), but in fact the constraint-sampling strategy does not seem so strange when we consider that the child learning constraints on closed class morphemes must search through a large space of possibilities while in possession of a limited capacity to process information. The nonconservatism of the strategy stems from the fact that simpler hypotheses (i.e., ones comprising a smaller number of feature constraints) are less restrictive than more complex ones.[8]

Enforcing Uniqueness

The mechanism discussed above can allow the child to acquire more complex and restrictive rules and entries in the absence of negative evidence. However, if the earlier, more liberal versions of those rules applied productively in the child's grammar and left a set of incorrect entries in their aftermath, the child must also possess the means of expunging that residue, or else he or she would still be left with an overly inclusive grammar. For example, consider a child who has overapplied the English past tense inflection rule to inappropriate stems, resulting in *bringed*, or one who has an incorrect rule of present inflection that inflects stems with -*s* plus the information that that is the form to be used in the third person present form, omitting mention of number (thus *walks* might be the form in the child's lexicon that stands for the third person form of *walk*). If certain "full entry" theories of inflectional morphology are correct, then the

---

[8] Some readers may feel uncomfortable with the idea that sooner or later the child hypothesizes, out of thin air, every possible feature constraint that a language could employ in its affixes. For example, nothing would prevent an English-speaking child from one day entertaining the notion that *wants* encodes the information that its object must have a globular shape, and until it occurs to a Cherokee child to entertain this notion, he or she will not have learned the language. For crosslinguistically prevalent features such as number and case this may be what happens, but for rarer features it seems less plausible that the child would spontaneously hypothesize them. In Chapter 5 of Pinker (1984) I address this problem in the following way. Imagine that the child operates under what I call the "Unique Entry Constraint" (a version of the "Uniqueness Principle" that I discuss later in this chapter): that every combination of grammatical features may be expressed by at most one form (e.g., there can be at most one past tense form of *go*, one general purpose past tense inflection, one plural marker, etc.). Then if the child receives direct positive evidence for distinct forms that encoded the same set of features (equivalently, that compete for the same "cell" in an inflectional paradigm), the child actively searches for some semantic or phonological feature that distinguishes the alternative entries. For example, upon closer examination the child might discover that all nouns in his or her lexicon bearing one form of plural ending refer to animate entities, whereas all nouns bearing an alternative form refer to inanimate entities. By adding the feature [± *animate*] to his or her inflectional paradigm for plural markers, and differentiating the alternative forms accordingly, the Unique Entry Constraint is satisfied. But more important for the present discussion, the child did not have to wait until the lucky moment when animacy was randomly hypothesized as a feature constraint. By examining the contrast between stored forms that hitherto existed in free variation, the child was able to discover the missing feature constraint more directly. This strategy, of course, does not make the procedure any less conservative. Note also that the principle that inspires the child to search actively for a missing feature constraint—namely, the proviso that feature combinations must be expressed by unique forms—also plays a role in the second mechanism I propose for recovering from overgeneration.

child will have saved in his or her lexicon the incorrectly inflected form. Learning additional feature constraints on the productive rule (e.g., "inflect a verb stem with -ed only if the stem does not end in -ing"; "inflect a verb stem with -s to obtain its third person singular version") will prevent the child from making errors with new verbs, but by itself it will do nothing to prevent the child from using the incorrect forms created earlier.

One solution to this problem comes from a suggestion made by Kenneth Wexler (1979) which has come to be known as the "Uniqueness Principle" (e.g., Roeper, 1982; Wexler & Culicover, 1980). According to this principle, there may be at most a single realization of a given form in a language, unless there is direct positive evidence in the input for more than one form, in which case both forms may be retained. Wexler originally stated this principle as a constraint on the number of surface structures that a given deep structure could map onto. But Grimshaw (1981), Roeper (1981), and Pinker (1984) (see also Anderson, 1977; Pinker, 1979; 1981) have proposed that the Uniqueness Principle can be extended to other domains of grammar, mandating that certain other types of underlying structures, such as lexical or inflectional forms, can have at most one realization barring direct evidence that the language sanctions more than one realization. The child could use the Uniqueness Principle in the following way: if a certain form has been created through the application of some productive mechanism, and then the input contains an alternative realization of that form, then the earlier form is "pre-empted" and hence expunged from the grammar. But if that earlier form is exemplified in the input (as opposed to owing its existence solely to the application of productive processes), it is immune to pre-emption by an alternative form, and both are retained.

Here are some examples of how the child could apply versions of the Uniqueness Principle to unlearn incorrect rules in the absence of negative evidence:

- Assume that the child operates under the constraint that for every lexical stem, there is at most one morphological realization of every cell in its inflectional paradigm (e.g., one third person singular present, one past tense, one past participle). Then if the child had created the past tense form *breaked* by applying a productive inflectional rule, the appearance of *broke* in the input, and the realization that *broke* is a past tense version of *break*, would be sufficient to eliminate *breaked*. For those relatively uncommon forms that do have alternative surface realizations (e.g., *has proved/proven; cactuses/cacti; dived/dove; leaped/leapt*), the child would hear evidence for both forms in the input, unlike the case of *breaked/broke*, and would retain both forms.[9]

---

[9] Readers familiar with language development might think that this account is at odds with the well-known developmental sequence whereby children first use the *irregular* form of a verb or noun, and *then* the overregularized form (e.g., Ervin, 1964). If the child has already learned the irregular form for a verb, shouldn't the Uniqueness Principle prevent him or her from applying the productive inflection rule to that verb's stem, hence preventing overregularization to begin with? There are two

Note that this procedure would help to explain the oft-noted fact that in adult grammars, productive rules of derivation and inflection are blocked when there is a lexical item that has a strong form fulfilling the same function as the output of the rule (e.g., Aronoff, 1976).

- A similar process could account for the elimination of any incorrect lexical entries that might be retained subsequent to the generation of overly productive lexical rules, such as the examples cited above in (1). Imagine that the child creates a paradigm for each verb in which cells are defined for the alternative surface forms corresponding to that verb (e.g., its active, passive, causative, reflexive, middle, inchoative, etc.). Furthermore, the Uniqueness Principle applies to these paradigm cells (as it does for inflectional paradigms), so that each paradigm cell may be realized in only one way. Then the acquisition of *kill*, and the realization that it corresponds to the causative version of *die*, could result in the deletion of the incorrect causative form of *dead* or *die* cited in (3); similar processes could eliminate the incorrect causative forms *stay*, *climb*, and *come*, when *keep*, *lift*, and *bring*, respectively, are acquired. Likewise, *sweep* could eliminate the verb *broom*, and so on for many other examples cited by Clark (1982).

- Children can assume that the default control relation for transitive verbs allowing subjectless complements (*tell, want, see, order*, etc.) is one where the matrix object is coreferential with the role of the missing complement subject (e.g., *I told him$_i$ [PRO$_i$ to go]*, and so on for the vast majority of complement-taking transitive verbs). However, for some exceptional verbs (e.g., *promise, strike*) the matrix subject is what controls the missing complement subject (e.g., *I$_j$ promised him [PRO$_j$ to go]*). Children are notorious for assuming that the default control relation holds for these exceptional verbs (Chomsky, 1969). When the child hears an adult use *promise NP to VP* in an interpretable context (one where it is patently clear that the referent of the matrix subject is intended to be coreferential with the subject of the complement verb), the child can acquire a correct lexical entry for *promise* in which subject control is mandated (Pinker, 1982, 1984). But what prevents the child

---

possible reasons why a strong form might fail to prevent the application of a productive rule despite the Uniqueness Principle, both with independent empirical support. First, in some cases the child may not recognize that an irregular form belongs to the same paradigm as the stem undergoing productive inflection (e.g., he or she might think that *go* and *went* are different verbs). Kuczaj (1981) makes this argument, and cites the fact that children often productively inflect the irregular forms themselves, as if they were independent stems (e.g., *wented, wenting*). Second, in cases where the child does possess information about which stem an irregular form belongs to, he or she may be unable to access that information for performance reasons (e.g., the pointer between the past tense cell of the inflectional paradigm of *break* and the item *broke*). Hence the child would not have the information necessary to block the productive rule in mind at the crucial moment. Evidence for this possibility is the fact that adults often make overregularization errors in their speech (Merrill Garrett, personal communication, 1983; Stemberger, 1982), and that irregular forms are almost always high in frequency.

from incorrectly retaining multiple possibilities for control in *promise* sentences, making it analogous to *ask* (cf. *the pupil asked the teacher to leave*, which is ambiguous, versus *the pupil promised/told the teacher to leave*, which is unambiguous)? If the child assumes that every verb may participate in at most one control relation (barring direct evidence to the contrary), then the acquisition of subject-control *promise* is sufficient for the child to expunge the object-control version. For *ask*, on the other hand, the child would have evidence from its use in different contexts (ones in which the matrix subject and matrix object, respectively, were interpreted as being coreferential with the complement subject role) that it violates the default assumption, and would not expunge either possibility of control but would retain both in his or her grammar.

These are some of the examples in which I have been able to appeal to various versions of the "Uniqueness Principle" in order to account for how children unlearn their mistakes in the absence of negative evidence. For further details and for justification of these accounts, and for analogous accounts of the unlearning of other types of mistakes (e.g., errors in the syntactic categorization of words, in determining the syntactic head of a phrase type, and in determining which verbs subcategorize for which types of complementizers), see Pinker (1984).

Implications of Uniqueness

There are three important but nonobvious corollaries to the use of uniqueness principles in theories of language acquisition. Recall that that there are counterexamples to the Uniqueness Principle (e.g., *dived/dove; ask*), and the child must have some way of learning them. But if we were simply to say that the child can learn both unique and nonunique realizations of forms, then the principle would not be of any value (for example, the child could learn *broke* from the input, and *breaked* from the application of a productive rule, and assume that that is one of the cases in the language in which the Uniqueness Principle is violated). Of course, there is a reliable diagnostic of whether or not the child should assume that the Uniqueness Principle holds. If alternative realizations of a form are both heard in the input, then the child should retain both—the input should be the final arbiter. However, if one realization is heard in the input and the other was created by some productive mechanism, then the child is safe in discarding the latter. The implication of this is that the child must have some way of distinguishing between rules or items directly exemplified in the input, and rules or items created by some productive mechanism, such as lexical or inflectional rules, canonical correspondences between semantics and syntax (e.g., Grimshaw, 1981; Macnamara, 1982; Pinker, 1982), or the default choice of unmarked parameter settings (Chomsky, 1981; see Pinker, in press). The child could append a special "pre-emptability" symbol to any rule, parameter setting, or item that was created by a productive mechanism; or he or she could append a special "pre-emption-proof" symbol to any rule, parameter setting, or item that was directly exemplified in the input (where the precise meaning of "directly exemplified in the input" would be specified by an explicit acquisition theory). Many people seem to find this proposal counterintuitive or implausible, but I see no way of making the Uniqueness Principle work unless it is adopted (see Pinker, 1984, for many examples).

The second corollary of the use of the Uniqueness Principle in an acquisition theory is that one must specify in the theory what the domains are in which Uniqueness holds. That is, there must be a specification of exactly what it is that there is a unique realization of. This can be done in two ways. One is to appeal to a general principle stating that languages avoid synonymity—the child could discard a form if it had the same meaning as an alternative form witnessed in the input. Dwight Bolinger (1975) has argued that some version of this claim is true: he has written that "when we say two things that are different we mean different things by them" (p. 127). Any theory that appealed to this principle would, of course, have to give some precise definition of "meaning" such that the Uniqueness Principle would apply in all the necessary cases without ruling out what appear to be genuine synonyms or cases of nonsemantically conditioned variation (e.g., grammatical gender or arbitrary declensional classes, or lexical synonyms such as *couch* and *sofa*, or the apparently free variation in word order allowed by languages such as Warlpiri; see Hale, 1981). Alternatively, there may not be a single Uniqueness Principle that can be applied to any theory of grammar without further specification; instead, theories might have to specify a set of analogous but separate instantiations of the Uniqueness Principle for the different components in which Uniqueness holds (e.g., Uniqueness applies to the contents of cells in inflectional and derivational paradigms, and to the control relations allowed for individual complement-taking predicates, but *not* to the alternative expansions of a phrase in a free-constituent order language or rule). A third possibility is that Uniqueness is not defined semantically, but does apply across the board within a grammar. In that case there would have to be some definition applying across components that would allow one to pick out what the "forms" would be that admitted of unique realizations. Conceivably such a theory might be highly similar to a theory of the components of a "core" or "basic" grammar that the child assumes to be the case in the absence of coun-terevidence. That is, many of the forms that the child expects there to be no more than one of may also be forms that the child expects there to be no *less* than one of. See Bickerton (1984) and Slobin (1984) for further discussion.

It is not clear to me which of these alternatives is correct, and it will not be a simple matter to decide among them. For one thing, since all formulations are likely to be faced with counterexamples, any such formulation must give the child the power to learn nonunique realizations of a form, and hence no set of counterexamples by themselves can torpedo a formulation of the Uniqueness principle. Instead, such formulations may be evaluated by crosslinguistic evidence (i.e., the counterexamples should be the rare cases) and by developmental evidence (i.e., the child should learn the true counterexamples more grudgingly). But what is clear to me is that the issue of which forms the child expects to have unique realizations is central to the problem of accounting for error recovery in the absence of negative evidence.

The third implication is that if the Uniqueness Principle supplies part of the solution to the no-negative-evidence problem, it does not contradict the conservatism hypothesis so much as it makes it irrelevant. Consider a case where the child hypothesizes form A, then hears form B in the input, where A and B are alternative realizations of some form that is subject to the Uniqueness Principle, and the child respects the principle by eliminating A the instant that B is acquired. The child has not progressed from a less restrictive to a more restrictive grammar; the two stand in an intersecting relation, not a subset-superset relation. It is only if the child temporarily admits of a grammar in which A and B are in free variation that two successive hypothesis grammars generate nested languages. In the account I suggested in the previous paragraph, the child should not entertain such hypotheses until he or she had heard *both* forms in the input, which would be consistent with the conservatism hypothesis, and that would only occur for rare cases such as *dived/dove* or *ask* (see also Footnote 9). Therefore if the account above is correct, the Uniqueness Principle would dictate that cases in which alternative hypotheses generate nested languages should in general not exist: the presence of one form in the language should be predictive of some other form not existing. Hence the conservatism hypothesis would not be applicable, and if the Uniqueness Principle is widespread, nonconservatism would not do much of the work in explaining language acquisition in the absence of negative evidence. The significant work would in most cases consist of showing how Uniqueness leads to non-nested hypothesis languages. In terms of the tree of hypotheses shown in Figure 2, Uniqueness would give the tree many roots and very short branches.

If my particular account of the ordering of children's hypotheses is incorrect, and children do hypothesize free variation of alternative forms in the absence of direct evidence in the input for each one, then we do have a case of nested languages. And in that case, Uniqueness would allow the child to progress from a less restrictive to a more restrictive hypothesis. That would be a case of the conservatism hypothesis being applicable, but false. In either case, the use of the Uniqueness Principle diminishes the role of conservatism in explaining acquisition.

Summary

In sum, I have made the following arguments. Because children do not receive information about what is not a sentence in their language, any theory of language acquisition must specify how children avoid acquiring languages that are supersets of the target language. One possibility is that in some domains of grammar children progress from more restrictive to less restrictive grammars as positive evidence comes in, never entertaining a grammar that generates both grammatical and ungrammatical sentences. However, this account is inconsistent with the fact that children's interim grammars seem to generate supersets of the target language in certain domains, and that children are undoubtedly productive in domains in which their productivity could lead them to generate all the grammatical sentences in the domain plus ungrammatical sentences. Two mechanisms are proposed that would allow the child to alter his or her grammar in the direction of generating fewer sentences, even in the absence of negative evidence. The first puts a rein on overly productive rules. It consists of a constraint sampling mechanism that hypothesizes features to be added to rules, lexical entries, and inflections, such that these features limit the domain of application of the entities they are appended to. These hypothesized constraints would be sampled from a space defined by universal grammar for that rule type, and would be discarded if counterexemplified by future inputs, retained otherwise. The sampling could be made more direct if the child hypothesized constraints that accounted for the contrast between alternative structures that appeared to exist in free variation. The second mechanism applies in cases in which an overly productive rule creates incorrect entries that remain in the grammar even after the rule itself has been made more conservative. This mechanism instantiates Wexler's Uniqueness Principle, and applies whenever the child finds alternative realizations of a single type of grammatical form. If one of those entries was directly exemplified in the input and the other was created by the application of a productive rule, the child expunges the latter entry; if both were directly exemplified in the input, the child retains both. This latter mechanism has implications for the representation of productively created structures in the child's grammar, for the type of mapping between syntax and semantics in adult grammars, for theories of core grammar, and for the question of the extent to which universal grammar ever allows the child to hypothesize grammars generating nested languages.

References

Anderson, J. R. (1977). Induction of augmented transition networks. *Cognitive Science, 1*, 125–157.
Aronoff, M. (1976). *Word formation in generative grammar*. Cambridge, MA: MIT Press.
Baker, C. L. (1979). Syntactic theory and the projection problem. *Linguistic Inquiry, 10*, 533–581.

Baker, C. L. (1981). Learnability and the English auxiliary system. In C. L. Baker & J. J. McCarthy, (Eds.), *The logical problem of language acquisition*. Cambridge, MA: MIT Press.

Berwick, R. C., & Weinberg, A. S. (1984). *The grammatical basis of linguistic performance*. Cambridge, MA: MIT Press.

Bickerton, D. (1984). The language bioprogram hypothesis. *Behavioral and Brain Sciences, 7*, 173–221.

Bloom, L., Lightbown, P., & Hood, L. (1975). Structure and variation in child language. *Monographs of the Society for Research in Child Development, 40*.

Bloom, L., Tackeff, J., & Lahey, M. (1984). Learning *to* in complement constructions. *Journal of Child Language, 11*, 391–406.

Bolinger, D. (1975). Meaning and form—Some fallacies of asemantic grammar. In E. F. K. Koerner, J. Odmark, & J. H. Shaw (Eds.), *Amsterdam studies in the theory and history of linguistic science*, series 4: Current Issues in Linguistic Theory, vol. 1: *The transformational-generative paradigm and modern linguistic theory*. Amsterdam: J. Benjamin.

Bowerman, M. (1982a). *Children's mental representation of events: some clues to structures and categories from recurrent speech errors*. Stanford University Psychology Department Colloquium, Stanford, CA, March, 29, 1982.

Bowerman, M. (1982b). Reorganizational processes in lexical and syntactic development. In E. Wanner & L. R. Gleitman (Eds.), *Language acquisition: The state of the art*. Cambridge: Cambridge University Press.

Bowerman, M. (1983). How do children avoid constructing an overgeneral grammar in the absence of feedback about what is not a sentence? *Papers and reports on child language acquisition*. Stanford University Department of Linguistics, Stanford, CA.

Braine, M. D. S. (1971). On two types of models of the internalization of grammars. In D. I. Slobin (Ed.), *The ontogenesis of grammar: A theoretical symposium*. New York: Academic Press.

Braine, M. D. S. (1976). Children's first word combinations. *Monographs of the Society for Research in Child Development, 41*.

Bresnan, J. (1978). A realistic transformational grammar. In M. Halle, J. Bresnan & G. Miller (Eds.), *Linguistic theory and psychological reality*. Cambridge, MA: MIT Press.

Bresnan, J. (1982). Control and complementation. In J. Bresnan (Ed.), *The mental representation of grammatical relations*. Cambridge, MA: MIT Press.

Brown, R. (1968). The development of *wh* questions in child speech. *Journal of Verbal Learning and Verbal Behavior, 7*, 279–290.

Brown, R. (1973). *A first language: The early stages*. Cambridge, MA: Harvard University Press.

Brown, R., & Hanlon, C. (1970). Derivational complexity and order of acquisition in child speech. In J. R. Hayes (Ed.), *Cognition and the development of language*. New York: Wiley.

Bush, R. R., & Estes, W. K. (Eds.) (1959). *Studies in mathematical learning theory*. Stanford, CA: Stanford University Press.

Chomsky, C. (1969). *Acquisition of syntax in children from 5–10*. Cambridge, MA: MIT Press.

Chomsky, N. (1981). *Lectures on government and binding*. Dordrecht, Netherlands: Foris.

Chomsky, N., & Lasnik, H. (1977). Filters and control. *Linguistic Inquiry, 8*, 425–504.

Clark, E. V. (1982). The young word maker: a case study of innovation in the child's lexicon. In E. Wanner & L. R. Gleitman (Eds.), *Language acquisition: The state of the art*. Cambridge: Cambridge University Press.

Clark, E. V., & Clark, H. H. (1979). When nouns surface as verbs. *Language, 55*, 767–811.

Dell, F. (1981). On the learnability of optional phonological rules. *Linguistic Inquiry, 12*, 31-37.

Erreich, A., Valian, V., & Winzemer, J. (1980). Aspects of a theory of language acquisition. *Journal of Child Language, 2*, 157–179.

Ervin, S. (1964). Imitation and structural change in children's language. In E. Lenneberg (Ed.), *New directions in the study of language*. Cambridge, MA: MIT Press.

Gergely, G., & Bever, T. G. (in press). *The mental representation of causative verbs. Cognition*.

Gold, E. M. (1967). Language identification in the limit. *Information and Control, 16*, 447–474.

Grimshaw, J. (1981). Form, function, and the language acquisition device. In C. L. Baker & J. J. McCarthy (Eds.), *The logical problem of language acquisition*. Cambridge, MA: MIT Press.

Hale, K. (1981). *On the position of Walbiri in a typology of the base*. Bloomington: Indiana University Linguistics Club.

Jakubowicz, C. (1983, October). *On markedness and binding principles*. Paper presented at the Eighth Annual Boston University Conference on Language Development.

Kuczaj, S. A. II. (1981). More on children's initial failure to relate specific acquisitions. *Journal of Child Language, 8*, 485–487.

Kuczaj, S. A. II, & Brannick, N. (1979). Children's use of the *wh* question modal auxiliary placement rule. *Journal of Experimental Child Psychology, 28*, 43-67.

Kuczaj, S. A. II, & Maratsos, M. (1979, March). *The initial verbs of yes-no questions: a different kind of general grammatical category*. Presented at the symposium "The Child's Formulation of Grammatical Categories and Rules," Biennial Meeting of the Society for the Research in Child Development. San Francisco.

Lapointe, S. (1981). Free order phrase structure rules. In W. Chao & D. Wheeler (Eds.), *University of Massachusetts Occasional Papers in Linguistics, 6*. Amherst: Graduate Linguistics Students Association, University of Massachusetts.

Lebeaux, D., & Pinker, S. (1981, October). *The acquisition of the passive*. Paper presented at the Sixth Annual Boston University Conference on Language Development.

Macnamara, J. (1982). *Names for things: A study of child language*. Cambridge, MA: Bradford Books/MIT Press.

Major, D. (1974). *The acquisition of modal auxiliaries in the language of children*. The Hague: Mouton.

Maratsos, M. P. (1978). New models in linguistics and language acquisition. In M. Halle, J. Bresnan, & G. Miller (Eds.), *Linguistic theory and psychological reality*. Cambridge, MA: MIT Press.

Maratsos, M. P. (1983). Some current issues in the study of the acquisition of grammar. In P. Mussen (Ed.), *Carmichael's manual of child psychology*, 4th Ed. New York: Wiley.

Maratsos, M. P., & Chalkley, M. (1981). The internal language of children's syntax: the ontogenesis and representation of syntactic categories. In K. Nelson (Ed.), *Children's language*, vol. 2. New York: Gardner.

Mazurkewich, I., & White, L. (1984). The acquisition of the dative alternation: Unlearning over-generalizations. *Cognition, 16*, 261–283.

Osherson, D. N., Stob, M., & Weinstein, S. (in press). *Introduction to formal learning theory*. Cambridge, MA: Bradford Books/MIT Press.

Pinker, S. (1979). Formal models of language learning. *Cognition, 7*, 217–283.

Pinker, S. (1981). Comments on the paper by Wexler. In C. L. Baker & J. J. McCarthy (Eds.), *The logical problem of language acquisition*. Cambridge, MA: MIT Press.

Pinker, S. (1982). A theory of the acquisition of lexical interpretive grammars. In J. Bresnan (Ed.), *The mental representation of grammatical relations*. Cambridge, MA: MIT Press.

Pinker, S. (1984). *Language learnability and language development*. Cambridge, MA: Harvard University Press.

Pinker, S. (in press). Markedness and language development. In R. Matthews, R. May, & W. Demopoulos (Eds.), *Learnability and language*. Dordrecht, Netherlands: Reidel.

Pinker, S., & Frost, L. A. (1984, October). *Constraining productivity: Children's passivization of verbs with different thematic roles*. Paper presented at the Ninth Annual Boston University Conference on Language Development.

Roeper, T. (1981). In pursuit of a deductive model of language acquisition. In C. L. Baker & J. J. McCarthy (Eds.), *The logical problem of language acquisition*. Cambridge, MA: MIT Press.

Slobin, D. I. (1973). Cognitive prerequisites for the development of grammar. In C. Ferguson &

D. I. Slobin (Eds.), *Studies of child language development*. New York: Holt, Rinehart and Winston.

Slobin, D. I. (1985). Crosslinguistic evidence for the language-making capacity. In D. I. Slobin (Ed.), *The crosslinguistic study of language acquisition*. Hillsdale, NJ: Erlbaum.

Stemberger, J. P. (1982). *The lexicon in a model of language production*. Doctoral dissertation. San Diego: University of California.

Talmy, L. (1978). The relation of grammar to cognition—a synopsis. In D. Waltz (Ed.), *Proceedings of TINLAP-2* (Theoretical Issues in Natural Language Processing). Urbana: University of Illinois.

Wasow, T. (1981). Comments on the paper by Baker. In C. L. Baker & J. J. McCarthy (Eds.), *The logical problem of language acquisition*. Cambridge, MA: MIT Press.

Weinstein, S. (1979, June). Untitled presentation at the Irvine Workshop on Learnability, Laguna Beach, CA.

Wells, G. (1979). Learning and using the auxiliary verb in English. In V. Lee (Ed.), *Language Development*. New York: Wiley.

Wexler, K. (1979, June). Untitled presentation at the Irvine Workshop on Learnability, Laguna Beach, CA.

Wexler, K. (1981). Some issues in the theory of learnability. In C. L. Baker & J. J. McCarthy (Eds.), *The logical problem of language acquisition*. Cambridge, MA: MIT Press.

Wexler, K., & Culicover, P. (1980). *Formal principles of language acquisition*. Cambridge, MA: MIT Press.

Williams, E. (1981). Argument structure and morphology. *Linguistic Review, 1*, 81–114.

Wilson, R., Pinker, S., Zaenen, A., & Lebeaux, D. (1981, October). *Productivity and the dative alternation*. Paper presented at the Sixth Annual Boston University Conference on Language Development.

Part II
Hypothesis Learning and Language Learning: Formal and Methodological Aspects

Chapter 4

Learning Machines*

John Case
State University of New York at Buffalo

Introduction

This chapter is a summary of my work (mostly) at Buffalo (with students) on the abstract, recursion theoretic approach to learning machines. I first describe the work on inductive inference machines which is about that part of algorithmic cognition related to doing inductive inference, the practice of explanatory hypothesis generation in science—of learning "rules" for phenomena. Next I discuss the work on what are called language learning machines.

So that the reader is not misled in expectations about this material let me say that the work here is *not* directly about how to build machines which are as smart as Einstein at theoretical physics or as clever at learning language as a child. The immediate goals are much more modest. The results I present are better interpreted philosophically than as guides to the engineer. Many of these results describe interesting *limitations* on algorithmic learning; they give us a picture of some of the "surface features" of the *boundaries* of this phenomenon.

I discuss some of the problems of applying this work to the case of human cognition, and I critically examine the relevance of language learning machines to humans. Occasionally I suggest mathematical or experimental questions that I believe are worth exploring.

Inductive Inference Machines

Consider the following model of (at least part of the practice of) science.

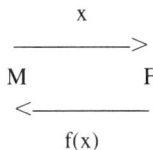

$$\begin{array}{ccc} & x & \\ & \xrightarrow{\hspace{2cm}} & \\ M & & F \\ & \xleftarrow{\hspace{2cm}} & \\ & f(x) & \end{array}$$

---

* Research supported in part by NSF grants MCS-7704388 and MCS 8010728.

In the diagram M represents an agent doing (discrete) scientific experiments on a phenomenon F. I think of F as definitionally circumscribed by the set of all possible experiments on it. x represents one of the possible experiments on F, and f(x) is the result of doing experiment x on F. For a suitable example chemical phenomenon F, an experiment x would be to mix together in certain proportions (different proportions for different x) two liquids, each of fixed chemical composition and temperature, and the corresponding experimental result f(x) would be the color of the resulting mixture.

Conceptually f is a behavioral summary of F. f is a function, that is, single-valued; this is to model the fact that in science we are concerned with replicable, *deterministic* outcomes—even, for example, in quantum mechanics where the replicable, deterministic outcome is a probability distribution or in more concrete terms, at least for some cases, a diffraction fringe pattern; the outcome is not the position and momentum of particular particles. For convenience and without loss of generality I take f to map N, the set of natural numbers, to N—without loss of generality because I am assuming the sets of experiments and experimental results are discrete and hence can be Gödel numbered. An implicit, but in some respects inessential assumption is that the set of possible experiments is algorithmically decidable. Blum and Blum (1975) consider the more general situation, but, it turns out, I have no need of that generality in this chapter.

Unless I say otherwise, "function" will refer to (total) maps from N to N.

I am concerned with the case that the agent M is a machine, machine in the sense of algorithmic device.

A word about the discreteness of experiments, etc., is in order. Even though many extant scientific theories make predictions about measurable values being particular *real* numbers, we can only measure a few rational values. While the reals are continuous, the (infinite) subsets of the rationals that correspond to values we can (in principle) measure are discrete. Of course it might be that the world is continuous, but we are restricted to making mere discrete measurements. It might also be that the world is discrete and its apparent continuity is, as I happen to suspect, an illusion, albeit a useful illusion, a beautiful invention for dealing with (among other things) discrete collections the discreteness of which we are unable to easily perceive. Whatever may be the correct metaphysics, scientists are stuck with discrete measurements, and the model I discuss here is based on discreteness. I conjecture that if *natural* extensions are developed to the continuous case(s), there will be no surprises. "natural" means in part that the interpretation of the results does not implicitly or explicitly assume people can measure a continuum of different values.

In the model M's goal is to learn or conjecture algorithmic, *predictive* explanations for F, that is, programs (in some fixed programming language) for computing f (or, as we shall see, some variant of f).

A paragraph about the choice of programming language is in order. An *acceptable* programming language (Rogers, 1958, 1967; Machtey & Young,

1978) is one such that there are effective translations back and forth between it and a standard Turing Machine formalism. The papers of my students Riccardi (1980, 1981) and Royer (1984) each contain my result that the acceptable programming languages are characterized as those in which *all* control structures *can* be implemented (while-loop and if-then-else are *example* control structures). Rogers (1958, 1967) showed the acceptable languages are characterized as being maximal with respect to effective translations: the acceptable programming languages are those into which all programming languages can be effectively translated (compiled). Rogers (1958) showed that any two acceptable languages are recursively isomorphic. Basically all general purpose programming languages used in the world are acceptable; non-acceptable languages are known only through mathematical constructions (Rogers, 1958; Friedberg, 1958; Pour-El, 1964; Machtey, Winklman, & Young, 1978; Riccardi, 1980, 1981; Royer, 1984). It can be shown that the theorems here are *independent* of the acceptable programming language employed, that is, the theorems hold for each fixed choice of acceptable programming language. We shall assume, then, that our fixed programming language is acceptable.

The theorems can be interpreted as being about the capabilities and limitations of science as it could be done by algorithmic devices. In one sense they are theorems in artificial intelligence. Now if *we* are algorithmic devices, at least the limitative theorems are also about us! Many people in learnability theory appear to make an unspoken and perhaps unconscious assumption that theorems about the limitations of *algorithmic* learnability tell us about human learnability. They make an implicit assumption of some perhaps weak form of mechanism! By mechanism I do not mean classical or Newtonian mechanism or variations on the theme. I mean what could be called *neomechanism*: discrete, algorithmic mechanism (see Webb, 1980, for a discussion of what is essentially this more modern form of mechanism). Some of the very interesting work of Pour-El and Richards (1979, 1981, 1983a, b, in press) can be thought of in part as about a more classical brand of mechanism. Reals, functions on reals, and operators on those are just higher type objects than, say natural numbers—Pour-El and Richards's work is about computability on these higher type objects; mine is about computability on the lowest type objects. Many people seem to make a, perhaps unconscious, assumption that there are actual metaphysical counterparts to real numbers in the physical world; I do not!

To supplement the discussion of randomness vis à vis neomechanism in Webb (1980), I cite a lovely result of deLeeuw, Moore, Shannon, and Shapiro (1956) (see also Gill, 1972, 1977). The partial functions defined by the *expected* output values of Turing machines with random oracle are again the partial recursive (algorithmically computable) functions provided the probability distribution is itself computable (for example, the coin tossing oracle satisfies the proviso). Furthermore, Gill (1972, 1977) showed that a class of Turing machines with a random oracle (defining partial functions by expected value of output), which class satisfies the proviso, actually constitutes an *acceptable* programming system for the partial recursive functions!

Definition (Gold, 1967; Blum & Blum, 1975). M is said to be an *inductive inference machine* (abbreviated: *IIM*) iff M is an algorithmic device which takes as its input the graph of a function f: N $\longrightarrow$ N an ordered pair at a time, and, from time to time between receiving inputs, M outputs a program (perhaps a program having something to do with computing f).

For such a machine M and a function f, the programs in the sequence of programs output by M on f may or may not have much to do with computing f; it depends on M and f.

It can be shown (Blum & Blum, 1975; Case & Smith, 1983) that for the theorems presented here we may assume without loss of generality any IIM takes the graph of an arbitrary input function f in the order (0, f(0)), (1, f(1)), (2, f(2)), ... That is, there is *no* gain in inferring power obtained by doing some "key" experiments first! There *may* be gains in the *speed* with which successful inferences are made, but this interesting possibility has not yet been well explored.

Next I present one of many possible meanings for "M is *successful* on f." The "*EX*" is for "*ex*planatorily."

Definition (Gold, 1967; Blum & Blum, 1975; Case & Smith, 1983). I say that M *EX-identifies* f iff M fed f outputs, for some n, only the *finite* sequence of programs $p_0, \ldots, p_n$ where p_n computes f.

NB: I said nothing about the value of n being algorithmically discoverable from the graph of f. If it were, the programs $p_0, \ldots, p_{n-1}$ could be eliminated.

Some examples follow.

Suppose f is any fixed computable function. Let M_f be an IIM which on any input g just outputs a fixed program for f. Then M_f *EX*-identifies f, but it fails to *EX*-identify any g not = f. The point of this example is that constructing IIMs which succeed on single functions is trivial and, hence, not very interesting. An interesting problem is to design IIMs which succeed on wide classes of functions.

Let M_{poly} be an IIM which, given n > 0 different data points about an input function, first applies standard curve fitting techniques to discover the lowest degree polynomial (if any) with coefficients in N which passes through the n data points; then M_{poly} outputs a program for that polynomial iff it hasn't already. Clearly M_{poly} *EX*-identifies each function in the entire class of such polynomials because if such a polynomial is of degree m, then a final, correct program is conjectured after m + 1 of its data points have been seen. I say that M_{poly} *EX-identifies* this *class* and that the class is *in EX*. Note that M_{poly} fails very badly to *EX*-identify non-polynomial functions. In general *no* IIM can algorithmically discover the degree of a polynomial just from an enumeration of its graph (I omit the proof). Hence, no IIM which *EX*-identifies all such polynomials can always *EX*-identify each polynomial with its *first* output program.

The *primitive recursive functions* (Rogers, 1967; Machtey & Young, 1978; Meyer & Ritchie, 1967) can be roughly thought of as the class of (total) functions computable with programs whose looping structure is restricted to Pascal-like *for-loops* (Fortran-like *do-loops*). They properly include the polynomials of the previous example. Gold (1967) essentially showed that the class of primitive recursive functions *is* in *EX*! It is well known (Gold, 1967; Brainerd & Landweber, 1974) that (with respect to an n-adic coding of strings) the characteristic functions of context sensitive languages are properly contained in the class of primitive recursive characteristic functions. Hence, the class of characteristic functions of context sensitive language *is* in *EX*. Quite a different result holds for the context sensitive languages vis à vis language learnability, the inference of grammars from mere *enumerations* of languages. This is discussed in the next section.

Gold (1967) also essentially showed that the entire class of (total) computable functions is *not* in EX. Hence, there is no IIM which can *EX*-identify *every* computable function! Case and Fulk (in preparation) showed, in answer to a question of R. Wiehagen, that, given any IIM M_1, there is an IIM M_2 that *EX*-identifies all the functions that M_1 does plus infinitely many more that M_1 does not. Freivalds and Kinber later independently showed this result. Case and Fulk also showed that such an M_2 cannot in general be algorithmically obtained from M_1. As we shall see in the next section, this result contrasts sharply with a result of Osherson, Stob, and Weinstein (1982) about maximality for language learning machines.

Next I turn briefly to two interesting special cases of *EX*-identification. In my terminology, an IIM is *postdictively complete* iff each of its conjectures correctly predicts all of the data points on which that conjecture is based; an IIM is *postdictively consistent* iff none of its conjectures explicitly outputs something contradicting the data about the input function on which that conjecture is based—a conjecture *may* fail to yield any output at all concerning data points on which it is based. In some literature postdictive completeness is (I believe misleadingly) referred to as *consistency*. Let *COMPEX* (respectively, *CONSEX*) stand for the collection of sets S of functions such that some postdictively complete (respectively, postdictively consistent) IIM *EX*-identifies each function in S. Blum & Blum (1975) essentially showed that, with respect to *EX*-identification, postdictive completeness limits the power of IIMs, that is, *COMPEX* is *properly* contained in *EX*. R. Wiehagen showed that so does postdictive consistency, that is, *CONSEX* is properly contained in *EX*. This latter result is particularly nice because it shows us that there is sometimes an advantage to making conjectures that explicitly contradict what we already know! In effect: it is *sometimes* good to unlearn something for awhile. In the light of the Blum and Blum and Wiehagen results I fully expected that, with respect to *EX*-identification, postdictive completeness would be even more limiting to the power of IIMs than postdictive consistency; however, my current doctoral student, M.

Fulk, showed that, with respect to *EX*-identification, postdictive completeness is no more limiting than postdictive consistency, that is, *CONSEX* = *COMPEX*. This work of Fulk's as well as that cited below will appear in his dissertation.

As I've already pointed out, the entire class of computable functions is *not* in EX (Gold, 1967). Hence, at least with respect to *EX*, there is no algorithmic learning device which is (in a sense) a perfect scientist; if we are machines (in the algorithmic sense), with respect to *EX*, we can't be perfect scientists either. I was motivated to consider to what extent one could get around this unfortunate limitation by considering criteria of success less strict than *EX*. Physics was my undergraduate major and I noticed that physicists sometimes knowingly use slightly incorrect explanations for phenomena; in physical optics they speak of a prediction failure in the classical explanation of dispersion as *anomalous dispersion*. Long after my physics experience it occurred to me that IIMs allowed to make a few mistakes in a final conjecture *might* be able to identify larger classes than they can under *EX*-identification. Thanks to Blum and Blum (1975) I already knew this was the case if the final conjecture is allowed to make an *unbounded*, finite number of mistakes in output behavior (see the material on *EX** below). Of course this *EX** criterion is an interesting mathematical reference point, but it is not a practical criterion—the finitely many mistakes may occur at all the data points about which one ever wants to make predictions. However, in most cases one *can* tolerate a small *bounded* number (1, 2, 3, . . .) of incorrect predictions; hence, EX^n below is for "small" n a "practical" criterion.

Definition (Case & Smith, 1978, 1983). Suppose a is in N or {*}. M EX^a-identifies f iff M fed f outputs, for some n, only the *finite* sequence of programs $p_0, \ldots p_n$ where p_n computes f *except* on no more than a inputs if a is in N—except on a finite number of inputs if a = *. EX^a = {S | for some IIM M M EX^a-identifies each function in S}.

Of course EX^0 = *EX*.

Imagine the programs in our fixed acceptable programming language to be Gödel numbered in some way (Rogers, 1967). The following hierarchy theorem done jointly with my student Smith vindicates in one respect the physicists' use of anomalous explanations!

Theorem (Case & Smith, 1978, 1983). Let S_a = {f | program number f(0) computes f except on no more than a inputs}. For all n > 0, S_n is in ($EX^n - EX^{n-1}$), that is, *some* IIM EX^n- identifies each function in S_n, but *no* IIM EX^{n-1}-identifies each function in S_n; furthermore, S_* is in *EX**, but in *no* EX^n, for n in N.

Hence, EX^0 is properly contained in EX^1, which is properly contained in $EX^2, \ldots$, each of which is properly contained in *EX**.

I consider the n = 1 case of the previous theorem. That S_1 above is nonempty follows from the Kleene recursion theorem (Rogers, 1967), a self-reference principle for algorithmic devices. The proof that S_1 is not in *EX* appears in Case and Smith (1978, 1983); it too employs the Kleene recursion theorem.

Let M_1 be the following peculiar IIM. On input f, M_1 outputs program number
f(0) as its only conjecture. Clearly M witnesses that S_1 is in EX^1—and does a
poor job on functions not in S_1. Here is a fanciful way to think of M_1. Suppose
experiment number 0 is to go out and catch a snowflake under certain well-
specified (and *result determining*) conditions, interpret the pattern of that snowflake according to some fixed coding of patterns into N, and use as the result
of experiment 0 that number which codes the pattern of the snowflake found.
Suppose the phenomenon F represents some global aspect of the universe so that
a program for the corresponding f might be thought of as the secret of the
universe. Now under EX^1-identification M_1 "expects" to discover the secret of
the universe (modulo no more than one mistake or anomaly) in a snowflake
pattern. Of course M_1 *might* be right (although it seems unlikely); nonetheless,
M_1 EX^1-identifies such a large class of computable functions (namely S_1) that
no IIM can EX^0-identify *every* function in it!

   Corollary (Non-Union Theorem, Blum & Blum, 1975). There are classes of
sets of recursive functions S and T each in EX^0 such that *no* IIM EX^0-identifies
the union of S and T!

   It follows that the classes in EX^0 are not closed under finite union! I interpret
this to mean that there must be diversity in the learning machines that do inductive
inference; there is no one cognitive style which, ever more perfected, handles
all cases of inductive inference. It is *not* possible for certain pairs of cognitive
styles to be melded into one which subsumes them both! A straightforward
generalization of the Non-Union Theorem in Smith (1982) can be interpreted to
mean that for each n $>$ 1, there are n cognitive styles which cannot be melded
into (n -1). I think this need for diversity of cognitive styles in learning machines
is a special case of the need for diversity within biological species to ensure their
survival.

   A strengthening of the Non-Union Theorem for more general criteria of
success appears in Case and Smith (1983). Smith (1982) and Daley (1984)
contain complex generalizations of the Non-Union Theorem for unions of arbitrary finite size and with respect to the criteria EX^a and BC^a (defined below),
respectively. Pitt (1984) recently showed that the power of *probabalistic* IIMs
(under *EX* and *BC* criteria) can be neatly characterized in terms of "teams"
(Smith, 1982) of *deterministic* IIMs!

   I give now a proof from Case and Smith (1983) that the Non-Union Theorem
itself follows from the preceding *EX*-hierarchy theorem.

   Let S = {f | program number f(0) computes f} and T = {f | program number
f(0) computes f *except* on *exactly one* input}. M_1 above obviously also *EX*-
identifies S. I define M_2 as follows.

   Begin M_2: on input f first output program number f(0) *patched* to be assuredly
correct on input 0. (I.e., this patched program outputs value f(0) on input 0, and
otherwise behaves like program f(0).) Next execute stage s = 0, where stage
s in general is described immediately below.

Stage s. Run program number f(0) on input s. If it's ever discovered that this program on input s outputs f(s), then output program number f(0) patched to be assuredly correct on input (s + 1) and execute stage (s + 1); otherwise, do not leave stage s. End stage s.

End M_2.

To show M_2 *EX*-identifies T. Suppose f is in T and s_0 is the unique input s on which program number f(0) does *not* output f(s). (NB: program number f(0) may fail to output at all on input s_0.) Then M_2 reaches and never leaves stage s_0. M_2's final conjecture is program number f(0) patched to be assuredly correct on input s_0. Program f(0) itself is already correct on all inputs different from s_0 by virtue of f's being in T. Hence, M_2 *EX*-identifies f.

Therefore, both S and T are in *EX*. Clearly the union of S and T is just S_1 above, which, by the previous theorem, is *not* in *EX*.[]

I next consider another infinite hierarchy of criteria of success. The "*BC*" stands for "*behaviorally correctly.*"

Definition (Case & Smith, 1978, 1983). M BC^a-identifies f iff M fed f outputs an *infinite* sequence of programs p_0, p_1, p_2, . . . such that, for some i, p_i, p_{i+2}, . . . each compute f *except* on no more than a inputs if a is in N—except on a finite number of inputs if a = *.

BC^a = the class of sets S of recursive functions such that some IIM BC^a-identifies each function in S.

NB: The value of i above cannot necessarily be algorithmically found from an enumeration of the graph of f. Even though in the a = 0 case the programs p_i, p_{i+1}, p_{i+2}, . . . *each* compute f, they may be so vastly different from one another that it is not possible to prove in ZF set theory of any two of them that they compute the same function! An open question is how to characterize BC in an insightful way in terms of the Program Equivalence Problem, the algorithmically unsolvable problem of deciding of a pair of programs whether they compute the same (partial) function. The criteria MEX^a (defined below) *have* been so characterized: first the a = 0 case by Freivalds (1975) and later the a > 0 cases by my student Chen (1981, 1982). See the notion of *a-limiting standardizable with a recursive estimate* in the latter references.

Theorem: (Harrington & Case: Case & Smith, 1978, 1983). Let S = {f | for some i, programs numbered f(i), f(i + 1), f(i + 2), . . . *each* compute f}. Then S is in (BC^0-EX^*).

S in the previous theorem is highly self-referential. Consider the IIM which on input f outputs (in order) the programs numbered f(0), f(1), f(2), ... Clearly this IIM BC^0-identifies S. In Case and Smith (1978, 1983) it is shown by an infinitary self-reference argument (based on my operator recursion theorem, Case, 1974) that S is not in EX^*. (Later I make some brief intuitive remarks about infinitary self-reference arguments.)

Barzdin (1974) independently and previously defined the notion of BC^0 based on an observation of Feldman (1972) and showed that EX^0 is properly contained in BC^0.

It is easy to argue (J. Steel: Case & Smith, 1983) that EX^* is contained in BC^0: suppose S is in EX^* as witnessed by M_1; let M_2 simulate M_1, but repeatedly output M_1's last output patched to be assuredly correct on the data points seen so far (M_2 is, then, postdictively complete!); past some point M_2 on f in S is always applying patches to M_1's *final* conjecture p_f, and past some point these patches more than cover the finitely many anomalies in p_f; hence, past some point all of M_2's conjectures on f in S correctly compute f; M_2 doesn't "know" *when* this is happening though and therefore outputs an infinite sequence of programs; M_2 BC^0-identifies S. In particular it is easy to argue from the construction of M_2 that postdictive completeness is no obstacle for BC^0-identification; it has a different problem. To understand the problem, first consider a variation on the theme of BC style criteria. Let FEX^a be defined just like BC^a except that the infinite sequence of output programs is restricted to contain only finitely many *different* programs (Case & Smith, 1983). It is shown in Case and Smith (1983) that $FEX^a = EX^a$. The a = 0 case is previously and independently due to Barzdin and Podnieks (1973). This means that the extra inferring power of BC style criteria over EX style criteria *depends* on machines outputting *infinitely* many *different* programs; the "warehouse" in which one stores the current last conjecture of such machines must grow without bound! A human cranium won't do for such a warehouse.

The next theorem shows that, for BC style inference criteria too, inferring power is enhanced by allowing slightly inaccurate predictive explanations. It too is proved by an infinitary self-reference argument. (These infinitary self-reference arguments can be thought of as exploiting the existence of a growing "network" of programs/machines such that each machine in the network at any time projects a quiescent copy of the entire network at that time into its external work space and takes that copy into account as data in its computations and decisions. I note, in this connection, that according to certain Eastern metaphysical principles and Leibniz's Monadology the world *is* a network, albeit not necessarily of algorithmic devices, each part of which "reflects" on the whole. I am not at all committed to such a view of the world; however, the seeming consistency of neomechanism with such a metaphysics and the fact that some of our theorems can be proved by means of multiply self-reflecting networks of machines intrigue me.)

Theorem (Case & Smith, 1978, 1983). Suppose n > 0. Let $S_n = \{f \mid$ for some i, programs numbered f(i), f(i + 1), f(i + 2), ... *each* compute f except on no more than n inputs$\}$. Then S_n is in $(BC^n - BC^{n-1})$.

It follows that EX^0 is properly contained in EX^1, which is properly contained in EX^2, which is properly contained in . . . , each of which is properly contained in EX^*, which is properly contained in BC^0, which is properly contained in BC^1, which is properly contained in BC^2, which is properly contained in . . . , each of which is properly contained in BC^*. In Case and Smith (1983) I interpret the proof of this hierarchy result to show there are some previously unnoticed problems with Popper's Refutability Principle (in philosophy of science).

It occurred to me to ask what criteria are there beyond BC^*. Surprisingly enough the answer supplied by L. Harrington is "none."

Theorem (Harrington: Case & Smith, 1983). The entire class of computable functions is in BC^*, that is, some IIM BC^*-identifies every recursive function!

BC^* is therefore an especially interesting mathematical reference point, and the EX - BC hierarchy (Case & Smith, 1978, 1983) is a natural one. It is shown, however, in the dissertation of Chen (1981), that if M is *any* IIM which BC^*-identifies the entire class of computable functions, then for any k > 0, for suitable computable functions f, if p_n is the program output by M based on the *first* n + 1 data points of f, although all but finitely many of the p_n's compute a finite variant of f, infinitely many of the p_n's fail to compute f at the *next* k data points! Hence, BC^* is not a practical inference criterion.

I became interested in whether it might be possible to construct IIMs that BC^*-identified all the computable functions and *simultaneously* identified a large class of computable functions by some more practical criterion. Again in Chen's dissertation (1981) it is shown that, while S = {f | program number f(0) computes f} is in EX, for any n, S cannot be BC^n-identified by any IIM which simultaneously BC^*-identifies the entire class of computable functions.

An IIM M is called *reliable* (Blum & Blum, 1975; Minicozzi, 1976) iff, for any computable f, if M outputs a final program on f, then that final program computes f. REX is EX restricted to reliable IIMs (Blum & Blum, 1975; Case & Smith, 1983). Blum & Blum (1975) show that REX contains many large and interesting classes of recursive functions. Fulk has shown that, for an appropriate notion of reliable, there is an REX anomaly hierarchy similar to the EX hierarchy above. In Chen's dissertation (1981) it is shown that, if S is in REX, then *some* IIM simultaneously BC^*-identifies every recursive function and *REX*-identifies S. Minicozzi (1976) shows that the classes inferred by reliable IIMs *are* closed under finite (and effective infinite) union.

So far I have mostly been concerned with the correctness (or approximate correctness) of conjectures output by an IIM. There are additional desirable features. For example it is desirable if the running time of a (nearly) correct conjecture is small. Let FS denote the class of functions with output value 0 on all but finitely many inputs. It is easy to show that some IIM M EX-identifies FS and M's final conjecture on any function in FS runs in time linear in the length of input (expressed in binary notation). A beautiful result of M. Sipser is generalized slightly in Chen's dissertation (1981). It is shown there that if M is any IIM which BC^n-identifies the class of polynomial time computable functions (this class properly includes FS) and p is any (possibly high degree) polynomial, then there is a function f in FS such that all but finitely many of M's output programs on input f run in time $> p$ of the length of the input. Hence, *easily* computable (approximate) explanations for easily computable functions cannot be inferred provided we also want to find (approximate) explanations for other easily computable, but not quite so easily computable, functions! It is further shown in Chen (1981) that this result does not extend to BC^*. Dana Angluin at Yale told me she has generalized Sipser's result in other directions. Much work remains to be done concerning the subject of runtime of inferred programs.

Another desirable feature of a (nearly) correct conjecture is that it be a small size program—possibly minimal size. One can think of the size of a program as the number of symbols in it. While in very strong senses there are computable functions possessing no minimal runtime programs (Blum, 1967a; Meyer & Fischer, 1972), there are always minimal *size* programs for any computable function. Blum (1967b) gives an axiomatic treatment of program size. Freivalds (1975) considered EX-identification with the additional requirement that the final conjecture be actually minimal size. Minimal size programs satisfy a variant of Occam's Razor. Freivalds (1975) nicely showed that this new criterion was *dependent* (dependent, I believe, in an inelegant, unprofound way) on the particular acceptable programming system employed! This motivated him to consider a slightly less strict criterion generalized by me below. Freivalds's less strict criterion is the $a = 0$ case in the following.

Definition (Chen, 1981, 1982). S is in MEX^a iff there is an IIM M and a recursive function h such that M EX^a-identifies S *and*, for all f in S, M's final conjecture on f has size no greater than h of the size of a *minimal* size program for f.

Informally the final program is restricted to have size within a computable "fudge factor," h, of minimal size.

It turns out that MEX^a is independent of the acceptable programming system (Freivalds, 1975; Chen, 1981, 1982). That is, for each fixed acceptable programming system, it is the same class of sets of recursive functions.

It is interesting to consider whether the pleasant restriction that final programs be nearly minimal size limits the inferring power of IIMs. Let Z be the collection of characteristic functions of finite sets, that is, the class of 0–1 valued functions which each equal 0 on all but a finite number of arguments. Since Z is contained (properly) in the class of primitive recursive functions, it is in EX. In fact, since Z is such a basic and simple class of functions, it is trivial to show directly Z is in EX. Kinber (1977) announced that Z is *not* in MEX^0! Chen shows further that:

Theorem (Chen, 1981, 1982). For each n in N, Z is not in MEX^n.

This suggests that the criteria MEX^n are too restricted to be practical. However, Chen showed that:

Theorem (Chen, 1981, 1982). $S_a = \{f \mid$ program number f(0) computes f except for up to a anomalies$\}$ *is* in MEX^a.

This is especially surprising since we know from above (Case & Smith, 1978, 1983) that, for example, S_1 is not in EX^0, yet by Chen's result it *is* in MEX^1! Hence, EX^0 and MEX^1 are just incomparable. Each contains a large class of functions the other does not! From Chen's result and Case and Smith (1978, 1983) it follows that:

Corollary (Chen, 1981, 1982). MEX^0 is properly contained in MEX^1, which is properly contained in MEX^2, which is properly contained in, . . . , each of which is properly contained in MEX^*.

Chen showed the following surprising:

Theorem (Chen, 1981, 1982). $MEX^* = EX^*$!

Hence, nearly minimal size programs *can* be inferred without loss of inferring power *provided* we are willing to tolerate an unbounded finite number of anomalies in the final program, but not if the finite number of anomalies is uniformly bounded by a constant.

Summarizing we have the following:

Theorem (Case & Smith, 1978, 1983; Chen, 1981, 1982). (An arrow from one criterion to another denotes containment, and lack of an equal sign or implicit or explicit arrow denotes lack of containment.)

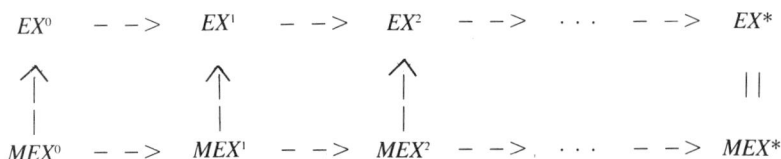

EX^0 $- ->$ EX^1 $- ->$ EX^2 $- ->$ $\cdots$ $- ->$ EX^*

MEX^0 $- ->$ MEX^1 $- ->$ MEX^2 $- ->$ $\cdots$ $- ->$ MEX^*

Chen obtained the following Non-Union Theorem for MEX.

Theorem (Chen, 1981, 1982). There are classes S and T in MEX^0 such that the union of S and T is not in EX^*.

It seems interesting to search for generalizations and strengthenings of this Theorem.

Another set of criteria to be explored is:

$MFEX^a$, that is, FEX^a, but with *each* final program within some recursive "factor" of minimal size.

Language Learning Machines

This section is *not* about machines that learn to talk sense. It is instead about machine inference of *formal* grammars from *texts* (arbitrary, not necessarily computable) enumerations of *formal* languages. There are at least two motivations for this work. One is that it is much easier than the study of machines that learn to talk sense. The other is that the inference of grammars from text seems to be a mathematically interesting and tractable *approximation* to the study of real language learning. Gold (1967) in his seminal paper on the subject pointed out that the psycholinguistic literature indicates that children are seemingly rarely informed of their grammatical errors; hence, their *formal* exposure to language consists in receiving some *enumeration* of the utterances in the language *without* much information about the non-elements of the language. Whence the interest in inference from *texts* of a language. Texts contain the positive information, but not (explicitly) the negative information about a language. Of course the characteristic function of a language contains (explicitly) both positive and negative information. A special case of what we studied in the previous section of this chapter is the inference of programs for characteristic functions of languages. For *formal* language learning it then seems more appropriate to study inference from texts rather than characteristic functions. Now a formal grammar for a language in the most general case (type 0, Hopcroft & Ullman, 1979) is equivalent to a program which enumerates the language. The languages enumerable by a program are just the *recursively enumerable* (*r.e.*) languages. It seems most natural to consider, then, inference of grammars from texts rather than inference of programs for characteristic functions from texts. In any case I do not treat the latter in this chapter. See Osherson and Weinstein (1982a), Pinker (1979), Wexler and Culicover (1980), and Wexler (1982) for discussion of the role of Gold's paradigm in contemporary theories of natural language. See Case and Lynes (1982) for some surprising comparisons between the inference of grammars and of decision procedures each from *characteristic functions* of formal languages.

I proceed more formally now. A *text* t for a language L is just a mapping from N into [N union {*}] such that [range of t $-$ {*}] = L. We shall sometimes refer to [range of t $-$ {*}] as the *content* of t. The "*" is from Blum & Blum (1975) to help us model gaps in texts and to facilitate handling the finite languages (including the empty language). Below we define a series of text identification criteria generalizing Gold's (1967) famous text identification. These criteria are from the paper I did with my student Lynes (Case & Lynes, 1982). Gold's criterion is the a = 0 case. Osherson and Weinstein (1982a, b) independently defined the a = * case.

Definition (Case & Lynes, 1982). We say a machine M *TXTEX^a-identifies* a language L iff for *all* texts t for L, M fed t outputs some finite, non-empty sequence of programs (equivalently, grammars) the last of which enumerates a language which differs from L by no more than a elements if a is in N, by no more than finitely many elements if a = *.

TXTEX^a = the class of sets S of r.e. languages such that some machine *TXTEX^a*-identifies each language in S.

We shall refer to *TXTEX^0* as just *TXTEX*. It is easy to show (Gold, 1967) that the class of all finite languages is in *TXTEX*. Gold (1967) showed that *no* class of languages in *TXTEX* contains both an infinite language and all its finite sublanguages! Clearly, then (Osherson, Stob, & Weinstein, 1982), the class of finite languages is in a very strong sense *maximal*. It also follows that none of the classes of languages in the Chomsky hierarchy (regular, context free, context sensitive, and r.e) are contained in *TXTEX*. This suggested to Gold that the classes in *TXTEX* are "small." He considered two plausible, alternative conclusions. One was that the class of natural languages is much "smaller" than previously thought—after all we can learn natural languages, but no machine can learn even the class of regular languages let alone any superclass of the regular languages (at least with respect to *TXTEX*). The other was that children are being given additional information in some perhaps subtle way. First I'll discuss "smallness" of classes in *TXTEX*, then additional information. If we take as evidence of smallness that no superclass of the puny regular languages can be learned (with respect to *TXTEX*), then the first conclusion is perhaps warranted. Dana Angluin provides an argument against this evidence of smallness. She (1980a, b) defines a natural class of languages called the *pattern languages* and shows that this class *is* in *TXTEX*, but it is incomparable (with respect to class inclusion) to the classes of regular and context free languages. Hence, the classes in *TXTEX* just divide up the "world" differently than low level Chomsky classes. Wiehagen (1977; Klette & Wiehagen, 1980) showed there is a class of self-referential languages in TXTEX so "large" that it contains a finite variant of each r.e. language! I argue that we have no evidence that the class of (past, present, and possible future) natural languages contains an infinite language and all its finite sublanguages. Furthermore, there is no experimental evidence that people could learn even the regular languages *by text presentation*. There is some experimental evidence that people can't learn much at all by *text presentation* unless there is also an accompanying semantics (Moeser & Bregman, 1972, 1973)! Clearly there is a need to determine just how sensitive these results are to the many parameters of interest. In any case it seems to me that children *are being given additional information—semantics*. Frankly that is not so subtle. It's just hard to formalize mathematically. I strongly recommend that future mathematical research in (machine) language learning attempt to describe formalisms that take semantics into account at least approximately. One mathematical trick is to assume that semantics is somehow providing grammatical (not text) information about the complement of a language and to consider criteria of success which assume that varying degrees of grammatical information about the complement are also presented. One can abstract away from the mechanism by which semantics provides this information. Under my direction Fulk is investigating such criteria. He has already shown, for example, that being given text for a language and a grammar for the complement is equivalent to being given text for it and an enumeration of a non-empty, finite sequence of grammars, the last of which is a grammar for the complement. Furthermore, he has exhibited hierarchies of criteria based on being given text and slightly erroneous grammars for the complement. I would frankly be happy to see some robust, recursion theoretic formalisms which do not abstract away from the mechanism by which semantics provides useful information.

I now move on to present some material which does not answer my criticisms, but which is still of interest; furthermore, some of it leads naturally to additional problems and directions.

Osherson, Stob, and Weinstein in reading the experimental, language learning literature found a (perhaps implicit) assumption that people have a "store" of grammars *for natural languages* and at any time in learning a natural language people conjecture one of these "stored" grammars. This led them to the following:

Definition (Osherson et al., 1983). A machine is called *prudent* iff any conjecture it ever outputs is a program for enumerating some language it *TXTEX*-identifies.

They posed the interesting question as to whether any S in *TXTEX* can be *TXTEX*-identified by some prudent machine. Fulk showed the surprising result that "prudence suffices":

Theorem (Fulk). For any M_1, there is an M_2 such that M_2 is prudent and *TXTEX*-identifies at least the classes of languages that M_1 does.

It is an interesting open question whether such an M_2 can be algorithmically found from M_1.

Definition (Case & Lynes, 1982). A machine M *TXTBC^a*-identifies a language L iff for all texts t for L, M fed t outputs an infinite sequence of programs (equivalently, grammars) all but finitely many of which enumerate a language which differs from L by no more than a elements if a is in N, by no more than finitely many elements if a = *.

TXTBC^a = the class of sets S of r.e. languages such that some machine *TXTBC^a*-identifies each language in S.

Osherson and Weinstein (1982a, b) independently defined our notions of *TXTBC^0* and *TXTBC**. They established the interconnections between these, *TXTEX,* and *TXTEX**. These interconnections are a part of the next theorem (mostly) due to myself and Lynes. We worked independently of Osherson and Weinstein except that we learned their nice result that *TXTEX** is *not* contained in *TXTBC^0* from them. It should be noted in this theorem that the *TXTBC* hierarchy is shifted by a factor of 2 in comparison to the *TXTEX* hierarchy! More specifically: *TXTEX^m* is contained in *TXTBC^n* iff m is less than or equal to 2n. Here is an intuitive comment on this factor of 2 result. Above I proved Steel's observation that *EX** *is* contained in *BC^0*. If one attempts to copy that argument in the case of text inference, one discovers that with essentially half the information in a characteristic function, that is, with text, one can, by resorting to an infinite sequence of output programs, patch but half the anomalies.

Theorem (Case & Lynes, 1982). (An arrow from one criterion to another denotes containment, and lack of an implicit or explicit arrow denotes lack of containment.)

$$TXTBC^0 \xrightarrow{\hspace{2cm}} TXTBC^1 \; \rightarrow \; \cdots \; \rightarrow \; TXTBC^*$$

$$\uparrow \qquad\qquad\qquad \uparrow \qquad\qquad\qquad\qquad\qquad \uparrow$$

$$TXTEX^0 \; \rightarrow \; TXTEX^1 \; \rightarrow \; TXTEX^2 \; \rightarrow \; \cdots \; \rightarrow \; TXTEX^*$$

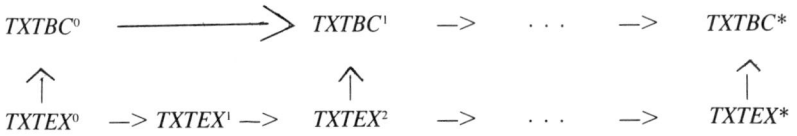

Recently with my student Henjin Chi I showed that there is a notion of $TXTMEX^a$-identification for text analogous to MEX^a-identification above and that similar hierarchy results hold. In particular this means for "practical" criteria there is a loss of learning power if nearly minimal size grammars are required.

One can define a notion of BC-*prudence* for $TXTBC$ analogous to the prudence notion above for $TXTEX$. It is open whether BC-prudent machines suffice for $TXTBC$!

Let $TXTFEX$ be defined just like $TXTBC$ except that the infinite sequence of output programs is restricted to contain only finitely many *different* programs. This notion is from Osherson and Weinstein (1982b). They show the extremely nice result that TXTEX is *properly* contained in $TXTFEX$ (which is properly contained in $TXTBC$). In particular, then, we again have the problem that to realize the full power of $TXTBC$ inference we would need a warehouse of unbounded size to store the most recent conjecture. Similarly we have this problem for $TXTFEX$ since there is no bound on the finite number of "final" programs. Let $TXTFEX_n$ denote $TXTFEX$ but with the restriction that the final *correct* programs be no more than n in number. My analysis of the proof in Osherson and Weinstein (1982b) that $TXTEX$ is properly contained in $TXTFEX$ enables me to conclude that $TXTEX$ is in fact properly contained in $TXTFEX_2$! Now $TXTFEX_2$ is a practical text criterion; furthermore, since it is strictly more powerful than $TXTEX$, if humans did not converge to a final grammar in their heads (per natural language learned), but rather converged to oscillating (perhaps in some highly non-periodic way) between up to two grammars, they could text-identify a larger class of "natural" languages. This argument has motivated me to investigate (work in progress) the obvious variations on the theme (with anomalies, etc.) of $TXTFEX_n$. It seems to me that if one is going to study text-identification criteria at all as a model of language learning, then criteria like $TXTFEX_n$ for "small" n and allowing a "small" number of anomalies are vastly more plausible than TXTEX!

The next theorem generalizes a result of Gold's I mentioned above. It contrasts sharply with Harrington's Theorem for BC^*.

Theorem (Case & Lynes, 1982). No class of languages which contains an infinite language and all its finite sublanguages is in $TXTBC^*$.

If (strict) neomechanism is true about the world, then children are never exposed to non-computable texts! It is interesting, then, to examine versions of the identification criteria we have discussed in which "for all texts t" is replaced by "for all recursive texts t." If I is a criterion of language learning above, then

RECI denotes I restricted to recursive texts. We (1982) noted that $RECTXTEX^a$ = $TXTEX^a$. The a = 0 case was announced by Wiehagen (1977). Hence, for TXTEX style criteria, demanding success even on non-computable texts does not affect learning power. We (1982) also pointed out that the entire class of r.e. languages *is* in $RECTXTBC*$! Hence, in a very strong sense, for TXTBC style criteria, demanding success on non-computable texts *does* affect learning power. I posed the question as to whether, for n in N, $RECTXTBC^n$ = $TXTBC^n$. In a letter dated August 18, 1983, R. Frievalds presented a proof that they are not! It can be shown that the classes $RECTXTBC^a$ form a hierarchy. Other work by me on RECI style criteria is in progress.

If neomechanism is true about the world, it is plausible that the texts children actually receive are not arbitrarily computationally complex (Machtey & Young, 1978) recursive texts. Let C denote a class of texts for the class of r.e. languages. Let CI denote text criterion I, restricted to texts in C. Let *PRIMREC* (respectively, *LINEARTIME*) denote the class of primitive recursive (respectively, linear time computable) texts (Machtey & Young, 1978). Gold (1967) adapted a theorem of Kleene's to show that any r.e. language is the content of some text in PRIM-REC. I can show the same for LINEARTIME. Gold showed that PRIM-RECTXTEX contains the entire class of r.e. languages! It is well known (Machtey & Young, 1978) that some primitive recursive texts are extraordinarily computationally complex. I can show that if C is LINEARTIME or any class of texts in EX which contains LINEARTIME, then CTXTEX contains the class of all r.e. languages. I think it would be interesting to investigate the tradeoffs (if any) between the computational complexity of a class of texts C for the r.e. languages and the "speed" of convergence of machines which CTXTEX-identify the class of r.e. languages. In general speed of convergence of learning machines has not been well explored. Daley and Smith have begun a preliminary exploration in the case of IIMs.

A subrecursive class of texts is, for our purposes, a class of recursive texts whose computational complexity is bounded above by a recursive function. We have the following generalization of an observation in Gold (1967). It is well known (Rogers, 1967) that any infinite r.e. language has a recursive text which is 1-to-1, that is, has no repetitions in it.

Theorem (Case). Suppose C is a subrecursive class of texts. Then there is an infinite r.e. set A such that *no* f in C is such that for some k > 0, f is "k (or less) to 1-valued" and the content of f = A. Moreover, we can take A to be a recursive language.

This means that if C is a subrecursive class of texts for the class of r.e. languages, all texts in C for some infinite r.e. language have to have an unbounded number of repetitions in them. Hence, either there will be infinitely many delays (*s) or, for *each* k > 0, some utterances will have to be repeated more than k times. If the texts we present to children contain a lot of repetitions, that would be consistent with a restriction in the world to subrecursive texts. I suspect the previous theorem can be strengthened to say something about when the repetitions must occur as a function of the complexity of C.

References

Angluin, D. (1980a). Finding patterns common to a set of strings. *Journal of Computer and Systems Science*, 21, 46–62.

Angluin, D. (1980b). Inductive inference of formal languages from positive data. *Information and Control*, 45, 117–135.

Blum, L., & Blum, M. (1975). Toward a mathematical theory of inductive inference. *Information and Control*, 28, 125–155.

Brainerd, W., & Landweber, L. (1974). *The theory of computation*. New York: Wiley.

Barzdin, J., & Podnicks, K. (1973) The theory of inductive inference. In *Proceedings of the mathematical foundations of computer science*. High Tatras, Czechoslovakia, pp. 9–15. (in Russian).

Barzdin, J. (1974). Two theorems on the limiting synthesis of functions. In *Theory of algorithms and programs*, Latvian State University, Riga, U.S.S.R., 210, 82–88 (in Russian).

Blum, M. (1967a). A machine-independent theory of the complexity of recursive functions. *Journal of the Association of Computing Machinery*, 14, 322–336.

Blum, M. (1967b). On the size of machines. *Information and Control*, 11, 257–265.

Case, J., & Fulk, M. (in preparation). *The non-existence of maximal machine-identifiable classes*.

Case, J., & Lynes, C. (1982). Machine inductive inference and language identification. In *Proceedings 9th colloquium automata, languages, and programming*. Aarhus, Denmark, July, 1982, *Lecture Notes in Computer Science*, 140, 77–115, Berlin: Springer.

Case, J., & Smith, C. (1978). Anomaly hierarchies of mechanized inductive inference. In *Proceedings of the 10th symposium on the theory of computing*, San Diego, CA, pp. 314–319.

Case, J., & Smith, C. (1983). Comparison of identification criteria for machine inductive inference. *Theoretical Computer Science*, 25, 193–220.

Case, J. (1974). Periodicity in generations of automata. *Mathematical Systems Theory*, 8, 15–32.

Chen, K. (1981). *Tradeoffs in machine inductive inference*. Ph.D. Dissertation, State University of New York.

Chen, K. (1982). Tradeoffs in the inductive inference of nearly minimal size programs. *Information and Control*, 52, 68–86.

Daley, R. (1983). On the error correcting power of pluralism in BC-type inductive inference. *Theoretical Computer Science*, 24, 95–104.

de Leeuw, E., Moore, C., Shannon, C., & Shapiro, N. (1956). Computability by probabilistic machines. *Automata Studies, Annals of Mathematical Studies*, 34. Princeton, NJ: Princeton University Press.

Feldman, J. (1972). Some decidability results on grammatical inference of best programs. *Information and Control*, 20, 244–262.

Freivalds, R. (1975). Minimal Gödel numbers and their identification in the limit. *Lecture notes in computer science*, 32, 219–225. Berlin/NY: Springer-Verlag.

Friedberg, R. (1958). Three theorems on recursive enumeration. *Journal of Symbolic Logic, 23*, 309–316.

Gill, J. (1972). *Probabilistic Turing machines and complexity of computation*. Ph.D. Dissertation, Berkeley, CA: University of California.

Gill, J. (1977). Computational complexity of probabilistic Turing machines. *SIAM Journal of Computing, 6*, 675–695.

Gold, M. (1967). Language identification in the limit. *Information and Control, 10*, 447–474.

Hopcroft, J., & Ullman, J. (1979). *Introduction to Automata Theory, Languages, and Computation.* Reading, MA: Addison-Wesley.

Klette, R., & Wiehagen, R. (1980). Research in the theory of inductive inference by GDR mathematicians—a survey. *Information Sciences, 22*, 149–169.

Kinber, E. (1977). On a theory of inductive inference. *Lecture notes in computer science, 56*, pp. 435–440. Berlin: Springer-Verlag.

Moeser, D., & Bregman, A. (1972). The role of reference in the acquisition of a miniature artificial language. *Journal of Verbal Learning and Verbal Behavior, 11*, 759–769.

Moeser, D., & Bregman, A. (1973). Imagery and language acquisition. *Journal of Verbal Learning and Verbal Behavior, 12*, 91–98.

Meyer, A., & Fischer, P. (1972). Computational speed-up by effective operators. *Journal of Symbolic Logic, 37*, 48–68.

Meyer, A., & Ritchie, D. (1967). Computational complexity and program structure. *IBM Research Report 1817.*

Machtey, M., Winklmann, K., & Young, P. (1978). Simple Gödel numberings. *SIAM Journal of Computing, 7*, 39–60.

Machtey, M., & Young, P. (1978). *An Introduction to the General Theory of Algorithms.* NY: North-Holland.

Minicozzi, E. (1976). Some natural properties of strong-identification in inductive inference. *Theoretical Computer Science, 2*, 345–360.

Osherson, D., Stob, M., & Weinstein, S. (1982). Ideal learning machines. *Cognitive Science, 6*, 277–290.

Osherson, D., Stob, M., & Weinstein, S. (1983). Learning strategies. *Information and Control, 5*, 34–97.

Osherson, D., & Weinstein, S. (1982). A note on formal learning theory. *Cognition, 11*, 77–88.

Osherson, D., & Weinstein, S. (1982). Criteria of language learning. *Information and Control, 52*, 123–138.

Pour-El, M. (1964). Gödel numberings versus Friedberg numberings. *Proceedings of the American Mathematical Society, 4*, 252–256.

Pour-El, M., & Richards, I. (1979). A computable ordinary differential equation which possesses no computable solution. *Annals of Mathematical Logic, 17*, 61–90.

Pour-El, M., & Richards, I. (1981). The wave equation with computable initial data such that its unique solution is not computable. *Advances in Mathematics, 39*, 215–239.

Pour-El, M., & Richards, I. (1983a). Computability and noncomputability in classical analysis. *Transactions of the American Mathematical Society, 275*, 539–560.

Pour-El, M., & Richards, I. (1983b). Noncomputability in analysis and physics: a complete determination of the class of noncomputable linear operators. *Advances in Mathematics, 48*, 44–74.

Pour-El, M., & Richards, I. (in press). The eigenvalues of an effectively determined self-adjoint operator are computable, but the sequence of eigenvalues is not. *Advances in Mathematics.*

Pinker, S. (1979). Formal models of language learning. *Cognition, 7*, 217–283.

Pitt, L. (1984, June). A characterization of probabilistic inference. *TR 319.* New Haven, CT: Yale University.

Riccardi, G. (1980). *The independence of control structures in abstract programming systems.* Ph.D. Dissertation. Buffalo: State University of New York.

Riccardi, G. (1981). The independence of control structures in abstract programming structures. *Journal of Computer and System Science, 22*, 107–143.

Rogers, H. (1958). Gödel numberings of the partial recursive functions. *Journal of Symbolic Logic,* *23,* 331–341.

Rogers, H. (1967). *Theory of recursive functions and effective computability.* New York: McGraw-Hill.

Royer, J. (1984). *A connotational theory of program structure.* Ph.D. Dissertation. Buffalo: State University of New York.

Smith, C. (1982). The power of pluralism for automatic program synthesis. *Journal of the Association for Computing Machinery, 29,* 1144–1165.

Wexler, K., & Culicover, P. (1980). *Formal principles of language acquisition.* Cambridge, MA: MIT Press.

Webb, J. (1980). *Mechanism, mentalism and metamathematics.* Boston: D. Reidel.

Wiehagen, R. (1977). Identification of formal languages. *Lecture notes in computer science, 53.* Berlin: Springer-Verlag.

Wexler, K. (1982). On extensional learnability. *Cognition, 11,* 89–95.

Chapter 5
An Analysis of a Learning Paradigm

Daniel N. Osherson
Massachusetts Institute of Technology

Michael Stob
Calvin College

Scott Weinstein
University of Pennsylvania

1 Introduction

In *Formal Principles of Language Acquisition*, Kenneth Wexler and Peter Culicover present a theory of the learnability of a certain collection of languages with transformational grammars. Their theory is the only sustained effort to show the learnability of a class of languages with some linguistic significance. In this respect alone, their theory is of considerable theoretical interest. Moreover, their theory demonstrates not only the learnability of a large collection of languages but also demonstrates that learning can take place in a feasible way—that is, under psychological constraints that seem to be plausible first hypotheses with respect to child language acquisition.

Underlying Wexler and Culicover's theory is a substantial body of work of a more abstract character on language acquisition. This "formal learning theory" began with investigations by Gold (1967) on the identifiability of various classes of languages and has been pursued by researchers in the theory of computation under the title "machine inductive inference." This theory seeks to provide mathematical models of the fixation of belief and to provide the tools necessary for a detailed study of learning.

In this paper we will apply the framework provided by formal learning theory to the learning theoretic paradigm embodied in the model of language acquisition proposed by Wexler and Culicover. This study will highlight several properties of the paradigm they investigate.

The paper is organized as follows. After a brief exposition of the notions of formal learning theory in Section 2, we proceed to an analysis of the

Wexler–Culicover learning paradigm in Section 3. Here, we isolate and discuss eight learning theoretic properties of their paradigm. In Section 4, we analyze these properties singly and in combination using the tools of formal learning theory. We provide information about the strength of each of these assumptions singly and about the role they play in achieving the overall learnability result. Section 5 is occupied with concluding remarks.

2 Formal Preliminaries

2.1 Languages and Texts

N is the set of natural numbers. We take the notions *finite sequence* (in N) and *infinite sequence* (in N) to be basic. The set of all finite sequences is denoted: SEQ. For ρ, $\tau \in$ SEQ, n $\in$ N, and infinite sequence, t: ρ is *in* t if ρ is an initial segment of t; ρ is *in* τ if ρ is an initial segment of τ; rng(ρ) is the set of numbers appearing in ρ; rng(t) is the set of numbers appearing in t; lh(ρ) is the length of ρ; finite sequences of length 1 are identified with their sole member; $\rho*\tau$ is the concatenation of ρ and τ; ρ(n) is the nth member of ρ; t(n) is the nth member of t; $\bar{\rho}$ (n) is the finite sequence of length n in ρ; and $\bar{t}$(n) is the finite sequence of length n in t. τ^n is the n-fold concantenation of τ with itself. τ^{-n} is the initial segment of τ of length lh(τ) $-$ n and $^{-n}\tau$ is the final segment of τ of length n.

Let ϕ_0, ϕ_1, . . . , ϕ_i, . . . be a fixed list of all partial recursive functions of one variable, and assume the list to be *acceptable* in the sense of Rogers (1967, Chapter 2). For i $\in$ N, let W_i = domain ϕ_i, the recursively enumerable subset of N with *index* i. *Languages* are identified with nonempty members of $\{W_i | i \in N\}$. The collection of all languages is denoted: *RE*. For L $\in$ *RE*, i $\in$ N, if L = W_i, then i is said to be *for* L. It can be shown that there are infinitely many indices for any given language, L. In contexts where languages themselves are (the graphs) of functions we will identify functions with languages and say that i is an index for f if W_i = graph (f) under a fixed recursive pairing function $<., .>$.

A *text for* L $\in$ *RE*, is any infinite sequence such that rng(t) = L. The class of all texts for L is denoted: T_L. Given a collection, *L*, of languages, "T_L" denotes $U_{L \in L} T_L$, the class of all texts for languages in *L*.

2.2 Learning Functions and Identification

Let G be a fixed computable isomorphism between SEQ and N. A *learning function* is any function from N into N; such a function will be thought of as operating on members of SEQ (via G), yielding indices for recursively enumerable sets.

Let F be a learning function and t be a text. We say that F *converges to* i *on* t just in case $F(\bar{t}(n)) = i$ for all but finitely many n. Intuitively, F converges to i on t if F eventually conjectures i and never departs from it thereafter. We say that F *converges on* t just in case F converges to i on t for some i. F is said to *identify* t just in case F converges to some i on t such that $W_i = \text{rng}(t)$. F *identifies* L ∈ RE just in case F identifies every t ∈ T_L; F identifies L ⊆ RE just in case F identifies every L ∈ L; in this case L is said to be identifiable.

We call a set of learning functions, S, a *strategy*. A strategy, S, is said to be *restrictive* if there is an identifiable L which cannot be identified by any F ∈ S.

2.3 Some Notations

$K = \{i | i \in W_i\}$. K is r.e. and $\bar{K}$ (the complement of K) is not r.e.
If $X \subseteq N$, $p^X = \{p^n | n \in X\}$.

2.4 Some Useful Facts

The following lemma, due to Blum and Blum (1975), is a very useful tool in learning theoretical studies. See Osherson, Stob, and Weinstein (1983) for a proof of the lemma and a discussion of its content and consequences in a topological setting.

Lemma 1: If F identifies L then ∃ ρ such that
(i) $\text{rng}(\rho) \subseteq L$;

(ii) $W_{F(\rho)} = L$; and

(iii) $\forall \tau (\text{rng}(\tau) \subseteq L \rightarrow F(\rho) = F(\rho * \tau))$.

If ρ satisfies the conditions (i) through (iii) we call ρ a *locking* sequence for F and L.

The following theorem gives a useful combinatorial characterization of identifiability. The result and its proof are based on the characterization theorem of Anguin (1980).

Theorem 2: (The Characterization Theorem)
(i) *L* is identifiable,

if and only if,

(ii) $\forall L \in L \ \exists D \ [D \text{ is finite} \wedge D \subseteq L \wedge \forall L' \in L(L' \subseteq L \rightarrow D \not\subseteq L')]$.
Proof: (ii→i) Suppose *L* satisfies (ii). Let $<D_i, W_{f(i)}>_{i \in N}$ be such that f is 1-1, $\{W_{f(i)} | i \in N\} = L$ and $\forall i \forall j (D_i \text{ is finite} \ D_i \subseteq W_{f(i)} \wedge (W_{f(i)} \subseteq W_{f(i)} \rightarrow D_i \not\subseteq W_{f(i)}))$ and $W_{f(i)} = W_{f(i)} \rightarrow D_i = D_i$.
Define a learning function, F, as follows: $F(\tau) = f(\mu i(D_i \subseteq \text{rng} (\tau) \subseteq W_{f(i)}))$ if there

exists such an i; = f(0) otherwise. We claim that F identifies L. Let t be a text for $L \in L$ and let $i_0 = \mu i(L = W_{t(i)})$. Let $X = \{j < i_0 | W_{t(i_0)} - W_{t(j)} \neq \emptyset\}$ and let $n_j \in W_{f(i_0)} - W_{t(j)}$ for every $j \in X$. Let $m = \mu n(D_i \cup \{n_j | j \in X\} \subseteq rng(\bar{t}(n)))$. We claim that $\forall n \geq m \ F(\bar{t}(n)) = f(i_0)$. Let $n \geq m$. Clearly, $D_i \subseteq rng(\bar{t}(n)) \subseteq W_{t(i_0)}$. If $j \in X$, then $rng(\bar{t}(n)) \not\subseteq W_{t(j)}$. If $j < i_0$ and $j \notin X$, then $W_{t(i_0)} \subseteq W_{t(j)}$. But then, $D_i \not\subseteq W_{t(i_0)}$, and hence $D_i \not\subseteq rng(\bar{t}(n))$. Hence $F(\bar{t}(n)) = f(i_0)$.

(i → ii) Suppose F identifies L and, for reductio, fix $L \in L$ such that $\forall D$ (D $\subseteq L \wedge$ D is finite $\rightarrow (L_D \in L \wedge D \subseteq L_D, CL))$. Let t be a text for L and let D_i enumerate the finite subsets of L. For each i, let t_i be a text for L_{D_i}. We define a text, t', for L on which F does not converge, contradicting the hypothesis that F identifies L. Let $\tau_0 = <t(0)>$ and let $\tau_{2i} = \tau_{2i-1} * t(i)$. Let $\tau_{2i+1} = \tau_{2i} * t_j(m)$ where $D_j = rng(\tau_{2i})$ and $m = \mu n(W_{F(\tau_{2i} * \bar{t}_j(n))} = L_{D_j})$. Let $t' = \bigcup_{i \in N} \tau_i$. t' is a text for L and F does not converge on t'.

The following theorem, due to Gold (1967), shows that certain simple collections of languages are not identifiable. It is a corollary of the Characterization Theorem.

Theorem 3: If L properly includes all finite languages then L is not identifiable.

3 Learning Theoretic Properties of the Wexler–Culicover Paradigm

In this section we consider eight learning theoretic properties of the paradigm which Wexler and Culicover invoke to demonstrate the learnability of their class of transformational languages. The first five of these are properties of the learner, that is, strategies in the terminology of the preceding section; the next two deal with the environment for learning; and the eighth concerns the criterion of success.

3.1 Strategies

The five strategies which Wexler and Culicover hypothesize about the learner are (1) memory limitation, (2) gradualism, (3) computability, (4) total function mindedness, and (5) degree 2 learning. We will describe each of these strategies in turn and discuss their plausibility.

3.1.1 Memory limitation. It is reasonable to suppose that a child engaged in the process of acquiring a language does not recall all the primary linguistic data she has been presented over time, or at least that the entire body of these data is not at each moment effective in determining the future course of her process of acquisition. This may be supposed to be so except insofar as this body of data has somehow shaped her current linguistic competence. This quite plausible hypothesis about the use which the child makes of the data for language acquisition may be formulated in terms of the child's mechanism for projecting her hypotheses, the strategy of memory limitation (due to Wexler & Culicover, 1980). This strategy states that the child's next grammatical hypothesis is a function of her current hypothesis, her current datum, and at most the last n of her preceding data, for some fixed n. Formally, F is an n-memory limited learning function if and only if $\forall \rho \forall \tau (F(\rho^{-n}) = F(\tau^{-n}) \wedge {}^{-n}\rho = {}^{-n}\tau \rightarrow F(\rho) = F(\tau))$.

3.1.2 Gradualism.
Memory limitation constrains the use to which the learner may put past data. In contrast, gradualism constrains the distance which the learner can move as a result of the presentation of a single datum. In order to make sense of such a constraint, we need to avail ourselves of the notion of a measure on the distance between grammars. In an intuitive sense, the hypothesis that the learner can only be driven to a grammar of nearby complexity to her current conjecture in a single step seems quite plausible. Children do not seem to fluctuate wildly in their states of grammatical competence through the course of acquisition but appear to experience gradual reorganizations of their grammar.

In the Wexler and Culicover paradigm gradualism is realized as the constraint that the learning procedure alter at most one rule of its hypothesized transformational component when presented with any single datum. One way of formalizing the notion of gradualism in the general setting of learning theory is to suppose that there is a fixed assignment, f, of complexity to grammars which maps them one to one onto the natural numbers. Then, a learning function, G, is said to be gradual with modulus k if and only if $\forall \tau |f(G(\tau)) - f(G(\tau^{-1}))| < k$.

3.1.3 Computability.
In contrast to the first two strategies which deal with use of past data and the relation between consecutive conjectures, computability constrains the manner in which grammatical hypotheses are projected on the basis of the primary linguistic data. The hypothesis of computability states that the learner's conjectures must be a computable function of the corpus of primary linguistic data to which she has been exposed, that is, a function which may be computed by a Turing machine. In the current intellectual climate, this seems like a plausible hypothesis since it just amounts to a specialization of the computational theory of the mind to the case of language acquisition. Below, in Section 4, we will consider learning theoretic results both with respect to this strategy and in its absence. The virtue of results about ineffective learning, that is, learning by non-computable hypothesis generators, is that they provide a means of prizing apart information theoretic and computation theoretic aspects of problems of inductive inference.

3.1.4 Total function mindedness.
Before proceeding to discuss this strategy it will be necessary to describe in more detail the learning situation which Wexler

and Culicover consider. Transformational languages are for Wexler and Culicover recursively enumerable sets of pairs consisting of a base phrase marker
and a surface string. The collection of base phrase markers is recursive. A text
for such a language consists, as in Section 2, of an enumeration of all and only
the pairs in the language. Thus, in the learning situation envisioned by Wexler
and Culicover the pairs of base phrase marker and surface string are construed
as the data available to the learner. In order to achieve their learning result
Wexler and Culicover place two special constraints on the character of the
transformational languages they consider. First, these languages are taken to be
single valued, that is, each base phrase marker is paired with at most one surface
string. This hypothesis of single valuedness is insured by the consideration only
of languages which are generated by deterministic transformational components,
that is, components which do not allow for optional application of designated
transformations. Second, the languages Wexler and Culicover consider are total,
that is, each base phrase marker is paired with some surface string or can be
effectively determined to fail to be so paired (and hence paired with an arbitrary
filter symbol). Thus, the transformational components which Wexler and Culicover consider do not exhibit the kind of arbitrary filtering which was crucial
to the results of Peters and Ritchie (1973) on the over-generativity of transformational grammars.

These two constraints on the transformational languages which Wexler and
Culicover investigate are transformed by them into a learning strategy in the
following way. Namely, the hypotheses of the learner are restricted to be grammars of single valued total languages, that is, languages which are the graphs
of total functions whose domain is the collection of phrase markers generated
by the universal base component. We may formalize this strategy as follows.
F is total function minded just in case $\forall i \in \text{rng}(F)$ (W_i is a total function).

3.1.5 Degree 2 learning.
This last strategy concerns the complexity of the
primary linguistic data to which the learner is responsive. Children in acquiring
their native language are not exposed to data of unlimited complexity. Moreover,
it seems plausible to suppose that there may be a bound on the complexity of
data which are effective in altering their conjectures. This last hypothesis may
be formulated in terms of a learning strategy, namely, ignore data of complexity
beyond a fixed bound. Formally, F is a C,n learner iff $\forall \tau \forall m$ ($C(m) > n \rightarrow F(\tau)$
$= F(\tau*m)$), where C is a function from N into N which measures the complexity
of a datum.

Clearly, the restrictiveness of this strategy depends heavily on the character
of C. In the Wexler–Culicover paradigm, C is chosen to measure the depth of
embedding of sentence nodes in a base phrase marker and n is set to 2. This
choice has the important consequence that $\{m | \ C(m) \leq 2\}$ is finite, that is, C,n
learners within the Wexler–Culicover paradigm are sensitive in framing their
grammatical hypotheses to only a finite collection of possible data.

3.2 Environments

Wexler and Culicover consider two hypotheses about the environments in which language acquisition occurs.

3.2.1 Stochastic environments. In some environments each potential element of a language is associated with a fixed probability of occurrence, invariant through time. Wexler and Culicover actually hypothesize that each sentence of a language has associated with it a fixed lower bound on the probability of its occurrence, which is invariant over time. The simplification considered here does not affect the plausibility considerations advanced below nor the results reported in Section 4. Such environments may be thought of as infinite sequences of stochastically independent events, the probability of a given element, e, appearing in the n + 1st position being independent of n and of the contents of positions 0 through n.

To study such environments, each $L \in RE$ is associated with a proability measure, m_L, on N such that for all $x \in N$, $x \in L$ if and only if $m_L(\{x\}) > 0$. (Recall that every $L \in RE$ is nonempty; see Section 2.1.) Next, we impose on T_{RE} its Baire topology, T_{RE}; that is, for each $\rho \in SEQ$, we take $B_\rho = \{t \in T_{RE} | \rho$ is in t$\}$ to be a basic open set of T_{RE}. For each $L \in RE$, we define the (unique) complete probability measure, M_L, on T_{RE} by stipulating that for all $\rho \in SEQ$, $M_L(B_\rho) = \Pi_{j < lh(\rho)} m_L(\rho(j))$. We now assume the existence of a fixed collection, $\{M_L | L \in RE\}$ of measures on corresponding members of $\{T_L | L \in RE\}$. Intuitively, for measurable $S \subseteq T_L$, $M_L(S)$ is the probability that an arbitrarily selected text for L is drawn from S.

This notion of stochastic environment does not seem to be a plausible hypothesis about the natural environment for language acquisition. For, it appears that the likelihood of the occurrence of any sentence could be made smaller and smaller without bound by manipulating the prior linguistic context. To give a somewhat whimsical example, the probability of occurrence of ''Snow is white'' at the n + 1st position in a text could be driven lower and lower by the occurrence of ''I'll give anyone who doesn't say, 'snow is white' m dollars'' at the nth position, for larger and larger values of m.

3.2.2 Infinity texts. An *infinity text* for a language, L, is one in which each sentence of L occurs infinitely often. As an environment for learning, infinity texts guarantee that the learner will encounter each construction of a language after any stage of her linguistic development. As we will see below, this feature of infinity texts relieves the restrictions imposed on memory limited learners.

3.3 Criterion of Success: Measure 1 Learning

In the stochastic context discussed in Section 3.2.1, the definition of language identification given above may be modified to a probabilistic notion of acquisition. As a criterion of success for acquiring a language, L, Wexler and Culicover require only that the learner identify a subset of T_L of sufficient probability, not necessarily all of T_L. F is said to *measure 1 identify* L if and only if M_L ({t ∈ T_L| F identifies t}) = 1. F *measure 1 identifies L* if and only if F measure 1 identifies each L ∈ L; in this case, L is said to be *measure 1 identifiable*. Notice that if F identifies every infinity text for L then F measure 1 identifies L, since M_L ({t ∈ T_L|∃ m ∈ L({n|t(n) = m} is finite)}) = 0 for any measure of the sort described above. In Section 4 we will see that measure 1 identification is a significantly weaker criterion of success than identification.

4 Learning Theoretical Analysis

In the preceding section we isolated and discussed several of the hypotheses underlying the Wexler–Culicover learning paradigm. In this section we will examine a number of results which demonstrate the strength of these hypotheses taken singly and in combination in order to determine their role in securing the Wexler–Culicover learnability result.

4.1 Gradualism, Memory Limitation, and Degree 2 Learning

A gradual learner experiences only modest reorganizations of her grammatical competence through the course of language acquisition. The following theorem shows that this style of learning is no handicap.

> **Theorem 4:** If L is (computably) identifiable, then L is (computably) identifiable by a gradual learning function.

A proof of this theorem may be found in Osherson, Stob, and Weinstein (1982).

Whereas gradualism places restrictions on neither computable nor noneffective learners, memory limitation restricts even the classes of total functions available to noneffective learners as compared to those available to computable learners whose memories are unconstrained.

> **Theorem 5:** There is a class of total recursive functions, F, such that F is computably identifiable, but F is not identifiable by any n-memory limited learner, computable or not.
>
> **Proof:** Let F = {f| ∀ x(f(x) = 0 V f(x) = 1) ∧ ({x|f(x) = 0} is finite V {x|f(x) = 0} = N)}. Clearly, F is identifiable by a computable learning function.
>
> Suppose, for *reductio*, that F is identifiable by a k-memory limited learning function, G. Let τ be a locking sequence for λn.0 and G. Let τ′ = τ*τ(0)^k. Let τ″ be such that τ′ * τ″ locks G onto the f ∈ F such that f(x) = 0 iff <x, 0> ∈ rng(τ). Let n be such that <n, 0>∉rng(τ) and <n, 1>∉rng(τ″). Let t be an enumeration of f − {<n, 1>}.

Then, by k-memory limitation, G converges on $t' = \tau * <n, 0> * \tau(0)^k * \tau'' * t$ to an index for f, but t' is a text for $(f - \{<n, 1>\}) \cup \{<n, 0>\}$. Hence, G does not identify F.

Memory limitation is thus a severe restriction on even noneffective learners, but its combination with gradualism is more restrictive still, as the next theorem shows.

Theorem 6: There is a collection of languages, L, such that L is computably, 1-memory limited identifiable, but L is not gradually, n-memory limited identifiable for any n, even noneffectively.

A proof of this theorem may be found in Osherson et al. (1982).

As noted in Section 3.1.5, if F is a degree 2 learner, then F is sensitive to only finitely many data in framing its conjectures, that is, $\exists n \forall m > n \forall \tau \ (F(\tau*m) = F(\tau))$. We call an F which satisfies this condition *finitely sensitive*. It is easily seen that any finitely sensitive F can identify only finitely many languages.

Conversely if L is a finite collection of languages then L can be identified by a finitely sensitive learner, which is, in addition, computable, 1-memory limited and gradual.

Theorem 7: If L is finite then L can be identified by a computable, 1-memory limited, gradual, finitely sensitive learner.
Proof: Let $L = \{L_i | 0 \leq i < n\}$. For $0 \leq i$, $j < n$, let $d_{ij} = \mu m(m \ \varepsilon \ L_i - L_j)$ if such an m exists; $= \mu m(m \ \epsilon \ L_i)$ otherwise. Let $D = \{d_{ij} | 0 \leq i, j < n\}$ and let $D_i = D \cap L_i$. It follows from the definitions that $i \neq j \rightarrow D_i \neq D_j$. Let h be a 1-1 computable function on $P(D)$ such that $W_{h(D_i)} = L_i$. Define a learning function, F, as follows. $F(<>) = h(\emptyset)$. $F(\tau*m) = h(h^{-1}(F(\tau)) \cup \{m\})$, if $m \ \epsilon \ D$; $= F(\tau)$, otherwise. Clearly, F is computable, 1-memory limited and identifies L. F is finitely sensitive with bound max(D) and F is gradual with modulus max $\{|f(h(D')) - f(h(D''))| \| D', D'' \subseteq D\}$ for complexity measure, f.

4.2 Stochastic Environments, Measure 1 Learning, and Infinity Texts

Measure 1 identification of a language differs from ordinary identification only by a set of measure zero. The next proposition reveals the significance of this small difference.

Theorem 8: *RE* is measure 1 identifiable.
Proof: We define $f \ \epsilon \ F$ such that for all $L \ \epsilon \ RE$, $M_L(\{t \ \epsilon \ T_L | f \text{ identifies } t\}) = 1$. Let $L_0, L_1, \ldots$ be an enumeration of *RE*, and let $M_0, M_1, \ldots$ be an enumeration of their associated measures. If $n \ \epsilon \ N$, $\rho \ \epsilon \ SEQ$, and W is an r.e. set, we say that ρ *agrees with* W *through* n just in case for all $x < n$, $x \ \epsilon \ W$ if and only if $x \ \epsilon \ \text{rng} \ (\rho)$. Intuitively,

if t is a text, as m gets large we want to define $f(\bar{t}(m)) = i$ only if $\bar{t}(m)$ agrees with L_i through some large number n, with n increasing as m does. Yet we want n to be small relative to m so that most texts, t, for L_i have the property that $\bar{t}(m)$ agrees with L_i through n. To make the definition of f precise, define for every $j,n,m \in N$, $A_{j.n.m}$ = $\{t \in T_{L_j} | \bar{t}(m)$ does not agree with L_j through n$\}$. It is easy to see that $M_j(A_{j.n.m})$ is defined and that for every $j,n \in N$, $\lim_{m \to \infty} M_j(A_{j.n.m}) = 0$.

Define a function $h:N \to N$ by $h(n) = \mu m[\max\{M_0(A_{0.n.m}), \ldots, M_n(A_{n.n.m})\} < 2^{-n}]$.

Notice that $\sum_{n \in N} M_i(A_{i.n.h(n)})$ is finite, for $i \in N$. Now let $X_i = \{t | t \in A_{i.n.h(n)}$ for infinitely many n$\} = \bigcap_{k \in N} \bigcup_{n > k} A_{i.n.h(n)}$. Then, by the Borel–Cantelli Lemma (Lamperti, 1966, p. 25), $M_i(X_i) = 0$ for $i \in N$.

Now, given a text, t, define f on t as follows. $f(\bar{t}(m)) = \mu i \leq m[\bar{t}(m)$ agrees with L_i through n, where n is the greatest integer such that $h(n) \leq m]$, if such exists; $= 0$, otherwise. With this definition of f, it is clear that if i is the smallest index for L then f converges to i on all texts $t \notin X_i$.

We say that F *identifies* L *on a set of texts*, T, just in case F identifies every $t \in T_L \cap T$. The following theorem shows the extent to which infinity texts relieve the burden of memory limitation. Recall that the set of infinity texts for L has measure 1. Hence, the following theorem shows that if *L* is identifiable then *L* is 1-memory limited measure 1 identifiable.

Theorem 9: If *L* is identifiable then *L* is 1-memory limited identifiable on infinity texts.

Proof: Suppose *L* is identifiable. Then *L* satisfies condition (ii) of the characterization theorem. Let $<D_i, W_{f(i)}>$ be as in the proof of the characterization theorem. Toward constructing a 1-memory limited learning function, F, which identifies *L* on infinity texts, we define the following function G.

$$G(<i,D,m>,n) = \begin{cases} <i,D,m>, & \text{if } n > m \wedge D_i \subseteq D \wedge D \cup \{n\} \subseteq W_{(i)}; \\ <i,D \cup \{n\},m>, & \text{if } n \leq m \wedge D_i \subseteq D \wedge D \cup \{n\} \subseteq W_{(i)}; \\ <\mu j(D_i \subseteq D \cup \{n\} \subseteq W_{(i)}, & \text{if } \neg(D_i \subseteq D \wedge D \cup \{n\} \\ D \cup \{n\}, m + 1>, & \subseteq W_{(i)}) \wedge \exists j(D_i \subseteq D \subseteq W_{(i)}); \\ <0, D \cup \{n\}, m + 1> & \text{otherwise} \end{cases}$$

Let $h(i,D,m)$ be a 1-1 function with $W_{(h.i.D.m)} = W_{f(i)}$ for every i, D, m. For $1 \leq k \leq 3$, let $h_k(n) = (h^{-1}(n))_k$. Define F as follows. $F(<>) = h(0,\emptyset,0)$. $F(\tau^*<n>) = h(G(<h_1(F(\tau)),h_2(F(\tau)),h_3(F(\tau))>,n)$. It is clear from the definition that F is 1-memory limited. We claim that F identifies *L* on infinity texts. Let t be an infinity text for L $\in L$ and $i_0 = \mu j(L = W_{f(j)})$. We claim that there is a D and m such that F converges to $h(i_0, D, m)$ on t. First note that if F converges on t then F converges correctly. For otherwise there exists a j such that $D_j \subseteq W_{f(i_0)} \subset W_{f(j)}$ since t is an infinity text for $W_{f(i_0)}$. But this contradicts the characteristic property of the enumeration $<D_i, W_{f(i)}>_{i \in N}$. Suppose, then, that F fails to converge on t. Then $\{h_1 (F(\bar{t}(n))) \mid n \in N\}$ is infinite. Let X and the n_j be as in the proof of the characterization theorem. There is an n such that $h_3(F(\bar{t}(n))) \geq max(D_{i_0} \cup \{n_j \mid j \in X\})$. Since t is an infinity text, there is then an m such that $D_{i_0} \cup \{n_j \mid j \in X\} \subseteq h_2 (F(\bar{t}(m)))$. But then $\forall n \geq m (F(\bar{t}(n)) = F(\bar{t}(m)) \wedge h_1(F(\bar{t}(m)) = i_0)$. The proof of this is parallel to the proof of correct convergence for the characterization theorem.

4.3 Computability

Computability is a restriction on the power of arbitrary learning functions.

Theorem 10: There is an L such that L is identifiable but L is not computably identifiable.

Proof: Let $L = \{KUD \mid D \text{ finite}\}$. A proof that L is identifiable but not computably identifiable may be found in Osherson and Weinstein (1982), modulo the observation that identifiability (as defined here) and extensional identifiability (as defined there) collapse into one another for noncomputable learners.

Computability also further restricts other strategies, as the following theorem shows.

Theorem 11: There is a collection of languages, L, such that L is computably identifiable and L is 1-memory limited identifiable, but L is not computably, n-memory limited identifiable for any n.

Proof: Let $L = 2^K$, $L_n = L \cup \{3^n\}$ and $L'_n = L \cup \{2^n, 3^n\}$. Let $L = \{L\} \cup \{L_n \mid n \in N\} \cup \{L'_n \mid n \in N\}$. It is clear that L is computably identifiable and that L is 1-memory limited identifiable (by a noncomputable learner). To show that L is not computably, 1-memory limited identifiable, we argue as follows. (The argument for arbitrary n is a straightforward generalization.)

Suppose for reductio that F is computable and 1-memory limited and identifies L. Let τ be a locking sequence for F and L. For every $n \in K$, $F(\tau^*<2^n>) = F(\tau)$. Hence, for some $m \in \bar{K}$, $F(\tau^*<2^m>) = F(\tau)$, else $\bar{K}$ would be recursively enumerable. Let s be an enumeration of K, and let $t = \tau^*<3^m>^*s$ and $t' = \tau^*<2^m, 3^m>^*s$. By 1-memory limitation, $F(\tau^*<3^m>) = F(\tau^*<2^m, 3^m>)$. But, t is a text for L_m and t' is a text for L'_m. Hence, F does not identify L.

The measure 1 criterion of success is liberating for computable learners as well as for arbitrary learners. Let $L = \{L_i \mid i \in N\}$ be an indexed collection of languages, and let $\{p_i \mid i \in N\}$ be the corresponding measures on them. L is said to be *uniformly measured* just in case the predicates ''$x \in L_y$'' and ''$p_x(\{y\}) =$

z'' are decidable (the decidability of the latter predicate actually implies that of the former). Minor modifications in the proof of Theorem 8 yield the following.

Theorem 12: Let L be a uniformly measured collection of languages. Then, some computable F measure 1 identifies L.

Note that many collections which properly include all the finite languages can be uniformly measured. Hence, by Theorem 3, there are computably, measure 1 identifiable collections which are not identifiable.

4.4 Total Function Mindedness

We next turn to consider total function mindedness. First, as noted by Wexler and Culicover, total function mindedness is not restrictive in the context of ineffective learning. Indeed, any denumerable collection of functions is identifiable by a noneffective learner using a simple enumeration procedure. Hence, the entire collection of total recursive functions is identifiable by a noneffective learner, all of whose conjectures are indices of total recursive functions. For computable learners, the situation is quite different. Gold (1967, Theorem I.5) shows that the collection of total recursive functions is not identifiable by any computable function, total function minded or not. (See Blum & Blum, 1975, the NonUnion Theorem, for an interesting alternative proof.)

The question remains whether every collection of total recursive functions which is identifiable by a computable learning function, is identifiable by a total function minded computable learning function, that is, whether the strategy of total function mindedness is restrictive with respect to the collections of total functions which are computably identifiable. It would be surprising were this so, since it would mean that in order to identify certain collections of total functions, the learner would be forced to conjecture indices of r.e. sets which were not the graphs of total fuctions—conjectures which must be mistaken if the given collection of total functions is her target for learning. But in fact, total function mindedness does restrict the collections of total functions available to the computable learner.

Theorem 13: There is a collection, F, of total recursive functions such that F is identifiable by a computable learning function, but F is not identifiable by any total function minded computable learning function.
Proof: Let F be the collection of self describing total recursive functions. (A recursive function, f, is self describing iff $\mu n\ f(n) = 0$ is itself an index for f.) Clearly, F is identifiable by a simple effective 1-memory limited learning procedure. Hence, we only need show that F cannot be identified by any total function minded computable function, G. This is a corollary of the following lemmas. If f and g are total functions we say f is equal to g almost everywhere iff $\{n | f(n) \neq g(n)\}$ is finite.

Lemma 14: For every total recursive function, f, there is a self describing total recursive function, g, such that f is equal to g almost everywhere.

Lemma 15: Let F be an r.e. indexable collection of total recursive functions and let $G = \{g \mid \exists f(f \epsilon F \wedge f$ is equal to g almost everywhere}. Then G is r.e. indexable. We leave the proofs of the lemmas as an exercise for the interested reader. (See Rogers, 1967, for useful information.) To prove the theorem from the lemmas, suppose for *reductio* that G is a total function minded computable learning function which identifies F. Then $F' = \{W_i \mid i \epsilon \text{rng}(G)\}$ is an r.e. indexable collection of total recursive functions containing all the self describing total recursive functions. Let $F'' = \{g \mid \exists f(f \epsilon F' \wedge f$ is equal to g almost everywhere}. By the first lemma, F'' is exactly the collection of all total recursive functions. By the second lemma, F'' is r.e. indexable. But this contradicts the fact that the set of total recursive functions is not r.e. indexable. (Note that the same proof shows that total mindedness, with the obvious definition, is restrictive with respect to the collections of computably identifiable total recursive relations, modulo an application of the uniformization theorem, cf. Rogers, 1967, sect. 5.8.)

5 Conclusion

In the preceding sections we have provided an analysis of the Wexler–Culicover learning paradigm. This analysis illustrates the basis upon which the learnability result of Wexler and Culicover (1980) rests (cf. Theorem 7), as well as the surprising strength of some of the individual assumptions there deployed (cf. Theorems 8 and 12). The analysis also exhibits the role that learning theory can play in the study of natural language. Learning theory provides the tools to study which classes of languages are available to the child under explicit hypotheses about the child's linguistic environment, the learning strategy she implements, and the criterion of successful learning. In this way, learning theory constitutes an approach to the study of natural language which complements the approach offered by comparative grammar. A lengthier discussion of the relation between learning theory and comparative grammar, as well as a study of a learning paradigm which implies strong nativism, that is, the thesis that there are only finitely many natural languages, may be found in Osherson, Stob, and Weinstein (1984).

References

Angluin, D. (1980). Inductive inference of formal languages from positive data. *Information and Control, 45*, 117–135.

Blum, L., & Blum, M. (1975). Toward a mathematical theory of inductive inference. *Information and Control, 28*, 125–155.

Gold, E. M. (1967). Language identification in the limit. *Information and Control, 10*, 447–474.

Lamperti, J. (1966). *Probability: A Survey of the Mathematical Theory.* New York: W. A. Benjamin.

Osherson, D., & Weinstein, S. (1982). A note on formal learning theory. *Cognition, 11*, 77–88.

Osherson, D., Stob, M., & Weinstein, S. (1982). Learning strategies. *Information and Control, 53*, 32–51.

Osherson, D., Stob, M., & Weinstein, S. (1983). Note on a central lemma of learning theory. *Journal of Mathematical Psychology, 27*, 86–92.

Osherson, D., Stob, M., & Weinstein, S. (1984). Learning theory and natural language. *Cognition, 17*, 1–28.

Peters, P. S., & Ritchie, R. W. (1973). On the generative power of transformational grammar. *Information Sciences, 6*, 49–83.

Rogers, H. (1967). *Theory of recursive functions and effective computability.* New York: McGraw-Hill.

Wexler, K., & Culicover, P. (1980). *Formal principles of language acquisition.* Cambridge, MA: MIT Press.

Chapter 6
The Rise of Selective Theories: A Case Study and Some Lessons from Immunology

Massimo Piattelli-Palmarini
Florence Center for the History and Philosophy of Science, Italy
and Massachusetts Institute of Technology

Can the truth (*the capability to synthesize an antibody*) by learned? If so, it must be assumed not to pre-exist; to be learned, it must be acquired. We are thus confronted with the difficulty to which Socrates calls attention in *Meno*, namely that it makes as little sense to search for what one does not know as to search for what one knows; what one knows one cannot search for, since one knows it already, and what one does not know one cannot search for, since one does not even know what to search for. Socrates resolves this difficulty by postulating that learning is nothing but recollection. The truth (*the capability to synthesize an antibody*) cannot be brought in, but was already inherent.

Soren Kierkegaard (as quoted and translated by Niels K. Jerne in 1966; the replacement of "truth" by antibody formation is, of course, Jerne's) in N. K. Jerne (1966).

It is becoming for a great Dane to quote from another great Dane. We will capitalize on Jerne's substitution of antibody synthesis for Kierkegaard's "truth." It is tempting to make the inverse substitution down into the immunological literature, from Ehrlich to Jerne. After all, the problems facing selective theories in all domains are very similar. The triumph of selective theories in immunology, though, is an almost perfect paradigm case, as Noam Chomsky has not failed to underline, because it exposes what precisely was wrong with the instructive theories that contested this triumph for over half a century. As early as 1897 Paul Ehrlich had proposed a selective mechanism to account for the formation of antibodies. As we will see, Ehrlich's theory was then abandoned for over 50 years, until Jerne, one evening in March 1954, while walking home from the Danish State Serum Institute in Copenhagen got "the idea of a selective mechanism of antibody formation." In September 1955 he submitted to the Proceedings of the National Academy of Sciences of the U.S. a literally epoch-making paper that opened the modern selective outlook in immunology, putting an end to the era of instructivism. In 1969 another leading biochemist and immunologist, Gerald M. Edelman, felt entitled to use the expression "selective dogma" to summarize the state of the art (Edelman & Gall, 1969). The dogma is happily still with us.

In this paper I will endeavor to show why it took so long to establish this dogma and, most of all, which were the core assumptions that misled at least two generations of biologists to think any selective theory in immunology obviously false, nay, "inconceivable." These assumptions had to be overturned not only in immunology, but in many fields of biology, from enzymatic adaptation to genetic regulation, from the theory of evolution to the growth of neuronal networks. Selective theories are now prevailing everywhere in biology and such presumptions as the economy of nature, the optimality of design and the strict adaptiveness of innately specified mechanisms have lost much of their plausibility. The a priori plausibility-rating of hypotheses in biology is overwhelmingly in favor of selective models, rather than instructive ones. The *Zeitgeist* is blowing, if not against, at least far from instructivism and from its underlying presumptions.

Jerne's quotation perfectly captures the main puzzle of all instructive theories, one that I will call the puzzle of the first encounter. In a nutshell: if there is no pre-existing specificity, how can recognition of, and matching between, forms take place at all? What *unspecific* mechanism can secure the initial encounter (and a very *close* encounter at that) between the inside and the outside partners? Yet such encounters, in immunology as well as in language acquisition and in concept formation, must be efficient, non-random, quick, but conducive to long-lasting effects. The obstacle seems unsurmountable for *any* instructive theory I am aware of. The history of empiricism and of all classic learning theories is largely the history of the failure to appreciate the devastating effects of the puzzle of the first encounter. We owe it to Noam Chomsky and to Jerry Fodor to have fully appreciated this fact in the domains of language acquisition and concept formation.

Immunologists had been facing this obstacle over and over again from roughly 1910 to 1955, when Jerne overcame it by taking a selective tack. The dilemma of the *Meno*, of which Jerne, through Kierkegaard, aptly reminds us, was solved in immunology by unravelling the nature of the *sources* of innate specificity. Selective theories have in fact to solve a different, less forbidding puzzle: the puzzle of the pre-existing variety. Immunologists have solved it to anyone's satisfaction. We have at least one notable solid case where novelty, specificity, variety, combinatorial build-up, and innateness are made perfectly compatible. Apparently "instructive" processes are explained away through a strictly selective theory. In cognitive science the situation is far less satisfactory, but the arguments in favor of selective theories are rationally quite cogent. At least it has been shown that no instructive theory of the old stock can possibly do the job. In the cognitive domains, as in immunology, I surmise one will have to overturn those naive assumptions that have bridled the scientific imaginations of past generations. The rise of selective theories is bound to redefine the very nature of the problems and to induce a reassessment of what we ought to explain in the first place. On this point too the case of immunology is very illuminating.

Immunology, 'That a Topic for Cognitive Science?'

It is by now a truism of epistemology that theories are under-determined by data and that, either one has stringent a priori criteria to restrict the class of testable hypotheses, or one gets no science at all. It is also next to a truism that some stock of innocent, seemingly plausible, background assumptions concerning the "baseline" mechanisms of nature play a pivotal role in setting the stage for the more specialized theories. However, these supposedly "innocent" assumptions have the embarrassing propensity to become too naive, or downright perverse, with the passing of time. Newer generations of scientists become less and less willing to constrain hypotheses under the spell of some core assumptions once acritically espoused by scientists of previous generations.

Since these *préjugés* tend to apply, so to speak, across the board, over and above the sectorial wisdom of single disciplines, it takes no less than the change of a whole *Zeitgeist*, a diffuse paradigm-shift in many fields, before they are questioned and eventually dismissed.

The kind of assumptions we will be challenging in the present paper bear upon the economy of nature, the optimality of design and the "no frills" scheme of orthodox Darwinian evolution. Another pervasive assumption, for which I have no name, is that which serves as a premise to the conclusion that whatever is innate *must* be raw, simple, primitive, unfinished, unspecific, not-quite-there, potential rather than actual.

Given what we now know about the innermost mechanisms of biological systems, these assumptions have been steadily and profitably waning in biology proper. I am a bit surprised to see very similar assumptions still doing heavy duty in many quarters of the psychological community, especially in Europe. That being so, I venture to anticipate that some interesting lessons could be drawn by the cognitive sciences from the history of ideas in fields such as immunology. A chapter of special relevance is precisely the rise of selective theories, and the demise of instructive theories, in immunology. The first obvious "innocent" hypotheses put forward and tested during the infancy of biological disciplines were all instructive. Almost invariably these instructive hypotheses have yielded to selective ones, which have proved to be conceptually more powerful, capable of explaining the apparently instructive superficial nature of phenomena, and, what counts most, to be basically *true* of living systems. These selective theories were long resisted under the spell of arguments dictated by considerations on the economy of nature, the thriftiness of the genome, the mere potentiality of innate structures. That these allegedly innocent and obvious assumptions went bankrupt in biology can be of interest to psychologists and linguists. Since some cognitive psychologists, especially those inspired by Piaget, pretend to derive their theories directly from overarching biological principles (such as equilibration, adaptation, self-organization, etc.), it should at least be relevant to *them* that biology has gone wildly selective. At any rate, it seems to me that the new and promising theories in cognitive psychology and linguistics are *now* being resisted with arguments ominously reminiscent of those of the old biology, under the spell of assumptions which look a lot like those once dearly held by natural scientists. My suggestion here is that these arguments could be wrong *in psychology*, that those assumptions should be dismissed *on cognitive grounds*, under the impact of discoveries and considerations very similar to those now prevailing in biology.

I will be done with truisms, at least momentarily, by stating that I am not for a moment suggesting that selective theories *are* right in cognition *because* they are right in biology. That is bad science and worse epistemology. I am not advocating the reliance on the new biology of the new cognitive psychology, as opposed to the reliance of the old psychology on the old biology. I recommend no reliance on *any* biology. Theories and hypotheses in linguistics and cognitive science must stand or crumble on linguistic and cognitive grounds alone. What I am recommending is justified suspicion of arguments in favor of instructive theories in linguistics and cognitive science that owe so much to core assumptions that have been abandoned by biologists. This is just mental hygiene through a "case study." The hint is that those arguments *can* be equally unfounded in cognition on grounds very similar to those that condemned their counterparts in biology.

This is, I think, responsible science and Kosher epistemology. Now the case itself.

"Unvorstellbar," or How Could Anyone Be a Selectivist?

Since time immemorial it has been well known to mankind that certain diseases, once contracted, leave the individual who successfully recovers immune from further contagion. It was, however, not before the second half of the 19th century that the *mechanisms* of the immune response were brought under systematic scientific scrutiny. It did not escape the attention of such giants as Pasteur, Koch, Bordet, Metchnikoff, and especially Paul Ehrlich that, in addition to their obvious clinical impact, these studies, by unravelling the mechanisms of acquired immunity, were illuminating one of the most basic problems of life: the nature and sources of cellular and molecular *specificity*. The agents responsible for the fine specificity of recognition were discovered to be globular proteins present in the so-called gamma fraction of the blood serum. These circulating antibodies or gamma-globulins offered a bewildering variety of highly specific sub-populations, each capable of "recognizing" and "binding" itself to a particular alien body or antigen. These "serological reactions" could be replicated *in vitro* under suitable conditions and they became the object of extensive, painstaking analysis both at the biochemical and the physiological level. The overall picture at the end of the 19th century was that the higher organisms (all mammals for instance), days or even hours after being injected with a pathogenic microorganism, release into the blood stream a high number of antibodies that are specifically aimed at *that* microorganism and at *no other*. This response leads to fixation of specific gamma-globulins to the pathogen, to the "agglutination" of the complex and to the subsequent "lysis" or destruction of the invader by means of phagocytosis carried out by specialized cells called macrophages.

Already by 1897 Paul Ehrlich, the father of modern immunology, had produced a systematic theory of the mechanisms of antibody formation. His theory, quite interestingly, was a *selective* theory. Ehrlich wanted to capture the fundamentals of the immune response by means of ordinary chemical reactions and in terms of current, more diffuse kinds of biological responsiveness. His "side chains" theory countenanced the presence, on the membrane of immuno-competent cells, of various chemical groupings (various side chains of different specificity) that performed an all-out recognition function. These multipotent cells, like most other cells, had to sift through incoming and outgoing nutrients, déchets, and metabolites. The side chains, in performing this routine janitoring, monitored the presence of foreign substances or antigens, fixated to them, and thereby got distorted. These side chains, which were already *present* on the membrane of the cells (lymphocytes), were then severed from the membrane and released into the blood or lymph, becoming antibodies. What is crucial to Ehrlich's selective theory is that the detachment from the membrane stimulated a synthesis of *more* side chains and therefore antibodies of *that* kind. Ehrlich's overall picture is strikingly modern and basically correct. The fate of his selective theory was however temporarily doomed.

Thanks to experiments performed by Obermayer, Pick, and most of all by Karl Landsteiner on *artificial* haptens (antigens not existing in nature), Ehrlich's selective theory was abandoned for more than half a century. Between 1914 and 1955 it was *inconceivable* that *any* selective theory of antibody formation could possibly be true. Ehrlich's theory was never "forgotten" in a trivial sense; it was dutifully mentioned in all the theoretical papers and in textbooks on immunology over those decades. It was mentioned and then categorically dismissed as inconceivable ("Unvorstellbar" in the original wording of two influential instructivists, F. Breinl and F. Haurowitz, in a 1930 paper; William W. C. Topley in his authoritative 1933 textbook says, with a typical British understatement, "it is difficult to believe").

Why was Ehrlich's selective theory inconceivable? The crux of the matter was that organisms could efficiently, quickly, and reliably produce antibodies, *very specific* antibodies, against substances that had never been encountered in evolutionary history. Topley had shown that organisms were likewise quick to produce antibodies against parasites typical of totally unrelated species (e.g., rabbits against parasites of the kangaroo, and vice versa). How could this be?

Breinl and Haurowitz deem it "unvorstellbar" (something one cannot picture to himself) "that the organism can deliver ready-made antibodies for thousands of artificial substances, obtainable at whim." There is practically *no argument* in the full sense of the word. All these authors just mention selective theories as *obviously* false, in the light of Landsteiner's results. When a true theory appears so obviously false to everyone for so long, there must be something quite peculiar at work. This something is, to all intents and purposes, some naive, apparently innocent set of assumptions which, combined with Landsteiner's experiments, do render selective theories obviously wrong. The above sentence quoted from the 1930 paper by Breinl and Haurowitz can be matched with a passage by Felix Haurowitz in a review of 1952:

> Ehrlich, one of the pioneers in the field of immunology, had originally assumed that traces of each type of antibody are preformed in the organism, and that injection of an antigen induces over-production of this type of antibody so that its excess passes into the blood. This view had to be abandoned when it was shown by Landsteiner that synthetic products of the chemical laboratory are able to act as antigens. We cannot immagine that the organism has preformed antibodies against p-, m- and o-azophenyl-sulphonic acid or similar synthetic substances never occurring in nature. ("The mechanism of the immunological response" (p. 269) in *Biological Review of the Cambridge Philosophical Society*, Vol. 27, (1952), pp. 247–280.)

There is hardly an argument at all, why the view "had to be abandoned," why "we cannot imagine" that antibodies can be preformed. All this literature takes the rationale as tacitly understood.

The core assumptions are something like the following:

1. Nature is economical, it allows no organism to drag behind thousands or even millions of molecular species that are of no use (the encounter with the organic chemical wizardries of early 20th century German labs are highly unlikely in nature's plans).
2. Darwinian selection awards survival and proliferation to the thrifty genotypes, not to genotypes that carry a heavy ballast of useless, non-adaptive genes.
3. What is in the organism at birth, or at any rate in the absence of active intercourse with the environment, is coarse, unspecific, rich in potentialities but not in actuality.

Now, assuming that these three core beliefs, or any notational variant, are true, then indeed Landsteiner's experiments make any selective theory of antibody formation not only false, but obviously so.

The organism *can* produce very specific, that is highly complex and refined, molecules aimed at artificial substances; *therefore* these cannot be present in the organism from the start (prior to its being exposed to the foreign substance). These antibodies can only be obtained under the impact of the foreign substance, that is, via an *instructive* process, a transfer of structure from the outside to the inside.

Given these core beliefs *and* Landsteinder's results, how could anyone be a selectivist in immunology? In fact, until the momentous paper of Niels K. Jerne in 1955, immunologists tried all conceivable instructive theories. Some of these, with hindsight, look just crazy, but hindsight is a perverse master.

Two Kinds of Instructivism

The main trend of instructivism in the 1930s was focussed on "directed synthesis." Antibodies were supposed to be built-up from *precursors* under the orienting influence of the foreign antigen on the innermost protein-synthesizing mechanisms of the cell.

Breinl, Haurowitz, Mudd, Alexander, and many others, long before the discovery of the role of DNA in protein synthesis, thought it possible that proteins could be built out of other proteins and/or smaller pieces through a kind of inverted enzymatic process. There were plenty of enzymes that could cleave proteins at specific sites. The idea was to make those enzymes work the other way around, to *assemble* proteins from scattered pieces. Details need not detain us here, nor the elaborate ways through which antigens were supposed to mix in the process. Genes were supposed to be proteins anyway, therefore those models were quite in tune with the molecular genetics of those years. Needless to say, no such "directed synthesis" theory proved any good, neither in immunology nor anywhere else.

In 1940 a great chemist, Linus Pauling, who had just discovered a characteristic architecture of the protein molecules (at the time he had assumed it to be *the* architecture of proteins), the α-helix, proposed a new kind of instructive theory. Pauling's "directed folding" theory invoked the plasticity of gamma-globulins to account for the formation of specific antibodies. The "complementarity of fit" between antigen and antibody, thanks to the plasticity of the latter, could account for the *imprinting* of the shape of the antigen (or rather of its negative mold) onto the surface of the antibody. Initially shapeless globulins became specific antibodies through this "coiling" of the molecule in close contact with the molecule of the antigen. Pauling typically makes an appeal to the rule of parsimony (the use of the minimum effort to achieve the result) to determine the mode of action of antibodies to form the precipitates. He rightly assumes that the antigen cannot interfere with the mechanism of protein synthesis (which he still believes to be due to enzymes and other "protein templates"), but that it does interfere with the coiling and folding of the molecule *after* its synthesis is completed. Through energetic considerations and a rough calculation of the number of possible, nearly equi-energetic, configurations, Pauling comes to the expected range of diversity for possible shapes of antibodies.

He was bound to make at least two major predictions that flew in the face of decades of the best immunological evidence: if antibodies were obtained by directed folding in contact with the antigen, then it was *mandatory* that specific antibodies could also be obtained *in vitro*. Moreover, the mechanism of directed folding ought to produce, at least occasionally, antibodies against two totally unrelated antigens (bi-specific antibodies, so to speak), given only that these two unrelated antigens are brought simultaneously in contact with one and the same globulin molecule. Pauling ventured both predictions against the opinion (and against the data) of two generations of immunologists, and two years later he and Campbell claimed to have obtained experimental results confirming both predictions. It will come as no surprise, even to the immunologically most incompetent reader, that what they had been doing was simply an *in vitro selection* of antibodies having by chance *some* specificity for the tested antigens. By and large their experiments proved irreproducible and were soon forgotten. Until 1955 the "directed synthesis" and the "directed folding" theories of antibody formation shared their popularity, with a slight preference for the former. Then came Watson and Crick and the non-overlapping code, and things started to change at a very high speed. Whatever the merit of the "directed folding" theory, the "directed synthesis" notion turned out to be totally untenable. The swing of the pendulum was towards selective theories.

What If a Selective Theory Were True, After All?

Niels Kaj Jerne, then working in Denmark and actively collaborating with the "Phage group" of Max Delbrück at Caltech proposed his "natural selection" theory of antibody formation in his justly famous paper, submitted to the *Proceedings of the National Academy of Sciences of the United States* in September 1955. A few excerpts from this paper will give the flavor of Jerne's theory and, what's more in our present context, the crucial points of his argumentation.

> The role of the antigen is neither that of a template nor that of an enzyme modifier. The antigen is *solely a selective carrier of a spontaneously circulating antibody* to a system of cells which can reproduce this antibody. Globulin molecules are continuously being synthesized in an *enormous variety of different configurations*. Among the population of circulating globulin molecules there will, *spontaneously*, be fractions possessing affinity toward any antigen to which the animal can respond. . . . The introduction of the antigen into the blood or into the lymph leads to the *selective attachment* to the antigen surface of those globulin molecules which *happen to have* a complementary configuration" (p. 849; emphases added)

Jerne, in order to sustain his bold claims, had then to show how his "natural selection theory" could explain all known facts about the immune response and all known facts about the structure of antibodies and the synthesis of proteins. The stumbling block was, obviously, still having to account for Landsteiner's experiments. "An immense body of experimental data testifies to the fact that normal sera from one animal species may contain antibodies against an enormous number of different bacteria, some of which are not known to be natural parasites of this species" (p. 851). These results and those obtained with artificial antigens were compatible with a selective theory if the diversity of specific kinds of antibodies present in the organism "in the absence of, and prior to, exposure to an antigen," was large enough. "Since normal mammalian serum contains more than 10^{17} globulin molecules per milliliter, these may include a million 10^{11} fractions of different specificity. This would seem an amply sufficient number" (p. 85). Jerne then points to the role of DNA and RNA in protein synthesis and to neat evidence that the antigen could not possibly interfere directly with such processes. The role of the antigen is to *select* those fractions that happen to have a complementary fit and thereby (with a process that Jerne leaves totally in the dark and which is being elucidated only now, in the early '80s, also thanks to his later work) triggers the synthesis of more antibodies of that specificity.

In the next few years, thanks to Lederberg and Burnet, such an amplification mechanism was correctly ascribed to a switching on and ensuing multiplication of the line(s) of cells bearing that antibody on its (their) surface. The full-blown selective theory was therefore called "clonal selection." More recent developments will be sketched at the end of this paper (the "internal image" theory which is, once again, due to Jerne).

Sixty years had elapsed since Ehrlich's selective theory had been put forward. After 50 years of instructivism a selective theory was again *vorstellbar*, conceivable and possibly true.

The breathtaking developments in molecular biology came to confirm and refine Jerne's insights. They were also destined to erode all confidence in the economy of nature, the thriftiness of the genome, and the unpolished, nonspecific nature of innate structures.

Some Highlights on Crucial Results of Modern Biology

It was chiefly through statistical reasoning that evolutionary biology managed to overcome the crudeness of early Darwinism. Naïve conceptions centered around the survival of the fittest and the struggle for life gave way to the elaborate mathematical analyses pioneered by J. B. S. Haldane, R. A. Fisher, and Sewall Wright. It soon became evident that the fixation of new alleles was a lengthy process captured by the vagaries of numerical fluctuations, whereby the "old" alleles mostly ended up by coexisting with the new ones (polymorphisms) and only rarely replaced them wholesale in a population. On the other hand slight variations of "fitness" (this notion being now translated by Haldane into precise probabilistic terms) could give rise to radical imbalances in relative frequencies in the long run. Genetic trends, as evidenced by statistical population genetics, often turned out to be remarkably counter-intuitive. At any rate the mathematical theory of evolution was far from justifying the belief in uniform, monotonic spreads of "better" genes that had characterized the rough-and-ready versions of over-confident Darwinians.

The more recent game-theoretical approach to statistical population genetics, notably through the work of Richard C. Lewontin, and the "hitch-hike" mechanisms described by John Maynard-Smith, countenance a lot of "serendipity" in evolution. Genes that "just" happen to be close to "useful" genes are likely to be co-selected, whatever their function. Tails, trails, and lucky neighborhoods become crucial processes in the maintenance and spread of genetic material. Functionally unrelated traits tend to co-occur and be co-selected (thanks to their fortuitous location along chromosomes) with truly adaptive genes. Needless to say, in the fullness of time, the indirectly selected genes can turn out to be as useful as those that had been "directly" selected. The concept of "strategy," borrowed from the theory of games, becomes more and more pervasive in evolutionary theory. The effects of lucky coincidences make sense of a lot of "nonsense." The actual genetic composition of any given organism mostly fails to be mapped *directly* onto the selective pressures of present or past environments. The term "adaptation" becomes murky, and words of skepticism are being preached concerning the orthodox Darwinian "rationalizations" of what there is. Motoo Kimura has rightly stressed the role of "genetic drift" (as distinct from that of selective pressures) in the change of gene frequencies, while the notion of neutral or quasi-neutral mutations divorces genetic constitution from any obvious, direct effect of the environment. Lastly, the emerging theory of "punctuative equilibria" in the origin of species, which is presently finding a good molecular basis in the theory of "molecular drive" (due to G. Dover), stresses the sudden, pervasive character of some genetic rearrangements that seem to be much more dramatic and widespread than anyone had imagined until a few years ago. Molecular drive, being rooted in "blind" molecular constraints at the chromosome level, removes one step further the facts of genome evolution from their net effects in terms of adaptation and survival. It does not deny drift, hitch-hiking, and Darwinian selection, but it adds crucial new complexity to the overall picture.

The "argument from design" loses whatever cogency it might have initially received from an older biology. The new outlook, basically, suggests that nothing is transparently "there" *to* perform such and such a function. When biological structures do, as a matter of fact, perform certain functions, their "design" resembles very little what a human engineer would have planned. The "tinkering" of evolution, as François Jacob acutely portrays it, is always bound to invent light bulbs out of some pre-existing wax candle. It usually manages to do so and it is a miracle, but a very messy miracle, offering little grounds to any argument from design.

Molecular biology, in its turn, is progressively nullifying any residual trust in the economy of nature. Genomes are on the average 40% filled with "junk DNA" (a technical term, mind you)—repeated sequences whose function (if any beyond the scaffolding level) remains to this day unknown. Moreover genes of higher organisms are split into introns and exons, with apparent high levels of waste, since only exons code for actual proteins. A baroque intricacy of regulations, presumably also involving introns, monitors the expression of genes in higher organisms. The hopes of earlier generations of molecular geneticists to be able to construct universal "models" by looking at bacteria or other suitable procaryotes are being baffled. Species-specificities down to the molecular level are becoming a nuisance to the general theories of regulation of the '60s and early '70s.

In immunology proper, things are changing at such a pace that anything stated now risks becoming obsolete within a year. However, a few basic facts do hold and they are salient in the context of this paper. The detailed knowledge of the nature of G.O.D. (generators of diversity) amply explains how the organism can indeed have "ready made" (*pace* Breinl and Haurowitz) very specific antibodies against *any* molecular configuration it can encounter. Selectivism is now a "dogma," down to the most minute details of the antibody-synthesizing machinery.

What is more, Niels Jerne postulates the *actual* presence in each organism of an "internal image" of *any possible molecular pattern*. Antibodies against other antibodies (anti-antibodies or rather antigen binding sites against other antigen binding sites) do constitute an "idiotypic network," a huge repertoire wherein copies of the "outside" molecular world are physically present. *Any* pattern is *already* in the actual repertoire of the organism. The demarcation between self and non-self is now conceived in terms of a very subtle *statistical (populational) imbalance within the network*.

As is so typical of the new outlook, the immune system *is not there to defend* the organism against outside invaders. The system is "just" a self-regulating generator of cellular and molecular diversity, subject to imbalances of various sorts. The immunodefensive reaction is a byproduct of such internal regulations. Almost leading Jerne's ideas to the extreme, some immunologists of the younger generation, such as A. Coutinho and P. A. Cazenave, openly welcome the birth of an "immunology without antigens."

Besides offering a clear example of *how*, in detail, selective theories can explain away all semblance of instructive processes, modern immunology is particularly illuminating in the way it thus re-defines the very nature of the problems at hand.

If, in order to account for the relatively crude phenomenon of the immuno-logical lock-and-key recognition between molecules, one must countenance such exotic entities as the "network" and the "internal image," one can only shudder to think what intricacies the "selective" explanation of learning processes in psychology may encompass. On the other hand, it is hard to find arguments to the effect that the case must be simpler in cognitive matters. It is hard, precisely unless one persists in appealing to the economy of nature, the optimality of design, and other core-assumptions. It has been the main burden of the present chapter to show why these arguments are better left in the science museum.

Conclusion

To anyone who is conversant with the progress of biology in the last few decades, some core assumptions once widely and stubbornly entertained in biology proper seem at best dubious. It is surprising to see these very assumptions still dog-matically invoked in the cognitive sciences, where they seem to sustain arguments to the effect that nothing more than "general intelligence" or "simple mental precursors" can be innate. It is held in some quarters that the innateness of a "language of thought" à la Fodor, or of the very specific language faculties à la Chomsky is unthinkable. The reasons (or alleged reasons) why this ought to be so are dangerously similar to those that were once wrongly invoked against selective theories in biology, more specifically in immunology. Some arguments in psychology are picked up *directly and explicitly* from the old biology. It is revealing, I think, that when modern biologists warn these cognitive scientists away from such arguments, the latter opt for a *biology of their own*, apparently to be substituted for the biology of biologists (witness the exchanges between Piaget, Jacob, Changeux, and Monod at the Royaumont meeting). The innateness of *plenty* of concepts and of *plenty* of specialized mental "organs" ought to be wiped away by considerations on the economy of nature, the orderliness and uniformity of natural design, the multi-purpose, undifferentiated, non-actual character of innate dispositions.

I have endeavored to show that such arguments proved wrong in immunology, and at best weak in most sectors of biology. In neurobiology, any such line of reasoning is nowadays being avoided, given the proliferation of neuro-trans-mitters and the terrific redundancies of neuronal networks (there seem to be up to twenty *complete* visual maps in the cortex of higher primates; why, it is not known). Selective theories in the build-up of neuronal networks are being very successfully proposed (what is more, including those elaborated by a Nobel prize winner for immunology, Gerald M. Edelman).

The "connecting link" from basic biology to the cognitive sciences ought to be precisely the neurosciences. It is of some importance that in this very field selective theories are rampant.

If one wants the cognitive sciences to be at least compatible with (or even based on) biology the selective outlook seems mandatory. If, on functionalist grounds, one rather wants the cognitive sciences to stand on their own two feet, it becomes no less than a useful exercise in mental hygiene to try to dismiss core assumptions that look a lot like those that *had* to be abandoned in biology.

The purpose of this paper is to suggest that the innateness of very complex, highly diversified, and quite specific mental setups is at least *conceivable*. Whether they are, as a matter of fact, innate, what they are, and how they interconnect is obviously an empirical problem. The mental hygiene here recommended ought to be conducive to the fresh outlook that in the cognitive sciences innatist hypotheses and selective theories are also the most, not the least, likely to be true. Such lessons to be drawn from biology could alter the *a priori* plausibility-rating of cognitive theories. Altogether a not totally irrelevant result. At the risk of being redundant, let me stress in closing that I do not advocate holding true the doctrine of modularity or the language of thought *because* selectiveness is the language of immunology. The moral of this story is only that there are independent historical and rational grounds to hold them conceivable and possibly true. What if they were indeed *true*? This "what-if-ism" has much to be recommended. The present paper, at any rate, intends to recommend it.

Bibliography

The general concepts of biology mentioned in this paper are to be found in:

Bona, C. A., & Kohler, H. (Eds.). (1983). *Annals of the New York Academy of Sciences, 418, Immune networks*, The New York Academy of Sciences.

Cavalli-Sforza, L. L., & Bodmer, W. F. (1971). *The genetics of human populations*. San Francisco: Freeman.

Changeux, J.-P. (1983). *L'homme neuronal*. Paris: Fayard.

Dover, G. A., & Flavell, R. B. (Eds.). (1982). *Genome evolution*. London: Academic.

Edelman, G. M. (1982). Through a computer darkly: Group selection and higher brain function. *Bulletin of the American Academy of Arts and Sciences, 36*, 20–49.

Edelman, G. M., & Reeke, G. N. (1982). Selective networks capable of representation, transformations, limited generalizations, and associative memory. *Proceedings of the National Academy of Sciences U.S.A., 79*, 2091–2095.

Golub, E. S. (1981). *The cellular basis of the immune response*. Sunderland, MA: Sinauer.

Gould, S. J. (1977a). *Ontogeny and phylogeny*. Cambridge, MA: Harvard University Press.

Gould, S. J. (1977b). Punctuated equilibria: The tempo and mode of evolution reconsidered. *Paleobiology, 3*, 115–151.

Hunt, T., Prentis, S., & Tooze, J. (Eds.), (1983). *DNA makes RNA makes PROTEIN*. Oxford and Amsterdam: Elsevier Biomedical Press (reprints from the journal *Trends in Biomedical Sciences*).

Jacob, F. (1977). Evolution and tinkering. *Science, 196*, 1161–1166.

Lewontin, R. C. (1982). *Organism and environment*. Privately circulated manuscript.

Piattelli-Palmarini, M. (1984). On the possibility of applying biological laws to social phenomena: An epistemological point of view. In N. Keyfits (Ed.), *Population and biology*, Liège: Ordina Editions.

Piattelli-Palmarini, M. (1981). Equilibria, crystals, programs, energetic models and organizational models. In M. L. Dalla Chiara (Ed.), *Boston studies in the philosophy of science*, Vol. 47, pp. 341–359. *Italian studies in the philosophy of science*. Dordrecht: D. Reidel.

Piattelli-Palmarini, M. (Ed.). (1980). *Language and learning: The debate between Jean Piaget and Noam Chomsky*. Cambridge, MA: Harvard University Press.

Provine, W. B. (1971). *The origins of theoretical population genetics*. Chicago: University of Chicago Press.

Classics of early selectivism

Burnet, F. M. (1959). *The clonal selection theory of acquired immunity*. Nashville, TN: Vanderbilt University Press.

Edelman, G. M., & Gall, W. E. (1969). The antibody problem. *Annual review of biochemistry, 38*, 699–766.

Ehrlich, P. (1900). On immunity with special reference to cell life. *Proceedings of the Royal Society*, Series B, Vol. 66, p. 424.

Ehrlich, P. (1906). *Collected studies on immunity* (trans. C. Boldvan). London: Wiley.

Jerne, N. K. (1955). The natural-selection theory of antibody formation. In *Proceedings of the National Academy of Sciences U.S.A., 41*, 849–856.

Jerne, N. K. (1966). The natural selection theory of antibody formation: Ten years later. In *Phage and the origins of molecular biology*. Cold Spring Harbor, NY: Cold Spring Harbor Laboratory of Quantitative Biology.

Lederberg, J. (1959). Genes and antibodies. *Science, 129*, 1669.

Classics of instructivism

Alexander, J. (1932). Some intracellular aspects of life and disease. *Protoplasma, 14*, 296–306.

Breinl, F., & Haurowitz, F. (1930). Chemische Untersuchung des Präzipitates aus Hämoglobin und Anti-Hämoglobin-Serum und Bemerkungen über die Natur der Antikörper. *Hoppe-Seyler's Zeitschrift für Physiologische Chemie, 192*, 45–57.

Haurowitz, F. (1952). The mechanism of the immunological response. *Biological Review of the Cambridge Philosophical Society, 27*, 247–280.

Landsteiner, K. (1936). *The specificity of serological reactions*. Springfield, IL: Charles C. Thomas.

Landsteiner, K., & Rothen, A. (1939). Absorption of antibodies by egg albumin films. *Science, 90*, 65–66.

Mudd, S. (1932). A hypothetical mechanism of antibody formation. *Journal of Immunology, 23*, 423–427.

Pauling, L. (1940). A theory of the structure and process of formation of antibodies. *Journal of the American Chemical Society, 62*, 2643–2657.

Topley, W. W. C. (1933). *An outline of immunity* (esp. Chap. 5). London: Edward Arnold.

Part III
Concept Acquisition

Chapter 7

The Acquisition of Natural Kind and Artifact Terms*

Frank C. Keil

Cornell University

For many years it has been claimed that children's knowledge of conceptual categories, and consequently of word meanings, undergoes dramatic qualitative changes with development. While there have been a wide variety of ways of describing these changes, one of the most common has been that young children's representations are instance bound (or concrete) and that these change with development into more principled, or abstract, representations. For example, more than 50 years ago Vygotsky (1934) observed that young children seem to think and talk about categories such as kinship terms in a markedly different manner than older children. Younger children referred to uncles in terms of familiar examples of uncles and seemed to decide whether a new entity was an uncle based on some metric of similarity to these exemplars, while older children referred to the strict kinship relation.

Of course Vygotsky is only one of several who made such observations about children (e.g., Bruner et al., 1966; Werner, 1948; Anglin, 1970), and if one goes outside psychology one can find abundant evidence for these views. Any elementary school teacher can provide several anecdotes illustrating the point. Nonetheless, despite these commonplace observations, a closer look at what has been said about how concepts and word meanings change with development reveals several problems and inconsistencies that make one wonder whether there is anything to the phenomenon at all. One set of problems centers around the notion that there is some sort of global across-the-board shift in the ways in which concepts are represented. For a variety of reasons this view has fallen into disfavor, and much of the most recent work in developmental psychology argues against such global representational shifts (see, e.g., Gleman & Baillargeon, 1983). Some of the most compelling criticisms were made in Fodor's (1972) retrospective review of Vygotsky's book where he argued that there are

---

* Preparation of this paper and much of the research described herein was supported by National Science Foundation Grant BNS-81-02655. Many thanks to Barbara Bauer, Lianne Ritter, and Cindy Hutton for assistance in all stages of this research project.

few reasons to believe such global shifts exist and a whole host of reasons to think they are very implausible. A second line of criticisms questions whether even adults usually represent concepts and word meanings in terms of such abstract principles that have the flavor of definitions. While they may do so for kinship terms and other special cases where a simple clear definition is available—that is, for the so-called "nominal kind terms"—most of our natural language terms don't seem to have anything remotely close to definitions. What reason is there to believe that adults have any more principled or abstract beliefs about these concepts than children?

Despite these problems, there may still be some truth to the observation that conceptual structures change from instance bound representations to deeper, principled ones. There is not, however, a global representational shift of the sort that most classic developmental theories have proposed. In fact, the shift is less related to differences between children and adults than it is to the way in which all of us come to acquire knowledge about various conceptual domains. Secondly, a change occurs as well for natural kind terms, not from instances to definitions but to something more complex, and ultimately much more interesting. The main purpose of this paper is to explore this change for natural kind terms and to contrast their use with that of artifact terms. An especially important issue concerns the presence of an underlying "core" of knowledge that exerts a powerful influence throughout the entire period of change.

A Characteristic to Defining Shift

The best place to start is not with natural kinds, but with nominal kinds where meanings most closely approximate definitions. These include kinship terms like "uncle," dimensional terms like "tall," and other terms often associated with social relations such as many financial terms, moral terms, and the like. It is becoming increasingly clear that, at least for these terms, there does seem to be a shift in how concepts are represented. Carey (1978) has referred to this shift as one from haphazard examples to feature based descriptions where the features seem to be necessary and sufficient. She suggests that the meaning of the word "tall" changes in this manner, from cases where children construe its meaning in terms of typically tall things to a more content independent (i.e., less instance bound) description in terms of geometric properties. Thus, early on, a child may know what it means for a man to be tall (e.g., head to toe extent) or for a house to be tall (e.g., roof to street extent), but the child may not have a content independent representation of the meaning that can be applied to any physical object.

To examine the shift in a more general manner for a wider range of nominal kinds than simply dimensional terms, I have developed a different methodology that borrows on a distinction commonly drawn in the semantic memory literature, namely that between characteristic and defining aspects of word meaning (cf. Smith, Shoben, & Rips, 1974). This distinction assumes that word meanings can be described as lists of features, a point of some controversy which is not necessary to the account that follows. Nonetheless, for expositional purposes I will talk about the meanings of these terms using features. Keil and Batterman (1984) provide alternative paraphrases for those who find such feature decomposition notions unpalatable.

The characteristic/defining contrast assumes that word meanings can be seen as a mix of these two types of features, where the characteristic features are merely typically associated with concepts, while the defining features are used to decide whether or not a given example is a valid instantiation of a concept. These features can be used to describe the developmental changes mentioned above if we assume that children who are just beginning to learn the meaning of a word tend to represent it primarily in terms of characteristic features and that only with time do they start to refer to defining features. The child who relies on characteristic features would then seem to represent meanings in terms of collections of properties associated with typical instances he or she has experienced, while the child who relies on defining features would seem to go beyond such instance bound knowledge.

We (Keil & Batterman, 1984) have now documented this shift for a wide range of terms that seem to have both clear definitions and salient characteristic features. The method is to simply present children with pairs of stories for each term that have either many characteristic features but incorrect defining ones or the reverse, highly uncharacteristic features but correct defining ones. For example, one story for a "museum" described an atypical but technically correct museum that was a shack in the countryside with displays of dirty T-shirts of movie stars while the other described a huge building in the city with columns and paintings and statues inside, but which was a private dwelling in which no guests were allowed.

The results are consistently observed for almost all of the nominal kind terms we have studied and can be summarized by the graph in Figure 1, which shows a clear shift from reliance on characteristic features to defining features.

A second equally important point is that the shift occurs at different times for different concepts, sometimes occurring as early as the preschool years and other times not occurring until after the 4th grade. In a later study we have shown that for terms from various semantic fields (e.g., immoral acts, kinship terms, and cooking terms) the shift occurs at roughly the same times for terms within each field, but at widely differing times for terms across fields. There is a great deal more to tell about this shift, such as how parents talk to children about such concepts, what happens when you try to explicitly teach these concepts, and whether and how the shift occurs in other cultures, but these issues go beyond the purpose of the present chapter.

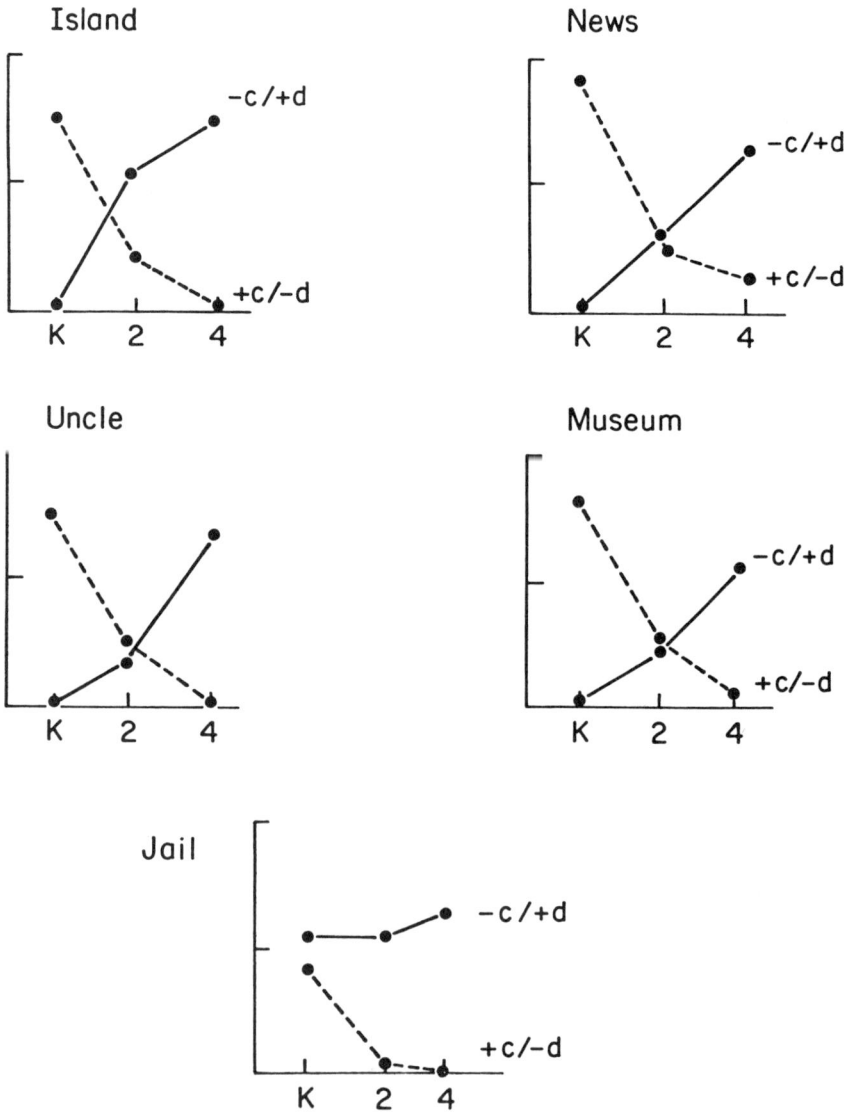

(Y-axis represents extent to which children judge story
to be valid instance of concept)

Figure 1. Examples of the Characteristic-to-Defining Shift in the Keil and Batterman
(1984) study.

Natural Kinds

The problem at hand is what this shift means for terms without clear definitions, those for natural kinds. Certainly one of the most important developments in the philosophy of language in the last 15 years has been the argument that terms applying to many naturally occurring classes of things may not have definitions. Both Putnam (1975) and Kripke (1972) have eloquently argued against there being necessary and sufficient features for these terms.

The argument against definitions seems to spell serious trouble for the characteristic to defining shift, and at its worst suggests that the shift for nominal kinds may be a curiosity that is confined to a relatively small subset of all natural language terms. The Putnam/Kripke view has been interpreted by some psychologists as arguing that natural kind concepts have only characteristic features, out of which prototypes develop, and that these features fully specify the meanings of these terms. If so, then there could be no characteristic to defining shift since there would be only characteristic features in even the most sophisticated representations of meaning.

Fortunately, both Putnam and Kripke to leave us with something else beyond the stereotype or prototype: the notion that there is a causal history underlying the usage of these terms, one that suggests a deeper more principled way of determining their meaning that can overrule characteristic features. It is not a definition, however, but a set of causal links going back to some sort of initial discovery procedure or naming occasion. This emphasis on causal structure as a potentially opposing force to characteristic features is an extremely important addition to theories of meaning. In this chapter, I will suggest that as we become more knowledgeable in a domain, we become increasingly dissatisfied with the notion that meaning is merely a set of characteristic features that happen to be probabilistically associated with a class of things. We start to assume and look for the presence of a richer underlying structure that is causal in nature. Thus, analogous to the characteristic to defining shift for nominal kinds, there may be a characteristic to underlying causal structure shift for natural kinds.

The obvious question at this point is whether the underlying causal structure is really so different; after all, aren't many underlying causal laws that apply to a class of objects also merely probabilistic in nature and thus really only characteristic features? Perhaps the meanings of natural kind terms are characteristic features all the way down, they just become more and more complicated and subtle and require more knowledge and experience to be understood. There may be some truth to this objection, but it misses a vital point: prototype based concepts built up out of characteristic features are surprisingly atheoretical sorts of things. By their very nature, they do not and cannot tell us, for example, why it is that the various features that are typical of birds (e.g., beaks, feathers, and eggs) tend to be so highly intercorrelated: they simply are. Features and prototypes, in short, give no explanation of the structure of conceptual categories.

The only knowledge one can have consists of the degree to which various properties are associated with categories. Underlying causal theories for natural kinds, by contrast, pay much less attention to typicality and more to mechanism or explanation.

But even while we might reject such characteristic features, we might not have much knowledge of the alternative. Putnam has observed that, for many terms, most users of those terms may have only a weak idea of what the deeper causal structure is or what the criteria are for deciding if a new entity is a valid instance. Thus, I am happy to use the term "robin" to refer to a class of birds that I usually pick out exclusively on the basis of characteristic features. Nonetheless, at the same time, I recognize that those characteristic features may be fallible and I know that some other body of knowledge, which I loosely call "avian biology," is the real basis for deciding if a given bird is a robin. I may have little of that knowledge myself: I merely need to believe that there is a community of experts who do possess that knowledge and who can make those decisions for me. This, crudely put, is Putnam's notion of division of linguistic labor.

Here I want to suggest that from an early age we have a natural bias to try to go beyond characteristic features, and believe that there is a deeper causal structure that is the essence of meaning, even when there sometimes may not be. As a result, even when there is no community of experts for a particular phenomenon and characteristic features are all we know of it, we usually do not consider those features to be final criteria for defining the phenomenon. In fact there may be phenomena for which we simultaneously believe (a) that they are so complex that humans could never grasp the explanations that tie them together and (b) that such an explanation does exist in principle and overrules any set of characteristic attributes.

Based on some of the comments that children have given us, it appears that this underlying causal structure is of a particular type: it describes a causal chain leading us back to an object's origin. In other words, the chain tells us how and why an object came into being. This is true for both natural kinds and artifacts, although there are important differences between the two in how the path is constructed.

Artifacts have often been contrasted with natural kinds because their "essences" seem to be of a different sort. Schwartz discusses the contrast in his 1978 *Cognition* article, where he talks about the sorts of natural changes that artifacts and natural kinds can undergo. A different sort of contrast is shown by the kinds of discoveries that can be made about the two sorts of things and how people react to those discoveries. Probably all of us have heard stories about scientists discovering that a class of things that have all the characteristic features associated with one natural kind are in fact really instances of another because of deeper principles. These sorts of accounts occur throughout the history of zoology: the glass "snake" that looks and acts just like a snake but which is really a lizard, the panda which is not a bear, and so on. And it still goes on today, although not so much in scientific circles as in popular reports to lay people. Tabloid newspapers frequently report discoveries about cats that are really dogs, pets that are really space aliens, etc.

By contrast, similar discoveries about artifacts have little consequence for the object's identity. Consider how one would react to a news story of the following sort: Scientists just discovered that a group of objects made in Syracuse to be chairs and which look just like chairs are not chairs at all; for when they looked at the chemical and molecular structure of these objects they discovered that they were really lecterns. Obviously such an account doesn't ring true and no one is convinced by it. This is because we regard the essences of artifacts to be the intended function of the creator, and we tend to think that this function is usually directly perceivable in their characteristic features. Not so for natural kinds. This is not to say that there are no discoveries about artifacts that could undermine the characteristic features. On the contrary, since virtually all artifacts do have underlying causal structures describing their origins, they too can be found to be really something else. The discovery, however, must be of a different sort and refers less to scientific properties of the object (i.e., its molecular or anatomical structure) than to the intended function of its creator. Thus, an archeologist might discover that a collection of chairlike things were in fact lecterns because they were found to be the products of individuals whose intentions were that they function as lecterns.

This contrast between discoveries about natural kinds and artifacts suggests a study to explore how this knowledge might change in children. If young children are much more prone to rely on characteristic features, then perhaps they react differently to stories about discoveries than more knowledgeable people and perhaps they will treat the natural kinds more like artifacts. To test this hypothesis we presented children with stories of the following sorts:

A Natural Kind Story

There are animals that live out on a farm near Dryden and they look just like this (show picture of raccoon). They prowl around houses a lot and sometimes eat garbage and they like to wash their food in streams. Well, some scientists went and studied these animals very carefully with microscopes and other sorts of stuff, and when they looked at them and their insides they found out that they weren't like most raccoons at all. The scientists found out that they had the blood of skunks, the bones of skunks, the brains of skunks, and all the other inside parts of skunks rather than those of raccoons. And they found out that these animals' mommies and daddies were skunks and that when they had babies their babies were skunks. So their mommies and daddies look just like this (point to pictures of skunk) and their babies look just like this (picture of skunk). What do you think they really are, raccoons or skunks?

An Artifact Story

There are these things that look just like this (show picture of coffeepot) and they are made in a big factory in Buffalo for people to make coffee in. They put the coffee grounds in here and then they add water and heat it all up on the stove and then they have coffee. A while ago some scientists looked at these things carefully and they found out that they aren't like most coffeepots at all, because when they looked at them under a microscope they found out that they were not made out of the same stuff as most coffeepots. Instead they came from birdfeeders like this (point to picture of birdfeeder) which had been melted down and then made into these (point to picture of coffeepot) and when people were all done making coffee with these they melted them down again and made birdfeeders out of them. What are they, birdfeeders or coffeepots?

An important advantage to this method is that, by contrasting artifacts with natural kinds, we can assess whether any developmental changes merely reflect some sort of changing response bias—for example, perhaps as children get older they tend to defer more to authority figures and decide that whatever the scientists say must be the case. If so then we would expect to see the same shift at the same time for both natural kinds and artifacts.

Figure 2 shows an overall summary of the results. There is a developmental trend wherein the younger children tend to treat artifacts and natural kinds alike

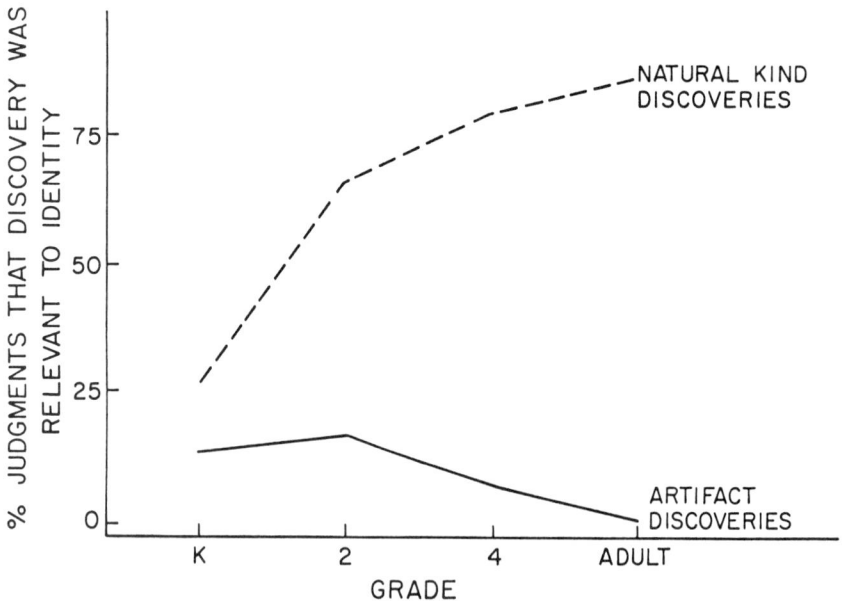

Figure 2. Results of the Discovery Study.

and cling to the characteristic features while the older children treat the artifacts and natural kinds very differently and are perfectly willing to let the discovery override the characteristic features for the natural kinds but not for the artifacts. (A two way analysis of variance program found significant main effects for grade and story type as well as a significant interaction, all of which would be expected.)

We have replicated this study with a second set of stories, and found essentially the same result, with a significant main effect for story type and a significant type $\times$ grade interaction. The main effect for grade was not significant, but this is not important when a large interaction is present.

One can get a much better feeling for what is going on here from a few excerpts from the transcripts. Here is a kindergartner (in the second study) on raccoons and skunks:

> Experimenter: So what is it really, a raccoon or a skunk?
>
> Child: Raccoon.
>
> E: Why?
> C: Because a raccoon is fatter and that (points to picture of skunk) . . . and that has black and white and that (raccoon) is black and dark black.
> E: So even though this special animal has the inside parts of a skunk and its mommy and daddy were skunks that looked just like this and its babies were skunks you think the best name for it is what? . . . a skunk or a raccoon?
> C: A raccoon.
> E: Why?
> C: Because the raccoon is fat and the skunk is skinny and it doesn't have the same skin because the skunk has black and white and the raccoon has light black and dark black.

Consider a different kindergartner about a thing that looks like a tiger but has inside parts of lions and parents and babies that are lions.

> Experimenter: What is it, lion or tiger?
> Child: Tiger.
> E: Why?
> C: Because it has stripes.
> E: Now even though this special animal has the inside parts of a lion and its mommies and daddies were lions and when it has babies they are lions . . . pause . . . the best name for this special animal is what? lion or tiger?
> C: Tiger.
> E: And what is your reason?
> C: Because of the stripes on it.

Similar patterns of responses are seen when the younger children are presented with stories about artifacts: the children attend almost exclusively to characteristic features. For example, a kindergartner discussed the coffeepot that was made from birdfeeders in the following manner:

> Experimenter: So what is it a coffeepot or a bridfeeder?
> Child: A coffeepot.
> E: Why?
> C: Because it doesn't look like a birdfeeder. I wouldn't put birdseed in it. . . .
>   I would put coffee in the coffeepot.
> E: So even though this special object was made from birdfeeders that look just
>   like this and when they are done with them, they melt them down and make
>   birdfeeders again you think the best name for it is what? . . . a birdfeeder or
>   a coffeepot?
> C: Coffeepot.
> E: And your reason?
> C: Because it doesn't look like a birdfeeder and I wouldn't put bird seed in it.

The same sorts of responses were given for the other artifacts.

As the children get older, they change in their judgments, and start to treat the artifacts and the natural kinds differently.

For example, a 4th-grader on the raccoon/skunk story:

> Experimenter: Is it a raccoon or a skunk?
> Child: I'd say a skunk . . . yes, a skunk.
> E: Why?
> C: Because it has everything that a skunk has only it doesn't . . . only the outside
>   parts of it doesn't look like that. And its babies were a skunk and its parents
>   were a skunk.
> E: Does it matter that it looks like that (picture of raccoon) or that it paws through
>   your trash or that it doesn't stink?
> C: Not really, not really.

Another example with a 4th-grader with the horse/zebra story:

> Experimenter: What is it really? A horse or a zebra?
> Child: Zebra.
> E: Why?
> C: Because it has the insides like a zebra, the blood like a zebra.
> E: Was it important what it looked like? Did it matter that it looked like this?
> C: Yes.
> E: Why?
> C: I don't know.
> E: (repeats story) . . . so what is the best name?
> C: Zebra.
> E: Why?
> C: Because it has the insides like a zebra and it has brains and cells and it's going
>   to have babies like it.

E: Is it important what the animal looks like:
C: Yes.
E: Why?
C: Because people will think it's a horse and it's not.

Despite promising results, these two studies also have problems that make any conclusions tentative. The most serious problem is that the stories given make certain presuppositions about the nature of the underlying causal structure, for example, that it involves blood and bones and brains and who the parents are. The suggestion that these are just other characteristic features, perhaps deeper less easily perceived ones, is hard to discount. Moreover, in principle the child need not adopt any of the notions of Western biological science to make the shift away from characteristic features; it is only necessary that the child think a deeper explanatory structure of some sort or another exists. Unfortunately, this study, by specifying what that structure is, may not be demonstrating as fully as possible differences in the ways children think about natural kinds and artifacts.

A second problem is that it would be nice to have a case where what the experts do or say is taken as irrelevant to the identify of natural kinds by knowledgeable users of these terms so as to have a contrast to the situation in the discovery study.

To address both these problems and to provide converging evidence for the shift, a different study was conducted that was concerned with transformations that were performed on objects rather than discoveries that were made about them. The objects involved and features described were the same as in the second discoveries study.

The Operations Study

Again, the general idea is to assess whether children, as they become more sophisticated about certain domains, start to treat artifacts and natural kinds differently with respect to the relative importance of characteristic features, where it is assumed that with artifacts one can usually perceive the maker's intention via the characteristic features and thus know its identity. The following two stories illustrate the new paradigm:

Raccoon/Skunk

The doctors took a raccoon (show picture of raccoon) and shaved away some of its fur. They dyed what was left all black. Then they bleached a single stripe all white down the center of its back. Then with surgery, they put in its body a sac of super smelly odor, just like a skunk has (we define odor for younger children as "super smelly yucky stuff"). When they were all done the animal looked like this (show picture of skunk). After the operation, was this a skunk or a raccoon? (Both pictures were present at the time of the final question.)

Coffeepot/birdfeeder

The doctors took a coffeepot that looked like this (picture of coffeepot). They sawed off the handle, sealed the top, took off the top knob, sealed closed the spout and sawed it off. They also sawed off the base and attached a flat piece of metal. They attached a little stick, cut a window and filled the metal container with bird food. When they were done, it looked like this (picture of birdfeeder). After the operation, was this a coffeepot or a birdfeeder? (Both pictures were present at the time of the final question.)

The results are consistent with those of the discoveries study, as can be seen in Figure 3. There is a clear shift and the distinction between artifacts and natural kinds becomes more dramatic with age (both main effects and the interaction

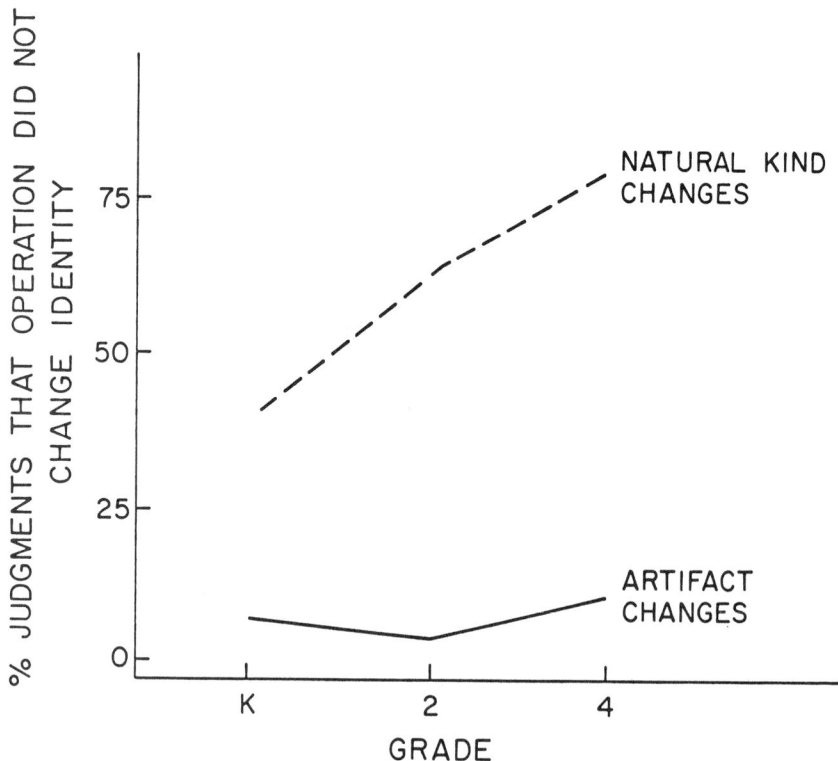

Figure 3. Results of the Operations Study.

are significant in a repeated measures 2-way ANOVA). The children also seem to make the shift a little earlier with the operations paradigm (the difference between the two story types is significant for kindergartners, here, but was not in the discoveries paradigm). This makes good sense if one assumes that the operations paradigm allowed a wider range of causal theories to undermine the characteristic features by not forcing one theory on the children as did the discoveries paradigm. As before the picture becomes clearer with a few examples from the transcripts:

A kindergartner on the skunk/raccoon story.

> Child: It's a skunk!
> Experimenter: Why do you think it's a skunk?
> C: It looks and stinks like a skunk.
> E: Can it be a skunk even if its mommies and daddies were raccoons and its babies are raccoons?
> C: (Nods yes emphatically)
> E: And so even though it started out like this (raccoon) and they did (etc. . . .) it's really a skunk?
> C: (Nods yes)

A kindergartner on the birdfeeder/coffeepot story.
> Child: Birdfeeder, because they changed it into a birdfeeder.
> E: Why isn't it a coffeepot anymore?
> C: They ruined it.
> E: How did they ruin it?
> C: Cutting the things off of it.
> E: So it couldn't be a coffeepot anymore?
> C: No, they ruined it.
> E: What couldn't it do if they cut off those parts?
> C: It would leak.

Again, as the children get older, they shift for the natural kinds but not for the artifacts.

A 4th-grader's notion on the skunk/raccoon story.
> Child: Raccoon, it's just like most of the others . . . they just made it look and smell like one and they made it act like one . . . but it's still a raccoon on the inside.
> Experimenter: Could it still be a raccoon even though it looked and smelled like a skunk?
> C: Well, people would think it's a skunk, but the people who made it into a skunk, they know it's still a raccoon.
> E: Did they really make it into a skunk or was it still a raccoon?
> C: They made it look like a skunk and smell like a skunk . . . but it's really a raccoon.

Finally, a different 4th-grader on the raccoon/skunk story:

> Child: It's a raccoon, because you can put anything on an animal, but it will be the same thing.
>
> E: So even though it looks and smells like a skunk, you think it's still a raccoon?
>
> C: Yes.

Summary of the Discoveries and Operations Studies

Children do shift with increasing knowledge in what they regard as important for determining the identity of objects, and the shift is reliably observed across a wide range of natural kind terms. Moreover, as was the case with the characteristic to defining shift, the shift seems to occur at different times for different domains with biological kinds shifting earlier than minerals. This is important as it again provides evidence against any simple strategy shifts. The nature of knowledge at the very early stages is quite different in kind from that seen in adults in that characteristic features predominate early on and causal structure later.

An important issue concerns the possible cultural universality of the shift for both natural and nominal kinds. Maybe the shifts do not represent the normal course of concept learning as much as the effects of socialization in Western society. There have been suggestions that literacy impels one to regard words as having definitions or essences (e.g., Olson, 1982) as well as accounts that Western schooling shapes children to think in a more rigid categorical way (e.g., Scribner & Cole, 1973). Perhaps characteristic features and their ensuing prototypes are the norms for adult cognition and the shifts uncovered here are anomalies created by the relatively unusual practices of our culture.

I cannot provide a fully definitive answer to this question now, but based on some work conducted by Sheila Jeyifous in Nigeria, there is good reason to expect such a shift in virtually all cultures. We have found strong evidence that non-literate, traditional members of the Yoruba people in Nigeria make both the characteristic to defining shift for nominal kinds and the corresponding shift for natural kinds. They may do so at different times depending on expertise, but they do make the shift. What is especially interesting is that their view of the causal structure underlying natural kinds is very different from that of Western science. Thus, when a Yoruba subject judges that a sheep which has acquired all the characteristic features of a goat is still a sheep, she may justify her response not be referring to evolution or biological laws, but by referring instead to what is loosely called Yoruba metaphysical logic, wherein she might discuss how the two animals were created by different gods in certain ways and how such origins override simple changes in characteristic features.

This is important because it illustrates the dangers of a prevalent kind of cultural chauvinism. We assume that if Western science is not used then reasoning must all be in terms of instance bound characteristic features, a view not so different from the old accounts of other cultures having primitive, unscientific, concrete thought. Almost 20 years ago the anthropologist Robin Horton (1967) made similar observations about tendencies to regard the thought of traditional peoples as unscientific. He described how the people of many traditional West African societies often go beyond the concrete here and now in attempts to explain and label various entities and appeal to elaborate underlying causal theories. They often recognize the need to override what Horton calls "common sense," which closely resembles knowledge based on characteristic features, by appeal to deeper theories.

The shift for natural kinds is unlikely to simply be a shift from what you can see to what you can't see or from perceptual features to conceptual features. In the closely analogous work with nominal kinds there are several cases where both the defining and characteristic features are perceptual (cooking terms, island) or both are conceptual (some immoral acts) and the shift is still observed. The best demonstration that the young children are not completely swayed by perceptual features, however, would be to find certain categorical distinctions that are especially dear to them, ones where their causal theories might first become elaborated. I will suggest that children's first attempts to attach underlying causal structure to natural kinds is at the level of what I have called elsewhere "ontological categories," certain fundamental categories such as plants, animals, artifacts, and non-biological natural kinds. In other work (Keil, 1979, 1983a, b) I have argued that these categories form a kind of conceptual skeleton or framework underlying our knowledge of concepts. Thus, even the youngest children may not be the unrepenting phenomenologists they appear in that they are essentialist from an early age with respect to ontological categories.

An Underlying Conceptual Skeleton

Throughout all the studies described above there have been signs that something above and beyond the relative importance of characteristic versus more principled aspects of meaning is guiding the children's responses. Even the youngest children often know what general sorts of things are being talked about and what sorts of properties they might conceivably have, such as that they were animals, artifacts, or minerals. In a different study (Keil, 1983a) when children were told, for example, that hyraxes are sleepy, even though they had no idea what hyraxes were, they nonetheless insisted that hyraxes must also be able to be hungry, excited, heavy, and not plugged in or broken down. Without any reference to specific instances, they nonetheless confidently made judgments about what sorts of properties are entailed by other properties of general categories such as animals, plants, and other physical objects.

To test more explicitly children's knowledge of such general categories, the operations study was repeated with the modification that some operations made an object cross not just species categories but ontological ones as well. So, for example, in addition to having operations that change tigers into lions, we have operations that change toy mice into what look like real mice and porcupines into cacti. In the first study there were three types of within category changes: animals into animals, plants into plants, and minerals into minerals; and three types of across category changes: artifacts into animals, animals into plants, and animals into minerals. In a second study, the additional category of artifacts into artifacts was also included. In both studies we used photographs to illustrate the before and after states. We reasoned that if young children still said that identity was preserved while looking at actual photographs, then we would have the strongest possible demonstration of their resistance to perceptual features. The perceptual similarity between objects for within category changes was no greater than that for across category changes.

We are still finishing up typing the transcripts for both studies, but preliminary analyses of the data in both cases reveal the same pattern.

The data shown in Figure 4 represent on the spot scores made by the experimenter in the second study while questioning the children. In the past, these sorts of rapid assessments have correlated very well with the scores from two independent raters of transcripts. Nonetheless, these results should be recognized as preliminary until final scorings have been done. An analysis of the data shown in Figure 4 does show a significant interaction between responses for within and across categories and the results strongly suggest that while the younger children tend to treat natural kinds more like artifacts for within category shifts, they maintain that identity is preserved for the across category shifts.

A brief excerpt or two illustrates the differences between within and across category responses:

Same Kindergartner on Within and Across Category Changes

Within: Horse into Zebra

Child: Where did they teach it to live?
Experimenter: They taught it to live in Africa instead of a stable.
C: Well, I don't think horses live in Africa and zebras do, so it's a zebra.
E: OK, you know what they did to it (goes over story). But now it's a zebra?
C: Yeah.
E: Even though it came from a horse?
C: Yeah.

Within: Oak into Pine

C: It has to be an oak tree, because I mean a pine tree because it has prickles and I don't think it will grow any more acorns.
E: OK, so you think it's a pine tree even though it came from an oak tree?
C: Yeah.

Across: Porcupine into Cactus

C: I think it's a porcupine still.

E: And why is it still a porcupine and not a cactus?

C: Because maybe it still moves and cactuses don't move.

E: OK . . . what they did is dyed it a yellowish-green and they injected with this stuff that makes it hibernate or go to sleep for years and then it looked like this. So what do you think?

C: It's a cactus. It looks like a cactus for years probably because they made it hibernate?

E: But do you think it's a cactus or do you think it's a porcupine?

C: Still a porcupine.

E: OK, why do you think it's still a porcupine? What makes it still a porcupine?

C: Cause, they made it hibernate for years and after those years are all over, it will start waking up again.

E: So even though it looks like this now . . . you think it's a porcupine?

C: Yes.

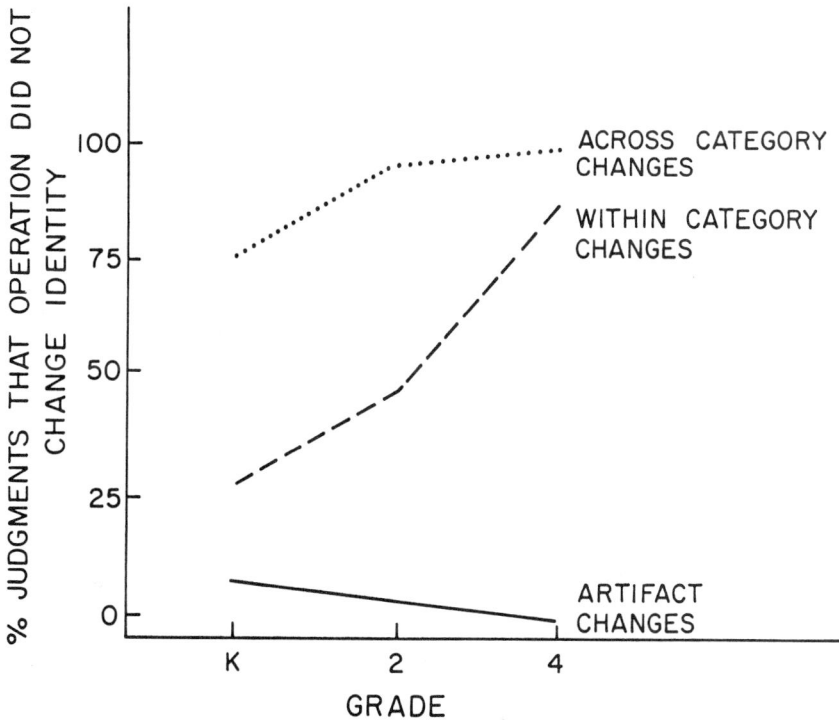

Figure 4. Results of the Study on Operations Within and Across Ontological Categories.

Across: Toy into Real Dog

C: A toy still.
E: And why is it a toy?
C: Because dogs don't have . . . what did you say?
E: Computer.
C: Because dogs don't have computers in their brains, or their head, and real dogs do.
E: Wait . . . you think it's a toy?
C: Yes.
E: Because real dogs don't have computers in their brains. What do they have in their brains?
C: I don't know.
E: But it's not a computer?
C: Yes, it's a toy.

Different Kindergartner

Within: Maple into Pine

C: Pine tree.
E: Even though it started out as a maple tree?
C: Yep.
E: Why is it a pine tree now?
C: Cause it doesn't have leaves.
E: It doesn't have leaves . . . so that makes it a real pine tree?
C: Yep.
E: OK, is it just like all the other pine trees?
C: Yep.

Across: Squirrel into Moss

C: Really a squirrel.
E: Still really squirrel . . . even though he looks like a moss plant?
C: Yeah.
E: Why is he still really a squirrel?
C: Cause he's just painted.
E: He's just painted, and he didn't make him into moss?
C: Yeah.
E: What is different about him, that's not like moss? How is he not like moss? (repeats story)
C: I'm pretty sure . . .
E: You can't think of a reason but you are pretty sure he's still a squirrel?
C: Yeah?

Across: Toy into Dog

C: It's still a remote control dog.
E: It's still a remote control dog, even though it looks like a real dog?
C: Yeah.

E: How come it's a remote control dog?
C: Because it has batteries in here (points).

These results, then, suggest that children are never completely overwhelmed by characteristic features, but that early on they have only the most skeletal distinctions at the causal level. It is difficult to imagine how it could be otherwise . . . how could they be expected to know in advance precisely what categories are and are not transformable by manipulation of what features? After all, there are some natural kinds such as male and female that many adults do think are transformable by sex change operations.

What must develop is an increasing knowledge of each natural kind domain such as biological knowledge or chemical knowledge, and, as that knowledge develops, it allows children to go beyond characteristic features in increasingly subtle ways. From the start they seem to have some global underlying principles that distinguish broad categories such as plants, animals, and artifacts, but they need to learn a great deal more to go beyond characteristic features in distinguishing a horse from a zebra. It's also clear that what develops is not merely a shift from the perceptual to the conceptual. Even kindergartners will use nonperceivable properties to overrule highly characteristic perceivable ones if the kinds are from ontologically distinct categories about which they seem to know principled distinctions at an early age.

These studies lend support for the presence of a level of conceptual representation corresponding to ontological knowledge. They do not require that it be represented in a particular way, but since in other work (Keil, 1979) I have claimed that such knowledge obeys a hierarchical structural constraint known as the M constraint, mention should be made of it as well as of some recent critiques of that constraint by Gerard and Mandler (1983) and Carey (1983). This is done in a later chapter in this volume written with Michael Kelly.

Conclusions

Overall, the main point of this chapter has been to explore the sorts of conceptual changes that occur in children's beliefs about the meanings of natural kind and artifact terms. While we may initially become acquainted with various natural domains through the most characteristic properties of their instances, we move beyond such representations to an increasingly rich causal structure that tells us how and why a thing came into being. Even the youngest children, however, are not totally overwhelmed by characteristic features and the prototypes that result from them. They seem to have a skeletal framework of knowledge that is more principled; and it is at this level that they first override characteristic features. There is increasing evidence that very young children can have sophisticated causal theories about the mechanisms underlying various objects and their behaviors (see, e.g., Gelman, 1983). Moreover, Gelman and Markman[1] have shown that even preschoolers can overrule characteristic features in making inductions about some natural kinds if they are provided with appropriate linguistic labels. Obviously, children cannot possibly know all the detailed principles that distinguish all the possible subclasses of natural kinds: adults cannot either. But the results described here suggest that they do establish foothold in these theories at the ontological level and gradually with increasing knowledge expand to other levels.

Taken as a whole, these findings have implications for theories about the nature of concepts in adults. Characteristic features and prototypes, while certainly associated with how we often use concepts and normally rapidly identify their instances, may not be the same as people's beliefs about what these concepts mean. With increasing knowledge we become more and more able to go beyond mere collections of characteristic features and discover the explanatory causal structure that lies beneath them.

References

Anglin, J. M. (1970). *The growth of word meaning*. Cambridge, MA: MIT Press.
Bruner, J. S., Olver, R. R., Greenfield, P. M., et al. (1966). *Studies in cognitive growth*. New York: Wiley.
Carey, S. (1978). The child as a word learner. In M. Halle, J. Bresnan, & G. Miller (Eds.), *Linguistic theory and psychological reality*. Cambridge, MA: MIT Press.
Carey, S. (1983). Constraints on the meanings of natural kind terms. In T. B. Seiler & W. Wannenmacher (Eds.), *Concept development and the development of word meaning*. New York: Springer-Verlag.
Fodor, J. (1972). Some reflections on L. S. Vygotsky's *Thought and language. Cognition, 1*, 83–95.
Gelman, R. (1983). Recent trends in cognitive development. In C. J. Sheirer & A. M. Rogers (Eds.), *The G. Stanley Hall lecture series* (Vol. 3). Washington, DC: American Psychological Association.
Gelman, R., & Baillargeon, R. (1983). A review of some Piagetian concepts. In J. H. Flavell & E. M. Markman (Eds.), *Handbook of child psychology: Vol. 3. Cognitive development*. New York: Wiley.
Gerard, A. B., & Mandler, J. M. (1983). Sentence anomaly and ontological knowledge. *Journal of Verbal Learning and Verbal Behavior, 22*, 105–120.
Horton, R. (1967). African traditional thought and Western science. *Africa, 37*, 50–71, Pt. 1, 159–187, Pt. 2.
Keil, F. C. (1979). *Semantic and conceptual development: An ontological perspective*. Cambridge, MA: Harvard University Press.
Keil, F. C. (1983a). Semantic inferences and the acquisition of word meaning. In T. Seiler & W. Wannenmacher (Eds.), *Concept development and the development of word meaning*. Berlin: Springer-Verlag.

---

[1] Gelman, S., & Markman, E. Natural kind terms and induction in young children, unpublished paper.

Keil, F. C. (1983b). On the emergence of semantic and conceptual distinctions. *Journal of Experimental Psychology: General, 112*, 357–385.

Keil, F. C., & Batterman, N. (1984). A characteristic-to-defining shift in the development of word meaning. *Journal of Verbal Learning and Verbal Behavior, 23*, 221–236.

Kripke, S. (1972). Naming and necessity. In D. Davidson & G. Harman (Eds.), *Semantics of natural language*. Dordrecht, Holland: Reidel.

Olson, D. (1982). Consequences of schooling. *The Quarterly Newsletter of the Laboratory of Comparative Human Cognition, 4*, 75–78.

Putnam, H. (1975). The meaning of meaning. In H. Putnam (Ed.), *Mind, language and reality* (Vol 2). London: Cambridge University Press.

Schwartz, Barry. (1978). *Psychology of Learning and Behavior*. New York: Norton.

Scribner, S., & Cole, M. (1973). Cognitive consequences of formal and informal education. *Science, 182*, 553–559.

Smith, E. E., Shoben, E. J., & Rips, L. J. (1974). Structure and process in semantic memory: A featural model for semantic decisions. *Psychological Review, 81*, 214–241.

Vygotsky, L. S. (1962). *Thought and language* (E. Hanfmann & G. Vakar, Trans.). Cambridge, MA: MIT Press. (Original work published 1924)

Werner, H. (1948). *Comparative psychology of mental development*, 2nd ed. New York: International Universities Press.

Chapter 8

Constraints on Semantic Development*

Susan Carey

Massachusetts Institute of Technology

As clearly recognized at least from the time of the British Empiricists, any theory of the nature of human knowledge must come to grips with the problem of how it is acquired. This problem, in turn, decomposes into two—the problem of specifying the initial state of the child and the problem of specifying the principles by which the initial state is modified. For any given domain of knowledge one cannot say, *a priori*, whether the study of human infants will bear on the solution to these problems. One reason is that the initial state may not be operative until after infancy. Some maturationally determined state of the central nervous system may be required; alternatively, certain intellectual achievements, themselves attained during infancy or early childhood, may be required to trigger the initial state in that domain. In this chapter I will argue that in spite of these very real possibilities, the empirical study of infants will be crucial to the understanding of the human semantic and conceptual system.

Recently, Keil (1979) has proposed a fragment of a theory of semantic development concerning the principles by which the initial state[1] is modified. I argue in this chapter that his proposal is both importantly right and importantly wrong. A diagnosis of what went wrong implicates a greater role for the specification of the initial state in the explanation of semantic development.

The Problem

Learning the meaning of a new word is an inductive process. The child must infer its meaning from the uses he hears others make of the word and from their

* *Editors' Note*: This paper was originally published in Jaques Mehler and Robin Fox, Eds., *Neonate Cognition*, Lawrence Earlbaum Associates, Inc., Hillsdale, NJ, 1984. It is reprinted here with the kind permission of the editors and the publisher.

[1] My use of the locution "initial state" in this paper is non-standard. I mean the state of the system when it first becomes active. More is innate than the initial state. On a parameter setting model, for example, the entire set of allowable configurations of parameters, plus the principles by which the environment fixes parameter values, are innate. On my usage, only the first setting of the parameters would constitute the initial state.

reactions to his usage. A major goal for the theorist trying to understand the process of meaning acquisition, like that for the theorist trying to understand any case of induction, is to specify the constraints on the hypotheses the child will entertain.

This point can be illustrated through Quine's (1960) well-known scenario, in which he asks us to imagine ourselves interrogating an informant who speaks an alien language. Our information about the meanings of words is to come from pointing to putative referents, saying the word, and observing assent or dissent on the part of our informant. The informant points to a rabbit and says *gavagai*. Our hypothesis is that *gavagai* means the same thing as the English word *rabbit*, and we proceed to test our hypothesis by pointing out other rabbits and other animals and quering of each one, *gavagai*? The informant assents in each case of a rabbit and demurs in each case of a non-rabbit. The problem is that there are infinitely many other hypotheses about the meaning of *gavagai* that are consistent with the data we have so far. *Gavagai* could designate a particular species of rabbit found in that glen. This is a hypothesis we might well entertain, and it is clear how we would rule it out (seek out other species of rabbits). But *gavagai* could also mean *rabbit or light bulb*. While it is clear how we would rule out that hypothesis too (query about a light bulb), there are an infinitude of such hypotheses, such that we could spend the rest of our lives and then forever after just learning the meaning of the word *gavagai*. The problem is still worse. Quine pointed out that there are some hypotheses we might entertain that it would be impossible to rule out from such information. *Gavagai* might mean, for example, *undetached rabbit part*, any part of a rabbit, its ear, tail, left leg, its body, and so on, as long as it is currently attached to a rabbit. Any pointing to a rabbit requires pointing somewhere, and so is a case of pointing to an undetached rabbit part.

Quine's example applies equally to the young child's learning the meaning of the word *rabbit*, where the hypotheses the child entertains are stated in terms of the concepts he represents in mentalese (*mentalese* is Fodor's term for the language of thought). Of course, neither we nor the child would ever entertain hypotheses like *undetached rabbit part* or *rabbit or light bulb*. The child's hypotheses are severely constrained to those that will converge on the correct meaning over a relatively short period (sometimes one-trial learning.)[2]

The problem of induction *is* the central problem of knowledge acquisition in any domain, including the domain of word meanings. Constraints on induction

---

[2] My use of this example is quite different from Quine's. He shows that the problem arises even if we allow information from other sources than the assent/dissent scenario imagined above, because of the "indeterminacy of translation." A skeptic about meaning, Quine endorses the consequences of this line of argument—that for us the meaning of *rabbit* is indeterminate between the animal, undetached parts of the animal, and a host of other possibilities. This is not the place to engage in a debate about Quine's skepticism. Here the example serves the much simpler point that our inductive processes must be highly constrained.

are provided by the initial state—the concepts first available to the child for hypothesis testing about word meanings—and from the nature of the processes by which those concepts are combined and modified. Keil's (1979) constraint is of the latter type, and would rule out a class of those unnatural concepts we considered above, those like *rabbit or light bulb*.

The M Constraint on Linguistic Categories

Keil's proposal is adapted from work by the philosopher Fred Sommers (1963). Sommers's thesis is that there is a level of concepts (the ontological level) that have a special status in our conceptual system and that there is a structural constraint on these concepts (they form a strict hierarchy). His argument depends upon a subsidiary thesis concerning the relation between language and ontological types, to which we now turn.

Ontology is that branch of philosophy that concerns what exists. There are myriad issues in the literature on ontology that Sommers's theory does not touch on (for instance, the hotly debated issues of whether our ontology admits properties, whether numbers exist, etc.). Sommers's theory concerns the categories in terms of which we conceptualize our world, categories named by terms such as *table, star, storm, woman, milk, country, Richard Nixon, love*, and so on. The level of ontologically important concepts is distinguished from other concepts in terms of the contrast between category mistakes and false statements. This is equivalent to the contrast between a predicate's spanning a term and a predicate's truly applying to a term. *The idea is green* is a category mistake; an idea is not the kind of thing that can be green or any other color. *The Empire State Building is green*, in contrast, is merely false. It could be green; it has some color that just happens not to be green. Spanning is the relation between a predicate and a term when the predicate could possibly truly apply to the term, whether or not it actually does. *Green* spans *building, table, animal, grass*, etc., but not *idea, hour, war*, etc. A category mistake results when a predicate that does not span a term is predicated of it. Truly applying is the relation between a predicate and a term such that a true sentence is formed by the predication. *Green* truly applies to *grass* and *gall bladder*, but not *Empire State Building*. A falsehood results when a predicate that does not truly apply to a term is predicated of it.

Some would deny that there is a true distinction between category mistakes and falsehoods. We will not enter this debate here. For the sake of argument, let us accept both the distinction *and* its importance for understanding semantic development. My criticisms of Sommers's theory lie elsewhere. His theory contains two theses: (1) ontological categories form a strict hierarchy and (2) predicates in natural language do not span different ontological types, where "different" here means on different branches of the ontological hierarchy. I argue below that both theses are false.

These two theses of Sommers's theory allow the production of a predicability tree, such as that in Figure 1 (adapted from Keil, 1979). Keil explains the predicability tree as follows:

> The general rule for interpreting a tree structure is that a predicate spans all those terms that every predicate below it spans. For example, the predicate *is sick* spans all terms spanned by *is asleep* and *is wilted*, namely, all living things. The highest node in the tree contains predicates that span all terms. Intuitively, this seems correct, since anything, physical or nonphysical, may be interesting or not. Every nonterminal node represents an indefinitely large class of predicates, although only

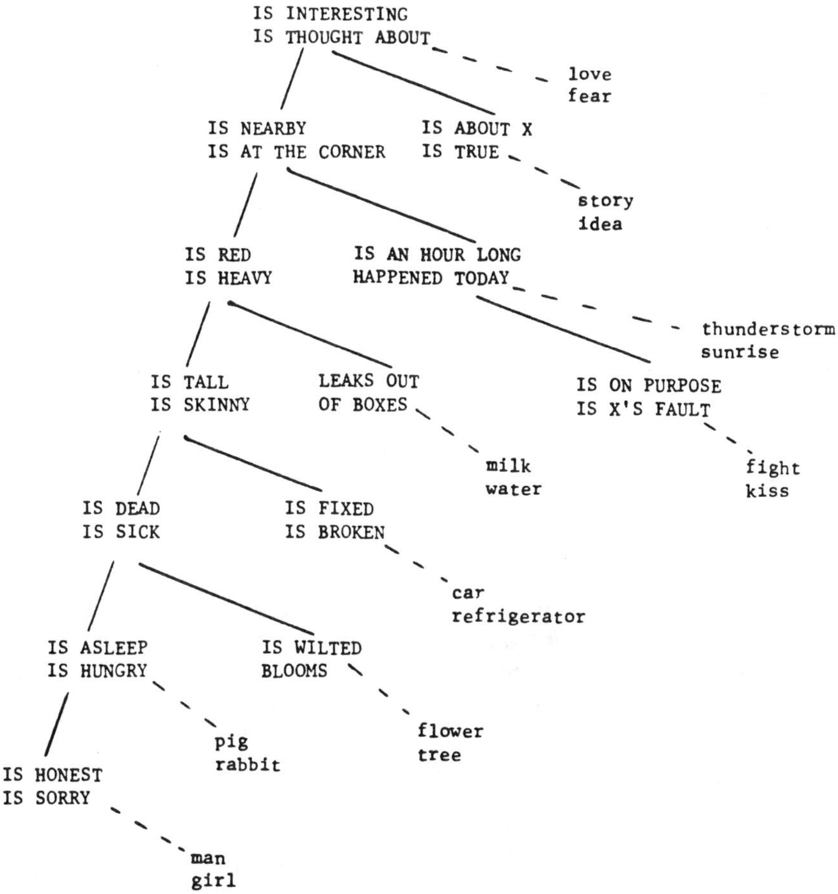

Figure 1. Sample predicability tree (redrawn from Keil, 1979).

a few examples are shown here. Thus, the node containing *is asleep* and *is hungry* would also include *is awake* and *is frightened*, among many other predicates. Similarly, terminal nodes represent indefinitely large classes of terms, so that in addition to *man* and *girl*, the node under *is honest* and *is sorry* would contain all terms denoting conscious beings. Nonterminal nodes also represent classes of terms, namely the supersets of all sets of terms under any such node. For example, the node with the predicate *is heavy* represents the union of several classes of terms that forms a superordinate class consisting of all physical objects. Every node in the tree represents a class of terms that in turn denotes members of an ontological category. Thus, isomorphic to the predictability tree is an ontological tree with a different ontological category at each node. (Keil, 1979, p. 14)

The claims that ontological categories form a strict hierarchy, and that predicates in natural language do not span different ontological types, are equivalent to the structural constraints Sommers and Keil propose for the ontological commitments of natural language: the M and W constraints. The M constraint is that different predicates cannot span intersecting sets of terms. One predicate can span a subset or superset of the terms spanned by another (as in the relation between *is tall* and *is dead*) or they may have no terms in common (as in the relation between *is fixed* and *is honest*), but they can never span terms in common and also have terms that are spanned by each alone. To use Keil's example again: Figure 2a shows an apparent violation of the M-constraint. *The bat* is spanned by both *is made by hand* and *was dead*, but each of those predicates spans some terms not spanned by the other. Sommers and Keil argue that this is not a true counterexample, for it depends upon ambiguity: *the bat* is ambiguous.

The W-constraint is the converse of the M constraint: two terms cannot be spanned by intersecting sets of predicates. Figure 2b shows an apparent counterexample. *Is rational* spans both *the man* and *the number*, but there are also predicates that span one term and not the other. Again, this counterexample hangs on the ambiguity of *is rational*. Sommers's thesis is that there are no violations of the M–W constraints, except those that depend upon ambiguity and metaphor.

The M–W constraint is structural in that it concerns the structure of the tree, irrespective of the particular terms and predicates on the tree. The constraint is domain independent with respect to particular fields of knowledge, such as knowledge of the physical world, the biological world, the social world. Terms and predicates from all these domains are represented on the tree, and are all subject to the M–W constraint. Sommers intended the M–W constraint to provide a test for true ambiguity, as opposed to vagueness. At this point in the research program, Keil and Sommers part company. Keil goes on to suggest that the M–W constraint actually limits hypotheses during word learning. Violation of the constraint is sufficient to rule out a candidate word meaning. *Rabbit or light bulb (rabbitebulb)*, for example, is ruled out by the violation of the M constraint in Figure 2c. Some of the predicates that span *the rabbitebulb* span *the car* but not *the worm* and, conversely, some that span *the rabbitebulb* span *the worm* but not *the car*.

In his writings Keil concentrates on the role of the structural constraint, the M–W constraint, in limiting hypotheses. But for the M constraint to work in any particular case, an equally important condition must also be met. The word learner must already represent nodes in the tree that are defined by predicate clusters like *is dead, has bones* . . . (animate objects) and *is broken, is made in a factory* . . . (artifacts). That is, particular spanning relations between predicates and terms must be represented such that an M violation could be generated. Let us call this source of constraint the *present state constraint*. According to Keil's theory, then, hypotheses as to possible word meanings are limited by the present state of the semantic system, at the time of encountering the word, and by the M–W constraint.

Keil (1979) offered several forms of evidence for his thesis. He showed that adults honor the M constraint when asked to make judgments about sensible predications. He then developed a technique by which very young children can

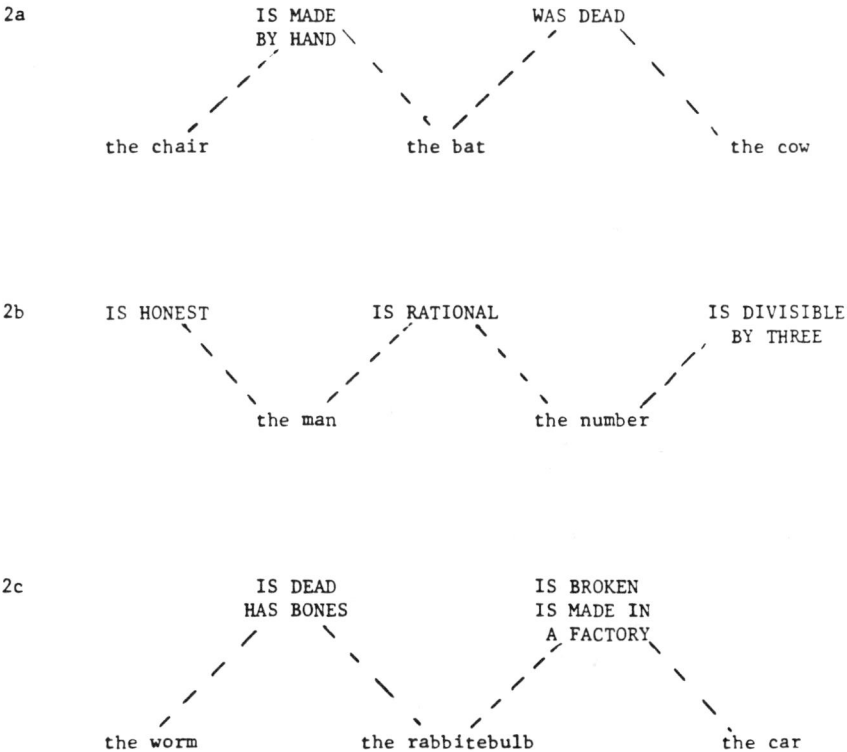

Figure 2. Three violations of the M–W constraint.

be induced to make spanning judgments. Children are asked to say whether sentences like "The table is happy," are silly or not. To check whether the child was using "silly" to indicate false statements or category mistakes, Keil probed with opposites. That is, the child would also be given "The table is unhappy." If he judged both to be silly, Keil credited him with the view that neither *happy* nor *unhappy* spans *table*. If a predicate–term combination is false, that predicate's opposite will be true of the term, whereas the opposite of a predicate that does not span a term also does not span that term. Keil also followed up all judgments with short interviews to clarify the child's beliefs.

Keil found that children's predicability trees were M-constrained. That is, children virtually never violated the M–W constraint. Their trees differed from those of adults, however, in being collapsed versions of the adult tree. The child made many fewer distinctions that did the adult. Figure 3 shows a typical 5-year-old's tree and a typical 7-year-old's tree. A collapsed tree means that the child accepts predicate–term combinations an adult would not. To give just one example, Keil reports the following exchange with a 6-year-old:

E: The squirrel is fixed.
S: That's O.K.
E: How could you fix a squirrel?
S: With a screwdriver—like if his stomach was broken or something.
E: How could you fix a squirrel's stomach with a screwdriver?
S: Very carefully.

This child's entire pattern of judgments indicated that he did not distinguish between animate objects and human artifacts.

By concentrating on the structural constraint, and by ignoring the role played by the present state constraint, Keil failed to see an undesirable consequence of his developmental work. A child with a collapsed tree such as Figure 3a or 3b would be blocked from positing *rabbit or light bulb* as a candidate word meaning, but not *light bulb or idea*. But children under 8 are prodigious word learners; surely they do not consider such hypotheses. Keil's theory cannot explain the fact that they do not. Whatever alternative account explains why 3-year-olds do not posit *light bulb or idea* as a candidate word meaning could also explain the constraint on adults' word learning as well.

In what follows I argue that the M–W constraint could not play the role Keil claims for it. The first, most important, step in the argument is a demonstration that the M–W constraint is not true. Secondly, I argue that even if it were largely true, there is positive evidence that it does not constrain hypotheses about word meanings. Finally, I argue that another way of viewing ontological categories, on which the M–W constraint is denied, accounts for the actual constraints on word learning.

Predicability tree showing a 5-year-old's intuitions

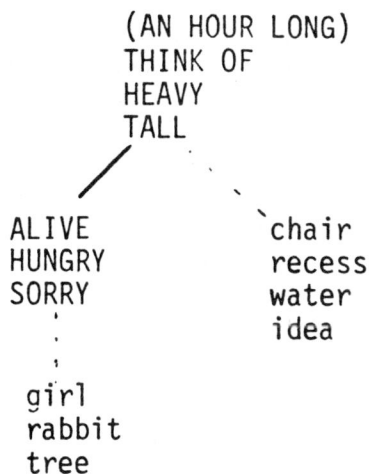

```
                (AN HOUR LONG)
                THINK OF
                HEAVY
                TALL

          /              `
    ALIVE              chair
    HUNGRY             recess
    SORRY              water
      .                idea
      :
      !
     girl
    rabbit
    tree
```

Predicability tree showing a 7-year-old's intuitions

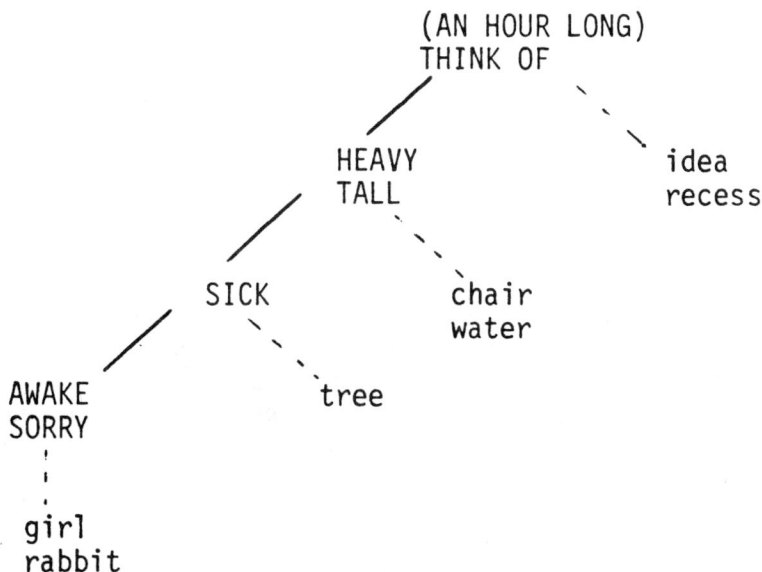

```
                      (AN HOUR LONG)
                      THINK OF
                 /              `
                /                 `
              HEAVY                 idea
          /   TALL                  recess
         /        `
        /           `
      SICK           chair
    /      `         water
   /         `
AWAKE        tree
SORRY
  !
  i
  .
 girl
rabbit
```

Figure 3. Sample predicability trees from children's intuitions.

The M Constraint—A Counterexample

In a masters thesis at the Massachusetts Institute of Technology, Davis (1979) presented a class of counterexamples involving predicates of spatial extent (*is long, is tall*) and other inherently comparative adjectives (*is heavy*). In his studies he duplicated Keil's (1979) procedures (with different terms and predicates, of course) and found that subjects' judgments of category mistakes were never consistent with M-constrained predicability trees. This was in marked contrast to Keil's subjects, who virtually never made predicability judgments inconsistent with M-constrained trees. I take this difference to show that Keil chose materials for his studies where the basic ontological types actually were hierarchically related, and where the subsidiary thesis that predicates do not span different ontological types held, but that there is no constraint on human conceptualization to construe language thus.

The example I will use differs from Davis's. For purposes of exposition I will trust that the reader's intuitions about spanning relations are the same as mine; like Davis, I have checked this with subjects, who all provide patterns of judgments that violate M-constrained trees. The predicates that force an M violation are *is long* and *contains gold*. Figure 4 shows the four possible placements of these predicates on an M-constrained tree. They could be co-nodal (Case 1), as are *is hungry* and *is awake*. They could be on entirely separate parts of the tree (Case 2), as are *is awake* and *is broken*. Finally, they could be hierarchically related, as are *is awake* and *is sorry*. If hierarchically related, *contains gold* could span more terms than *is long* (Case 3) or vice-versa (Case 4). To show that the M constraint is not respected, one must find counterexamples to all four possible arrangements. These are provided on Figure 4, as in the M constraint violation in which these predicates participate.[3]

These are true counterexamples to the M constraint. *Long* is not ambiguous, meaning something different when it spans grave and when it spans table. Things of different ontological types may share a geometry, and terms of spatial extent refer to geometrical properties. Thus, the subsidiary thesis (Thesis 2) about the relation between natural language and ontological types that allows construction of predicability trees is clearly not true. Natural language predicates *may* span different ontological types without implicating ambiguity or metaphor. That holes, surfaces, three-dimensional objects, and types of matter are different ontological types, and that this will be reflected in their different roles in category

---

[3] In order to establish a counterexample to the Sommers/Keil claims one must find terms that violate, without ambiguity, each of the four possible placements of the terms on an M-constrained tree. These are provided on Figure 4. For example, *is long* and *contains gold* could not be co-nodal (Case 1) if a term can be found that only one spans.

mistakes, is not here being denied. So far, all that is being denied is that these patterns of category mistakes are M-constrained.

Even though Thesis 2 is false, the basic claim that ontological types form a strict hierarchy (Thesis 1) may still be true. However, the above counterexample allows us to see that Thesis 1 fails as well. Two ontologically important distinctions—between material and non-material things and between dimensionless and bounded things—cross-classify, as can be seen in Table 1. Stuff, as named by prototypical mass nouns, is inherently dimensionless, with the consequence that mass terms such as *water* or *copper* are not spanned by *is big*. Similarly, while a region of space can be big or little, space itself cannot. Conversely, as we saw above, classes of both material and non-material things are spanned by *is big* and its variants.

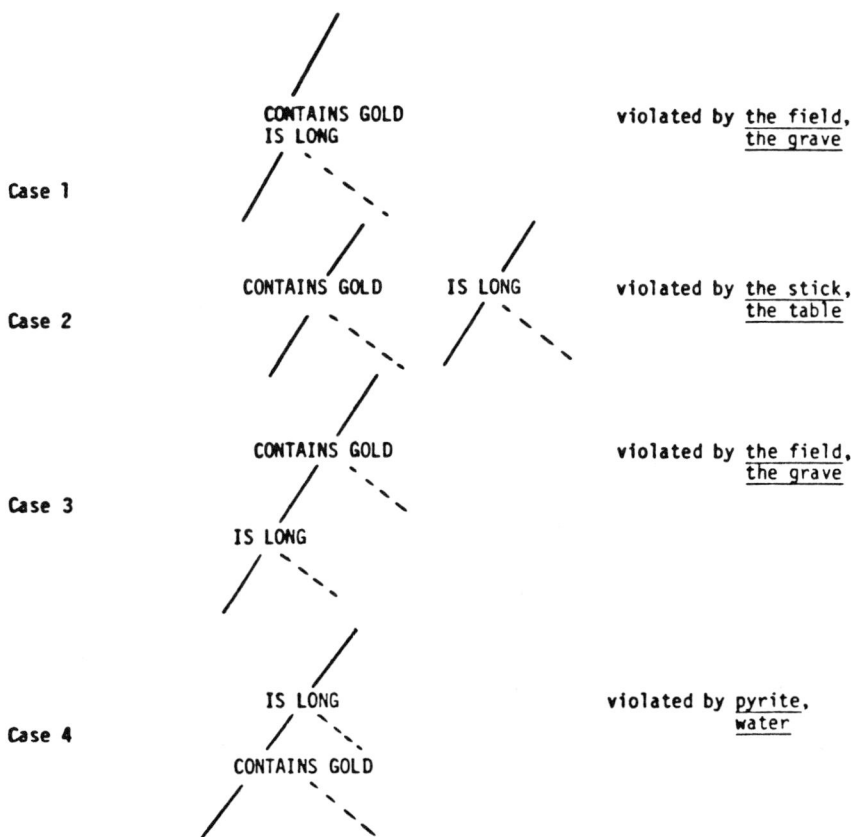

Figure 4. An example of a violation of the M constraint that does not depend upon ambiguity.

Table 1 Cross-classification of two ontologically important distinctions

Bounded	Material	
spatially	yes	no
Yes	the table	the shadow
	the snake	the field
	the tower	the hole
No	the gold	the sky
	the water	the space

Does the M Constraint Constrain Word Learning?

Keil might reply to these counterexamples that they are special, affecting only
a small part of the tree, and that the M constraint holds in general, in enough
cases to be useful as a source of constraint on word learning. This response
requires that children would have an inordinate difficulty learning the concepts,
terms, and predicates implicated in the violations.[4] However, many other counterexamples can be found, implicating other parts of the tree.

If the M constraint limits hypothesis testing about the meanings of words,
languages would be expected to resist systematic and productive violations of
it. Rather than showing resistance, languages appear profligate in the ease with
which different ontological types are lexicalized with single words. Keil (1979)
and Sommers (1963) both discuss a class of apparent counterexamples such as
those in Figure 5. *Is sunny* and *is democratic* span any term denoting a country,
but *is democratic* spans *senate* but not *isthmus* while the reverse is true for *is
sunny*. Keil and Sommers point out that such cases involve ambiguities, as can
be seen by a paraphrase test. *Russia* can be paraphrased *the government of Russia*
and also *the land Russia*. Governments do not have climates and geographic
entities do not have governments, hence the apparent M violation. A similar
ambiguity is involved in the second counterexample in figure 5. *Book* can be
paraphrased by *story the author spun* or *material object in which the story is
printed*. Physical objects (geographical or literary) are clearly different ontological types than governmental institutions or than abstract entities such as ideas,

---

[4] It is true that the meanings of these words are worked out late. Spatial adjectives become fully
specified only by age 6 or so (see Carey, 1982, for a review), and words for material kinds, like
wood and *gold*, attain their adult meaning only after age 8 or 9 (Dickinson, 1982). However, the
meanings of many words not involved in M violations, such as *alive*, are attained just as late (Carey,
1985.) Other explanations for late acquisition can be given that encompass both those that are and
are not involved in M violations.

stories, and arguments. These apparent counterexamples, then, depend upon ambiguity, just as did the earlier examples involving *is rational* and *the bat*.

As mentioned above, Sommers's goal was to provide a criterion for ambiguity. According to him, violation of the M constraint is, in itself, a test for the ambiguity of terms like *the country* and *the story*. These are not counterexamples, then, to Sommers's theory, as long as the two terms are indeed ambiguous, as the theory requires.[5] No, the problem here is for Keil's claim that the M constraint limits hypotheses about the meanings of words. These are not like the accidental and unique ambiguities of *is rational* and *the bat*. There are hundreds of cases like *Russia* and *the book*. Every name for a country, city, or state participates in cases like Figure 5a; every abstract representational entity routinely instantiated by physical tokens participates in cases like Figure 5b. A song can be loud and about a princess, and a sentence can be blurred and about a princess.

It is clear what is going on here. Geographically specified entities have physical properties, such as terrain and climate, and their institutions have non-physical properties. While there is no ontological necessity to this conjunction (economic and political institutions *could* be defined over kinship networks, for examples, irrespective of geography), the conjunction holds and is captured in

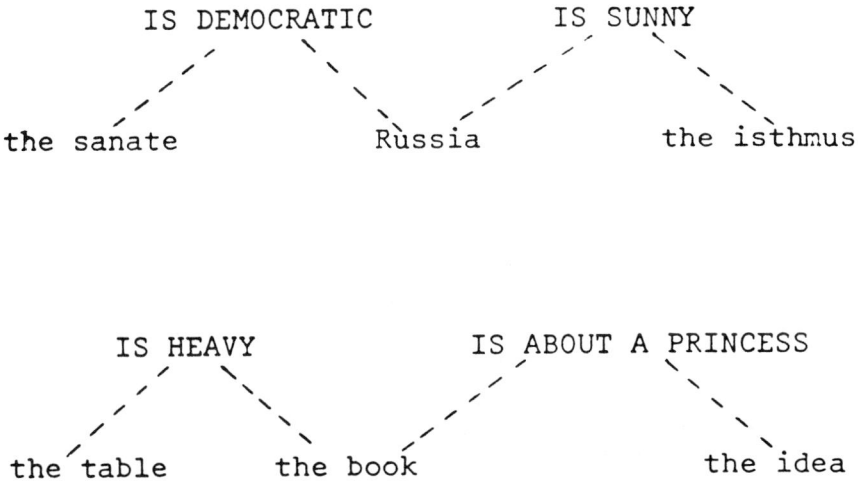

Figure 5. Examples of systematic violations of the M constraint—top of the tree.

[5] There is, in these waters, a true counterexample to Sommers's claim. *The story* is a term that refers to both types and tokens. The discussion in the text concerns its ambiguity when referring to two different types. However, on standard semantic analyses, a particular token can have both semantic and physical properties, thus actually violating the M constraint. This caveat does not apply to examples such as *the country*, and for the purposes of my present argument I am willing to grant the ambiguity of *the story* as well.

language by the use of one term *Russia* to refer to both the government and the land. Similarly, given that people express ideas, arguments, stories, etc., in order to communicate them, there is a regular, non-necessary, conjunction between the abstract entities and physical tokens that represent them. Many other types of systematic ambiguities that produce M violations could be cited. To give one additional example: the process/product distinction often ignored in our lexicon. *The drawing* refers both to the act of drawing (an event) and to the product that can be framed (an object). Rather than being constrained *against* ambiguities of these types, natural languages opportunistically exploit accidental coincidences of ontological types if it is convenient to do so.

Such systematic ambiguities make dubious the claim that there is any constraint against a single term's referring to two different ontological types. Let me reiterate my argument so far. In the previous section I showed that Sommers's theory is false. Predicates do apply to different ontological types without ambiguity. In the present section I argued that language's ready acceptance of terms that systematically refer (even with ambiguity) to different ontological types militates against Keil's claim that avoiding M violations constrains hypothesis testing during word learning.

A Second True Counterexample

This counterexample, also discussed by Keil (1979), concerns yet another part of the tree (Figure 6). Many people have the intuition that *The man is pregnant* is not merely false, it is a category mistake. *Is pregnant* does not span *man; is impotent does not span woman*. This would seem to motivate a branching of the tree below the cluster of predicates that specifies the ontological type *human* (*is sorry, is wealthy . . .* , Figure 6). But *is pregnant* also spans *cow, ewe, chicken*, etc. This counterexample, like that involving *is long* and *contains gold*, shows that basic ontological types are not hierarchically organized; the ontological distinction male/female cross-classifies the ontological distinction person/animal. *Is pregnant* is not ambiguous; it does not mean something different when it applies to women from when it applies to gerbils.

Keil's response to this and similar counterexamples is to deny that *The man is pregnant* is a category error. It is simply false, just as *The man is not pregnant* is true. So too for *The woman is impotent*; this is merely false. The distinction male/female is not at the ontological level. What are we to do when an important point hangs on a clash of intuitions? As Keil rightly points out, a well-confirmed theory may decide the unclear cases. Unfortunately, the other classes of counterexamples discussed above show that we are not in such a situation. We may not appeal to the well-confirmed M constraint and the well-confirmed hierarchy of ontological types to overrule our intuitions that *The man is pregnant* is a category error and to decide in favor of Case 3 on Figure 6.

An Alternative View of the Ontological Level

If, as I have argued, both of Sommers's theses are false, are we left with nothing to say about the ontological level, other than that there is one and it is implicated in category errors? Happily, there is another way of thinking about ontologically important concepts on which the denial of the Sommers–Keil claims is expected.

In explicating the ontological commitments of a language, we specify the basic types of entities presupposed by that language. Ontology, we have said, is the study of the basic categories of what exists. What can we do to find out about these basic categories? We have no *choice* other than to use our theories of the world. Ontology rides on the back of scientific theory.

A theory consists of three interrelated components: a set of phenomena that are in its domain, the causal laws and other explanatory mechanisms in terms of which the phenomena are accounted for, and the concepts in terms of which the phenomena and explanatory apparatus are expressed. Some concepts within theories are extraordinarily important—those that figure in the important laws of the theory, those that are involved in the explanatory work of the theory. As theories develop, changes in these central concepts have ramifications for the whole theory. For example, the change from the Newtonian to the Einsteinian conception of mass dictated that kinetic energy is *not* $mv^2/2$. Such core concepts

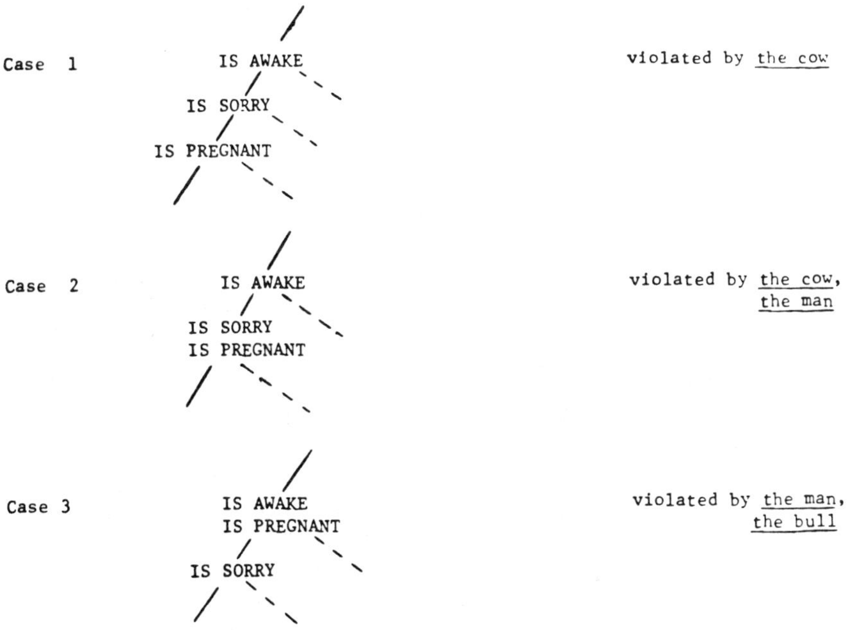

Figure 6. A bottom of the tree violation of the M constraint.

participate in what empiricists and logical positivists held to be the analytic truths in that theory (see Quine, 1953, and Putnam, 1966, for arguments that there are no analytic truths of the sort sought by empiricists).

If there is an ontological level of concepts, the set of core concepts in our theories is the best candidate. On this view, the clearest cases of category mistakes occur when predicates from one theoretical domain are applied to terms from another. *The sun ate a banana* is a category error because eating is in the domain of biological theory and the sun is not a biological entity like an animal or a plant. There will also be within-theory category mistakes, as *The man is pregnant* may be. Category errors within a theory occur when predicates are applied across subdomains of fundamentally different types. *Has positive charge* spans *the electron*, but not *the temperature*, even though both terms and the predicate come from the domain of physics. Subatomic particles and average kinetic energy of a collection of molecules, in current physical theory, are fundamentally different kinds of things. Only the former can have electrical charges.

If ontological commitments are to be explicated relative to theories, the conceptual structures that have the status of theories must be distinguished from those that do not. All concepts are embedded in several relatively organized conceptual structures, called in the psychological and artificial intelligence literatures *schemas, scripts, frames*, etc. If all of these conceptual structures can play a role in determining a person's fundamental ontological commitments, that is, if all conceptual structures act like theories in this regard, then making the move of collapsing the study of ontology with the study of theories has not gained much.

It is possible to distinguish our naive physics, in terms of which our concepts of objects, space, time, and physical causality are constrained, and our restaurant script, even if this script plays some role in explicating our conceptions of waitresses. A central component of theories is their explanatory apparatus. If one queries the events in the restaurant script (Why does one order the food before it comes? Why does one pay for the food? etc.), the explanations given lie outside the script itself. The answer to why one pays for food lies in the theoretical domain of economics, where questions of exchange of goods and services sit. The answer to why one must order first lies partly in the domain of physics, where questions of time and physical causality sit, and also in the domain of psychology, where questions of communication and action sit. There is reason to hope that there are relatively few theoretical domains organizing our causal knowledge, and it is to these that we should turn to explicate our basic ontological commitments.

Viewing category mistakes (and the ontological level of concepts) this way accommodates the insights of the Sommers–Keil theory and also its failures. The hierarchical relations person–animal–living thing–physical object follow from the fact that the very same object participates in different theories by virtue of different properties. People are physical objects, so the laws of physics apply to them; they are also biological entities of two ontologically important, nested, types—animals and humans. Different theoretical domains are not always hierarchically related. Mathematics, for example, cross-cuts many other theoretical domains. Thus, that basic ontological categories do not form a strict hierarchy is no surprise. A final consequence of this view is that the distinction between category errors and falsehoods will not be clear cut. The distinction between the core concepts of a theory and the peripheral ones is a matter of degree, as is the distinction between conceptual structures that play major explanatory roles and those that do not. While the distinction between male and female is well entrenched in biological theory, it is probably less so than that between animal and plant. Such considerations predict unclear cases, such as whether *The man is pregnant* is a category mistake or merely false.

Implications for Semantic Development

While I heartily endorse the project of infusing questions of ontology into psychological research, we have made little progress on the question of constraints on semantic development. The Keil–Sommers proposal for a structural constraint on ontological categories fails. We are left with the present state constraint. Theories held at the moment of induction constrain inductive practices. If we had thought about the lessons of another example from the philosophical literature, Goodman's (1955) *grue* example, we might have expected this outcome. To psychologize Goodman's discussion, the problem is what makes *green* a natural concept while *grue* is not. (*Grue* means *green if examined before the year 2000 A.D., otherwise blue.*) Goodman considered at length the possibility of stating a structural constraint on concepts that makes *green* natural and *grue* unnatural. A first suggestion that comes to mind is that *grue* is more complex than *green*; perhaps there are simplicity constraints. A second immediate suggestion is that *grue* contains a proper name in its definition ("2000 A.D."); perhaps there is a constraint against property concepts being defined in terms of specific individuals (call this the deictic constraint). Goodman constructed the *grue* example precisely to rule out structural constraints of these sorts. There is no way of specifying complexity on which *grue* comes out more complex than *green*; further, *green* is as much a deictic property as is *grue*. For a flavor of Goodman's argument, consider the obvious fact that *grue* and *green* are symmetric with respect to complexity and deicticality, depending upon the primitives in terms of which the definitions are stated. That is, *green* can be defined as *grue if examined before the year 2000 A.D.—otherwise bleen*, where *bleen* is a concept analogous to *grue*. Of course, we want to say why *green* and *blue* are candidates for being primitives, while *grue* and *bleen* are not, but we cannot appeal again to complexity or deicticality. Goodman concluded that there are no structural constraints on conceptual naturalness that would do the required work. Rather, what makes *green* more natural than *grue* is that it is more entrenched in our conceptual systems. That is, it plays an important role in the theories we hold to be true, while *grue* does not.

I pointed out before the obvious point that the M constraint can do no work alone, but only in conjunction with the present state of the conceptual system. In fact, there are still other ways in which Keil fails to acknowledge the role of non-structural constraints on induction. He gives the child the semantically interpreted concept *object* out of which other ontological categories become differentiated. Where does this come from? Further, Figure 1 represents, I believe, Keil's best guess as to the ontological tree underlying all languages. But if the M constraint were the only source of constraint on ontological categories, infinitely many M-constrained hierarchies should be possible. Keil must allow that there are theory-specific constraints on ontological categories, as well as the structural M constraint; I am arguing here that most probably these are the only constraints on ontological categories.

If the only constraints on the learner's hypotheses about word meanings are the concepts held at the time of encounter, then the search for an account of word meaning leads inexorably to an account of the initial state. And since word learning begins in earnest in the second year of life, studies of infants will be necessary in order to specify that initial state.

Quine (1960) used the phrase *innate feature space* to denote the features in terms of which the young child sees his world and in terms of which he forms hypotheses about its nature. One problem with Quine's *innate feature space*, like the behaviorist's set of discriminative stimuli, like the empiricist's sense data, is that no structure in this space is posited that might provide constraints on hypothesis formation. The line of argument presented here has one clear implication: if interested in constraints on the child's inductive practices, look for the theories the child is born with. And if I may hazard a guess, there are exactly two—a naive physics embodying a physical causality and a naive psychology embodying an intentional causality. Central to the former is the concept *object*, and to the latter the concept *person*.

Spelke (1984) underlines two points about the infant's conception of objects. First, empirical research on infants is necessary; some aspects of the adult's concept are present very early on, guiding further knowledge acquisition; others, like many of the Gestalt principles, are not evident at all, so far, in the first year of life. Second, and more important to us here, the infant's concept of *object* cannot be specified apart from related concepts such as *space, number*, and *physical causality*. Spelke shows that bounded entities that occupy a unique position in space, or maintain a single trajectory through space, are seen as single objects. The 4-month-old infant knows that objects out of sight persist, and that a solid object cannot pass through the space occupied by another solid object. Spelke shows that we cannot diagnose the infant's concept of object without examining the expectations the child has about the behavior of objects. More crucially, she shows that the child's concept cannot be explicated except relative to other concepts that articulate a set of physical beliefs.

While there are claims in the infancy literature that young babies have very different expectations about the behavior of people than about the behavior of inanimate objects (e.g., Tronick, Adamson, Wise, Als, & Brazelton, 1975), much less systematic work has been done on the infant's naive psychology than on his naive physics. There is evidence that biological knowledge differentiates out of knowledge of human activities and does not become a separate theoretical domain from psychology until after age 6 (Carey, 1985), but we do not know just when the initial psychological theory becomes available as an inductive base, nor do we know its nature.

Conclusions

Considerations of constraints on word learning, on concept acquisition, and on induction in general suggest a research program organized around ontological issues. The view of ontology defended here requires that theory-like conceptual structures be few in number and distinguishable from non-theory-like structures. We must ask whether very young children represent theory-like structures, we must find out which ones are represented early, and we must characterize the ontological commitments of these first theories. We must also spell out just *how* these early theories constrain inductive projection. A host of empirical issues are raised; the work is yet to be done.

References

Carey, S. (1982). Semantic development, state of the art. In L. Gleitman & E. Wanner (Eds.), *Language acquisition: State of the art*. London: Cambridge University Press.

Carey, S. (1985). *Conceptual change in childhood*. Cambridge, MA: Bradford Books.

Davis, S. (1979). *Of ontology and mental representation*. Unpublished masters thesis. Cambridge, MA: MIT.

Dickinson, D. (1982). *The child's concept of material kind*. Unpublished Ph.D. dissertation. Cambridge, MA: Harvard.

Goodman, N. (1955). *Fact, fiction and forecast*. Indianapolis, IN: Bobbs-Merrill.

Keil, F. C. (1979). *Semantic and conceptual development: An ontological perspective*. Cambridge, MA: Harvard University Press.

Putnam, H. (1966). The analytic and the synthetic. In *Minnesota studies in the philosophy of science, Vol. III*. Minneapolis: University of Minnesota Press.

Quine, W. V. O. (1953). Two dogmas of empiricism. In W. V. O. Quine (Ed.), *From a logical point of view*. Cambridge, MA: Harvard University Press.

Quine, W. V. O. (1960). *Word and object*. Cambridge, MA: MIT Press.

Sommers, F. (1963). Types and ontology. *Philosophical Review, 72*, 327–363.
Spelke, E. S. (1984). Perception of unity, persistence, and identity: Thoughts on infants' conceptions of objects. In J. Mehler (Ed.), *Neonate cognition*. Hillsdale, NJ: Erlbaum.
Tronick, E., Adamson, L., Wise, S., Als, H., & Brazelton, T. B. (1975, April). *The infants' entrapment between contradictory messages in face to face interaction*. Paper presented at the Meeting of the Society for Research in Child Development, Denver.

Chapter 9

Theories of Constraints and Constraints on Theories*

Frank C. Keil
Michael H. Kelly
Cornell University

Arguments for the importance of constraints on the hypothesis space of the learner have now been made in several disciplines: in the linguistic and philosophical literature (Chomsky, 1980), the cognitive sciences (Osherson, 1978), and in cognitive development in particular (e.g., Keil, 1981; Gelman, 1983). In evaluating such arguments, of course, the researcher must identify *prima facie* plausible constraints, and then determine empirically their psychological relevance. Drawing on the philosophical work of Sommers, Keil (1979) has provided evidence for a natural restriction on co-predication known as the M constraint. In re-examining a number of possible violations to the M constraint that were initially discussed by Sommers and Keil and introducing another exception involving spatial terms and predicates, Carey (this volume) concludes that patterns of co-predication are not governed by the M constraint. Carey goes on to speculate that the failure to demonstrate the existence of the M constraint is not attributable to the specific nature of the constraint. Rather it derives from the broader possibility that "The only constraints on natural concepts come from the entrenchment of concepts in theories currently held" (p. 000). In this chapter we seek to explore some alternatives to Carey's pessimistic assessment of the M constraint in particular and the notion of constraints on conceptual structure in general.

Carey's main criticisms of the M constraint can be summarized as follows:

1. The original selections of terms and predicates in earlier work by Keil and Sommers are not arbitrary and in fact are selected in such a way as to favor the constraint.

* Preparation of this paper and much of the research described herein was supported by National Science Foundation Grants BNS-81-02655 and BNS-83-18076 to the first author, and by a National Science Foundation predoctoral fellowship to the second author. This paper was revised while the first author was a Fellow of the Center for advanced Study in the Behavioral Sciences and where he was grateful for financial support from the John D. and Cotherine T. MacArthur Foundation, the Alfred P. Sloan Foundation, and the Exxon Education Foundation.

2. There are several particular exceptions to the M constraint, that in the aggregate, make it untenable. They are:
    a. Problems with spatial entities with no mass.
    b. Problems with entities that appear to be both physical and abstract objects.
    c. Problems with entities that appear to be both events and physical objects.
    d. Problems with entities at the lowest levels of the predicability tree that seem to cause violations because of local inconsistencies.
3. In general there are unlikely to be epistemological constraints on conceptual structure independent of the theories one currently holds about the structure of the world.
4. There is no reason to believe that something like the M constraint plays a role in guiding induction about the meanings of new words.

Carey agrees with the account of Keil (1979, 1981) to the extent that some constraints must guide induction and to the extent that she agrees upon the importance of an ontological level of representation.

To reply to these criticisms it will help first to summarize what we see the M constraint to be about:

First, it is never claimed that the M constraint is absolutely inviolate. Sommers (e.g., 1963) has made such a suggestion, but we see no more reason for it to be absolute than other accepted constraints on natural language, such as those on syntax.

Second, we do differ somewhat from the original account in Keil (1979) in that we now emphasize more that the constraint arises out of conceptual structure at the level of ontological knowledge. Consequently, the constraint is only approximately reflected in linguistic structure via predicability. Thus we view predicability as a helpful, but nonetheless potentially fallible, clue to the structure of underlying ontological knowledge.

Third, because the constraint is at the level of conceptual structure, we regard it as a language independent universal structuring tendency on patterns of thinking which only indirectly affects word meaning.

Let us now turn to consider the points raised by Carey.

On Picking of Predicates and Terms

Carey and others (Gerard & Mandler, 1983) are certainly right in observing that the predicates and terms used to originally construct the predicability trees in Keil (1979) were not selected at random. It is not at all obvious, however, whether the exceptions she offers are even more selected to make the opposite point. Clearly, once the issue reaches a point where examples and counterexamples are volleyed back and forth, it is necessary to employ more objective means of selecting terms and predicates to see to what extent, if any, the constraint holds. To this end we decided to assess the magnitude of some exceptions to the M constraint that Carey discusses by using a more objective method of selecting stimuli items.

Problems of Spatial Entities without Mass

Carey puts the most emphasis on the M constraint violations that seem to arise when predicates such as "long," "tall," and "heavy" are applied to objects such as shadows, holes, and fields, objects that seem to have spatial extent and therefore accept spatial predicates, but which do not have mass and therefore cannot accept predicates referring to weight or mass. It does seem that legitimate M constraint violations do arise with such examples, as Keil (1979) concedes. The question here is how widespread those violations are. A few violations do not make a criminal, and a few criminals do not demonstrate that most members of a domain do not follow general laws. Thus, in responding to Carey we must ask if a wide variety of terms are randomly selected, how many of them will result in violations?

To answer this question we conducted a study in which 165 nouns were selected at random from *The Random House Dictionary of the English Language* (1969). The list of terms so selected are shown in Table 1. The only restrictions on selection of terms were that they be listed in the word frequency norms of Kucera and Francis (1967).

All the nouns were paired with each of the predicates "long," "tall," and "heavy" in sentences of the form "The x is y." The sentences were then randomly arranged and presented to the subjects who were to judge each sentence as sensible or anomalous. If a subject did not know the meaning of a word s/he was encouraged to consult the definition in the dictionary and use that definition to guide the requested judgment of anomaly. In other respects the procedure for eliciting anomaly judgments was basically the same as that used in Keil (1979). Eight college undergraduates participated as subjects.

The results are straightforward. On the average, 95% of the judgments made by our subjects conformed to an M-constrained tree in which the predicate "heavy" dominates "tall" and "long." The results would have been even stronger except for one subject who produced M-constrained responses to 83% of the terms. Most of the violations for this subject can be accounted for by an unwillingness to attribute the predicate "is long" to human beings. We should note that, unlike Carey (1983), this was our only subject who resisted the application of "long" to pragmatically awkward objects such as persons. That Carey should find more of these cases is most likely a consequence of her subjects confusing the pragmatically odd with the semantically odd. The two are not the same and the difference has been argued for elsewhere (cf. McCawley, 1978).

One new finding from this study concerns those cases where subjects looked up the definitions of unfamiliar words (they were asked to keep a record of this).

Table 1 Terms used in spatial predicate experiment

Account	Fog	Podium
Adolescence	Foundation	Porridge
Ague	Frivolity	Preamble
Alliance	Galaxy	Prestige
Amphetamine	Generality	Project
Annihilation	Glamour	Pseudomonas
Apocrypha	Goody	Pyramid
Argon	Greed	Quicksilver
Assertion	Gullet	Ranch
Authority	Halo	Recommendation
Badge	Haulage	Reign
Bargain	Helping	Reservation
Bean	Highball	Rhyme
Bequest	Homogeneity	Rock 'N' Roll
Biplane	Hoy	Rubber
Blood	Hypertrophy	Safeguard
Booklist	Illegitimacy	Sassafras Tree
Brandy	Incident	Secularism
Brown	Inflammation	Sense
Bus	Interconnectedness	Shame
Calculus	Involution	Shot
Capitol Building	Jack	Sincerity
Cast	Joiner	Sleet
Centrifuge	Kas	Soap
Chasm	Kit	Soup
Chocolate	Lack	Spike
Citizen	Latex	Square
Closet	Lemon	Statute
Collection	Lightyear	Stole
Congressman	Load	Structure
Compassion	Lowlands	Suds
Conversion	Madam	Supply
Cost	Management	Syllable
Crate	Martin	Talent
Crust	Medal	Telegraph
Cyclorama	Metabolism	Theater
Day	Millenium	Throttle
Deformity	Moccasin	Today
Derrick	Mop	Townsman
Dichondra	Nap	Tremor
Discontinuance	Nest	True
Divinity	Nodule	Twilight
Dove	Nonresident	Uncle
Duchess	Nurse	Unification
Eave	Offense	Upheaval
Electrolysis	Opinion	Vanity
Enchantment	Otter	Veteran
Epilogue	Palm	Volition
Etiquette	Parlor	Warranty
Exile	Pea	Well
Factory	Perfection	Whole
Feast	Phase	Withdrawal
Figment	Picture	X-Ray
Flap	Plagiarism	Zeal

The vocabularies of our subjects were surprisingly good so we only obtained 20 such cases. However, for 19 of the 20 occasions in which subjects did look up the definition of a word, they gave responses that honored the M constraint. Since most dictionary entries do not mention whether the referent of a word is a physical object, event, or abstract object, subjects had to infer this classification from the more specific definition. When they did so, the subjects clearly did not classify a term as referring to BOTH a physical object and event, or BOTH a physical object and an abstract object. If they did so, we would have found a great many more M-constraint violations. This pattern of results suggests that when individuals attempt to learn the meanings of novel words, an initial bias is to assume that the physical object, event, and abstract object categories are non-intersecting sets, just as the M constraint would predict. The existence of some terms that seem to have both physical object and abstract object senses, such as "book," does not detract from this initial cognitive bias.

This study would therefore seem to support the existence of an M-constrained structure even at that part of the ontological tree where Carey argues that it is most problematic. Clearly the ratio of terms causing violations to those that do not is very small; and therefore the vastly predominant pattern of language use would honor the constraint. This result may also indicate that spatially extended massless entities are conceptually unusual or perhaps even cognitively awkward in comparison to the normal order of things in the tree. Incidentally, "heavy," "long," and "tall" were used in this study as they were the predicates used in an earlier version of Carey's chapter (Carey, 1983). We see no reason, however, why similar, if not even more constrained results should be obtained with "contains gold" instead of "heavy," since fewer metaphorical extensions are suggested.

Carey's other major exceptions revolve around cases in which abstract object and event terms also take physical object predicates. As pointed out in some detail in Keil (1979) these cases have been known about for some time, and Sommers (1965, 1971) presents several reasons for assuming that they are not true violations. Carey herself acknowledges that the paraphrase criterion for cases like "Italy" and "story" do seem to point to an ambiguity in what is being denoted. Nonetheless she sees these terms as exceptions to the M constraint by arguing that if it were a true constraint, it should force our language to avoid creating such ontologically ambiguous terms. This conclusion does not follow automatically from the existence of the constraint; and it is important to see why not before evaluating Carey's claim.

The constraint is originally and fundamentally one on conceptual structure and can only constrain word meaning via that structure. The most basic consequence of the constraint is that words such as "Italy" and "story" refer to two conceptually distinct entities; that is, at the ontological level, something cannot be both an event and an abstract object or both an event and a physical object. Thus, most offending linguistic terms of this sort should be ambiguous;

not necessarily all, however, as the constraint does allow occasional legitimate exceptions. It does not follow from this conceptual constraint that the two parts of the ambiguity should always be represented by a unique lexical item.

The constraint could still indirectly influence word meanings in that, when one hears a term such as "Italy," one knows that the speaker is referring to either the physical, geographical region, or the abstract political institutions, but not both simultaneously. Thus, only the physical region is (or could be) mountainous, and only the political institution is (or could be) democratic. In fact, one could argue that pressure to have unique terms for potentially ambiguous words should be strongest for just those cases where the two meanings are relatively close together and likely to be confusable in various pragmatic settings. If the same predicates apply to both and if both are likely to be encountered in similar situations, it is of course very useful to have distinct terms. Ambiguous words such as "story," however, refer to some of the most conceptually disparate entities possible, sharing only predicates at the very top of the ontological tree such as "interesting" and "good." Thus while, all other things being equal, it might be desirable to have no ambiguity in our terms, the risk of confusing the intended referents is not likely to be very high.

All other things are not equal, however, in terms of reasons for words to be ambiguous. In the real world it is very common for propositional entities such as stories and wills to have corresponding physical tokens. Similarly, many events are closely associated with the physical objects that normally participate in those events. Indeed, without the participants there would be no event. This is partly why children who do not have a good grasp on these non-physical categories tend to interpret words for events and abstract objects as referring to the physical objects that are most closely associated with them. Even in adult language there is frequently a striking shortage of predicates and terms that uniquely apply to non-physical objects, and so we extend physical predicates and terms either metaphorically or via ellipses in order to cover for such systematic lexical gaps.

As adults, therefore, we may inherit from childhood a shortage of non-physical object predicates and terms. One natural recourse is to frequently use ellipses so as to refer to the non-physical via the associated physical objects. As a matter of convenience we adopt the same word such as "book" to refer to both since it is so rare to have one independent of the other and because confusions of what we are talking about are so unlikely. Incidentally, since young children do not seem to think about the existence of non-physical entities when evaluating such terms, the M constraint influences their word meanings even more so than for adults, since those terms will not be ambiguous for them.

These considerations aside, there might still be more conceptual difficulty associated with words that take predicates from differing ontological categories; and it is therefore useful to see to what extent this is true. A second study was therefore conducted that explored whether in general constructions such as "It is warm and democratic'' are conceptually more awkward than ''It is warm and blue'' or ''It is democratic and capitalistic.'' We felt that if we made the term less concrete by using a pronoun such as ''it,'' a more sensitive measure of the unnaturalness of the various co-predications would be attained. With a specific term such as ''Italy'' it seems likely that we have, over the years, learned that such terms point to two different ontological categories and we more or less automatically disambiguate the referents of physical and non-physical object predicates.

Seventeen subjects were asked to choose which sentence of a pair was more cognitively awkward or required more conceptual labor to think about. One sentence had predicates from different ontological categories (e.g., warm and democratic), the other predicates from the same categories (e.g., warm and blue or democratic and capitalistic). The modal pattern of responses was to pick 17 out of 18 times the sentence with predicates from the same category as referring to something that was more cognitively natural or easier to think about (the mean was 16.6). These results clearly show that subjects consistently regard cross-category predications as more awkward than within-category predications.

Terms such as ''Italy'' and ''book'' raise the more general issues of heterotypical entities, discussed extensively by Sommers (1965, 1971). When elements from two ontologically distinct categories frequently co-occur in the real world, language users often adopt the convention of using one term to refer to both, especially when one of the two categories is developmentally much more basic than the other. We have suggested that the constraint is still in evidence with such terms given the different meanings of paraphrases and the increased conceptual awkwardness of cross category co-predications that apply to pronouns. We are currently engaged in followup studies to show other ways in which these co-predications are cognitively more awkward. The most important point here, however, is the recognition that the M constraint primarily affects concepts and only secondarily word meanings.

Local Inconsistencies

Carey's final exception to the M constraint, ''The man is pregnant,'' serves to illustrate the special nature of early ontological knowledge and its differences from other kind of conceptual and semantic knowledge. This particular example, among others, was discussed at length in Keil (1979), and Carey herself concedes that the strength of this violation rests upon the degree to which the previous examples are clear violations. Given the results and arguments made above, we feel that the previous examples are not nearly as compelling as they might appear at first. ''The man is pregnant'' is not an ontological category mistake and is in fact much closer to a contradiction. Several lines of argument support this claim.

First, it does not seem that such a phrase has anything like the inconceivability of category mistakes where a complete incompatibility of conceptual domains is at work. One anecdotal piece of evidence in support of conceivability is the existence of a film entitled "The Rabbit Test" in which a man became pregnant and yet clearly remained a man throughout the rest of the film. By contrast, one would not even know how to go about making a film about a red idea or a chair that happened yesterday.

Examples such as pregnant men have the air of contradiction about them rather than anomaly (see also Drange, 1966, and McCawley, 1968, for arguments that distinguish between contradictions and anomalies). They seem to represent local conflicts of features that are specifically attached to people and animals (e.g., type of sex) and not to broader categories. Thus, no one considers "the square is round" or "the forest was treeless" to be conceptual anomalies. Rather, they represent linguistic conflicts in the specific meanings of the terms involved, a clash at the level of definitions rather than broad conceptual structure.

If one regards any local clash as a category mistake, one quickly has to deal with "touchtone chairs," "stick-shift refrigerators," and "deciduous mushrooms." Chairs are neither touchtone nor dial, but one doesn't want to equate this with ontology. This again illustrates the dangers of looking too shallowly at the linguistic clues to conceptual structure.

Finally, there is some recent evidence that the philosophical distinction between contradictions and anomalies has psychological reality. In a recent thesis, Baynes (1984) has shown a double disassociation of contradictions and anomalies in Broca's and fluent aphasics. In rough terms, Broca's aphasics are considered to have intact conceptual representation, but damage to specifically linguistic structures. The reverse is (very roughly) the case for fluent aphasics. Based on these differences, one would predict Broca's aphasics to have much more difficulty than the fluents at distinguishing between contradictions and plausible sentences, and yet have less difficulty than the fluents at distinguishing between anomalies and plausible sentences. Indeed, such predictions were supported by Baynes's experiments. These findings buttress the idea that contradictions occur at the level of the lexicon and anomalies at the level of conceptual structure. It seems as if these two types of information are represented in different ways and perhaps even in different parts of the brain. Since the M constraint is fundamentally conceptual in nature, the existence of contradictions does not stand as a relevant violation.

Life without Constraints?

Carey, while using the same Quinean and Goodmanian arguments for constraints on induction as appear in Keil (1979, 1981) nonetheless comes to a different conclusion. She acknowledges that there must be constraints on induction but ends up arguing that the only constraint on natural concepts is the relative entrenchment of our various theories about the world in which those concepts participate, the "present state constraint." This proposal doesn't really help very much since it only pushes the question of constraints to another level. Just as there must be constraints for us to be able to induce concepts, so also must there be constraints for us to be able to induce theories. What then are the constraints on the theories? We are happy to call concepts "theories about categories" but we fail to see how this helps us. The M constraint could be discussed as a constraint on natural theories rather than natural concepts. Surely, some constraints must be needed, and it seems like a reasonable candidate. Carey partially addresses this issue by saying that the only non present state constraints on natural concepts are the theories we are born with; but she is mistaken in assuming that these constraints will be always discoverable in research on the perceptions and cognitions of young infants, as she implies. Surely that is not the case for constraints on syntax; why must it be so for other conceptual domains? We think it is unlikely that all a priori constraints on conceptual structure can be reduced to those of the infant's naive physics and naive psychology.

If one goes beyond the single criterion of predicability in explorations of ontological knowledge and the M constraint, as one should for a constraint on conceptual structure, it becomes clear that the particular structure of ontological knowledge guides our cognitions, and frequently our language, in many ways. Consider a recent study by Kelly and Keil (1985) on metamorphoses and conceptual structure. When we looked at the patterns of transformations across ontological categories described in Ovid's *Metamorphoses* and Grimms' fairy tales, we discovered that in both cases we could predict quite accurately the likelihood of transformations based on the distance between two ontological categories in the tree, with members from categories that were further apart being less likely to be changed into each other. These predictions would not have been possible had the ontological categories been arranged in a non-hierarchical manner (i.e., violating the M constraint).

Carey describes very briefly a study done by Keil (1983) in which children were asked to make inferences about the meanings of unfamiliar words based on simple predications about them (e.g., "hyraxes are sleepy"). The patterns of results are too extensive to fully describe here, but the most pertinent point is that children seemed to use their ontological knowledge in a surprisingly effective manner to guide their inductions about the meanings of the words. Thus, when told "Hydraxes are sleepy" the child will infer that hydraxes can be sick or hungry, but not plugged in or an hour long. If the M constraint is still viable, this study can be regarded as providing strong support for its role in aiding the induction of new word meanings.

It may be that part of our disagreement with Carey arises from talking about different things. As described in Keil (in press), there are many ways in which learning could be constrained: *a priori* domain specific constraints of the M-constraint sort, *a priori* domain general constraints, and constraints imposed by the knowledge that one already has. These are not mutually exclusive and evidence for one doesn't negate the others. In fact they all should be regarded as participating extensively in most natural learning situations.

Hierarchies are wonderful things, they grant us a tremendous cognitive economy and freedom (cf. Simon, 1969). Unfortunately much of the world is not hierarchical in nature and we distort it when we try to rigidly hierarchicalize it throughout. It may be, however, that at the level of ontological knowledge, we can get by with this hierarchical simplification, even though it may not be completely accurate, and thereby reap the large cognitive benefits. Perhaps the most compelling reason to believe in the M constraint is the enormous contrast between the tree structures suggested by predicability relations and the lattice structures generated by truth relations. This cannot be an accidental fact, nor merely a fact about the world, but a property of human conceptual structure.

References

Baynes, K. M. (1984). *Detection of anomaly and contradiction by agrammatic and fluent aphasics.* Unpublished doctoral dissertation. Ithaca, NY: Cornell.

Carey, S. (1983). Constraints on the meanings of natural kind terms. In T. Seiler & W. Wannenmacher (Eds.), *Concept development and the acquisition of word meaning.* Berlin: Springer-Verlag.

Chomsky, N. (1980). *Rules and representations.* New York: Columbia University Press.

Drange, T. (1966). *Type crossings.* The Hague: Mouton.

Gelman, R. (1983). Recent trends in cognitive development. In C. J. Scheirer & A. M. Rogers (Eds.), *The G. Stanley Hall lecture series* (Vol. 3). Washington, DC: American Psychological Association.

Gerard, A. B., & Mandler, J. M. (1983). Sentence anomaly and ontological knowledge. *Journal of Verbal Learning and Verbal Behavior, 22,* 105–120.

Keil, F. C. (1979). *Semantic and conceptual development: An ontological perspective.* Cambridge, MA: Harvard University Press.

Keil, F. C. (1981). Constraints on knowledge and cognitive development. *Psychological Review, 88,* 197–227.

Keil, F. C. (1983). Semantic inferences and the acquisition of word meaning. In T. Seiler & W. Wannenmacher (Eds.), *Concept development and the development of word meaning.* Berlin: Springer-Verlag.

Keil, F. C. (in press). On the structure dependent nature of stages of cognitive development. In I. Levin (Ed.), *Stage and structure.* Norwood, NJ: Ablex.

Kelly, M., & Keil, F. C. (1985). The more things change . . . : Metamorphoses and conceptual structure. *Cognitive Science, 9,* 403–416.

Kucera, H., & Francis, W. N. (1967). *Computational analysis of present-day American English.* Providence, RI: Brown University Press.

McCawley, J. D. (1968). The role of semantics in a grammar. In E. Bach & R. T. Harms (Eds.), *Universals in linguistic theory.* New York: Holt.

McCawley, J. D. (1978). Conversational implicatures and the lexicon. In P. Cole (Ed.), *Syntax and semantics, Vol. 9.* New York: Academic.

Osherson, D. N. (1978). Three conditions on conceptual naturalness. *Cognition, 6*, 263–289.

Simon, H. A. (1969). *The sciences of the artificial.* Cambridge, MA: MIT Press.

Sommers, F. (1963). Types and ontology. *Philosophical Review, 72*, 327–363.

Sommers, F. (1965). Predicability. In M. Black (Ed.), *Philosophy in America.* Ithaca, NY: Cornell University Press.

Sommers, F. (1971). Structural ontology. *Philosophia, 1*, 21–42.

Chapter 10
Children's Acquisition of Metalinguistic and Metacognitive Verbs

David R. Olson
Janet W. Astington
Ontario Institute for Studies in Education, Toronto, Canada

The structure of mental states such as believing, desiring, and intending has come to occupy a central place in theories of cognition. Rozeboom (1972), for example, points out that "the literal meaning of 'cognitive' is, after all, *pertaining to knowledge*; so any version of 'cognitive' psychology with a legitimate claim to this title must significantly address something which differentiates believings from infracognitive events" (p. 36). But once "believings" are admitted into a psychological theory, we are apt to be swept away by the rich array of alternative mental states that humans both entertain and express in language, including the following: suspect, doubt, disbelieve, want, desire, fear, contemplate, wonder, decide, try, dream, hypothesize, imagine, intend, pretend, perceive, remember, know, and many others.

Cognitive theories which are primarily concerned with the representation and acquisition of knowledge, whether that knowledge is described as schemata, networks, or scripts, at least implicitly acknowledge that a certain proposition—say, *Birds have feathers*, or simply *p*—is held in a certain mental state, namely, that of knowing, as opposed to, for example, doubting. But while the propositional structure of cognition has come in for detailed analysis (Anderson, 1980), less attention has been given to the "propositional attitude" to these propositions. To incorporate these attitudes or mental states, the cognitive representation of an idea or belief must have a more general form, such as, *John knows that birds have feathers* or simply (X)(*mental verb*)(p), where p is some proposition, *mental verb* is some cognitive orientation to that proposition, and X is the holder or entertainer of that mental state. The mental state, sometimes called the intentional state (Dennett, 1978; Searle, 1979), incorporates both the mental attitude verb and the object of that verb. The verb and its object are called the propositional attitude and the propositional content by some writers (Fodor, 1978) or the psychological mode and the representative content by others (Searle, 1979). To Fodor, "propositional attitudes are relations between organisms and formulae in an internal language'' (1978, p. 508). To Carnap (1947) and Vendler (1970), they are attitudes to sentences. We should note that grammatically mental verbs occur in complex sentences; the matrix verb denotes the propositional attitude and its object complement is the propositional content.

Propositional attitudes and their propositional contents are also important in the analysis of speech acts. Mental states are closely and directly tied to speech acts, and this relation permits a new formulation of the ancient problem of the relation between language and thought. The formulation of this problem begins with Descartes, for it was Descartes who first claimed that mental states were at the center of human nature:

> What then am I? A thing which thinks. What is a thing which thinks? It is a thing which doubts, understands, (conceives), affirms, denies, wills, refuses, which also imagines and feels. (*Meditations, II*, Haldane & Ross, 1973, vol. I, p. 153)

For Descartes, it is not language which makes us human, it is thought. But in a careful reanalysis of the cognitive activities that Descartes took as characterizing ''a thing which thinks,'' Vendler (1972) noted that Descartes's list was not homogeneous. Mixed in with pure mental states such as doubting, understanding, believing, willing, imagining, wanting, and feeling are some acts like affirming, denying, and refusing, which could more appropriately be classified as speech acts. Vendler points out that Descartes's list is a mixture of what in today's terminology would be called both mental state and speech act verbs. Vendler (1970) uses a grammatical criterion to differentiate the two sets, and then points out that for each speech act verb there is a corresponding mental state verb: ''the same things that can be asserted, suggested, or denied in words, can be realized and understood, believed, suspected or doubted in thought . . . what you can wonder about in thought, you can ask about in speech'' (pp. 87–89). Thus, for example, if one can say ''I believe that it is raining,'' one can also say ''I assert that it is raining.'' Similarly, if one can say ''I want you to come,'' one can also say ''I ask you to come.'' And, if one can say ''I promise to do it,'' one can also say ''I intend to do it.'' Finally, if one can say ''I regret hurting you,'' one can also say ''I apologize for hurting you.'' In each case there is a close correspondence between the speech act and the corresponding mental state.

Searle takes the argument one step further within a generalized theory of speech acts and mental states. Searle (1969, 1983), building on the work of Austin (1962), classifies all utterances into five general types of speech acts: assertives, directives, commissives, expressives, and declarations. The successful performance of any of these speech acts depends upon their meeting certain criteria of intention and context, which Austin called *felicity conditions*. The most important of these felicity conditions, Searle calls the *sincerity condition*. In order to assert *that p* sincerely (an assertive speech act), the speaker must believe *that p*; in order to request *p* sincerely (a directive speech act), the speaker must want or desire *p*; in order to promise sincerely *to do p* (a commissive speech act) the speaker must intend *to do p*; and in order to apologize sincerely *for p* (an expressive speech act) the speaker must regret *p*. There is a variety of propositional attitudes for expressive speech acts (e.g., regret, forgiveness, gratitude) to which we have given the general name "sentiment" (see Table 1). It is not clear whether or not declarations "I declare . . . ." and "I pronounce . . . ." have sincerity conditions: Searle (1975) said they did not, but more recently he has said that declarations presuppose a belief and a desire; for example, if I declare the meeting adjourned, I must want it to be so, and believe it to be so (Searle, 1983).

Hence we require beliefs and desires for the explanation of intentional behavior, and these beliefs and desires are expressed in speech acts. Although one may entertain a mental state such as *wanting x* and perform a speech act such as *asking for x* without knowledge of the concepts representing these speech acts and mental states, these concepts and the metalinguistic and metacognitive verbs denoting them mark out in a precise way the structure of intentional states and as a result may provide one line of access to these states and to their role in action, talk, and thought.

Table 1 Classification of Speech Act Verbs and Corresponding Mental State Verbs

SPEECH ACTS			MENTAL STATES		
Speech Act Type	Verbs of Saying	Example	Propositional Attitude = Sincerity Condition	Verbs of Meaning	Example
Assertive	assert explain predict deny	I assert that it is raining	Belief	believe under- stand guess doubt	I believe that it is raining
Directive	ask order request command	I ask you to come	Desire	want wonder wish desire	I want you to come
Commissive	promise guarantee vow pledge	I promise to do it	Intention	intend plan propose try	I intend to do it
Expressive	apologize pardon praise thank	I apologize for hurting you	Sentiment	regret forgive approve appreciate	I regret hurting you

Our concern in this paper is with this set of metalinguistic and metacognitive concepts and the verbs denoting them, their developmental histories, and their effects on the mental life of children and adults. Although all behavior is intentional and is based upon goals or desires and directed by beliefs and knowledge, what is the role of such concepts as intending, thinking, knowing, wanting, saying, and promising in the cognitive processes of children and how are these concepts related to the metalinguistic and metacognitive verbs denoting them?

As we have said, the possession of mental states and the performance of speech acts may be quite unrelated to the comprehension of metacognitive and metalinguistic verbs. However our hypothesis is that children's concepts of mental states and speech acts are dependent on their comprehension of the verbs that denote them. That is, children may have beliefs and intentions without knowing the terms *believe* and *intend*, but their awareness of beliefs and intentions in themselves and others—in other words, their concept of belief and intention—may be dependent on their comprehension of these (or some synonymous) terms. Further we suggest that it is the use of these terms which enables distinctions to be made between different speech acts (e.g., *suggest* vs. *claim*) and different mental states (e.g., *believe* vs. *guess*) and between a speech act and its corresponding mental state (e.g., *promise* vs. *intend*); children's understanding of the difference between an intention and a promise, we suggest, depends on their comprehension of the metacognitive verb *intend* and the metalinguistic verb *promise*. Only when children comprehend such pairs of terms will they understand that a person may express one mental state while actually holding another. Only then will they realize that what is asserted is not necessarily what is believed, or what is promised is not necessarily what is intended, that is, only then will they understand the nature of lies and false promises.

Literature Review

As we have mentioned, then, our concern is with the concepts denoted by metalinguistic and metacognitive verbs, including say/mean, ask/want, promise/intend, thank/appreciate, apologize/regret, and the like. Although we are also concerned with the speech acts and mental states underlying talking and thinking, we have directed our research towards the concepts denoted by metalinguistic and metacognitive verbs. In this section we shall review studies which have examined children's competence with these verbs.

There is remarkably little information concerning the spontaneous use of mental state and speech act verbs, but what there is suggests that children use some of these verbs from a very early age. The following metacognitive verbs are reported to have been produced in natural situations by children under 3 years of age: *decide, forget, guess, hope, like, love, know, mean, miss, need, pretend, remember, think, try, understand, want, wish*, and *wonder*; only three metalinguistic verbs are reported: *ask, say,* and *tell* (Bretherton & Beeghly, 1982; Brown, 1973; Kagan, 1981; Limber, 1973). The data are somewhat limited: Brown's and Limber's data are each from only three subjects, and there is no record of how many subjects used a particular verb nor how frequently it was used. Bretherton and Beeghly studied 30 children, aged 2 years 4 months, and they do record the percentage of children using each verb. Their data come from mothers' reports of their children's utterances, supplemented by tests of comprehension and production given to the children: *want* was used by 93% of their sample; *know* by 66%; and *think, remember, forget, pretend,* and *dream* by 30%. Bretherton and Beeghly characterized all these words as cognitive terms, except for *want,* and they found that cognitive terms were mastered significantly less well by this age group than all other terms expressing internal states including perceptual terms (e.g., *watch, listen*), physiological terms (e.g., *be tired, be thirsty*), and volitional terms (e.g., *want, need*). These latter terms do express internal states but without the use of the complement constructions which are necessary for the expression of propositional attitudes. Incidentally, Bretherton and Beeghly report that the high percentage for *know* was due to the frequency of ''I don't know,'' which does not involve a complement construction. On the other hand Limber (1973), who recorded one hour per month of children's interaction with their mothers and with an experimenter, reported 26 complement-taking verbs used by his subjects during their third year, and said that once one of these verbs appeared in the child's speech, it took complements, unless the child had not produced any four-word utterances: *want,* for example, may appear very early in utterances like ''want juice,'' ''want cookie,'' etc. Limber suggests that it is not surprising that these verbs occur with complements immediately, because it is the only way that many of them can be used. It should be remembered that these data come from only three subjects.

Brown's (1973) study focuses on morphological development, but he does mention the occurrence of object complements with certain verbs ''including *think, know, guess, tell, hope* and *mean*'' (p. 22). He also reports that, at about 2 years, children start to modify the generic verb with *wanna, gonna,* and *hafta* which he described as ''a statement of the child's wish or intention'' (p. 318). Indeed, *want* is the earliest and most frequent verb reported in all the studies; more than half of Kagan's (1981) sample of 14 children first used *want* between 18 and 22 months of age. Hall and Nagy (1979) have shown that by the middle school years children have an enormous stock of these words of ''internal report'' at their disposal and that their use depends upon class, ethnicity, and social situation.

The fact that many of these verbs are used from age 2 onwards is interesting when one looks at empirical studies of children's comprehension of the same verbs. As we shall see, the results of more detailed experimental analysis of these verbs show that children's knowledge of them is far from complete. Experiments using the following verbs are reported in the literature: *believe, desire, figure* (= guess), *forget, guess, know, pretend, remember, say, think, want,* and *wish*. In addition, Chomsky (1969) studied the syntactic development of constructions using *ask, tell,* and *promise,* and her work was followed by a number of other studies which confirmed and extended her results. We shall not discuss those studies here, except to mention that Chomsky distinguished between "knowing the meaning or concept of a word, and knowing the syntactic structures associated with it" (p. 40) and suggested that the former may be acquired years before the latter. But perhaps not; we would argue that syntactic knowledge is part of the meaning of a word even though it can be described separately, and until children comprehend all the syntactic structures associated with a verb, although they know something of its meaning, they do not know the full meaning.

The experiments we shall discuss can be considered in two groups: those concerned with the child's ability to distinguish between related verbs and those concerned with the factive, non-factive, or counter-factive uses of these verbs. Experiments in the first group test children's comprehension of the precise meaning of a verb, by testing their ability to use a set of related terms appropriately. For example, 4-year-olds, but not 3-year-olds, were able to distinguish between someone's knowing (if he had evidence) and thinking (if he did not) that a hidden object was under a certain box (Johnson & Maratsos, 1977). Children 3 to 4 years old could not distinguish between knowing and guessing a hidden object's location; children 5 and 6 years old would say that they had guessed if they chose the wrong location, and would say that they had known if they chose correctly, even though they had no evidence prior to choosing. It was not until 6 to 7 years of age that they used the terms appropriately (Miscione, Marvin, O'Brien, & Greenberg, 1978). A somewhat similar study showed that not until 7 years of age would children distinguish appropriately between *remember, know,* and *guess* (Johnson & Wellman, 1980). No study has tested more than three verbs at the same time. The general finding is that the youngest children do not comprehend the precise meaning of these verbs, even though, as we have reported above, children younger than those tested here use the verbs in natural situations. Perhaps it should be noted that in ordinary conversation even adults may not use the terms precisely, saying, for example, "I knew that it would be a typical Hollywood movie" even though they had no prior evidence for knowing.

The second group of experiments is concerned with children's understanding of factivity; that is, their understanding that a speaker using a factive verb presupposes the truth of the complement clause, and that its truth conditions are unchanged if the factive verb is negated. For example, in the sentence "John knows that the tire is flat," the complement clause "the tire is flat" is presupposed. As a result, negating the matrix clause to produce "John doesn't know that the tire is flat" leaves the truth of the complement clause unaltered. The experiments are hard to compare because they tested different sets of verbs, used very different tasks, and reported different aspects of the data. The ages at which children respond appropriately varies enormously, depending on the particular verb and the particular task. A general conclusion is hard to come by, but children seem to respond correctly at a younger age in situations where they are required to manipulate toys (Hopmann & Maratsos, 1978) than in tests where they are required to make a yes/no/maybe judgment of the truth of the complement clause (Harris, 1975; Scoville & Gordon, 1980). In most studies young children do not use *maybe* which is the correct response when the main verb is non-factive; the use of *maybe* develops with age.

A further problem arises in those studies that find adults making "incorrect" responses: should children's performance be compared with that of adults, or with the response expected by the experimenter on the basis of a linguistic description of factivity? For example, Scoville and Gordon found that only 54% of the adults in their sample judged the complement to be true for both "X knows that . . ." and "X does not know that . . ." despite the fact that the speaker obviously had knowledge of the neutral event described in the complement and the subject did not. One is uncertain whether to criticize the experimental design or the subjects' performance, or to acknowledge that pragmatically adults treat *X does not know that p* as telling them nothing concerning the truth or falsity of *p*.

Say is the only speech act verb used in this group of experiments. Harris (1975) found that children up to 12 years old, but not adults, treated *say* as a factive verb. The complement clauses in these sentences described neutral events about which the subjects could be assumed to have no knowledge or opinion, and it seems that under those circumstances children are prepared to judge what was said as true. Indeed, Scoville and Gordon found that some adults treated *say* as factive, or to be more accurate, treated it like *know* in the same experiment reported above: if *X* says that *p*, then *p* is true, and if *X* does not say that *p*, then the truth value of *p* is unknown. Further, Harris found that not just the verb but the plausibility of the complement was a major factor in children's judgments of truth and anomaly.

We have found a similar pattern of results in a study of second grade children's comprehension of the verbs *think, know*, and *pretend* (Olson & Torrance, 1986). Subjects' judgment of the truth of the complement was determined primarily by the plausibility of the complement and only secondarily by the factivity of the verb. Thus, if told: "John knows that snow is black" and asked: "If John *knows* that snow is black, is snow black?" most subjects replied, "No," thereby disregarding the factive verb. Conversely, if told: "John pretends that snow is white. If John *pretends* that snow is white, is snow white?" again most subjects disregard the counter-factive verb, *pretend*, and respond on the basis of the plausibility of the complement. Hence, they tended to make correct judgments for the counter-factive verb, *pretend*, when it had a complement which was implausible on its own, and they tended to make correct judgments for the factive verb, *know*, when it had a plausible complement. With neutral complement clauses, the mental state verb was more likely to be taken literally. Children made fewer correct judgments for *think* because (as we noted above) they are reluctant to say *maybe* which is the correct response for *think*. These results are shown in Table 2. Pilot studies with adults revealed much the same pattern; the verb is treated secondarily to the complement. We are currently exploring children's reactions to mildly implausible sentences such as "The girls know that *the* icecream tastes bad."

Thus these studies indicate that while many important speech act and mental state verbs occur in children's early language, the full meaning of these terms, as indicated by their contrastive uses—say/know, know/guess—is not completely mastered until well on into the school years. Indeed, only some adults use these verbs precisely, and then, only on occasions of "considered" speech or writing. Finally, the development of children's competence with these verbs may reflect directly the syntactic complexity of the sentences in which they occur; semantic and syntactic complexity are closely related.

Competence with these mental states or propositional attitudes may be related to what in the developmental literature is referred to as "metacognition." Flavell (1981) defines it broadly as "knowledge or cognition that takes as its object, or regulates any aspect of, any cognitive endeavor . . . a 'cognition about cognition' " (p. 37). Flavell's concern, however, is not with the conditions under which such mental states as deciding, understanding, believing, knowing, or the like can be inferred or with children's knowledge of the verbs denoting these mental states, but rather with the cognitive procedures that children or adults can bring to bear intentionally to alter their cognitive processes. Central to the management of these processes is what Brown (1980), Flavell (1981), Markman (1981), and others refer to as "monitoring," namely keeping track of cognitive goals, experiences, and actions.

Although this concern and ours undoubtedly cover much of the same ground, it is important to notice the differences. *Monitor*, unlike *perceive, remember, believe*, or *intend*, is not a mental state verb. To illustrate this difference, consider the mental state verb *understand*. No doubt young children understand, in some sense, the world around them and the language directed to them. This under-

Table 2 Percentage of Correct Responses for Each Verb and Each Complement Type

Complement Type	Matrix Verb			
	Think	Know	Pretend	Total
Plausible	44	96	49	63
Neutral	50	84	72	69
Implausible	43	56	83	60
Total	46	79	68	

standing is captured in Piaget's concepts of assimilation and accommodation. If neither assimilation nor accommodation occur, that is, if understanding in this general sense fails to occur, there has been no experience; to understand is to assimilate an event to a schema or to accommodate in such a way as to represent that event appropriately. But whether or not children realize that they *understand that p*, that is whether they have a concept of understanding before they acquire the verb *understand* which denotes that concept, is not at all certain. It is clear that young school-age children fail to "monitor" their comprehension, in the sense that they do not look for omissions, incongruities, or irrelevancies in texts (Markman, 1981) even when asked if they understand them, and there is some evidence that children's concept of understanding, as marked by the verb *understand* in such contexts as "I hear what you say but I don't understand" develops only at about 6 or 7 years of age (Robinson, Goelman, & Olson, 1983). Hence, it is possible that the operations described as metacognitive are dependent upon the child's comprehension and use of metacognitive verbs.

Acquisition of Metalinguistic and Metacognitive Verbs

As the review of children's language indicated, in the early years their only speech act verbs are *say, tell,* and *ask*, while there is a greater variety of mental state verbs including *think* and *mean*. Our studies have examined the beginnings of the contrastive use of *say* and *mean*. A few 3-year-olds begin to use *mean* in questions such as "What means old-fashioned?" In a systematic study of 36 Bristol pre-school children, Robinson (1980) found that those children who in their early years had heard the verb *mean* being used contrastively with *say* as in "I heard what you said, but I don't know what you mean" at age 6 showed a full understanding of ambiguous messages and their role in communication failure. Contrastive use thus both appears later and depends upon the speaking practices of parents.

What are children learning when they begin to contrast what is *said* and what is *meant*? *Say* may be used not only to mark assertives but also any other speech act and in this sense it may be considered as the prototypical speech act verb; *say* may take the place of *assert, request, promise,* and *declare*. *Mean* plays a somewhat analogous role for denoting the mental states expressed by speech acts. It indicates that the sincerity conditions for those speech acts hold. So if one says it and means it, one believes it; if one asks for it and means it, one wants it; if one promises it and means it, one intends it. Nonetheless, *mean* is not simply a mental state verb as it cannot stand alone: one may think that verbs are fascinating but one cannot mean that verbs are fascinating except as an explanation of some other utterance.

Our studies have examined children's understanding of the contrast between what is *said* and what is *meant* in a variety of contexts. In one study (Olson

& Hildyard, 1981) a story was read to 5- to 8-year-old children who were then asked questions about it. The story was about two children, Kevin and Susie, who went to a movie and bought and shared some popcorn; it concluded with Kevin complaining to Susie, "You have more than me." When asked what Kevin had said, more than half of the kindergarten children replied, "He said, give me some" or its equivalent. By age 8 the majority reported verbatim what had been said, and when asked, they indicated that they knew what was meant as well. From such observations we infer that pre-school children fail to differentiate what is said and what is meant, that is, they tend to confuse the speech act with the meaning expressed by the speech act. It is the concepts denoted by the verbs *say* and *mean* which permit the child to treat both language and meaning in a new way.

The cognitive implications of the failure to make this distinction are shown in an experiment which followed on some earlier studies of Robinson and Robinson (1977). They had found that if pre-school children in a communication-game task either produced or received an ambiguous message, they tended not to blame the speaker or his message but rather to blame the listener. In this task, the experimenter and the child have an identical set of pictures and there is a screen between them so they can see only their own set. The game is to pick a picture and describe it so that the other person can pick the same one. The pictures are so designed that it is likely that an incomplete description will sometimes cause the partner to choose the wrong one; for example, if there are pictures of a big red flower, a small red flower, a big blue flower and a small blue flower, both adjectives are needed to identify each picture uniquely. If an incomplete description is given and the wrong picture is chosen, the experimenter asks the child what went wrong. Consistently, 5-year-olds blame the listener for choosing wrongly, whereas 7-year-olds blame the speaker for his or her faulty message. This pattern of blaming holds whether the child is speaker or listener. In our collaborative experiment (Robinson et al., 1983), each time the inadequate message resulted in a communication failure, we simply asked, "What did I/you say?" The older children reported the inadequate message, what was said, and added "You meant . . ." or "You should have said . . ." while the younger listener blamers answered with the intended sentence, rather than the actual sentence. That is, the sentence meaning, if it is not simply false, seems not to be accessible to them. When sentences do go wrong, the child appears not to recognize the distinction between what was said and what was meant, and to assume that the speaker is simply mistaken, or later, to be lying.

A recent study by Newman (1982) reports a similar finding in children's interpretation of lies. He showed first- to sixth-grade children (6- to 11-year-olds) a "Sesame Street" television segment in which Ernie says to Bert: "I'm going to divide this banana up so both of us can have some" whereupon he eats the whole banana and gives the skin to Bert, saying: "See, I took the inside part and here's the outside part for you." Newman then asked the children whether

Ernie had lied or not. First-grade children think that he did; but by the third grade children begin to notice that the claim is both true and false. It is true by virtue of what was actually said, its "sentence meaning," it is false by virtue of its putative intended meaning. In terms of the hypothesis described above, children come to notice that the language may be treated either in terms of sentence meaning or speaker's intended meaning and in some cases the two may be discrepant. But both come to be noticed, in part, because the child is attempting to construct meanings for the metalinguistic and metacognitive terms *say* and *mean* and to use those terms to represent contrastive concepts for speech acts and the mental states they express.

In some earlier work Olson (1977) attempted to show that the differentiation of what is said and what is meant is of particular importance to writing and the interpretation of text, the traditional problem of hermeneutics. For written, archival texts problems of interpretation become formidable. Not only does the written text preserve only the surface form, the very words, from which the meanings and intentions must be recovered but the interpretation itself may be open to dispute. In speech, one may simply ask "What?" if one fails to understand; in reading written texts, one must work up and perhaps discuss what was meant. Congruent with this interpretation it may be mentioned that the child's acquisition of the say/mean distinction is usually acquired in the context of reading and being read to. It is in reading contexts that a parent may say to a child: "Do you know what 'persevere' means?"

There is some parallel information that helps to support the argument that the elaboration of the concepts of speech acts and mental states represented by the metalinguistic and metacognitive verbs is indeed tied to literacy. Hundert (in preparation) points out that in the 17th century there developed "increasing lexical distinctions in many European languages between the verbs employed for knowing, for acquaintance, and for the possession of moral virtue or prudence" and that this development "struck Vico as a significant transformation in human consciousness" (p. 2). We recently looked up the earliest known occurrences of some of these verbs, the verbs for assertive speech acts and those for the corresponding mental states. The dates for the introduction of these verbs into English is shown in Table 3. This table shows that in Old English (OE) there were four basic mental state verbs: *know, mean, think,* and *understand.* The two OE assertive speech act verbs are *say* and *tell.* While all of the other mental state verbs listed are of Middle English origin, the corresponding speech act verbs are from the 16th and 17th centuries, the period during which attempts were made, as the Royal Society of London put it, "to improve English as a medium of prose" (Sprat, 1966). Presumably, when written English had to serve the needs of science and government, it became important to make the differentiations marked by these terms.

Our suggestion is that a child in learning this metalanguage comes to make the conceptual distinctions marked by these terms. Conversely, he or she is unable to make these distinctions if the terms are not known. If it becomes important for some purpose to make conceptual differentiations, for example, between saying it and meaning it, he or she will learn the distinction by means of learning the words marking this distinction. Once acquired, the concepts marked by these words may be used for various conceptual purposes, as we saw from the experiments mentioned; the child is able among other things to criticize inadequate messages, to lie, and to make false promises!

Now let us turn to a consideration of a more interesting speech act, promising. Whereas it may be argued that a child may make assertions without knowing what assertions are, it is more difficult to make that case for promising. It may be impossible to make a promise unless you actually have a concept of promising, and that in turn may be dependent upon knowing the word *promise*. As we mentioned earlier, the sincerity condition for promising x is the intention to do x. While it is self-evident that children have intentions, it is not clear that they know what intentions are, that is that they have a concept of intention. Moreover, if making promises depends upon knowing what a promise is, and that in turn depends upon knowing what an intention is, it follows that to make a promise one must not only have intentions but know what an intention is. These are some of the possibilities that Janet Astington has been examining in her recent studies.

In one study Astington (in press) tested 4- to 9-year-olds' comprehension of verbs that are used to express intention (e.g., *intend, mean, plan*, and *try*). She showed the child three pictures—for example, a boy getting undressed, a boy

Table 3 Earliest Known Occurrences of Verbs Denoting Assertive Speech Acts and Corresponding Mental States (from *The Shorter Oxford English Dictionary,* 3rd edition)

Speech Act Verbs (Assertives)	Mental State Verbs
assert, 1604	believe, ME
argue ME, but argue that . . . , 1548	decide, ME
admit (= concede as true), 1532	discover, ME
concede, 1632	doubt, ME
contradict, 1570	guess, ME
deny, ME	hope, OE
explain, 1513	imagine, ME
mention, 1530	know, OE
predict, 1546	mean, OE
remark, 1633	remember, ME
remind, 1645	suppose, ME
report, late ME	think, OE
state, 1641	understand, OE
say, OE	
tell, OE	

Note: OE = before 1150, ME = 1150–1450, late ME = 1350–1450.

sitting in a bath tub, and a boy sitting fishing—and said, "Which picture shows 'The boy intends to take a bath'?" There were eight different sets of pictures and eight different expressions of intention (e.g., "The girl plans to carry the box" and "The boy is going to have a swing"). She found that the younger children (up to about age 7) chose the picture that showed performance of the action to illustrate the sentence; the older children chose the picture that showed preparation for the action, which is the closest we could get to illustrating an intention. From this study we infer that children do not fully comprehend verbs denoting prior intention until about 7 years of age.

Some of the verbs used in this study (e.g., *will, is going to*) may express intention, or may simply make a prediction concerning future behavior, whereas the metacognitive verbs *intend, plan*, and *mean* mark intention explicitly. However an explicit expression of intention is not a promise; a promise is more than an expression of intention. In saying "I promise to do it" you undertake an obligation, and you make this explicit using the speech act verb *promise*. Making a false promise involves knowing that you are committed to act, and knowing at the same time that you do not intend to perform. But even though you do not intend to act, you have expressed an intention to do so—speech act verbs express mental states, even though they may not be the mental states that the speaker holds. This is why it is odd to say "I say that it's raining but I don't believe that it's raining" or "I promise to come but I don't intend to" (Moore's paradox). The speaker expresses a mental state which he then denies holding. In pilot work we have looked to see whether children find these sentences odd. A 9-year-old who comprehended *intend, plan*, etc. (from the previous task), and who defined *promise* as "it means to do something or to not do something that you said you would do or you said you wouldn't do," did not think "I promise to come but I don't intend to" was odd, although she understood the task, and had rejected other sentences. For this sentence she said, "That's O.K. 'cause you can promise to come and not keep it if you don't have time." But adults do find these sentences odd, and an 11-year-old responded to "I promise to come but I don't intend to" with "Not O.K. I promise to come means I will come—I have to. But I don't intend to . . . I will but I won't. You can't say that." And this child's definition of *promise* was more sophisticated because it introduced the element of commitment, "If you say *promise* it means they can trust you." For her promising is not just predicting a future event, nor just expressing an intention, but also undertaking an obligation. In future work we hope to demonstrate that this is a developmental sequence.

Summary

In this chapter we have addressed some of the relations between language and thought. Whether we think of that relation as holding between words and ideas, as was typical for the British associationists, or in terms of sentences and propositions, as has been the case since Frege, or in terms of speech acts and mental states that we have pursued here, the common issue is whether language merely expresses existing ideas, propositions, and mental states or whether the language provides the occasion for the construction of these mental structures. For simple natural kind concepts such as cats and trees, it does indeed seem likely that the concept is formed and the child goes on a search for its representation or expression in a natural language. Macnamara (1982) gives the most recent expression of this view. When it comes to concepts such as those appropriate to the various uses of language such as saying and meaning generally, or to asserting, requesting, and, perhaps most clearly, promising, thanking, apologizing, it is not clear that the mental state has any existence except as the sincerity condition for the performance of certain speech acts. It seems plausible that a child cannot make a promise unless he or she knows what a promise is and has a word to express that concept. But then what about an intention? In this case, the child seems not to have the concept of intending but it seems unreasonable to claim that he does not have intentions. Similarly, it seems clear that children can say things, and even mean things by what they say, but there is no evidence that they know this, that is, that they have concepts of saying and meaning. The acquisition of contrasting concepts said/meant permits the child to do a variety of things that were previously inconceivable, lying and false promising being two of the more prominent. It permits children to adjudicate arguments in which they accuse each other of saying x when in fact that was not the intended meaning, it permits them to criticize the speaker and the message rather than the listener in cases of communication failure, and it permits them to derive "literal" or sentence meaning in school-like tasks. Hence, these are important concepts for the mental life of children. And they are concepts that are expressed and acquired, we have argued, through an elaborate set of metalinguistic and metacognitive verbs.

But if these concepts are dependent for their formation on the presence of a language for expressing them, that is, if these concepts are essentially "linguistic concepts," one is led to reconsider the status of the pre-linguistic concepts of children and non-linguistic animals and machines. It is clearly inappropriate to say that children have the concept of *say* and the concept of *mean* or the concept of *promise* but they simply do not know the terms for expressing those concepts. Our argument has been that if they do not know the word, they do not possess the concept. True they can say and mean things, but they do not have concepts of saying and meaning. So too they can, perhaps, recognize cats and trees but whether or not they have concepts which represent cats and trees, concepts which can represent those objects in their absence, without the language for expressing those concepts, seems, to us, to remain an open question.

Intentions are crucial to the analysis of behavior and of speaking. Without intention, action reduces to mere movement; without intention, language reduces to linguistic form. Although intention is an integral part of talk and action, an important part of conceptual development results from the acquisition of concepts for representing actions and intentions as marked by the terms in the metalanguage. The acquisition of these concepts permits the development of new kinds of actions, insincere actions as well as deliberate actions, and new uses of language—lies and false promises—on one hand and indirect speech acts—metaphor and literal meaning—on the other. These conceptual distinctions denoted by the metalanguage are just the beginning of the elaborated set of concepts such as *claim, hypothesize, infer,* and *conclude* which make up such an important part of the language of literature, science, and philosophy into which children are inducted during the school years.

References

Anderson, J. R. (1980). *Cognitive psychology and its implications.* San Francisco: Freeman.
Astington, J. W. (in press). Children's comprehension of expressions of intention. *British Journal of Developmental Psychology, 3.*
Austin, J. L. (1962). *How to do things with words.* Cambridge, MA: Harvard University Press.
Bretherton, I., & Beeghly, M. (1982). Talking about internal states: The acquisition of an explicit theory of mind. *Developmental Psychology, 6,* 906–921.
Brown, A. L. (1980). Metacognitive development and reading. In R. J. Spiro, B. C. Bruce, & W. F. Brewer (Eds.), *Theoretical issues in reading comprehension.* Hillsdale, NJ: Erlbaum.
Brown, R. (1973). *A first language: The early stages.* Cambridge, MA: Harvard University Press.
Carnap, R. (1947). *Meaning and necessity.* Chicago: University of Chicago Press.
Chomsky, C. (1969). *The acquisition of syntax in children from 5 to 10.* Cambridge, MA: MIT Press.
Dennett, D. C. (1978). *Brainstorms.* Montgomery, VT: Bradford Books.
Descartes, R. (1973). *The philosophical works of Descartes* (trans. & ed., E. S. Haldane & G. R. T. Ross). Cambridge, England: Cambridge University Press.
Flavell, J. H. (1981). Cognitive monitoring, In W. P. Dickson (Ed.), *Children's oral communication skills.* New York: Academic.
Fodor, J. A. (1978). Propositional attitudes. *Monist, 61,* 501–523.
Hall, W. S., & Nagy, W. E. (1979, October). *Theoretical issues in the investigation of words of internal report* (Tech. Rep. No. 146). Urbana: University of Illinois, Center for the Study of Reading.
Harris, R. J. (1975). Children's comprehension of complex sentences. *Journal of Experimental Child Psychology, 19,* 420–433.
Hopmann, M. P., & Maratsos, M. P. (1978). A developmental study of factivity and negation in complex syntax. *Journal of Child Language, 5,* 295–309.
Hundert, E. J. (in preparation). Enlightenment and the decay of common sense. In F. Holthoon & D. R. Olson (Eds.), *Common sense: The foundation for the social sciences.*
Johnson, C. N., & Maratsos, M. P. (1977). Early comprehension of mental verbs: Think and know. *Child Development, 48,* 1743–1747.
Johnson, C. N., & Wellman, H. M. (1980). Children's developing understanding of mental verbs: Remember, know and guess. *Child Development, 51,* 1095–1102.
Kagan, J. (1981). *The second year: The emergence of self-awareness.* Cambridge, MA: Harvard University Press.

Limber, J. (1973). The genesis of complex sentences. In T. E. Moore (Ed.), *Cognitive development and the acquisition of language*. New York: Academic.

Macnamara, J. T. (1982). *Names for things*. Cambridge, MA: MIT Press.

Markman, E. M. (1981). Comprehension monitoring. In W. P. Dickson (Ed.), *Children's oral communication skills*. New York: Academic.

Miscione, J. L., Marvin, R. S., O'Brien, R. G., & Greenberg, M. T. (1978). A developmental study of preschool children's understanding of the words "know" and "guess." *Child Development, 49*, 1107–1113.

Newman, D. (1982). Perspective-taking versus content in understanding lies. *Quarterly Newsletter of the Laboratory of Comparative Human Cognition, 4*, 26–29.

Olson, D. R. (1977). From utterance to text: The bias of language in speech and writing. *Harvard Educational Review, 47*, 257–281.

Olson, D. R., & Hildyard, A. (1981). Assent and compliance in children's language. In W. P. Dickson (Ed.), *Children's oral communication skills*. New York: Academic.

Olson, D. R., & Torrance, N. G. (1986). Some relations between children's knowledge of metalinguistic and metacognitive verbs and their linguistic competencies. In I. Gopnik & M. Gopnik (Eds.), *From models to modules: Studies in cognitive science from the McGill workshops*. Norwood, NJ: Ablex.

Robinson, E. J. (1980). Mother-child interaction and the child's understanding about communication. *International Journal of Psycholinguistics, 7*, 85–101.

Robinson, E. J., Goelman, H., & Olson, D. R. (1983). Children's understanding of the relationship between expressions (what was said) and intentions (what was meant). *British Journal of Developmental Psychology, 1*, 75–86.

Robinson, E. J., & Robinson, W. P. (1977). Development in the understanding of causes of success and failure in verbal communication. *Cognition, 5*, 363–378.

Rozeboom, W. W. (1972). Problems in the psycho-philosophy of knowledge. In J. R. Royce & W. W. Rozeboom (Eds.), *The psychology of knowing*. New York: Gordon & Breach.

Scoville, R. P., & Gordon, A. M. (1980). Children's understanding of factive presuppositions: An experiment and a review. *Journal of Child Language, 7*, 381–399.

Searle, J. R. (1969). *Speech acts: An essay in the philosophy of language*. Cambridge, England: Cambridge University Press.

Searle, J. R. (1975). A taxonomy of illocutionary acts. In K. Gunderson (Ed.), *Language, mind and knowledge (Minnesota Studies in the Philosophy of Science*, vol. VII). Minneapolis: University of Minnesota Press.

Searle, J. R. (1979). What is an Intentional state? *Mind, 88*, 74–92.

Searle, J. R. (1983). *Intentionality: An essay in the philosophy of mind*. Cambridge, England: Cambridge University Press.

Sprat, T. (1966). *History of the Royal Society of London for the improving of natural knowledge* (J. I. Cope and H. W. Jones, Eds.). St. Louis: Washington University Press. (Originally published, London, 1667.)

Vendler, Z. (1970). Say what you think. In J. L. Cowan (Ed.), *Studies in thought and language*. Tucson: University of Arizona Press.

Vendler, Z. (1972). *Res cogitans: An essay in rational psychology*. Ithaca, NY: Cornell University Press.

Author Index

Italics indicate bibliographic citations.

Subject Index

A

Apes, 29–50
  ape language, 30–46
    comparison with humans, 37–46
    gesture (sign) language projects, 33–37
    naming, 37–39
    question answering, 39
  cognitive capacities, 44–48
  general intelligence, 46–47
  lack of neuro-physiology for speech, 33
  performance of cognitive tasks, 46–47
Aphasia, 10, 180
  Broca's aphasia, 10, 180
  Wernicke's aphasia, 10
Artifacts, 138–139, 141–142, 143–145, 147–148
  essence, 139–140
  vs. natural kinds, 140
Artifact terms, 133–134
Auxiliary verb, 7

B

Bilingualism, 24–25
  acquired, 24
  native, 24–25
Biological basis of language, 3–25, 29–30, 50
  (*see also* Innateness)
  autonomous language faculty, 29–30, 50
  biological dispositions, 7–8
  domain-specific capacities, 29
Biological program, 4, 22–25
  ceiling of accomplishments, 23
  evidence from neurological defects, 22–24
  limiting factors in growth, 24
  low-level automatic processes, 23
Blind children, 20–21
Brain injury, 6
  any capacity for language learning, 6

C

Categories, 9–10, 19, 60–62, 133, 138, 147–148, 150–151
  acquisition pattern, 9–10

basic level categories, 19
category changes, 148–150
ontological categories, 148–150
verb subcategorization, 60–62
Causal structure, 137–138, 143
Causal theories, 149–152
  and explanatory structure, 149, 152
Characterization theorem, 105–106
Cognition and language, 46–50
  cognitive prerequisites, 46–47
Competence, grammatical, 106–107, 110–111
Computability, 85, 103–115
  and language identifiability, 113–115
  of learning functions, 114–115
  and probability distribution, 85
  by Turing machine, 107
Concepts, 133–135, 137, 152, 156–157
  conceptual anomalies, 179–180
  conceptual change, 133–134, 147–150
  conceptual contradictions, 180
  conceptual structures, 168, 180
  prototype-based, 137
  structural constraints, 156
Conservatism hypothesis, 55–76
  developmental evidence, 58–65
  versions of, 55–57
Constraints on cognitive semantic development, 154–171, 173–182
  epistemological constraints, 155–156, 173–174
  M constraint, 156–166, 170, 173–182
  W constraint, 158–160

D

Deaf children, 16–17, 48–49
  learning "home sign," 16–17
  indexical referencing (pointing), 48
Degree-2 learning, 108
Developmental shifts, 134–135, 140, 143–145, 146, 147
  cultural universality, 146–147
  and treatment of natural kinds and artifacts, 140–141
Downs Syndrome, 22–23

Charles Péguy

Notre jeunesse

précédé par

De la raison

Préface et notes
de Jean Bastaire

Gallimard

Si la philosophie cartésienne fut une dénonciation du désordre et si la philosophie bergsonienne a commencé par une dénonciation du *tout fait,* la pensée de Péguy (1873-1914) fut peut-être avant tout une dénonciation de l'angélisme ou d'un certain kantisme, aux mains si pures qu'il n'en a plus. De mains. Il n'y a qu'une histoire (« culminante, suprême, limite »), celle d'un Dieu qui paria sur l'homme au point de *risquer* son être dans un visage humain. Quand l'homme manque Dieu, Dieu manque l'homme. Il y a ce risque, ce risque infini. Aussi est-ce dans le temps que l'homme qui se perd se trouve, s'il ne dégrade pas la mystique en politique.

Les sigles renvoient aux publications suivantes :

- CQ, III-4 : *Cahiers de la Quinzaine*. Le chiffre romain indique le numéro de la série, le chiffre arabe le numéro du Cahier dans la série.

- OEPC, I, II et III : *Œuvres en prose complètes*, édition Robert Burac, Gallimard, Pléiade, tome I, 1987, tome II, 1988, tome III, 1992.

- FACP : *Feuillets de l'Amitié Charles Péguy*, publication périodique, 1948-1977.

- ACP : *L'Amitié Charles Péguy*, bulletin trimestriel, paraît depuis 1978.

PRÉFACE

On trouvera dans ce volume deux textes polémiques de Péguy. L'un bref, peu connu, parut en décembre 1901 dans les *Cahiers de la Quinzaine* édités par l'auteur[1]. L'autre long, très célèbre, fut publié dans ces mêmes *Cahiers* en juillet 1910[2]. Leur regroupement n'est pas l'effet d'une décision arbitraire. Ils ont le même objet. A deux moments de la vie de Péguy, ils traitent de la décomposition du dreyfusisme, vaste propos auquel le publiciste a consacré plusieurs milliers de pages.

Dans *De la raison*, un an après la loi d'amnistie qui clôturait officiellement l'affaire Dreyfus, Péguy lance une mise en garde solennelle aux vainqueurs, ses récents compagnons de lutte : ne faisons pas à nos adversaires ce que nous n'avons pas admis qu'ils nous fissent. Soyons fidèles à la raison. Dans *Notre jeunesse*, la suite des événements n'ayant que trop justifié ses

1. *De la raison*, CQ, III-4, 5 décembre 1901, OEPC, I, 1987, p. 834-853.
2. *Notre jeunesse*, CQ, XI-12, 17 juillet 1910, OEPC, III, 1992, p. 5-159.

craintes, il exalte l'immortelle Affaire en dénonçant la
dérive politicienne qui l'a défigurée aux yeux de
l'opinion et en dressant au cœur de son livre le
portrait de Bernard-Lazare, âme du dreyfusisme.

*

De la raison se présente explicitement comme un
« avertissement » mis en tête d'un *Cahier* de Jaurès
intitulé *Études socialistes*. Jaurès a rassemblé là une
vingtaine d'articles qu'il avait donnés les mois précé-
dents au quotidien *La Petite République*. Il les publie
dans les *Cahiers* à la demande de Péguy. Ce n'est pas
la première fois que celui-ci est l'éditeur de Jaurès.
Deux ans avant, en 1899, il s'est en partie ruiné à
sortir un épais volume de presque six cents pages, tiré
à dix mille exemplaires et intitulé *Action socialiste*, qui
recueillait des articles plus anciens du tribun [1].
S'il récidive en 1901, c'est que l'accord subsiste
entre les deux hommes, du moins sur la doctrine.
Mais de larges fissures se sont introduites sur la
tactique. Autant qu'un homme de pensée, Jaurès est
un homme de terrain. Responsable politique d'un des
principaux courants socialistes, il privilégie souvent
l'action et subordonne parfois dangereusement, aux
yeux de Péguy, la fin aux moyens. Ainsi en a-t-il été en
décembre 1899, lors du premier congrès de l'unité

---

1. Jean Jaurès, *Action socialiste*, Georges Bellais éditeur, 1899,
558 p. Fondée par Péguy le 1er mai 1898, la Librairie Georges
Bellais sera suivie des *Cahiers de la Quinzaine*, fondés le 5 janvier
1900. Péguy considérera toujours qu'il s'agit d'une seule et même
entreprise.

socialiste où fut prévue une censure à l'intérieur de l'organisation à venir. Cela motiva la première rupture de Péguy avec Jaurès et la création des *Cahiers de la Quinzaine,* fondés pour dire toute la vérité, rien que la vérité, fût-ce « envers et contre nous » [1].

Avec *De la raison,* une seconde rupture s'annonce. Cette fois Jaurès a en tête l'union du Bloc de défense républicaine contre un retour menaçant de la droite antidreyfusiste. Tous les moyens sont bons pour barrer la route à cette droite, même ceux que les dreyfusistes reprochaient naguère à leurs adversaires d'employer. Péguy s'inquiète de ces complaisances tactiques. Au cours d'une réunion de plusieurs heures qu'il a avec Jaurès pour l'établissement du volume d'*Études socialistes,* il constate que l'action du tribun est « beaucoup plus établie, beaucoup plus constante, beaucoup plus tenue que je ne le croyais. Elle est ainsi plus contraire encore à ce que je me représente » [2].

De cette discussion a sans doute jailli l' « avertissement » jeté à la cantonade, d'une manière impersonnelle, sous le titre *De la raison.* Péguy n'y vise pas Jaurès en tant que penseur politique. Il lui rend au contraire hommage dès la première phrase, prévenant que l'auteur des *Études socialistes* « n'y fait appel qu'à la raison ». Mais toute la philippique ultérieure frémit de l'inquiétude qu'éprouve Péguy de voir Jaurès cautionner, sur le plan pratique, un déni total de raison qu'il est urgent de dénoncer.

1. *Lettre au provincial,* CQ, I-I, 5 janvier 1900, OEPC, I, 1987, p. 295.

2. CQ, III-3, 26 octobre 1901, quatrième page de la couverture, OEPC, I, 1987, p. 1693.

Nous sommes à quelques mois du ministère Combes qui va être formé en mai 1902, à la suite des élections marquées par la victoire du Bloc républicain, et dont Jaurès, élu vice-président de la Chambre, soutiendra la politique sans défaillance. Cette politique, Péguy en fait le procès six mois à l'avance, ou plutôt en dégage l'idéologie sous-jacente. Idéologie entièrement contraire à la raison pour un motif très simple : « La raison ne procède pas par la voie de l'autorité. C'est donc trahir la raison que de vouloir assurer le triomphe de la raison par les moyens de l'autorité. »

Suit une série de considérations rigoureuses et proprement axiomatiques où Péguy, en « véritable libertaire », défend la liberté de pensée contre les libres penseurs. La raison ne procède pas de l'autorité gouvernementale (« en aucun sens la raison n'est la raison d'État »), ni de l'autorité parlementaire (« elle n'est pas soumise à la loi de la majorité »), ni de l'autorité militaire (« elle ignore totalement l'obéissance passive »), ni de l'autorité intellectuelle (« le gouvernement des intellectuels serait le plus insupportable des gouvernements »), ni de l'autorité démagogique (« le peuple n'est pas souverain de la raison »).

Elle ne procède pas non plus de l'autorité religieuse. « Athée de tous les dieux », Péguy retourne contre les anticléricaux l'accusation de fanatisme qu'ils ont l'habitude de lancer contre les tenants du cléricalisme. Il ne saurait y avoir de religion de la raison. Le culte de la déesse Raison était une « insanité inouïe ». « Un catéchisme de la raison tiendrait en ses pages la plus effroyable tyrannie. » « Une république de cuistres ne serait pas moins inhabitable qu'une république de moines. »

La raison ne procède pas de l'autorité socialiste, « en supposant qu'il y ait une autorité socialiste », ce que Péguy conteste. « Attacher au socialisme, fût-ce au nom de la raison, un système de science, ou d'art, ou de philosophie, c'est littéralement commettre un abus de confiance envers l'humanité, et c'est recommencer en laïque la prévarication de l'Église, qui vend aux pauvres le pain pour le billet de confession. » Péguy a déjà crié *Casse-cou* à Jaurès là-dessus, neuf mois plus tôt, en lui reprochant de louer inconsidérément la philosophie matérialiste et athée d'Édouard Vaillant, « ramassis d'insanités par quoi le citoyen Vaillant maintient son autorité soupçonneuse »[1].

Avec *De la raison*, Péguy enfonce le clou et révoque en droit, d'une façon prémonitoire, les cours de marxisme-léninisme qui vont étouffer pendant soixante-quinze ans, en URSS et ailleurs, tout effort de pensée libre. « C'est l'effet d'une ambition naïve et mauvaise que de vouloir clore l'humanité par la révolution sociale. Faire un cloître de l'humanité serait l'effet de la plus redoutable survivance religieuse. Loin que le socialisme soit définitif, il est préliminaire, préalable, nécessaire, indispensable mais non suffisant. Il est avant le seuil. »

Pas plus qu'elle ne procède de l'autorité de la tradition, la raison ne procède de l'autorité de la révolution. Et elle est doublement étrangère à l'autorité de la tradition révolutionnaire, qui crée des

---

1. *Casse-cou*, CQ, II-7, 2 mars 1901, OEPC, I, 1987, p. 702.

« traditions surencombrantes ». Imiter les anciens
révolutionnaires ne consiste pas à les répéter dans un
monde qui a changé, mais c'est avoir « en face du
monde que nous connaissons le même sentiment de
liberté, de raison, qu'ils avaient en face de leur
monde ». La révolution consiste en un nouveau
regard. « Vu d'ailleurs, attaqué d'ailleurs, le réel
recommence brusquement à couler à pleins bords. »

Il n'est pas jusqu'à l'autorité des médias que la
raison ne conteste résolument. Lui-même journaliste,
animateur d'une revue qui s'efforce d'obéir aux seules
règles de la raison, Péguy dénonce dans la presse un
« quatrième pouvoir » non moins nocif que les autres.
Les journalistes y ajoutent d'ordinaire l'hypocrisie
d'un double jeu. Ils ameutent en effet « toutes les
libertés, toutes les licences, toutes les révoltes contre
les autorités gouvernementales officielles ». Mais ils
ont les mêmes mœurs et pratiquent les mêmes
méthodes, également attentatoires à la raison. Ils ne
sauraient donc se plaindre que les autorités officielles
les traitent de la même façon.

« La raison ne procède pas enfin de la pédagogie » :
formule par laquelle Péguy arrive au cœur de ce qui le
préoccupe, « au plus grave danger du temps présent ». Éducateur-né, il souffre de voir les exigences
mal entendues de la démocratie tourner à une dégradation de la raison. Là aussi, la raison exige de réagir
contre une autorité déjà signalée sur le plan politique,
mais encore plus désastreuse sur le plan culturel : la
démagogie. « Il ne faut pas que la pédagogie soit de la
démagogie. Il ne faut pas qu'après avoir souffert de
notre négligence le peuple aujourd'hui soit déformé
par notre complaisance. Il ne faut pas qu'ayant

souffert de l'ignorance où il était laissé, il soit aujour-
d'hui déformé par un demi-savoir, qui est toujours un
faux savoir. Ce qu'on doit enseigner au peuple, ce
n'est ni une vanité ni un orgueil, c'est la modestie
intellectuelle, et cette justesse qui est la justice de la
raison. »

Sous une forme ramassée et pourrait-on dire kan-
tienne, bien que s'y manifestent déjà les reprises
patientes et les répétitions perforantes propres au
grand style péguyste, *De la raison* est un texte essentiel
où, à travers les contingences de l'action, Péguy
élabore un véritable traité sur le bon usage de la
raison, bien différent du bréviaire ordinaire des rationalistes scientistes.

Autant qu'une dénonciation de la dérive politique
dreyfusienne, c'est une salubre leçon de logique qui
s'achève en rappelant les limites de la raison : « Elle
n'épuise pas la vie et même le meilleur de la vie ; les
instincts et les inconscients sont d'un être plus profondément existant sans doute. » Mais n'oublions pas
que « la question même de savoir ce qui revient à la
raison et ce qui ne revient pas à la raison, ce n'est que
par le travail de la raison que nous pouvons nous la
poser ». Aussi ne devons-nous pas laisser fausser cet
indispensable outil de discrimination.

*

Comme *De la raison*, *Notre jeunesse* débute sous la
forme d'une préface. Il s'agit d'introduire une série de
onze *Cahiers* qui vont s'échelonner d'août 1910 à
décembre 1911 sous le titre : *Une famille de républicains*

fouriéristes, Les Milliet [1]. Péguy a le goût du document brut. Depuis le début des *Cahiers,* il aime rassembler des archives et, en élève de Michelet, affectionne particulièrement les témoins modestes, inconnus, qui n'ont pas « fait » l'histoire, mais à travers lesquels l'histoire s'est faite.

Les souvenirs de la famille Milliet s'étendent sur une longue et riche période qui, de 1830 à 1874, englobe la Monarchie de Juillet, la Révolution de 1848, le Second Empire, la Guerre de 1870 et la Commune. Le narrateur Paul Milliet est un jeune peintre bourgeois, républicain socialiste, qui mange du curé comme son père franc-maçon et, disciple de Victor Considérant, fréquente avec sa famille le phalanstère de Condé-sur-Vègre, dans la forêt de Rambouillet, avant de se rallier à la Commune pour défendre la République.

Dans ses papiers de famille, il offre plus et mieux que des lettres de Victor Hugo et de Bérenger : une documentation sur les obscurs et les sans-grade qui, derrière les chefs du parti républicain, constituent les troupes. Sur les grands patrons, on a toujours des renseignements. Mais la connaissance défaille à un niveau plus humble et pourtant capital. « Ce que nous voulons savoir, dit Péguy, ce n'est point une histoire endimanchée, mais l'histoire de tous les jours de la semaine. »

Le gérant des *Cahiers* esquisse alors ce qui sera plus

1. Sur cette série, cf. Alfred Saffrey, « Paul Milliet, une famille de républicains fouriéristes », dans FACP, n° 166, 15 mars 1971, p. 9-28, et Jean Bastaire, « Péguy et les Milliet », dans *Littérature et société,* recueil d'études en l'honneur de Bernard Guyon, Desclée de Brouwer, 1973, p. 149-160.

tard le programme de l'école des *Annales* de Lucien
Febvre et Marc Bloch : « comment vivait une famille
républicaine *ordinaire,* moyenne pour ainsi dire, obscure, prise au hasard, ce qu'on y croyait, ce qu'on y
pensait, — ce qu'on y faisait, car c'étaient des
hommes d'action, — ce qu'on y écrivait ; comment on
s'y mariait, comment on y vivait, de quoi, comment
on y élevait les enfants ; comment on y naissait,
d'abord ; — comment on y travaillait ; comment on y
parlait ». En somme de « l'histologie ethnique », qui
permette de savoir quel était le « tissu » même de
cette bourgeoisie et de ce peuple qui ont fondé la
République.

Mais ce commencement de préface tourne à la
fausse entrée, car Péguy délaisse bien vite Paul
Milliet, ou plutôt prend rapidement prétexte de son
évocation des origines de la vie républicaine pour en
venir au véritable sujet et au véritable interlocuteur
que le gérant des *Cahiers* entend se donner. L'essai
devient une postface à l'avant-dernier *Cahier* publié
par Daniel Halévy, en avril 1910, sous le titre *Apologie
pour notre passé*[1].

Comme *De la raison, Notre jeunesse* illustre une autre
caractéristique des œuvres de Péguy. Celui-ci les
définit ordinairement comme des dialogues, bien
qu'elles aient l'apparence de monologues où l'on
n'entend que la voix véhémente, comique, érudite,
intarissable de l'auteur. En fait, ces monologues sont
très souvent des réponses. Péguy réagit à un événement ou à un texte. Il dialogue avec un fait ou avec un

---

1. Daniel Halévy, *Apologie pour notre passé*, CQ, XI-10, 10 avril
1910.

homme qui le provoque et dont il ne donne pas toujours explicitement la référence.

Quand il s'agit d'un texte, celui-ci est souvent un *Cahier* précédent que Péguy a l'élégance de publier en premier et avec lequel il engage ensuite la discussion. Ainsi *Notre Patrie*[1] répond sans doute à *Leur Patrie,* pamphlet de Gustave Hervé, mais également à *La paix et la guerre,* plaidoyer pacifiste que les *Cahiers* ont donné juste avant sous la plume de Charles Richet[2]. De même les deux *Notes* sur Bergson et sur Descartes[3] répondent à *Une philosophie pathétique*[4], essai anti-bergsonien publié aux *Cahiers* par Julien Benda.

Notre jeunesse est une protestation lancée contre un *Cahier* dont Péguy a pourtant, en cours d'élaboration, longuement parlé avec l'auteur Daniel Halévy. Deux ans avant, en 1908, les deux amis, anciens compagnons de lutte dans l'affaire Dreyfus, avaient songé à commémorer le dixième anniversaire de l'événement. D'où le titre donné à l'ouvrage : *Apologie pour notre passé.* Dans l'esprit de Péguy, l'essai devait jouer sur deux registres : exaltation du dreyfusisme et condamnation de ses suites.

Il s'agissait d'une célébration qui, par la dénonciation de l'avilissement ultérieur, aurait valeur d'exem-

1. *Notre Patrie,* CQ, VII-3, 22 octobre 1905, OEPC, II, 1988, p. 10-61.

2. Charles Richet, *La paix et la guerre,* CQ, VII-2, 8 octobre 1905.

3. *Note sur M. Bergson et la philosophie bergsonienne,* CQ, XV-8, 26 avril 1914, OEPC, III, 1992, p. 1246-1277. *Note conjointe sur M. Descartes et la philosophie cartésienne,* texte posthume, OEPC, III, 1992, p. 1278-1477.

4. Julien Benda, *Une philosophie pathétique,* CQ, XV-2, 23 novembre 1913.

ple et de ressourcement. Lisant l'ouvrage d'Halévy
sur épreuves, Péguy déchante : « Je ronchonnais, je
marmonnais, je marmottais, et plus je trouvais que le
cahier est beau, plus je me révoltais. » Halévy adopte
en effet le ton d'une confession douloureuse, « péni-
tente », dira Péguy, comme si les dreyfusistes avaient
quelque chose à se reprocher.

En fait, ce dont l'auteur écrit l'histoire, c'est du
parti dreyfusiste qui, de compromissions en délations
et démissions, a dégénéré en démagogie combiste.
Mais ce parti ne représente que les « apparents »,
hélas très puissants et actifs, nullement les plus nombreux dreyfusistes restés purs et qui ne sont pas du
tout des « exceptions », des « fantaisistes ». Halévy ne
les oublie pas et les admire toujours, mais ne les croit
pas représentatifs. Il accorde ainsi presque tout aux
antidreyfusistes, dans une espèce de désenchantement
rétrospectif.

Réagissant avec violence, Péguy rédige *Notre jeunesse*. Il y emploie des mots durs qui, par ricochet,
atteignent sans qu'il le veuille son collaborateur. « Je
ne me sens nullement ce poil de chien battu, de chien
mouillé. Dans ces *confessions d'un dreyfusiste* qui feront
une part importante de nos *confessions* générales, il y
aura de nombreux cahiers qui s'intituleront *mémoires
d'un âne*. Il n'y en aura aucun qui s'intitulera *mémoires
d'un lâche, ou d'un pleutre*. »

Touché au vif, Daniel Halévy demande réparation
sous forme d'une lettre de protestation qu'il envoie à
Péguy et que celui-ci accepte d'abord de publier dans
les *Cahiers*, puis qu'il décide de remplacer par un plus
long texte d'excuse dû à sa plume et qu'il intitule
Solvuntur objecta : soixante-dix-huit pages où la fonc-

tion dialogique se manifeste une fois de plus chez l'auteur de *Notre jeunesse*.

Dans le cas présent, le dialogue prend l'allure d'un duel qui reste à l'intérieur de limites littéraires, quoi qu'en aient dit les Tharaud dans *Notre cher Péguy* [1]. La paire de témoins échangés est constituée par deux amis communs qui, loin d'arrêter les conditions d'un combat, négocient les termes de certains passages du nouveau texte péguyste. Démesurément accru par des ajouts successifs qui introduisent d'autres thèmes dans ce qui voulait être au départ un simple chant de l'amitié, l'ouvrage paraît en octobre 1910 sous le titre *Victor-Marie comte Hugo* avec en épigraphe — ultime touche duellistique — l'hémistiche cornélien : « A moi, comte, deux mots » [2].

*

Contre le pessimisme dépressif de Daniel Halévy, *Notre jeunesse* est une réhabilitation de l'affaire Dreyfus, une remontée de pente à l'occasion de laquelle Péguy analyse justement le mouvement inverse : comment, en exploitant un grand moment historique, on dégringole de l'héroïsme à la combine.

C'est tout le problème de la dégradation de la mystique en politique. A propos de ce thème devenu banal et souvent mal compris, on a travesti Péguy en idéaliste : quelqu'un qui veut garder les mains pures,

1. Jérôme et Jean Tharaud, *Notre cher Péguy*, Plon, 1926, II, p. 155.
2. *Victor-Marie comte Hugo*, CQ, XII-I, 23 octobre 1910, OEPC, III, 1992, p. 161-357.

mais qui comme les kantiens n'a pas de mains, pour reprendre ses propres mots à la fin de *Victor-Marie comte Hugo*[1]. Gardien des immortels principes, Péguy n'accepterait pas de descendre dans les eaux louches du quotidien et, à l'inverse d'un Jaurès courageusement égoutier, sermonnerait les autres depuis les hauteurs d'une virginité stérile.

Il s'agit de bien autre chose et le plus engagé n'est pas celui qu'on imagine. Péguy ne s'en prend évidemment pas à la politique comme science, comme étude et mise en œuvre des moyens nécessaires à l'administration de la cité. Il a trop le respect de la compétence pour mépriser l'homme politique qui fait son métier et travaille de son mieux au bien-être général. S'il dénonce dans *De la raison* l'autorité gouvernementale et parlementaire, c'est lorsqu'elle est une autorité de commandement et de force contraire à la raison. On ne fera pas de Péguy un ennemi de la raison politique et des décisions et démarches qu'elle engage.

L'ennemi de Péguy est non pas la science politique ou l'action politique, mais ce que nous appelons aujourd'hui la politique politicienne, une politique déconnectée de son inspiration, coupée de sa justification, détournée de sa source. Une politique libérée de ses obligations et qui peut ainsi être facilement captée par des intérêts privés ou par des appétits de puissance étrangers au bien commun.

Loin d'être contre la politique, Péguy est contre son affaissement, son aliénation, processus d'entropie inévitable lorsque la politique n'est plus soutenue, animée, portée par un élan, ou pour parler plus précisé-

1. *Idem*, p. 331.

ment lorsque *LE* politique cesse d'être un instrument au service de tous pour ne plus être qu'un moyen commode de garder des places. « La mystique républicaine, c'était quand on mourait pour la République, la politique républicaine, c'est à présent qu'on en vit. »

Aux yeux de Péguy, la politique ainsi dénoncée est nécessairement corruption, mensonge, cynisme, car elle ne procède d'aucune foi ni n'engendre aucun dévouement. En se ramenant à une lutte autour de l'assiette au beurre, elle se nie elle-même par son refus de tout altruisme. Elle est « le monde de ceux qui ne croient à rien, pas même à l'athéisme, qui ne se dévouent, qui ne se sacrifient à rien. *Exactement :* le monde de ceux qui n'ont pas de mystique. Et qui s'en vantent ».

A l'inverse, la mystique est le monde de ceux qui s'engagent vraiment. Les politiques ne font que se prêter. Ils jouent avec le réel, fricotent avec lui pour sauver leurs petits profits de pouvoir et d'argent. Mais ils ne sont animés par aucune conviction profonde, de celles qui viennent du cœur de l'être et vont au cœur des choses. Ce sont eux les superficiels, les légers, les évanescents, et c'est pourquoi immanquablement leur action tourne à la catastrophe. Seuls les mystiques touchent à la racine et par leur élan bouleversent l'histoire.

Il ne faut pas céder au chantage à l'efficacité qu'exercent les politiques. « C'est nous qui sommes pratiques, *qui faisons quelque chose,* et c'est eux qui ne le sont pas, *qui ne font rien.* Le peu même qu'ils sont, ils ne le sont que par nous. La misère, la vanité, le vide, l'infirmité, la frivolité, la bassesse, le néant qu'ils sont, cela même ils ne le sont que par nous. »

Péguy étend sa réflexion au-delà du champ civique jusqu'au champ religieux et, dans sa critique, déborde les élites pour atteindre le peuple : « Qu'on ne s'y trompe pas. Le mouvement de *dérépublicanisation* de la France est profondément le même mouvement que le mouvement de sa *déchristianisation*. C'est ensemble un même, un seul mouvement de *démystication*. C'est du même mouvement profond, d'un seul mouvement, que ce peuple ne croit plus à la République et qu'il ne croit plus à Dieu. Une même stérilité dessèche la cité politique et la cité chrétienne. C'est proprement la stérilité moderne. »

Cassandre implacable, l'auteur de *Notre jeunesse* n'annonce pourtant pas la fin des temps. Il n'est pessimiste que pour le temps présent. Il sait très bien qu'un peuple a d'infinies ressources, que des remontées de sève sont toujours possibles. Il voit même de nouvelles fécondités se dessiner autour de lui. Il croit que la génération de ses enfants sera une génération mystique. Ingénu retour d'espérance chez un pamphlétaire qui n'a rien d'un Léon Bloy apocalyptique et qui ne soupçonne pas que le mysticisme des années trente sera le mysticisme totalitaire du nazisme et du stalinisme.

Mais quand n'est pas retrouvée une mystique humaine, raisonnable, véritablement « personnaliste et communautaire », selon l'expression chère à Emmanuel Mounier, grand disciple de Péguy durant les années trente, quand à sa place se creuse le vide de la désinvolture, de l'affairisme et du scepticisme, il ne faut pas s'étonner que des mystiques sauvages se développent et déraisonnent là où la raison n'a pas été accueillie dans son rôle de clarificatrice des valeurs et d'éducatrice du souffle.

Loin d'entretenir une attitude d'esquive et de fuite, la mystique exige une vigilance extrême pour saisir le moment où l'on prolonge dans la politique une action commencée dans la mystique. « L'action suit son train. On regarde par la portière. Il y a un mécanicien qui conduit. Pourquoi s'occuper de la conduite ? » Mais « prendre son billet au départ, dans un parti, dans une faction, et ne plus jamais regarder comment le train roule et surtout sur quoi le train roule, c'est se placer résolument dans les meilleures conditions pour se faire criminel ».

Péguy l'affirme solennellement, et c'est une nouvelle forme de son irréductible opposition à toute contrainte qui ne procède pas de la raison, à toute autorité fondée seulement sur la force, fût-ce la force de l'habitude : « Quand par impossible un homme de cœur discerne au point de discernement, s'arrête au point d'arrêt, refuse de muer à ce point de mutation, quand un homme de cœur, pour demeurer fidèle à une mystique, refuse d'entrer dans le jeu de la politique correspondante, les politiciens ont accoutumé de le nommer d'un petit mot bien usé aujourd'hui : volontiers ils nous nommeraient traître. Qu'on le sache bien, c'est ce traître que nous avons toujours été et que nous serons toujours. »

Il suffit de recourir à l'étymologie pour savoir ce qu'est un véritable traître. Trahir vient du latin « tradere » qui signifie remettre, céder, livrer. « Le traître au sens plein, au sens ancien de ce mot, c'est celui qui vend sa foi, qui vend son âme, qui livre son être même, qui *perd* son âme, qui trahit ses principes, son idéal, son être même. » C'est donc justement « celui qui trahit sa mystique pour entrer dans la politique correspondante, passant complaisamment par-dessus le point de discrimination ».

La vigilance est d'autant plus requise qu'on se heurte à une loi commune, à laquelle n'échappe aucun secteur de l'opinion : « Tout commence par *LA* mystique et tout finit par *DE LA* politique. » Aussi la question décisive n'est-elle pas « de savoir qui l'emportera de toutes les politiques », mais de faire en sorte que dans chaque système de pensée et d'action « la mystique ne soit pas dévorée par la politique à laquelle elle a donné naissance ». C'est une question de « niveau des vies », de hauteur d'exigence et d'intériorité d'engagement.

On mesure à cela la vanité de bien des luttes qui consistent à opposer des réalités qui ne sont pas du même niveau. La mystique républicaine s'oppose alors à la politique royaliste comme la mystique royaliste s'oppose à la politique républicaine. On obtient de la sorte des victoires à peu de frais, car les postulats en sont biaisés et suent la mauvaise foi.

Péguy nous avertit : « Quand on veut comparer un ordre à un autre ordre, un système à un autre système, il faut les comparer par des plans et sur des plans du même étage. Il faut comparer les mystiques entre elles ; et les politiques entre elles. Il ne faut pas comparer une mystique à une politique ; ni une politique à une mystique. » Autrement « on ne s'entendra jamais. Mais c'est peut-être ce que demandent les partis ».

Une autre conséquence est que selon les plans

l'antagonisme n'est pas de même espèce. « Les mystiques sont beaucoup moins ennemies entre elles que les
politiques. Parce qu'elles n'ont point comme les
politiques à se partager sans cesse une matière
temporelle, un monde temporel, une puissance temporelle incessamment limitée. Et quand elles sont
ennemies, elles le sont tout autrement, à une profondeur infiniment plus essentielle, avec une noblesse
infiniment plus profonde. »

Aucun camp n'a donc à se vanter. « Quand on voit
ce que la politique cléricale a fait de la mystique
chrétienne, comment s'étonner de ce que la politique
radicale a fait de la mystique républicaine ? » Mais au
niveau mystique peut se nouer entre chaque camp une
alliance féconde, « la mystique du salut » ne s'oppo-
sant pas aujourd'hui à « la mystique de la liberté »
comme la politique cléricale s'oppose à la politique
radicale. Péguy en fait lui-même l'expérience : « Il est
aisé d'être ensemble bon chrétien et bon citoyen, *tant
qu'on ne fait pas de la politique* », tant qu'on n'est pas
réactionnaire catholique ou républicain combiste.

*

Selon l'auteur de *Notre jeunesse*, l'affaire Dreyfus est
un exemple éminent du « recoupement » et de la
« culmination » de trois mystiques : hébraïque, chrétienne, française. Sous prétexte de ne pas faire de
cadeau aux antisémites, pourquoi nier qu'elle fut
d'abord une affaire juive, de mystique et de politique
juives, de mystique juive affrontée à une politique
juive ?

Au départ, il y eut « une *minorité agissante*, une

bande de forcenés, groupés autour de quelques têtes qui sont très précisément les prophètes d'Israël ». Ces énergumènes se dressèrent contre la prudence séculaire de leur race, contre ses peurs, ses atermoiements, ses démissions. Pour défendre la justice et sauver un innocent, ils remirent en cause un précaire équilibre. o non ! ce ne fut pas la politique juive ni le parti juif qui soulevèrent des tumultes. La politique juive ne demandait qu'à se taire et à « acheter la paix en livrant le bouc ».

On ne saurait jeter la pierre à ce peuple. Comme tous les peuples, il cherche sa tranquillité. Il en est d'autant plus anxieux qu'il incarne à travers les siècles le peuple martyr par excellence. « Il n'a pas sur la peau un point qui ne soit pas douloureux, où il n'y ait un ancien bleu, une ancienne contusion, une meurtrissure d'Orient ou d'Occident. » Aussi ne veut-il avoir d'histoire avec personne, fût-ce au prix d'une abstention coupable.

Qui le lui reprochera ? Ses prophètes justement. Ils lui mettent l'épée dans les reins, le forcent à marcher. La mystique juive oblige la politique juive à céder, à se laisser emporter. « C'est en Israël que le dreyfusisme naissant rencontra les plus vives résistances. Beaucoup disaient *à quoi bon*. Dans les familles on traitait communément de folie cette tentative. Une fois de plus la folie devait l'emporter. Plus tard, bientôt tous, ou presque tous, marchèrent, parce que quand un prophète a parlé, en Israël, tous le haïssent, tous l'admirent, tous le suivent. »

Ce prophète fut Bernard-Lazare. Péguy semble ne l'avoir connu personnellement qu'en 1901. Mais grâce à Lucien Herr, son maître en dreyfusisme, lui-même rallié à la cause de Dreyfus par Bernard-Lazare, Péguy en entendit parler et le lut dès 1897, de sorte qu'il se réclame à bon droit de sa filiation, dans *Notre jeunesse*[1].

On oublie trop souvent que le portrait qu'il en trace date des dernières années de la vie de son héros (1901-1903). Le Bernard-Lazare de Péguy n'est plus l'homme de l'affaire Dreyfus, mais celui de la décomposition du dreyfusisme. Ainsi s'explique la réaction de certains de ses premiers compagnons qui ne l'ont pas reconnu dans le visage pathétique que lui prête Péguy, taxé d'exagération poétique et mystique.

L'homme que fréquente le gérant des *Cahiers* et dont il devient l'intime est un combattant vaincu par sa victoire. Les lendemains de l'Affaire sont à l'opposé de ce qu'il en attendait. Miné par la maladie, il l'est aussi par la désillusion. L'une et l'autre n'altèrent pas sa lucidité, ses convictions, son courage. Elles leur donnent seulement une nouvelle profondeur spirituelle et un arrière-fond d'éternité.

Rejeté par son peuple qui l'a un moment suivi et qui maintenant le trahit, Bernard-Lazare manifeste sa pleine stature de prophète. On va « le laisser tomber dans la solitude, l'oubli, le mépris ». On va l'y laisser mourir de « l'effroyable surmenage qu'il avait assumé pour sauver Dreyfus », aussi de l'incroyable tension que lui procure un peu partout le sort misérable des Juifs. Car souffrant pour les autres une passion de salut où il investit ses dernières forces, il a « un cœur qui saigne dans tous les ghettos du monde ».

1. Cf. Nelly Wilson, « L'amitié de Péguy et de Bernard-Lazare », dans ACP, n° 13, janvier-mars 1981, p. 5-6.

C'est à ce double titre : dénonciateur de la décomposition dreyfusienne et champion des Juifs opprimés, qu'il devint en ces années-là « l'inspirateur secret et très exactement le patron des *Cahiers* ». « Très sincèrement athée », il participait à l'air du temps. « Il était positiviste, scientificiste, intellectuel, moderne, enfin tout ce qu'il faut. » Mais cet athée « ruisselait de la parole de Dieu », « le feu au cœur, une tête ardente, *et le charbon ardent sur la lèvre prophète* ».

« Il avait indéniablement, poursuit Péguy, des parties de saint. Et quand je parle de saint, je ne suis pas suspect de parler par métaphore. Il avait une douceur, une bonté, une tendresse mystique, une digestion parfaite de l'amertume et de l'ingratitude. » Mais dans ses deux bons gros yeux de myope, derrière le binocle, brillait le feu allumé il y a cinquante siècles.

Pour ce prophète, tout l'appareil des puissances d'État, des autorités de toute sorte, ne pesait pas une once devant la révolte d'une conscience, qui est « la suprême juridiction, la seule ». Les puissances temporelles n'existaient littéralement pas. Seules existaient les puissances spirituelles avec lesquelles il se sentait une affection secrète, « même avec les catholiques qu'il combattait délibérément. Mais il ne voulait les combattre que par des armes spirituelles dans des batailles spirituelles ».

On le vit bien lors de l'avant-dernier texte que Péguy publia de lui, en août 1902 : une consultation sur *La loi et les congrégations* [1]. En février 1902, Bernard-Lazare avait pris dans les *Cahiers* la défense des Juifs

---

1. Bernard-Lazare, *La loi et les congrégations*, CQ, III-21, 16 août 1902, p. 207-231.

persécutés en Roumanie[1]. Six mois plus tard, il intervint en faveur des écoles catholiques victimes en France, toute proportion gardée, d'une semblable oppression mise en place par Combes.

Péguy brandit dans *Notre jeunesse* le texte de cette consultation. Il en cite des extraits qu'il fait précéder de quelques libres propos tenus en privé par Bernard-Lazare. « Les cléricaux nous ont embêtés pendant des années, il ne s'agit pas à présent d'embêter les catholiques. » « On ne peut pas poursuivre par des lois des gens qui s'assemblent pour faire leur prière. Si on trouve qu'ils sont dangereux, qu'ils ont trop d'argent, qu'on les poursuive, qu'on les atteigne par des mesures générales, comme tout le monde. »

« On n'a jamais vu, commente Péguy, un Juif aussi peu partisan, aussi peu concevant du talion. Il ne voulait pas rendre précisément le bien pour le mal, mais très certainement le juste pour l'injuste. » C'est ainsi qu'il employait pour les catholiques la même expression, « *comme tout le monde* », dont il se servait pour Dreyfus.

Dans les extraits de sa consultation que reproduit *Notre jeunesse*, Bernard-Lazare reproche justement à Jaurès, fidèle appui de Combes, d'appliquer la loi du talion. Citation de Jaurès : « Il y a des crimes politiques et sociaux qui se paient, et le grand crime collectif commis par l'Église contre la vérité, contre l'humanité, contre le droit et contre la République, va enfin recevoir son juste salaire. » Commentaire de Bernard-Lazare : « Parce qu'il est Jaurès, parce qu'il

1. Bernard-Lazare, *L'oppression des Juifs en Europe orientale. Les Juifs en Roumanie*, CQ, III-8, 13 février 1902.

a été notre compagnon dans une bataille qui n'est pas finie, il doit nous donner d'autres raisons que des raisons théologiques. »

Bernard-Lazare ne veut pas admettre « des justifications semblables, même et surtout quand elles sont données par Jaurès, car, au-dessous, d'autres sont prêts à les interpréter dans un sens pire, à en tirer des conséquences redoutables pour la liberté », en particulier la liberté d'enseignement. « Nous nous refuserons aussi bien à accepter les dogmes formulés par l'État enseignant, que les dogmes formulés par l'Église. Nous n'avons pas plus confiance en l'Université qu'en la Congrégation. »

Bernard-Lazare exprime ici la même attitude que celle dont Péguy a fixé les traits quelques mois avant, dans *De la raison*. Au terme de sa consultation, le publiciste juif conclut par des mots que *Notre jeunesse* ne reprend pas, mais qui sont rigoureusement conformes à la pensée péguyste : « Il ne nous faut exiger qu'une chose : toute liberté pour la raison. Cependant, si nous avions si peu de foi en elle que nous dussions faire appel à la contrainte pour la faire triompher, nous serions peu dignes de la servir, et nous serions vaincus. Car la raison est malhabile à employer la force, et le droit sait parfois se servir de la force pour se défendre, jamais pour s'imposer »[1].

*

« Culmination » de la mystique juive, l'affaire Dreyfus l'a été aussi de la mystique chrétienne. Péguy

---

1. *La loi et les congrégations, op. cit.,* p. 231.

parle en connaissance de cause, lui qui vient de publier le *Mystère de la charité de Jeanne d'Arc.* Depuis ce moment, certains s'interrogent sur la nature de ses sentiments religieux. Est-il vraiment devenu chrétien, ou s'agit-il seulement d'un christianisme d'emprunt, de sympathie, nécessaire pour exprimer l'âme de la Pucelle ?

L'ami et le disciple de l'athée Bernard-Lazare ne laisse aucun doute à ce sujet. « Comment le nier, à présent que nous sommes à douze et quinze ans de notre jeunesse et qu'enfin nous voyons clair dans notre cœur ? Notre dreyfusisme était une religion. » Il renchérit : « Aujourd'hui nous pouvons avouer que de toutes les passions qui nous poussèrent dans cette ardeur et dans ce bouillonnement, une vertu était au cœur, et c'était la vertu de charité. »

Il prononce enfin les mots décisifs que souligne l'emploi des majuscules : « La Justice et la Vérité que nous avons tant aimées n'étaient point des justices et des vérités de concept, elles étaient organiques, elles étaient chrétiennes, elles étaient éternelles et non point temporelles seulement, elles étaient des Justices et des Vérités, *une* Justice et *une* Vérité *vivantes.* » Peut-on mieux désigner le Christ ?

Exprimant ce qui a toujours été sa conviction profonde et qui était aussi celle de Jaurès au temps de l'affaire Dreyfus, à savoir que le dreyfusisme n'était qu'un cas particulier du socialisme, le recouvrement d'une justice particulière dans le cadre du recouvrement d'une justice collective, Péguy remonte de l'un à l'autre et replace la mystique dreyfusiste à l'intérieur de la mystique socialiste, mystique proprement chrétienne.

« Ce qui a pu donner le change, c'est que toutes les forces *politiques* de l'Église étaient contre le dreyfusisme. Mais les forces politiques de l'Église ont toujours été contre la mystique. Notamment contre la mystique chrétienne. » Si elles ont tellement été contre le dreyfusisme et le socialisme, c'est qu'elles ont perdu le sens du christianisme comme « religion du salut temporel », religion d'une Justice et d'une Vérité incarnées dans le temps et l'histoire, aussi bien pour les individus que pour les sociétés.

Au-delà de son attitude ponctuelle envers Dreyfus, l'Église n'a pas voulu voir et continue d'être aveugle au fait que « le christianisme, qui est la religion du salut éternel, est embourbé dans la boue des mauvaises mœurs économiques, industrielles ». Ainsi la politique chrétienne oppose-t-elle à la mystique socialiste, qui dérive de la mystique et des exigences du Christ, « une religion de bourgeois, une religion de riches, une espèce de religion supérieure pour classes supérieures de la société, une misérable sorte de religion distinguée pour gens censément distingués ».

C'est là proprement « le modernisme du cœur et de la charité » dont se rend coupable le catholicisme et où se vérifie la dégradation actuelle de la mystique chrétienne en politique chrétienne. L'Église ne veut pas « *faire les frais* d'une révolution économique, d'une révolution sociale, d'une révolution industrielle, pour dire le mot d'une révolution *temporelle* pour le salut *éternel* ».

Il ne faut pas se leurrer sur les effets bénéfiques de la séparation de l'Église et de l'État. Cette séparation ne favorise que partiellement une reconquête de la mystique sur la politique. Sans doute l'Église est-elle plus libre. « Sous toutes les duretés de la liberté, d'une certaine pauvreté, elle est autrement elle-même. Jamais on n'obtiendra sous le nouveau régime des évêques aussi mauvais que les évêques concordataires. Mais il ne faut pas se dissimuler non plus que si l'Église a cessé de faire la religion officielle de l'État, elle n'a point cessé de faire la religion officielle de la bourgeoisie de l'État. »

Qu'ils soient cléricaux catholiques ou radicaux antichrétiens, les bourgeois de l'un et l'autre côté, les capitalistes de l'un et l'autre bord, les politiques de l'une et l'autre tendance se retrouvent au coude à coude pour *ne pas payer*, ne pas *faire les frais*. Et ils tombent d'accord pour déplacer le débat sur le terrain moins brûlant de controverses intellectuelles et philosophiques, les bourgeois cléricaux oubliant pour leur part « les effrayantes réprobations sur l'argent dont l'Évangile est comme saturé » et demeurant « moelleusement assis dans la paix du cœur, dans la paix sociale ».

A travers ces lignes féroces, on mesure à quel point le chrétien Péguy de 1910 n'a rien renié des convictions du Péguy socialiste et dreyfusiste de 1898. Par déception de ce que la politique socialiste a fait de la mystique socialiste, il ne s'est pas rallié à ce que la politique chrétienne a fait de la mystique chrétienne. Sa mystique est restée la même, et c'est elle qui lui fait dénoncer maintenant « cette tension à l'argent contaminant le monde chrétien et lui faisant sacrifier sa foi et ses mœurs au maintien de la paix économique et sociale ».

*

« Recoupement » des mystiques juive et chrétienne, l'affaire Dreyfus l'a été aussi de ces deux mystiques avec la mystique française. Pour le nationalisme comme pour le christianisme, Péguy remonte aux racines socialistes de son dreyfusisme. A l'inverse de ce que pensaient les antidreyfusistes, ce socialisme péguyste, conforme à celui du Jaurès d'alors, « n'était nullement antifrançais, nullement antipatriote, nullement *anti*national. Il était exactement *inter*national ».

Loin d'affaiblir ou d'effacer la nation, il l'exaltait, car il la rendait saine en la guérissant des mauvaises mœurs industrielles. Son objectif était de restaurer la qualité du travail en commençant par le monde ouvrier et en gagnant de proche en proche jusqu'à une restauration de toute la société. « C'était cette philosophie des producteurs qui devait trouver en M. Sorel, moraliste et philosophe, son expression la plus haute. J'ajoute même que ce ne pouvait être que cela. »

Dans ces conditions, non seulement le socialisme ne portait pas atteinte aux droits légitimes de nations, mais il en servait les intérêts essentiels. « Ce n'était point violer, effacer les nations, mais au contraire, que de travailler à remplacer d'une substitution organique, moléculaire, un champ clos, une concurrence anarchique de peuples forcenés, frénétiques, par une forêt saine, par une forêt grandissante de peuples prospères, par tout un peuple de peuples florissants. »

Tel était le socialisme des dreyfusistes socialistes, celui de Jaurès et de Péguy, auquel s'opposait justement le socialisme des antidreyfusistes socialistes, celui de Guesde et de Vaillant, militants marxistes qui

ne voulaient rien avoir de commun avec la défense
d'un officier d'état-major bourgeois, et qui faisaient
passer les intérêts économiques de classe avant l'intérêt moral de la nation.

A l'inverse, les dreyfusistes socialistes parlaient au
fond le même langage que les antidreyfusistes antiso-
cialistes. S'il y avait désaccord entre eux, c'était à
partir des mêmes prémisses, du même postulat patriotique. « Qu'en fait eux ou nous nous fussions les
meilleurs patriotes, c'était précisément l'objet du
débat. » Pour les uns comme pour les autres, la
trahison militaire était un crime contre la patrie. La
seule question était de savoir si Dreyfus avait vraiment trahi et, une fois introduit le doute, si l'intérêt
supérieur de la nation exigeait qu'on sacrifiât quand
même un innocent probable.

Non moins patriotes que Barrès et Maurras, Jaurès
et Péguy soutenaient que l'honneur de la France ne
pouvait reposer sur l'injustice et le mensonge. L'idée
qu'ils se faisaient de leur pays autant que leur
conception de l'émancipation humaine par la révolution sociale les écartait de toute concession sur ce
point fondamental. On ne sauve personne, nation ou
classe, en méprisant les lois de la conscience.

Dans les années qui suivirent la conclusion de
l'affaire Dreyfus, Jaurès se démentit là-dessus ou du
moins permit qu'on le démentît en couvrant de son
autorité une position absolument contraire à ses
sentiments personnels et constamment réaffirmés.
Après la rupture en 1900 sur la liberté de la presse et
celle en 1902 sur la liberté de conscience, ce fut avec
Péguy la troisième et définitive rupture en 1905 sur le
patriotisme, à l'occasion de l'affaire Hervé, ce socia-

liste antimilitariste auteur de *Leur Patrie* auquel Péguy
répliqua par *Notre Patrie*.

En avril 1905, au terme d'inlassables efforts, Jaurès
animait un nouveau parti socialiste enfin réunifié, la
SFIO. Dans son pamphlet, en pleine crise de Tanger,
Gustave Hervé choisit de prôner la grève générale et
l'insurrection, en cas de guerre avec l'Allemagne.
Jaurès n'était pas d'accord et le fit savoir. Mais par
souci d'unité et pour ne pas affaiblir les forces de paix,
il préféra engager le dialogue avec le courant hervéiste
plutôt que de l'exclure.

En août 1907, au congrès socialiste national de
Nancy, toujours pour préserver l'unité et la paix,
Jaurès développa une analyse subtile selon laquelle le
fameux « drapeau dans le fumier » planté par Hervé
signifiait le contraire de ce qu'on avait cru. D'après
Jaurès, Hervé s'indignait de ce qu'en célébrant la
bataille de Wagram on glorifiât une « abominable
tuerie césarienne ». « En sorte que c'est pour protéger
contre la profanation militariste la majesté du drapeau que vous avez écrit votre article. C'est la religion
blessée du drapeau qui a protesté en vous »[1].

Une telle interprétation fut accueillie par les rires
de la salle et les protestations réitérées de Gustave
Hervé. Mais du coup, au congrès socialiste international de Stuttgart qui se tint quelques jours plus tard, le
courant hervéiste se rallia à Jaurès, du moment qu'on
lui laissait toute liberté de se propager à l'intérieur du
parti.

Il faut avoir présent à l'esprit cette tactique de

---

1. Jean Jaurès, *Œuvres,* édition Max Bonnefous, Rieder, V-3,
1933, p. 104-105.

Jaurès pour comprendre la fureur qu'elle suscita en 1910 chez Péguy. Jaurès n'était certes pas devenu antipatriote. Mais pour des raisons d'opportunisme, il sacrifiait la fin aux moyens et optait une fois de plus pour une morale de situation contre une morale de conviction. C'est là précisément ce que Péguy appelle une dégradation de la mystique en politique.

Avec une rare violence, l'auteur de *Notre jeunesse* se livre à une évocation cruelle des motivations pychologiques de Jaurès où, à travers l'injustice des propos, se manifeste l'intensité d'un amour déçu. Ce n'est plus de la satire, mais un réglement de comptes où tout est bon pour ridiculiser l'ancien ami dont on estime qu'il a trahi. Dans un monologue digne de Molière, Péguy lui fait dire : « Quand quelqu'un m'aime et me sert, le sot, me prodigue les preuves les plus incontestables de l'amitié la plus dévouée, du dévouement le plus absolu, aussitôt je sens s'élever dans ce qui me sert de cœur un commencement, un mépris invincible pour cet imbécile. »

Autant qu'il déteste ses amis, Jaurès admire ses ennemis. Ainsi colle-t-il à Hervé qui se joue de lui. L'esprit de conciliation se mue chez le tribun socialiste en une complaisance perpétuelle, une démission inlassable. Il est imbattable dans l'art de lâcher du lest et d'avaler des couleuvres. Il ne se plaît à rien tant qu'à transiger avec ceux qui le bafouent, au lieu de les empêcher de nuire.

A cette critique très subjective du caractère ou plutôt du manque de caractère de Jaurès, Péguy en joint une autre plus objective qui met en cause les qualités manœuvrières du tribun. Celui-ci se croit malin à pratiquer d'une certaine façon la technique de l' « entrisme » : entrer dans le camp ennemi pour le ruiner en douceur. « Quand je suis resté dans un parti pendant un certain temps, au bout de ce temps on voit, tout le monde comprend que je les ai trahis. Comprenez-vous enfin, gros bête, me dit-il me poussant du coude. »

Péguy s'indigne de ce procédé déloyal. D'abord pour une raison « assez basse », « politique », selon laquelle est parfois pris celui qui croyait prendre, comme dans les histoires de contre-espionnage. Ensuite pour une raison «de bonne compagnie, tirée de la vieille morale : on n'a pas le droit de trahir les traîtres mêmes. Les traîtres, il faut les combattre, et non pas les trahir ».

Le résultat de tous ces petits complots, combinaisons et manigances, c'est qu'on a réussi à déshonorer rétroactivement les partisans socialistes de Dreyfus. « Par son endossement, par son invention, par son imposition du combisme Jaurès a créé *en arrière* cette illusion que le dreyfusisme était anticatholique, antichrétien. Par son endossement de l'hervéisme il a créé *en arrière* cette illusion que le dreyfusisme était *anti*nationaliste, antipatriote, antifrançais. »

*

Péguy se tourne alors vers les antidreyfusistes et, parmi eux, vers ceux qu'il considère encore — il déchantera en 1914, dans la *Note conjointe* — comme des adversaires situés sur le même plan que lui. N'at-il pas signalé, au début de *Notre jeunesse*, « un déchirement continuel entre la mystique royaliste et la politique royaliste » telles qu'en témoignent les deux

principaux journaux monarchistes, « la mystique
étant naturellement à *l'Action française,* sous des formes
rationalistes qui n'ont jamais trompé qu'eux-mêmes,
et la politique étant au *Gaulois,* comme d'habitude
sous des formes mondaines » ?

Approchant du terme de son ouvrage, Péguy
s'adresse directement aux théoriciens de *l'Action française* et réplique point par point à leurs arguments.
L'affaire Dreyfus a-t-elle été dès l'origine un complot
monté par le *parti intellectuel*? Illusion rétrospective qui
est bien le propre, chez les monarchistes, d'une sorte
de connivence avec ceux qu'ils dénoncent. *L'Action
française* regroupe « un parti de logiciens, un parti
logique ». Aussi ses doctrinaires ne perçoivent-ils pas
les vrais mouvements de fond. Ils prennent les
profiteurs pour les fondateurs et commettent l'erreur
typiquement moderne qui consiste, en histoire, à
reporter le présent sur le passé.

L'affaire Dreyfus a-t-elle été l'expression d'un *parti
de l'étranger*? Autre erreur née de l'hervéisme qui, lui
aussi, cache le véritable paysage et fait qu'on mélange
les profiteurs avec les fondateurs. « On reporte sur
nous antécédents la trahison de Hervé suivant, de
Hervé successeur. » Ce faisant, « par une sorte de
sympathie de trouble, une secrète amitié de désordre,
une secrète complaisance de démagogie », les gens
d'*Action française* ne sont pas mécontents d'utiliser
Hervé pour diffamer un gouvernement qu'ils haïssent
parce qu'il est formé d'anciens dreyfusistes.

L'affaire Dreyfus a-t-elle été enfin la création d'un
parti juif? Péguy s'étend plus longuement sur cette
imputation calomnieuse et en profite pour attaquer de
front l'antisémitisme. Il rappelle d'abord ce qu'il a

déjà dit, combien l'Affaire a été montée *contre* le parti juif et combien Bernard-Lazare a eu à vaincre de résistance dans son milieu. « Ensuite ceux qui lui pardonnèrent le moins ce furent encore les Juifs. »

Plus généralement, l'erreur d'appréciation sur Israël vient de ce que « LES ANTISÉMITES NE CONNAISSENT POINT LES JUIFS ». Conscient de dire une « énormité », Péguy l'écrit en lettres capitales. Les antisémites prétendent que « tous les Juifs sont riches ». Où ont-ils vu cela ? Péguy a l'expérience inverse. « Je ne connais guère que des Juifs pauvres et des Juifs misérables. Il y en a tant que l'on n'en sait pas le nombre. J'en vois partout. »

Qui se ressemble s'assemble, fût-ce pour se détester. Les antisémites riches connaissent les sémites riches, les antisémites capitalistes les sémites capitalistes, les antisémites d'affaires les sémites d'affaires. Pour sa part, Péguy avoue que le seul créancier qui l'ait traité « avec une dureté balzacienne n'était point un Juif. C'était un Français, un chrétien, trente fois millionnaire. *Que n'aurait-on pas dit s'il avait été Juif ?* »

Chrétien lui-même, Péguy se sent obligé de porter témoignage en faveur de la pauvreté juive, de la fidélité juive, de l'amitié juive. Il argumente contre son jeune ami maurrassien Jean Variot : « Vous leur faites toujours des reproches contradictoires. Quand leurs riches ne les soutiennent pas, quand leurs riches sont durs vous dites : *C'est pas étonnant, ils sont Juifs.* Quand leurs riches les soutiennent, vous dites : *C'est pas étonnant, ils sont Juifs. Ils se soutiennent entre eux.* »

Et d'ajouter une remarque mystérieuse et angoissante : « Au fond, ce que vous voudriez, c'est qu'ils n'existent pas. Mais cela, c'est une autre question. »

A quoi Péguy pense-t-il ? A un délire raciste mettant en cause aussi bien la France et sa culture que le christianisme et sa foi, qu'il faudrait libérer tous les deux du virus hébraïque ?

Pour l'instant, l'auteur de *Notre jeunesse* se borne à noter que l'antisémitisme vient « pour un tiers des antisémites professionnels, et pour les deux autres tiers de mécanismes ». En d'autres termes, il y entre un tiers de fantasmes et deux tiers de déterminismes. Mais on ne remarque aucune intention nocive chez les Juifs pris comme Juifs. Ils ne sont ni plus ni moins mauvais que les autres hommes. Ils sont « comme tout le monde », pour reprendre l'expression de Bernard-Lazare.

Ce qui fausse le débat, c'est qu'ils sont victimes d'une illusion d'optique bien connue « qui nous fait voir un carré *blanc sur noir* beaucoup plus grand que le même carré *noir sur blanc*, qui paraît tout petit ». Ainsi « tout carré *juif sur chrétien* nous paraît beaucoup plus grand que le même carré *chrétien sur juif* ». Péguy se promet « d'examiner quelque jour dans un plus grand détail » cette illusion d'optique historique, politique et sociale. Il ne l'a malheureusement pas fait.

Afin de corriger l'illusion d'une façon empirique, il recommande seulement « un exercice salutaire, une sorte de gymnastique suédoise de l'esprit ». Elle consiste à « faire la preuve par le contraire ». On retient « certains faits, nombreux, à mesure qu'ils passent, et on se demande, de l'auteur, ce que nous venons de nous demander : *Qu'est-ce qu'on dirait s'il était Juif ?* » Cette inversion du jugement produit des effets merveilleux, car « on voit vite alors que les plus grands scandales et les plus nombreux ne sont point des scandales juifs. Et il s'en faut ».

Délaissant intellectuels, antimilitaristes et juifs, Péguy en vient pour finir à la question de fond qui permet selon lui de départager antidreyfusistes et dreyfusistes. Conformément à sa règle initiale, il ne se livre pas au petit jeu des oppositions frauduleuses entre la politique d'un bord et la mystique de l'autre bord. Il confronte mystique à mystique, mystique réactionnaire et maurrassienne à mystique républi-caine et chrétienne. Ce faisant, vingt ans avant la condamnation de *l'Action française* par Pie XI, il met en contradiction sur leur propre terrain les maurras-siens chrétiens, qui imposent au spirituel la primauté du temporel.

Qu'a-t-on vu en effet durant l'affaire Dreyfus ? D'un côté, des gens qui affirmaient que, Dreyfus coupable ou innocent, « on ne *compromettait* pas pour un homme, pour un seul homme, la vie et le salut d'un peuple, l'énorme salut de tout un peuple. On sous-entendait : le salut *temporel* ». De l'autre côté, des gens qui, contre toute sagesse et toute loi humaines, dans une opéra-tion « de l'ordre de la folie ou de l'ordre de la sainteté », se plaçaient à rien moins « qu'au point de vue DU SALUT ÉTERNEL DE LA FRANCE ».

« Nos adversaires, poursuit Péguy, parlaient le lan-gage de la raison d'État, qui n'est pas seulement le langage de la raison politique et parlementaire, du méprisable intérêt politique et parlementaire, mais beaucoup plus haut le très respectable langage de la continuité temporelle du peuple et de la race, du salut temporel du peuple et de la race. Et nous par un mouvement chrétien profond, par une poussée très profonde révolutionnaire et ensemble traditionnelle du christianisme, nous n'allions pas à moins qu'à nous élever je ne dis pas à la conception mais à la passion, mais au souci d'un salut éternel de ce peuple. Tout au fond nous ne voulions pas que la France fût constituée en état de péché mortel. »

On relèvera l'importante nuance introduite par Péguy dans la notion de raison d'État qu'il dénonçait naguère, dans *De la raison*, comme contraire à la raison. Il semble aujourd'hui renverser la perspective lorsqu'il reconnaît « qu'on ne perd point une cité, qu'une cité ne se perd point pour un seul citoyen ». Et il insiste en prenant l'exemple de la cité grecque. « C'est le langage même du véritable civisme et de la sagesse antique. C'est le langage de la raison. »

Péguy rejoint-il à présent Maurras ? Il n'en est rien. S'il lui concède que la raison d'État peut dans certaines circonstances non seulement ne pas être méprisable mais être raisonnable, s'il lui accorde qu'elle peut entrer dans une mystique, encore est-ce dans une mystique non chrétienne et non révolutionnaire, une mystique de conservation, qui manque de cette fraîcheur et de cette innovation créatrice qui sont les marques de toute révolution authentique.

Péguy continue d'être avec Antigone contre Créon, car il n'y a pas qu'une, mais deux sagesses antiques. Pour lui, « une seule injustice, surtout si elle est officiellement enregistrée, un seul crime suffit à rompre tout le pacte social, un seul déshonneur suffit à déshonorer tout un peuple ». Nous sommes comptables de l'honneur de notre peuple, l'honneur dont nous avons hérité et que nous avons à transmettre, « Plus nous avons de passé et, comme dit *l'Action française*, de responsabilité, plus il nous faut défendre ce passé, le garder pur. » C'est « la vieille poussée cornélienne : *Je rendrai mon sang pur comme je l'ai reçu* ».

C'est aussi la vieille « poussée chrétienne ». A un ami chrétien venu le visiter au moment le plus douloureux de l'affaire Dreyfus et qui lui objectait qu'on ne peut pas sacrifier tout un peuple pour un homme, Péguy se souvient d'avoir répondu en citant simplement une page de Joinville. Le chroniqueur rapporte un propos de saint Louis selon lequel mieux vaut souffrir de la lèpre que d'être en état de péché mortel. En 1910, Peguy répond de même à Maurras et à ses disciples que, pour un peuple comme pour un individu, mieux vaut risquer sa vie temporelle que sa vie éternelle.

*

Si l'on considère le retentissement de *Notre jeunesse*, il faut noter que dès le départ, comme on pouvait s'y attendre, les réactions divergent, parfois avec violence. L'examen de la correspondance privée reçue par Péguy est significatif à cet égard, car les sentiments s'y expriment souvent plus à découvert.

Le 12 juillet, dès la sortie du volume, Romain Rolland envoie un bref billet : « C'est très beau. Voilà un Cahier qui survivra au temps. Du bon travail pour la France » [1]. Le 18, un autre ami, Louis Gillet, déborde d'enthousiasme, et sa réaction est d'autant plus intéressante qu'elle émane d'un catholique :

1. *Pour l'honneur de l'esprit,* correspondance Péguy-Rolland, présentée et annotée par Auguste Martin, Albin Michel, 1973, p. 291.

« Livre sublime. Les cinquante pages sur Lazare, les prophètes juifs, la psychologie des Juifs, le métro, la tente, la vie nomade, sont naturellement le chef-d'œuvre. Certainement ce qu'a fait sortir de plus beau cette étonnante affaire »[1].

Le 22 août, le protestant Charles-Marie Garnier, éminent angliciste, est aussi admiratif : « Vous avez atteint de votre coutre le roc d'une grande loi et toute la terre encore chaude de notre jeunesse en est profondément remuée. De l'Affaire et de Bernard-Lazare vous écrivez des pages qui fixeront la physionomie de l'une et de l'autre dans cette histoire »[2]. Le 16 septembre, Alexandre Millerand, ministre des travaux publics, des postes et des télégraphes, avoue : « J'ai dévoré l'ouvrage dans mon après-midi. Il y a dans vos 220 pages plus de pensée et de substance que dans toute une bibliothèque. Votre passage sur Bernard-Lazare et la Cour de Cassation est une petite merveille »[3].

Le 2 décembre, Henri Bergson s'excuse d'une grande fatigue qui l'a empêché de féliciter plus tôt Péguy pour son cahier « sur la mystique et la politique » : « Certains de vos jugements sont peut-être un peu sévères ; mais vous n'avez rien écrit de

1. Jérôme Gillet, « Autour de Péguy et Louis Gillet », dans FACP, n° 190, octobre 1973, p. 31.
2. « Péguy et Charles-Marie Garnier », correspondance présentée par Auguste Martin, dans FACP, n° 83, avril 1961, p. 5-6.
3. « Péguy et Alexandre Millerand », correspondance présentée et annotée par Auguste Martin, dans FACP, n° 179, 15 juillet 1972, p. 26.

meilleur que ce cahier, ni de plus émouvant »[1]. Le
même jour, l'abbé Henri Bremond suggère : « Votre
philosophie du dreyfusisme, cette distinction entre la
mystique et la politique, mais cela va loin, très loin.
Au fond il faut le dire tout bas, mais enfin on peut le
dire — au fond c'est toute l'histoire de l'Église »[2].

Le ton change avec les antidreyfusistes ou avec ceux
qui, tel Georges Sorel, le sont devenus après la victoire
dreyfusienne et se sont rapprochés de Maurras. Le 22
juillet, Sorel se défoule dans une lettre à Daniel
Halévy dont il se déclare solidaire : « Je crois que
Péguy a été fort mal inspiré quand il a voulu aborder
la psychologie des dreyfusistes ; qu'est-ce que c'est
que cette *grandeur* qu'il s'attribue, tout en disant qu'il
a été *berné* ? Il est difficile d'accorder ces deux choses ;
il a appartenu à la catégorie des gens qui se sont jetés
dans l'Affaire par légèreté d'esprit, désir de vivre des
aventures, esprit de chimères ; vous avez appartenu à
la catégorie peu nombreuse des gens qui ont bien
accompli un devoir douloureux ; vous avez le beau
lot »[3].

Pour Georges Valois, le rejet est catégorique, et le
27 juillet ce virulent antisémite retourne contre Péguy
une des considérations de *Notre jeunesse* : « Comment
pouvez-vous donner les preuves d'une absolue inaptitude à concevoir la question juive, comme vous le
faites à partir de la page 178 ? Les Juifs sont une

1. « Bergson-Péguy », correspondance présentée et annotée par
Auguste Martin, dans FACP, n° 155, janvier 1970, p. 32.
2. André Blanchet, « Péguy et Bremond », dans FACP, n° 171,
10 septembre 1971, p. 4.
3. Christine Beaulieu, « Le conflit de 1910 entre Péguy et Daniel
Halévy », dans ACP, n° 12, octobre-décembre 1980, p. 209.

nation opposée à la nôtre. Ils ne peuvent pas être Français, parce que, vous l'avez dit, partout, dans nos maisons de pierre, ils sont sous la tente. Voilà pourquoi nous sommes antisémites, lorsque les nomades tiennent l'État dans notre pays » [1].

Plus agressif encore est Paul Claudel qui, par l'entremise de Gide, avait demandé à connaître autre chose que le *Mystère de la charité de Jeanne d'Arc* qu'il venait de lire avec plaisir. *Notre jeunesse* le prend à rebrousse-poil, bien qu'il confesse dans une lettre du 10 août à Péguy : « Toute cette partie du livre si belle, si éloquente, où vous parlez des Juifs et de Bernard-Lazare, a arraché de force mon admiration. Quel dommage de trouver un vrai Français, un soldat de Saint Louis (je pense à vos admirables pages sur le péché mortel) combattant avec des gens qui ne sont pas de sa race contre la sienne, avec des gens tout primitifs et imbus de la malédiction de Dieu ! » [2].

Suit une réfutation en règle « dont l'intensité est la mesure même de l'impression subie » [3]. Si elle ne compte sûrement pas au nombre des meilleures pages de Claudel, elle offre une verdeur abrupte qui situe bien le débat au niveau requis par Péguy. Claudel ne prend pas de gants et, hors des précautions que vont adopter durant un premier temps les gens d'*Action française*, désireux de ménager l'auteur de *Notre jeunesse*, il oppose frontalement et sur les points mêmes

1. Éric Cahm, *Péguy et le nationalisme français,* Cahiers de l'Amitié Charles Péguy, 1972, p. 100-101.
2. Henri de Lubac et Jean Bastaire, *Claudel et Péguy,* Aubier, 1974, p. 131.
3. *Idem,* p. 131.

soulevés par Péguy sa mystique chrétienne réactionnaire et antisémite à la mystique chrétienne républicaine et philosémite du gérant des *Cahiers*.

Il refuse de distinguer entre mystique et politique.
« L'un n'est-il pas lié à l'autre comme l'acte à la
puissance ? Le combisme est lié au dreyfusisme
comme les massacres de septembre aux principes de
89. » Quant à parler d'une politique cléricale, « à
quel moment l'Église a-t-elle eu le dessus dans le
gouvernement depuis cinq ou six siècles » ? Aujour-
d'hui, « la politique de l'Église, c'est l'héroïque et
l'admirable Pie X qui la représente, elle n'a rien à
craindre d'aucune critique » [1].

Dire que le mouvement dreyfusiste fut un mouvement chrétien n'est pas moins inacceptable. « Il n'y a
rien de si opposé à l'esprit chrétien que la préférence
du sens propre. Cela est protestant, c'est-à-dire abominable à tout cœur catholique [2]. »

Claudel établit là-dessus une série d'équivalences
révélatrices du christianisme dont il se réclame : « Si
vous êtes chrétien, vous êtes ami de l'ordre ; si vous
aimez l'ordre, vous reconnaissez l'autorité ; et quelle
autorité y a-t-il, si vous la jugez comme ayant vous-
même autorité sur elle ? » [3]. C'est très exactement
l'inverse du christianisme péguyste qui, dans la droite
ligne du « prophète » Bernard-Lazare, place la
conscience au-dessus des institutions.

Comment nier, poursuit Claudel, « l'action de la
juiverie dans cette affaire ? J'ai vécu dans tous les pays

1. *Idem*, p. 131.
2. *Idem*, p. 132.
3. *Idem*, p. 133.

du monde et partout j'ai vu les journaux et l'opinion entre les mains des Juifs. J'étais à Jérusalem en décembre 1899 et j'ai vu au moment de la seconde condamnation [de Dreyfus] la rage de ces punaises à face humaine qui vivent en Palestine par centaines de mille des razzias que leurs congénères opèrent sur la chrétienté » [1].

Enfin Claudel part en guerre contre « les intellectuels, ceux qui sont en Chine les lettrés et dont on retrouve la main dans tous les troubles, ceux que j'appellerai les *inadaptés* ». Le dreyfusisme est l'œuvre de ces marginaux anarchistes. « Un homme qui a une tâche, un devoir précis, a le cœur satisfait, il est trop intéressé par son devoir immédiat pour s'occuper de ce qui ne le regarde pas. Il sait que Dieu ne le jugera pas pour ces choses dans lesquelles il n'a pas compétence ni élection et s'en remet aux gens qui ont autorité [2]. »

*

Pour ce qui regarde les réactions publiques sous la forme d'articles publiés dans la presse, on notera qu'elles sont moins abondantes que celles suscitées six mois plus tôt par le *Mystère de la charité de Jeanne d'Arc*. Comme le *Mystère* repris chez Plon, *Notre jeunesse* sort pourtant en même temps qu'aux *Cahiers* chez Ollendorff et bénéficie d'un accroissement de diffusion identique.

Dans le relatif manque d'écho que rencontre le

1. *Idem*, p. 133.
2. *Idem*, p. 133.

livre, il y a plus et autre chose qu'un phénomène d'usure lié à la parution trop rapprochée de deux titres. La situation de Péguy n'a pas changé. Il reste isolé entre deux camps : les politiciens dreyfusistes qu'il a lâchés et les politiciens antidreyfusistes qui espèrent le récupérer.

Les seconds ont cru triompher avec le *Mystère de la charité de Jeanne d'Arc*, œuvre d'un dreyfusard qu'ils ont imaginé « repenti » et auquel ils ont ménagé un accueil flatteur. Ils déchantent à la lecture de *Notre jeunesse* où, sans se réconcilier avec ses anciens camarades de lutte, Péguy maintient son hostilité envers ses anciens adversaires. Il ne regagne donc rien d'un côté et perd ce qu'il avait acquis de l'autre. C'est ce que Georges Sorel, furieux, déplore dans sa lettre à Daniel Halévy : « Il est bien plus facile de faire le plongeon que de se hisser sur le rocher de l'Acropole [1]. »

Chez Péguy, la démarche est parfaitement délibérée. A travers sa réplique à Daniel Halévy, il veut remettre les choses au point et dissiper toute équivoque. Il ne se repent nullement. A présent autant que naguère, il est fier de l'affaire Dreyfus. Avec une simplicité qui plus qu'orgueilleuse est un défi, il répète : « Nous fûmes des héros. La technique même de l'héroïsme, et nommément de l'héroïsme militaire. Nous fûmes cette poignée de Français qui sous un feu écrasant enfoncent des masses, conduisent un assaut, enlèvent une position. » De quoi faire grincer des dents aux partisans de l'État-Major, surtout lorsque

---

1. Christine Beaulieu, « Le conflit de 1910 entre Péguy et Daniel Halévy », *op. cit.*, p. 209.

Péguy en rajoute et célèbre « la *discipline* des *anarchistes* ».

Le premier article important vient d'un dreyfusiste aussi peu « repenti » que Péguy, Marcel Drouin, beau-frère de Gide. Il publie sous son pseudonyme habituel, Michel Arnauld, une critique dans la *Nouvelle revue française* de septembre 1910. Il y a été incité par un propos de lui que rapporte *Notre jeunesse* et sur lequel s'achève le livre. Compagnon du jeune Péguy pendant les années de l'affaire Dreyfus, il n'a pas de peine à se rappeler que le futur auteur du *Mystère de la charité de Jeanne d'Arc* avait déjà dédié une première *Jeanne d'Arc* « à toutes celles et à tous ceux qui auront vécu, qui seront morts pour l'établissement de la République universelle ». Il ne voit pas deux hommes en Péguy, mais un seul chez qui mystique républicaine et mystique chrétienne vont ensemble.

Rationaliste convaincu, Michel Arnauld craint pourtant que l'antagonisme entre mystique et politique n'encourage une dangereuse confusion entre « mystique et sentimentalisme ». Ce qui sépare les dreyfusistes des antidreyfusistes « n'est pas seulement une question de vie intérieure, de perfection, de salut personnel. Si nous opposons mystique à mystique, encore faut-il que chacune d'elles enveloppe la vision et le choix d'une certaine *politique* »[1].

Michel Arnauld reconnaît qu'il ne prend pas ici le mot dans le sens péjoratif où le prend Péguy. Mais

1. Michel Arnauld, « *Notre jeunesse* de Charles Péguy », *Nouvelle revue française*, 1er septembre 1910, dans Éric Cahm, *Péguy et le nationalisme français,* Cahiers de l'Amitié Charles Péguy, 1972, p. 187.

l'auteur de *Notre jeunesse* « oublie que le mot a deux sens, et néglige des deux le plus essentiel. Être royaliste, ce n'est pas seulement se rattacher à une tradition de dévouement et de sacrifice ; c'est attribuer au régime monarchique une vertu d'ordre et de prospérité sociale. Être républicain, ce n'est pas seulement se ranger sous une autre tradition de dévouement et de sacrifice ; c'est surtout croire à l'efficace, aux bienfaits du régime démocratique » [1].

Comme nous l'avons montré, les craintes du critique de la *NRF* ne sont pas fondées en ce qui concerne Péguy. Celui-ci n'a jamais négligé ni encore moins ignoré, dans sa vie et son œuvre, la politique comme art d'administrer la cité. Quand la politique refuse d'être une carrière et se contente d'être une réflexion et un métier, il la respecte et y participe. Encore faut-il que la politique ainsi entendue soit vivifiée par une mystique. Michel Arnauld en convient, lorsqu'il se réfère à une « foi républicaine » prête au combat, si besoin était. C'est ce que Péguy lui a précisément fait dire, aux dernières lignes de *Notre jeunesse*.

En ce même mois de septembre 1910, les *Annales de la Jeunesse laïque* publient un long article d'un autre dreyfusiste, Georges Guy-Grand, proche de Daniel Halévy. C'est un partisan du juste milieu, « à mi-chemin entre la politique froidement cynique d'un Maurras et le mysticisme éperdu d'un Péguy » [2]. On ne s'étonnera pas que celui-ci ait fort mal reçu l'article et y ait relevé, non sans abus, une « certaine bassesse

1. *Idem,* p. 188.
2. Georges Guy-Grand, « Un épilogue », *Les Annales de la Jeunesse laïque,* septembre 1910, dans Éric Cahm, *op. cit.,* p. 197.

d'âme »[1]. Une tiédeur indéniable s'y exprimait envers l'affaire Dreyfus.

Péguy ne pouvait supporter cela. Le même scénario de brouille et de réparation se renouvela, comme avec Halévy. Après une attaque en règle dans un court texte, les *Amis des Cahiers*, paru le 20 novembre, Péguy fit machine arrière trois semaines plus tard en publiant sans commentaire une lettre fort digne de la victime outragée[2]. Le commentaire vint l'année suivante, au détour d'une page d'*Un nouveau théologien M. Fernand Laudet*. Le gérant des *Cahiers* s'y félicitait d'avoir publié intégralement le rectificatif, « me donnant ainsi, et bien gratuitement, toutes les apparences d'avoir tort »[3]. Le bougonnement s'accompagnait pourtant d'une ouverture en vue d'une éventuelle collaboration future.

Dans son article, Georges Guy-Grand balance perpétuellement entre mystique et politique. « Incontestablement, le premier mouvement du dreyfusien fut mystique[4]. » Faut-il s'indigner qu'il ne le soit pas resté ? « La mystique se dégrade en politique, mais la politique n'est que l'application de la mystique : application difficile, obscure, sans gloire et souvent sans joie, mais nécessaire[5]. » Si la mystique n'accepte

1. *Les Amis des Cahiers*, CQ, XII-2, 20 novembre 1910, OEPC, III, 1992, p. 348-349.

2. CQ, XII-4, 13 décembre 1910, OEPC, III, 1992, p. 1572-1573.

3. *Un nouveau théologien M. Fernand Laudet*, CQ, XIII-2, 24 septembre 1911, OEPC, III, 1992, p. 522.

4. Georges Guy-Grand, « Un épilogue », dans Éric Cahm, *op. cit.*, p. 191.

5. *Idem*, p. 195.

pas de se compromettre, elle risque de demeurer dans les nuées, d'entretenir un rêve évangélique, spiritualiste, idéaliste, sans effet sur le réel.

Guy-Grand continue de louvoyer entre Péguy et Maurras en accordant au premier que, dans l'affaire Dreyfus, il fallait songer au « salut éternel » de la France, mais en ne refusant pas au second la préoccupation du « salut temporel ». Comment associer les deux ? En comprenant que non seulement l'intérêt mystique, mais l'intérêt politique du pays était de ne pas admettre que dans une société moderne le droit des individus fût bafoué. Péguy dit-il autre chose quand il affirme que seule la mystique est pratique, concrète, tandis que la politique s'en tient aux apparences ?

Le chroniqueur des *Annales de la Jeunesse laïque* s'enferre de plus en plus lorsqu'il décèle une contradiction chez les partisans de la mystique. « Ces anti-politiques, ces adversaires acharnés de la politique des partis sont parmi les plus grands admirateurs de l'Église [1] », qui est elle-même un parti. Guy-Grand reconnaît certes que sa critique ne vise pas Péguy. Celui-ci est logique avec lui-même, puisqu'il condamne précisément le cléricalisme autant que le combisme. N'a-t-il pas tort cependant ? « Il y a un cléricalisme nécessaire, comme un anticléricalisme nécessaire. Ces deux politiques peuvent et doivent se combattre ; mais, bien comprises, elles doivent se respecter [2]. »

On imagine la réaction de Péguy devant de tels

1. *Idem*, p. 196.
2. *Idem*, p. 196.

propos. Au fond, la ligne de rupture se dessine parfaitement autour de la figure emblématique de *Notre jeunesse*. « Ce Bernard-Lazare qu'on nous fait admirer, quel effroyable nihiliste ! Conseils de guerre, magistrature, institutions, État, nation, rien de ces misérables choses temporelles n'a de prix à ses yeux. Il y a Lui et l'Éternel, et sans doute aussi Charles Péguy. Cela est inouï. Cela dénote une perversion du sens individuel devant quoi nous sommes stupides. Si l'individualisme c'était ça, il n'y aurait rien à répondre à Maurras [1]. »

Maurras jubile, en effet, lorsqu'il voit un dreyfusiste laïque, adhérent du parti républicain, surprendre d'autres dreyfusistes — et parmi eux Bernard-Lazare, le fondateur — en flagrant délit d'anarchisme. Dans trois numéros successifs, du 24 octobre au 8 novembre 1910, *l'Action française* se fait largement l'écho du différend entre Halévy, « demi-juif converti au protestantisme maternel », Péguy, « ancien normalien, ancien admirateur et disciple de Jaurès dont il est aujourd'hui l'ennemi le plus intime », et Guy-Grand, « rédacteur aux rouges *Annales de la Jeunesse laïque* » [2].

Bien entendu, le journaliste anonyme de *l'Action française* commence par marquer les distances au sujet du couple mystique-politique. « M. Péguy donne à ce mot de *politique*, auquel ici on a restitué sa vieille noblesse, un sens assez bas, comme tyrannie de

1. *Idem,* p. 193.
2. « La décomposition dreyfusienne », *L'Action française,* 24 octobre, 7 novembre et 8 novembre 1910, dans Éric Cahm, *op. cit.,* p. 201.

parti ou trafic d'intérêts. La mystique, au contraire, est l'idée pure et désintéressée. Il nous paraît qu'en affranchissant ce qu'il appelle la *mystique* de toute responsabilité en quelque sorte *terrestre,* M. Péguy lui ravit aussi toute sa grandeur et son honneur [1]. »

Une fois de plus, on reproche à Péguy, philosophe du charnel et théologien de l'incarnation, son « idéalisme », son manque de sens « terrestre » et « terrien ». Par un malentendu obstiné, on ne veut pas voir qu'à l'inverse il proteste contre la désubstantialisation, la déperdition de force que connaît la mystique lorsqu'elle se dégrade, s'affaisse en politique. C'est un élan qu'il soutient, alors qu'on le tance de ne pas admettre une retombée, une chute.

Mais le plus grave n'est pas là, poursuit le chroniqueur de *l'Action française.* Le pire, « c'est que M. Péguy, après s'être dégagé de toute compromission dans la politique de Dreyfus, se roule comme un furieux aux pieds de son idole, la mystique dreyfusienne. Il compose alors du juif Bernard-Lazare un éloge qui nous couvre de honte, nous, les compatriotes de M. Péguy. La joie frénétique avec laquelle il exalte la mémoire du pire d'entre les Juifs destructeurs nous fait mal » [2].

En somme, l'auteur de *Notre jeunesse* a beau « être dangereusement véridique sur l'éternel nomadisme juif », exécrer à bon droit les suites de l'Affaire qui

1. *Idem,* p. 203-204.
2. *Idem,* p. 204.

constituent autant de « crimes », dénoncer excellemment comme « un coup de force judiciaire » l'arrêt de la Cour de Cassation qui achève d'innocenter Dreyfus en 1906[1]. Toutes ces vues justes n'empêchent pas le « sombre fanatisme » de Péguy d'exprimer « une mystique immolatoire et anarchique » tout à fait condamnable[2].

A l'autre extrémité du champ politique, parmi les syndicalistes révolutionnaires de *L'École émancipée* qui regroupe les instituteurs libertaires, cette même mystique emporte l'acquiescement le plus cordial, comme en témoigne un long article d'Élie Reynier, paru les 25 février et 4 mars 1911 dans leur bulletin. Les seules réserves portent, chez ces adeptes de l'hervéisme et de la guerre sociale, sur « l'incompréhension calomnieuse » que Péguy affiche envers Gustave Hervé. On lui abandonne par contre Jaurès avec « ses faiblesses, ses concessions, ses finasseries politiciennes, son adhésion enthousiaste à la démagogie combiste, ses réticences emberlificotées devant la propagande hervéiste »[3].

Honnêtement, ces instituteurs d'extrême gauche reconnaissent la justesse de la critique faite à l'enseignement laïque, coupable de masquer la mystique de l'Ancien Régime. Athées ou libres penseurs, ils ne se scandalisent pas du rapprochement effectué entre mystique républicaine et mystique chrétienne, se sentant tenus par là de considérer « non pas avec

1. *Idem,* p. 203-204.
2. *Idem,* p. 204 et 206.
3. Élie Reynier, « Notre jeunesse », *L'École émancipée,* 25 février et 4 mars 1911, dans FACP, n° 128, 20 février 1967, p. 39.

tolérance, avec curiosité, mais avec une réelle et
sincère sympathie tout mouvement politique ou religieux, si différent soit-il du nôtre, qui est vraiment
vivant, intérieur, inspirateur de dévouement et d'ardeur » [1].

L'accord fondamental porte sur cette parenté de
toutes les mystiques s'unissant contre toutes les
politiques. Il y a bien opposition irréductible entre
« l'idéal et l'exploitation de cet idéal par les habiles,
les arrivistes, roublards et autoritaires ». Remplis de
« l'indomptable orgueil dreyfusiste », ces instituteurs
se félicitent de n'avoir pas versé dans la politique.
« Nous nous sommes refusés à toute démagogie, y
compris combiste ; à toute intolérance et à toute
oppression, même anticléricales ; à toute compromission politicienne. Et au nom de nos principes dreyfusistes, nous protestons comme il y a douze ans contre
le monstrueux jugement de Rouen (condamnant à
mort le syndicaliste Jules Durand), contre la mobilisation et la révocation des cheminots parce que gré-
vistes, contre les persécutions aux révolutionnaires de
Russie et d'ailleurs [2]. »

Une autre approbation sans réserve vise « les
admirables pages sur le socialisme, conçu comme un
assainissement de la nation et du peuple, une philosophie du travail, de la *restauration du travail*. Tout notre
syndicalisme est tel. Nous faisons de notre travail le
centre même de notre vie, nous rapportons à lui tous
nos efforts et toute notre pensée, ou plutôt nous
dérivons notre pensée de notre travail consciencieuse-

1. *Idem,* p. 37-38.
2. *Idem,* p. 36-37.

ment, joyeusement accompli. Ajoutons que cette *morale des producteurs,* nous la devons en grande partie à Péguy, à Charles Guieysse, à Sorel, Berth, Lagardelle, et aussi à quelques maîtres, à quelques isolés, Séailles, Payot »[1].

Après ce bel hommage, sera-t-on surpris qu'en 1916, un autre socialiste d'extrême gauche écrive : « Nous relisons un livre que nous aimons beaucoup, *Notre jeunesse* de Charles Péguy, et nous nous enivrons de ce sens mystique et religieux du socialisme, de la justice, qui tout entier l'anime. Nous sentons en nous une vie nouvelle, une foi plus vibrante que d'habitude, et les misérables polémiques de petits politiciens lourdement matérialistes dans leurs motivations ont pour seul effet de nous rendre plus fiers »[2]. Ce socialiste allait être un des fondateurs du parti communiste italien : il s'appelait Antonio Gramsci.

*

Péguy l'inclassable, l'insaisissable, ne se manifeste jamais mieux que dans *Notre jeunesse.* Aucun parti, de droite ou de gauche, ne saurait l'annexer, car s'il n'arrête pas de prendre parti, il ne se situe pas au niveau des partis. La pétrification partisane, commode pour les pensées médiocres et les actions aveugles, relève de cette politique qu'il dénonce. Pour lui, le monde est chaque matin à inventer. L'événe-

---

1. *Idem,* p. 39-40.
2. Antonio Gramsci, « I moventi e Coppoleto », *L'Avanti,* 19 avril 1916, dans *Sotto la mole, 1916-1920,* OC-X, 1960, p. 118.

ment incite inépuisablement à rebondir. Face à l'inattendu, l'homme vivant est celui qui, porté par l'espérance, ne cesse d'engendrer du nouveau. C'est cela en fin de compte, la mystique : une création permanente.

Jean Bastaire

DE LA RAISON

Avant qu'on étudie à leur tour ces études [1], avant qu'on y soit même introduit par l'auteur, il est indispensable que l'on soit averti que l'auteur n'y fait appel qu'à la raison. Cela est indispensable en un temps où la raison a presque autant que jamais des ennemis, qui sont dangereux, où elle a plus que jamais des faux amis, qui sont plus dangereux. On doit nommer ennemis de la raison les déments qui exercent leur démence contre la raison. Et on doit nommer les faux amis de la raison les déments qui veulent que la raison procède par les voies de la déraison.

La raison ne procède pas par la voie de l'autorité. Comme elle n'admet de celui qui enseigne aucune intimidation, chantage ni menace, comme elle ne reçoit aucun exercice de force, aucun excès de pouvoir, aucun pouvoir, commandement, abus ni coup d'État, elle ne suppose de celui qui est enseigné aucune lâcheté. C'est donc trahir la raison, c'est faire déraisonner la raison que de vouloir assurer le triomphe de la raison par les moyens de l'autorité.

La raison ne procède pas de l'autorité gouvernementale. C'est donc trahir la raison que de vouloir assurer le triomphe de la raison par des moyens gouvernementaux. C'est manquer à la raison que de vouloir établir un gouvernement de la raison. Il ne peut y avoir, il ne doit y avoir ni ministère, ni préfecture, ni sous-préfecture de la raison, ni consulat, ni proconsulat de la raison. La raison ne peut pas, la raison ne doit pas commander au nom d'un gouvernement. Faire ou laisser opérer par un préfet des perquisitions dans la chambre d'une institutrice, quand même le préfet serait un préfet républicain, quand même l'institutrice ne serait pas une institutrice républicaine, ce n'est pas attenter à la liberté seulement, c'est attenter à la raison. La raison ne demande pas, la raison ne veut pas, la raison n'accepte pas qu'on la défende ou qu'on la soutienne ou qu'on agisse en son nom par les moyens de l'autorité gouvernementale. En aucun sens la raison n'est la raison d'État. Toute raison d'État est une usurpation déloyale de l'autorité sur la raison, une contrefaçon, une malfaçon.

En particulier la raison ne procède pas de l'autorité militaire. Elle ignore totalement l'obéissance passive. C'est trahir la raison que de vouloir assurer la victoire de la raison par la discipline qui fait la force principale des armées [1]. C'est faire déraisonner la raison que de l'enseigner par les moyens militaires. La raison ne demande pas, n'accepte pas l'obéissance. On ne commande pas au nom de la raison comme on commande à la manœuvre. Il n'y a aucune armée de la raison, aucuns soldats de la raison, et surtout il n'y a aucuns chefs de la raison. Il n'y a même, à parler proprement, aucune guerre de la raison, aucune campagne, aucune expédition. La raison ne fait pas la guerre à la déraison. Elle réduit tant qu'elle peut la déraison par des moyens qui ne sont pas les moyens de la guerre, puisqu'ils sont les moyens de la raison. La raison ne donne pas des assauts ; elle ne forme pas des colonnes d'attaque ; elle n'enlève pas des positions ; elle ne force pas des passages ; elle ne fait pas des entrées solennelles ; ni elle ne couche comme le vainqueur militaire sur le champ de bataille.

La raison ne procède pas de l'autorité religieuse. Il fallait une insanité inouïe pour oser instituer le culte de la déesse Raison[1]. Et si l'on peut excuser une insanité dans un temps d'affolement, déclarons-le haut : la froide répétition politique de cette insanité, la commémoration concertée de cette insanité constitue l'indice le plus grave d'incohérence ou de démence, de déraison. Non la raison ne procède pas par la voie du culte. Non la raison ne veut pas d'autels. Non la raison ne veut pas de prières. Non la raison ne veut pas de prêtres. C'est trahir le plus gravement la raison, c'est faire déraisonner le plus gravement la raison que de la déguiser en déesse, en cabotinage et musique ; c'est la trahir que de lui fabriquer des fêtes religieuses, des imitations en simili-culte, avec tout ce qu'il faut. Et même l'admirable prière que Renan fit sur l'Acropole[2] après qu'il fut parvenu à en comprendre la parfaite beauté n'a plus aucun sens, lue ou déclamée sur les planches devant la foule inépuisablement trompée.

Déclarons-le sans peur. Et sachons nous faire les ennemis qui voudront. La raison ne veut aucune Église. Il ne peut pas, il ne doit pas y avoir une Église de la raison. Les pratiques cérémonielles, cultuelles et rituelles sont totalement étrangères à l'honnêteté de la

raison. Les pratiques surhumaines, religieuses, infernales ou divines, inhumaines, sont totalement étrangères à l'humanité de la raison. La raison est honnête
homme. Il n'y a pas un clergé de la raison. Nous
n'avons pas renoncé, nous n'avons pas dénoncé les
religions d'hier pour annoncer la religion de demain,
pour prêcher quelque religion nouvelle. Nous sommes
irréligieux de toutes les religions. Nous sommes athées
de tous les dieux. Dans le douloureux débat de la
raison et de la foi nous n'avons pas laissé la foi pour la
foi dans la raison, mais pour la raison de la raison. La
raison n'admet ni prophéties ni déclamations ni
proclamations, — ni dogmes ni décrets des conciles ni
brefs des papes. Et c'est tromper lamentablement le
peuple perpétuel que de lui présenter les vérités de la
raison sur le même ton et comme on lui annonçait les
vérités prétendues révélées.

La raison ne procède pas de l'autorité parlementaire. Elle ne tient ni de ces longues assemblées, que
nous nommons parlements, ni de ces assemblées
courtes, que nous nommons congrès. La raison n'a ni
président, ni assesseurs, ni secrétaire, ni aucun
bureau. Elle manque souvent de sténographes. Elle
n'a pas toujours un procès-verbal, un compte rendu.
Elle ne constitue aucun comité directeur. Elle ne
procède pas par votation. Elle n'est pas soumise à la
loi de majorité. Elle n'est pas proportionnelle au
nombre. Beaucoup peuvent se tromper. Il se peut
qu'un seul ait raison. Même il se peut que pas un n'ait
raison. La raison ne varie pas avec le nombre. Elle ne
flatte pas plus les foules qu'elle ne flattait les grands.
Elle ne flatte pas plus les peuples qu'elle ne flattait les
rois. Elle ne flatte pas plus les démocraties qu'elle ne

flattait les monarchies ou les oligarchies. Nous savons qu'il y a eu dans le passé de longs temps et de vastes régions où la raison ne résidait qu'en des minorités, en des unités. Même il y a eu des nations où la raison ne résidait pas. Elle peut s'absenter aujourd'hui encore.

La raison ne procède pas de l'autorité démagogique. Ameuter les masses, lancer les foules est un exercice d'autorité non moins étranger à la raison que d'amasser quelque majorité, de lancer quelque régiment. Nous sommes aujourd'hui sous le gouvernement de la démagogie beaucoup plus que sous le gouvernement de la démocratie. Les tribuns, les avocats et les journalistes nous gouvernent lourdement. Libre de la monarchie, de l'oligarchie et de la démocratie, gouvernements réguliers, la raison est libre aussi de la démagogie, gouvernement de fait. Elle n'est pas plus soumise aux nouveaux courtisans qu'elle n'était soumise aux anciens. Ni les manifestations de la rue ni les manifestations des meetings ne valent au regard de la raison. La raison ne monte sur aucuns tréteaux. Les mouvements des masses ne pèsent pas plus que les révolutions de palais. Le peuple abusé ne peut pas faire que la raison ne soit pas la raison, et que la déraison devienne la raison. La foule abusée ne peut pas plus que ne pouvait le monarque abusé. Le peuple n'est pas souverain de la raison.

La raison ne procède pas de l'autorité manuelle. Autant il est vrai que la raison n'exerce aucune autorité, autant il est vrai que le gouvernement des intellectuels serait le plus insupportable des gouvernements, — autant il est réciproquement vrai que la raison, qui n'accepte aucune autorité, qui ne subit aucun gouvernement, n'accepte pas une autorité manuelle, ne subit pas un gouvernement manuel. C'est fausser la raison que d'imaginer, comme l'a rêvé Renan [1], un gouvernement spirituel de la terre habitée, un gouvernement des intellectuels omnipotent. Une république de cuistres ne serait pas moins inhabitable qu'une république de moines. Si on la laissait se former, une caste intellectuelle serait plus agaçante et pèserait plus lourd sur le monde que toute caste. Mais c'est aussi manquer à la raison que d'ameuter contre les intellectuels sérieux les autorités grossières des travailleurs manuels mal renseignés. La justice, la raison, la bonne administration du travail demandent que les intellectuels ne soient ni gouvernants ni gouvernés. Qu'ils soient modestement libre, comme tout le monde.

Dans la société présente, où le jeu de la spécialisation s'est outré automatiquement, les fonctions intellectuelles et les fonctions manuelles ne sont presque jamais attribuées aux mêmes ouvriers ; les ouvriers intellectuels délaissent presque tout le travail des mains ; les ouvriers manuels délaissent presque tout travail de l'esprit, presque tout exercice de la raison. Dans la cité harmonieuse [2], dont nous préparons la naissance et la vie, les fonctions intellectuelles et les fonctions manuelles se partageront harmonieusement les mêmes hommes. Et la relation de l'intellectuel au manuel, au lieu de s'établir péniblement d'un individu à l'autre, s'établira librement au cœur du même homme. Le problème sera transposé. Car nous n'avons jamais dit que nous supprimerions les problèmes humains. Nous voulons seulement, et nous espérons les transporter du terrain bourgeois, où ils ne peuvent recevoir que des solutions ingrates, sur le terrain humain, libre enfin des servitudes économiques. Nous laissons les miracles aux praticiens des anciennes et des nouvelles Églises. Nous ne promettons pas un Paradis. Nous préparons une humanité libérée.

Les chefs audacieux et les foules blasées, les meneurs menés, les candidats et les électeurs trouveront sans doute que ce programme est insuffisant. Mais nous savons par l'histoire de l'humanité, par l'histoire des sciences, des arts, de la philosophie, qu'un changement de plan est un événement, une opération considérable. Dans tous les genres de travail deux progrès sont ouverts. On peut d'abord avancer par évolution en continuant dans le même sens. Mais il vient presque toujours un moment où le travailleur a l'impression que le sens est épuisé : aucune application, aucune insistance ne peut plus tirer du réel ce que le réel n'a plus dans le sens commencé. Des vies entières consommées dans un travail ingrat ne rendraient plus ce qu'elles coûteraient. Alors intervient la révolution. Vu d'ailleurs, attaqué d'ailleurs, le réel recommence brusquement à couler à pleins bords. Et pourtant le réel est le même qu'il était. Mais il n'est plus vu du même regard, il n'est plus vu le même, il n'est plus connu le même. C'est ainsi que nous sommes révolutionnaires. Nous voulons que la même humanité se donne la liberté nouvelle.

Nous ne méprisons pas les humanités passées, nous n'avons ni cet orgueil, ni cette vanité, ni cette insolence, ni cette imbécillité, cette faiblesse. Nous ne

méprisons pas ce qu'a d'humain l'humanité présente.
Au contraire nous voulons conserver ce qu'avaient
d'humain les anciennes humanités. Nous voulons
sauver ce qu'a d'humain l'humanité présente. Nous
évitons surtout de faire à l'humanité présente la plus
grave injure, qui est de la vouloir dresser. Nous
n'avons pas la présomption d'imaginer, d'inventer, de
fabriquer une humanité nouvelle. Nous n'avons ni
plan ni devis. Nous voulons libérer l'humanité des
servitudes économiques. Libérée, libre, l'humanité
vivra librement. Libre de nous et de tous ceux qui
l'auront libérée. Ce serait commettre la prévarication
maxima, le détournement le plus grave que d'utiliser
la libération pour asservir les libérés sous la mentalité
des libérateurs. Ce serait tendre à l'humanité comme
un guet-apens universel que de lui présenter la
libération pour l'attirer dans une philosophie, quand
même cette philosophie serait étiquetée philosophie
de la raison.

  Attacher au socialisme un système, lier au socialisme, fût-ce au nom de la raison, un système de
science, ou d'art, ou de philosophie, c'est littéralement
commettre un abus de confiance envers l'humanité.
Attirer l'humanité vers sa libération pour la précipiter
dans un système, c'est commettre au nom de la raison
la malversation que l'Église a commise au nom de la
foi. C'est vendre à l'humanité ce que nous devons lui
donner. C'est vendre un objet que nous ne devons pas
laisser tomber dans le commerce économique. Par une
libération c'est introduire à un asservissement. Disons
plus : vendre à l'humanité sa libération économique
pour l'établissement d'un système, ce n'est pas seulement tromper et voler l'humanité, ce n'est pas seule-

ment trahir l'humanité, ce n'est pas seulement vendre l'invendable, ce n'est pas seulement laïciser la malversation de l'Église, recommencer en laïque la prévarication de l'Église, qui vend aux pauvres le pain pour le billet de confession, pour la respectable prière et pour la sainte communion, c'est commettre le crime le plus grave pour un socialiste : c'est monnayer à son avantage la servitude économique même.

Attacher au socialisme libérateur une augmentation de système pour que ça passe avec n'est pas seulement une opération inélégante, laide, mufle, de mauvais ton, de mauvaise tenue, de mauvaise culture, de mauvais goût, de mauvaise allure ; ce n'est pas seulement une opération immorale, injuste, perverse, inverse, et de mauvaise administration ; c'est une opération proprement, particulièrement contraire au socialisme. L'idéalisme ou le matérialisme, l'idéaliste ou le matérialiste, le déterministe ou le libéraliste qui feraient du socialisme avec l'arrière-pensée plus ou moins confuse que leur système en soit avantagé ne joueraient pas seulement un jeu laidement déloyal, mais leur jeu serait un perpétuel reniement du socialisme ; ils ne joueraient pas seulement faux, ils joueraient bourgeois. Utilisant à leurs fins intéressées le désir, le besoin, la passion de libération économique, ils utiliseraient en effet, au second degré, l'asservissement précédent, la servitude même à laquelle on veut échapper. Ils n'exerceraient pas seulement un chantage, mais ils exerceraient précisément le chantage économique, vice propre de la société bourgeoise, du régime bourgeois.

Nous n'avons pas plus à vendre la terre que les

chrétiens n'avaient à vendre le ciel. Nous n'avons pas
à laïciser les marchandages des clercs. Bien loin que le
socialisme repose officiellement sur un système d'art
ou de science ou de philosophie, loin qu'il tende à
l'établissement, à la glorification d'un système, loin
qu'il soit matérialiste ou idéaliste, athéiste ou théiste,
au contraire le socialisme est ce qui laissera l'humanité libérée libre enfin de travailler, d'étudier, de
penser librement. C'est l'effet d'une singulière inintel-
ligence que de s'imaginer que la révolution sociale
serait une conclusion, une fermeture de l'humanité
dans la fade béatitude des quiétudes mortes. C'est
l'effet d'une ambition naïve et mauvaise, idiote et
sournoise que de vouloir clore l'humanité par la
révolution sociale. Faire un cloître de l'humanité
serait l'effet de la plus redoutable survivance religieuse. Loin que le socialisme soit définitif, il est
préliminaire, préalable, nécessaire, indispensable
mais non suffisant. Il est avant le seuil. Il n'est pas la
fin de l'humanité, il n'en est pas même le commencement. Il est, selon nous, avant le commencement.
Avant le commencement sera le Verbe [1].

Il ne faut pas que les idées soient arrivistes ni qu'on
les fasse passer en contrebande. Il ne faut pas qu'elles
soient parasitaires, qu'elles s'attachent au socialisme
ainsi que de malheureux jeunes gens deviennent les
secrétaires des hommes influents. L'écœurement que
nous avons des petits ambitieux qui se veulent pousser
dans les emplois du socialisme ministériel et dans les
identiques emplois du socialisme antiministériel, nous
l'aurons des systèmes qui voudraient arriver par le
socialisme et dans le socialisme. Enfin c'est un
insupportable abus de l'autorité paternelle que de

vouloir imposer aux générations neuves les radotages des générations fatiguées, vieilles, que nous sommes. Justement parce que nous les aurons libérées, elles sauront beaucoup mieux que nous ce qu'elles auront à penser. La raison ne procède pas de l'autorité paternelle. Ne faisons pas au nom de la raison des vœux perpétuels pour nous-mêmes. Et n'en faisons pas pour les perpétuelles générations. Laissons l'humanité tranquille. Une révolution qui entend nous débarrasser des intérêts doit être absolument désintéressée.

Réciproquement c'est trahir la raison, comme on trahissait le socialisme, que d'introduire dans les débats de la raison des poids additionnels. Dans le débat des systèmes rationnels, ajouter à certains systèmes, au matérialisme, à l'athéisme, le surpoids des volontés socialistes, leur infuser la sève et le sang des passions révolutionnaires, c'est fausser le jeu de l'action par des interventions étrangères à l'action ; mais réciproquement c'est fausser le jeu de la raison par des interventions étrangères à la raison. C'est procurer à certains systèmes une importance démesurée dans l'histoire de la pensée. La raison ne procède pas de l'autorité socialiste, en supposant qu'il y ait une autorité socialiste. La raison ne procède pas de l'autorité révolutionnaire, en admettant que les jacobins aient vraiment institué une autorité révolutionnaire. La raison ne dépend pas plus des masses révolutionnaires que des masses réactionnaires ou des masses inertes. Elle ne dépend d'aucunes forces. Elle ne dépend pas plus des armées révolutionnaires que des armées militaires. Elle ne dépend pas des masses populaires. Elle ne dépend pas de l'autorité manuelle.

C'est trahir la raison et c'est trahir le peuple que de

vouloir établir sur le peuple un gouvernement, un commandement, une autorité de la raison. Mais c'est trahir aussi la raison et c'est trahir aussi le peuple que de vouloir établir sur la raison, par la démagogie ou par la pédagogie, un gouvernement, un commandement, une autorité des ouvriers manuels. Entendons-nous : les ouvriers manuels, parce qu'ils sont des hommes, et qu'ils ont leur part de la raison commune, ont le droit et le devoir de penser dans la mesure de leur compétence. Mais c'est un des modes les plus dangereux de la démagogie que de masquer au peuple ses incompétences inévitables, provisoires, mais provisoirement inévitables. Dénoncer au peuple des ouvriers manuels un ouvrage de philosophie parce qu'il se vend sept cinquante chez Alcan, dénoncer au peuple un ouvrage de métaphysique parce qu'il y a quinze fois le mot Dieu à la page 28 et quatre-vingt-douze fois le mot Dieu à la page 31, dénoncer au peuple cet ouvrage comme entaché de cléricalisme, je dis que c'est du jésuitisme, et je dis que c'est de l'Inquisition [1].

C'est du jésuitisme et c'est de la duplicité, car le journal a deux clientèles, deux régions. Si le journal n'était lu que par des intellectuels, une inculpation de cléricalisme intentée à une thèse de philosophie, — échafaudée sur ce que le mot Dieu y paraît, ne serait pas dangereuse, parce que le lecteur, avisé, y reconnaîtrait un amusement. Un amusement d'un goût douteux, assez pervers, mais un amusement enfin. Si le journal n'était lu que par des ouvriers manuels, si l'auteur de l'accusation était lui-même un manuel, cette accusation serait dangereuse, mais elle serait sincère. Ce qui fait la duplicité, c'est qu'un auteur intellectuel délibérément jette cette accusation devant un double public. L'auteur, intellectuel, sait ce que c'est que la métaphysique et la théodicée. L'auteur ne peut pas croire que son accusation existe. Et parce qu'il a du talent l'accusation insidieuse est énoncée en termes attentivement violents. Les intellectuels verront bien que c'est une bonne blague et ne mépriseront pas le journaliste comme ignorant. Les ouvriers manuels prendront pour argent comptant. La réputation littéraire sera sauve auprès des premiers, la réputation morale sera sauve auprès des seconds.

Je ne crois pas que rien soit aussi dangereux pour le peuple et pour la raison que ces malentendus à double malentente. M. le marquis de Rochefort y excellait [1]. Il savait admirablement inventer la calomnie qui ferait sourire les gens d'esprit et qui soulèverait l'émotion du peuple. Faire la calomnie assez grosse pour que sa grosseur même avertisse les gens avertis qu'on est averti soi-même; et utiliser cette même grosseur pour soulever une grosse émotion du peuple : c'est à ce double jeu que M. de Rochefort était un joueur que l'on croyait inimitable. De toutes les solutions que l'on peut imaginer au problème intellectuel-manuel, celle-ci est la plus injurieuse à la fois pour les intellectuels et pour les manuels, car elle suppose que les intellectuels sont si sensibles aux plaisirs douteux d'un amusement pervers qu'ils en oublient les plus simples éléments de la moralité commune, et elle suppose que les ouvriers manuels sont si empressés d'indignation grossière qu'ils ne se renseignent jamais sur le bien-fondé, sur la vérité, sur la justice des réquisitoires que des procureurs de

complaisance, que des avocats généraux de journa-
lisme leur jettent.

Ce n'est pas cette solution injurieuse, douteuse,
double, que nous acceptons. En attendant que par le
changement préliminaire de plan qui nous paraît
capital dans la future, dans la prochaine histoire de
l'humanité, la santé du travail manuel avec la santé
du travail intellectuel soit dévolue à tous les hommes,
en attendant que la relation du manuel à l'intellectuel
se pose librement en tout homme, puisque dans la
société présente les répartitions sont faites entre
individus et non entre élaborations du même individu,
de la même personne, du même homme, puisque le
travail manuel et le travail intellectuel sont distribués
à des individus différents, sans communication normale, puisque, sauf exceptions, peu nombreuses, les
uns ne travaillent guère que de leurs mains, et les
autres de la raison, notre solution sera la simple
solution de la liberté professionnelle. Pour la même
raison que les boulangers ne font pas les maisons, et
que les laboureurs ne font pas les habits, pour la
même raison les ouvriers manuels, boulangers et
maçons, moissonneurs, tisseurs et tailleurs n'ont à
faire ni à défaire les thèses de philosophie.

Exactement comme on n'admet pas l'autorité professionnelle de l'ouvrier manuel sur l'ouvrier manuel
dans des corps de métiers différents, exactement ainsi
on ne doit admettre aucune autorité professionnelle de
l'ouvrier manuel sur l'ouvrier intellectuel. Comme les
boulangers sont ignorants de la bâtisse et les moissonneurs de la taille et du tissage, exactement ainsi les
boulangers et les maçons, les moissonneurs et les
tisseurs, comme tels, sont ignorants de la théodicée.

On peut la leur enseigner, s'il y a des raisons pour qu'on la leur enseigne. On peut ne pas la leur enseigner, s'il y a des empêchements ou des raisons contraires. Mais c'est les flatter bassement que de leur dénoncer par des accusations politiques un travail où ils n'ont pas encore acquis la compétence. Déclarons-le hautement : un professeur de philosophie peut et doit faire de la théodicée quand et comme la raison le demande. Et il n'est responsable et comptable de sa théodicée que devant la raison, devant la raison raisonnante, devant la raison en travail, devant la raison critique.

Ne fondons pas, ne laissons pas fonder une religion de la raison. Nous avons renoncé une religion qui nous commandait de faire maigre le vendredi saint ; ne fondons pas une religion qui nous forcerait à faire gras ce même jour. Nous avons renoncé une religion qui nous commandait de croire en un Dieu personnel, en trois personnes, souverainement bon, souverainement aimable, tout-puissant, créateur du ciel et de la terre, et souverain seigneur de toutes choses ; ne fondons pas une religion qui nous interdirait de prononcer même un nom dont le moins que l'on puisse dire est qu'il a eu quelque fortune dans l'histoire de l'humanité. La raison ne procède pas de l'autorité presbytérale. Une religion de la raison cumulerait tous les vices religieux avec tous les envers des vertus rationnelles. Ce serait un cumul rare, singulier, culminant, unique de vices communément inconciliables, habituellement séparés, logiquement contradictoires. Ce serait comme une gageure de cumulation. Un catéchisme est insupportable. Mais un catéchisme de la raison tiendrait en ses pages la plus effroyable tyrannie. À la fois parodie et texte.

La raison ne procède pas plus des autorités officieuses que des autorités officielles. Ni le publiciste, ni le journaliste, ni le tribun, ni l'orateur, ni le conférencier ne sont aujourd'hui de simples citoyens. Le journaliste qui a trente ou cinquante ou quatre-vingts milliers de lecteurs, le conférencier qui a régulièrement douze ou quinze cents spectateurs exercent en effet, comme le ministre, comme le député, une autorité gouvernementale. On conduit aujourd'hui les lecteurs comme on n'a pas cessé de conduire les électeurs. La presse constitue un quatrième pouvoir. Beaucoup de journalistes, qui blâment avec raison la faiblesse des mœurs parlementaires, feraient bien de se retourner sur soi-même et de considérer que les salles de rédaction se tiennent comme les Parlements. Il y a au moins autant de démagogie parlementaire dans les journaux que dans les assemblées. Il se dépense autant d'autorité dans un comité de rédaction que dans un conseil des ministres; et autant de faiblesse démagogique. Les journalistes écrivent comme les députés parlent. Un rédacteur en chef est un président du conseil, aussi autoritaire, aussi faible. Il y a moins de libéraux parmi les journalistes que parmi les sénateurs.

C'est le jeu ordinaire des journalistes que d'ameuter toutes les libertés, toutes les licences, toutes les révoltes, et en effet toutes les autorités, le plus souvent contradictoires, contre les autorités gouvernementales officielles. « Nous, simples citoyens », vont-ils répétant. Ils veulent ainsi cumuler tous les privilèges de l'autorité avec tous les droits de la liberté. Mais le

véritable libertaire sait apercevoir l'autorité partout
où elle sévit ; et nulle part elle n'est aussi dangereuse
que là où elle revêt les aspects de la liberté. Le
véritable libertaire sait qu'il y a vraiment un gouvernement des journaux et des meetings, une autorité des
journalistes et des orateurs populaires comme il y a un
gouvernement des bureaux et des assemblées, une
autorité des ministres et des orateurs parlementaires.
Le véritable libertaire se gare des gouvernements
officieux autant que des gouvernements officiels. Car
la popularité aussi est une forme de gouvernement, et
non des moins dangereuses. La raison ne se fait pas de
clientèle. Un journaliste qui joue avec les ministères et
qui arguë du simple citoyen n'est pas recevable. Cela
aussi est double, et cela est trop commode.

Quand un journaliste exerce dans son domaine un
gouvernement de fait, quand il a une armée de
lecteurs fidèles, quand il entraîne ces lecteurs par la
véhémence, l'audace, l'ascendant, moyens militaires,
par le talent, moyen vulgaire, par le mensonge, moyen
politique, et ainsi quand le journaliste est devenu
vraiment une puissance dans l'État, quand il a des
lecteurs exactement comme un député a des électeurs,
quand un journaliste a une circonscription lectorale,
souvent beaucoup plus vaste et beaucoup plus solide,
il ne peut pas venir ensuite nous jouer le double jeu ; il
ne peut pas venir pleurnicher. Dans la grande bataille
des puissances de ce monde, il ne peut pas porter des
coups redoutables au nom de sa puissance et quand les
puissances contraires lui rendent ses coups, dans le
même temps il ne peut pas se réclamer du simple
citoyen. Qui renonce à la raison pour l'offensive ne

peut se réclamer de la raison pour la défensive. Il y aurait là déloyauté insupportable, et encore duplicité.

La raison ne procède pas de la terreur, qui est la forme aiguë de la force. La raison ne procède pas de la suspicion, qui est la forme sournoise de la terreur. Le régime de la terreur, que ce soit de la terreur gouvernementale ou de la terreur populaire non moins gouvernementale, quand même ce régime dresserait des autels à la raison, et surtout si ce régime dressait des autels à la raison, n'est pas un régime de la raison. Le régime des suspects, où l'exercice de la force exercée est mystérieusement agrandi par la peur de la force exerçable, quand même les suspects seraient les ennemis de la raison, et surtout si les suspects étaient les ennemis de la raison, le régime des suspects est le plus contraire à la raison. Mais il n'y a pas seulement à redouter pour la raison un régime officiel des suspects, agrandissant quelque terreur officielle. Plus redoutable encore, plus odieux, plus ennemi de la raison, plus haïssable un régime officieux des suspects, comme celui auquel nous soumet le gouvernement de la presse. Ni les dénonciations calomnieuses, ni les allégations sans preuves ne sont de la raison. La raison n'est pas policière. Elle n'est pas plus policière de presse que policière d'État.

La raison ne procède pas même de cette popularité plus fine et plus aérée qui s'obtient dans les régions de culture. Ni les décorations d'État, ni les distinctions corporatives, ni les cooptations, ni les grades professionnels, ni les académies, ni les fêtes scientifiques, ni les cinquantenaires, ni les centenaires, ni les statues, ni les bustes, ni les noms inscrits aux plaques des rues, ni les banquets, quand même on les nommerait dîners, ni la renommée, ni la gloire ne sont proprement de la raison. Tout cela suppose quelque émulation. Or la raison ne procède pas par l'émulation. Tout cela suppose une application aux travaux de la raison de grandeurs qui ne sont pas du même ordre. La raison n'admet pas la rivalité, mais la seule collaboration, la coopération. Toute idée de récompenses ou de punitions, de sanctions, fussent-elles élégantes, spirituelles et psychologiques, est étrangère à la raison. Dans les sciences mêmes il est souvent difficile de proportionner les cérémonies aux travaux dont elles sont la consécration. Dans les lettres, dans les arts et dans la philosophie, cela est littéralement impossible. Au contraire les œuvres les plus fortes sont aussi les plus inattendues, les moins entourées, ou les plus enviées. Enfin les cérémonies laïques ressemblent toujours à des cérémonies religieuses.

La raison ne procède pas de l'autorité historique. Pas plus que les majorités contemporaines les majorités historiques des générations mortes ne peuvent commander à la raison. Pas plus qu'elle n'est toujours et proprement révolutionnaire, la raison n'est toujours et proprement traditionnelle. Mais elle est proprement rationnelle, et raisonnable. C'est la méconnaître que de l'assimiler ou de l'identifier à la révolution; c'est la méconnaître aussi que de l'assimiler ou de l'identifier à la tradition. Elle est la raison. Et n'obéissant pas à la révolution, n'obéissant pas à la tradition, elle n'obéit pas non plus à la coïncidence des deux, à la tradition révolutionnaire. Car par un accouplement singulier, par un retour inattendu, nous voyons de plus en plus les poussées révolutionnaires se cristalliser en formes traditionnelles. De plus en plus la révolution, qui est la rupture de la tradition, tend à constituer elle-même un appareil traditionnel. Et en face de ces nouvelles traditions révolutionnaires, doublement nouvelles, comme étant des traditions, puisqu'elles sont révolutionnaires, et comme étant révolutionnaires, puisqu'elles sont des traditions, la raison n'a pas trop de ses deux libertés propres : liberté qu'elle sait garder en face de la tradition, liberté qu'elle sait garder en face de la révolution.

De tout temps les mouvements révolutionnaires, les ruptures de tradition, essentiellement libres d'origine, ont eu de la tendance à retomber dans l'ancien automatisme. Ainsi la conservation recommençait, la tradition renaissait avec la matière même que lui fournissait la révolution. Mais jamais comme aujourd'hui le mouvement révolutionnaire n'a été amorti en des formes aussi traditionnelles, aussi conservatoires. Par une étrange inconséquence, ou par une étrange insuffisance de pensée, le précédent constitué par la Révolution française, par la grande révolution bourgeoise, a fasciné les révolutionnaires socialistes, les fascine aujourd'hui plus que jamais[1]. Les journées de 1830, les doubles journées de 1848, les mois de la Commune ont contribué à former, ont complété comme un code révolutionnaire. Jamais comme aujourd'hui les partis révolutionnaires, les comités, les commissions, les congrès, les conseils n'ont été liés, ne se sont liés, ne se sont figés, n'ont lié leurs commettants et leurs commis par autant de cérémonial, par autant d'étiquette, par autant d'habitude, par autant de protocole, par autant de tradition, par autant de conservation.

Par une ingratitude mentale singulière, les gouver-

nements révolutionnaires, les autorités socialistes
opposent à la raison, à la liberté, dont ils sont nés, des
traditions supplémentaires, des conservations surencombrantes. La raison ne doit se soumettre à ces
traditions onéreuses ni parce qu'elles sont traditionnelles, ni parce qu'elles sont révolutionnaires. Imiter
les anciens révolutionnaires, les vieux révoltés, ne
consiste pas à penser en face du monde que nous
connaissons identiquement les pensées qu'ils avaient
en face du monde qui leur était contemporain. Mais
c'est les imiter bien que d'avoir en face du monde que
nous connaissons la même attitude, le même sentiment de liberté, de raison, qu'ils avaient en face de
leur monde. Imiter servilement, ponctuellement leurs
idées, comme on accepterait un héritage inerte, mort,
avoir en face du monde présent les idées qu'ils avaient
en face du monde passé, recommencer nos anciens,
qui étaient justement des révolutionnaires parce qu'ils
ne recommençaient pas leurs anciens, calquer leurs
idées, ce serait n'imiter ni leur conduite, ni leur
méthode, ni leur action, ni leur vie. Ce serait n'imiter
pas l'usage qu'ils ont fait de la raison.

Imiter bien les anciens révolutionnaires, c'est nous
placer librement en face du monde comme ils se
plaçaient librement en face du monde. Ce n'est pas
nous placer servilement en face de leur monde. C'est
user de la raison comme ils en usaient, sans aucun
artifice d'école ni retard factice. Pas plus que nous ne
devons attacher à la révolution sociale et imposer aux
humanités futures nos systèmes, nous ne devons pas
plus leur imposer des systèmes hérités, fussent-ils
hérités de révolutionnaires. Nous ne devons pas leur
imposer, leur communiquer en passant par nous des

systèmes anciens. Nous ne devons pas plus transmettre des autorités que nous ne devons en instituer.
L'opération serait la même. Que le système imposé
plus tard au nom de la révolution soit né parmi nous
ou que nous l'ayons nous-mêmes reçu de nos aînés, le
résultat serait le même. Ce serait toujours marquer
l'humanité au lieu de la libérer. Ce serait toujours
marchander et fausser l'affranchissement. Ce serait
toujours opprimer la raison, faire sur la raison libre
peser les anciennes œuvres d'une raison moins libre.
Ce serait toujours monnayer la servitude économique
pour avantager déloyalement le personnel révolutionnaire.

Nous n'apportons pas avec nous, nous n'apportons
ni comme une invention ni comme un héritage des
sentiments inédits, fabriqués exprès pour nous, et
portant la marque de cette fabrication. Nous n'entendons pas remplacer, suppléer, remettre au magasin les
vieux sentiments qui ont fait la joie ou la consolation,
le bonheur et la beauté du monde. Nous n'avons pas
des sentiments nouveaux qui remplaceraient l'antique
amour, l'amitié, les affections, les sentiments et les
passions de l'amour, les sentiments et les passions de
l'art, des sciences, de la philosophie. Nous ne sommes
pas des dieux qui créons des mondes. Nous voulons
devenir des économes utiles, des gérants avisés, des
ménagers diligents. Nous ne demandons pas à créer
des animalités ni des humanités, mais modestes nous
demandons que les biens économiques de la présente
humanité soient administrés pour le mieux, afin que
la servitude économique étant soulevée des nuques,
les têtes libres se redressent, les corps vivent en santé,
les âmes aussi. Nous sommes avant tout modestes. Un

socialisme orgueilleux serait une aberration. Un métaphysique serait criminel ou fou.

La raison ne procède pas de la pédagogie. Nous touchons ici au plus grave danger du temps présent. Malgré la complicité des mots mêmes, il ne faut pas que la pédagogie soit de la démagogie. C'est la pédagogie qui doit s'inspirer de la raison, se guider sur la raison, se modeler sur la raison. Il ne faut pas qu'après avoir souffert de notre négligence le peuple aujourd'hui soit déformé par notre complaisance. Il ne faut pas qu'ayant souffert de l'ignorance où il était laissé, il soit aujourd'hui déformé par un demi-savoir, qui est toujours un faux savoir. C'est l'immense danger de l'enseignement primaire, à programmes encyclopédiques indigestes, c'est encore plus l'immense danger de l'enseignement primaire supérieur, c'est au plus haut degré l'immense danger et l'immense difficulté des universités populaires [1]. Des individus admirablement dévoués, parfaitement sages, des personnes entendues, préviennent, évitent le danger, tournent, surmontent la difficulté, mais elles sont aussi les premières à les avoir mesurés. Ceux qui aiment le primaire, les instituteurs et le peuple, au lieu de les exploiter, en sont justement soucieux.

Ce serait fausser irréparablement l'esprit du peuple, ce serait donc trahir la raison la plus nombreuse, faire déraisonner la raison la plus nombreuse, encourager l'insanité générale, cultiver la démence et semer à pleines mains la déraison que de faire ou de laisser croire au peuple des travailleurs manuels, aux différents degrés de l'enseignement primaire, que le travail de la raison obtient ses résultats sans peine, sans effort et sans apprentissage. D'autant plus que le peuple sait fort bien, le peuple admet fort bien, mieux que les bourgeois, le peuple connaît par son expérience professionnelle que dans aucun ordre du travail manuel on n'obtient des résultats gratuits, donnés. Dans tous les métiers manuels tout le monde sait qu'il faut qu'on travaille et qu'il faut qu'on ait appris. Par quelle injuste infériorité, ou par quelle complaisance au fond démagogique, par quelle flatterie ferait-on croire ou laisserait-on croire au peuple que la science, que l'art et que la philosophie, que les travaux intellectuels, que les travaux de la raison ne sont pas aussi sérieux.

Ce serait rendre à la démocratie le pire des mauvais services que de vulgariser, d'étendre au peuple des ouvriers l'ancien préjugé nobiliaire. Il ne faut pas que le peuple non plus veuille tout savoir sans avoir jamais rien appris. Il ne faut pas que le peuple non plus ne se soit donné la peine que de naître peuple. Jamais on n'aurait l'idée de faire du pain sans avoir appris la boulangerie, ni de labourer sans savoir le labourage. Pourquoi veut-on traiter des grands problèmes sans avoir fait l'apprentissage indispensable. On accorde à peu près à la science qu'elle exige un apprentissage; mais on le dénie trop souvent aux lettres, aux arts, à la philosophie. On introduirait ainsi la présomption la plus dangereuse; on se préparerait les déceptions les plus graves, les plus méritées. Ce qu'on doit enseigner au peuple, ce n'est ni une vanité, ni un orgueil, c'est la modestie intellectuelle, et cette justesse qui est la justice de la raison. Au lieu de le lancer sur l'existence, ou, ce qui revient au même, sur l'inexistence de Dieu, sur l'immortalité de l'âme ou sur sa survivance ou sur sa mortalité, sur le déterminisme ou l'indéterminisme, sur le matérialisme ou la philosophie de l'histoire, enseignons-lui modestement des matières plus prêtes. Cela seul sera probe. Et c'est seulement ainsi que nous le respecterons.

Non pas que nous voulions interdire au peuple l'accès de la raison. C'est nous au contraire qui ne voulons pas qu'il aille se casser le nez à de fausses portes. Nous demandons qu'il avance raisonnablement, sagement, rationnellement dans les voies de la raison, aussi loin qu'il peut, mais en toute probité. La raison n'use pas du mensonge, quand même le faux serait plus court. Si l'on est en face d'un auditoire qui n'entend pas la démonstration du théorème afférent au carré de l'hypoténuse, il ne faut pas fabriquer une démonstration fausse mais saisissable aboutissant à la même proposition et la présenter au peuple avec cette arrière tranquillité que ça ne fait rien puisque la vraie démonstration fournit une assurance éternellement valable, une certitude. Non, mais on dit honnêtement à ceux qui ne sont pas géomètres : Les géomètres démontrent que le carré construit sur l'hypoténuse est équivalent à la somme des carrés construits sur les côtés de l'angle droit. — Il ne faut pas oublier que la plupart des grands problèmes sont plus difficiles et demandent plus de préparation que le théorème du carré de l'hypoténuse.

Non pas que pour assurer l'indépendance, la pleine liberté de la raison, nous voulions lui instituer quelque royaume en dehors et au-dessus de l'humanité. C'est dans l'humanité même et pour l'humanité que nous entendons que la raison fonctionne. C'est l'intérêt commun de la raison et de l'humanité que l'humanité entende la voix de la raison. Les deux intérêts sont ici

inséparables. Mais le fonctionnement, le travail de la
raison a ceci de propre, que dans ce travail on ne doit
rien sacrifier à la réussite extérieure. Il faut que la
raison pénètre de plus en plus l'humanité ; il faut que
la raison s'insère de plus en plus dans l'action, mais à
cette condition que par cette pénétration, par cette
insertion la raison ne soit jamais entamée. Les avantages que la raison tire de son travail propre et les
avantages que la raison et l'humanité tirent de sa
propagation ne sont pas des avantages du même ordre
qui se balancent et peuvent s'équivaloir. Mais les
avantages propres de la raison travaillant sont rigoureusement conditionnels, constituent la condition
indispensable sans quoi l'avantage extérieur est
annulé.

On doit travailler de son mieux à faire avancer la
raison dans son travail propre ; on doit travailler de
son mieux à faire entrer la raison dans l'action de
l'humanité, mais ces deux efforts ne sont pas du même
ordre ; le deuxième est rigoureusement conditionné
par le premier. Le premier est absolument libre du
deuxième.

La raison n'est pas tout le monde. Nous savons, par
la raison même, que la force n'est pas négligeable, que
beaucoup de passions et de sentiments sont vénéra-
bles ou respectables, puissants, profonds. Nous savons
que la raison n'épuise pas la vie et même le meilleur
de la vie ; nous savons que les instincts et les
inconscients sont d'un être plus profondément existant sans doute. Nous estimons à leur valeur les
pensées confuses, les impressions, les pensées obs-
cures, les sentiments et même les sensations. Mais
nous demandons que l'on n'oublie pas que la raison

est pour l'humanité la condition rigoureusement indispensable. Nous ne pouvons sans la raison estimer à sa juste valeur tout ce qui n'est pas de la raison. Et la question même de savoir ce qui revient à la raison et ce qui ne revient pas à la raison, ce n'est que par le travail de la raison que nous pouvons nous la poser.

Ce que nous demandons seulement, mais nous le demandons sans aucune réserve, sans aucune limitation, ce n'est pas que la raison devienne et soit tout, c'est qu'il n'y ait aucun malentendu dans l'usage de la raison. Nous ne défendons pas la raison contre les autres manifestations de la vie. Nous la défendons contre les manifestations qui, étant autres, veulent se donner pour elle et dégénèrent ainsi en déraisons. Nous ne la défendons pas contre les passions, contre les instincts, contre les sentiments comme tels, mais contre les démences, contre les insanités. Nous demandons que l'on ne fasse pas croire au peuple qu'on parle au nom de la raison quand on emploie des moyens qui ne sont pas les moyens de la raison. La raison a ses moyens propres, qu'elle emploie dans les arts, dans les lettres, dans les sciences et dans la philosophie. Ces moyens ne sont nullement disqualifiés pour l'étude que nous devons faire des phénomènes sociaux. Ce n'est pas quand la matière de l'étude est particulièrement complexe, mouvante, libre, difficile, que nous pouvons nous démunir d'un outil important, ou que nous devons le fausser.

NOTRE JEUNESSE

Une famille de républicains fouriéristes. — **les Milliet.**
— Après tant d'heureuses rencontres, après les
cahiers de Vuillaume [1] c'est une véritable bonne
fortune pour nos *cahiers* que de pouvoir commencer
aujourd'hui la publication de ces archives d'une
famille républicaine. Quand M. Paul Milliet m'en
apporta les premières propositions, avec cette ingué-
rissable modestie des gens qui apportent vraiment
quelque chose il ne manqua point de commencer par
s'excuser, disant : Vous verrez. Il y a là-dedans des
lettres de Victor Hugo, de Béranger. (Il voulait par là
s'excuser d'abord sur ce qu'il y avait, dans les papiers
qu'il m'apportait, des *documents* sur les grands
hommes, provenant de grands hommes, des documents *historiques,* sur les hommes *historiques,* et, naturellement, des documents inédits.) Il y a des lettres de
la conquête de l'Algérie, de l'expédition du Mexique,
de la guerre de Crimée. (Ou peut-être plutôt de la
guerre d'Italie.) (Il voulait s'excuser par là, alléguer
qu'il y avait, dans ces papiers, des documents *historiques,* sur les grands événements de l'*histoire,* provenant,
venant directement des grands événements, et natu-

rellement des documents authentiques, et naturellement des documents inédits.) Je lui répondis non.

Je lui dis non vous comprenez. Ne vous excusez pas.
Glorifiez-vous au contraire. Des lettres de Béranger,
des lettres de Victor Hugo, il y en a plein la chambre.
Nous en avons par-dessus la tête. Il y en a plein les
bibliothèques et c'est même de cela (et pour cela) que
les bibliothèques sont faites. C'est même de cela que
les bibliothécaires aussi sont faits. Et nous autres aussi
les amis des bibliothécaires. Nous en avons nous en
avons nous en avons. On nous en publie encore tous
les jours. Et quand il n'y en aura plus on en publiera
encore. Parce que, dans le besoin, nous en ferons. Que
dis-je, nous en faisons, on en fait. Et la famille nous
aidera à en faire. Parce que ça fera toujours des droits
d'auteur à toucher.

Mais ce que nous voulons avoir, *ce que nous ne pouvons
pas faire,* c'est précisément les lettres de gens qui ne
sont pas Victor Hugo. Quinet, Raspail, Blanqui, —
Fourier, — c'est très bien. Mais ce que nous voulons
savoir, c'est exactement, c'est précisément quelles
troupes avaient derrière eux, quelles admirables
troupes, ces penseurs et ces chefs républicains, ces
grands fondateurs de la République.

Voilà ce que nous voulons avoir, ce que nul ne peut
faire, ce que nul ne peut controuver.

Sur les grands patrons, sur les chefs l'histoire nous
renseignera toujours, tant bien que mal, plutôt mal
que bien, c'est son métier, et à défaut de l'histoire les
historiens, et à défaut des historiens les professeurs
(d'histoire). Ce que nous voulons savoir et ce que
nous ne pouvons pas inventer, ce que nous voulons
connaître, ce que nous voulons apprendre, ce n'est

point les premiers rôles, les grands masques, le grand
jeu, les grandes marques, le théâtre et la représentation ; ce que nous voulons savoir c'est ce qu'il y avait
derrière, ce qu'il y avait dessous, comment était fait ce
peuple de France, enfin ce que nous voulons savoir
c'est quel était, en cet âge héroïque, le *tissu* même du
peuple et du parti républicain. Ce que nous voulons
faire, c'est bien de l'*histologie* ethnique. Ce que nous
voulons savoir c'est de quel tissu était tissé, tissu ce
peuple et ce parti, comment vivait une famille républicaine *ordinaire,* moyenne pour ainsi dire, obscure, prise
au hasard, pour ainsi dire, prise dans le tissu ordinaire, prise et taillée à plein drap, à même le drap, ce
qu'on y croyait, ce qu'on y pensait, — ce qu'on y
faisait, car c'étaient des hommes d'action, — ce qu'on
y écrivait ; comment on s'y mariait, comment on y
vivait, de quoi, comment on y élevait les enfants ; —
comment on y naissait, d'abord, car on naissait, dans
ce temps-là ; — comment on y travaillait ; comment
on y parlait ; comment on y écrivait ; et si l'on y faisait
des vers quels vers on y faisait ; dans quelle terre enfin,
dans quelle terre commune, dans quelle terre ordinaire, sur quel terreau, sur quel terrain, dans quel
terroir, sous quels cieux, dans quel climat poussèrent
les grands poètes et les grands écrivains. Dans quelle
terre de pleine terre poussa cette grande République.
Ce que nous voulons savoir, c'est ce que c'était, c'est
quel était le tissu même de la bourgeoisie, de la
République, du peuple quand la bourgeoisie était
grande, quand le peuple était grand, quand les
républicains étaient héroïques et que la République
avait les mains pures. Pour tout dire quand les
républicains étaient républicains et que la république

était la république. Ce que nous voulons voir et avoir
ce n'est point une histoire endimanchée, c'est l'histoire de tous les jours de la semaine, c'est un peuple
dans la texture, dans la tissure, dans le tissu de sa
quotidienne existence, dans l'acquêt, dans le gain,
dans le labeur du pain de chaque jour, *panem quotidianum* [1], c'est une race dans son réel, dans son épanouis-
sement profond.

Maintenant s'il y a des lettres de Victor Hugo et des
vers de Béranger, nous ne ferons pas exprès de les
éliminer. D'abord Hugo et Béranger sortaient de ces
gens-là. Mais avec ces familles-là il faut toujours se
méfier des procès.

Comment vivaient ces hommes qui furent nos
ancêtres et que nous reconnaissons pour nos maîtres.
Quels ils étaient profondément, communément, dans
le laborieux train de la vie ordinaire, dans le laborieux
train de la pensée ordinaire, dans l'admirable train du
dévouement de chaque jour. Ce que c'était que le
peuple du temps qu'il y avait un peuple. Ce que
c'était que la bourgeoisie du temps qu'il y avait une
bourgeoisie. Ce que c'était qu'une race du temps qu'il
y avait une race, du temps qu'il y avait cette race, et
qu'elle poussait. Ce que c'était que la conscience et le
cœur d'un peuple, d'une bourgeoisie et d'une race. Ce
que c'était que la République enfin du temps qu'il y
avait une République : voilà ce que nous voulons
savoir ; voilà très précisément ce que M. Paul Milliet
nous apporte.

Comment travaillait ce peuple, qui aimait le travail, *universus universum,* qui tout entier aimait le travail
tout entier, qui était laborieux et encore plus travailleur, qui se délectait à travailler, qui travaillait tout

entier ensemble, bourgeoisie et peuple, dans la joie et dans la santé; qui avait un véritable culte du travail; un culte, une religion du travail bien fait. Du travail fini. Comment tout un peuple, toute une race, amis, ennemis, tous adversaires, tous profondément amis, était gonflée de sève et de santé et de joie, c'est ce que l'on trouvera dans les archives, parlons modestement dans les papiers de cette famille républicaine.

On y verra ce que c'était qu'une culture, comment c'était infiniment autre (infiniment plus précieux) qu'une science, une archéologie, un enseignement, un renseignement, une érudition et naturellement un système. On y verra ce que c'était que la culture du temps que les professeurs ne l'avaient point écrasée. On y verra ce que c'était qu'un peuple du temps que le primaire ne l'avait point oblitéré.

On y verra ce que c'était qu'une culture du temps qu'il y avait une culture; comment c'est presque indéfinissable, tout un âge, tout un monde dont aujourd'hui nous n'avons plus l'idée.

On y verra ce que c'était que la moelle même de notre race, ce que c'était que le tissu cellulaire et médullaire. Ce qu'était une famille française. On y verra des caractères. On y verra tout ce que nous ne voyons plus, tout ce que nous ne voyons pas aujourd'hui. Comment les enfants faisaient leurs études du temps qu'il y avait des études.

Enfin tout ce que nous ne voyons plus aujourd'hui.

On y verra dans le tissu même ce que c'était qu'une cellule, une famille; non point une de ces familles qui fondèrent des dynasties, les grandes dynasties républicaines; mais une de ces familles qui étaient comme des dynasties de peuple *républicaines*. Les dynasties du tissu commun de la République.

Ces familles qui justement comptent pour nous parce qu'elles sont du tissu commun.

Un certain nombre, un petit nombre peut-être de ces familles, de ces communes dynasties, s'alliant généralement entre elles, se tissant elles-mêmes entre elles comme des fils, par filiation, par alliance ont fait, ont fourni toute l'histoire non pas seulement de la République, mais du peuple de la République. Ce sont ces familles, presque toujours les mêmes familles, qui ont tissé l'histoire de ce que les historiens nommeront le mouvement républicain et que nous nommerons résolument, qu'il faut nommer la publication de la mystique républicaine. L'affaire Dreyfus aura été le dernier sursaut, le soubresaut suprême de cet héroïsme et de cette mystique, sursaut héroïque entre tous, elle aura été la dernière manifestation de cette race, le dernier effort, d'héroïsme, la dernière manifestation, la dernière publication de ces familles.

Halévy croirait aisément, et je croirais bien volontiers avec lui qu'un petit nombre de familles fidèles, ayant fondé la République, l'ont ainsi maintenue et sauvée, la maintiennent encore. La maintiennent-elles autant? A travers tout un siècle et plus, en un certain sens, presque depuis la deuxième moitié du dix-huitième siècle. Je croirais bien volontiers avec lui qu'un petit nombre de fidélités familiales, dynastiques, héréditaires ont maintenu, maintiennent la tradition, la mystique et ce que Halévy nommerait très justement la *conservation* républicaine. Mais où je ne croirais peut-être pas avec lui, c'est que je crois que nous en sommes littéralement les derniers représentants, et à moins que nos enfants ne s'y mettent, presque les survivants, posthumes.

En tout cas les derniers *témoins*.

Je veux dire très exactement ceci : nous ne savons pas encore si nos enfants renoueront le fil de la tradition, de la conservation républicaine, si se joignant à nous par-dessus la génération intermédiaire ils maintiendront, ils retrouveront le sens et l'instinct de la mystique républicaine. Ce que nous savons, ce que nous voyons, ce que nous connaissons de toute certitude, c'est que pour l'instant nous sommes l'arrière-garde.

Pourquoi le nier. Toute la génération intermédiaire a perdu le sens républicain, le goût de la République, l'instinct, plus sûr que toute connaissance, l'instinct de la mystique républicaine. Elle est devenue totalement étrangère à cette mystique. La génération intermédiaire, et ça fait vingt ans.

Vingt-cinq ans d'âge et au moins vingt ans de durée.

Nous sommes l'arrière-garde ; et non seulement une arrière-garde, mais une arrière-garde un peu isolée, quelquefois presque abandonnée. Une troupe en l'air. Nous sommes presque des *spécimens*. Nous allons être, nous-mêmes nous allons être des archives, des archives et des tables, des fossiles, des témoins, des survivants de ces âges historiques. Des tables que l'on consultera.

Nous sommes extrêmement mal situés. Dans la chronologie. Dans la succession des générations. Nous sommes une arrière-garde mal liée, non liée au gros de la troupe, aux générations antiques. Nous sommes la dernière des générations qui ont la mystique républicaine. Et notre affaire Dreyfus aura été la dernière des opérations de la mystique républicaine.

Nous sommes les derniers. Presque les après-derniers. Aussitôt après nous commence un autre âge, un tout autre monde, le monde de ceux qui ne croient plus à rien, qui s'en font gloire et orgueil.

Aussitôt après nous commence le monde que nous avons nommé, que nous ne cesserons pas de nommer le monde moderne. Le monde qui fait le malin. Le monde des intelligents, des avancés, de ceux qui savent, de ceux à qui on n'en remontre pas, de ceux à qui on n'en fait pas accroire. Le monde de ceux à qui on n'a plus rien à apprendre. Le monde de ceux qui font le malin. Le monde de ceux qui ne sont pas des dupes, des imbéciles. Comme nous. *C'est-à-dire :* le monde de ceux qui ne croient à rien, pas même à l'athéisme, qui ne se dévouent, qui ne se sacrifient à rien. *Exactement :* le monde de ceux qui n'ont pas de mystique. Et qui s'en vantent. Qu'on ne s'y trompe pas, et que personne par conséquent ne se réjouisse, ni d'un côté ni de l'autre. Le mouvement de *dérépublicanisation* de la France est profondément le même mouvement que le mouvement de sa *déchristianisation*. C'est ensemble un même, un seul mouvement profond de *démystication*. C'est du même mouvement profond, d'un seul mouvement, que ce peuple ne croit plus à la République et qu'il ne croit plus à Dieu, qu'il ne veut plus mener la vie républicaine, et qu'il ne veut plus mener la vie chrétienne, (qu'il en a assez), on pourrait presque dire qu'il ne veut plus croire aux idoles et qu'il ne veut plus croire au vrai Dieu. *La même* incrédulité, *une seule* incrédulité atteint les idoles et Dieu, atteint ensemble les faux dieux et le vrai Dieu, les dieux antiques, le Dieu nouveau, les dieux anciens et le Dieu des chrétiens. Une même stérilité dessèche la cité et la chrétienté. La cité politique et la cité chrétienne. La cité des hommes et la cité de Dieu. C'est proprement la stérilité moderne. Que nul donc ne se réjouisse, voyant le malheur qui arrive à l'ennemi, à l'adversaire, au voisin. Car *le même* malheur, *la même* stérilité lui arrive. Comme je l'ai mis tant de fois dans ces cahiers, du temps qu'on ne me lisait pas, le débat n'est pas proprement entre la République et la Monarchie, entre la République et la Royauté, surtout si on les considère comme des formes politiques, comme deux formes politiques, il n'est point seulement, il n'est point exactement entre l'ancien régime et le nouveau régime français, le monde moderne ne s'oppose pas seulement à l'ancien régime français, il s'oppose, il se contrarie à toutes les anciennes cultures ensemble, à tous les anciens régimes ensemble, à toutes les anciennes cités ensemble, à tout ce qui est culture, à tout ce qui est cité. C'est en effet la première fois dans l'histoire du monde que tout un monde vit et prospère, *paraît* prospérer *contre toute culture*.

Que l'on m'entende bien. Je ne dis pas que c'est pour toujours. Cette race en a vu bien d'autres. Mais enfin c'est pour le temps présent.

Et nous y sommes.

Nous avons même des raisons très profondes d'espérer que ce ne sera pas pour longtemps.

Nous sommes extrêmement mal situés. Nous sommes en effet historiquement situés à un point critique, à un point de discernement, à ce point de

discrimination. Nous sommes situés juste entre les
générations qui ont la mystique républicaine et celles
qui ne l'ont pas, entre celles qui l'ont encore et celles
qui ne l'ont plus. Alors personne ne veut nous croire.
Des deux côtés. *Neutri*, ni les uns ni les autres des
deux. Les vieux républicains ne veulent pas croire
qu'il n'y a plus des jeunes républicains. Les jeunes
gens ne veulent pas croire qu'il y a eu des vieux
républicains.

Nous sommes entre les deux. Nul ne veut donc nous
croire. Ni les uns ni les autres. Pour tous les deux nous
avons tort. Quand nous disons aux vieux républicains : Faites attention, après nous il n'y a personne,
ils haussent les épaules. Ils croient qu'il y en aura
toujours. Et quand nous disons aux jeunes gens :
Faites attention, ne parlez point si légèrement de la
République, elle n'a pas toujours été un amas de
politiciens, elle a derrière elle une mystique, elle a en
elle une mystique, elle a derrière elle tout un passé de
gloire, tout un passé d'honneur, et ce qui est peut-être
plus important encore, plus près de l'essence, tout un
passé de race, d'héroïsme, peut-être de sainteté,
quand nous disons cela aux jeunes gens, ils nous
méprisent doucement et déjà nous traiteraient de
vieilles barbes.

Ils nous prendraient pour des maniaques.

Je répète que je ne dis point que c'est pour toujours.
Les raisons les plus profondes, les indices les plus
graves nous font croire au contraire, nous forcent à
penser que la génération suivante, la génération qui
vient après celle qui vient immédiatement après nous,
et qui bientôt sera la génération de nos enfants, va être
enfin une génération mystique. Cette race a trop de

sang dans les veines pour demeurer l'espace de plus
d'une génération dans les cendres et dans les moisis-
sures de la critique. Elle est trop vivante pour ne pas
se réintégrer, au bout d'une génération, dans l'organique.

Tout fait croire que les deux mystiques vont
refleurir à la fois, la républicaine et la chrétienne. Du
même mouvement. D'un seul mouvement profond,
comme elles disparaissaient ensemble, (momentané-
ment), comme ensemble elles s'oblitéraient. Mais
enfin ce que je dis vaut pour le temps présent, pour
tout le temps présent. Et dans l'espace d'une génération il peut se produire tout de même bien des
événements.

Il peut arriver des malheurs.

Telle est notre maigre situation. Nous sommes
maigres. Nous sommes minces. Nous sommes une
lamelle. Nous sommes comme écrasés, comme aplatis
entre toutes les générations antécédentes, d'une part,
et d'autre part une couche déjà épaisse des générations suivantes. Telle est la raison principale de notre
maigreur, de la petitesse de notre situation. Nous
avons la tâche ingrate, la maigre tâche, le petit office,
le maigre devoir de faire communiquer, par nous, les
uns avec les autres, d'assurer la communication entre
les uns et les autres, d'avertir les uns et les autres, de
renseigner les uns sur les autres. Nous serons donc
généralement conspués de part et d'autre. C'est le sort
commun de quiconque essaie de dire un peu de
vérité(s).

Nous sommes chargés, comme par hasard, de faire
communiquer par nous entre eux des gens qui précisé-

ment ne veulent pas communiquer. Nous sommes chargés de renseigner des gens qui précisément ne veulent pas être renseignés.

Telle est notre ingrate situation.

Nous retournant donc vers les anciens, nous ne pouvons pourtant dire et faire, nous ne pouvons que répéter à ces républicains antécédents : Prenez garde. Vous ne soupçonnez pas, vous ne pouvez pas imaginer à quel point vous n'êtes pas suivis, à quel point nous sommes les derniers, à quel point votre régime se creuse en dedans, se creuse par la base. Vous tenez la tête, naturellement, vous tenez le faîte. Mais toute année qui vient, toute année qui passe vous pousse d'un cran, fait de votre faîte une pointe plus amincie, plus tremblante, plus seulette, plus creusée en dessous. Et déjà dix, quinze, bientôt vingt annuités, annualités de jeunes gens vous manquent à la base.

Vous tenez la pointe, vous tenez le faîte, vous tenez la tête, mais ce n'est qu'une position de temps, une situation comme géographique, historique, temporelle, temporaire, chronologique, chronographique. Ce n'est qu'une situation par le fait de la situation. Ce n'est pas, ce n'est nullement une situation organique. La situation à la pointe, la situation de pointe du bourgeon qui organiquement, végétalement mène l'arbre, tire tout l'arbre à lui. Et par où il a passé tout l'arbre passera.

Je suis épouvanté quand je vois, quand je constate simplement ce que nos anciens ne veulent pas voir, ce qui est l'évidence même, ce qu'il suffit de vouloir bien regarder : combien nos jeunes gens sont devenus étrangers à tout ce qui fut la pensée même et la

mystique républicaine. Cela se voit surtout, et naturellement, comme cela se voit toujours, à ce que des
pensées qui étaient pour nous des pensées sont
devenues pour eux des idées, à ce que ce qui était pour
nous, pour nos pères, un instinct, une race, des
pensées, est devenu pour eux des *propositions,* à ce que
ce qui était pour nous organique est devenu pour eux
logique.

Des pensées, des instincts, des races, des habitudes
qui pour nous étaient la nature même, qui allaient de
soi, dont on vivait, qui étaient le type même de la vie,
à qui par conséquent on ne pensait même pas, qui
étaient plus que légitimes, plus qu'indiscutées : irrai-
sonnées, sont devenues ce qu'il y a de pire au monde :
des thèses, historiques, des hypothèses, je veux dire ce
qu'il y a de moins solide, de plus inexistant. Des
dessous de thèses. Quand un régime, d'organique est
devenu logique, et de vivant historique, c'est un
régime qui est par terre.

On prouve, on démontre aujourd'hui la République. Quand elle était vivante on ne la prouvait pas.

On la vivait. Quand un régime se démontre,
aisément, commodément, victorieusement, c'est qu'il
est creux, c'est qu'il est par terre.

Aujourd'hui la République est une thèse, acceptée,
par les jeunes gens. Acceptée, refusée ; indifféremment ; cela n'a pas d'importance ; prouvée, réfutée. Ce
qui importe, ce qui est grave, ce qui signifie, ce n'est
pas que ce soit appuyé ou soutenu, plus ou moins
indifféremment, c'est que ce soit une thèse.

C'est-à-dire, précisément, *qu'il faille* l'appuyer ou la
soutenir.

Quand un régime est une thèse, parmi d'autres,

(parmi tant d'autres), il est par terre. Un régime qui est debout, qui tient, qui est vivant, n'est pas une thèse.

— Qu'importe, nous disent les politiciens, professionnels. Qu'est-ce que ça nous fait, répondent les politiciens, qu'est-ce que ça peut nous faire. Nous avons de très bons préfets. Alors qu'est-ce que ça peut nous faire. Ça marche très bien. Nous ne sommes plus républicains, c'est vrai, mais nous savons gouverner. Nous savons même mieux gouverner, beaucoup mieux que quand nous étions républicains, disent-ils. Ou plutôt quand nous étions républicains nous ne savions pas du tout. Et à présent, ajoutent-ils modestement, à présent nous savons un peu. Nous avons désappris la République, mais nous avons appris de gouverner. Voyez les élections. Elles sont bonnes. Elles sont toujours bonnes. Elles seront meilleures. Elles seront d'autant meilleures que c'est nous qui les faisons. Et que nous commençons à savoir les faire. La droite a perdu un million de voix. Nous lui en eussions aussi bien fait perdre cinquante millions et demi. Mais nous sommes mesurés. Le gouvernement fait les élections, les élections font le gouvernement. C'est un prêté rendu. Le gouvernement fait les électeurs. Les électeurs font le gouvernement. Le gouvernement fait les députés. Les députés font le gouvernement. On est gentil. Les populations regardent. Le pays est prié de payer. Le gouvernement fait la Chambre. La Chambre fait le gouvernement. Ce n'est point un cercle vicieux, comme vous pourriez le croire. Il n'est point du tout vicieux. C'est un cercle, tout court, un circuit parfait, un cercle fermé. Tous les cercles sont fermés. Autrement ça ne serait pas des cercles. Ce n'est pas tout à fait ce que nos fondateurs avaient prévu. Mais nos fondateurs ne s'en tiraient pas déjà si bien. Et puis enfin on ne peut pas fonder toujours. Ça fatiguerait. La preuve que ça dure, la preuve que ça tient, c'est que ça dure déjà depuis quarante ans. Il y en a pour quarante siècles. C'est les premiers quarante ans qui sont les plus durs. C'est le premier quarante ans qui coûte. Après on est habitué. Un pays, un régime n'a pas besoin de vous, il n'a pas besoin de mystiques, de mystique, de sa mystique. Ce serait plutôt embarrassant. Pour un aussi grand voyage. Il a besoin d'une bonne politique, c'est-à-dire d'une politique bien gouvernementale.

Ils se trompent. Ces politiciens se trompent. Du haut de cette République quarante siècles (d'avenir) ne les contemplent pas. Si la République marche depuis quarante ans, c'est parce que tout marche depuis quarante ans. Si la République est solide en France, ce n'est pas parce que la République est solide en France, c'est parce que tout est solide partout. Il y a dans l'histoire moderne, et non pas dans toute l'histoire, il y a pour les peuples modernes de grandes vagues de crises, généralement parties de France (1789-1815, 1830, 1848) qui font tout trembler d'un bout du monde à l'autre bout. Et il y a des paliers, plus ou moins longs, des calmes, des bonaces qui apaisent tout pour un temps plus ou moins long. Il y a les *époques* et il y a les *périodes*. Nous sommes dans une période. Si la République est assise, ce n'est point

parce qu'elle est la Rébulique, (cette République), ce
n'est point par sa vertu propre, c'est parce qu'elle est,
parce que nous sommes dans une période, d'assiette.
La durée de la République ne prouve pas plus la
durée de la République que la durée des monarchies
voisines ne prouve la durée de la Monarchie. Cette
durée ne signifie point qu'elles sont durables, mais
qu'elles ont commencé, qu'elles sont dans une
période, durable. Qu'elles se sont trouvées comme ça,
dans une période, de durée. Elles sont contemporaines, elles trempent dans le même temps, dans le
même bain de durée. Elles baignent dans la même
période. Elles sont du même âge. Voilà tout ce que ça
prouve.

Quand donc des républicains arguënt de ce que la
République dure pour dire, pour proposer, pour faire
état, pour en faire cette proposition qu'elle est durable, quand ils arguënt de ce qu'elle dure depuis
quarante ans pour inférer, pour conclure, pour proposer qu'elle est durable, pour quarante ans, et plus,
qu'elle était au moins durable pour quarante ans,
qu'elle était valable, qu'elle avait un *bon* au moins
pour quarante ans, ils ont l'air de plaider l'évidence
même. Et pourtant ils font, ils commettent une
pétition, de principe, un dépassement d'attribution.
Car dans la République, qui dure, ce n'est point la
République, qui dure. C'est la durée. Ce n'est point
elle la République qui dure en elle-même, en soi-
même. Ce n'est point le régime qui dure en elle. Mais
en elle c'est le temps qui dure. C'est son temps, c'est
son âge. En elle ce qui dure c'est tout ce qui dure.
C'est la tranquillité d'une certaine période de l'huma-

nité, d'une certaine période de l'histoire, d'une certaine période, d'un certain palier historique.

Quand donc les républicains attribuent à la force propre du régime, à une certaine vertu de la République la durée de la République ils commettent à leur profit et au profit de la République un véritable dépassement de crédit, moral. Mais quand les réactionnaires par contre, les monarchistes nous montrent, nous font voir avec leur complaisance habituelle, égale et contraire à celle des autres, nous représentent, au titre d'un argument, la solidité, la tranquillité, la durée des monarchies voisines (et même, en un certain sens, leur prospérité, bien qu'ici, en un certain sens, ils aient quelquefois beaucoup plus raison), ils font exactement, de leur côté, non pas même seulement un raisonnement du même ordre, mais le même raisonnement. Ils font, ils commettent la même anticipation, une anticipation contraire, la même, une anticipation, une usurpation, un détournement, un débordement, un dépassement de crédit symétrique, antithétique, homothétique : la même anticipation, la même usurpation, le même détournement, le même débordement, le même dépassement de crédit.

Quand les républicains attribuent à la République, (aux républicains), (au peuple, aux citoyens), à l'assiette, à la tranquillité, à la solidité, à la durée de la République la durée de la République, ils attribuent à la République ce qui n'est pas d'elle mais du temps où elle se meut. Quand les monarchistes attribuent aux monarchies voisines, (aux monarques), (aux monarchistes, aux peuples, aux sujets), à leur assiette, à leur tranquillité, à leur solidité, à leur durée leur durée, ils attribuent à ces monarchies ce qui n'est pas d'elles mais du temps où elles se meuvent. Du même temps. Qui est le temps de tout le monde. Et cet escalier à double révolution centrale, cette symétrie, cet antithétisme homothétique des situations, cet appareillement des attributions n'a rien qui doive nous étonner. Les républicains et les monarchistes, les gouvernants républicains et les théoriciens monarchistes font le même raisonnement, commettent la même attribution, des attributions contraires, complémentaires, homothétiques, la même fausse attribution parce que tous les deux ils ont la même conception, les uns et les autres ils sont des intellectuels, tous les deux ensemble et séparément, tous les deux contrairement et ensemble ils sont des politiques, ils croient en un certain sens à la politique, ils parlent le langage politique, ils sont situés, ils se meuvent sur le plan (de la) politique. Ils parlent donc le même langage. Ensemble les uns et les autres. Ils se meuvent donc sur le même plan. Ils croient aux régimes, et qu'un régime fait ou ne fait pas la paix et la guerre, la force et la vertu, la santé et la maladie, l'assiette, la durée, la tranquillité d'un peuple. La force d'une race. C'est comme si l'on croyait que les châteaux de la Loire font ou ne font pas les tremblements de terre.

Nous croyons au contraire (au contraire des uns et des autres, au contraire de tous les deux ensemble) qu'il y a des forces et des réalités infiniment plus profondes, et que ce sont les peuples au contraire qui font la force et la faiblesse des régimes ; et beaucoup moins les régimes, des peuples.

Nous croyons que les uns et les autres ensemble ils ne voient pas, ils ne veulent pas voir ces forces, ces réalités infiniment plus profondes.

Si la République et les monarchies voisines jouissent de la même tranquillité, de la même durée, c'est qu'elles trempent, qu'elles baignent dans le même bain, dans la même période, qu'elles parcourent ensemble le même long palier. C'est qu'elles mènent la même vie, au fond, la même diète. Là-dessus les républicains et les monarchistes font des raisonnements contraires, le même raisonnement contraire, ils font des raisonnements conjugués. Nous au contraire, nous autres, nous plaçant sur un tout autre terrain, descendant sur un tout autre plan, essayant d'atteindre à de tout autres profondeurs, nous pensons, nous croyons au contraire que ce sont les peuples qui font les régimes, la paix et la guerre, la force et la faiblesse, la maladie et la santé des régimes.

Les républicains et les monarchistes ensemble, premièrement font des raisonnements, deuxièmement font des raisonnements conjugués, appariés, couplés, géminés.

Nous tournant donc vers les jeunes gens, nous tournant d'autre part, nous tournant de l'autre côté nous ne pouvons que dire et faire, nous ne pouvons que leur dire : Prenez garde. Vous nous traitez de vieilles bêtes. C'est bien. Mais prenez garde. Quand vous parlez à la légère, quand vous traitez légèrement, si légèrement la République, vous ne risquez pas seulement d'être injustes, (ce qui n'est peut-être rien, au moins vous le dites, dans votre système, mais ce qui, dans notre système, est grave, dans nos idées, considérable), vous risquez plus, dans votre système, même dans vos idées vous risquez d'être sots. Pour entrer dans votre système, dans votre langage même. Vous oubliez, vous méconnaissez qu'il y a eu une mystique républicaine ; et de l'oublier et de la méconnaître ne fera pas qu'elle n'ait pas été. Des hommes sont morts pour la liberté comme des hommes sont morts pour la foi. Ces élections aujourd'hui vous paraissent une formalité grotesque, universellement menteuse, truquée de toutes parts. Et vous avez le droit de le dire. Mais des hommes ont vécu, des hommes sans nombre, des héros, des martyrs, et je dirai des saints, — et quand je dis *des saints* je sais peut-être ce que je dis, — des hommes ont vécu sans nombre, héroïquement, saintement, des hommes ont souffert, des hommes sont morts, tout un peuple a vécu pour que le dernier des imbéciles aujourd'hui ait le droit d'accomplir cette formalité truquée. Ce fut un terrible, un laborieux, un redoutable enfantement. Ce ne fut pas toujours du dernier grotesque. Et des peuples autour de nous, des peuples entiers, des races travaillent du même enfantement douloureux, travaillent et luttent pour obtenir cette formalité dérisoire. Ces élections sont dérisoires. Mais il y a eu un temps, mon cher Variot [1], un temps héroïque où les malades et les mourants se faisaient porter dans des chaises pour aller *déposer leur bulletin dans l'urne*. Déposer son bulletin dans l'urne, cette expression vous paraît aujourd'hui du dernier grotesque. Elle a été préparée par un siècle d'héroïsme. Non pas d'héroïsme à la manque, d'un héroïsme à la littéraire. Par un siècle du plus incontestable, du plus authentique héroïsme. Et je dirai du plus français. Ces élections sont dérisoires.

Mais il y a eu une élection. C'est le grand partage du monde, la grande élection du monde moderne entre l'Ancien Régime et la Révolution. Et il y a eu un sacré ballottage, Variot, Jean Variot. Il y a eu ce petit ballottage qui commença au moulin de Valmy et qui finit à peine sur les hauteurs de Hougoumont. D'ailleurs ça a fini comme toutes les affaires politiques, par une espèce de compromis, de cote mal taillée entre les deux partis qui étaient en présence.

Ces élections sont dérisoires. Mais l'héroïsme et la sainteté avec lesquels, moyennant lesquels on obtient des résultats dérisoires, *temporellement* dérisoires, c'est tout ce qu'il y a de plus grand, de plus sacré au monde. C'est tout ce qu'il y a de plus beau. Vous nous reprochez la dégradation temporelle de ces résultats, de nos résultats. Voyez vous-mêmes. Voyez vos propres résultats. Vous nous parlez toujours de la dégradation républicaine. La dégradation de la mystique en politique n'est-elle pas une loi commune.

Vous nous parlez de la dégradation républicaine, c'est-à-dire, proprement, de la dégradation de la mystique républicaine en politique républicaine. N'y a-t-il pas eu, n'y a-t-il pas d'autres dégradations. Tout commence en mystique et finit en politique. Tout commence par *la* mystique, par une mystique, par sa (propre) mystique et tout finit par *de la* politique. La question, importante, n'est pas, il est important, il est intéressant que, mais l'intérêt, la question n'est pas que telle politique l'emporte sur telle ou telle autre et de savoir qui l'emportera de toutes les politiques. L'intérêt, la question, l'essentiel est que *dans chaque ordre, dans chaque système* **la mystique ne soit point dévorée par la politique à laquelle elle a donné naissance.**

L'essentiel n'est pas, l'intérêt n'est pas, la question n'est pas que telle ou telle politique triomphe, mais que dans chaque ordre, dans chaque système chaque mystique, cette mystique ne soit point dévorée par la politique issue d'elle.

En d'autres termes il importe peut-être, il importe évidemment que les républicains l'emportent sur les royalistes ou les royalistes sur les républicains, mais cette importance est infiniment peu, cet intérêt n'est rien en comparaison de ceci : que les républicains demeurent des républicains ; que les républicains soient des républicains.

Et j'ajouterai, et ce ne sera pas seulement pour la symétrie, complémentairement j'ajoute : que les royalistes soient, demeurent des royalistes. Or c'est peut-être ce qu'ils ne font pas en ce moment-ci même, où très sincèrement ils croient le faire le plus, l'être le plus.

Vous nous parlez toujours de la dégradation républicaine. N'y a-t-il point eu, par le même mouvement, n'y a-t-il point une dégradation monarchiste, une dégradation royaliste parallèle, complémentaire, symétrique, plus qu'analogue. C'est-à-dire, proprement parlant, une dégradation de la mystique monarchiste, royaliste en une certaine politique, issue d'elle, correspondante, en une, en la politique monarchiste, en la politique royaliste. N'avons-nous pas vu pendant des siècles, ne voyons-nous pas tous les jours les effets de cette politique. N'avons-nous pas assisté pendant des siècles à la dévoration de la mystique royaliste par la politique royaliste. Et aujourd'hui même, bien que ce parti ne soit pas au pouvoir, dans ses deux journaux principaux nous voyons, nous lisons tous les jours les effets, les misérables résultats d'une politique ; et même, je dirai plus, pour qui sait lire, un déchirement continuel, un combat presque douloureux, même à voir, même pour nous, un débat presque touchant, vraiment touchant entre une mystique et une politique, entre leur mystique et leur politique, entre la mystique royaliste et la politique royaliste, la mystique étant naturellement à l'*Action française,* sous des formes rationalistes qui n'ont jamais trompé qu'eux-mêmes, et la politique étant au *Gaulois,* comme d'habitude sous des formes mondaines. Que serait-ce s'ils étaient au pouvoir. (Comme nous, hélas.)

On nous parle toujours de la dégradation républicaine. Quand on voit ce que la politique cléricale a fait de la mystique chrétienne, comment s'étonner de ce que la politique radicale a fait de la mystique républicaine. Quand on voit ce que les clercs ont fait généralement des saints, comment s'étonner de ce que nos parlementaires ont fait des héros. Quand on voit ce que les réactionnaires ont fait de la sainteté, comment s'étonner de ce que les révolutionnaires ont fait de l'héroïsme.

Et alors il faut être juste, tout de même. Quand on veut comparer un ordre à un autre ordre, un système à un autre système, il faut les comparer par des plans et sur des plans du même étage. Il faut comparer les mystiques entre elles ; et les politiques entre elles. Il ne faut pas comparer une mystique à une politique ; ni une politique à une mystique. Dans toutes les écoles primaires de la République, et dans quelques-unes des secondaires, et dans beaucoup des supérieures on compare inlassablement la politique royaliste à la mystique républicaine. Dans l'*Action française* tout revient à ce qu'on compare presque inlassablement la politique républicaine à la mystique royaliste. Cela peut durer longtemps.

On ne s'entendra jamais. Mais c'est peut-être ce que demandent les partis.

C'est peut-être le jeu des partis.

Nos maîtres de l'école primaire nous avaient masqué la mystique de l'ancienne France, la mystique de l'ancien régime, ils nous avaient masqué dix siècles de l'ancienne France. Nos adversaires d'aujourd'hui nous veulent masquer cette mystique d'ancien régime, cette *mystique de l'ancienne France que fut la mystique républicaine.*

Et nommément la mystique révolutionnaire.

Car le débat n'est pas, comme on le dit, entre l'Ancien Régime et la Révolution. L'Ancien Régime était un régime de l'ancienne France. La Révolution est éminemment une opération de l'ancienne France. La date discriminante n'est pas le premier janvier 1789, entre minuit et minuit une. La date discriminante est située aux environs de 1881 [1].

Ici encore les républicains et les royalistes, les gouvernements, les gouvernants républicains et les théoriciens royalistes font le même raisonnement, un raisonnement en deux, complémentaires, deux raisonnements conjugués, complémentaires, conjugués.

Couplés ; géminés. Nos bons maîtres de l'école primaire nous disaient sensiblement : jusqu'au premier janvier 1789 (heure de Paris) notre pauvre France était un abîme de ténèbres et d'ignorance, de misères les plus effrayantes, des barbaries les plus grossières, (enfin ils faisaient leur leçon), et vous ne pouvez pas même vous en faire une idée ; le premier janvier 1789 on installa partout la lumière électrique. Nos bons adversaires de l'École d'en face nous disent presque : jusqu'au premier janvier 1789 brillait le soleil naturel ; depuis le premier janvier 1789 nous ne sommes plus qu'au régime de la lumière électrique. Les uns et les autres exagèrent.

Le débat n'est pas entre un ancien régime, une ancienne France qui finirait en 1789 et une nouvelle France qui commencerait en 1789. Le débat est beaucoup plus profond. Il est entre toute l'ancienne France ensemble, païenne (la Renaissance, les humanités, la culture, les lettres anciennes et modernes, grecques, latines, françaises), païenne et chrétienne, traditionnelle et révolutionnaire, monarchiste, royaliste et républicaine, — et d'autre part, et en face, et au contraire une certaine domination primaire, qui s'est établie vers 1881, qui n'est pas la République, qui se dit la République, qui parasite la République, qui est le plus dangereux ennemi de la République, qui est proprement la domination du parti intellectuel.

Le débat est entre toute cette culture, toute la culture, et toute cette barbarie, qui est proprement la barbarie.

Le débat n'est pas entre les héros et les saints ; le

combat est contre les intellectuels, contre ceux qui méprisent également les héros et les saints.

Le débat n'est point entre ces deux ordres de (la) grandeur. Le combat est contre ceux qui haïssent la grandeur même, qui haïssent également l'une et l'autre grandeurs, qui se sont faits les tenants officiels de la petitesse, de la bassesse, et de la vilenie.

C'est ce que l'on verra, ce qui éclate avec une évidence saisissante dans les *papiers* de cette *famille républicaine fouriériste*. Ou plutôt, car c'est un peu moins compact, un peu moins tassé, dans les *cahiers* de cette *famille de républicains fouriéristes*. Mon Dieu, s'il y a des lettres de Victor Hugo, eh bien, oui, nous les publierons. Nous ne serons pas méchants. Nous ne ferons pas exprès d'embêter cette grande mémoire. Mais ce que nous publierons surtout, ce sont les dossiers, ce sont les papiers des Milliet. On y verra comment le tissu même du parti républicain était héroïque, et ce qui est presque plus important combien il était cultivé ; combien il était classique ; en un mot, pour qui sait voir, pour qui sait lire, combien il était ancienne France, et, au fond, ancien régime.

On y verra ce que c'était que la pâte même dont le pain était fait.

Notre collaborateur M. Daniel Halévy a fort bien indiqué, dans ces cahiers mêmes, dans son dernier cahier, il a marqué seulement mais il a fort bien marqué que l'histoire de ce siècle ne va pas pour ainsi dire tout de go. Qu'elle n'est pas simple, unique, unilatérale, univoque, bloquée, blocarde, enfin elle-même qu'elle n'est pas un bloc; qu'elle ne va point toute et toujours dans le même sens; qu'elle n'est point d'un seul tenant. Il n'y a pas eu un ancien régime qui a duré des siècles; puis un jour une révolution qui a renversé l'ancien régime; puis des retours offensifs de l'ancien régime; et une lutte, un combat, un débat d'un siècle entre la révolution et l'ancien régime, entre l'ancien régime et la révolution. La réalité est beaucoup moins simple. Halévy a fort bien montré que la République avait, était une tradition, une conservation, elle aussi, (elle surtout peut-être), qu'il y avait une tradition, une conservation républicaine. La différence, la distance entre les deux hypothèses, entre les deux théories se voit surtout, surgit comme d'elle-même naturellement à certains points critiques, par exemple aux coups d'État. Dans la première théorie, dans la première hypothèse, dans l'hypothèse du bloc et de la rigidité, les deux coups d'État sont des mouvements du même ordre, du même sens, du même gabarit, de la même teneur. C'est un mouvement, le même mouvement en deux fois. Le deuxième coup d'État est le recommencement, le double, la réduplication du premier. La reprise du premier. Décembre est comme une deuxième édition de Brumaire. Brumaire était la première édition de Décembre. C'est ce qu'enseignent par un double enseignement, conjugué, par le même enseignement, par un enseignement conjugué, géminé, d'une part les instituteurs, d'autre part les réactionnaires. Pour les instituteurs et dans l'enseignement des instituteurs (notamment de Victor Hugo) les deux coups d'État sont deux crimes, un même crime, redoublé, le même crime, en deux temps. Pour les réactionnaires et dans l'enseignement des réactionnaires les deux coups d'État sont deux opérations de police, deux heureuses opérations de police, renouvelées l'une de l'autre, recommencées l'une de l'autre, redoublées l'une de l'autre. Recommandées l'une de l'autre.

Un mouvement en deux temps. Brumaire et Décembre. C'est la double idée de Hugo et des bonapartistes.

La réalité est beaucoup moins simple, beaucoup plus complexe et peut-être même beaucoup plus compliquée. La Révolution française fonda une tradition, amorcée déjà depuis un certain nombre d'années, une conservation, elle fonda un ordre nouveau. Que cet ordre nouveau ne valût pas l'ancien, c'est ce que beaucoup de bons esprits ont été amenés aujourd'hui à penser. Mais elle fonda certainement un ordre nouveau, non pas un désordre, comme les réactionnaires le disent. Cet ordre ensuite dégénéra en désordre(s), qui sous le Directoire atteignirent leur plus grande gravité. Dès lors si nous nommons, comme on le doit, *restaurations* les restaurations d'ordre, quel qu'il soit, d'un certain ordre, de l'un ou de l'autre ordre, et si nous nommons *perturbations* les introductions de désordre(s), le 18 Brumaire fut certainement une restauration (ensemble, inséparablement républicaine et monarchiste, ce qui lui confère un intérêt tout particulier, un ton propre, un sens propre, ce qui en fait une opération réellement très singulière, comparable à nulle autre, et qu'il faudrait étudier de près, à laquelle surtout il ne faut rien comparer dans toute l'histoire du dix-neuvième siècle français, et même et autant dans toute l'histoire de France, à laquelle enfin il ne faut référer, comparer nulle autre opération française, à laquelle on ne trouverait d'analogies que dans certaines opérations peut-être d'autres pays) ; (et surtout à qui il faut bien se garder de comparer surtout le 2 Décembre) ; 1830 fut une restauration, républicaine ; ah j'oubliais, on oublie toujours Louis XVIII ; la Restauration fut une restauration, monarchiste ; 1830 fut une restauration, républicaine ; 1848 fut une restauration républicaine, et une explosion de la mystique républicaine ; les journées de juin même furent une deuxième explosion, une explosion redoublée de la mystique républicaine ; au contraire le 2 Décembre fut une perturbation, une introduction d'un désordre, la plus grande perturbation peut-être qu'il y eut dans l'histoire du dix-neuvième siècle français ; il mit au monde, il introduisit, non pas seulement à la tête, mais dans le corps même, dans la nation, dans le tissu du corps politique et social un personnel nouveau, nullement mystique, purement politique et démagogique ; il fut proprement l'introduction d'une démagogie ; le 4 septembre fut une restauration, républicaine ; le 31 octobre, le 22 janvier même fut une journée républicaine ; le 18 mars même fut une journée républicaine, une restauration républicaine en un certain sens, et non pas seulement un mouvement de température, un coup de fièvre obsidionale, mais une deuxième révolte, une deuxième explosion de la mystique républicaine et nationaliste ensemble, républicaine et ensemble, inséparablement patriot(iqu)e ; les journées de mai furent certainement une perturbation et non pas une restauration ; la République fut une restauration jusque vers 1881 où l'intrusion de la tyrannie intellectuelle et de la domi-

nation primaire commença d'en faire un gouvernement de désordre.

C'est en ce sens, et en ce sens seulement, que le
2 Décembre fut *le Châtiment, l'Expiation*[1] du 18 Brumaire, et que le deuxième Empire fut *le Châtiment* du
premier. Mais loin d'être la réplique du premier le
second Empire fut en un sens tout ce qu'il y eut de
plus contraire au premier. Le premier Empire fut un
régime d'ordre, d'un certain ordre. Il fut même, sous
beaucoup d'indisciplines, même militaires, comme
une sorte d'apothéose de la discipline, éminemment
de la discipline militaire. Il fut un régime d'un très
grand ordre et d'une très grande histoire. Le
deuxième Empire fut un régime de tous les désordres.
Il fut réellement l'introduction d'un désordre, d'un
certain désordre, l'introduction, l'installation au pouvoir d'une certaine bande, déconsidérée, très *moderne*,
très *avancée*, nullement ancienne France, nullement
ancien régime. Ou encore on peut dire que le
deuxième Empire est le plus gros boulangisme que
nous ayons eu, et aussi le seul qui ait réussi.

La Révolution au contraire, la grande, avait été une
instauration. Une instauration plus ou moins heu-
reuse, mais enfin une instauration.

Une instauration, c'est-à-dire ce dont toute restauration même n'est déjà plus qu'une répétition, une
image affaiblie, un essai de recommencement.

En d'autres termes encore, en un autre terme, le
premier Empire ne fut point ce que nous nommons un
césarisme. Le deuxième Empire fut ce que nous

nommons un césarisme. Le boulangisme fut un césarisme. Il y eut beaucoup de césarisme dans l'antidrey-
fusisme. Il n'y en eut point dans le dreyfusisme. La
domination combiste fut très réellement un césarisme,
le plus dangereux de tous, parce que c'était celui qui
se présentait le plus comme républicain. La domination radicale et radicale-socialiste est proprement un
césarisme, nommément un multicésarisme de comités
électoraux.

Il faut si peu suivre les noms, les apparences, les
aspects, il faut tant se méfier des noms que de même
que le deuxième Empire, historiquement, réellement,
ne *continue* pas l'Empire premier, de même la troisième
République, historiquement, réellement, ne se *continue*
pas elle-même. La suite, la continuation de la troisième République ne *continue* pas le commencement de
la troisième République. Sans qu'il y ait eu en 1881
aucun grand événement, je veux dire aucun événement inscriptible, à cette date la République a
commencé de se discontinuer. De républicaine elle est
notamment devenue césarienne.

Il ne faut pas dire seulement : Tout s'explique, je
dirai : Tout s'éclaire par là. Les difficultés incroyables
de l'action publique et privée s'éclairent soudainement, d'un grand jour, d'une grande lumière, quand
on veut bien donner audience pour ainsi dire, quand
on veut bien considérer, quand on veut bien seulement faire attention à cette distinction, à cette récri-
mination, je veux dire à cette discrimination remontante que nous venons de reconnaître. Tous les
sophismes, tous les paralogismes de l'action, tous les
parapragmatismes, — ou du moins tous les nobles, tous

les dignes, les seuls précisément où *nous* puissions
tomber, les seuls que nous puissions commettre, les
seuls innocents, — si coupables pourtant —, viennent
de ce que nous prolongeons indûment dans l'action
politique, dans la politique, une ligne d'action dûment
commencée dans la mystique. Une ligne d'action était
commencée, était poussée dans la mystique, avait
jailli dans la mystique, y avait trouvé, y avait pris sa
source et son point d'origine. Cette action était bien
lignée. Cette ligne d'action n'était pas seulement
naturelle, elle n'était pas seulement légitime, elle était
due. La vie suit son train. L'action suit son train. On
regarde par la portière. Il y a un mécanicien qui
conduit. Pourquoi s'occuper de la conduite. La vie
continue. L'action continue. Le fil s'enfile. Le fil de
l'action, la ligne de l'action continue. Et continuant,
les mêmes personnes, le même jeu, les mêmes institutions, le même entourage, le même appareil, les
mêmes meubles, les habitudes déjà prises, on ne
s'aperçoit pas que l'on passe par-dessus ce point de
discernement. D'autre part, par ailleurs, extérieure-
ment l'histoire, les événements ont marché. Et l'ai-
guille est franchie. Par le jeu, par l'histoire des
événements, par la bassesse et le péché de l'homme la
mystique est devenue politique, ou plutôt l'action
mystique est devenue action politique, ou plutôt la
politique s'est substituée à la mystique, la politique a
dévoré la mystique. Par le jeu des événements, qui ne
s'occupent pas de nous, qui pensent à autre chose, par
la bassesse, par le péché de l'homme, qui pense à
autre chose, la matière qui était matière de mystique
est devenue matière de politique. Et c'est la perpétuelle et toujours recommençante histoire. Parce que

c'est la même matière, les mêmes hommes, les mêmes comités, le même jeu, le même mécanisme, déjà automatique, les mêmes entours, le même appareil, les habitudes déjà prises, nous n'y voyons rien. Nous n'y faisons pas même attention. Et pourtant la même action, qui était juste, à partir de ce point de discernement devient injuste. La même action, qui était légitime, devient illégitime. La même action, qui était due, devient indue. La même action, qui était celle-ci, à partir de ce point de discernement ne devient pas seulement autre, elle devient généralement son contraire, son propre contraire. Et c'est ainsi qu'on devient innocemment criminel.

La même action, qui était propre, devient sale, devient une autre action, sale.

C'est ainsi qu'on devient innocent criminel, peut-être les plus dangereux de tous.

Une action commencée sur la mystique continue sur la politique et nous ne sentons point que nous passons sur ce point de discernement. La politique dévore la mystique et nous ne sautons point quand nous passons sur ce point de discontinuité.

Quand par impossible un homme de cœur discerne au point de discernement, s'arrête au point d'arrêt, refuse de muer à ce point de mutation, rebrousse à ce point de rebroussement, refuse, pour demeurer fidèle à une mystique, d'entrer dans les jeux politiques, dans les abus de cette politique qui est elle-même un abus, quand un homme de cœur, pour demeurer fidèle à une mystique, refuse d'entrer dans le jeu de la politique correspondante, de la politique issue, de la parasitaire, de la dévorante politique, les politiciens ont accoutumé de la nommer d'un petit mot bien usé aujourd'hui : volontiers ils nous nommeraient traître.

D'ailleurs ils nous nommeraient traître sans conviction, pour mémoire, pour les électeurs. Parce qu'il faut bien mettre quelque mot dans les programmes et dans les polémiques.

Qu'on le sache bien c'est ce traître que nous avons toujours été et que nous serons toujours. C'est ce traître, notamment, éminemment, que nous avons toujours été dans l'affaire Dreyfus et dans l'affaire du dreyfusisme. Le véritable traître, le traître au sens plein, au sens fort, au sens ancien de ce mot, c'est celui qui vend sa foi, qui vend son âme, qui livre son être même, qui *perd* son âme, qui trahit ses principes, son idéal, son être même, qui trahit sa mystique pour entrer dans la politique correspondante, dans la politique issue, passant complaisamment par-dessus le point de discrimination.

Je ne suis pas le seul. Les abonnés de ces cahiers, même aujourd'hui, après douze ans de morts, et de renouvellements annuels, se composent aujourd'hui encore pour les deux tiers, sont encore pour les deux tiers des anciens dreyfusards, des nouveaux dreyfusards, des dreyfusards perpétuels, des dreyfusards impénitents, des dreyfusards *mystiques,* des hommes de cœur, des petites gens, généralement obscurs, généralement pauvres, quelques-uns très pauvres, pour ainsi dire misérables, qui ont sacrifié deux fois leur carrière, leur avenir, leur existence et leur pain : une première fois pour lutter contre leurs ennemis, une deuxième fois pour lutter contre leurs amis ; et combien n'est-ce pas plus difficile ; une première fois pour résister à la politique de leurs ennemis, une deuxième fois pour résister à la politique de leurs amis ; une première fois pour ne pas succomber à leurs ennemis, une deuxième fois pour ne pas succomber à leurs amis.

C'est ce traître-ci que nous entendons être.

Une première fois pour ne pas succomber à la démagogie de leurs ennemis, une deuxième fois pour ne pas succomber à la démagogie de leurs amis ; une première fois pour ne pas succomber à l'inimitié, une deuxième fois pour ne pas succomber à la plus difficile amitié.

Tous nous savons ce que ça nous a coûté. Et c'est pour cela que nous exigerons toujours de nos amis un respect que nos ennemis ne nous ont jamais refusé.

Les politiciens veulent que nous endossions leurs politiques, que nous marchions dans leurs politiques, dans leurs combinaisons, que nous entrions dans leurs vues, politiques, que nous trahissions nos mystiques pour leurs politiques, pour les politiques correspondantes, pour les politiques issues. Mais nous ne sommes pas sous leurs ordres.

Alors les politiciens veulent décerner l'honneur et le droit. Mais ils n'en sont peut-être pas maîtres.

Ils veulent décerner l'obéissance et l'obédience, confirmer la firme, distribuer l'honneur, déclarer la règle. Mais ils n'en sont peut-être pas maîtres.

Ils ne sont pas nos maîtres. Tout le monde n'est pas sous leurs ordres. Ils ne sont pas même leurs propres maîtres.

Parlons plus simplement de ces grands hommes. Et moins durement. Leur politique est devenue un manège de chevaux de bois. Ils nous disent : Monsieur, vous avez changé, vous n'êtes plus à la même place. *La preuve, c'est que vous n'êtes plus en face du même chevau de bois.* Pardon, monsieur le député, ce sont les chevaux de bois qui ont tourné.

Il faut rendre d'ailleurs cette justice à ces malheureux qu'ils sont généralement très gentils avec nous, *excepté* la plupart de *ceux qui* sortant du personnel enseignant *constituent le parti intellectuel.* Tous les autres, les députés propres, les politiciens proprement dits, les parlementaires professionnels ont bien autre chose à faire que de s'occuper de nous, et surtout que de nous ennuyer ou de nous être désagréables : les concurrents, les compétiteurs, les électeurs, la réélection, les compétitions, les affaires, la vie. Ils aiment mieux nous laisser tranquilles. Et puis nous sommes si petits (en volume, en masse) pour eux. En masse politique et sociale. Ils ne nous aperçoivent même pas. Nous n'existons pas pour eux. Ne nous gonflons pas jusqu'à croire que nous existons pour eux, qu'ils nous voient. Ils nous méprisent trop pour nous haïr, pour nous en vouloir de nous être infidèles, je veux dire de ce qu'ils nous sont infidèles, à nous et à notre mystique, *leur* mystique, la mystique qui nous est commune, censément, réellement commune, (à nous parce que nous nous en nourrissons et qu'inséparablement nous vivons pour elle, à eux parce qu'ils en profitent et qu'ils la parasitent), pour même nous (en) tenir rigueur. Quand nous sollicitons, à notre tour de bêtes, ils mettent même souvent une sorte de dilection, secrète, un certain point d'honneur, d'un certain honneur, une coquetterie à nous rendre service. Ils ont l'air de dire : Vous voyez bien. Nous faisons ce métier-là. Nous savons très bien ce qu'il vaut. Il faut bien gagner sa vie. Il faut bien faire une carrière. Au moins rendez-nous cette justice que quand il le faut, quand on le peut, quand l'occasion s'en présente, nous sommes encore compétents, nous sommes encore capables de nous intéresser aux grands intérêts spirituels, de les défendre.

Ils ont raison. Et il faut bien que nous leur fassions cette justice. C'est une espèce de coquetterie qu'ils ont, fort louable, une dilection, (un remords), une sorte de garantie intérieure qu'ils prennent, un regret qui leur vient, comme une réponse qu'ils font à un avertissement secret. Ceux qui sont intraitables, ceux qui sont bien fermés, ce ne sont que les anciens intellectuels devenus députés, notamment les anciens professeurs, nommément les anciens normaliens. Ceux-là en veulent véritablement à la culture. Ils ont contre elle une sorte de haine véritablement démoniaque.

Il faut d'ailleurs bien faire attention. Quand on parle de parti intellectuel et de l'envahissement de la domination du primaire il faut prendre garde. Il ne suffit pas de dire primaire, primaire. Il faut bien voir aujourd'hui que le primaire n'est pas tout, (tout entier), dans le primaire. Il s'en faut. Il n'est point tant dans le primaire. Il s'en faut, et ce n'est même pas là qu'il est le plus. Il faut prendre garde que c'est sans aucun doute dans le supérieur aujourd'hui qu'il y a le plus de primaire, de contamination primaire, de domination primaire. Pour moi j'ai la conviction qu'il se distribue beaucoup plus de véritable culture, aujourd'hui même encore, dans la plupart des écoles primaires, dans la plupart des écoles des villages de France, entre les carrés de vignes, à l'ombre des

platanes et des marronniers, qu'il ne s'en distribue
entre les quatre murs de la Sorbonne. Voici quelle est
à peu près aujourd'hui, dans la réalité, la hiérarchie
des trois enseignements : Un très grand nombre
d'instituteurs encore, même radicaux et radicaux-
socialistes, même francs-maçons, même libre-pen-
seurs professionnels, pour toutes sortes de raisons de
situation et de race continuent encore d'exercer,
généralement à leur insu, dans les écoles des provinces
et même des villes un certain ministère de la culture.
Ils sont encore, souvent malgré eux, des ministres, des
maîtres de la distribution de la culture. Ils exercent
cet office. L'enseignement secondaire donne un admirable exemple, fait un admirable effort pour maintenir, pour (sauve)garder, pour défendre contre l'envahissement de la barbarie cette culture antique, cette
culture classique dont il avait le dépôt, dont il garde
envers et contre tout la tradition. C'est un spectacle
admirable que (celui que) donnent tant de professeurs
de l'enseignement secondaire, pauvres, petites gens,
petits fonctionnaires, exposés à tout, sacrifiant tout,
luttant contre tout, résistant à tout pour défendre
leurs *classes*. Luttant contre tous les pouvoirs, les
autorités temporelles, les puissances constituées.
Contre les familles, ces électeurs, contre l'opinion ;
contre le proviseur, qui suit les familles, qui suivent
l'opinion ; contre *les parents des élèves* ; contre le proviseur, le censeur, l'inspecteur d'Académie, le recteur
de l'Académie, l'inspecteur général, le directeur de
l'enseignement secondaire, le ministre, les députés,
toute la machine, toute la hiérarchie, contre les
hommes politiques, contre leur avenir, contre leur
carrière, contre leur (propre) avancement ; littérale-

ment contre leur pain. Contre leurs chefs, contre leurs maîtres, contre l'administration, la grande Administration, contre leurs supérieurs hiérarchiques, contre leurs défenseurs naturels, contre ceux qui devraient naturellement les défendre. Et qui les abandonnent au contraire. Quand ils ne les trahissent pas. Contre tous leurs propres intérêts. Contre tout le gouvernement, notamment contre le plus redoutable de tous, contre le gouvernement de l'opinion, qui partout est toute moderne. Pourquoi. Par une indestructible probité. Par une indestructible piété. Par un invincible, un insurmontable attachement de race et de liberté à leur métier, à leur office, à leur ministère, à leur vieille vertu, à leur fonction sociale, à un vieux civisme classique et français. Par un inébranlable attachement à la vieille culture, qui en effet était la vieille vertu, qui était tout un avec la vieille vertu, par une continuation, par une sorte d'héroïque attachement au vieux métier, au vieux pays, au vieux lycée. Pour quoi. Pour tâcher d'en sauver un peu. C'est par eux, par un certain nombre de maîtres de l'enseignement secondaire, par un assez grand nombre encore heureusement, que toute culture n'a point encore disparu de ce pays. Je connais, je pourrais citer moi tout seul, moi tout petit cent cinquante professeurs de l'enseignement secondaire qui font tout, qui risquent tout, qui bravent tout, même et surtout l'ennui, le plus grand risque, la petite fin de carrière, pour maintenir, pour sauver tout ce qui peut encore être sauvé. On trouverait difficilement cinquante maîtres de l'enseignement supérieur, et même trente, et même quinze, qui se proposent autre chose (outre la carrière, et l'avancement, et pour commencer précisément d'être de l'enseignement supérieur) qui se proposent autre chose que d'ossifier, que de momifier la réalité, les réalités qui leur sont imprudemment confiées, que d'ensevelir dans le tombeau des fiches la matière de leur enseignement.

Je citerais cent cinquante professeurs de l'enseignement secondaire qui font tout ce qu'ils peuvent, et même plus, pour essayer seulement de sauvegarder un peu, dans ce vieux pays, un peu de bon goût, un peu de tenue, un peu d'ancien goût, un peu des anciennes mœurs de l'esprit, un peu de ce vieil esprit de la liberté de l'esprit.

Les instituteurs ne font point tant partie du parti intellectuel. Ni tant qu'ils le croient. Ni tant qu'ils le voudraient bien. Ils ont tant d'autres attaches encore dans le pays réel, quoi qu'ils fassent. Ils sont beaucoup plus les agents de la culture qu'ils ne le voudraient. Les professeurs de l'enseignement secondaire n'en font pour ainsi dire aucunement partie, excepté les politiciens, les quelques-uns qui ont chauffé leur avancement, leur rapide acheminement sur Paris. Autrement, pour tout le reste, pour tous les autres, pour tout le corps, on peut dire, il faut dire que l'enseignement secondaire, tout démantelé qu'il soit, tout défait que l'on l'ait fait, est encore la citadelle, le réduit de la culture en France.

On fait quelquefois grand état, dans le supérieur, au moins dans le commencement, dois-je dire pour épater les nouveaux, les jeunes gens, de ce que les professeurs de l'enseignement secondaire font des *classes,* tandis que messieurs les maîtres et professeurs de l'enseignement supérieur *au contraire* font des *cours.* Il faut malheureusement le leur dire : Dans l'état actuel de l'enseignement, c'est dans les *classes* que se distribue encore beaucoup de culture, et c'est dans les *cours* qu'il n'y en a plus.

Ceux qui sont acharnés surtout, comme parti politique, comme parti intellectuel, ceux qui sont forcenés, ce sont ces jeunes gens qui passent directement de l'ancienne et de la nouvelle École Normale au Parti Socialiste Unifié. Les dernières élections viennent de nous envoyer encore tout un paquet de ces jolis garçons. Les *enfants de chœur,* notamment celui qui est si joli et joufflu. Comme c'est son devoir d'enfant de chœur.

Notre première règle de conduite, ou, si l'on préfère, la première règle de notre conduite sera donc, étant dans l'action, de ne jamais tomber dans la politique, c'est-à-dire, très précisément, suivant une ligne de l'action, de nous défier, de nous méfier de nous-mêmes et de notre propre action, de faire une extrême attention à distinguer le point de discernement, et ce point reconnu, de rebrousser en effet à ce point de rebroussement. Au point où la politique se substitue à la mystique, dévore la mystique, trahit la mystique, celui-là seul qui laisse aller, qui abandonne, qui trahit la politique est aussi le seul qui demeure fidèle à la mystique, celui-là seul qui trahit la politique est aussi le seul qui ne trahit pas la mystique.

Au point de rebroussement il ne faut rien garder de la vieille analyse, de la vieille idée. De l'habitude. Il faut être prêt à recommencer, il faut recommencer *de plano* l'analyse.

Si notre première règle d'action, de conduite sera de
ne point continuer aveuglément par-dessus le point de
discernement une action commencée en mystique et
qui finit en politique, pareillement, parallèlement
notre première règle de connaissance, de jugement, de
connaissement sera de ne point continuer aveuglément
par-dessus le point de discernement un jugement, un
connaissement sur une action commencée en mystique et qui finit en politique. Il faut avant tout et
surtout se défier, se méfier de soi, de son propre
jugement, de son propre connaissement. Il faut sur
tout se donner garde de continuer. Continuer, persévérer, en ce sens-là, c'est tout ce qu'il y a de plus
dangereux pour la justice, pour l'intelligence même.
Prendre son billet au départ, dans un parti, dans une
faction, et ne plus jamais regarder comment le train
roule et surtout sur quoi le train roule, c'est, pour un
homme, se placer résolument dans les meilleures
conditions pour se faire criminel.

Tout le fatras des propos et des conversations, les
embarras, les apparentes contradictions, les embrous-
saillements, les inextricables difficultés du jugement,
les apparentes incompréhensions et impossibilités de
comprendre et de suivre, les bonnes fois contraires et
les mauvaises fois entrelacées, les bonnes et les
mauvaises fois adverses, le recommencement perpétuel et fatigant de la vanité des mêmes propos, la
répétition, l'exécrable répétition des mêmes incohé-
rents et infatigables propos seraient beaucoup éclairés
si l'on faisait seulement attention de quoi on parle, si,
sur toute action, dans chaque action, dans chaque
ordre, on parle de la mystique ou, plus généralement,

de la politique. Ainsi s'explique q̶
polémiques, dans tant de débats les
les deux ennemis paraissent avoir égale̶
également tort. Une des principales causes en est q̶
l'un parle de la mystique, et l'autre répond de la
politique correspondante, de la politique issue. Ou
l'un parle de la politique, et l'autre répond de la
mystique antérieure. Ce n'est pas seulement la justice,
dans l'ordre du jugement moral, qui demande que
l'on compare toujours deux actions aux mêmes étages
et non point en deux étages différents, la mystique à la
mystique et la politique à la politique, et non point la
mystique à la politique ni la politique à la mystique,
c'est aussi la justesse, dans l'ordre du jugement
mental, qui a exactement la même exigence.

Quand nos instituteurs comparent incessamment la
mystique républicaine à la politique royaliste et
quand tous les matins nos royalistes comparent la
mystique royaliste à la politique républicaine, ils font,
ils commettent le même manquement, deux manque-
ments mutuellement complémentaires, deux manquement mutuellement contraires, mutuellement
inverses, mutuellement réciproques, deux manque-
ments contraires, le même, un manquement conjugué ; ensemble ils manquent à la justice et à la justesse
ensemble.

Une première conséquence de cette distinction, une
première application de ce reconnaissement, de ce
discernement, de cette redistribution, c'est que les
mystiques sont beaucoup moins ennemies entre elles
que les politiques, et qu'elles le sont tout autrement. Il
ne faut donc pas faire porter aux mystiques la peine
des dissensions, des guerres, des inimitiés politiques, il

faut pas reporter sur les mystiques la malendu-
rance des politiques. Les mystiques sont beaucoup
moins ennemies entre elles que les politiques ne le
sont entre elles. Parce qu'elles n'ont point comme les
politiques à se partager sans cesse une matière,
temporelle, un monde temporel, une puissance temporelle incessamment limitée. Des dépouilles temporelles. Des dépouilles mortelles. Et quand elles sont
ennemies, elles le sont tout autrement, à une profondeur infiniment plus essentielle, avec une noblesse
infiniment plus profonde. Par exemple jamais la
mystique civique, la mystique antique, la mystique de
la cité et de la supplication antique ne s'est opposée,
n'a pu s'opposer à la mystique du salut comme la
politique païenne s'est opposée à la politique chrétienne ; aussi grossièrement, aussi bassement, aussi
temporellement, aussi mortellement que les empereurs païens se sont opposés aux empereurs chrétiens,
et réciproquement. Et la mystique du salut aujour-
d'hui ne peut pas s'opposer à la mystique de la liberté
comme la politique cléricale s'oppose par exemple à la
politique radicale. Il est aisé d'être ensemble bon
chrétien et bon citoyen, *tant qu'on ne fait pas de la
politique*.

Les politiciens, au moment qu'ils *changent* la mystique en politique, une mystique en une politique, si on
ne les suit pas, alors c'est eux qui vous accusent de
changer.

Nous en avons eu un exemple éminent dans l'affaire
Dreyfus continuée en affaire Dreyfusisme. On peut
dire que les politiciens introduisent et dans l'action et

dans la connaissance (où déjà il y en a tant, où il y en a tant de naturelles), des difficultés artificielles, des difficultés supplémentaires, des difficultés surérogatoires, des difficultés plus qu'il n'y en a. Et il y en a déjà tant. Ils veulent toujours, quelquefois par politique, mais généralement par incompréhension naturelle, par insuffisance, par incapacité d'aller profondément, que les serviteurs des mystiques deviennent les agents des politiques. Ils introduisent partout, ils découpent, des déchirures temporelles gratuites, des déchirures politiques artificielles. Comme si ce n'était pas assez déjà des grands déchirements mystiques. Ils créent ainsi des enchevêtrements.

Nous en avons eu un exemple éminent dans cette immortelle affaire Dreyfus continuée en affaire Dreyfusisme. S'il y en eut une qui sauta par-dessus son point de discernement, ce fut celle-là. Elle offre, avec une perfection peut-être unique, comme une réussite peut-être unique, comme un exemple unique, presque comme un modèle un raccourci unique généralement de ce que c'est que la dégradation, l'abaissement d'une action humaine, mais non pas seulement cela : particulièrement, proprement un raccourci unique, (comme) une culmination de ce que c'est que la dégradation d'une action mystique en action politique passant (aveuglément ?) par-dessus son point de rupture, par-dessus son point de discernement, par-dessus son point de rebroussement, par-dessus son point de continuité discontinue.

Faut-il noter une fois de plus qu'il y eut, qu'il y a dans cette affaire Dreyfus, qu'il y aura longtemps en elle, et peut-être éternellement, une vertu singulière. Je veux dire une force singulière. Nous le voyons bien

aujourd'hui. A présent que l'affaire est finie. Ce
n'était pas une illusion de notre jeunesse. Plus cette
affaire est finie, plus il est évident qu'elle ne finira
jamais. Plus elle est finie plus elle prouve. Et d'abord
il faut noter qu'elle prouve qu'elle avait une *vertu*
singulière. Dans les deux sens. Une singulière vertu de
vertu tant qu'elle demeura dans la mystique. Une
singulière vertu de malice aussitôt qu'elle fut entrée
dans la politique. C'est un des plus grands mystères
qu'il y ait dans l'histoire et dans la réalité, et
naturellement aussi, naturellement donc l'un donc de
ceux sur qui l'on passe le plus aveuglément, le plus
aisément, le plus inattentivement, le plus sans sauter,
que cette espèce de différence absolue, (irrévocable,
irréversible, comme infinie), qu'il y a dans le *prix* des
événements. Que certains événements soient d'un
certain prix, aient un certain prix, un prix propre; que
des événements différents du même ordre ou d'ordres
voisins, ayant la même matière ou des matières du
même ordre et de même valeur, ayant la même forme
ou des formes du même ordre et de même valeur,
aient pourtant des prix, des valeurs infiniment différentes; que chaque événement, opérant une même
matière, faisant devenir une même matière, sous une
même forme, dans une même forme, que tout événement ait pourtant un prix propre, mystérieux, une
force propre en soi, une valeur propre, mystérieuse;
qu'il y ait des guerres et des paix qui aient une valeur
propre, qu'il y ait des *affaires* qui aient une valeur
propre, absolue; qu'il y ait des héroïsmes qui aient
une valeur propre; qu'il y ait des saintetés même qui
aient une valeur propre, c'est assurément un des plus
grands mystères de l'événement, un des plus poi-

gnants problèmes de l'histoire ; qu'il y ait non seulement des hommes (et des dieux) qui comptent plus
que d'autres, infiniment plus, mais qu'il y ait des
peuples, qui sont comme marqués, qu'il y ait comme
une destination, comme une évaluation, comme une
mesure non pas seulement des hommes et des dieux,
mais des peuples mêmes ; qu'il y ait des peuples tout
entiers qui aient un prix, une valeur propre, qui soient
marqués pour l'histoire, pour toute l'histoire temporelle, et (par suite) peut-être sans doute pour l'autre,
et que des peuples tout entiers, tant d'autres peuples,
l'immense majorité des peuples, la presque totalité
soient marqués au contraire pour le silence et l'ombre,
pour la nuit et le silence, pour tomber dans un silence,
ne se lèvent que pour tomber, c'est un mystère que
nous ne voyons pas, comme tous les plus grands
mystères, précisément parce que nous y baignons,
comme dans tous les plus grands mystères ; enfin qu'il
y ait non seulement des hommes et pour ainsi dire des
dieux temporellement élus, mais des peuples entiers
temporellement élus et peut-être plus, c'est certainement peut-être le plus grand mystère de l'événement,
le plus poignant problème de l'histoire. Qu'il y ait
même comme des événements élus. C'est le plus
grand problème de la création. Nous ne manquerons
point, nous n'éviterons point de le considérer, de le
méditer longuement dans les études que nous avons
commencées de la situation faite à l'histoire et à la
sociologie dans la philosophie générale du monde
moderne [1].

Il faut donc le dire, et le dire avec solennité :
l'affaire Dreyfus fut une affaire élue. Elle fut une crise
éminente dans trois histoires elles-mêmes éminentes.

Elle fut une crise éminente dans l'histoire d'Israël. Elle fut une crise éminente, évidemment, dans l'histoire de France. Elle fut surtout une crise éminente, et cette dignité apparaîtra de plus en plus, elle fut surtout une crise éminente dans l'histoire de la chrétienté. Et peut-être de plusieurs autres. Ainsi par un recoupement, par une élection peut-être unique elle fut triplement critique. Elle fut triplement éminente. Elle fut proprement une affaire culminante. Pour moi, si je puis continuer ces études que nous avons commencées de la situation faite à l'histoire et à la sociologie dans la philosophie générale du monde moderne, suivant cette méthode que nous gardons de ne jamais rien écrire que de ce que nous avons éprouvé nous-mêmes, nous prendrons certainement cette grande crise comme exemple, comme référence de ce que c'est qu'une crise, un événement qui a une valeur propre éminente.

Ce prix, cette valeur propre de l'affaire Dreyfus apparaît encore, apparaît constamment, quoi qu'on en ait, quoi qu'on fasse. Elle revient malgré tout, comme un revenant, comme une revenante. Ce qui double la preuve, ou plutôt ce qui fait la preuve, c'est qu'elle ne se manifeste pas seulement dans un sens, dans l'un des deux sens, mais ce qui fait la preuve (rien ne prouve autant que le mal), c'est hélas qu'elle prouve, qu'elle se manifeste également dans tous les deux sens. Elle a dans le bon sens, dans le sens mystique, une force incroyable de vertu, une vertu de vertu incroyable. Et dans le mauvais sens, dans le sens politique, elle a une force, une vertu de vice incroyable. Aujourd'hui encore, aujourd'hui comme toujours, aujourd'hui plus que jamais on ne peut pas en parler à la légère, on ne peut pas en traiter légèrement, on ne peut pas en parler d'un air détaché. On ne peut pas en parler sans se passionner, aussitôt. Aujourd'hui comme jamais tout propos qui se tient, tout article de revue ou de journal, tout livre, tout cahier qui s'écrit de l'affaire Dreyfus a en lui, porte en lui on ne sait quel virus, quel point de virus qui nous travaille infatigable. On n'en peut point toucher un mot qui ne soit nocif et sacré. Nous n'en souffrons que trop, quelquefois, aux cahiers, le jeudi[1]. Mais c'est la marque même et le signe de la valeur, du prix propre, le signe de l'élection.

Pour moi si ayant achevé une œuvre infiniment plus grave je viens à l'âge des *Confessions,* qui est, comme on sait, cinquante ans révolus, à neuf heures du matin, c'est ce que je me proposerai certainement d'y représenter. J'essaierai, reprenant, achevant mon ancienne *décomposition du dreyfusisme en France* de donner non pas une idée, mais j'essaierai de donner une représentation de ce que fut dans la réalité cette immortelle affaire Dreyfus. Elle fut, comme toute affaire qui se respecte, une affaire essentiellement mystique. Elle vivait de sa mystique. Elle est morte de sa politique. C'est la loi, c'est la règle. *C'est le niveau des vies*[2]. Tout parti vit de sa mystique et meurt de sa politique. C'est ce que j'essaierai de représenter. J'avoue, je commence à croire que ce ne sera pas inutile. Je soupçonne qu'il y a sur cette affaire Dreyfus de nombreux malentendus. J'avoue que je ne me reconnais pas du tout dans le *portrait* que Halévy a tracé ici même *du dreyfusiste.* Je ne me sens nullement

ce poil de chien battu. Je consens d'avoir été vainqueur, je consens (ce qui est mon jugement propre)
d'avoir été vaincu (ça dépend du point de vue auquel
on se place), je ne consens point d'avoir été battu. Je
consens d'avoir été ruiné, (dans le temporel, et fort
exposé dans l'intemporel), je consens d'avoir été
trompé, je consens d'avoir été berné. Je ne consens
point d'avoir été mouillé. Je ne me sens point ce poil
de chien mouillé. Je ne me reconnais point dans ce
portrait. Nous étions autrement fiers, autrement
droits, autrement orgueilleux, infiniment fiers, portant haut la tête, infiniment pleins, infiniment gonflés
des vertus *militaires*. Nous avions, nous tenions un tout
autre ton, un tout autre air, un tout autre port de tête,
nous portions, à bras tendus, un tout autre propos. Je
ne me sens aucunement l'humeur d'un pénitent. Je
hais une pénitence qui ne serait point une pénitence
chrétienne, qui serait une espèce de pénitence civique
et laïque, une pénitence laïcisée, sécularisée, tempora-
lisée, désaffectée, une imitation, une contrefaçon de *la*
pénitence. Je hais une humiliation, une humilité qui
ne serait point une humilité chrétienne, l'humilité
chrétienne, qui serait une espèce d'humilité civile,
civique, laïque, une imitation, une contrefaçon de
*l'*humilité. Dans le civil, dans le civique, dans le
laïque, dans le profane je veux être bourré d'orgueil.
Nous l'étions. Nous en avions le droit. Nous en avions
le devoir. Non seulement nous n'avons rien à regretter. Mais nous n'avons rien, nous n'avons rien fait
dont nous n'ayons à nous glorifier. Dont nous ne
puissions, dont nous ne devions nous glorifier. On
peut commencer demain matin la publication de mes
œuvres complètes. On pourrait même y ajouter la

publication de mes propos, de mes paroles complètes.
Il n'y a pas, dans tous ces vieux cahiers, un mot que je
changerais, excepté quatre ou cinq mots que je
connais bien, sept ou huit mots de théologie qui
pourraient donner matière à un malentendu, être
interprétés à contresens, parce qu'ils sont au style
indirect et que l'on ne voit pas assez dans la phrase
qu'ils sont au style indirect. Non seulement nous
n'avons rien à désavouer, mais nous n'avons rien dont
nous n'ayons à nous glorifier. Car dans nos plus
ardentes polémiques, dans nos invectives, dans nos
pamphlets nous n'avons jamais perdu le respect du
respect. Du respectable respect. Nous n'avons, nous
n'avons à avoir ni regret ni remords. Dans ces
confessions d'un dreyfusiste qui feront une part importante de nos *Confessions* générales, il y aura, je l'ai
promis, de nombreux cahiers qui s'intituleront
Mémoires d'un âne[1], ou peut-être, plus platement,
mémoires d'un imbécile. Il n'y en aura aucun qui
s'intitulera *mémoires d'un lâche,* ou *d'un pleutre* (nous
laisserons ceux-ci à faire à M. Jaurès et ils ne seront
certainement pas mal faits). (Il est si bon maquignon.) Il n'y en aura aucun qui s'intitulera *cahiers,
mémoires d'un faible; d'un repentant.* Il n'y en aura aucun
qui s'intitulera *mémoires d'un homme politique.* Ils seront
tous, dans le fond, les mémoires d'un homme mystique.

On peut publier demain matin nos œuvres
complètes. Non seulement il n'y a pas une virgule que
nous ayons à désavouer, mais il n'y a pas une virgule
dont nous n'ayons à nous glorifier.

C'est bien l'idée de Halévy, qu'en effet je ne m'y reconnaisse pas. Plusieurs fois il nous le dit expressément. Mais je ne sais pas si son lecteur voit bien toujours que c'est son idée.

Notre collaborateur a bien marqué, dans tout son cahier, qu'en effet il ne s'agit point de nous. Ce qu'il a voulu faire, ce qu'il a si parfaitement réussi à nous donner, c'est bien plutôt l'histoire du dreyfusisme, le *portrait* du dreyfusisme que le portrait du dreyfusiste ; que l'histoire ou le portrait d'un dreyfusiste ; ou encore ce serait, je crois, dans sa pensée, le portrait, l'histoire et le portrait d'un dreyfusiste moyen ; ou plutôt c'est l'histoire et le portrait d'un parti, du parti dreyfusiste ; ou plus exactement d'un dreyfusiste qui était dans le parti dreyfusiste. Mais je crois qu'il y a un abîme entre l'histoire et le portrait d'un dreyfusiste qui était dans le parti dreyfusiste et l'histoire et le portrait d'un dreyfusiste qui n'était pas dans le parti dreyfusiste. C'est pour cela que quand je lisais en épreuves le cahier de notre collaborateur je voyais venir ce malentendu, je voyais prendre corps ce contresens. Je voyais poindre ce double sens et la confusion de ce double sens. C'est pour cela que j'avais une sourde révolte, sourde naturellement parce que je ne suis pas éloquent. Je ronchonnais, je marmonnais, je marmottais, tout en lisant mes épreuves, et plus je trouvais que le cahier est beau, plus je trouvais qu'il est bon, plus je me révoltais. Parce que plus je pensais qu'il serait écouté. Plus je pensais qu'il porterait. C'est pourquoi ce que je **veux** contester à notre collaborateur, c'est la proportion, c'est la *quotité* même, la quotité respective, dans l'ensemble du dreyfusisme et du parti dreyfusiste, de ceux que son cahier habille, et de ceux qu'il n'habille pas. De ceux à qui son cahier convient, et de ceux à qui il ne convient pas. Il a bien pensé lui-même, il a fait une réserve, il a fait une distinction utile en marquant bien qu'il fallait mettre à part ceux des dreyfusistes qui n'étaient point entrés dans les démagogies politiques, notamment dans la démagogie combiste. Mais où je conteste à notre collaborateur, c'est quand il paraît admettre que nous ne représentons pas le dreyfusisme et que les autres le représentent, quand il nous classe et nous met à part comme une exception, comme une sorte d'exception, quand toute son attention se porte sur les autres, sur ceux que nous sommes autorisés à nommer les *politiciens*. Nous prétendons au contraire que nous les mystiques nous sommes et nous fûmes, que nous avons toujours été le cœur et le centre du dreyfusisme, et que nous seuls nous le représentons.

Halévy a quelquefois l'air de dire que les autres auraient comme suivi une courbe légitime et que nous autres nous serions des sauvages, presque comme des fantaisistes, que nous aurions fait une rupture, brusque, un saut illégitime. Ce seraient les autres qui seraient pour ainsi dire de droit et nous qui serions comme de travers. Ce seraient les autres qui seraient la règle, le commun, l'ordinaire, le naturel, et nous qui serions non pas seulement l'extraordinaire, mais l'exception, et surtout une exception artificielle. On veut toujours que ce soit la faiblesse et la dégradation qui soit la règle, l'ordinaire le commun, qui soit comme de droit, qui aille de soi. C'est précisément ce que je conteste dans tous les ordres, au moins pour cette race française. En France le courage et la droiture vont très bien de soi.

Sans doute les *apparences* donneraient raison à Halévy, les apparents seraient pour lui. Je veux dire que si l'on (ne) considère (que) les dreyfusistes apparents, les hommes en vue, journalistes, publicistes, conférenciers, Universités Populaires, parlementaires, candidats, hommes politiques, tout ce qui parle et tout ce qui cause, tout ce qui écrit et tout ce qui publie, l'immense majorité des hommes en vue, la presque totalité des *apparents* s'empressèrent d'entrer dans les démagogies dreyfusistes, je veux dire dans les démagogies politiques issues de la mystique dreyfusiste. Mais ce que je conteste précisément, ce que je nie, c'est que ceux qui sont *apparents* pour l'histoire (et que l'histoire, en retour, saisit avec tant d'empressement) aient une grande importance dans les profondeurs de la réalité. Atteignant donc à des réalités profondes, seules importantes, je prétends que *tous* les dreyfusistes mystiques sont demeurés dreyfusistes, qu'ils sont demeurés mystiques, et qu'ils sont demeurés les mains pures. Qu'importe que tous les *apparents*, tous les *phénomènes,* tous les officiels, tous les avantageux aient abandonné, aient raillé, aient renié, aient trahi cette mystique pour la politique issue, pour toutes sortes de politiques, pour toutes les démagogies politiques. Cela, mon cher Halévy, vous l'avez dit vous-même : *C'est le niveau des vies.* Qu'importe qu'ils nous raillent. Seuls nous représentons et eux ils ne représentent pas. Qu'importe qu'ils nous tournent en dérision. Eux-mêmes ils ne vivent que par nous, ils ne sont que par nous. Les vanités mêmes qu'ils sont, sans nous ils ne le seraient pas.

Et non seulement je prétends que les dreyfusistes mystiques sont demeurés dreyfusistes et qu'ils sont demeurés mystiques. Mais j'atteste en plus, en surcroît, qu'ils étaient le nombre et qu'ils sont demeurés le nombre. Même au grossier point de vue, non plus de la qualité, de la vertu, mais de la quotité même et de la quantité, c'est eux qui comptaient, c'est eux qui comptent.

La politique se moque de la mystique, mais c'est encore la mystique qui nourrit la politique même.

Car les politiques se rattrapent, croient se rattraper en disant qu'au moins ils sont pratiques et que nous ne le sommes pas. Ici même ils se trompent. Et ils trompent. Nous ne leur accorderons pas même cela. Ce sont les mystiques qui sont même pratiques et ce sont les politiques qui ne le sont pas. C'est nous qui sommes pratiques, *qui faisons quelque chose,* et c'est eux qui ne le sont pas, *qui ne font rien.* C'est nous qui amassons et c'est eux qui pillent. C'est nous qui bâtissons, c'est nous qui fondons, et c'est eux qui démolissent. C'est nous qui nourrissons et c'est eux qui parasitent. C'est nous qui faisons les œuvres et les hommes, les peuples et les races. Et c'est eux qui ruinent.

Le peu même qu'ils sont, ils ne le sont que par nous. La misère, la vanité, le vide, l'infirmité, la frivolité, la bassesse, le néant qu'ils sont, cela même ils ne le sont que par nous.

C'est pour cela qu'il ne s'agit point qu'ils nous regardent comme des inspecteurs (comme eux-mêmes étant des inspecteurs). Il ne s'agit point qu'ils nous examinent et nous jugent, qu'ils nous passent en revue et en inspection. Qu'ils nous demandent des comptes, eux à nous, vraiment ce serait risible. Tout le droit qu'ils ont, avec nous, c'est de se taire. Et de tâcher de se faire oublier. Espérons qu'ils en useront largement.

Ce que je prétends, c'est que tout le corps mystique du dreyfusisme est demeuré intact. Qu'importe que les politiciens aient trahi cette mystique. C'est leur office même.

Après vous me direz que ni les États-Majors ni les comités ni les ligues n'étaient donc de cette mystique. Naturellement qu'ils n'en étaient pas. Vous n'auriez tout de même pas voulu qu'ils en fussent. Qu'importe toute la Ligue des Droits de l'Homme ensemble, et même du Citoyen, que représente-t-elle, en face d'une conscience, en face d'une mystique. Qu'importe une politique, cent politiques, au prix d'une mystique. Tout détestables qu'ils soient, ils ne sont encore que par nous, ils sont encore et toujours nos débiteurs. Toute mystique est créancière de toutes politiques.

Leur détestation même est de nous, est notre œuvre, nous parasite.

Vous ajouterez que la victime elle-même n'était donc point de sa mystique. De sa propre mystique.

Cela est devenu évident. Nous fussions morts pour Dreyfus. Dreyfus n'est point mort pour Dreyfus. Il est de bonne règle que la victime ne soit point de la mystique de sa propre affaire.

C'est le triomphe de la faiblesse humaine, le couronnement de notre vanité, la plus grande preuve ; le plus grand effort, le chef-d'œuvre, la démonstration la plus haute, suprême, culminante de notre infirmité.

Il fallait que ce fût ainsi pour que le chef-d'œuvre de notre misère fût achevé, pour que toute l'amertume fût bue, pour que l'ingratitude fût vraiment couronnée.

Pour que ce fût complet. Pour que le désabusement fût achevé.

L'affaire Dreyfus, le dreyfusisme, la mystique, le mysticisme dreyfusiste fut une culmination, un recoupement en culmination de trois mysticismes au moins : juif, chrétien, français. Et comme je le montrerai ces trois mysticismes ne s'y déchiraient point, ne s'y meurtrissaient point, mais y concouraient au contraire par une rencontre, par un recoupement, en une rencontre, en un recoupement peut-être unique dans l'histoire du monde.

Je suis en mesure d'affirmer que tous les mystiques dreyfusistes sont demeurés mystiques, sont demeurés dreyfusistes, sont demeurés les mains pures. Je le sais, j'en ai la liste aux cahiers. Je veux dire que tout ce qu'il y avait de mystique, de fidèle, de croyant dans le dreyfusisme s'est réfugié, s'est recueilli aux cahiers, dès le principe et toujours, guidés par un instinct sûr,

par le plus profond des instincts, comme dans la seule
maison qui eût gardé le sens et la tradition, le dépôt,
sacré pour nous, et peut-être pour l'histoire, de la
mystique dreyfusiste. Tel fut le premier fond, le
premier corps de nos amis et de nos abonnés.
Beaucoup déjà sont morts. Tous ceux qui ne sont pas
morts nous sont restés invariablement fidèles. Ou
plutôt ce fut ce premier fond, ce premier corps, tout ce
qu'il y avait de mystique, de fidèle, de croyant dans le
dreyfusisme qui fut, qui devint non point seulement
nos amis et nos abonnés, mais nos cahiers mêmes, le
corps et l'institution de nos cahiers. Je puis donc le
dire. Les hommes qui se taisent, les seuls qui impor-
tent, les silencieux, les seuls qui comptent, les tacites,
les seuls qui compteront, tous les mystiques sont
restés invariables, infléchissables. Toutes les petites
gens. Nous enfin. J'en ai encore eu la preuve et reçu le
témoignage aux vacances de Pâques, aux dernières, et
à ces vacances de la Pentecôte, où tant de nos amis et
de nos abonnés des départements, notamment des
professeurs, nous ont fait l'amitié de venir nous voir
aux cahiers. Ils sont comme ils étaient, ce qu'ils
étaient, ils sont les mêmes hommes qu'il y a dix ans.
Qu'il y a douze ans. Qu'il y a quinze ans. Et moi aussi
j'ose dire qu'ils m'ont trouvé le même homme qu'il y a
dix ans. Douze ans. Quinze ans. Ce qui est peut-être
plus difficile.

Ceux qui se taisent, les seuls dont la parole compte.

Voilà quel était le cœur et la force du dreyfusisme.
Ce cœur, ce centre, cette force est demeurée intacte.
Il s'était même créé un honneur dreyfusiste, ce qui

est la marque même de la consécration d'une mystique, de la création d'une mystique. Quand une
mystique en vient à créer un honneur, son honneur,
un honneur propre, particulier, c'est qu'elle existe
bien, comme mystique. Elle a donné, elle a trouvé sa
marque. Cet honneur, dreyfusiste, est demeuré intact.

Cette fidélité même que nos amis et que nos
abonnés nous ont gardée depuis quinze ans à travers
tant d'épreuves, à travers toutes les misères, toutes les
détresses, à travers, dessous tous les malentendus
politiques, toutes les hontes politiques, cette amitié
impeccable, cette fidélité d'un autre âge, cette fidélité
ancienne, antique, d'un autre temps, cette amitié,
cette fidélité unique dans tout le monde moderne ne
s'explique elle-même que comme une amitié, une
fidélité de l'ordre mystique. Elle nous récompense
nous-mêmes d'une fidélité toute mystique à notre
mystique.

Il n'est pas mort, pour lui; mais plusieurs sont
morts pour lui. Cela fait, cela consacre, cela sanc-
tionne une mystique.

D'autres sont morts pour lui.

Il ne s'est pas ruiné pour lui-même. Il ne se ruinera
pour nul autre. Mais beaucoup se sont ruinés pour lui.
Beaucoup ont sacrifié pour lui leur carrière, leur pain,
leur vie même, le pain de leurs femmes et de leurs
enfants. Beaucoup se sont jetés pour lui dans une
misère inexpiable. Cela fait, cela consacre, cela sanc-
tionne une mystique.

La misère, le seul incurable des maux.

D'autres se sont ruinés, se sont temporellement perdus pour lui.

Le plus grand de tous, Bernard-Lazare, quoi qu'on en ait dit, quoi qu'on en ait, plus lâchement, laissé dire, a vécu pour lui, est mort pour lui, est mort pensant à lui.

Ce qu'il y a de plus fort, c'est que cette mystique, que nos amis ont ignorée, plus que méconnue, ignorée, (nos *amis*, j'entends ici ce mot au sens politique, au sens des combats politiques, nos amis politiques, nos politiciens, nos parasites), nos adversaires eux-mêmes l'ont soupçonnée. M. Barrès a fort bien noté plusieurs fois que le mouvement dreyfusiste fut un mouvement religieux. Il a même écrit, et il y a longtemps, qu'il fallait regretter que cette force religieuse fût perdue [1]. Sur ce point au moins nous sommes en mesure de le rassurer. Cette force religieuse ne sera point perdue. Aux reconstructions qui s'imposent, aux restitutions, nous avons dit le mot aux *restaurations* qui s'annoncent nous venons la tête haute ; fiers et tout pleins de notre passé, battus de tant d'épreuves, forgés par nos misères mêmes. Aux restaurations qui s'annoncent nous venons la mémoire pleine, le cœur plein, les mains pleines et pures.

Moi-même si depuis bientôt quinze ans (en comptant tout) mal doué de ressources, mal doué de forces de tout ordre, mal doué de talents, à travers des difficultés de toutes sortes, à travers des traverses sans nombre j'ai pu tenir le coup, si j'ai pu continuer cette œuvre, persévérer dans cette œuvre, dans cette opération incessante c'est certainement que je suis attaché à ces cahiers, à cette institution, à cette œuvre d'un attachement, d'une liaison qui est de l'ordre mystique.

Je le disais précisément à Isaac[1] pendant les vacances de Pâques. Nous déjeunions ensemble, une fois par an. Je lui disais : Vous croyez, vous dites que nous sommes purs, que nous avons les mains pures. Vous le croyez, vous le dites. Mais vous ne savez pas ce que vous dites. Vous ne pouvez pas mesurer ce que vous croyez. Il faut vivre à Paris, dans ce que l'on a fait de la République, pour savoir, pour mesurer ce que c'est que d'être pur.

J'ai la certitude en effet que nos amis de province nous font confiance. Mais ils ne peuvent pas savoir, ils ne peuvent pas soupçonner *de quoi* ils nous font confiance, quelle est la matière, le terrain de la confiance qu'ils nous font.

L'affaire Dreyfus fut un recoupement, une culmination de trois mystiques au moins. Premièrement elle fut sur le chemin de la mystique hébraïque. Pourquoi le nier. Ce serait le contraire au contraire qui serait suspect.

Il y a une politique juive. Pourquoi le nier. Ce serait le contraire au contraire qui serait suspect. Elle est sotte, comme toutes les politiques. Elle est prétentieuse, comme toutes les politiques. Elle est envahissante, comme toutes les politiques. Elle est inféconde, comme toutes les politiques. Elle fait les affaires d'Israël comme les politiciens républicains font les affaires de la République. Elle est surtout occupée, comme toutes les politiques, à étouffer, à dévorer, à supprimer sa propre mystique, la mystique dont elle est issue. Et elle ne réussit guère qu'à cela.

Loin donc qu'il faille considérer l'affaire Dreyfus comme une combinaison, politique, un agencement, comme une opération de la politique juive, il faut *au contraire* la considérer comme une opération, comme une œuvre, comme une explosion de la mystique juive. Les politiciens, les rabbins, les communautés d'Israël, pendant des siècles et des siècles de persécutions et d'épreuves, n'avaient que trop pris l'habitude, politique, le pli de sacrifier quelques-uns de leurs membres pour avoir la paix, la paix du ménage politique, la paix des rois et des grands, la paix de leurs débiteurs, la paix des populations et des princes, la paix des antisémites. Ils ne demandaient qu'à recommencer. Ils ne demandaient qu'à continuer. Ils ne demandaient qu'à sacrifier Dreyfus pour conjurer l'orage. La grande majorité des Juifs est comme la grande majorité des (autres) électeurs. Elle craint la guerre. Elle craint le trouble. Elle craint l'inquiétude. Elle craint, elle redoute plus que tout peut-être le simple dérangement. Elle aimerait mieux le silence, une tranquillité basse. Si on pouvait s'arranger moyennant un silence entendu, acheter la paix en livrant le bouc, payer de quelque livraison, de quelque trahison, de quelque bassesse une tranquillité précaire. Livrer le sang innocent, elle sait ce que c'est. En temps de paix elle craint la guerre. Elle a peur des coups. Elle a peur des affaires. Elle est forcée à sa propre grandeur. Elle n'est conduite à ses grands

destins douloureux que forcée par une poignée de
factieux, une *minorité agissante,* une bande d'énergumènes et de fanatiques, une bande de forcenés,
groupés autour de quelques têtes qui sont très précisément les prophètes d'Israël. Israël a fourni des
prophètes innombrables, des héros, des martyrs, des
guerriers sans nombre. Mais enfin, en temps ordinaire, le peuple d'Israël est comme tous les peuples, il
ne demande qu'à ne pas entrer dans un temps
extraordinaire. Quand il est dans une période, il est
comme tous les peuples, il ne demande qu'à ne pas
entrer dans une époque. Quand il est dans une
période, il ne demande qu'à ne pas entrer dans une
crise. Quand il est dans une bonne plaine, bien grasse,
où coulent les ruisseaux de lait et de miel, il ne
demande qu'à ne pas remonter sur la montagne, cette
montagne fût-elle la montagne de Moïse. Israël a
fourni des prophètes innombrables; plus que cela elle
est elle-même prophète, elle est elle-même la race
prophétique. Tout entière, en un seul corps, un seul
prophète. Mais enfin elle ne demande que ceci : c'est
de ne pas donner matière aux prophètes à s'exercer.
Elle sait ce que ça coûte. Instinctivement, historiquement, organiquement pour ainsi dire elle sait ce que
ça coûte. Sa mémoire, son instinct, son organisme
même, son corps temporel, son histoire, toute sa
mémoire le lui disent. Toute sa mémoire en est pleine.
Vingt, quarante, cinquante siècles d'épreuves le lui
disent. Des guerres sans nombre, des meurtres, des
déserts, des prises de villes, des exils, des guerres
étrangères, des guerres civiles, des captivités sans
nombre. Cinquante siècles de misères, quelquefois
dorées. Comme les misères modernes. Cinquante

siècles de détresses, quelquefois anarchistes, quelquefois masquées de joies, quelquefois masquées, maquil-
lées de voluptés. Cinquante siècles peut-être de neurasthénie. Cinquante siècles de blessures et de cica-
trices, des points toujours douloureux, les Pyramides
et les Champs-Élysées, les rois d'Égypte et les rois
d'Orient, le fouet des eunuques et la lance romaine, le
Temple détruit et non rebâti, une inexpiable dispersion leur en ont dit le prix pour leur éternité. Ils
savent ce que ça coûte, eux, que d'être la voix
charnelle et le corps temporel. Ils savent ce que ça
coûte que de porter Dieu et ses agents les prophètes.
Ses prophètes les prophètes. Alors, obscurément, ils
aimeraient mieux qu'on ne recommence pas. Ils ont
peur des coups. Ils en ont tant reçu. Ils aimeraient
mieux qu'on n'en parle pas. Ils ont tant de fois payé
pour eux-mêmes et pour les autres. On peut bien
parler d'autre chose. Ils ont tant de fois payé pour
tout le monde, pour nous. Si on ne parlait de rien du
tout. Si on faisait des affaires, de(s) bonnes affaires.
Ne triomphons pas. Ne triomphons pas d'eux.
Combien de chrétiens ont été poussés à coups de
lanières dans la voie du salut. C'est partout pareil. Ils
ont peur des coups. Toute l'humanité a généralement
peur des coups. Au moins avant. Et après. Heureusement elle n'a quelquefois pas peur des coups pendant.
Les plus merveilleux soldats peut-être du grand
Napoléon, ceux de la fin, ne provenaient-ils pas
généralement de bandes de déserteurs et d'insoumis
que les gendarmes impériaux avaient poussés,
menottes aux mains, avaient refoulés comme un
troupeau jusqu'en cette île de Walcheren. De là sortit

pourtant Lutzen, Bautzen, la Bérésina, le glorieux Walcheren-Infanterie, 131ᵉ de l'arme [1].

Ils ont tant fui, tant et de telles fuites, qu'ils savent le prix de ne pas fuir. Campés, entrés dans les peuples modernes, ils voudraient tant s'y trouver bien. Toute la politique d'Israël est de ne pas faire de bruit, dans le monde (on en a assez fait), d'acheter la paix par un silence prudent. Sauf quelques écervelés prétentieux, que tout le monde nomme, de se faire oublier. Tant de meurtrissures lui saignent encore. Mais toute la mystique d'Israël est qu'Israël poursuive dans le monde sa retentissante et douloureuse mission. De là des déchirements incroyables, les plus douloureux antagonismes intérieurs qu'il y ait eu peut-être entre une mystique et une politique. Peuple de marchands. Le même peuple de prophètes. Les uns savent pour les autres ce que c'est que des calamités.

Les uns savent pour les autres ce que c'est que des ruines; toujours et toujours des ruines; un amoncellement de ruines; habiter, passer dans un peuple de ruines, dans une ville de ruines.

Je connais bien ce peuple. Il n'a pas sur la peau un point qui ne soit pas douloureux, où il n'y ait un ancien bleu, une ancienne contusion, une douleur sourde, la mémoire d'une douleur sourde, une cicatrice, une blessure, une meurtrissure d'Orient ou d'Occident. Ils ont les leurs, et toutes celles des autres. Par exemple on a meurtri *comme Français* tous ceux de l'Alsace et de la Lorraine annexée.

C'est bien mal connaître la politique juive, au moment même qu'on en parle, que de supposer que ce soit la politique juive et le parti juif qui aient jamais

soulevé une affaire comme l'affaire Dreyfus. Au
contraire. Ce ne sont jamais eux qui soulèvent les
tumultes. Ils ne demandent, ils ne recherchent que le
silence. Ils ne demandent qu'à se faire oublier. Sauf
quelques écervelés, ils ne recherchent que l'ombre et
le silence.

En fait et dans le détail même c'est ne pas connaître
un mot de l'affaire Dreyfus et du dreyfusisme et
notamment de la manière dont elle a commencé que
de croire, que de s'imaginer qu'elle est comme une
invention, une fabrication, une forgerie du parti juif,
de la politique juive, que le parti juif, la politique juive
ait vu de bon cœur poindre le commencement de cette
affaire. C'est très exactement le contraire. Ils ne
savaient pas bien, mais ils se méfiaient. Ils avaient
raison de se méfier. Au point de vue des intérêts. Cette
affaire, somme toute, et sous des victoires apparentes,
sous des aspects de conquête(s), sous des surfaces de
triomphe, leur a fait (beaucoup) plus de mal que de
bien.

Au point où en est tombée aujourd'hui la courbe de
l'histoire de cette affaire, nous pouvons dire en effet
aujourd'hui qu'une première fois nous fûmes vainqueurs des antidreyfusistes antidreyfusistes; qu'une
deuxième fois nous fûmes vaincus par les antidreyfusistes dreyfusistes; qu'aujourd'hui enfin nous sommes
en train d'être vaincus par les deux ensemble.

Ils se méfiaient. Prévoyaient-ils ce tumulte énorme,
cet énorme ébranlement. On ne prévoit jamais tout.
En tout cas ils n'aiment pas soulever des tumultes.

Quand donc la famille de M. Dreyfus, pour obtenir
une réparation individuelle, envisageait un chambar-
dement total de la France, et d'Israël, et de toute la

chrétienté, non seulement elle allait contre la politique française, mais elle n'allait pas moins contre la politique juive qu'elle n'allait évidemment contre la politique cléricale. Une mystique peut aller contre toutes les politiques *à la fois*. Ceux qui apprennent l'histoire ailleurs que dans les polémiques, ceux qui essaient de la suivre dans les réalités, dans la réalité même, savent que c'est en Israël que la famille Dreyfus, que l'affaire Dreyfus naissante, que le dreyfusisme naissant rencontra d'abord les plus vives résistances. La sagesse est aussi une vertu d'Israël. S'il y a les Prophètes il y a l'Ecclésiaste. Beaucoup disaient *à quoi bon*. Les sages voyaient surtout qu'on allait soulever un tumulte, instituer un commencement dont on ne verrait peut-être jamais la fin, dont surtout on ne voyait pas quelle serait la fin. Dans les familles, dans le secret des familles on traitait communément de folie cette tentative. Une fois de plus la folie devait l'emporter, dans cette race élue de l'inquiétude. Plus tard, bientôt tous, ou presque tous, marchèrent, parce que quand un prophète a parlé en Israël, tous le haïssent, tous l'admirent, tous le suivent. Cinquante siècles d'épée dans les reins les forcent à marcher.

Ils reconnaissent l'épreuve avec un instinct admirable, avec un instinct de cinquante siècles. Ils reconnaissent, ils saluent le coup. C'est encore un coup de Dieu. La ville encore sera prise, le Temple détruit, les femmes emmenées. Une captivité vient, après tant de captivités. De longs convois traîneront dans le désert. Leurs cadavres jalonneront les routes d'Asie. Très bien, ils savent ce que c'est. Ils ceignent leurs reins pour ce nouveau départ. Puisqu'il faut y passer ils y passeront encore. Dieu est dur, mais il est Dieu. Il punit, et il soutient. Il mène. Eux qui ont obéi, impunément, à tant de maîtres extérieurs, temporels, ils saluent enfin le maître de la plus rigoureuse servitude, le Prophète, le maître intérieur.

Le prophète, en cette grande crise d'Israël et du monde, fut Bernard-Lazare [1]. Saluons ici l'un des plus grands noms des temps modernes, et après Darmesteter [2] l'un des plus grands parmi les prophètes d'Israël. Pour moi, si la vie m'en laisse l'espace, je considérerai comme une des plus grandes récompenses de ma vieillesse de pouvoir enfin fixer, restituer le portrait de cet homme extraordinaire.

J'avais commencé d'écrire un *portrait de Bernard-Lazare* [3]. Mais pour ces hommes de cinquante siècles il faut bien peut-être un recul de cinquante ans. D'énormes quantités d'imbéciles, et en Israël et en Chrétienté, croient encore que Bernard-Lazare fut un jeune homme, un homme jeune, on ne sait pas bien, un jeune écrivain, venu à Paris comme tant d'autres, pour s'y pousser, pour y faire sa fortune, dans les lettres, comme on disait encore alors, dans le théâtre, dans les contes, dans les nouvelles, dans le livre, dans la nouvelle, dans le recueil, dans le conte, dans le fatras, dans le journal, dans la politique, dans toute la misère temporelle, venu au Quartier, comme tous les jeunes gens de ces pays-là, un jeune juif du Midi, d'Avignon et de Vaucluse, ou des Bouches du Rhône, ou plutôt du Gard et de l'Hérault. Un jeune juif de Nîmes ou de Montpellier. Je ne serais pas surpris, j'ai même la certitude que le jeune Bernard-Lazare le croyait lui-même. Le prophète d'abord ne se connaît point. On trouverait encore des gens qui feraient tout un travail sur Bernard-Lazare symboliste et jeune poète ou ami des symbolistes ou ennemi des symbolistes. On ne sait plus. Et dans l'affaire Dreyfus même je ne serais pas surpris que l'État-Major dreyfusiste, l'entourage de Dreyfus, la famille de Dreyfus et Dreyfus lui-même aient toujours considéré Bernard-Lazare comme un agent, que l'on payait, comme une sorte de conseil juridique, ou judiciaire, non pas seulement dans les matières juridiques, comme un faiseur de mémoires, salarié, comme un publiciste, comme un pamphlétaire, à gages, comme un polémiste et un polémiqueur, comme un journaliste sans journal, comme un avocat officieux, honoré, comme un officieux, comme un avocat non plaidant. Comme un faiseur, comme un établisseur de mémoires et dossiers, comme une sorte d'avocat consultant en matières juridiques et surtout en matières politiques, enfin comme un folliculaire. Comme un écrivain professionnel. Par conséquent comme un homme que l'on méprise. Comme un homme qui travaillait, qui écrivait sur un thème. Qu'on lui donnait, qu'on lui avait donné. Comme un homme qui gagnait sa vie, qui gagnait ce qu'il pouvait, qui gagnait ce qu'il gagnait. Par conséquent comme un homme que l'on méprise. Comme un homme à la suite. Peut-être comme un agent d'exécution. Israël passe à côté du Juste, et le méprise. Israël passe à côté du Prophète, le suit, et ne le voit pas.

La méconnaissance des prophètes par Israël et pourtant la conduite d'Israël par les prophètes, c'est toute l'histoire d'Israël.

La méconnaissance des saints par les pécheurs et

pourtant le salut des pécheurs par les saints, c'est toute l'histoire chrétienne.

La méconnaissance des prophètes par Israël n'a d'égale, n'a de comparable, bien que fort différente, que la méconnaissance des saints par les pécheurs.

On peut même dire que la méconnaissance des prophètes par Israël est une *figure* de la méconnaissance des saints par les pécheurs.

Quand le prophète passe, Israël croit que c'est un publiciste. Qui sait, peut-être un sociologue.

Si on pouvait lui faire une situation en Sorbonne. Ou plutôt à l'École *pratique (?)* (!) des Hautes Études. Quatrième section. Ou cinquième. Ou troisième. Enfin section des **sciences** *religieuses*. A la Sorbonne, *au bout de la galerie des Sciences*, escalier E, au premier étage. On pourra toujours. On est si puissant dans l'État français.

L'un des documents les plus effrayants de l'ingratitude humaine, (ici ce fut particulièrement de l'ingratitude juive, mais généralement aussi ce fut l'ingratitude de tant d'autres, sinon la nôtre, une ingratitude commune), fut la situation faite à Bernard-Lazare aussitôt après le déclenchement et le triomphe apparent, le faux triomphe de l'affaire Dreyfus. La méconnaissance totale, l'ignorance même, la solitude, l'oubli, le mépris où on le laissa tomber, où on le fit tomber, où on le fit périr. Où on le fit mourir.

— C'est de sa faute aussi s'il est mort, disent-ils dans leur incroyable, dans leur incurable bassesse, dans leur grossière promiscuité révoltante. Il ne faut jamais mourir. On a toujours tort de mourir. — Il faut donc dire, il faut donc écrire, il faut donc publier que comme il avait vécu pour eux, littéralement il est mort

par eux et pour eux. Oui, oui, je sais, il est mort de
ceci. Et de cela. On meurt toujours de quelque chose.
Mais le mal terrible dont il est mort lui eût laissé un
délai, dix, quinze, vingt ans de répit sans l'effroyable
surmenage qu'il avait assumé pour sauver Dreyfus.
Tension nerveuse effrayante et qui dura des années.
Effroyable surmenage de corps et de tête. Surmenage
de cœur, le pire de tous. Surmenage de tout.

On meurt toujours de quelque(s) atteinte(s).

Je ferai le portrait de Bernard-Lazare. Il avait,
indéniablement, des parties de saint, de sainteté. Et
quand je parle de saint, je ne suis pas suspect de
parler par métaphore. Il avait une douceur, une
bonté, une tendresse mystique, une égalité d'humeur,
une expérience de l'amertume et de l'ingratitude, une
digestion parfaite de l'amertume et de l'ingratitude,
une sorte de bonté à qui on n'en remontrait point, une
sorte de bonté parfaitement renseignée et parfaitement apprise d'une profondeur incroyable. Comme
une bonté à revendre. Il vécut et mourut pour eux
comme un martyr. Il fut un prophète. Il était donc
juste qu'on l'ensevelît prématurément dans le silence
et dans l'oubli. Dans un silence fait. Dans un oubli
concerté.

Il ne faut pas lui alléguer sa mort. Car sa mort
même fut pour eux. Il ne faut pas lui reprocher sa
mort.

On lui en voulait surtout, les juifs lui en voulaient
surtout, le méprisaient surtout parce qu'il n'était pas
riche. Je crois même qu'on disait qu'il était dépensier.
Cela voulait dire qu'on n'avait plus besoin de lui, ou
que l'on croyait que l'on n'avait plus besoin de lui.

Peut-être en effet leur coûtait-il un peu ; leur avait-il coûté un peu plus. C'était un homme qui avait la main ouverte.

Seulement il faudrait peut-être considérer qu'il était sans prix.

Car il était mort avant d'être mort. Israël une fois de plus, Israël poursuivait ses destinées temporellement éternelles. Il est extrêmement remarquable que le seul journal où on ait jamais traité dignement notre ami, je veux dire selon sa dignité, selon sa grandeur, selon sa mesure, dans son ordre de grandeur, où on l'ait traité en ennemi sans doute, violemment, âprement, comme un ennemi, mais enfin à sa mesure, où on l'ait considéré à la mesure de sa grandeur, où on ait dit, en termes ennemis, mais enfin où on ait dit combien il aimait Israël et combien il était grand fut *la Libre Parole*, et que le seul homme qui l'ait dit fut M. Édouard Drumont [1]. C'est une honte pour nous que le nom de Bernard-Lazare, depuis cinq ans, sept ans qu'il est mort, n'ait jamais figuré que dans son journal ennemi. Je ne parle pas des cahiers, dont il demeure l'ami intérieur, l'inspirateur secret, je dirai très volontiers, et très exactement, le patron. En dehors de nous, je dis très limitativement, comme on dit dans le droit, en dehors de nous des cahiers, il n'y a que M. Édouard Drumont qui ait su parler de Bernard-Lazare, qui ait voulu en parler, qui lui ait fait sa mesure.

Les autres, les nôtres se taisaient dès avant sa mort, se sont tus depuis avec un soin honteux, avec une perfection, avec une patience, avec une réussite extraordinaire.

Et il était mort avant d'être mort.

Ils avaient comme honte de lui. Mais en réalité c'étaient eux qui avaient honte d'eux devant lui.

C'étaient les politiciens, c'était la politique même qui avait honte de soi devant la mystique.

Combien de fois n'ai-je pas monté cette rue de Florence. Il y a pour tous les quartiers de Paris non seulement une personnalité constituée, mais cette personnalité a une histoire comme nous. Il n'y a pas bien longtemps et pourtant tout date. Déjà. Le propre de l'histoire, c'est ce changement même, cette *génération et corruption*[1], cette abolition constante, cette révolution perpétuelle. Cette mort. Il n'y a que quelques années, huit ans, dix ans, et quelle méconnaissance déjà, quelle méconnaissance immobilière.
— *Le vieux Paris n'est plus (la forme d'une ville*

Change plus vite, hélas ! que le cœur d'un mortel)[2] ;

On demeurait alors dans ce haut de Paris où personne aujourd'hui ne demeure plus. On bâtit tant de maisons partout, boulevard Raspail. M. Salomon Reinach[3] devait demeurer encore 36 ou 38 rue de Lisbonne. Ou un autre numéro. Mais enfin Bernard-Lazare y passait, y pouvait passer comme en voisin, en passant. Le quartier Saint-Lazare. La rue de Rome et la rue de Constantinople. Tout le quartier de l'Europe. Toute l'Europe. Des résonances de noms qui secrètement flattaient leur besoin de voyager, leur aisance à voyager, leur résidence européenne. Un quartier de gare qui flattait leur besoin de chemin de fer, leur goût du chemin de fer, leur aisance en chemin de fer. Tout le monde a déménagé. Quelques-uns dans la mort. Et même beaucoup. Zola demeurait rue de Bruxelles, 81 ou 81 *bis* ou 83 rue de Bruxelles. *Première audience. — Audience du 7 février. — Vous vous appelez Émile Zola? — Oui, monsieur. — Quelle est votre profession? — Homme de lettres. — Quel est votre âge? — Cinquante-huit ans. — Quel est votre domicile? — 81 bis, rue de Bruxelles*[1]. M. Ludovic Halévy[2] ne demeurait-il pas rue de Douai, qui doit être dans le même quartier, 22, rue de Douai, et encore aujourd'hui 62, rue de Rome, 155, boulevard Haussmann, c'étaient des adresses de ce temps-là. Dreyfus même était de ce quartier. Labori[3] seul demeure encore 41 ou 45 rue Condorcet. On me dit qu'il vient seulement d'émigrer 12, rue Pigalle, Paris IXe. Toute une population, tout un peuple demeurait ainsi sur les hauteurs de Paris, dans le flanc des hauteurs de Paris, dans ce haut Paris serré, tout un peuple, amis, ennemis, qui se connaissaient, ne se connaissaient pas, mais se sentaient, se savaient voisins de campagne dans cet immense Paris.

Combien de fois n'ai-je point monté, dans les jours douloureux, jusqu'à cette rue de Florence. Jours douloureux pour lui et pour moi, ensemble, également, car tout était perdu, que la politique, notre politique, (je veux dire la politique des nôtres), commençait à dévorer notre mystique. Lui le sentait si je puis dire avec plus de renseignement, je le sentais avec plus d'innocence. Mais il avait encore une innocence désarmante. Et j'avais déjà beaucoup de renseignements.

Je puis dire, pour qu'il n'y ait aucun malentendu, je dois dire que pendant ces dernières années, pendant cette dernière période de sa vie je fus son seul ami. Son dernier et son seul ami. Son dernier et son seul confident. A moi seul il disait alors ce qu'il pensait, ce qu'il sentait, ce qu'il savait enfin. Je le rapporterai quelque jour.

Je suis forcé d'y insister, je fus son seul ami et son seul confident. J'y insiste parce que quelques amis de contrebande qu'il avait, ou plutôt qu'il avait eus, des amis littéraires enfin, entreprenaient de se faire croire, et de faire croire au monde, qu'ils étaient restés ses amis, même après qu'ils avaient saboté, dénaturé, méconnu, inconnu, empolitiqué sa mystique.

Des amis de Quartier enfin, d'anciens amis d'étudiants, peut-être de Sorbonne. Des amis qui tutoient.

Et lui il était si bon que par cette incurable, par cette inépuisable bonté il le leur laissait croire aussi, et il le laissait croire au monde. Mais il m'en parlait tout autrement, parce que j'étais son seul confident, parce qu'il me confiait tous les secrets, tout le secret de sa pensée.

Il avait de l'amitié non pas une idée mystique seulement, mais un sentiment mystique, mais une expérience d'une incroyable profondeur, une épreuve, une expérience, une connaissance mystique. Il avait cet attachement mystique à la fidélité qui est au cœur de l'amitié. Il faisait un exercice mystique de cette fidélité qui est au cœur de l'amitié. Ainsi naquit entre lui et nous cette amitié, cette fidélité éternelle, cette amitié que nulle mort ne devait rompre, cette amitié parfaitement échangée, parfaitement mutuelle, parfaitement parfaite, nourrie de la désillusion, de toutes les autres, du désabusement de toutes les infidélités.

Cette amitié que nulle mort ne rompra.

Il avait au plus haut degré, au plus profond, cette morale de bande, qui est peut-être la seule morale.

Or pour sa mystique même il avait cette fidélité mystique, cette amitié mystique.

Cette amitié, cette morale de bande.

Il avait cette fidélité à soi-même qui est tout de même l'essentiel. Beaucoup peuvent vous trahir. Mais c'est beaucoup, c'est déjà beaucoup que de ne pas se trahir soi-même. Beaucoup de politiques peuvent trahir, peuvent dévorer, peuvent absorber beaucoup de mystiques. C'est beaucoup que les mystiques ne se trahissent point elles-mêmes.

Beaucoup de maréchaux ont pu trahir Napoléon. Mais au moins Napoléon ne s'est pas trahi lui-même. Le maréchal Napoléon n'a pas trahi Napoléon Empereur.

On peut dire que ses dernières joies, tant qu'il marchait, tant qu'il allait encore, furent de venir comme se réchauffer parmi nous aux jeudis des cahiers, ou, pour parler plus exactement, le jeudi aux cahiers. Il aimait beaucoup deviser avec M. Sorel [1]. Je dois dire que leurs propos étaient généralement empreints d'un grand désabusement.

Il avait un goût secret, très marqué, très profond, et presque très violent, pour M. Sorel. Un goût commun de désabusement; de gens à qui on n'en contait point. Quand ils riaient ensemble, quand ils éclataient, au même moment, car tous les deux avaient le rire jailli, c'était avec une profondeur d'accord, une complicité incroyable. Cet accord saisissant de l'esprit, du rire, qui n'attend pas, qui ne calcule pas, qui d'un coup atteint au plus profond, au dernier point, éclate et révèle. Qui d'un mot atteint au dernier mot. Tout ce que disait M. Sorel le frappait tellement qu'il m'en parlait encore tous les autres matins de la semaine. Ils étaient comme deux grands complices. Deux grands enfants terribles. Deux grands enfants complices qui eussent très bien connu les hommes.

L'amitié qu'il avait pour ces cahiers naissants, pour moi, avait quelque chose de désarmant. C'était toute la sollicitude, toute la tendresse, tout le renseignement, tout l'avertissement d'un grand frère aîné qui en a beaucoup vu.

Qui a été très éprouvé par la vie. Par l'existence.

Dès lors il était suspect. Dès lors il était isolé. L'honneur d'avoir fait l'affaire Dreyfus lui collait aux épaules comme une chape inexpiable. Suspect surtout, solitaire surtout dans son propre parti. Pas un journal, pas une revue n'acceptait, ne tolérait sa signature. On eût pris peut-être à la rigueur un peu de sa copie, en la maquillant, en l'avachissant, en la

sucrant. Surtout en enlevant, en effaçant cette dia-
blesse de signature. Il revenait naturellement vers
nous. Il n'y avait plus qu'aux cahiers qu'il pût parler,
écrire, publier, — causer même. Quand on faisait des
pourparlers pour créer un grand quotidien (dans ce
temps-là on pourparlait toujours pour créer un grand
nouveau quotidien) et qu'on demandait de l'argent
aux Juifs (ils en donnaient alors, ils s'en laissaient
arracher beaucoup trop, M. Jaurès en sait quelque
chose) les capitalistes, les commanditaires juifs n'y
mettaient guère qu'une condition : c'était que Bernard-Lazare n'y écrivît pas [1].

On s'organisait fort proprement de toutes parts
pour qu'il mourût tout tranquillement de faim.

Il revenait vers nous comme par sa pente naturelle.
Il était comme sacré, c'est-à-dire qu'on le comptait
pour son compte, on le mesurait à sa mesure, on le
prisait à sa valeur et en même temps et surtout on ne
voulait plus entendre parler de lui. Tout le monde le
taisait. Ceux qu'il avait sauvés le taisaient plus
obstinément, plus silencieusement que tous, l'enfon-
çaient dans un silence plus sourd, plus obstiné.
Quelques-uns, dans la criminelle pénombre de l'arrière-pensée, commençaient à laisser se penser en eux
qu'il était peut-être bien heureux, qu'il mourait peut-
être juste à temps pour sa gloire. Quelques-uns le
pensaient peut-être, quelques-uns le pensaient sans
doute. Le fait est, il faut lui rendre cette justice, qu'il
mourait opportunément ; commodément pour beaucoup. Presque pour tout le monde. Quelques personnes qu'il avait fait abonner aux cahiers pendant la

crise de l'affaire Dreyfus attendaient impatiemment qu'il mourût pour nous envoyer leur désabonnement, se débarrasser de cet énorme tribut de vingt francs par an qu'il leur avait imposé *pendant l'affaire Dreyfus*, comme on disait déjà. Nous reçûmes le désabonnement de M. Louis Louis-Dreyfus [1] dans la quinzaine ou dans le mois, peut-être dans la semaine qui suivit la mort de Bernard-Lazare.

Ceux qu'il avait sauvés étaient les plus pressés. Lui-même le savait très bien. On a beau savoir aussi que c'est la règle. A chaque fois c'est toujours nouveau. Et c'est toujours dur à avaler.

Lui-même il ne se faisait aucune illusion sur les hommes qu'il avait défendus. Il voyait partout les politiques, les hommes politiques arriver, dévorer tout, dévorer, déshonorer son œuvre. Je dirai tout ce qu'il m'a dit. Il atteignait, il obtenait une profondeur de sentiment(s), une profondeur de regret incroyable, il parvenait à ces profondeurs de bonté douce incroyables qui ne peuvent être qu'à base de désabusement.

Une petite minorité, un petit groupe, une immense majorité de juifs pauvres (il y en a, beaucoup), de misérables (il y en a, beaucoup), lui demeuraient fidèles, lui étaient attachés d'un attachement, d'un amour fanatique, qu'exaspéraient de jour en jour les approches de la mort. Ceux-là l'aimaient. Nous l'aimions. Les riches ne l'aimaient déjà plus.

Je dirai donc quel fut son enterrement.

Je dirai quelle fut toute sa fin.

Je dirai combien il souffrit.

Je dirai, dans ces *confessions*, combien il se tut.

Je vois encore sur moi son regard de myope, si
intelligent et ensemble si bon, d'une si invincible, si
intelligente, si éclairée, si éclairante, si lumineuse
douceur, d'une si inlassable, si renseignée, si éclairée,
si désabusée, si incurable bonté. Parce qu'un homme
porte un binocle bien planté sur un nez gras barrant,
vitrant deux bons gros yeux de myope, le moderne ne
sait pas reconnaître, il ne sait pas voir le regard, le feu
allumé il y a cinquante siècles. Mais moi je l'ai
approché. Seul j'ai vécu dans son intimité et dans sa
confidence. Il fallait écouter, il fallait voir cet homme
qui naturellement se croyait un moderne. Il fallait
regarder ce regard, il fallait entendre cette voix.
Naturellement il était très sincèrement athée. Ce
n'était pas alors la métaphysique dominante seulement, c'était la métaphysique ambiante, celle que l'on
respirait, une sorte de métaphysique climatérique,
atmosphérique ; qui allait de soi, comme d'être bien
élevé ; et en outre il était entendu, positivement,
scientifiquement, victorieusement, que ce n'était pas,
qu'elle n'était pas une métaphysique ; il était positiviste, scientificiste, intellectuel, moderne, enfin tout ce
qu'il faut ; surtout il ne voulait pas entendre parler de
métaphysique(s). Un de ses arguments favoris, celui
qu'il me servait toujours, était qu'Israël étant de tous
les peuples celui qui croyait le moins en Dieu, c'était
évidemment celui qu'il serait le plus facile de débarrasser des anciennes superstitions ; et ainsi ce serait
celui qui montrerait la route aux autres. L'excellence
des Juifs était selon lui, venait de ce qu'ils étaient
comme d'avance les plus libres penseurs. Même avec
un trait d'union. Et là-dessous, et là-dedans un cœur

qui battait à tous les échos du monde, un homme qui
sautait sur un journal et qui sur les quatre pages, sur
les six, huit, sur les douze pages d'un seul regard
comme la foudre saisissait une ligne et dans cette ligne
il y avait le mot Juif, un être qui rougissait, pâlissait,
un vieux journaliste, un routier du journal(isme) qui
blêmissait sur un écho, qu'il trouvait dans ce journal,
sur un morceau d'article, sur un filet, sur une
dépêche, et dans cet écho, dans ce journal, dans ce
morceau d'article, dans ce filet, dans cette dépêche il y
avait le mot Juif; un cœur qui saignait dans tous les
ghettos du monde, et peut-être encore plus dans les
ghettos rompus, dans les ghettos diffus, comme Paris,
que dans les ghettos conclus, dans les ghettos forclus;
un cœur qui saignait en Roumanie et en Turquie, en
Russie et en Algérie, en Amérique et en Hongrie,
partout où le Juif est persécuté, c'est-à-dire, en un
certain sens, partout; un cœur qui saignait en Orient
et en Occident, dans l'Islam et en Chrétienté; un
cœur qui saignait en Judée même, et un homme en
même temps qui plaisantait les Sionistes; ainsi est le
juif; un tremblement de colère, et c'était pour quelque
injure subie dans la vallée du Dniepr. Aussi ce que nos
Puissances ne voulaient pas savoir, qu'il fût le prophète, le juif, le chef, — le dernier colporteur juif le
savait, le voyait, le plus misérable juif de Roumanie [1].
Un tremblement, une vibration perpétuelle. Tout ce
qu'il faut pour mourir à quarante ans. Pas un muscle,
pas un nerf qui ne fût tendu pour une mission secrète,
perpétuellement vibré pour la mission. Jamais homme
ne se tint à ce point chef de sa race et de son peuple,
responsable pour sa race et pour son peuple. Un être
perpétuellement tendu. Une arrière-tension, une sous-

tension inexpiable. Pas un sentiment, pas une pensée, pas l'ombre d'une passion qui ne fût tendue, qui ne fût commandée par un commandement vieux de cinquante siècles, par le commandement tombé il y a cinquante siècles ; toute une race, tout un monde sur les épaules, une race, un monde de cinquante siècles sur les épaules voûtées ; sur les épaules rondes, sur les épaules lourdes ; un cœur élevé de feu, du feu de sa race, consumé du feu de son peuple ; le feu au cœur, une tête ardente, *et le charbon ardent sur la lèvre prophète* [1].

Quand je viens en relation avec quelqu'un de nos anciens adversaires (c'est un phénomène de plus en plus fréquent, inévitable, désirable même, car il faut bien qu'un peuple se refasse, et se refasse de toutes ses forces), je commence par lui dire : Vous ne nous connaissez pas. Vous avez le droit de ne pas nous connaître. Nos politiciens ont fait une telle *Foire sur la Place* que vous ne pouviez pas voir ce qui se passait *dans la maison* [2]. Nos politiciens n'ont pas dévoré seulement, absorbé notre mystique. Ils la masquaient complètement, au moins au public, à ce qu'on nomme le grand public. Vous n'étiez pas abonné aux cahiers. C'est tout naturel. Vous aviez autre chose à faire. Vous ne lisiez pas les cahiers. Mais cette mystique dont nous parlons, nous ne l'inventons pas aujourd'hui pour les besoins de la cause, nous ne l'improvisons pas aujourd'hui. Elle fut pendant dix et quinze ans la mystique même de ces cahiers en toutes ces matières et nous l'avons assez souvent manifestée. La seule différence qu'il y avait, c'est que masqués par les politiciens nos cahiers ne parvenaient point alors auprès du grand public et qu'aujourd'hui, dans le désarroi des politiciens, et sans doute pour une autre cause, et au moins même pour deux, ils y parviennent.

La seule différence qu'il y a, c'est qu'on ne nous lisait point ; et que l'on commence à nous lire.

Et d'autre part il est certain que nous sommes les seuls, qu'il n'y a que nous qui depuis quinze ans ayons tenu rigoureusement, impeccablement, infailliblement cette mystique. Là était notre force. Et aujourd'hui, obscure avec nous, ignorée avec nous, conservée avec nous, par nos soins, aujourd'hui par nos soins, avec nous cette mystique naturellement apparaît.

Elle était notre force, à nous autres faibles, à nous autres pauvres. La mystique est la force invincible des faibles.

Mais toute la différence qu'il y a, c'est qu'elle était inconnue ; et qu'aujourd'hui, avec nous, en nous elle est connue.

C'est pour cela que je veux bien qu'il y ait une *apologie pour notre passé,* et que je la trouve très bien faite, pourvu qu'il soit bien entendu seulement qu'il ne s'agit pas de *notre* passé, à nous, mais du passé des autres. Mon passé n'a besoin d'aucune apologie. Autrement il y aurait, il se produirait un effet, une illusion d'optique, extrêmement injurieuse pour nous ; et injuste ; et sotte. Un certain nombre, un petit nombre de dreyfusards, le dessus, ont fait, ont subi des démagogies, toute une démagogie, toute une *politique* dreyfusiste. Un certain nombre, un très grand nombre d'autres, nous les dessous, les profondeurs, les sots, nous avons tout fait, tout exposé pour demeurer fidèles à notre mystique, pour nous opposer à l'établissement de la domination de cette politique. C'est nous qui comptons. C'est nous qui représentons. C'est nous qui témoignons. C'est nous qui sommes la preuve. Nous voulons bien que les autres fassent des défenses et des apologies, des remords, des regrets et des soucis, qu'ils fassent des repentirs et des pénitences, laïques, qu'ils demandent et qu'ils obtiennent des absolutions, laïques, civiques, civiles et obligatoires. Nous leur en donnerons même les formules. Mais nous demandons qu'ils ne les demandent pas et ne les obtiennent pas pour nous ; qu'ils ne les exercent pas pour nous ; et deuxièmement qu'ils ne les demandent pas et ne les obtiennent pas et ne les exercent pas pour l'affaire Dreyfus elle-même et pour le dreyfusisme. Je ne veux point d'une *apologie pour Péguy,* ni *pour le passé de Péguy,* ni d'une *apologie pour les cahiers* ni *pour le passé des cahiers.* Je ne veux pas qu'on me défende. Je n'ai pas besoin d'être défendu. Je ne suis accusé de rien.

Je ne redoute rien tant que ceci : qu'on me défende.

Voilà tout le désaveu que j'ai le courage de m'infliger.

Je ne suis pas accusé. *Nous* ne sommes pas accusés. *Notre* affaire Dreyfus n'est pas accusée. Sous ce nom commun d'affaire Dreyfus, comme il arrive si souvent en histoire, sous ce nom presque générique il y a eu au moins, dans la réalité, deux affaires parfaitement

distinctes, extrêmement différentes. Deux affaires ont
couru, ont poussé leur carrière, ont suivi leur fortune.
Ont poussé leur chemin. La nôtre n'a rien à se
reprocher. Il y a eu des dreyfusistes purs et des
dreyfusistes impurs. C'est le niveau de l'humanité. Il
y a eu une affaire Dreyfus pure et une affaire Dreyfus
impure. C'est le niveau de l'événement. Nous ne
souffrirons pas que la première fasse des excuses,
donne des pénitences pour la deuxième. Ou si l'on
préfère, que la deuxième en fasse et en donne pour la
première. Avec la première. Ensemble. Nous n'avons
rien à nous faire pardonner. Nous ne souffrirons pas
que ceux qui ont à demander pardon, ou qui ont le
goût de demander pardon, demandent pardon aussi
ensemble pour nous.

Nous ne voulons pas du tout qu'on nous pardonne.

Nous qui avons tout sacrifié pour nous opposer
notamment à la démagogie combiste, issue de notre
dreyfusisme, politique issue de notre mystique, nous
ne sommes point dans le dreyfusisme une quantité
négligeable, qu'il faille ni que l'on puisse négliger
dans les comptes, éliminer et mépriser dans et pour les
opérations de l'histoire. C'est nous au contraire qui
sommes le centre et le cœur du dreyfusisme, qui le
sommes restés, c'est nous qui sommes l'âme. L'axe
passe par nous. C'est à notre montre qu'il faudra lire
l'heure.

Il y a eu, il y a un honneur dreyfusiste. Ceux qui
n'ont pas été fidèles à cet honneur, ceux qui n'ont pas
suivi cet honneur n'ont point à demander pardon
pour ceux qui l'ont suivi, qui le suivent.

Quand de loin en loin je viens en relation avec
quelqu'un de ces anciens adversaires, je lui dis : Vous

ne nous connaissez pas. Vous ne nous soupçonnez
peut-être pas. Vous en avez le droit. Tant des nôtres
ne nous connaissent pas. Nos politiciens ont tout fait
pour nous dérober à vous, pour nous masquer à vous,
pour nous désavouer, pour nous renier, pour nous
trahir, notre mystique et nous. Il est tout naturel que
placés en face d'eux dans la bataille vous n'ayez vu
que le dessus, la politique, qui se manifestait, et que
vous ne nous ayez pas vus, que vous n'ayez pas vu le
dessous, les profondeurs, qui nourrissaient. Vous avez
vu les manifestations et pendant que nous suivions les
règles de notre honneur vous n'avez pas vu les forces.
C'est la loi même du combat. Aujourd'hui vous ne
pouvez pas tout lire. En arrière, en remontant. Vous
ne pouvez pas tout nous connaître. On ne se rattrape
pas, on ne se refait pas, on ne se remet pas de dix,
douze ou quinze ans. Prenez seulement ceci. Et alors
je leur donne ou je leur envoie un exemplaire du III-
21, Jean Deck, *pour la Finlande*[1], non point seulement
pour qu'ils lisent ce gros et beau travail de notre
collaborateur, au moment même où la Finlande, qui
avait tout de même un peu résisté à l'autocratie pure,
à la bureaucratie autocratique, ne peut plus résister à
l'autocratie parlementaire, ne peut plus se défendre
contre la bureaucratie autocratique déguisée, mas-
quée d'un vague appareil parlementaire, mais parce
qu'à la fin de ce cahier, dans ce désastreux mois
d'août de 1902, nous avions, dans le désastre et dans
le désarroi de notre zèle, dans le deuil de notre
désastre, groupé hâtivement à la fin de ce cahier tout
ce que nous avions pu grouper hâtivement de dreyfusiste, tout ce que nous avions pu ramasser contre la
politique, contre la démagogie de la *loi des congréga-*

tions. Lisez seulement, leur dis-je, à la fin du cahier, ce
dossier de trente ou quarante pages *pour et contre les
congrégations.* Lisez même seulement, à la fin de ce
dossier, cette *consultation* de Bernard-Lazare datée du
6 août 1902, intitulée *la loi et les congrégations.* Vingt-
cinq pages. Les dernières vraiment qu'il ait données.
Un an après il était mort ou mourait.

Il faut leur faire cette justice qu'ils sortent de cette
lecture généralement stupéfaits. Ils ne soupçonnaient
point qui nous étions. Et surtout ils ne soupçonnaient
point que nous l'étions dès le principe. Que nous
l'avions été depuis si longtemps, depuis le principe. Ils
ne soupçonnaient point cette longue, cette initiale,
cette impeccable fidélité. Cette fidélité de toute une
vie. Notamment, éminemment ils ne soupçonnaient
point ce que c'était qu'un homme comme Bernard-
Lazare.

Il faut penser que dans ce *dossier,* dans cette
consultation, qu'il faut lire, qui n'est pas seulement un
admirable monument mais un monument inoublia-
ble, Bernard-Lazare s'opposait de tout ce qu'il avait
encore de force à la dénégation, à la déviation du
dreyfusisme en politique, en démagogie combiste.
Que ceux qui ont succombé, qui ont cédé, si peu que
ce fut, à la pire de toutes les démagogies, à la
démagogie combiste, fassent des *apologies,* ou qu'on en
fasse pour eux. Mais pour ceux qui ont été inébranla-
bles, pour ceux qui n'ont pas cédé d'une ligne, de
grâce, que l'on n'en fasse point. Quand on relit cet
admirable mémoire de Bernard-Lazare, on est comme
choqué, il vient une rougeur à cette idée seulement

que l'idée viendrait qu'un tel homme fût englobé, pût être englobé inconsidérément par des tiers, par le public, par les ignorants, dans les grâciés, dans les bénéficiaires d'une apologie.

Opérant, travaillant la même matière, évoluant dans la même matière il y a eu au moins deux affaires Dreyfus, élaborant la matière de la même histoire. Celle de Bernard-Lazare, la nôtre, était innocente et n'a pas besoin d'être défendue. Et en un autre sens encore il y avait très notamment deux affaires Dreyfus, celle qui était sortie de Bernard-Lazare, et celle qui était sortie du colonel Picquart[1]. Celle qui était sortie du colonel Picquart était très bien. Celle qui était sortie de Bernard-Lazare était infinie.

Il faut penser que, notamment dans cette *consultation*, qui fut littéralement son testament mystique, il ne s'opposait pas seulement au combisme, qui fut l'abus, la démagogie du système. Il s'était opposé, non moins vigoureusement, au waldeckisme, qui en était censément l'usage et la norme. Il n'était point allé seulement à l'abus, mais il était remonté à la racine même de l'usage. Il était allé, il était remonté à la racine, jusqu'à la racine. Naturellement, d'un mouvement, d'une requête, d'une réquisition naturelle, comme tout homme de pensée profonde. Il avait discerné l'effet dans la cause, l'abus dans l'usage. Il faut penser donc qu'il s'était opposé, de toutes ses forces, de tout ce qui lui restait de forces, non point au développement seulement, et aux promesses de développement, mais à l'origine même, au principe de la *politique* dreyfusiste. Il faut relire ce dossier, cette consultation, cette adjuration éloquente à Jaurès, presque cette mise en demeure, certainement déjà cette menace.

Il faut penser que c'était un homme, j'ai dit très précisément un prophète, pour qui tout l'appareil des puissances, la raison d'État, les puissances temporelles, les puissances politiques, les autorités de tout ordre, politiques, intellectuelles, mentales même ne pesaient pas une once devant une révolte, devant un mouvement de la conscience propre. On ne peut même en avoir aucune idée. Nous autres nous ne pouvons en avoir aucune idée. Quand nous nous révoltons contre une autorité, quand nous marchons contre les autorités, au moins nous les soulevons. Enfin nous en sentons le poids. Au moins en nous. Il faut au moins que nous les soulevions. Nous savons, nous sentons que nous marchons contre elles et que nous les soulevons. Pour lui elles n'existaient pas. Moins que je ne vous dis. Je ne sais même pas comment représenter à quel point il méprisait les autorités, temporelles, comment il méprisait les puissances, comment en donner une idée. Il ne les méprisait même pas. Il les ignorait, et même plus. Il ne les voyait pas, il ne les considérait pas. Il était myope. Elles n'existaient pas pour lui. Elles n'étaient pas de son grade, de son ordre de grandeur, de sa grandeur. Elles lui étaient totalement étrangères. Elles étaient pour lui moins que rien, égales à zéro. Elles étaient comme des dames qui n'étaient point reçues dans son salon. Il avait pour l'autorité, pour le commandement, pour le gouvernement, pour la force, temporelle, pour l'État, pour la raison d'État, pour les messieurs habillés d'autorité, vêtus de raison d'État une telle haine, une telle aversion, un ressentiment constant tel que cette haine les annulait, qu'ils n'entraient point, qu'ils n'avaient point l'honneur d'entrer dans son entendement. Dans cette affaire des congrégations, de cette loi des congrégations, ou plutôt de ces lois successives et de l'application de cette loi, où il était si évident que le gouvernement de la République, sous le nom de gouvernement Combes, manquait à tous les engagements que sous le nom de gouvernement Waldeck il avait pris, dans cette affaire, cette autre affaire, cette nouvelle affaire où il était si évident que le gouvernement faussait la parole d'un gouvernement et par conséquent du gouvernement, faussait enfin la parole de l'État, s'il est permis de mettre ces deux mots ensemble, Bernard-Lazare avait jugé naturellement qu'il fallait acquitter la parole de la République. Il avait jugé qu'il fallait que la République tînt sa parole. Il avait jugé qu'il fallait appliquer, interpréter la loi comme le gouvernement, les deux Chambres, l'État enfin avaient promis de la faire appliquer, s'étaient engagés à l'appliquer, à l'interpréter eux-mêmes. Avaient promis qu'on l'appliquerait. Cela était pour lui l'évidence même. La Cour de Cassation, naturellement aussi, n'hésita point à se ranger à l'avis (de ces messieurs) du gouvernement. Je veux dire du deuxième gouvernement. Un ami (comme on dit) vint lui dire, triomphant : *Vous voyez, mon cher ami, la Cour de Cassation a jugé contre vous.* Les dreyfusards devenus combistes crevaient déjà d'orgueil, et de faire les malins, et de la pourriture politicienne. Il faut avoir vu alors son œil pétillant de malice, mais douce, et de renseignement. Qui n'a pas vu son œil noir n'a rien vu, son œil de myope ; et le pli de sa lèvre. Un peu grasse. — *Mon cher ami*, répondit-il doucement, *vous vous trompez. C'est moi qui ai jugé autrement que la Cour de Cassation.* L'idée qu'on pouvait un instant lui comparer, à lui Bernard-Lazare, la Cour de Cassation, toutes chambres éployées, lui paraissait bouffonne. Comme l'autre était tout de même un peu suffoqué. — *Mais, mon garçon*, lui dit-il très doucement, *la Cour de Cassation, c'est des hommes.* Il avait l'air souverain de parler très doucement, très délicatement comme à un petit imbécile d'élève. Qui n'aurait pas compris. Pensez que c'était le temps où tout dreyfusard politicien cousinait avec la Cour de Cassation, disait *la Cour de Cassation* en gonflant les joues, crevait d'orgueil d'avoir été historiquement, juridiquement authentiqué, justifié par la Cour de Cassation, roulait des yeux, s'assurait au fond de soi sur la Cour de Cassation que Dreyfus était bien innocent. Il était resté gamin, d'une gaminerie invincible, de cette gaminerie qui est la marque même de la grandeur, de cette gaminerie noble, de cette gaminerie aisée qui est la marque de l'aisance dans la grandeur. Et surtout de cette gaminerie homme qui est rigoureusement réservée aux cœurs purs. Non jamais je n'ai vu une aisance telle, aussi souveraine. Jamais je n'ai vu un spirituel mépriser aussi souverainement, aussi sainement, aussi aisément, aussi également une compagnie temporelle. Jamais je n'ai vu un spirituel annuler ainsi un corps temporel. On sentait très bien que pour lui la Cour de Cassation ça ne lui en imposait pas du tout, que pour lui c'étaient des vieux, des vieux bonshommes, que l'idée de les opposer à lui Bernard-Lazare comme autorité judiciaire était purement baroque, burlesque, que lui Bernard-Lazare était une tout autre autorité judiciaire, et politique, et tout. Qu'il avait un tout autre ressort, une tout autre juridiction, qu'il disait un

tout autre droit. Qu'il les voyait parfaitement et
constamment dévêtus de leur magistrature, dépouillés
de tout leur appareil et de ces robes mêmes, qui
empêchent de voir l'homme. Qu'il ne pouvait pas les
voir autrement. Même en y mettant de la bonne
volonté, toute sa bonne volonté. Parce qu'il était bon.
Même en s'y efforçant. Qu'il ne concevait même pas
qu'on pût les voir autrement. Que lui-même il ne
pouvait les voir qu'en vieux singes tout nus. Nullement, comme on pourrait le croire, d'abord, comme
un premier examen, superficiel, hâtif, pourrait
d'abord le laisser supposer, en vieux singes revêtus de
la simarre et de l'hermine. On sentait si bien qu'il
savait que lui Bernard-Lazare il avait fait marcher ces
gens-là, qu'on les ferait marcher encore, et que lui
Bernard-Lazare on ne le ferait jamais marcher, que
ces gens-là surtout ne le feraient jamais marcher.
Qu'il avait temporellement fait marcher tout le
monde ; et que tout le monde ne le ferait jamais
spirituellement marcher. Pour lui ce n'était pas, ce ne
serait jamais la plus haute autorité du royaume, la
plus haute autorité judiciaire, la plus haute juridiction
du royaume, le plus haut magistrat de la République.
C'étaient des vieux juges. Et il savait bien ce que
c'était qu'un vieux juge. On sentait si bien qu'il savait
qu'il avait fait marcher ces gens-là, et qu'ils ne le
feraient jamais marcher. Quand l'autre fut parti : *Vous
l'avez vu*, me dit-il en riant. *Il était rigolo avec sa Cour de
Cassation.* Notez qu'il était, et très délibérément,
contre les lois Waldeck même. Contre la loi Waldeck.
Mais enfin, puisqu'il y avait une loi Waldeck, il
voulait, il fallait qu'on s'y tînt juridiquement. Et
même loyalement. Qu'on l'appliquât, qu'on l'inter-

prêtât comme elle était. Il n'aimait pas l'État. Mais enfin puisqu'il y avait un État, et qu'on ne pouvait pas faire autrement, il voulait au moins que le même État qui fît une loi fût le même aussi qui l'appliquât. Que l'État ne se dérobât point et ne changeât point de nom et de statut entre les deux, qu'il ne fît point ceci sous un nom et qu'il ne le défît point sous un autre, sous un deuxième nom. il voulait au moins que l'État fût, au moins quelques années, constant avec lui-même. L'autre voulait dire évidemment qu'il était d'un très grand prix, d'un prix suprême, d'un prix de cour suprême que la Cour de Cassation eût innocenté Dreyfus. Pour lui ce n'était d'aucun prix. Il considérait cette sorte de consécration juridique comme une consécration purement judiciaire, et uniquement comme une victoire temporelle, surtout sans doute comme une victoire de lui Bernard-Lazare sur la Cour de Cassation. Il ne lui venait point à la pensée qu'une Cour de Cassation pût faire ou ne pas faire, fît ou ne fît pas l'innocence de Dreyfus. Mais il sentait, il savait parfaitement que c'était lui Bernard-Lazare qui faisait l'autorité d'une Cour de Cassation, qui faisait ou ne faisait pas une Cour de Cassation même, parce qu'il en faisait la nourriture et la matière, et qu'ainsi et en outre il en faisait la forme même. Qu'en un sens, qu'en ce sens il en faisait la magistrature. Ce n'était pas la Cour de Cassation qui lui faisait bien de l'honneur. C'était lui qui faisait bien de l'honneur à la Cour de Cassation. Jamais je n'ai vu un homme croire, savoir à ce point que les plus grandes puissances temporelles, que les plus grands corps de l'État ne tiennent, ne sont que par des puissances spirituelles intérieures. On sait assez qu'il était tout à fait opposé à faire jouer l'article 445 [1] comme on l'a fait jouer (Clemenceau aussi y était opposé), et tous les embarras que nous avons eus du jeu de cet article, les embarras insurmontables qui se sont produits, qui sont résultés du jeu de cet article, ou plutôt de ce jeu de cet article étaient évités si on lui avait laissé le gouvernement de l'affaire. Il ne fait aucun doute qu'il considérait ce jeu comme une forfaiture, comme un abus, comme un coup de force judiciaire, comme une illégalité. En outre, avec son clair bon sens, bien français, ce juif, bien parisien, avec son clair regard juridique il prévoyait les difficultés inextricables où elle nous jetterait, qu'elle rouvrirait éternellement l'affaire ou plutôt qu'elle empêcherait éternellement l'affaire de se clore. Il me disait : *Dreyfus passera devant cinquante conseils de guerre, s'il faut,* ou encore : *Dreyfus passera devant des conseils de guerre toute sa vie. Mais il faut qu'il soit acquitté comme tout le monde.* Le fond de sa pensée était d'ailleurs que Dreyfus était bien sot de se donner tant de mal pour faire consacrer son innocence par les autorités constituées ; que ces gens-là ne font rien à l'affaire ; puisqu'on l'avait arraché à une persécution inique le principal était fait, tout était fait ; que les revêtements d'autorité, les consécrations judiciaires sont bien superflues, n'existent pas, venant de corps négligeables ; que c'est faire beaucoup d'honneur à ces messieurs ; qu'on est bien bon, quand on est innocent, en plus de le faire constater. Qu'on apporte ainsi, à ces autorités, une autorité dont elles ont grand besoin. Mais alors, au deuxième degré, si on y avait recours, il fallait y avoir recours droitement, il ne fallait point biaiser, il ne fallait point tricher, *surtout sans doute parce que c'était se donner les apparences, et peut-*

être la réalité, de s'incliner devant elles, de les redouter.
Puisqu'on y allait, puisqu'on s'en servait, il fallait s'en
servir, et y aller droitement. C'était encore un moyen
de leur commander. Si c'était de la politique, il fallait
au moins qu'elle fût droite. Il avait un goût incroyable
de la droiture, surtout dans ce qu'il n'aimait pas, dans
la politique et dans le judiciaire. Il se rattrapait pour
ainsi dire ainsi d'y aller malgré lui en y étant droit
malgré eux. Je n'ai jamais vu quelqu'un savoir aussi
bien garder ses distances, être aussi distant, aussi
doucement, aussi savamment, aussi horizontalement
pour ainsi dire. Je n'ai jamais vu une puissance
spirituelle, quelqu'un qui se sent, qui se sait une
puissance spirituelle garder aussi intérieurement pour
ainsi dire des distances horizontales aussi méprisantes
envers les puissances temporelles. Et donc il avait une
affection secrète, une amitié, une affinité profonde
avec *les autres* puissances spirituelles, même avec les
catholiques, qu'il combattait délibérément. Mais il ne
voulait les combattre que par des armes spirituelles
dans des batailles spirituelles. Sa profonde opposition
intérieure et manifestée au waldeckisme même venait
ainsi de deux origines. Premièrement, par une sorte
d'équilibre, de balancement, d'équité, d'égalité, de
justice, de santé politiques, de répartition équitable il
ne voulait pas qu'on fît aux autres ce que les autres
vous avaient fait, mais qu'on ne voulait pas qu'ils
vous fissent. *Les cléricaux nous ont embêtés pendant des
années*, disait-il, et plus énergiquement encore, *il ne
s'agit pas à présent d'embêter les catholiques*. On n'a jamais
vu un Juif aussi peu partisan, aussi peu pensant, aussi
peu concevant du talion. Il ne voulait pas rendre
précisément le bien pour le mal, mais très certaine-

ment le juste pour l'injuste. Il avait aussi cette idée que vraiment ça n'était pas malin, qu'il ne fallait guère se sentir fort pour avoir recours à de telles forces. Or il se sentait fort. Qu'il ne fallait guère avoir confiance en soi. Or il avait confiance en soi. Comme tous les véritables forts. Comme tous les véritables forts il n'aimait point employer des armes faciles, avoir des succès faciles, des succès diminués, dégradés, des succès qui ne fussent point du même ordre de grandeur que les combats qu'il voulait soutenir.

Deuxièmement il avait certainement une sympathie secrète, une entente intérieure avec les autres puissances spirituelles. Sa haine de l'État, du temporel se retrouvait là tout entière. *On ne peut pas poursuivre,* disait-il, *par des lois, des gens qui s'assemblent pour faire leur prière. Quand même ils s'assembleraient cinq cent mille. Si on trouve qu'ils sont dangereux, qu'ils ont trop d'argent, qu'on les poursuive, qu'on les atteigne par des mesures générales, comme tout le monde,* (ce même mot, cette même expression, *comme tout le monde,* dont il se servait toujours, dont il se servait précisément pour Dreyfus), *par des lois, économiques générales, qui poursuivent, qui atteignent tous ceux qui sont aussi dangereux qu'eux, qui ont de l'argent comme eux.* Il n'aimait pas que les partis politiques, que l'État, que les Chambres, que le gouvernement lui enlevât la gloire du combat qu'il voulait soutenir, lui déshonorât d'avance son combat.

D'une manière générale il n'aimait pas, il ne pouvait pas supporter que le temporel se mêlât du spirituel. Tous ces appareils temporels, tous ces organes, tous ces appareils de levage lui paraissaient infiniment trop grossiers pour avoir le droit de mettre leur patte grossière non seulement dans les droits mais même dans les intérêts spirituels. Que des organes aussi grossiers que le gouvernement, la Chambre, l'État, le Sénat, aussi étrangers à tout ce qui est spirituel, missent les doigts de la main dans le spirituel c'était pour lui non pas seulement une profanation grossière, mais plus encore, un exercice de mauvais goût, un abus, l'exercice, l'abus d'une singulière incompétence. Il se sentait au contraire une secrète, une singulière complicité de compétence spirituelle au besoin avec le pape.

Jamais je n'ai vu un homme je ne dis pas croire, je dis savoir à ce point je ne dis pas seulement qu'une conscience est au-dessus de toutes les juridictions, mais qu'elle est, qu'elle exerce elle-même dans la réalité une juridiction, qu'elle est la suprême juridiction, la seule.

Si on l'avait suivi, si on avait au moins suivi son enseignement et son exemple, si on avait continué dans son sens, si on avait seulement suivi le respect que l'on devait à sa mémoire, aujourd'hui la révision même du procès Dreyfus ne serait pas en danger, *comme elle l'est*. Elle ne serait pas exposée, comme elle l'est.

Aussi nous avons vu son enterrement [1]. Je dirai quel fut son enterrement. Qui nous étions, combien peu dans ce cortège, dans ce convoi, dans cet accompagnement fidèle gris descendant et passant dans Paris. En pleines vacances. Dans ce mois d'août ou plutôt dans ce commencement de mois de septembre. Quelques-

uns, les mêmes forcenés, les mêmes fanatiques, Juifs et
chrétiens, quelques Juifs riches, très rares, quelques
chrétiens riches, très rares, des Juifs et des chrétiens
pauvres et misérables, eux-mêmes en assez petit
nombre. Une petite troupe en somme, une très petite
troupe [1]. Comme une espèce de compagnie réduite qui
traversait Paris. De misérables Juifs étrangers, je veux
dire étrangers à la nationalité française, car il n'était
pas un Juif roumain, je veux dire un Juif de Roumanie, qui ne le sût prophète, qui ne le tînt pour un
véritable prophète. Il était pour tous ces misérables,
pour tous ces persécutés, un éclair encore, un rallu-
mage du flambeau qui éternellement ne s'éteindra
point. Temporellement éternellement. Et comme
toutes ces marques mêmes sont de famille, comme
tout ce qui est d'Israël est de race, comme ces choses-
là restent dans les familles, comment ne pas se
rappeler, comment ne point voir cet ancien enterrement quand on voyait si peu de monde, il y a quelques
semaines encore, à l'enterrement de sa mère. Relative-
ment peu de monde. Et pourtant ils connaissaient
beaucoup de monde. Je dirai sa mort, et sa longue et
sa cruelle maladie, et tout le lent et si prompt
acheminement de sa mort. Cette sorte de maladie
féroce. Comme acharnée. Comme fanatique. Comme
elle-même forcenée. Comme lui. Comme nous. Je ne
sais rien de si poignant, de si saisissant, je ne connais
rien d'aussi tragique que cet homme qui se roidissant
de tout ce qui lui restait de force se mettait en travers
de son parti victorieux. Qui dans un effort désespéré,
où il se brisait lui-même, essayait, entreprenait de
remonter cet élan, cette vague, ce terrible élan,
l'insurmontable élan de la victoire et des abus, de

l'abus de la victoire. Le seul élan qu'on ne remontera jamais. L'insurmontable élan de la victoire acquise. De la victoire faite. De l'entraînement de la victoire. L'insurmontable, le mécanique, l'automatique élan du jeu même de la victoire. Je le revois encore dans son lit. Cet athée, ce professionnellement athée, cet officiellement athée en qui retentissait, avec une force, avec une douceur incroyable, la parole éternelle ; avec une force éternelle ; avec une douceur éternelle ; que je n'ai jamais retrouvée égale nulle part ailleurs. J'ai encore sur moi, dans mes yeux, l'éternelle bonté de ce regard infiniment doux, cette bonté non pas lancée, mais posée, renseignée. Infiniment désabusée ; infiniment renseignée ; infiniment insurmontable elle-même. Je le vois encore dans son lit, cet athée ruisselant de la parole de Dieu. Dans la mort même tout le poids de son peuple lui pesait aux épaules. Il ne fallait point dire qu'il n'en était point responsable. Je n'ai jamais vu un homme ainsi chargé, aussi chargé d'une charge, d'une responsabilité éternelle. Comme nous sommes, comme nous nous sentons chargés de nos enfants, de nos propres enfants dans notre propre famille, tout autant, exactement autant, exactement ainsi il se sentait chargé de son peuple. Dans les souffrances les plus atroces il n'avait qu'un souci : que *ses* Juifs de Roumanie ne fussent point omis *artificieuse-ment,* pour faire réussir le mouvement, dans ce mouve-ment de réprobation que quelques publicistes euro-péens entreprenaient alors contre les excès des persé-cutions orientales. Je le vois dans son lit. On montait jusqu'à cette rue de Florence ; si rive droite, pour nous, si loin du Quartier. Les autobus ne marchaient pas encore. On montait par la rue de Rome, ou par la

rue d'Amsterdam, cour de Rome ou cour d'Amsterdam, je ne sais plus laquelle des deux se nomme
laquelle, jusqu'à ce carrefour montant que je vois
encore. Cette maison riche, pour le temps, où il vivait
pauvre. Il s'excusait de son loyer, disant : J'ai un bail
énorme sur le dos. Je ne sais pas si je pourrai sous-
louer comme je le voudrais. Quand j'ai pris cet
appartement-là, je croyais que je ferais un grand
journal et qu'on travaillerait ici. J'avais des plans. Il
en était loin, de faire un grand journal. Les journaux
des autres se faisaient, des autres mêmes, à condition
qu'il n'y fût pas. Je revois encore cette grande
chambre, rue de Florence, 5, (ou 7), rue de Florence,
la chambre du lit, la chambre de souffrance, la chambre
de couchée, la chambre d'héroïsme, (la chambre de
sainteté), la chambre mortuaire. La chambre du lit
d'où il ne se releva point. L'ai-je donc tant oublié moi-
même que ce 5, (ou ce 7), ne réponde plus mécanique-
ment à l'appel de ma mémoire, que ce 5 et ce 7 se
battent comme des chiffonniers dans le magasin de
ma mémoire, que chacun s'essaye et fasse valoir ses
titres. Et pourtant j'y suis allé. Et nous disions
familièrement entre nous : Est-ce que tu es allé rue de
Florence. Dans la grande chambre rectangulaire, je
vois le grand lit rectangulaire. Une, ou deux, ou trois
grandes fenêtres rectangulaires donnaient de grands
jours de gauche obliques rectangulaires ; tombant,
descendant lentement ; lentement penchés. Le lit
venait du fond, non pas du fond opposé aux fenêtres,
où étaient les portes, et, je pense, les corridors, mais
du fond qu'on avait devant soi quand on avait les
fenêtres à gauche. De ce fond le lit venait bien au
milieu, bien carrément, la tête au fond, jointe le fond,

les pieds vers le milieu de la chambre. Lui-même juste
au milieu de son lit, sur le dos, symétrique, comme
l'axe de son lit, comme un axe d'équité. Les deux bras
bien à gauche et à droite. C'étaient dans les derniers
temps. La maladie approchait de sa consommation.
Une profonde, une vigilante affection fraternelle, la
diligence d'une affection fraternelle pensait déjà à lui
faire, à lui préparer une mort qui ne fût point la
consommation de cette cruauté, qui fût plus douce, un
peu adoucie, qui n'eût point toute la cruauté, toute la
barbarie de cette maladie forcenée [1]. Qui ne fût point
le couronnement de cette cruauté. On lui avait conté
des histoires sur sa maladie, des histoires et des
histoires. Qu'en croyait-il ? Il faisait, comme tout le
monde, semblant de les croire. Qu'en croyait-il, c'est
le secret des morts. *Morientium ac mortuorum* [2]. Dans
cette incurable lâcheté du monde moderne, où nous
osons tout dire à l'homme, excepté ce qui l'intéresse,
où nous n'osons pas dire à l'homme la plus grande
nouvelle, la nouvelle de la seule grande échéance nous
avons menti nous-mêmes tant de fois, nous avons tant
menti à tant de mourants et à tant de morts qu'il faut
bien espérer que quand c'est notre tour nous ne
croyons pas nous-mêmes tout à fait aux mensonges
que l'on nous fait. Il faisait donc semblant d'y croire.
Mais dans ses beaux yeux doux, dans ses grands et
gros yeux clairs il était impossible de lire. Ils étaient
trop bons. Ils étaient trop doux. Ils étaient trop
beaux. *Ils étaient trop clairs.* Il était impossible de savoir
si c'était pas un miracle d'espérance (temporelle) (et
peut-être plus) qu'il espérait encore ou si c'était par
un miracle de charité, pour nous, qu'il faisait semblant d'espérer. Son œil même, son œil clair, d'une

limpidité d'enfant, était comme un binocle, comme un deuxième verre, comme une deuxième vitre, comme un deuxième binocle de douceur et de bonté, de lumière, de clarté. Impénétrable. Parce qu'on y lisait comme on voulait. C'étaient les derniers temps. Peu de gens pouvaient encore le voir, des parents mêmes. Mais il m'aimait tant qu'il me maintenait sur les dernières listes. J'étais assis au long de son lit à gauche au pied. A sa droite par conséquent. Il parlait de tout comme s'il dût vivre cent ans. Il me demanda comment je venais. Il me dit, avec beaucoup d'orgueil, enfantin, que le métro Amsterdam était ouvert. Ou quelque autre. Il se passionnait ingénument pour tout ce qui était voies et moyens de communications. Tout ce qui était allées et venues, géographiques, topographiques, télégraphiques, téléphoniques, aller et retour, circulations, déplacements, replacements, voyages, exodes et deutéronomes lui causait un amoncellement de joie enfantine inépuisable. Le métro particulièrement lui était une victoire personnelle. Tout ce qui était rapidité, accélération, fièvre de communication, déplacement, circulation rapide l'emplissait d'une joie enfantine, de la vieille joie, d'une joie de cinquante siècles. C'était son affaire, propre. *Être ailleurs*, le grand vice de cette race, la grande vertu secrète ; la grande vocation de ce peuple. Une renommée de cinquante siècles ne le mettait point en chemin de fer que ce ne fût quelque caravane de cinquante siècles. Toute traversée pour eux est la traversée du désert. Les maisons les plus confortables, les mieux assises, avec des pierres de taille grosses comme les colonnes du temple, les maisons les plus immobilières, les plus immeubles, les immeubles les

plus écrasants ne sont jamais pour eux que la tente
dans le désert. *Le granit remplaça la tente aux murs de
toile* [1]. Qu'importe ces pierres de taille plus grosses
que les colonnes du temple. Ils sont toujours sur le dos
des chameaux. Peuple singulier. Combien de fois n'y
ai-je point pensé. Pour qui les plus immobilières
maisons ne seront jamais que des tentes. Et nous au
contraire, qui avons réellement couché sous la tente,
sous des vraies tentes, combien de fois n'ai-je point
pensé à vous, Lévy [2], qui n'avez jamais couché sous
une tente, autrement que dans la Bible, au bout de
quelques heures ces tentes du camp de Cercottes [3]
étaient déjà nos maisons. *Que vos pavillons sont beaux, ô
Jacob ; que vos tentes sont belles, ô Israël* [4]. Combien de fois
n'y ai-je point pensé, combien de fois n'ai-je point
pensé à vous, combien de fois ces mots ne me
remontaient-ils pas sourdement comme une remontée
d'une gloire de cinquante siècles, comme une grande
joie secrète de gloire, dont j'éclatais sourdement par
un ressouvenir sacré quand nous rentrions au camp,
mon cher Claude [5], par ces dures nuits de mai. Peuple
pour qui la pierre des maisons sera toujours la toile
des tentes. Et pour nous au contraire c'est la toile des
tentes qui était déjà, qui sera toujours la pierre de nos
maisons. Non seulement il n'avait donc pas eu pour le
métropolitain cette aversion, cette distance qu'au fond
nous lui gardons toujours, même quand il nous rend
les plus grands services, *parce qu'il nous transporte trop
vite,* et au fond qu'il nous rend trop de services, mais
au contraire il avait pour lui une affection propre
toute orgueilleuse, comme un orgueil d'auteur. On le
perçait alors, la ligne numéro 1 seulement je crois était
en exploitation. Il avait un orgueil local, un orgueil de

quartier, qu'il eût abouti, déjà, jusqu'à lui, un des premiers, qu'il eût percé jusqu'à lui, qu'il eût commencé à monter vers ces hauteurs. Il me l'avait dit, quelques mois auparavant, quand on avait essayé de l'envoyer, comme tout le monde, vers les réparations du Midi. Il était allé d'hôtel en hôtel[1]. Il était heureux comme un enfant. Jusqu'à ce qu'il trouva une espèce de petite maison de paysan ; qu'il me présenta dans une lettre comme le paradis réalisé. Et d'où naturellement il revint rapidement, il rentra à Paris. Il me l'avait dit alors, dans un de ces mots qui éclairent un homme, un peuple, une race. *Voyez-vous*, *Péguy*, me disait-il, *je ne commence à me sentir chez moi que quand j'arrive dans un hôtel*. Il le disait en riant, mais c'était vrai tout de même.

En somme, dans l'action, dans la politique, puisqu'il en faut une, puisqu'il fallait y descendre, il était partisan du droit commun. Droit commun dans l'affaire Dreyfus, droit commun dans l'affaire Congrégations. Droit commun *pour* Dreyfus, droit commun *contre* les congrégations. Cela n'a l'air de rien, cela peut mener loin. Cela le mena jusqu'à l'isolement dans la mort.

Il était essentiellement pour la justice, pour l'équité, pour l'égalité (non point naturellement au sens démocratique, mais au sens d'équilibre parfait, d'horizontalité parfaite dans la justice). Il était contre l'exception, contre la loi d'exception, contre la mesure d'exception, qu'elle fût pour ou contre, persécution ou grâce. Il était pour le *niveau* de la justice.

Je le regardais donc ce matin-là, 7, rue de Florence.

Et je l'écoutais. J'étais assis au pied de son lit à gauche comme un disciple fidèle. Tant de douceur, tant de mansuétude dans une si cruelle situation me désarmait, me dépassait. Tant de douceur pour ainsi dire inexpiable. J'écoutais dans une piété, dans un demi-silence respectueux, affectueux, ne lui fournissant que le propos pour se soutenir. Le *Beethoven* de Romain Rolland [1] venait de paraître. Nos abonnés se rappellent encore quelle soudaine révélation fut ce cahier, quel émoi il souleva d'un bout à l'autre, comme il se répandit soudainement, comme une vague, comme en dessous, pour ainsi dire instantanément, comme il fut soudainement, instantanément, dans une révélation, aux yeux de tous, dans une entente soudaine, dans une commune entente, non point seulement le commencement de la fortune littéraire de Romain Rolland, et de la fortune littéraire des cahiers, mais infiniment plus qu'un commencement de fortune littéraire, une révélation morale, soudaine, un pressentiment dévoilé, révélé, la révélation, l'éclatement, la soudaine communication d'une grande fortune morale. Mais tout ce mouvement se gonflait, n'avait pas encore eu le temps de se manifester. Le cahier, je le répète, venait tout juste de paraître. Bernard-Lazare me dit : *Ah j'ai lu votre cahier de Romain Rolland. C'est vraiment très beau. Il faut avouer que l'âme juive et l'âme hellénique ont été deux grands morceaux de l'âme universelle.* Je ne manifestai rien, parce que j'ai dit que quand on va voir un malade on est résolu à ne rien manifester. On est donc gardé par une cuirasse, invincible, par un masque impénétrable. Mais je fus saisi, je me sentis poursuivi jusque dans les vertèbres. Car j'étais venu pour voir, je m'étais attendu à voir les avancées de la mort. Et c'est déjà beaucoup. Et je voyais brusquement les avancées des au-delà de la mort. Pour mesurer la profondeur, la nouveauté d'un tel mot, *l'âme éternelle*, et même *l'âme juive*, et *l'âme hellénique*, il faut savoir à quel point, avec quel scrupule religieux ces hommes, les hommes de cette génération évitaient d'employer le moindre mot du jargon mystique. On parlait alors de *recommencer* l'affaire Dreyfus, de *reprendre* l'affaire Dreyfus. Il faut se rappeler qu'entre l'affaire Dreyfus elle-même et la deuxième affaire Dreyfus il y eut un long temps de calme plat, de silence, d'une solitude totale. On ne savait pas alors, du tout, pendant tout ce temps, si l'affaire recommencerait ; jamais. Mieux eût valu qu'elle ne recommençât point. Nous n'eussions point été acquittés par la Cour de Cassation. Mais nous demeurions ce que nous étions, nous demeurions purs devant le pays et devant l'histoire. Mais tout pantelants de cette grande Affaire, de cette première grande histoire, tout suants et tout bouillants de la bataille, tout déconcertés du repos, du calme, du plat, de la paix fourrée, du repos louche, du traité louche, de l'inaction, de la paix des dupes, tout anxieux de n'avoir point obtenu, atteint tous les résultats temporels que nous espérions, que nous attendions, que nous escomptions, de n'avoir point réalisé le royaume de la justice sur la terre et le royaume de la vérité, tout anxieux surtout de voir notre mystique nous échapper, nous ne pensions dans le secret de nos cœurs qu'à une reprise de l'affaire, à ce que nous nommions entre nous, comme des conjurés, la *reprise*. Nous ne prévoyions pas, hélas, que cette reprise n'en serait que la plus basse dégradation, un détournement total, un détournement grossier de la mystique en politique.

Nous en parlions. Lui, dans son lit, m'en parlait
doucement. Je vis rapidement qu'il m'en parlait
comme d'une conjuration, mais comme d'une conjuration étrangère, à laquelle il demeurait étranger. De
gré, de force ? Je lui dis : Mais enfin qu'est-ce qu'ils
vont faire. Ils ne vous ont donc pas demandé conseil ?
Il me répondit doucement : *Ils ont préféré s'adresser à
Jaurès.* **Ils sont si contents de faire quelque chose
sans moi.**

Ils, c'était tout, c'étaient tous les autres, c'était
Dreyfus qu'il aimait comme un jeune frère.

Il ne fait aucun doute que pour nous la mystique
dreyfusiste fut non pas seulement un cas particulier de
la mystique chrétienne, mais qu'elle en fut un cas,
éminent, une accélération, une crise temporelle, une
sorte d'exemple et de passage que je dirai nécessaire.
Comment le nier, à présent que nous sommes à douze
et quinze ans de notre jeunesse et qu'enfin nous
voyons clair dans notre cœur. Notre dreyfusisme était
une religion, je prends le mot dans son sens le plus
littéralement exact, une poussée religieuse, une crise
religieuse, et je conseillerais même vivement à quiconque voudrait étudier, considérer, connaître un mouvement religieux dans les temps modernes, bien caractérisé, bien délimité, bien taillé, de saisir cet exemple
unique. J'ajoute que pour nous, chez nous, en nous ce
mouvement religieux était d'essence chrétienne, d'origine chrétienne, qu'il poussait de souche chrétienne,
qu'il coulait de l'antique source. Nous pouvons
aujourd'hui nous rendre ce témoignage. La Justice et

la Vérité que nous avons tant aimées, à qui nous avons donné tout, notre jeunesse, tout, à qui nous nous sommes donnés tout entiers pendant tout le temps de notre jeunesse n'étaient point des vérités et des justices de concept, elles n'étaient point des justices et des vérités mortes, elles n'étaient point des justices et des vérités de livres et de bibliothèques, elles n'étaient point des justices et des vérités concep-tuelles, intellectuelles, des justices et des vérités de parti intellectuel, mais elles étaient organiques, elles étaient chrétiennes, elles n'étaient nullement modernes, elles étaient éternelles et non point tempo-relles seulement, elles étaient des Justices et des Vérités, *une* Justice et *une* Vérité *vivantes*. Et de tous les sentiments qui ensemble nous poussèrent, dans un tremblement, dans cette crise unique, aujourd'hui nous pouvons avouer que de toutes les passions qui nous poussèrent dans cette ardeur et dans ce bouillon-nement, dans ce gonflement et dans ce tumulte, une vertu était au cœur et que c'était la vertu de charité. Et je ne veux pas rouvrir un ancien débat, aujour-d'hui, désormais historique, mais dans nos ennemis, chez nos ennemis, chez nos adversaires d'alors, histo-riques comme nous, devenus historiques, je vois beaucoup d'intelligence, beaucoup de lucidité même, beaucoup d'acuité : ce qui me frappe le plus, c'est certainement un certain manque de charité. Je ne veux pas anticiper sur ce qui est le propre des *confessions*. Mais il est incontestable que dans tout notre socialisme même il y avait infiniment plus de christianisme que dans toute la Madeleine ensemble avec Saint-Pierre de Chaillot, et Saint-Philippe du Roule, et Saint-Honoré d'Eylau. Il était essentiellement une religion de la pauvreté temporelle. C'est donc, c'est assurément la religion qui sera jamais la moins célébrée dans les temps modernes. Infiniment, d'infiniment la moins chômée. Nous en avons été marqués si durement, si ineffaçablement, nous en avons reçu une empreinte, une si dure marque, si indélébile que nous en resterons marqués pour toute notre vie temporelle, et pour l'autre. Notre socialisme n'a jamais été ni un socialisme parlementaire ni un socialisme de paroisse riche. Notre christianisme ne sera jamais ni un christianisme parlementaire ni un christianisme de paroisse riche. Nous avions reçu dès lors une telle vocation de la pauvreté, de la misère même, si profonde, si intérieure, et en même temps si historique, si éventuelle, si événementaire que depuis nous n'avons jamais pu nous en tirer, que je commence à croire que nous ne pourrons nous en tirer jamais.

C'est une sorte de vocation.

Une destination.

Ce qui a pu donner le change, c'est que toutes les forces *politiques* de l'Église étaient contre le dreyfusisme. Mais les forces politiques de l'Église ont toujours été contre la mystique. Notamment contre la mystique chrétienne. C'est l'application la plus éminente qu'il y ait jamais eu de cette règle générale que nous posions plus haut.

On pourrait même dire que l'affaire Dreyfus fut un *beau cas* de religion, de mouvement religieux, de commencement, d'origine de religion, un cas rare, peut-être un cas unique.

La mystique dreyfusiste enfin fut pour nous essentiellement une crise de (la) mystique française. Cette affaire fut pour nous et par nous très exactement dans la ligne française. Comme elle avait été très exactement pour nous et par nous dans la ligne chrétienne. Nous-mêmes nous y fûmes très exactement dans la ligne française comme nous y avions été très exactement dans la ligne chrétienne. Nous y fûmes de qualité française comme nous y avions été de qualité chrétienne.

Nous y déployâmes proprement les vertus, les qualités françaises, les vertus de la race : la vaillance claire, la rapidité, la bonne humeur, la constance, la fermeté, un courage opiniâtre, mais de bon ton, de belle tenue, de bonne tenue, fanatique à la fois et mesuré, forcené ensemble et pleinement sensé ; une tristesse gaie, qui est le propre du Français ; un propos délibéré ; une résolution chaude et froide ; une aisance, un renseignement constant ; une docilité et ensemble une révolte constante à l'événement ; une impossibilité organique à consentir à l'injustice, à prendre son parti de rien [1]. Un délié, une finesse de lame. Une acuité de pointe. Il faut dire simplement que nous fûmes des héros. Et plus précisément des héros à la française. (La preuve, c'est que nous ne nous en sommes pas relevés, que nous ne nous en sommes pas retirés.) (Toute notre vie peut-être nous serons des demi-soldes.) Il faut bien voir en effet comment la question se posait. La question ne se posait nullement alors, pour nous, de savoir si Dreyfus était innocent ou coupable. Mais de savoir si on n'aurait pas le courage de le déclarer, de le savoir innocent.

Quand nous écrirons cette *histoire de l'affaire Dreyfus* qui sera proprement les *mémoires d'un dreyfusiste* il y aura lieu d'examiner, d'étudier de très près et nous établirons très attentivement, dans le plus grand détail, ce que je nommerai la *courbe de la croyance publique à l'innocence de Dreyfus*. Cette courbe a subi naturellement les variations les plus extraordinaires. Naturellement aussi les antidreyfusistes ont tout fait pour la faire *monter* et il faut rendre cette justice aux dreyfusistes qu'ils ont généralement tout fait pour la faire *descendre*. Partie des environs de *zéro* en 1894 (la famille et quelques très rares personnes exceptées), on peut dire qu'elle monta, qu'à travers des soubresauts de toute sorte, des fluctuations politiques et histori- ques comme il ne manque jamais de s'en produire pour ces sortes de courbes elle monta constamment jusqu'au jour où le bateau qui ramenait Dreyfus en France introduisit parmi nous le corps même du débat. Dès lors, malgré les apparences, malgré un palier apparent, malgré une apparence d'horizonta- lité, en réalité elle commença de baisser lentement, régulièrement. Malgré des fortunes diverses, malgré des apparences de fortunes en réalité elle commença de tomber. Cette descente, cette chute, cette baisse est arrêtée aujourd'hui, on peut croire qu'elle est arrêtée pour toujours, parce qu'elle ne peut guère aller plus avant, tomber plus bas, parce que beaucoup de monde aujourd'hui s'en moquent totalement, et sur- tout parce que nous sommes retombés à un certain équilibre, dans un certain équilibre très tentant, très solide, très commun, le même où nous nous étions

arrêtés si longtemps à la montée : la France, le
monde, l'histoire coupés en deux, en deux partis bien
distincts, bien coupés, bien arrêtés, croyant professionnellement, officiellement, l'un à la culpabilité et
l'autre à l'innocence, faisant profession de croire l'un
à la culpabilité et l'autre à l'innocence. C'est la
situation, c'est la position commune, usuelle, fami-
lière, pour ainsi dire classique, c'est la situation
connue, le monde coupé en deux sur une question.
C'est la situation commode, car c'est la situation de
guerre, la situation de haine, mutuelle. C'est la
situation à laquelle tout le monde est habitué. C'est
donc celle qui durera, qui déjà faillit durer pendant la
montée de notre courbe, qui s'est retrouvée, qui s'est
reçue, qui s'est recueillie elle-même au même niveau
dans la descente, qui ne se reperdra plus, qui sera
définitive. Avec les amortissements successifs naturellement par la successive arrivée des nouvelles générations ; avec les amortissements croissants et l'extinction finale, l'extinction historique. Ce qu'il y a de
remarquable, c'est combien cette situation, ce palier
intermédiaire est commode, du pays coupé en deux,
combien nous nous y sommes arrêtés complaisamment, commodément, à la montée, comment,
combien nous nous y sommes retrouvés aisément,
rapidement à la descente. Commodément. Combien
nous nous y mouvions aisément, naturellement à la
montée, en pleine bataille, combien nous y bataillions
aisément, naturellement, comme chez nous, et
combien nous nous y sommes même attardés. Et
combien au retour, à la descente nous l'avons retrouvé
aisément, combien rapidement nous nous y sommes
retrouvés chez nous. Mais ce qui est incontestable

c'est que cette courbe, dans ces soubresauts, à l'issue de cette montée atteignit plusieurs fois un *maximum* qui était même un *universum*. Je veux dire que dans ces fluctuations, dans ces agitations, dans cette crise, dans ces sautes, dans ces coups de force et dans ces coups de théâtre il y eut au moins deux ou trois fois quarante-huit heures où *tout* le pays (nos adversaires mêmes et je dis même leurs chefs) crut à l'innocence de Dreyfus. Par exemple, notamment dans ce coup de foudre, instantanément après ce coup de théâtre du colonel Henry au Mont-Valérien (mort ou simulation de mort, assassinat, meurtre, suicide ou simulation de suicide.) (Enfin disparition.) Comment nous sommes retombés, redescendus de ce *summum,* qui ce jour, qui dans cet éclair paraissait définitivement acquis, comment on nous en a fait redescendre, comment on a ainsi, autant réussi à faire redescendre cette courbe, c'est le secret des politiciens. C'est le secret des politiques. C'est le secret de la politique même. C'est le secret de Dreyfus même, dans la mesure, et elle est totale, où nous quittant il s'est remis tout entier aux mains des politiques [1]. Comment on a réussi à tenir cette gageure, à nous faire tomber de ce *maximum* total, c'est la grande habileté, c'est le secret des politiciens. Comment on perd une bataille qui était gagnée, demandez-le à Jaurès. Aujourd'hui nous sommes condamnés à la contestation, perpétuelle, jusqu'à cet émoussement, cette hébétude, cette oblitération, inévitable, qui vient du temps, des générations suivantes, qu'on nomme proprement l'histoire, la position, l'acquisition de l'histoire. Quand nos ennemis, quand nos adversaires nous reprochaient d'être le parti de l'étranger, ils avaient totalement tort, absolument tort sur nous et contre nous (sur notre mystique et contre nos mystique; ils avaient partiellement raison sur et contre notre État-Major, qui précisément nous masquait à eux, qui faisait même tout ce qu'il pouvait pour nous masquer, devant le monde, et qui y a si parfaitement, si complètement réussi; ils avaient partiellement raison, (peut-être pour un tiers, en quotité), sur et contre nos chefs, sur et contre notre politique, sur et contre nos politiciens, l'adhésion à Hervé [1] et à l'hervéisme, la flatterie pour Hervé et pour l'hervéisme, la lâcheté, le tremblement de Jaurès, la platitude, l'aplatissement devant Hervé et devant le hervéisme, plus que cela l'empressement, la sollicitude empressée pour Hervé et l'hervéisme l'ont bien prouvé); mais enfin ils avaient le droit de ne pas nous connaître, dans le fatras de la bataille ils pouvaient à la rigueur, historiquement, à la rigueur historique ils pouvaient ne pas nous connaître; la Foire sur la Place pouvait leur masquer l'intérieur de la maison; ils pouvaient ne voir que la parade politique; mais enfin au pis aller, à l'extrême, à la limite, à l'extrême rigueur quand nos ennemis, quand nos adversaires nous accusaient d'être le parti de l'étranger, ils ne pouvaient jamais que nous faire un tort temporel; un tort extrême temporel, un tort capital temporel, mais en fin un tort temporel. Ils ne pouvaient pas nous déshonorer. Ils pouvaient nous faire perdre nos biens, ils pouvaient nous faire perdre la liberté, ils pouvaient nous faire perdre la vie, ils pouvaient nous faire perdre la terre même de la patrie. Ils ne pouvaient pas nous faire perdre l'honneur. Au contraire quand Jaurès, par une suspecte, par une lâche complaisance à tout le hervéisme, et à Hervé lui-

même, à Hervé personnellement, d'une part, pour la
patrie, laissait dire et laissait faire qu'il fallait renier,
trahir et détruire la France; créant ainsi cette illusion
politique, que le mouvement dreyfusiste était un
mouvement antifrançais; et quand d'autre part, pour
la foi, quand mû par les plus bas intérêts électoraux,
poussé par la plus lâche, par la plus basse complaisance aux démagogies, aux agitations radicales il
disait, il faisait que l'affaire Dreyfus et le dreyfusisme
entrassent, comme une partie intégrante, dans la
démagogie, dans l'agitation radicale anticléricale,
anticatholique, antichrétienne, dans la séparation des
Églises et de l'État, dans la loi des Congrégations,
waldeckiste, dans la singulière application, dans l'application combiste de cette loi; créant ainsi cette
illusion, politique, que le mouvement dreyfusiste était
un mouvement antichrétien; il ne nous trahissait pas
seulement, il ne nous faisait pas seulement dévier, il
nous déshonorait. Il ne faut jamais oublier que le
combisme, le système combiste, la tyrannie combiste,
d'où sont venus tous ces maux, a été une invention de
Jaurès, que c'est Jaurès qui par sa détestable force
politique, par sa force oratoire, par sa force parlementaire a imposé cette invention, cette tyrannie au pays,
cette domination, que lui seul l'a maintenue et a pu la
maintenir; que pendant trois et même quatre ans il a
été, sous le nom de M. Combes, le véritable maître de
la République. « *Quand Jaurès,* disait déjà Bernard-
Lazare dans cet admirable dossier, dans cet admirable mémoire, dans cette admirable consultation, datée
de *Paris, 6 août 1902*[1], quand on voulait que la loi
Waldeck eût un effet global, et qu'elle eût un effet
rétroactif. *Quand Jaurès se présente devant nous pour soutenir*

une œuvre qu'il approuve, à laquelle il veut collaborer, il doit,
parce qu'il est Jaurès, parce qu'il a été notre compagnon dans
une bataille qui n'est pas finie, (ce qu'il y avait d'admirable en effet, même au point de vue politique, au seul
point de vue politique, et Bernard-Lazare, avec sa
grande lucidité *politique,* l'avait aperçu instantanément, c'était qu'on n'avait même pas attendu la fin de
l'affaire Dreyfus, la conclusion pour opérer la contamination, la dégénération, le déshonneur, la déviation, la dégradation de mystique en politique, mais
c'était entre les deux affaires Dreyfus même que l'on
se préparait à la commettre, à l'accomplir, avant
même d'avoir liquidé l'affaire, au moment même où
on se préparait à la rouvrir, à la reprendre), (c'est-à-
dire qu'on avait commencé d'opérer la dégénération
de mystique en politique au moment même où l'on se
préparait à faire appel de nouveau à toutes les forces,
aux forces incalculables de la mystique).

C'est pour cela que nos politiciens, que nos politiques furent les derniers des criminels, qu'ils furent des
criminels au deuxième degré. S'ils n'avaient fait que
leur politique, pour ainsi dire professionnellement,
s'ils n'avaient fait qu'exercer leur métier de politiciens, ils pouvaient n'être coupables qu'au premier
degré, criminels qu'au premier degré. Mais ils voulaient en même temps conserver tous les avantages de
la mystique. Et c'est cela très précisément qui constitue le deuxième degré. Ils voulaient bien en même
temps trahir la mystique et en même temps non pas
seulement s'en réclamer, non pas seulement s'en
revêtir et s'en servir et apparaître avec, mais continuer à l'exciter. Ils voulaient, ils entendaient jouer le
double jeu, ils voulaient jouer ensemble les deux jeux

contraires, et le mystique, et le politique, qui exclut le mystique, ils se préparaient à jouer le double jeu, ils entendaient jouer ensemble de *leur* politique et de *notre* mystique, cumuler les avantages de leur politique et de notre mystique, s'avantager ensemble de leur politique et de notre mystique, jouer toujours ensemble le temporel et l'éternel.

Jouer le temporel avec les puissants de ce monde et en même temps faire appel à la mystique et à l'argent des pauvres gens, puiser toujours dans le cœur et dans la bourse des pauvres gens.

C'est ce qui fait que la responsabilité de Jaurès dans ce crime, dans ce double crime, dans ce crime au deuxième degré est culminante. Lui entre tous, lui au chef de l'opération il était un politicien comme les autres, pire que les autres, un retors entre les retors, un fourbe entre les fourbes ; mais lui il faisait semblant de n'être pas un politicien. De là sa nocivité culminante. De là sa responsabilité culminante. Quand les nationalistes, professionnels, disaient que nous étions *le parti de l'étranger,* ils ne pouvaient que nous calomnier, ils ne pouvaient que nous faire un tort temporel, à la limite un tort temporel limite, à l'extrême un tort temporel extrême. Quand Jaurès au contraire parlait pour nous, s'avouait pour nous, quand à ce titre, à notre titre, il intercalait le dreyfusisme et l'affaire Dreyfus d'une part dans l'antipatriotisme, politique, dans l'antipatriotisme hervéiste, dans la politique antipatriotique, hervéiste, dans l'agitation, dans la démagogie antipatriotique, hervéiste, quand il l'intercalait d'autre part dans cette autre démagogie politique, dans la démagogie antichrétienne, il atteignait, il touchait, il blessait au cœur le dreyfusisme même.

Ce qui fait à Jaurès dans ce double crime, dans ce crime au deuxième degré, une responsabilité culminante, c'est que lui entre tous il était un politique, un politicien comme les autres et que lui il disait qu'il était un mystique. Il me chicanerait naturellement sur ce mot, car c'est un homme de marchandage, et de plus maquignon que je connaisse. Mais il sait très bien ce que nous voulons dire.

Par son passé universitaire, intellectuel, par son commencement de carrière universitaire, intellectuelle, par ses relations, par tout son ton, par le grand nombre, par le faisceau d'amitiés *ardentes* qui montaient vers lui et qu'il encourageait, complaisamment, qu'il excitait constamment à monter vers lui, amitiés de pauvres, de petites gens, de professeurs, de nous, et qu'il récapitulait pour ainsi dire en lui, qu'il ramassait comme un foyer ramasse un faisceau de lumière et de chaleur, Jaurès faisait figure d'une sorte de professeur délégué dans la politique, mais qui n'était pas politique, d'un intellectuel, d'un philosophe (dans ce temps-là tous les agrégés de philosophie étaient philosophes, comme aujourd'hui ils sont tous sociologues). D'un homme qui travaillait, qui savait ce que c'est que de travailler. Qui avait un métier. Il faisait essentiellement figure d'un impolitique, d'un homme qui était comme chargé de nous représenter, de nous transmettre dans la politique. Au contraire c'était un politicien qui avait fait semblant d'être un professeur, qui avait fait semblant d'être un intellectuel, qui avait fait semblant de travailler et de savoir travailler, d'avoir un métier, qui avait fait semblant d'être des nôtres, qui avait fait semblant de tout. Quand les politiciens, quand ceux qui font métier et profession de la politique font leur métier, exercent leur profession, quand ils jouent, quand ils fonctionnent professionnellement, officiellement, sous leur nom, ceux qui sont connus comme tels, il n'y a rien à dire. Mais quand ceux qui font métier et profession d'être impolitiques font, sous ce nom, de la politique, il y a le double crime de ce détournement perpétuel. Faire de la politique et la nommer politique, c'est bien. Faire de la politique et la nommer mystique, prendre de la mystique et en faire de la politique, c'est un détournement inexpiable. Voler les pauvres, c'est voler deux fois. Tromper les simples, c'est tromper deux fois. Voler ce qu'il y a de plus cher, la croyance. La confidence. La confiance. Et Dieu sait si nous étions des âmes simples, des pauvres gens, des petites gens. C'est bien ce qui les fait rire aujourd'hui. *Quels sont,* dit-il, *quels sont ces imbéciles qui croyaient ce que je disais?* Qu'il se rassure, qu'il attende. Les vies sont longues, les mouvements contraires, qu'il ne nous tombe jamais dans les mains. Il ne rirait peut-être pas toujours.

Quoi de plus poignant que ce témoignage, que cette adjuration de Bernard-Lazare condamné, de Bernard-Lazare destiné, quoi de plus redoutable que ce témoignage, redoutable, par sa mesure même. *Quand Jaurès,* écrivait Bernard-Lazare, *se présente devant nous pour soutenir une œuvre qu'il approuve, à laquelle il veut collaborer, il doit, parce qu'il est Jaurès, parce qu'il a été notre compagnon dans une bataille qui n'est pas finie, nous donner d'autres raisons que des raisons théologiques.* (Il voyait très nettement combien il y avait de théologie grossière dans Jaurès, dans toute cette *mentalité* moderne, dans ce radicalisme politique et parlementaire, dans cette pseudométaphysique, dans cette pseudophilosophie, dans cette sociologie.) *Or c'est une raison théologique que de nous dire* (Ici je préviens que c'est du Jaurès, cité par Bernard-Lazare) : « *Il y a des crimes politiques et sociaux qui se payent, et le grand crime collectif commis par l'Église contre la vérité, contre l'humanité, contre le droit et contre la République, va enfin recevoir son juste salaire. Ce n'est pas en vain qu'elle a révolté les consciences par sa complicité avec le faux, le parjure et la trahison.* » (Fin du Jaurès, de la citation de Jaurès.) Bernard-Lazare disait plus simplement : *On ne peut pas embêter des hommes parce qu'ils font leur prière.* Il les avait, celui-là, les mœurs de la liberté. Il avait la liberté dans la peau ; dans la moelle et dans le sang ; dans les vertèbres. Non point, non plus, une liberté intellectuelle et conceptuelle, une liberté livresque, une liberté toute faite, une liberté de bibliothèque. Une liberté d'enregistrement. Mais une liberté, aussi, de source, une liberté toute organique et vivante. Je n'ai jamais vu un homme croire, à ce point, avoir à ce point la certitude, avoir conscience à ce point qu'une conscience d'homme était un absolu, un invincible, un éternel, un libre, qu'elle s'opposait victorieuse, éternellement triomphante, à toutes les grandeurs de la terre. *Il ne faut pas recevoir des justifications semblables,* écrivait encore Bernard-Lazare, *même et surtout quand elles sont données par Jaurès, car, au-dessous, d'autres sont prêts à les interpréter dans un sens pire, à en tirer des conséquences* **redoutables pour la liberté.** Il énumérait, sur quelques exemples éclatants, dans un style éclatant, coupant, bref, quelques-unes de ces antinomies, les capitales, quelques-uns de ces antagonismes. Il te prévoyait, Bernus [1], et la *résistance du peuple polonais aux exactions de la germanisation prussienne.* Dès lors il écrivait en effet, et ces paroles sont claires, elles sont capitales, elles sont actuelles comme au premier jour : *Si nous n'y prenons garde, demain on nous mettra en demeure d'applaudir le gendarme français qui prendra l'enfant par le bras pour l'obliger à entrer dans l'école laïque, tandis que nous devrons réprouver le gendarme prussien contraignant l'écolier polonais de Wreschen.* Voilà l'homme, voilà l'ami que nous avons perdu. Il écrivait encore, et ces paroles sont à considérer, elles sont à méditer aujourd'hui comme hier, aujourd'hui comme alors, elles seront à méditer toujours, car elles sont d'une hauteur de vues, d'une portée incalculable : « *Que demain on nous propose les moyens de résoudre la question de l'enseignement et nous la discuterons. Dès aujourd'hui on peut dire que le monopole universitaire n'en est pas la solution.* **Nous nous refuserons aussi bien à accepter les dogmes formulés par l'État enseignant, que les dogmes formulés par l'Église. Nous n'avons pas plus confiance en l'Université qu'en la Congrégation.** » Mais il faut que je m'arrête de citer. Je ne peux pourtant pas citer toute cette admirable *consultation,* citer tout un cahier dans un cahier, refaire les cahiers dans les cahiers, mettre tout le III-21 dans le XI-12 [2].

Voilà l'homme, voilà l'ami que nous avons perdu. Pour un tel homme nous ne ferons jamais une apologie, nous ne souffrirons jamais qu'on en fasse une.

Ce sont de tels hommes qui comptent, et qui comptent seuls. C'est nous qui comptons, seuls. Non seulement les autres n'ont point à parler pour nous. Mais c'est nous qui avons à parler, pour tout.

Il fut un héros et en outre il eut de grandes parties de sainteté. Et avec lui nous fûmes, obscurément, des héros.

Comment ne pas noter dans les quelques mots que nous avons cités, dans ces quelques phrases seulement que nous avons rapportées, je ne me retiens pas de noter non pas seulement ce sens de la liberté, et cette aisance dans la liberté, dans le maniement de la liberté, mais ce sens beaucoup plus curieux, beaucoup plus imprévu, apparemment plus imprévu, de la théologie, cet avertissement de la théologie. Instantanément il la voyait poindre partout où en effet elle point, elle-même ou quelque imitation, quelque contrefaçon, elle-même ou contrefaite.

Comment ne pas noter aussi son exact, son parfait, son réel internationalisme, Israël excepté, l'exactitude, l'aisance, l'allant de soi de son internationalisme, qui était beaucoup plus simple, beaucoup trop naturel, nullement appris, nullement forcé, nullement livresque, beaucoup trop aisé, beaucoup trop allant de soi pour jamais être un antinationalisme. Quand il parlait des Polonais pour les Bretons, ce n'était point un amusement, un rapprochement piquant. Ce n'était point un jeu d'esprit et pour jouer un bon tour. C'était naturellement qu'il voyait sur le même plan les Bretons et les Polonais. Il voyait vraiment la Chrétienté comme l'Islam, ce que nul de nous, même ceux qui le voudraient le plus, ne peut obtenir. Parce qu'il était bien réellement également en dehors des deux. Vue, angle du regard que nul de nous ne peut obtenir. Au moment où on faisait, même et peut-être surtout autour de lui, tout ce que l'on pouvait humainement pour évincer ses Juifs de Roumanie, par politique pour ne pas compromettre, pour ne pas charger le mouvement arménien, et qu'il y voyait très clair, dans cet assourdissement, un vieil ami de Quartier venait de le quitter [1]. Il me dit doucement, haussant doucement les épaules, comme il faisait, me le montrant pour ainsi dire des épaules, par-dessus le haut de ses épaules : *Il veut encore me rouler avec ses Arméniens. C'est toujours la même chose. Ils en...treprennent le Grand Turc parce qu'il est Turc et ils ne veulent pas qu'on dise un mot du roi de Roumanie parce qu'il est chrétien.* **C'est toujours la collusion de la chrétienté.**

Comment ne pas noter enfin comme c'est bien écrit, posé, mesuré, clair, noble, *français. Il ne faut pas recevoir des justifications semblables.* Une certaine proposition, un certain propos. Une certaine délibération. Un certain ton, une certaine résonance cartésienne même.

Apologie pour Bernard-Lazare. — Nourris, abreuvés, de notre mystique, la déformant, la dégradant aussitôt, la détournant instantanément en politique nos politiciens, Jaurès en tête, Jaurès le premier, créèrent cette double illusion, politique, premièrement que le dreyfusisme était antichrétien, deuxièmement qu'il était antifrançais. Il faut s'arrêter quelques instants à la deuxième.

Notre socialisme même, notre socialisme antécédent, à peine ai-je besoin de le dire, n'était nullement antifrançais, nullement antipatriote, nullement *anti-*

national. Il était essentiellement et rigoureusement, exactement *inter*national. Théoriquement il n'était nullement antinationaliste. Il était exactement internationaliste. Loin d'atténuer, loin d'effacer le peuple, au contraire il l'exaltait, il l'assainissait. Loin d'affaiblir, ou d'atténuer, loin d'effacer la nation, au contraire il l'exaltait, il l'assainissait. Notre thèse était au contraire, et elle est encore, que c'est au contraire la bourgeoisie, le bourgeoisisme, le capitalisme bourgeois, le sabotage capitaliste et bourgeois qui oblitère la nation et le peuple. Il faut bien penser qu'il n'y avait rien de commun entre le socialisme d'alors, notre socialisme, et ce que nous connaissons aujourd'hui sous ce nom. Ici encore la politique a fait son œuvre, et nulle part autant qu'ici la politique n'a *défait,* dénaturé la mystique. La politique, je dis la politique des politiques, professionnels, des politiciens, des politiques parlementaires. Mais plus encore, sans aucun doute, par l'invention, par l'intervention, par l'intercalation du sabotage, qui est une invention politique, au même titre que le vote, *plus encore que le vote,* pire, je veux dire plus politique, plus profondément politique, plus encore sans aucun doute les antipolitiques professionnels, les antipoliticiens, les syndicalistes, les antipolitiques antiparlementaires. Nous pensions alors, nous pensons toujours, mais il y a quinze ans tout le monde pensait comme nous, pensait avec nous, ou affectait de penser avec nous, il n'y avait sur ce point, sur ce principe même pas l'ombre d'une hésitation, pas l'ombre d'un débat. Il est de toute évidence que ce sont les bourgeois et les capitalistes qui ont commencé. Je veux dire que les bourgeois et les capitalistes ont cessé de faire leur

office, social, avant les ouvriers le leur, et longtemps
avant. Il ne fait aucun doute que le sabotage d'en haut
est de beaucoup antérieur au sabotage d'en bas, que le
sabotage bourgeois et capitaliste est antérieur, et de
beaucoup, au sabotage ouvrier; que les bourgeois et
les capitalistes ont cessé d'aimer le travail bourgeois et
capitaliste longtemps avant que les ouvriers eussent
cessé d'aimer le travail ouvrier. C'est exactement dans
cet ordre, en commençant par les bourgeois et les
capitalistes, que s'est produite cette désaffection générale du travail qui est la tare la plus profonde, la tare
centrale du monde moderne. Telle étant la situation
générale du monde moderne, il ne s'agissait point,
comme nos politiciens syndicalistes l'ont inventé,
d'inventer, d'*ajouter* un désordre ouvrier au désordre
bourgeois, un sabotage ouvrier au sabotage bourgeois
et capitaliste. Il s'agissait *au contraire*, notre socialisme
était essentiellement et en outre officiellement une
théorie, générale, une doctrine, une méthode générale,
une philosophie de l'organisation et de la réorganisa-
tion du travail, de la *restauration* du travail. Notre
socialisme était essentiellement et en outre officiellement une restauration, et même une restauration
générale, une restauration universelle. Nul alors ne le
contestait. Mais depuis quinze ans les politiciens ont
marché. Les doubles politiciens, les politiciens propres et les antipoliticiens. Les politiciens ont passé. Il
s'agissait au contraire d'une restauration générale,
d'une restauration totale, d'une restauration universelle *en commençant par le monde ouvrier*. Il s'agissait d'une
restauration totale fondée sur une restauration préalable du monde ouvrier; sur une restauration totale
préalable du monde ouvrier. Il s'agissait très exacte-

ment, et nul alors ne le contestait, tous au contraire
l'enseignaient, tous le déclaraient, il s'agissait au
contraire d'effectuer un assainissement général du
monde ouvrier, une réfection, un assainissement
moléculaire, organique, et commençant par cet assainissement de proche en proche un assainissement de
toute la cité. C'était déjà cette morale, cette méthode,
générale, cette philosophie des producteurs qui devait
trouver en M. Sorel [1], moraliste et philosophe, son
expression la plus haute, son expression définitive.
J'ajoute même que ce ne pouvait être que cela.

Et qu'il ne pouvait nullement, aucunement être
question que ce fût rien d'autre. Disons-le; pour le
philosophe, pour tout homme philosophant notre
socialisme était et n'était pas moins qu'une religion du
salut temporel. Et aujourd'hui encore il n'est pas
moins que cela. Nous ne cherchions pas moins que le
salut temporel de l'humanité par l'assainissement du
monde ouvrier, par l'assainissement du travail et du
monde du travail, par la restauration du travail et de
la dignité du travail, par un assainissement, par une
réfection organique, moléculaire du monde du travail,
et par lui de tout le monde économique, industriel.
C'est ce que nous nommons le monde industriel,
opposé au monde intellectuel et au monde politique,
au monde scolaire et au monde parlementaire; c'est
ce que nous nommons *l'économie*; la morale des
producteurs; la morale industrielle; le monde des
producteurs; le monde économique; le monde
ouvrier; la structure (organique, moléculaire) économique, industrielle; c'est ce que nous nommons
l'industrie, le régime industriel; c'est ce que nous
nommons le régime de la production industrielle. Le

monde intellectuel et le monde politique au contraire, le monde scolaire et le monde parlementaire vont ensemble. Par la restauration des mœurs industrielles, par l'assainissement de l'atelier industriel nous n'espérions pas moins, nous ne cherchions pas moins que le salut temporel de l'humanité. Ceux-là seuls s'en moqueront qui ne veulent pas voir que le christianisme même, qui est la religion du salut éternel, est embourbé dans cette boue, dans la boue des mauvaises mœurs économiques, industrielles ; que lui-même il n'en sortira point, qu'il ne s'en tirera point à moins d'une révolution économique, industrielle ; qu'enfin il n'y a point de lieu de perdition mieux fait, mieux aménagé, mieux outillé pour ainsi dire, qu'il n'y a point d'outil de perdition mieux adapté que l'atelier moderne.

Et que toutes les difficultés de l'Église viennent de là, toutes ses difficultés réelles, profondes, populaires : de ce que, malgré quelques prétendues œuvres ouvrières, sous le masque de quelques prétendues œuvres ouvrières et de quelques prétendus ouvriers catholiques, de ce que l'atelier lui est fermé, et de ce qu'elle est fermée à l'atelier ; de ce qu'elle est devenue dans le monde moderne, subissant, elle aussi, une modernisation, presque uniquement la religion des riches et ainsi qu'elle n'est plus socialement si je puis dire la communion des fidèles. Toute la faiblesse, et peut-être faut-il dire la faiblesse croissante de l'Église dans le monde moderne vient non pas comme on le croit de ce que la Science aurait monté contre la Religion des systèmes soi-disant invincibles, non pas de ce que la Science aurait découvert, aurait trouvé contre la Religion des arguments, des raisonnements censément victorieux, mais de ce que ce qui reste du monde chrétien socialement manque aujourd'hui profondément de charité. Ce n'est point du tout le raisonnement qui manque. C'est la charité. Tous ces raisonnements, tous ces systèmes, tous ces arguments pseudo-scientifiques ne seraient rien, ne pèseraient pas lourd s'il y avait une once de charité. Tous ces airs de tête ne porteraient pas loin si la chrétienté était restée ce qu'elle était, une communion, si le christianisme était resté ce qu'il était, une religion du cœur. C'est une des raisons pour lesquelles les modernes n'entendent rien au christianisme, au vrai, au réel, à l'histoire vraie, réelle du christianisme, et à ce que c'était réellement que la chrétienté. (Et combien de chrétiens y entendent encore. Combien de chrétiens, sur ce point même, sur ce point aussi, ne sont-ils pas modernes.) Ils croient, quand ils sont sincères, il y en a, ils croient que le christianisme fut toujours moderne, c'est-à-dire, exactement, qu'il fut toujours comme ils voient qu'il est dans le monde moderne, où il n'y a plus de chrétienté, au sens où il y en avait une. Ainsi dans le monde moderne tout est moderne, quoi qu'on en ait, et c'est sans doute le plus beau coup du modernisme et du monde moderne que d'avoir en beaucoup de sens, presque en tous les sens, rendu moderne le christianisme même, l'Église et ce qu'il y avait encore de chrétienté. C'est ainsi que quand il y a une éclipse, tout le monde est à l'ombre. Tout ce qui passe dans un âge de l'humanité, par une époque, dans une période, dans une zone, tout ce qui est dans un monde, tout ce qui a été placé dans une place, dans

un temps, dans un monde, tout ce qui est situé dans
une certaine situation, temporelle, dans un monde,
temporel, en reçoit la teinte, en porte l'ombre. On fait
beaucoup de bruit d'un certain modernisme intellectuel qui n'est pas même une hérésie, qui est une sorte
de pauvreté intellectuelle moderne, un résidu, une lie,
un fond de cuve, un bas de cuvée, un fond de tonneau,
un appauvrissement intellectuel moderne à l'usage
des modernes des anciennes grandes hérésies. Cette
pauvreté n'eût exercé aucun ravage, elle eût été
purement risible si les voies ne lui avaient point été
préparées, s'il n'y avait point ce grand modernisme du
cœur, ce grave, cet infiniment grave modernisme de la
charité. Si les voies ne lui avaient point été préparées
par ce modernisme du cœur et de la charité. C'est par
lui que l'Église dans le monde moderne, que dans le
monde moderne la chrétienté n'est plus peuple, ce
qu'elle était, qu'elle ne l'est plus aucunement ;
qu'ainsi elle n'est plus socialement un peuple, un
immense peuple, une race, immense ; que le christianisme n'est plus socialement la religion des profondeurs, une religion peuple, la religion de tout un
peuple, temporel, éternel, une religion enracinée aux
plus grandes profondeurs temporelles mêmes, la religion d'une race, de toute une race temporelle, de toute
une race éternelle, mais qu'il n'est plus socialement
qu'une religion de bourgeois, une religion de riches,
une espèce de religion supérieure pour classes supérieures de la société, de la nation, une misérable sorte
de religion distinguée pour gens censément distingués ; par conséquent tout ce qu'il y a de plus
superficiel, de plus officiel en un certain sens, de
moins profond ; de plus inexistant ; tout ce qu'il y a de

plus pauvrement, de plus misérablement formel; et d'autre part et surtout tout ce qu'il y a de plus contraire à son institution; à la sainteté, à la pauvreté, à la forme même la plus formelle de son institution. A la vertu, à la lettre et à l'esprit de son institution. De sa propre institution. Il suffit de se reporter au moindre texte des Évangiles.

Il suffit de se reporter à tout ce que d'un seul tenant il vaut mieux nommer l'Évangile.

C'est cette pauvreté, cette misère spirituelle et cette richesse temporelle qui a tout fait, qui a fait le mal. C'est ce modernisme du cœur, ce modernisme de la charité qui a fait la défaillance, la déchéance, dans l'Église, dans le christianisme, dans la chrétienté même qui a fait la dégradation de la mystique en politique.

On mène aujourd'hui grand bruit, je vois qu'on fait un grand état de ce que depuis la séparation le catholicisme, le christianisme n'est plus la religion officielle, la religion d(e l)'État, de ce que, ainsi, l'Église est libre. Et on a raison en un certain sens. La position de l'Église est évidemment tout autre, tout à fait autre sous le nouveau régime. Sous toutes les duretés de la liberté, d'une certaine pauvreté, l'Église est autrement elle-même sous le nouveau régime. Jamais on n'obtiendra sous le nouveau régime des évêques aussi mauvais que les évêques concordataires. Mais il ne faut point exagérer non plus. Il ne faut pas se dissimuler que si l'Église a cessé de faire la religion officielle de l'État, elle n'a point cessé de faire la religion officielle de la bourgeoisie de l'État. Elle a perdu, elle a laissé politiquement, mais elle n'a guère perdu, elle n'a guère laissé socialement toutes les charges de servitude qui lui venaient de son officialité. C'est pour cela qu'il ne faut pas triompher. C'est pour cela que l'atelier lui est fermé, et qu'elle est fermée à l'atelier. Elle fait, elle est la religion officielle, la religion formelle du riche. Voilà ce que le peuple, obscurément ou formellement, très assurément sent très bien. Voilà ce qu'il voit. Elle n'est donc rien, voilà pourquoi elle n'est rien. Et surtout et elle n'est rien de ce qu'elle était, et elle est, devenue, tout ce qu'il y a de plus contraire à elle-même, tout ce qu'il y a de plus contraire à son institution. Et elle ne se rouvrira point l'atelier, et elle ne se rouvrira point le peuple à moins que de faire, elle aussi, elle comme tout le monde, à moins que de *faire les frais* d'une révolution économique, d'une révolution sociale, d'une révolution industrielle, pour dire le mot d'une révolution *temporelle* pour le salut *éternel*. Tel est, éternellement, temporellement, (éternellement temporellement et temporellement éternellement), le mystérieux assujettissement de l'éternel même au temporel. Telle est proprement l'inscription de l'éternel même dans le temporel. Il faut faire les frais économiques, les frais sociaux, les frais industriels, *les frais temporels.* Nul ne s'y peut soustraire, non pas même l'éternel, non pas même le spirituel, non pas même la vie intérieure. C'est pour cela que notre socialisme n'était pas si bête, et qu'il était profondément chrétien.

C'est pour cela que lorsqu'on leur met sous les yeux la vieille chrétienté, quand on les met en face de ce que c'était dans la réalité qu'une paroisse chrétienne, une paroisse française au commencement du quinzième siècle, du temps qu'il y avait des paroisses françaises, quand on leur montre, quand on leur fait voir ce que c'était dans la réalité que la chrétienté, du temps qu'il y avait une chrétienté, ce que c'était qu'une grande sainte, la plus grande peut-être de toutes, du temps qu'il y avait une sainteté, du temps qu'il y avait une *charité,* du temps qu'il y avait des saintes et des saints, tout un peuple chrétien, tout un monde chrétien, tout un peuple, tout un monde de saints et de pécheurs, aussitôt quelques-uns de nos catholiques modernes, modernes à leur insu, mais profondément modernes, jusque dans les moelles, intellectuels à leur insu et qui se vantent de ne pas l'être, intellectuels tout de même, profondément intellectuels, intellectuels jusqu'aux moelles, bourgeois et fils de bourgeois, rentiers et fils de rentiers, pensionnés du gouvernement, pensionnés de l'État, fonctionnaires, pensionnés des autres, des autres citoyens, des autres électeurs, des autres contribuables, et qui fort ingénieusement ont préalablement fait inscrire sur le Grand-Livre de la Dette Publique les assurances d'ailleurs modestes de leur pain quotidien, ainsi armés quelques-uns de ces contemporains catholiques, devant une soudaine révélation de l'antique, de la vieille, de la chrétienté ancienne se hâtent de pousser quelques cris, comme de pudeur outragée [1]. Dans un besoin ils renieraient Joinville, comme trop grossier, comme trop peuple. *Le sire* de Joinville. Ils renieraient peut-être bien saint Louis. Comme trop roi de France.

Il faut faire les frais temporels. C'est-à-dire que nul, fût-ce l'Église, fût-ce n'importe quelle puissance spirituelle, ne s'en tirera à moins d'une révolution temporelle, d'une révolution économique, d'une révolution sociale. D'une révolution industrielle. A moins de payer cela. Pour ne pas payer, pour ne pas les faire un singulier concert s'est accordé, une singulière collusion s'est instituée, s'est jouée, se joue entre l'Église et le parti intellectuel. Ce serait même amusant, ce serait risible si ce n'était aussi profondément triste. Ce concert, cette collusion consiste à décaler, à déplacer le débat, le terrain même du débat. L'objet du débat. A dissimuler dans un coin le modernisme du cœur, le modernisme de la charité pour mettre en valeur, en fausse valeur, en lumière, en fausse lumière, pour mettre en surface, en vue, dans toute la surface le modernisme intellectuel, l'appareil du modernisme intellectuel, le solennel, le glorieux appareil. Ainsi tout le monde y gagne, car ça ne coûte plus rien, ça ne coûte plus aucune révolution économique, industrielle, sociale, temporelle, et nos bourgeois de l'un et l'autre côté, nos capitalistes de l'un et l'autre bord, de l'une et l'autre confession, les cléricaux et les radicaux, les cléricaux radicaux et les radicaux cléricaux, les intellectuels et ies clercs, les intellectuels clercs et les clercs intellectuels ne veulent rien tant, ne veulent que ceci : *ne pas payer*. Ne point faire de frais. Ne point faire les frais. Ne point lâcher les cordons de la bourse. On me pardonnera cette expression grossière. Mais il en faut une, il la faut dans cette situation grossière. Concert merveilleux, merveilleuse collusion. Tout le monde y gagne tout. Non seulement que ça ne coûte rien, mais aussi, en surplus, naturellement la gloire, qui ne vient jamais jusqu'à ceux qui la méritent. Tout le monde y trouve son compte, et même le nôtre. Une fois de plus deux partis contraires sont d'accord, se sont trouvés, se sont mis d'accord non pas seulement pour fausser le débat qui les divise ou paraît les diviser, mais pour fausser, pour transporter le terrain même du débat là où le débat leur sera le plus avantageux, leur coûtera le moins cher à l'un et à l'autre, poussés par la seule considération de leurs intérêts temporels. L'opération consiste à effacer, à tenir dans l'ombre cet effrayant modernisme du cœur et à mettre en première place, en seule place, le modernisme intellectuel, à tout attribuer, tout ce qui se passe, à la feinte toute-puissance, à l'effrayante, à la censément effrayante puissance du modernisme intellectuel. C'est un décalage, une substitution, un transfert, un transport, une transposition merveilleuse. Un déplacement perfectionné. Les intellectuels sont enchantés. *Voyez*, s'écrient-ils, *comme nous sommes puissants. Nous en avons une tête. Nous avons trouvé des arguments, des raisonnements si extraordinaires que par ces seuls raisonnements nous avons ébranlé la foi. La preuve que c'est vrai*, **c'est que ce sont les curés qui le disent.** Et les curés ensemble et les bons bourgeois cléricaux, censés catholiques, prétendus chrétiens, oublieux des anathèmes sur le riche, des effrayantes réprobations sur l'argent dont l'Évangile est comme saturé, moelleusement assis dans la paix du cœur, dans la paix sociale, tous nos bons bourgeois se récrient : *Tout ça aussi*, se récrient-ils, *c'est de la faute à ces sacrés professeurs, qui ont inventé, qui ont trouvé des arguments, des raisonnements si extraordinaires. La preuve que c'est vrai*, **c'est que c'est nous, curés, qui le disons.** Alors ça va bien, et non seulement tout le monde est en République, mais tout le monde est content. Les porte-monnaie restent dans les poches, et les argents restent dans les porte-monnaie. On ne met pas la main au porte-monnaie. C'est l'essentiel. Mais je le redis en vérité, tous ces raisonnements ne pèseraient pas lourd, s'il y avait une once de charité.

Le monde clérical bourgeois affecte de croire que ce sont les raisonnements, que c'est le modernisme cérébral qui est important uniquement pour n'avoir point à dépenser une révolution industrielle, une révolution économique.

Tel étant notre socialisme, et cela ne faisait alors aucun secret, comme cela ne faisait aucun doute, il est évident que non seulement il ne portait aucune atteinte et ne pouvait porter aucune atteinte aux droits légitimes des nations, mais qu'étant, que faisant un assainissement général, et par cela même, en dedans de cela même un assainissement du nationalisme et de la nation même, il servait, il sauvait les intérêts les plus essentiels, les droits les plus légitimes des peuples. Les droits, les intérêts les plus sacrés. Et qu'il n'y avait que lui qui le faisait. Ce n'était point violer, effacer les nations et les peuples, ce n'était point les fausser, les violenter, les oblitérer, les forcer, leur donner une entorse, mais au contraire, que de travailler à remplacer d'une substitution, d'un remplacement organique, moléculaire, un champ clos, une concurrence anarchique de peuples forcenés, frénétiques, par une forêt saine, par une forêt grandis-

sante de peuples prospères, par tout un peuple de
peuples florissants. Montants dans leur sève, dans
leur essence, dans la droiture et la lignée de leur
végétale race, libres de l'écrasement des servitudes
économiques, libres de la corruption organique, moléculaire des mauvaises mœurs industrielles. Ce n'était
point annuler les nations et les peuples. Au contraire
c'était les fonder, les asseoir enfin, les faire naître, les
faire et les laisser pousser. C'était les *faire*. Nous
avions dès lors la certitude, que nous avons, que le
monde souffre infiniment plus du sabotage bourgeois
et capitaliste que du sabotage ouvrier. Non seulement
c'est le sabotage bourgeois et capitaliste qui a
commencé, mais il est devenu rapidement presque
total. Et il est si je puis dire entré dans le monde
bourgeois comme une seconde race. Il est fort loin au
contraire d'avoir pénétré aussi profondément dans le
monde ouvrier, à cette profondeur, aussi totalement.
Et surtout il n'y est pas du tout le même. Il est fort
loin d'y être entré comme une race. Contrairement à
ce que l'on croit généralement, à ce que croient
communément les écrivains, les publicistes, les sociologues, qui sont des intellectuels et des bourgeois, le
sabotage dans le monde ouvrier ne vient pas des
profondeurs du monde ouvrier; il ne vient pas du
monde ouvrier lui-même. Il n'est point ouvrier. Il est,
essentiellement, bourgeois. Il ne vient pas du bas, par
une remontée des boues, des bas-fonds ouvriers, il
vient du haut. C'est le socialisme qui seul pouvait
l'éviter, éviter cette contamination. C'est le sabotage
bourgeois, le même, le seul, qui par contamination de
proche en proche descend par nappes horizontales
dans le monde ouvrier. Ce n'est point le monde

ouvrier qui exaspère des vices propres. C'est le monde
ouvrier qui s'embourgeoise graduellement. Contrairement à ce que l'on croit, le sabotage n'est point inné,
né dans le monde ouvrier. Il y est appris. Il y est
enseigné dogmatiquement, intellectuellement, comme
une invention étrangère. C'est une invention bourgeoise, une invention politique, parlementaire, essentiellement intellectuelle, qui pénètre par contamination et enseignement, intellectuel, par en haut dans le
monde ouvrier. Elle y rencontre des résistances qu'elle
n'avait jamais rencontrées dans le monde bourgeois.
Elle n'y a point bataille gagnée. Elle n'y a point ville
prise. Elle y est, somme toute, artificielle. Elle s'y
heurte à des résistances imprévues, à des résistances
d'une profondeur incroyable, à cet amour séculaire du
travail qui enrichissait le cœur laborieux. Le monde
bourgeois et capitaliste est presque tout entier, pour
ainsi dire tout entier consacré au plaisir. On trouverait encore un très grand nombre d'ouvriers, et non
pas seulement des vieux, qui *aiment* le travail.

Tel étant notre socialisme, il est évident qu'il était,
qu'il faisait un assainissement de la nation et du
peuple, un renforcement encore inconnu, une prospérité, une floraison, une fructification. Bien loin d'en
conjurer, d'en conspirer la perte. Nous avions déjà la
certitude, que nous avons, que le peuple qui entrerait
le premier dans cette voie, qui aurait cet honneur, qui
aurait ce courage, et en un sens cette habileté, en
recevrait une telle force, une telle prospérité organique et moléculaire, constitutionnelle, histologique, un
tel renforcement, un tel accroissement, un tel assainis-

sement de tous les ordres de sa force que non
seulement il marcherait à la tête des peuples, mais
qu'il n'aurait plus rien à redouter jamais, ni dans le
présent ni dans l'avenir, ni de ses concurrents économiques, industriels, commerciaux, ni de ses concurrents militaires.

Ainsi l'embourgeoisement par le sabotage suit une
marche exactement inverse de celle que nous voulions
suivre. Et faire suivre. Nous voulions qu'un assainissement du monde ouvrier, remontant de proche en
proche, assainît le monde bourgeois et ainsi toute la
société, toute la cité même. Et il s'est produit au
contraire, en fait il s'est produit qu'une démoralisa-
tion du monde bourgeois, en matière économique, en
matière industrielle et en toute autre matière, dans
l'ordre du travail et dans tout autre ordre, descendant
de proche en proche, a démoralisé le monde ouvrier,
et ainsi toute la société, la cité même. Loin d'ajouter,
de vouloir ajouter un désordre à un désordre, nous
voulions instaurer, restaurer un ordre, un ordre
nouveau, ancien ; nouveau, antique ; nullement
moderne ; un ordre laborieux, un ordre du travail, un
ordre ouvrier ; un ordre économique, temporel, industriel ; et par la contamination pour ainsi dire remontante de cet ordre réordonner le désordre même. Par
une contamination descendante c'est le désordre qui a
désordonné l'ordre. Qui a désorganisé l'organisation
de l'organisme. Mais nous avons le droit de dire que
ce désordre, que ce mauvais exemple a été introduit
dans le monde ouvrier par une sorte d'insertion
intellectuelle, par une opération en un sens aussi

artificielle qu'a pu l'être par exemple cette autre invention des Universités Populaires.

Ce serait une erreur de croire qu'il n'y a que le bien, l'effort au bien, la morale qui soit artificielle. Le mal, surtout dans une race comme la nôtre, l'effort au mal, l'effort d'avilissement, de contamination peut aussi bien être artificiel. Appris.

Autant que personne je sais combien ces efforts d'instruction et de moralisation, ces Universités Populaires et toutes autres, et tous autres, autant que personne je sais combien ces efforts bourgeois, intellectuels, distillés d'en haut sur le monde ouvrier, étaient factices, vides, vains; creux; combien ils ne rendaient pas et ne pouvaient pas rendre. Combien ils étaient artificiels, superficiels. Mais ce que je peux dire, c'est que au contraire, par contre les enseignements du sabotage étaient aussi des enseignements bourgeois et intellectuels; qu'ils étaient aussi des enseignements, donnés, reçus; versés, reçus; enseignés, appris. Des enseignements et des apprentissages. Ils ont plus rendu, ils ont mieux porté, ils ont plus et mieux entré, ils sont entrés beaucoup plus profond parce que le mal entre toujours plus que le bien, mais ce que je veux dire et que l'on ne dit pas, ce que je tiens à dire, ce qu'il faut dire c'est qu'ils étaient bien des enseignements du même ordre, venus, descendus du même lieu, du même monde. Aussi bourgeois, aussi intellectuels, aussi artificiels. Peut-être un peu moins superficiels, parce que le mal est toujours moins superficiel que le bien. Au fond aussi étrangers au monde ouvrier.

C'étaient des enseignements de (la) même sorte. Étant donné ce qu'était le monde ouvrier, c'était une erreur de croire que le mal y était naturel et que le bien seul, par une sorte de disgrâce, y était artificiel.

Ainsi dans ce monde moderne tout entier tendu à l'argent, tout à la tension à l'argent, cette tension à l'argent contaminant le monde chrétien même lui fait sacrifier sa foi et ses mœurs au maintien de sa paix économique et sociale.

C'est là proprement ce modernisme du cœur, ce modernisme de la charité, ce *modernisme des mœurs*.

Il y a deux sortes de riches : les riches *athées,* qui *riches* n'entendent rien à la religion. Ils se sont donc mis à l'histoire *des* religions, et ils y excellent (et d'ailleurs il faut leur faire cette justice qu'ils ont tout fait pour n'en point faire une histoire *de la* religion. C'est eux qui ont inventé les *sciences* religieuses ;

et les riches *dévots,* qui *riches* n'entendent rien au christianisme. Alors ils le professent.

Tel est, il faut bien voir, il faut bien mesurer, tel est l'effrayant modernisme du monde moderne ; l'effrayante, la misérable efficacité. Il a entamé, réussi à entamer, il a modernisé, entamé la chrétienté. Il a rendu véreux, dans la charité, dans les mœurs il a rendu véreux le christianisme même.

Ai-je besoin de dire, pour mémoire, de noter et de faire noter combien ce socialisme même était dans la pure tradition française, combien il était dans la ligne, dans la lignée française. L'assainissement, l'éclaircissement du monde a toujours été la destination, la vocation française, l'office français même. L'assainissement de ce qui est malade, l'éclaircissement de ce qui est trouble, l'ordination de ce qui est désordre, l'organisation de ce qui est brut. Faut-il noter combien ce socialisme à base de générosité, combien cette générosité claire, combien cette générosité pleine et pure était dans la tradition française ; plus que dans la tradition française même, plus profondément, dans le génie français. Dans la sève et dans la race même. Dans la sève et le sang de la race. Une générosité à la fois abondante et sobre, généreuse et pourtant renseignée, pleine et pure, féconde et nette, pleine et fine, abondante sans niaiserie, renseignée sans stérilité. Un héroïsme enfin plein et sobre, gai et discret, un héroïsme à la française.

Tel étant notre socialisme, un socialisme français, quel devait être notre dreyfusisme, un dreyfusisme éminemment français. La plus grande erreur sur ce point, la plus grande illusion, sur ce chef de la patrie, est venue sans aucun doute de l'affaire Hervé. De l'hervéisme ; de la démagogie hervéiste. Et surtout et sans aucun doute beaucoup plus de la complaisance suspecte à la démagogie hervéiste. Je ne parlerai qu'avec un grand respect d'un homme qui vient de rentrer en prison pour la troisième ou quatrième fois, peut-être plus [1]. Au moins il va en prison. On n'en saurait dire autant de M. Jaurès qui s'est toujours arrangé pour ne pas aller en prison. Et pourtant ce

n'est point tant Hervé qui a fait le virus de l'hervéisme, de la démagogie hervéiste. C'est sans aucun
doute M. Jaurès, nul autre, ce sont les louches
conversations, les intrigues, les compromissions, les
négociations de groupes et de congrès, de parti et
d'unification, ce sont les troubles ententes, les
avances, les platitudes, les plates capitulations de
Jaurès à Hervé et à tout le hervéisme. Ce qui fut
dangereux dans Hervé et dans le hervéisme, mortellement dangereux, ce ne fut point tant Hervé lui-même,
ce ne fut point tant le hervéisme. Ce fut Jaurès et le
jauressisme, car ce fut cette incroyable capitulation
perpétuelle de Jaurès devant Hervé, cet aplatissement, cette platitude infatigable. Cette capitulation en
quelque sorte autorisée, officielle, revêtue d'un grand
nom et du nom d'un grand parti, qui seule par
conséquent pouvait lui donner quelque autorité et le
lui donna, quelque vêtement, quelque consécration.
Cette capitulation constante qui ne gonfla pas seulement Hervé d'orgueil, mais qui le revêtit très authen-
tiquement d'une autorité morale, d'une autorité politique, d'une autorité sociale. Car l'homme qui l'auto-
risait ainsi, et de la meilleure des autorisations, en
capitulant perpétuellement devant lui, et presque
solennellement, en causant même avec lui, avait lui-
même une haute autorité morale, celle précisément
que nous lui avions conférée, il avait une grosse
autorité politique, une grosse autorité sociale. Il ne
faut jamais oublier que pendant toute cette période
cet homme, par cette invention qu'il avait faite du
combisme, et qu'il maintenait, patronnait, protégeait,
représentait le gouvernement même de la République.
Il y eut ainsi ici un des plus beaux cas qu'il y eût

jamais eu de détournement d'autorité morale, politique et sociale. Et ainsi de report de la responsabilité. Sans Jaurès, Hervé n'était rien. Par Jaurès, avec Jaurès il devint autorisé, il devint authentique, il devint (comme) un membre, et secrètement à beaucoup près le plus redouté, du gouvernement de la République. Par Jaurès, par le jauressisme, par le combisme, c'était le gouvernement même pour ainsi dire qui recevait, qui endossait Hervé.

Cela étant, il faut serrer de plus près, d'un peu plus près, il faut serrer au plus près cette affaire Hervé. Il faut bien voir ce que cela veut dire, ce qu'il y avait dedans. Et la serrant, il faut bien dire que ceux qui ont fait et endossé Hervé, fait et endossé le hervéisme sont ceux qui ont fait une atteinte mortelle, qui ont porté un coup incalculable, un coup mortel à la *croyance publique à l'innocence de Dreyfus.* C'est par eux, surtout par eux, par Jaurès dans la mesure où il a autorisé Hervé, par Dreyfus même dans la mesure où il a autorisé Jaurès, que nous sommes retombés sur ce palier moyen, sur ce palier sans fin, à mi-côte, dont nous avons dit que nous ne sortirions, que nous ne remonterons jamais, dont nous avons dit que l'histoire ne remonterait jamais.

Car il faut enfin, en quelques mots, démonter le mécanisme de cette dangereuse, de cette démagogie mortelle. Il me semble bien, si ma mémoire est bonne, si mes souvenirs sont justes, que pendant toute l'affaire Dreyfus nous nous efforcions de démontrer

que Dreyfus *n'était pas* un traître. Autant que je me
rappelle c'étaient nos adversaires qui s'efforçaient de
démontrer ou enfin qui prétendaient *qu'il était* un
traître. Ce n'était pas nous. Autant que je me
rappelle. Nous nous prétendions qu'il *n'était pas* un
traître. Les uns et les autres, autant qu'il me sou-
vienne, nous avions un postulat commun, un lieu
commun, c'est ce qui faisait notre dignité, commune,
c'est ce qui faisait la dignité de toute cette bataille,
c'est ce qui fit bientôt notre force, et cette proposition
commune initiale, qui allait de soi, sur laquelle on ne
discutait même pas, sur laquelle tout le monde était,
tombait d'accord, dont on ne parlait même pas, tant
elle allait de soi, qui était sous-entendue partout,
qu'on a honte à dire, tant elle allait de soi, c'était *qu'il
ne fallait pas* trahir, que la trahison, nommément la
trahison militaire, était un crime monstrueux. Tout a
changé de face, depuis que sur ces bords [1]. Tout le
mécanisme a été démonté, détourné, remonté à l'envers, depuis que Hervé est venu, de ce que Hervé est
venu. Hervé est un homme qui dit au contraire.

Les antidreyfusistes et nous les dreyfusistes nous
parlions le même langage. Nous parlions sur le même
plan. Nous parlions exactement le même langage
patriotique. Nous parlions sur le même plan patriotique. Nous avions les mêmes prémisses, le même
postulat patriotique. Qu'en fait eux ou nous nous
fussions des meilleurs patriotes, c'était précisément
l'objet du débat, mais que ce fût l'objet du débat, c'est
précisément ce qui prouve que les uns et les autres
nous étions patriotes. Qu'en droit, en intention ce fût
l'objet du débat. Nous autres, de ce côté-ci, nous ne
l'étions pas seulement sincèrement, nous l'étions

profondément d'abord, d'autant plus qu'on nous le contestait. Nous l'étions ensuite frénétiquement, peut-être avec une sorte de rage, parce qu'on nous le niait publiquement, et surtout peut-être parce que notre situation géographique dans la carte mentale et sentimentale, parce que les circonstances, les événements historiques nous avaient plusieurs fois donné les apparences de ne pas l'être.

Fondés sur le même postulat, partant du même postulat nous parlions le même langage. Les antidreyfusistes disaient : La trahison militaire est un crime et Dreyfus a trahi militaire. Nous disions : La trahison militaire est un crime et Dreyfus n'a pas trahi. Il est innocent de ce crime. Tout a changé de face depuis que Hervé est venu. La même conversation eut l'air de se poursuivre. L'affaire continue. Mais elle n'était plus la même affaire, la même conversation. Elle n'était plus la même. Elle en était une tout autre, infiniment autre, parce que le langage même était autre, infiniment autre parce que le plan même du débat n'était plus le même. Hervé est un homme qui dit : Il faut trahir.

Nommément il faut trahir militairement.

Les antidreyfusistes professionnels disaient : Il ne faut pas être un traître et Dreyfus est un traître. Nous les dreyfusistes professionnels nous disions : Il ne faut pas être un traître et Dreyfus n'est pas un traître. Hervé est un qui dit, et Jaurès laisse dire à Hervé, et Dreyfus même laisse Jaurès laisser dire à Hervé, et en un sens, et en ce sens au moins Dreyfus même laisse dire à Jaurès même : *Il faut être* un traître.

Nommément il faut être un traître militaire.

Par cet entraînement de proche en proche, par cette

sorte de dérapage de proche en proche, par cette dérivation, par ce détournement, par ce déglinguement Jaurès est entré dans le crime de Hervé ; par cette réversion, par cette réversibilité des responsabilités ; et de la plus basse façon que l'on y pût entrer, non point même par une complicité active, qui a ses risques, qui a son efficience, qui peut avoir même pour ainsi dire sa grandeur, mais obliquement, mais bassement, par une complicité tacite, sournoise, par une complicité de laisser faire et de laisser passer, par une complicité les yeux baissés. La plus basse de toutes. Et Dreyfus, faute de marquer les temps, est entré, s'est laissé entrer dans le crime Jaurès.

Quelle fut la répercussion de cette double dérivation, de cette double décadence, de ce double détournement, de ce détournement à deux temps sur l'efficacité de nos démonstrations dreyfusistes, il était aisé de le prévoir. Quand on s'efforce de démontrer qu'un homme n'est point un traître pensant profondément qu'*il ne faut pas* être un traître, on est au moins écouté. Mais quand on s'efforce de démontrer qu'un homme n'est point un traître laissant dire et disant qu'*il faut* être un traître, l'opération, la démonstration devient extrêmement suspecte. Car alors, dans l'hypothèse hervéiste, qu'il faut trahir, qu'il faut être un traître, s'il n'a pas trahi, il a eu les plus grands torts, ce Dreyfus. Et alors pourquoi le défendre. Par une sorte de gageure, de suprême élégance on le défendrait d'avoir commis un crime que précisément il faudrait commettre, on le défendrait d'avoir fait ce que précisément il fallait faire : c'est bien de l'honneur, c'est bien de la politesse. C'est trop poli pour être honnête. S'il faut être un traître militaire, Dreyfus a eu les plus grands torts de ne le point être. Et on le défendrait précisément d'avoir fait ce qu'il faut faire. On dirait : Il n'a pas trahi. Il a eu tort, car il faut trahir. Aussi nous le défendons. Ce serait, ce ferait un retournement de politesse bien acrobatique, une galanterie bien française, un retournement diagonal, diamétral de politesse. Une opération bien suspecte. Ces gens ne vous avaient point habitués à ces gageures de politesse. Tant de politesse devient extrêmement suspecte. Dans le raisonnement hervéiste en effet, s'il est permis de le nommer ainsi, Dreyfus, *tant qu'il ne trahit pas,* est un bien grand coupable. Il est un grand criminel. D'autant plus criminel et d'autant plus coupable qu'il était mieux situé, militairement, qu'il avait une admirable situation pour trahir. Militairement. Hervé, lui, n'avait pas cet honneur, il n'avait pas ce bonheur d'avoir, de pouvoir avoir à sa disposition les graphiques des chemins de fer. Comment, voilà un homme, Dreyfus, qui pouvait avoir en main les graphiques des chemins de fer et il ne les aurait pas instantanément sabotés. Quel être. Il ne faut pas oublier que Hervé est un monsieur qui le premier jour de la mobilisation, plus précisément dans la première heure du premier jour, c'est-à-dire, je pense, de minuit 01 à 1 heure 00 fusillera les cinq cent trente-sept mille hommes de l'armée (française) active ; plus les treize cent cinquante-sept mille hommes de la réserve de l'armée active, qui forment avec elle le premier ban ; puis les cinq cent soixante-seize mille hommes de l'armée territoriale ; puis les sept cent cinquante et un mille hommes de la réserve de l'armée territoriale, qui forment avec elle le deuxième ban ; sans compter le premier et le

deuxième ban des volontaires; et si on ne l'arrête il
fusillera aussi les troupes noires, de récente formation,
la célèbre, la fameuse *division noire,* les Toucouleurs,
Ouolofs, Sarakollés, Malinkés, et les autres populations, Djermas, Bellas, Baribas, Baoulés, Bobos, Sous-
sous, et Nagots et les Tourelourous et mesdames leurs
épouses. Tout ça avec des revolvers *américains,* car il ne
veut point encourager la production nationale. Je me
garderai de dire que ce sont des *Brownings,* on leur a
déjà assez fait de publicité. A cette marque. Auprès de
ce grand massacre, bien connu sous le nom de *massacre
des deux bans,* que pèse la tradition d'un graphique des
chemins de fer. Hervé parle souvent de l'affaire
Dreyfus, il en écrit dans son journal. S'il était
conséquent, constant avec lui-même, s'il était logique,
— et logicien, mais les plus rigoureux, les plus cruels
logiciens, pour les autres, ne sont pas toujours ceux
qui sont les plus impitoyables pour soi, — s'il était
logique avec lui-même il dirait : Nous avons défendu
ce Dreyfus, nous avons eu tort. Pensez donc : Il était
capitaine; capitaine d'État-Major; enfin il travaillait
dans les bureaux de l'État-Major de l'armée. Il était
merveilleusement outillé, merveilleusement situé pour
trahir. Et malheureusement il n'a pas trahi. Cet
homme insuffisant n'a pas trahi.

Voilà ce que Hervé dirait, s'il était logique et s'il
était libre. Voilà ce que les événements, ce que la
réalité dit pour lui. On voit assez quelle est pour nous
la conséquence, quelle est sur notre situation historique la répercussion de ce changement de situation
géographique. Quand je dis nous, naturellement, je
veux dire notre parti, nos politiciens. Car il ne s'agit
pas de nous mêmes. C'est un retour en arrière, une

répercussion en arrière, une répercussion remontante, reportée en arrière, réversible, réversée, reportée sur tout ce que nous avions dit, sur tout ce que nous avions fait, sur tout ce que nous avions été. Quand nous repoussions l'accusation d'être un traître repoussant profondément l'idée même d'être un traître, on pouvait nous combattre, mais au moins nous nous faisions écouter. Quand au contraire nous repoussons l'accusation d'être un traître accueillant profondément l'idée d'être un traître, comment ne pas voir que nous devenons instantanément suspects. Que nous perdons l'audience même.

Et même l'audience que nous avions déjà, eue, obtenue. L'ancienne audience.

Une audience qui paraissait acquise.

Une audience aujourd'hui annulée.

On peut se déshonorer en arrière.

Jaurès ici intervient, au débat, et se défend. Si je reste avec Hervé, dit-il, dans le même parti, si j'y suis resté constamment, toujours, si longtemps, malgré les innombrables couleuvres que Hervé m'a fait avaler, c'est pour deux raisons également valables. Premièrement c'est précisément, c'est à cause de ces innombrables couleuvres mêmes. Il faut bien songer que ce Hervé est l'homme du monde qui m'a administré le plus de coups de pied dans le derrière. En public et en particulier. Dans les congrès et dans les meetings. Dans son journal. Publiquement et privément, comme dit Péguy. Il faut l'en louer. Et comme il me connaît bien. Il faut l'en récompenser. Il faut que tant de zèle soit récompensé. Comme il sait que je ne marche *jamais* qu'avec ceux qui me maltraitent. Qui me poussent. Qui me tirent. Qui me bourrent. Et que je ne marche jamais avec les imbéciles qui m'aimaient. Comme il connaît bien le fond, si je puis dire, de mon caractère. Il faut aussi, il faut bien que tant de perspicacité soit récompensée. Il me connaît si bien. Il me connaît comme moi-même. Il sait que quand quelqu'un m'aime et me sert, le sot, me prodigue les preuves les plus incontestables de l'amitié la plus dévouée, du dévouement le plus absolu, aussitôt je sens s'élever dans ce qui me sert de cœur d'abord un commencement, un mépris invincible pour cet imbécile. Faut-il qu'il soit bête en effet, d'aimer un ingrat comme moi, de s'attacher à un ingrat comme moi. Comme je le méprise, ce garçon. En outre, en deuxième, ensemble, en même temps un sentiment de jalousie, de la haine envieuse la plus basse contre un homme qui est capable de concevoir les sentiments de l'amitié. Enfin un tas d'autres beaux sentiments, fleurs de boue, plantes de vase, qui poussent dans la boue politique comme une bénédiction de défense républicaine. Hervé sait si bien tout cela que je l'en admire moi-même. Comme il connaît bien ma *psychologie,* si vous permettez. Et qu'au contraire quand je reçois un bon coup de pied dans le derrière, je me retourne instantanément avec un sentiment de respect profond, avec un respect inné pour ce pied, pour ce coup, pour la jambe qui est au bout du pied, pour l'homme qui est au bout de la jambe ; et même pour mon derrière, qui me vaut cet honneur. Un bon coup de pied dans le *Hinterland,* dans mon *Hinterland*[1]. Et quand je pense qu'il y a des gens qui disent que je n'ai pas de fond. Je hais mes amis. J'aime mes ennemis.

On ferait une belle comédie avec mon *caractère*. Je hais mes amis parce qu'ils m'aiment. Je méprise mes amis parce qu'ils m'aiment. Parce qu'ils m'aiment j'ai en moi pour eux, je sens monter en moi contre eux une jalousie bassement envieuse, l'invincible sentiment d'une incurable haine. Je trahis mes amis parce qu'ils m'aiment. J'aime, je sers, je suis, j'admire mes ennemis parce qu'ils me méprisent (ils ne me haïssent même pas), parce qu'ils me maltraitent, parce qu'ils me violentent, parce qu'ils me connaissent enfin, parce qu'ils me connaissent donc. Et ils savent si bien comment on me fait marcher. Quand un me trahit, je l'aime double, je l'admire, j'admire sa compétence. Il me ressemble tant. J'ai un goût secret pour la lâcheté, pour la trahison, pour tous les sentiments de la trahison. Je suis double. Je m'y connais. J'y suis chez moi. J'y suis à l'aise. On ferait une grande tragédie, une triste comédie avec mon *caractère*. Hervé ne la ferait peut-être pas mal. Il me connaît si bien. Il y a des exemples innombrables que j'aie trahi mes amis. Depuis trente ans que je fonctionne, il n'y a pas un exemple que j'aie trahi mes ennemis. C'est vous dire que j'excelle dans tous les sentiments politiques. On ferait un beau roman de l'histoire des soumissions que j'ai faites à notre camarade, au citoyen Hervé.

Ce vice, secret, ce goût secret que j'ai pour l'avanie. J'encaisse, j'encaisse. Ce goût infâme que j'ai pour l'avanie. Pour le déshonneur, de l'avanie. Je suis l'homme du monde qui reçoit, qui encaisse le plus d'avanies. A mon banc. Dans mon journal même. A mon banc Guesde n'en rate pas une. Il ne manque point, il ne manque jamais de s'adresser à la Chambre au long de mes oreilles. Aussi comme je respecte,

comme j'admire, comme j'estime, comme je vénère ce
grand Guesde, ce dur Guesde. De cette vénération qui
est pour moi le même sentiment que l'effroi. Comme
je me sens petit garçon à côté de ces hommes, à côté
d'un Guesde, à côté surtout d'un Hervé.

Et ce goût de l'ingratitude que j'ai, qui est au fond
le même que le goût de l'avanie. Voyez comme
aujourd'hui je traite et laisse traiter (ou fais traiter)
Gérault-Richard qui pendant huit ans s'est battu pour
moi [1].

Ainsi parle Jaurès. Deuxièmement, dit-il, si je suis
resté avec Hervé, c'est précisément pour l'affaiblir,
pour l'énerver, pour lui oblitérer sa virulence. C'est
ma méthode. Quand je vois une doctrine, un parti
devenir pernicieux, dangereux, autant que possible je
m'en mets. Mais généralement comme j'en suis j'y
reste. Mais alors j'y reste complaisamment. J'y
adhère. Je m'y colle. Je parle. Je parle. Je suis
éloquent. Je suis orateur. Je suis oratoire. Je redonde.
J'inonde. Je reçois précisément ces coups de pied au
quelque part que fort ingratement vous me reprochez.
(Pourquoi me les reprochez-vous, vous à moi, puisque
moi je ne les reproche pas à ceux qui me les donnent.)
Mais ces coups de pied, ça n'empêche pas de parler,
au contraire. Ça lance pour parler. Enfin bref, ou
plutôt long, après un certain temps de cet exercice (et
je ne parle pas seulement, j'agis en outre, j'agis en
dessous) (j'excelle dans le travail des commissions,
dans les (petits) complots, dans les combinaisons,
dans le jeu des ordres du jour, dans les petites
manigances, dans les commissions et compromissions

et ententes, dans tout le travail souterrain, sous la main, sous le manteau. Dans le jeu, dans l'invention des majorités, factices; faites, obtenues par un savant compartimentage des scrutins. Dans tout ce qui est le petit et le grand mécanisme politique et parlementaire) enfin, au bout d'un certain temps de cet exercice il n'y a plus de programme, il n'y a plus de principe, il n'y a plus de parti, il n'y a plus rien, il n'y a plus aucune de ces virulences. Quand je me suis bien collé à eux pendant un certain temps, supportant pour cela les avanies qu'il faut, quand je suis resté dans un parti pendant un certain temps, pendant le temps voulu, au bout de ce temps on voit, on s'aperçoit, tout le monde comprend que je les ai trahis. Comprenez-vous enfin, gros bête, me dit-il me poussant du coude.

Quand je suis, quand je me mets dans un parti, ça se connaît tout de suite, presque tout de suite, à ce que c'est un parti qui devient malade. Quand je me mets quelque part, ça se voit, ça se reconnaît à ce que ça va mal. Ça ne marche plus. Quand je me mets dans une idée, elle devient véreuse.

Je l'ai fait au dreyfusisme; je l'avais fait et je l'ai fait au socialisme; je l'ai fait et je le fais à l'hervéisme; je l'ai fait et je le fais au syndicalisme. C'est encore le radicalisme que j'ai trahi le moins. Il n'y a que le combisme que je n'ai jamais pas trahi du tout.

Je crois Jaurès très capable de trahir tout le monde, et les traîtres mêmes. Mais ici encore il souffrira que nous ne l'accompagnions pas. Pour deux raisons, nous aussi. La première est assez basse et je m'en excuse d'avance. Elle est politique. C'est qu'on a beau être

Jaurès, en pareille matière on ne sait jamais où l'on va, jusqu'où l'on entre, jusqu'où on réussit, ou au contraire jusqu'où l'événement réussit contre vous, jusqu'où les autres, ceux où l'on entre, réussissent contre vous, sur vous, en vous-même. J'entends bien que c'est une espèce de contre-espionnage. Mais justement on sait assez combien les services du contre-espionnage (on l'a su notamment par l'affaire Dreyfus même, on l'a vu par tant d'autres) sont bizarrement mais naturellement embarbouillés, imbriqués dans les services contraires du droit espionnage. On ne sait jamais bien jusqu'où on trahit les traîtres. Jusqu'où on y réussit. Et jusqu'où au contraire la trahison, l'habitude, le goût de la trahison s'infiltre, pénètre dans les veines mêmes. On voit bien ce qu'on fait pour eux. On voit moins bien ce qu'on fait contre eux. Quand on va officiellement, formellement avec eux, parmi eux, on voit bien la force qu'on leur apporte. On voit beaucoup moins bien le tort qu'on leur fait.

La trahison de tous que l'on fait avec eux, à leur exemple, dans leur compagnie, on voit bien ce qu'elle rapporte, ce qu'elle leur apporte de trahison réelle. On voit bien ce qu'elle est de trahison. Au contraire la trahison d'eux que l'on est censé faire, on ne voit pas du tout toujours à quoi elle aboutit, ce qu'elle rend. Ce qu'elle est.

Quand une fois on a lâché, une fois qu'on a rendu la main, on ne sait plus jusqu'où elle se rend.

Deuxièmement, et celle-ci est une raison de bonne compagnie, tirée de la vieille morale, et je suis heureux de la dire : On n'a pas le droit de trahir les traîtres mêmes. On n'a jamais le droit de trahir, personne. Les traîtres, il faut les combattre, et non pas les trahir.

Hervé même, qui fait tant le fendant depuis que ça lui rapporte, fût-ce des mois de prison, et des années, quatre années aujourd'hui, mais c'est toujours un rapport, Hervé au contraire, qui fait profession de tout dire, lui, et de n'avoir peur de rien, Hervé était au contraire d'une sorte de prudence consommée, même cauteleuse, il ne faut pas dire bretonne pendant tout le temps de son introduction. Tout eût été si simple, si direct, s'il nous eût dit directement : Mesdames et messieurs, citoyennes et citoyens, j'arrive de Sens [1]. Vous voyez en moi le traître. Ce que Dreyfus n'a malheureusement pas été, je le suis. Ce que Dreyfus n'a malheureusement pas fait, je le veux faire, je suis venu à Paris pour le faire. *Je me suis fait venir de Sens pour être traître.* Je suis celui qui enseignerai désormais la trahison militaire, techniquement parlant. On s'était trompé jusqu'ici. Il faut être un traître, et nommément un traître militaire.

Comme le disaient nos maîtres, nos communs maîtres, j'ai *renouvelé la question.*

S'il nous eût dit tout simplement cela.

Mais dans ce temps-là je le connaissais beaucoup. Ce pacifiste s'avançait avec une prudence extraordinaire dans le sentier.

Le hervéisme a ainsi dénaturé en retour, déformé en arrière, disqualifié en remontant le dreyfusisme par une rétroactivité, une rétroaction, une rétroversibilité, une rétrospectivité, une rétroversion, une rétrospection, une responsabilité remontante. Une rétroresponsabilité.

On peut se démentir en arrière. C'est même ce que l'on fait le plus souvent. Dans la décomposition du dreyfusisme cette rétroaction, cette rétroversion fut au moins triple, elle fut peut-être quadruple. Par son endossement, par son invention, par son imposition du combisme Jaurès créa *en arrière* cette illusion que le dreyfusisme était anticatholique, antichrétien. Par son endossement de l'hervéisme il créa *en arrière* cette illusion que le dreyfusisme était *anti*nationaliste, antipatriote, antifrançais. Par son endossement (dans le combisme) de la démagogie primaire et laïque il créa *en arrière* cette illusion que le dreyfusisme était barbare, était contre la culture. Par son endossement (dans le socialisme) du syndicalisme démagogique, je veux dire de ce qu'il y a de démagogique dans le syndicalisme, dans l'invention et dans l'enseignement du sabotage, il créa *en arrière* cette illusion que le dreyfusisme était un élément important, peut-être capital, du désordre, de la désorganisation industrielle, de la désorganisation nationale.

Nous fûmes des héros. Il faut le dire très simplement, car je crois bien qu'on ne le dira pas pour nous. Voici très exactement en quoi et pourquoi nous fûmes des héros. Dans tout le monde où nous circulions, dans tout le monde où nous achevions alors les années de notre apprentissage, dans tout le milieu où nous circulions, où nous opérions, où nous croissions encore et où nous achevions de nous former, la question qui se posait, pendant ces deux ou trois années de cette courbe montante, n'était nullement de savoir si *en réalité* Dreyfus était innocent (ou coupable). C'était de savoir si on aurait le courage de le reconnaître, de le déclarer innocent. De le manifester innocent. C'était de savoir si on aurait le double courage. Premièrement le premier courage, le courage extérieur, le grossier courage, déjà difficile, le courage social, public de le manifester innocent dans le monde, aux yeux du public, de l'avouer au public, (de le glorifier), de l'avouer publiquement, de le déclarer publiquement, de témoigner pour lui publiquement. De risquer là-dessus, de *mettre* sur lui tout ce que l'on avait, tout un argent misérablement gagné, tout un argent de pauvre et de misérable, tout un argent de petites gens, de misère et de pauvreté ; tout le temps, toute la vie, toute la carrière ; toute la santé, tout le corps et toute l'âme ; la ruine du corps, toutes les ruines, la rupture du cœur, la dislocation des familles, le reniement des proches, le détournement (des regards) des yeux, la réprobation muette ou forcenée. muette et forcenée, l'isolement, toutes les quarantaines ; la rupture d'amitiés de vingt ans, c'est-à-dire, pour nous, d'amitiés commencées depuis toujours. Toute la vie sociale. Toute la vie du cœur, enfin tout. Deuxièmement le deuxième courage, plus difficile, le courage intérieur, le courage secret, s'avouer à soi-même en soi-même qu'il était innocent. Renoncer pour cet homme à la paix du cœur.

Non plus seulement à la paix de la cité, à la paix du foyer. A la paix de la famille, à la paix du ménage. Mais à la paix du cœur.

Au premier des biens, au seul bien.

Le courage d'entrer pour cet homme dans le royaume d'une incurable inquiétude.

Et d'une amertume qui ne se guérira jamais.

Nos adversaires ne sauront jamais, nos ennemis ne pouvaient pas savoir ce que nous avons sacrifié à cet homme, et de quel cœur nous l'avons sacrifié. Nous lui avons sacrifié notre vie entière, puisque cette affaire nous a marqués pour la vie. Nos ennemis ne sauront jamais, nous qui avons bouleversé, retourné ce pays nos ennemis ne sauront jamais combien peu nous étions, et dans quelles conditions nous nous battions, dans quelles conditions ingrates, précaires, dans quelles conditions de misère et de précarité. Combien par conséquent pour vaincre, puisque enfin nous vainquîmes, il nous fallut déployer, manifester, retrouver en nous, dans notre race, les plus anciennes, les plus précieuses qualités de la race. La technique même de l'héroïsme, et nommément de l'héroïsme militaire. Il ne faut pas se prendre aux mots. La *discipline* des *anarchistes,* par exemple, fut notamment admirable. Il n'échappe point à tout homme avisé que c'était en nous qu'étaient les vertus militaires. En nous et non point, nullement dans l'État-Major de l'armée. Nous étions, une fois de plus nous fûmes cette poignée de Français qui sous un feu écrasant enfoncent des masses, conduisent un assaut, enlèvent une position.

Comment nos ennemis, comment nos adversaires le sauraient-ils, quand nos amis (je veux dire ceux de notre parti, de notre bord, les politiques, les historiens de notre bord) quand nos amis mêmes ne s'en aperçoivent même pas. Sur ce point particulier des anarchistes, par exemple, ne leur demandez point à eux-mêmes des renseignements sur eux-mêmes. Ils vous jureraient leurs grands dieux, si je puis dire, qu'ils n'ont jamais été aussi indisciplinés. Les gens sont tous et si profondément intellectualistes qu'ils aiment mieux trahir, se trahir eux-mêmes, trahir, abandonner, renier leur histoire et leur propre réalité, renier leur propre grandeur et tout ce qui fait leur prix, tout plutôt que de renoncer à leurs formules, à leurs tics, à leurs manies intellectuelles, à l'idée intellectuelle qu'ils veulent avoir d'eux et qu'ils veulent que l'on ait d'eux.

Les théoriciens de l'*Action française* veulent que l'affaire Dreyfus ait été dans son principe même, dans son origine non seulement une affaire pernicieuse, une affaire véreuse, mais une affaire intellectuelle, une invention, une construction intellectuelle; un complot intellectuel. Je me permettrai de dire à mon tour, et en retour, que cette idée même me paraît être le résultat d'une construction intellectuelle. Si l'on engageait la conversation, je dis une conversation un peu suivie avec les hommes de ce parti, on (dé)montrerait peut-être aisément, on en viendrait, je crois, rapidement à poser qu'ils sont et surtout qu'ils se croient les grands ennemis du parti intellectuel et du monde moderne, mais qu'en réalité ils sont eux-mêmes une certaine sorte de parti intellectuel et de parti moderne. Très notamment un parti de logiciens, un parti logique.

C'est ce qu'il y aurait à dire sur eux de plus probant. Sinon de plus profond. Aussi on ne le dit pas. Cela se voit notamment à la forme de leur bataille même, notamment à l'idée qu'ils ont, qu'ils se font du parti intellectuel, de leurs adversaires intellectuels du parti intellectuel. Ils s'en font une idée, une représentation toute intellectuelle. Elle-même. Ils soutiennent contre eux, on serait tenté de dire avec eux un combat, une bataille intellectuelle, sur un plan, sur le plan intellectuel, en langage intellectuel, avec des armes intellectuelles. Ainsi généralement ils se font de leurs adversaires une idée intellectuelle, parce qu'étant eux-mêmes intellectuels ils se font une idée intellectuelle de tout, et deuxièmement, par un recoupement, par un secret accord du mécanisme des mentalités, ils se font des intellectuels, du parti intellectuel, une idée comme doublement intellectuelle; intellectuelle dans son corps et dans son mode; dans sa matière et dans sa forme; dans son auteur et dans son objet; dans son point d'origine et dans son point d'application; dans tout son trajet.

Sur cette question historique particulière de l'origine de l'affaire Dreyfus quand je lis dans l'*Action française* les souvenirs notamment de M. Maurice Pujo je vois qu'il croit (et naturellement qu'il croit se rappeler, mais je crois, moi, que c'est une opération purement intellectuelle, un phénomène très connu, en ce siècle de domination intellectuelle, une sorte de report de l'intellectuel sur la mémoire même, une introduction de l'intellectuel dans la mémoire, d'obumbration [1], une ombre portée, sur la mémoire, de l'idéation intellectuelle) il croit se rappeler que l'affaire Dreyfus a été préparée de toutes pièces, qu'elle a été comme montée dès l'origine, dès le principe, par le parti intellectuel.

Il obéit ainsi, il obéit ici à la plus grande illusion intellectuelle peut-être, je veux dire et à celle qui est la plus grande en nombre, en quotité, la plus nombreuse, à celle qui s'exerce le plus fréquemment, et à celle qui est la plus grande en quantité, dont l'effet est le plus grand, et plus grave ; non pas seulement à cette illusion intellectuelle pour ainsi dire générale, de substituer partout, dans tout l'événement historique, la formation organique ; mais très particulièrement à cette illusion d'optique historique intellectuelle qui consiste à reporter incessamment le présent sur le passé, l'ultérieur incessamment sur l'antérieur, tout l'ultérieur incessamment sur tout l'antérieur ; illusion pour ainsi dire technique ; et organique elle-même, je veux dire organique de l'intellectuel ; illusion de perspective, ou plutôt substitution totale, essai de substitution totale de la perspective à l'épaisseur, à la profondeur, essai de substitution totale du regard de perspective à la connaissance réelle, au regard en profondeur, au regard de profondeur ; essai de substitution totale du regard de perspective, à deux dimensions, à la connaissance réelle à trois dimensions d'un réel, d'une réalité à trois dimensions ; illusion d'optique, illusion de regard, illusion de recherche et de connaissance que j'essaie d'approfondir lui-même, entre toutes les illusions, (car elle est capitale, et d'une importance capitale), dans la thèse *de la situation faite à*

l'histoire dans la philosophie générale du monde moderne [1] ;
illusion qui consiste à substituer constamment au
mouvement organique réel de l'événement de l'histoire, qui se meut perpétuellement du passé vers le
futur en passant, en tombant perpétuellement par
cette frange du présent, une sorte d'ombre dure
angulaire portée à chaque instant du présent sur le
passé, l'ombre du coin du mur et du coin de la
maison, du pignon que nous croyons avoir sur la rue.

Quand on effectue ce report il semble en effet que le
parti intellectuel a monté toute l'affaire Dreyfus. Mais
quand on ne l'effectue pas on se rappelle qu'il n'a rien
monté du tout. D'abord généralement en histoire on
ne monte rien du tout. Ou enfin on ne monte pas tant
que ça. Ce qu'il y a de plus imprévu, c'est toujours
l'événement. Il suffit d'avoir un peu vécu soi-même
hors des livres des historiens pour savoir, pour avoir
éprouvé que tout ce qu'on monte est généralement ce
qui arrive le moins, et que ce qu'on ne monte pas est
généralement ce qui arrive. Sans doute il y a des
préparations, mais il faut qu'elles soient générales, il
n'y a guère de montages particuliers, de montages de
détail. Et quand il y a des montages de détail, il faut
qu'ils soient bien immédiats, presque instantanés,
qu'ils précèdent de bien peu l'effet. Autrement la
déconvenue s'intercale. Napoléon sans doute a bien
monté Austerlitz. Mais il ne le montait pas le jour du
18 Brumaire. Et pourtant il était un autre prépara-
teur, un autre monteur que le parti intellectuel. C'est
la plus fréquente, la plus générale erreur intellectuelle,
et elle (pro)vient précisément de ce report du présent

sur le passé, que de croire que tout a été monté et que c'est ce qui a été monté qui a réussi. Si le parti intellectuel avait été si malin, (si fort), que de faire une aussi grande affaire que l'affaire Dreyfus, que de la monter, mais alors il aurait précisément les vertus que nous lui nions, et il n'y aurait plus, messieurs, qu'à lui rendre les armes. Rassurez-vous, il ne les a point. Il est venu pour profiter, comme tous les profiteurs viennent ensuite. Il est venu en parasite, en suiveur. Il n'était point venu pour combattre, il n'était point venu pour fonder. C'est précisément la commune erreur historique, la commune erreur intellectuelle en matière d'histoire, que de reporter, en toute affaire historique, sur les vertus des fondateurs l'ombre portée des abusements des profiteurs.

Les fondateurs viennent d'abord. Les profiteurs viennent ensuite.

On peut préparer toute une carrière, toute une vie, on ne peut pas la monter. On peut préparer une guerre, une révolution, (et encore), (il faut être beaucoup, et encore), on ne peut pas la monter. A l'autre extrémité de la ligne, de la série, comme toujours, dans le détail on peut monter une journée, une bataille, une émeute, bataille de rues, et encore. Mais au milieu de la ligne, de la série, comme toujours, on ne peut pas monter à distance dans le détail une affaire. On peut monter une journée, un coup d'État, une émeute, un coup de force. D'une préparation, d'un montage immédiat. On ne peut pas monter à quelque distance, au milieu, de loin, d'ensemble une aussi grosse affaire. Ou si on la montait elle n'*arriverait* pas.

C'est à peine déjà si on peut monter une affaire, au sens industriel et commercial de ce mot.

C'est précisément ce qui est en cause. Si le parti intellectuel était assez malin, assez fort, assez pénétrant dans la réalité pour avoir monté, pour avoir su, pour avoir pu monter une aussi grosse affaire, s'il avait été de taille et d'une profondeur à soulever ainsi un gros mouvement de la réalité, un aussi gros mouvement, s'il avait été capable de malaxer ainsi, de triturer, de manier, d'élaborer, de pétrir un aussi gros morceau de la réalité, justement alors, alors précisément ils ne seraient pas ce que nous nommons le parti intellectuel, ils n'auraient point ces défauts, ces vices que nous nommons précisément du parti intellectuel, cette stérilité, cette incapacité, cette débilité; cette sécheresse, cet artificiel, ce superficiel; cet intellectuel. Ils seraient au contraire des gens qui auraient travaillé, connu, malaxé, pétri de la réalité. Ils seraient des gens qui auraient trempé dans la réalité même. Et pour avoir trituré un aussi gros morceau de la réalité ils seraient de singulièrement gros hommes, d'action, d'un rude calibre, d'un rude gabarit, d'un rude volume, de(s) grands réalistes, des maîtres. Enfin tout ce que précisément nous leur nions. Ils seraient des Richelieu et des Napoléon. Ils seraient peut-être, sans doute des tyrans encore. Mais ils seraient des grands tyrans, des tyrans considérables, des maîtres, des réalistes. Tout ce que précisément nous leur nions. Ils

seraient des tyrans comme Richelieu et Napoléon. Ils
baigneraient, ils tremperaient, ils commanderaient
dans la réalité.

On nous abuse beaucoup, les historiens, sur la
valeur des préparations historiques. En 1870 même,
au mois d'août, si une armée française, comme elle
était, avait été remise aux mains d'un Napoléon
Bonaparte, tous les tiroirs et toutes les préparations,
toutes les fiches et tous les registres d'un de Moltke
seraient aujourd'hui la risée des historiens mêmes.

Ils commettent une erreur du même ordre, plus
qu'une erreur analogue, une erreur inverse et parallèle quand ils nous nomment *le parti de l'étranger*. Ils
reportent sur nous les abusements de Hervé. Ou
plutôt ils commettent une erreur parallèle et non point
de sens contraire, mais de même sens, car en un sens
Hervé est lui aussi un profiteur. Il est un parasite. Il
est même un parasite de nous. Sur ce point particulier
c'est encore nous qui avons été des fondateurs, les
fondateurs, et c'est Hervé qui en un sens a été un
profiteur. Il n'eût point atteint en quelques jours, en
quarante-huit heures, cette sorte non pas seulement
de réputation, de célébrité, mais de gloire propre qu'il
a s'il ne s'était pas fondé sur nos propres, sur nos
lentes fondations, s'il n'avait pas profité, abusé de nos
grandes préparations. Nos adversaires feraient bien,
ils auraient le droit, et même le devoir, ils auraient
raison de nommer Hervé *le parti de l'étranger*. Ils ne le
font généralement point, pour des raisons fort honora-

bles, comme de respecter un prisonnier, et aussi pour
un fort honorable compagnonnage de prison, pour
avoir été en prison ensemble, pour d'autres aussi qui
le sont peut-être moins, comme par une sorte de
sympathie de trouble, une secrète amitié de désordre,
une secrète complaisance de démagogie. Une
complaisance à l'opposition, quelle qu'elle soit, quand
même elle est au fond encore plus une opposition à
eux-mêmes; une complaisance à tout ce qui trouble
un régime détesté. A tout ce qui embête un gouvernement haï. Alors ils se rattrapent, de cette indulgence
et de ce compagnonnage et de cette sympathie et de
cette complaisance en nous nommant, nous, *le parti de
l'étranger*. C'est une sorte de virement. C'est aussi le
même report. On reporte sur nous fondateurs la
trahison de Hervé profiteur. On reporte sur nous
antécédents la trahison de Hervé suivant, de Hervé
successeur. C'est un transfert. On reporte sur nous
fondateurs la trahison de Hervé parasite. L'attention
que l'on préfère ne point accorder à Hervé, on nous
l'accorde à nous généreusement. Seulement, passant
de Hervé à nous son contraire elle change de signe.
Puisqu'elle passe au contraire gardant le même signe.
Alors que, passant au contraire, elle devrait prendre le
signe contraire. Il faut donc que par une opération
intérieure, purement arbitraire, elle change de signe.
On la fasse arbitrairement changer de signe. Le grief
que l'on devrait faire à Hervé, c'est précisément celui-
là que l'on nous fait à nous son contraire.

Ils commettent une erreur non pas seulement du
même ordre, mais de la même tribu, de la même *gens,*

une erreur voisine, alliée, une erreur apparentée, une erreur de la même famille quand ils attribuent, quand ils nous représentent l'affaire Dreyfus comme montée par le parti juif. Il ne faudrait pas beaucoup me pousser pour me faire déclarer ce que je pense, que l'affaire Dreyfus, dans la mesure où elle fut montée, fut montée *contre* le parti juif. De toutes les résistances que Bernard-Lazare eut à refouler, pour commencer, dans le principe, les premières furent naturellement les résistances juives, puisque c'étaient celles de son propre milieu. Mais elles ne furent pas seulement les premières, elles furent aussi les plus énergiques peut-être. Les plus profondes, je crois. Sans doute les plus agissantes. Et ensuite ceux qui lui pardonnèrent le moins ce furent encore les Juifs. J'entends les politiciens juifs, le parti (politique) juif. De même que du côté intellectuel, dans le camp, dans le clan intellectuel, même dans le clan universitaire cette affaire Dreyfus fut commencée, fut engagée par quelques forcenés contre la résistance, contre la réprobation du parti, contre les résistances sourdes ou avouées, contre le silence et la peur et l'activité politique du parti. Le parti (politique) intellectuel ne s'y engagea lui-même que quand il crut que l'heure des dépouilles était venue.

Il est certain qu'il y a eu une trahison au moins dans l'affaire Dreyfus, et c'est la trahison du dreyfusisme même. Mais c'est commettre une erreur totale que de s'imaginer que cette trahison a été montée, délibérément commise, délibérément exercée par des Juifs sur des chrétiens. Dans l'État-Major de cette trahison il y avait Jaurès, qui n'est pas juif, il y eut, il vint Hervé, qui n'est pas juif. Jaurès est toulousain, Hervé est breton. Dans *le parti de l'étranger* je vois Hervé; si Hervé avait du courage (non point du courage moral si je puis dire et sentimental, je suis assuré qu'il en a, mais du courage mental et intellectuel même, de la conséquence), il dirait : Voyez, je suis *en fait le parti de l'étranger*; dans le parti de l'étranger je vois Hervé; par endossement de Hervé nous avons vu Jaurès. Par endossement de Jaurès nous en atteindrions, j'en ai bien peur, quelque autre. Mais enfin je ne vois dans ce parti, dans cet État-Major aucun Juif qui ait la taille, le volume social de Jaurès.

Ce que nos adversaires par contre ne peuvent pas savoir, ce que sincèrement ils ne peuvent pas imaginer, ce qu'ils ne peuvent pas compter, ce qu'ils ne connaissent pas, ce qu'ils ne peuvent pas se représenter, ce qu'ils ne soupçonnent pas, ce qu'ils ne peuvent pas même supposer, c'est combien de Juifs ont été irrévocablement enveloppés dans le désastre de l'affaire Dreyfus, combien de Juifs ont été les victimes, les réelles victimes, et sont demeurés les victimes de l'affaire Dreyfus, de cette trahison, de cette livraison de l'affaire Dreyfus. Combien de carrières, combien de vies juives ont été irréparablement ruinées, brisées, cela, nous le savons, combien de misères juives, nous le savons, nous qui étions de ce côté-ci de la bataille et pour le savoir il fallait être de ce côté-ci de la bataille [1], combien en sont restés marqués de misère pour leur vie entière; sans recompter celui qui est mort, sans compter ceux qui sont morts, comme des nôtres. Car enfin c'est une prétention qui fait sourire, que cette prétention des antisémites, que tous les Juifs sont riches. Je ne sais pas où ils le prennent, comment ils font leur compte. Ou plutôt je le sais trop, quand ils sont sincères. Mettons que je le sais bien. L'explication est bien simple. C'est que dans le monde moderne, comme je l'ai indiqué si souvent dans ces cahiers mêmes, nul pouvoir n'existe, n'est, ne compte auprès du pouvoir de l'argent, nulle distinction n'existe, n'est, ne compte auprès de l'abîme qu'il y a entre les riches et les pauvres, et ces deux classes, malgré les apparences, et malgré tout le jargon politique et les grands mots de solidarité, s'ignorent comme à beaucoup près elles ne se sont jamais ignorées. Infiniment autrement, infiniment plus elles s'ignorent et se méconnaissent. Sous les apparences du jargon politique parlementaire il y a un abîme entre elles, un abîme d'ignorance et de méconnaissance, de l'une à l'autre, un abîme de non communication. Le dernier des serfs était de la même chrétienté que le roi. Aujourd'hui il n'y a plus aucune cité. Le monde riche et le monde pauvre vivent ou enfin font semblant comme deux masses, comme deux couches horizontales séparées par un vide, par un abîme d'incommunication. Les antisémites bourgeois ne connaissent donc que les Juifs bourgeois, les antisémites mondains ne connaissent et haïssent que les Juifs mondains, les antisémites qui font des affaires ne connaissent et ne haïssent que les Juifs qui font des affaires. Nous qui sommes pauvres, comme par hasard nous connaissons un très grand nombre de Juifs pauvres, et même misérables. Dans cette région des Juifs pauvres l'affaire Dreyfus, la trahison politique et politicienne, la trahison parlementaire, la banqueroute frauduleuse de l'affaire Dreyfus et du dreyfusisme a causé des ravages effroyables et qui ne seront jamais réparés. Ravages d'argent, de travail, de situations, de carrière, — de santé, — mais aussi ravages de cœur, désabusement qui est venu se joindre à l'éternel désabusement de la race.

Ils sont comme nous, ils sont parmi nous, ils sont nos amis, ils ont été éprouvés, ils ont souffert, ils ont été maltraités autant que nous, plus que nous. Car ils s'en relèvent plus malaisément encore.

Comme nous ils sont des demi-soldes, ils sont et ils seront toute leur vie dans cette situation ingrate de demi-soldes qui n'auraient point fait de grandes campagnes historiques.

Ce qu'il faut dire, c'est qu'un État-Major de juifs et de chrétiens a trahi des troupes excellentes de juifs et de chrétiens. Et ce qu'il faut dire aussi, c'est que c'est toujours comme ça.

Voici exactement ce que je veux dire de Bernard-Lazare. Dans *le Temps* du vendredi 27 mai 1910 je lis ce simple filet, dans les petits caractères de la dernière heure : *Dernière heure. — L'expulsion des Juifs de Kief. — Saint-Pétersbourg, 26 mai. — Les autorités de Kief ont procédé à l'expulsion de 1 300 familles israélites condamnées par une récente circulaire du ministère de l'intérieur, à quitter la ville. — La misère des expulsés est très grande.* (Havas) — Ce qu'il y a de poignant dans cette dépêche, ce n'en est point seulement la sécheresse et la brièveté. C'est à quel point de telles dépêches passent aujourd'hui inaperçues. Ce que je veux dire, c'est que sous Bernard-Lazare elles ne passaient point inaperçues.

Le même *Temps*, — du mercredi 15 juin 1910 : *Les travaux de la Douma. — On a déposé sur le bureau de l'Assemblée un projet de loi tendant à abolir la séquestration des Juifs dans des quartiers spéciaux. Ce projet a l'appui de 166 députés de l'opposition et de quelques octobristes.*

Dans *le Matin* du dimanche 12 juin 1910, car il y en a presque tous les jours : *Les droits électoraux de la Pologne russe. — Saint-Pétersbourg, 11 juin. —* Dépêche particulière du « Matin ». — *La Douma a voté aujourd'hui une loi créant des zemstvos électifs dans six provinces du sud-ouest et assurant aux paysans un minimum du tiers des conseillers et aux propriétaires polonais un maximum qui est également fixé à un tiers. Les Polonais sont éligibles comme membres des comités exécutifs et reconnus qualifiés pour servir comme employés des zemstvos.* **Les juifs, par contre** (c'est moi qui souligne), *les Juifs par contre sont entièrement exclus,* **sauf comme employés.**

Le projet présenté par le gouvernement privait les Polonais de la majeure partie de ces droits ; mais l'opposition, soutenue par les octobristes, a imposé ces amendements.

Dans *le Matin* du lundi 13 juin 1910 : *Six mille israélites sont expulsés de Kieff. — Saint-Pétersbourg, 12 juin. — D'après la* Rietch, *près de six mille israélites ont été expulsés de Kieff. La plupart sont de pauvres gens.*

*Beaucoup d'entre eux, sans foyer et dans la plus grande misère,
errent aux environs de la ville.*

*Un fait à peine croyable est que leur expulsion a eu lieu en
vertu de la circulaire de 1906 de M. Stolypine, circulaire qui
accordait à tous les israélites alors à Kieff sans droit légal de
résidence la permission d'y rester. Tous les israélites pouvant
prouver qu'en 1906 ils résidaient légalement à Kieff sont
laissés tranquilles ; mais ceux au contraire qui s'y trouvaient
alors illégalement tombent sous le coup d'arrêtés d'expulsion.
Chaque jour, de nouveaux groupes de victimes sont chassés de la
ville.* (Times.)

Et *dans le même* numéro du *Matin,* pour que ce soit
complet, cette extraordinaire nouvelle, cette extraordinaire annonce de Salonique : les bateliers *juifs*
exerçant un boycottage *turc* des marchandises *grecques.*
C'est assez bien. *Le boycottage antigrec à Salonique. —
Constantinople, 12 juin. — Les bateliers de Salonique,* **qui
pour la plupart sont des israélites,** (c'est encore
moi qui souligne), *ont décrété le boycottage des steamers
grecs.*

*Ici, cependant, l'agitation antigrecque semble devenir moins
violente et on espère que le gouvernement prendra les mesures
nécessaires pour empêcher toute nouvelle propagation du
mouvement.* (Times.) Singulier peuple, qui a toutes ses
querelles, propres, et qui épouse les querelles des
autres, qui a toutes ses infortunes propres et qui
épouse les fortunes et les infortunes des autres.

Par un mouvement parallèle, comparable, analogue, assimilable à plusieurs mouvements que nous

avons déjà trouvés, dans cette matière même, sur ce point même les antisémites sont beaucoup trop modernes. Ils sont beaucoup plus modernes que nous. Ils sont beaucoup plus modernes qu'ils ne le veulent. Ils sont beaucoup plus modernes qu'ils ne le croient. Ils sont beaucoup plus enfoncés dans le monde moderne qu'ils ne le veulent et qu'ils ne le croient et que nous ne le sommes, ils en sont beaucoup plus teintés. C'est faire beaucoup d'honneur au monde moderne, c'est aussi pour ainsi dire en un certain sens le méconnaître, méconnaître justement son modernisme, sa modernité, ce qu'il est, c'est en méconnaître le virus que de dire : Le monde moderne est une invention, une forgerie, une fabrication, le monde moderne est inventé, a été inventé, monté, de toutes pièces, par les Juifs sur nous et contre nous. C'est un régime qu'ils ont fait de leurs mains, qu'ils nous imposent, où ils nous dominent, où ils nous gouvernent, où ils nous tyrannisent ; où ils sont parfaitement heureux, où nous sommes, où ils nous rendent parfaitement malheureux.

C'est bien mal connaître le monde moderne, que de parler ainsi. C'est lui faire beaucoup d'honneur. C'est le connaître, c'est le voir bien superficiellement. C'est en méconnaître bien gravement, (bien légèrement), le virus, toute la novicité. C'est bien en méconnaître toute la misère et la détresse. Premièrement le monde moderne est beaucoup moins monté. Il est beaucoup plus une maladie naturelle. Deuxièmement cette maladie naturelle est beaucoup plus grave, beaucoup plus profonde, beaucoup plus *universelle*.

Nul n'en profite et tout le monde en souffre. Tout le monde en est atteint. Les modernes mêmes en souffrent. Ceux qui s'en vantent, qui s'en glorifient, qui s'en réjouissent, en souffrent. Ceux qui l'aiment le mieux, aiment leur mal. Ceux mêmes que l'on croit qui n'en souffrent pas en souffrent. Ceux qui font les heureux sont aussi malheureux, plus malheureux que les autres, plus malheureux que nous. *Dans le monde moderne tout le monde souffre du mal moderne.* Ceux qui font ceux que ça leur profite sont aussi malheureux, plus malheureux que nous. *Tout le monde est malheureux dans le monde moderne.*

Les Juifs sont plus malheureux que les autres. Loin que le monde moderne les favorise particulièrement, leur soit particulièrement avantageux, leur ait fait un siège de repos, une résidence de quiétude et de privilège, au contraire le monde moderne a ajouté sa *dispersion* propre moderne, sa dispersion intérieure, à leur dispersion séculaire, à leur dispersion ethnique, à leur antique dispersion. Le monde moderne a ajouté son trouble à leur trouble ; dans le monde moderne ils cumulent ; le monde moderne a ajouté sa misère à leur misère, sa détresse à leur antique détresse ; il a ajouté sa mortelle inquiétude, son inquiétude incurable à la mortelle, à l'inquiétude incurable de la race, à l'inquiétude propre, à l'antique, à l'éternelle inquiétude.

Il a ajouté l'inquiétude universelle à l'inquiétude propre.

Ainsi ils cumulent. Ils sont à l'intersection. Ils se
recoupent sur eux-mêmes. Ils recoupent l'inquiétude
juive, qui est leur, par l'inquiétude moderne, qui est
nôtre et leur. Ils subissent, ils reçoivent ensemble, à
cette intersection, l'inquiétude verticale et l'inquiétude horizontale ; l'inquiétude descendante verticale
et l'inquiétude étale horizontale ; l'inquiétude verticale de la race, l'inquiétude horizontale de l'âge, du
temps.

Dans cette âpre, dans cette mortelle concurrence du
monde moderne, dans cette compromission, dans
cette compétition perpétuelle ils sont plus chargés que
nous. Ils cumulent. Ils sont doublement chargés. Ils
cumulent deux charges. La charge juive et la charge
moderne. La charge de l'inquiétude juive et la charge
de l'inquiétude moderne. Le mutuel appui qu'ils se
prêtent (et que l'on a beaucoup exagéré, car il y a
aussi, naturellement, des inquiétudes intérieures, des
haines, des rivalités, des compétitions, des ressenti-
ments intérieurs ; et pour prendre tout de suite un
exemple éclatant, l'exemple culminant la personne et
la si grande philosophie de M. Bergson, qui demeu-
rera dans l'histoire, qui sera comptée parmi les cinq
ou six grandes philosophies, de tout le monde, ne sont
point détestées, haïes, combattues par personne, dans
le parti intellectuel, autant que par certains, par
quelques professeurs juifs notamment de philosophie), le mutuel appui qu'ils se prêtent est amplement
compensé, plus que compensé par cette effrayante,
par cette croissante poussée de l'antisémitisme qu'ils

reçoivent tous ensemble. Qu'ils ont constamment à repousser, à réfuter, à rétorquer tous ensemble. Combien n'ai-je point connu de carrières de Juifs, de pauvres gens, fonctionnaires, professeurs, qui ont été brisées, qui sont encore brisées, pour toujours, par le double mécanisme suivant : pendant toute la poussée de l'antisémitisme victorieux et gouvernemental on a brisé leur carrière parce qu'ils étaient juifs ; (et les chrétiens parce qu'ils étaient dreyfusistes). Et aussitôt après pendant toute la poussée du dreyfusisme victorieux mais gouvernemental on a brisé leurs carrières parce qu'on était combiste et qu'avec nous ils étaient demeurés dreyfusistes purs. C'est ainsi, par ce double mécanisme, qu'ils partagent avec nous, *fraternellement,* une misère double, une double infortune inexpiable.

Dans cette course du monde moderne ils sont comme nous, plus que nous ils sont lourdement, doublement chargés.

Les antisémites parlent des Juifs. Je préviens que je vais dire une énormité : **Les antisémites ne connaissent point les Juifs.** Ils en parlent, mais ils ne les connaissent point. Ils en souffrent, évidemment beaucoup, *mais ils ne les connaissent point*[1]. Les antisémites riches connaissent peut-être les Juifs riches. Les antisémites capitalistes connaissent peut-être les Juifs capitalistes. Les antisémites d'affaires connaissent peut-être les Juifs d'affaires. Pour la même raison je ne connais guère que des Juifs pauvres et des Juifs misérables. Il y en a. Il y en a tant que l'on n'en sait pas le nombre. J'en vois partout.

Il ne sera pas dit qu'un chrétien n'aura pas porté

témoignage pour eux. Il ne sera pas dit que je n'aurai pas témoigné pour eux. Comme il ne sera pas dit qu'un chrétien ne témoignera pas pour Bernard-Lazare.

Depuis vingt ans je les ai éprouvés, nous nous sommes éprouvés mutuellement. Je les ai trouvés toujours solides au poste, autant que personne, affectueux, solides, d'une tendresse propre, autant que personne, d'un attachement, d'un dévouement, d'une piété inébranlable, d'une fidélité, à toute épreuve, d'une amitié réellement mystique, d'un attachement, d'une fidélité inébranlable à la mystique de l'amitié.

L'argent est tout, domine tout dans le monde moderne à un tel point, si entièrement, si totalement que la séparation sociale horizontale des riches et des pauvres est devenue infiniment plus grave, plus coupante, plus absolue si je puis dire que la séparation, verticale de race des juifs et des chrétiens. La dureté du monde moderne sur les pauvres, contre les pauvres, est devenue si totale, si effrayante, si impie ensemble sur les uns et sur les autres, contre les uns et contre les autres.

Dans le monde moderne les connaissances ne se font, ne se propagent que horizontalement, parmi les riches entre eux, ou parmi les pauvres entre eux. Par couches horizontales.

Pauvre je porterai témoignage pour les Juifs pauvres. Dans la commune pauvreté, dans la misère commune pendant vingt ans je les ai trouvés d'une sûreté, d'une fidélité, d'un dévouement, d'une solidité, d'un attachement, d'une mystique, d'une piété dans l'amitié inébranlable. Ils y ont d'autant plus de mérite, ils y ont d'autant plus de vertu qu'en même temps, en plus de nous, ils ont sans cesse à lutter contre les accusations, contre les inculpations, contre les calomnies de l'antisémitisme, qui sont précisément toutes les accusations du contraire.

Que voyons-nous ? Car enfin il ne faut parler que de ce que nous voyons, il ne faut dire que ce que nous voyons ; que voyons-nous ? Dans cette galère du monde moderne je les vois qui rament à leur banc, autant et plus que d'autres, autant et plus que nous. Autant et plus que nous subissant le sort commun. Dans cet enfer temporel du monde moderne je les vois comme nous, autant et plus que nous, trimant comme nous, éprouvés comme nous. Épuisés comme nous. Surmenés comme nous. Dans les maladies, dans les fatigues, dans la neurasthénie, dans tous les surmenages, dans cet enfer temporel j'en connais des centaines, j'en vois des milliers qui aussi difficilement, plus difficilement, plus misérablement que nous gagnent péniblement leur misérable vie.

Dans cet enfer commun.

Des riches il y aurait beaucoup à dire. Je les connais beaucoup moins. Ce que je puis dire, c'est que depuis

vingt ans j'ai passé par beaucoup de mains. Le seul de
mes créanciers qui se soit conduit avec moi non pas
seulement comme un usurier, mais ce qui est un peu
plus, comme un créancier, comme un usurier de
Balzac, le seul de mes créanciers qui m'ait traité avec
une dureté balzacienne, avec la dureté, la cruauté
d'un usurier de Balzac n'était point un Juif. C'était un
Français, j'ai honte à le dire, on a honte à le dire,
c'était hélas un « chrétien », trente fois millionnaire.
Que n'aurait-on pas dit s'il avait été juif[1].

Jusqu'à quel point leurs riches les aident-ils ? Je
soupçonne qu'ils les aident un peu plus que les nôtres
ne nous aident. Mais enfin il ne faudrait peut-être pas
le leur reprocher. C'est ce que je disais à un jeune
antisémite, joyeux mais qui m'écoute[2]; sous une
forme que je me permets de trouver saisissante. Je lui
disais : *Mais enfin, pensez-y,* **c'est pas facile d'être
Juif.** *Vous leur faites toujours des reproches contradictoires.*
*Quand leurs riches ne les soutiennent pas, quand leurs riches
sont durs vous dites :* **C'est pas étonnant, ils sont Juifs.**
Quand leurs riches les soutiennent, vous dites : **C'est
pas étonnant, ils sont Juifs. Ils se soutiennent
entre eux.** — *Mais, mon ami, les riches chrétiens n'ont qu'à
en faire autant. Nous n'empêchons pas les chrétiens riches de
nous soutenir entre nous.*

C'est pas facile d'être juif. Avec vous. Et même sans vous.
Quand ils demeurent insensibles aux appels de leurs
frères, aux cris des persécutés, aux plaintes, aux
lamentations de leurs frères meurtris dans tout le
monde vous dites : *C'est des mauvais Juifs.* Et s'ils
ouvrent seulement l'oreille aux lamentations qui mon-

tent du Danube et du Dniepr vous dites : *Ils nous trahissent. C'est des mauvais Français.*

Ainsi vous les poursuivez, vous les accablez sans cesse de reproches contradictoires. Vous dites : *Leur finance est juive, elle n'est pas française.* — Et la finance française, mon ami, est-ce qu'elle est française.

Est-ce qu'il y a une *finance* qui est française.

Vous les accablez sans cesse de reproches contradictoires. Au fond, ce que vous voudriez, c'est qu'ils n'existent pas. Mais cela, c'est une autre question.

Que n'aurait-on pas dit s'il avait été juif? Ils sont victimes d'une illusion d'optique très fréquente, très connue dans les autres ordres, dans l'ordre de l'optique même. De l'optique propre. Comme on pense toujours à eux, à présent, comme on ne pense qu'à eux, comme l'attention est toujours portée sur eux, depuis que la question de l'antisémitisme est soulevée (et sur cette question même de l'antisémitisme il faudrait (en) faire toute une histoire, il faudrait en faire l'histoire, voir comment il vient pour un tiers d'eux, pour un tiers des antisémites, professionnels, *et pour les deux autres tiers*, comme disait un professeur, pour les deux autres tiers de mécanismes), depuis que la question de l'antisémitisme est ainsi posée, comme on ne pense qu'à eux, comme toute l'attention est toujours sur eux, comme ils sont toujours dans le faisceau de lumière, comme ils sont toujours dans le blanc du regard ils sont très exactement victimes de cette illusion d'optique bien connue qui nous fait voir un carré *blanc sur noir* beaucoup plus grand que le même carré *noir sur blanc,* qui paraît tout petit. Tout carré *blanc sur noir* paraît *beaucoup* plus grand que le même carré *noir sur blanc.* Tout ainsi tout acte, toute opération, tout carré *juif sur chrétien* nous paraît, nous le voyons beaucoup plus grand que le même carré *chrétien sur juif.* C'est une pure illusion d'optique historique, d'optique pour ainsi dire géographique et topographique, d'optique politique et sociale qu'il y aura lieu quelque jour d'examiner dans un plus grand détail.

Pour mesurer toute la valeur, toute la grandeur, toute l'amplitude, tout l'angle de cette illusion, pour corriger cet angle d'erreur, pour faire la correction, les corrections nécessaires, pour nous redonner, pour retrouver la ligne, la direction, pour nous redonner, pour retrouver la justice et la justesse, il est un exercice salubre, excellent pour la justice, pour la justesse, pour la bonne santé intellectuelle et morale, excellent pour l'hygiène intellectuelle et mentale, un exercice salutaire, une sorte de gymnastique suédoise de l'esprit, un *Müller*[1] mental. Il consiste à faire la meilleure des preuves, qui est la preuve par le contraire. Est-ce Pesloüan[2], est-ce moi qui l'avons inventé. Les questions d'origine se perdent toujours dans la nuit des temps. C'est plutôt nous deux. Ce que je sais c'est que nous le pratiquons souvent ensemble, dans nos pourparlers d'expérience. Les résultats sont toujours merveilleux. Il consiste à faire le contraire. C'est un exercice d'assouplissement, de rectification merveilleux. Il consiste à retenir certains faits, nombreux, à mesure qu'ils passent, et à dire, à se demander, de l'auteur, ce que nous venons par exemple de nous demander une fois : *Qu'est-ce qu'on dirait s'il était juif ?* Non seulement cet exercice rend toujours, mais on est surpris de voir comme il rend, comme il rectifie. *Combien* il rend. On voit vite alors, on compte aisément que les plus grands scandales et les plus nombreux ne sont point des scandales juifs. Et il s'en faut.

Sans nous livrer délibérément ici à cet exercice, n'est-il pas frappant déjà, au premier abord, que nos grandes hontes, nos hontes nationales, Jaurès, Hervé, Thalamas, ne sont point juives, ne sont point des Juifs. Il est même très remarquable au contraire, une fois que l'on compte ainsi, combien peu de nos hontes sont juives, il est remarquable que parmi les protagonistes de nos hontes nationales il n'y a aucun Juif. *Qu'est-ce que l'on dirait si Jaurès était juif ? Qu'est-ce que l'on dirait,* surtout, *si Hervé était juif ?* C'est-à-dire, précisément, si un Juif avait été lâche le vingtième de ce que Jaurès l'a été, si un Juif avait dit contre la patrie, française, avait prononcé, contre *notre patrie,* le vingtième des monstruosités que *notre compatriote* Hervé a si superbement sorties, *qu'est-ce qu'on aurait dit.* Et pareillement *qu'est-ce que l'on dirait* si Thalamas était juif.

Pour prendre un exemple d'épisode, tout petit, mais d'autant mieux dessiné peut-être, d'autant mieux caractérisé, d'autant mieux (dé)limité, d'autant plus aisé, plus facile à saisir, qu'est-ce qu'on aurait dit dans un débat récent, dans un monde très spécial, si c'eût été M. Bataille qui eût été juif et madame Bernhardt qui ne l'eût pas été[1].

Dans l'affaire Dreyfus même, sans y revenir, ou plutôt sans y entrer, dans l'État-Major même du dreyfusisme et de l'affaire Dreyfus il est fort notable que ce sont les Juifs, les grands Juifs qui ont encore le moins faibli. L'exemple de M. Joseph Reinach[1] est caractéristique. On peut dire que dans l'affaire Dreyfus, dans l'État-Major de l'affaire Dreyfus et du parti dreyfusiste il représentait en un certain sens, et même pour ainsi dire officiellement, ce que l'on a nommé le parti juif. Dans le parti politique dreyfusiste il représentait pour ainsi dire le parti politique juif. Seul en outre il était d'un volume politique et social, d'un ordre de grandeur au moins égal à celui d'un Jaurès Or que voyons-nous. Il faut toujours dire ce que l'on voit. Surtout il faut toujours, ce qui est plus difficile, voir ce que l'on voit. Nous voyons que de tout notre État-Major il est le seul qui n'ait point faibli devant les démagogies dreyfusistes, devant les démagogies politiques issues de notre mystique dreyfusiste. Il est le seul notamment qui n'ait pas faibli, qui n'ait pas plié devant la démagogie combiste, devant la démagogie de la tyrannie combiste. Il est le seul nommément, et ceci est d'autant plus remarquable qu'il est par toute sa carrière un homme politique, il est le seul qui un des premiers se soit résolument opposé à la *délation* aux *Droits de l'Homme*[2], comme on le voit dans le dossier que nous avons constitué en ce temps. Si l'on voulait bien prendre la peine de lire les six ou sept gros volumes de son *Histoire de l'affaire Dreyfus* et si on ne laissait pas au seul M. Sorel[3] tout le soin de les lire, on verrait aussitôt que nul (historien) ne fut aussi sévère que lui pour toutes les démagogies dreyfusistes,

issues du dreyfusisme, pour toutes les déviations
politiques, pour toutes les dégradations du dreyfusisme. On en est même surpris. Il y a là comme une
sorte de stoïcisme politique assez curieux. Et même
quelquefois comme une espèce de gageure. On est
surpris, et c'est bien le plus grand éloge que je
connaisse d'un homme, on est surpris que cet homme
politique, riche et puissant, ait eu plusieurs fois les
vertus politiques d'un pauvre. *De quel non-Juif pourrait-
on en dire autant.*

De Dreyfus même, pour aller au cœur du débat, à
l'objet, à la personne même, de Dreyfus il est évident
que je n'ai rien voulu dire, que je n'ai rien dit ni rien
pu dire qui atteignît l'homme privé. Je me rends bien
compte de tout ce qu'il y a de tragique, de fatal dans
la vie de cet homme. Mais ce qu'il y a de plus
tragique, de plus fatal c'est précisément qu'il n'a pas
le droit d'être un homme privé. C'est que nous avons
incessamment le droit de lui demander des comptes,
le droit, *et le devoir* de lui demander les comptes les plus
sévères. Les plus rigoureux.

Autrement je saurais bien tout ce qu'il y a de
tragique, de fatal dans la vie privée de cet homme. Ce
que je sais de plus touchant de lui est certainement cet
attachement profond, presque paternel, qu'il a inspiré
à notre vieux maître M. Gabriel Monod[1]. M. Monod
me le disait encore aux cahiers il n'y a que quelques
semaines. A peine. Dreyfus venait encore d'avoir un
deuil, très proche, très douloureux, très *fatal,* dans sa
famille. M. Monod nous le rapportait, nous le contait
avec des larmes dans la voix. Il nous disait en même
temps, ou plutôt il ne nous le disait pas, mais il nous
disait beaucoup plus éloquemment que s'il nous l'eût

dit, combien il l'aimait, nous assistions un peu
surpris, un peu imprévus, un peu dépassés, parce
qu'on ne le croit pas, on ne s'y attend pas, à cette
affection profonde, à cette affection sentimentale, à
cette affection *privée*, à cette affection quasi paternelle,
paternelle même qu'il a pour Dreyfus. Nous en étions
presque un peu gênés, comme d'une découverte,
toujours nouvelle, et comme si on nous ouvrait des
horizons nouveaux, comme si on nous avait fait entrer
dans une famille sans bien nous demander notre avis,
un peu inconsidérément, un peu indiscrètement, tant
nous avons pris l'habitude de ne vouloir connaître en
Dreyfus que l'homme public, de ne vouloir le traiter
qu'en homme public, durement comme un homme
public. Laissant de côté, non seulement devant une
réalité, mais devant une aussi saisissante, aussi tragique, aussi poignante réalité laissant de côté tout
l'appareil des méthodes prétendues scientifiques, censément historiques, laissant de côté tout l'appareil des
métaphysiques métahistoriques notre vieux maître,
assis, disait, avec des larmes intérieures : *On dirait qu'il*
y a une fatalité. On dirait que c'est un homme qui est marqué
d'une fatalité. Il ne sort point constamment du malheur. Je
viens de le quitter encore. (Et il nous contait cette dernière
entrevue, ce dernier deuil, cette sorte d'embrasse-
ment, ce deuil familial, privé.) *Je l'ai vu*, nous disait-il,
ce héros, ce grand stoïcien, cette sorte d'âme antique. (C'est
ainsi qu'il parle de Dreyfus, une âme inflexible, un
héros, douloureux, mais antique.) *Je viens de le voir. Cet*
homme héroïque, cette âme stoïque, ce stoïcien que j'ai vu
impassible et ne jamais pleurer dans les plus grandes épreuves.
Je viens de le voir. Il était courbé, il pleurait sur cette mort. Il
me disait : « Je crois qu'il y a une fatalité sur moi. Toutes les

fois que nous nous attachons à quelqu'un, que nous voyons un peu de bonheur, que nous pourrions un peu commencer d'être heureux, ils meurent. » Nous étions saisis, dans cette petite boutique, de cette révélation soudaine. *Quand nous pourrions un peu commencer d'être heureux,* n'était-ce point le mot même, le cri d'Israël, plus qu'un symbole, la destination même d'Israël. Et en outre nous voyions passer, venant d'un historien, passant par-dessus un historien, par-dessus les épaules d'un historien, rompant toutes les méthodes, rompant toutes les métaphysiques positivistes, rompant toutes les disciplines modernes, rompant toutes les histoires et toutes les sociologies nous voyions passer les au-delà de l'histoire. L'arrière-pensée, l'arrière-intention, la mystérieuse arrière-inquiétude, arrière-pensée de tant de peuples, des peuples antiques nous était ramenée, la même, intacte, intégrale, toute neuve, nous était reconduite entière par le plus vieux maître vivant de nos historiens modernes, par le plus respecté, par le plus considéré. Et c'était toujours *l'histoire,* plus que l'histoire, *la destination du peuple d'Israël.* L'émotion des autres était décuplée pour moi par cette sorte d'affection presque filiale, par cette sorte de piété secrète que depuis mes années de normalien j'ai toujours gardée pour notre vieux maître. Affection, piété un peu rude, on l'a vu [1]. Mais d'autant plus secrètement profonde. D'autant plus filiale, d'autant plus comme personnelle, d'autant plus jalousement gardée. Je me sentais dans son affection un peu frère en pensée de Dreyfus, frère en affection, et cela me gênait beaucoup. Nous étions là. Nous étions des hommes. Le même souffle nous courbait, qui courba les peuples antiques. Le même problème nous soulevait, qui souleva les peuples antiques. Ce problème, cet anxieux problème de la fatalité, qui se pose pour tout peuple, pour tout homme non livresque. Et associant dans sa pensée, dans sa parole, sans même s'en apercevoir, tant c'était naturel, tant on voyait que c'était l'habitude, son habitude, associant l'homme et l'œuvre, le héros et l'histoire, l'objet et l'entreprise, partant déjà il nous disait s'en allant : *Quelle affaire. Quel désastre. Quand on pense à tout ce qui pouvait sortir de bien de cette affaire-là pour la France.* Et en effet on ne savait plus si c'était Dreyfus ou l'affaire Dreyfus qui était malheureuse, qui était fatale, qui était mal douée pour le bonheur, incapable de bonheur, marquée de la fatalité. Car c'étaient bien tous les deux ensemble, inséparablement, inséparément, indivisément, indivisiblement, l'un portant l'autre, l'une dans l'autre. Et déjà il partait (il était venu acheter une *Antoinette* [1], dans l'édition des cahiers), et nous nous serrions la main, repartant vers nos travaux différents, vers nos soucis différents, vers nos préoccupations différentes. Et nous nous serrions bien la main comme à un enterrement. Nous étions les parents du défunt. Et même les parents pauvres.

La plus grande fatalité, c'est précisément que cet homme ait été cette affaire, qu'il ait été jeté irrévocablement dans l'action publique, et même la plus publique. Il avait peut-être toutes les vertus privées. Il aurait fait sans doute un si bon homme d'affaires. Qu'est-ce qu'il est allé faire capitaine. Qu'est-ce qu'il est allé faire dans les bureaux de l'État-Major. Là est la fatalité. Qu'est-ce qu'il est allé faire dans une

réputation, dans une célébrité, dans une gloire mon-
diale. Victime malgré lui, héros malgré lui, martyr
malgré lui. Glorieux malgré lui il a trahi sa gloire. Là
est la fatalité. *Invitus invitam adeptus gloriam* [1]. Parce
qu'il était devenu capitaine, parce qu'il était entré
dans les capitaines, parce qu'il était entré dans les
bureaux de l'État-Major cet homme fut contraint de
revêtir une charge, une gloire inattendue, une charge,
une gloire inexpiable. Mystérieuse destination du
peuple d'Israël. Tant d'autres, qui voudraient la
gloire, sont forcés de se tenir tranquilles. Et lui, qui
voudrait bien se tenir tranquille, il est forcé à la
vocation, il est forcé à la charge, il est forcé à la gloire.
Là est sa fatalité même. Voilà un homme qui était
capitaine. Il pensait monter colonel ou peut-être
général. Il est monté Dreyfus. Comment voulez-vous
qu'il s'y reconnaisse. Il fallait pourtant qu'il s'y
reconnût, il devait pourtant s'y reconnaître. On l'a
improvisé pilote, gouverneur, *gubernator* d'un énorme
bateau qu'il n'a pas su conduire, qu'il n'a pas su
gouverner. Et pourtant il en est responsable. Là est la
fatalité. Là est la mystérieuse destination d'Israël.
Brusquement revêtu, revêtu malgré lui d'une énorme
magistrature, d'une magistrature capitale, de la
magistrature de victime, de la magistrature de héros, de
la magistrature de martyr il s'en est lamentablement
tiré. Et ce qu'il y a de fatal, ce qu'il y a de douloureux,
ce qu'il y a de tragique, c'est que nous ne pouvons pas
ne pas lui en demander compte.

Celui qui est désigné doit marcher. Celui qui est
appelé doit répondre. C'est la loi, c'est la règle, c'est le
niveau des vies héroïques, c'est le niveau des vies de
sainteté. Investi victime malgré lui, investi héros

malgré lui, investi victime malgré lui, investi martyr
malgré lui il fut indigne de cette triple investiture.
Historiquement, réellement indigne. Insuffisant; au-
dessous; incapable. Impéritie et incurie. Incapacité
profonde. Indigne de ce triple sacre, de cette triple
magistrature. Et ce qu'il y a de pire, ce qu'il y a de
fatal, ce qu'il y a de plus tragique, c'est qu'à moins
d'entrer dans son crime et sous peine de participer de
son indignité, de cette indignité même nous ne
pouvons pas ne pas lui en demander compte. Quiconque a eu le monde en main, est responsable du monde.
Nous ne pouvons pas entrer dans son jeu. Nous
n'avons pas le droit d'entrer dans ses raisons, fussent-
elles légitimes; privément légitimes. Et c'est surtout si
elles sont légitimes qu'il faut nous en défier. Car elles
nous tenteraient. Nous devons tout oublier, le bien
que nous savons de lui, l'affection que nous aurions
pour lui, que nous serions tentés d'avoir pour lui, la
touchante, la paternelle affection de ce vieil homme
pour lui; de ce vieil homme que lui-même nous
respectons tant, que nous aimons tant. Nous *devons*
tout oublier et nous ne pouvons que lui demander
compte. Compte de cette immense bataille qu'il a
perdue. Il s'est trouvé engagé sans le vouloir général
en chef, plus que cela, drapeau d'une immense armée
dans une immense bataille contre une immense
armée. Et il a perdu cette immense bataille. Et nous
ne pouvons lui parler que de cela. Nous n'avons le
droit que de lui parler de cela. Nous n'avons le droit
d'engager, d'accepter de lui, avec lui nulle autre
conversation, aucun autre entretien. Nul autre
propos.

Nous devons taire, nous devons faire taire tous nos

autres sentiments. Il a été constitué un homme public. Il a été constitué un homme de gloire, d'un retentissement universel. Nous ne pouvons que lui demander compte de son action publique, de ses sentiments publics, de ce désastre public. Celui qui perd une bataille, en est responsable. Et il a perdu cette immense bataille. Nous ne pouvons que lui demander compte de tout ce qui était engagé dans cette bataille, dans cette action publique. Nous ne pouvons que lui demander compte des mœurs publiques, de la France, *d'Israël même,* de l'humanité dont il fut un moment.

Singulière destinée. Il fut investi, institué malgré lui homme public. Tant d'autres ont voulu devenir hommes publics, et y ont mis le prix, et en ont été implacablement refoulés par l'événement. Il fut investi, institué malgré lui homme de gloire. Tant d'autres ont voulu la gloire, et y ont mis le prix, et en ont été implacablement refoulés par l'événement. Et lui il a eu tout cela. Il a eu tout malgré lui. Il a eu tout ce qu'il ne voulait pas. Mais il faut que celui qui est investi marche.

Tant d'hommes, des milliers et des milliers d'hommes, soldats, poètes, écrivains, artistes, hommes d'action (victimes), héros, martyrs, tant d'hommes, des milliers et des milliers d'hommes ont voulu entrer dans l'action publique, devenir, se faire des hommes publics; et ils y ont mis le prix. Tant d'hommes ont brigué la gloire, temporelle, des milliers et des milliers d'hommes, et d'être immortels, temporellement immortels dans la mémoire des hommes. Et ils y ont mis le prix. Ils y ont mis le génie, l'héroïsme, des efforts sans nombre, des efforts effrayants; des souffrances effrayantes; des vies entières, et quelles vies, de véritables martyres. Et rien, jamais rien. Et lui, sans rien faire, malgré lui en quelques semaines il est devenu l'homme dont l'humanité entière a le plus retenti, son nom est devenu le nom, il est devenu l'homme dont tout le monde a le plus répété, a le plus célébré le nom depuis la mort de *notre maître Napoléon*[1]. Ce que cent batailles avaient donné à l'autre, il l'a eu malgré lui. Et il n'en était pas plus fier. C'est bien pour cela que nous ne pouvons écrire et parler de lui que comme nous l'avons fait dans les deux premiers tiers de ce cahier[2].

Cette situation tragique me rappelle un mot de Bernard-Lazare. Il faut toujours en revenir, on en revient toujours à un mot de Bernard-Lazare. Ce mot-ci sera le mot décisif de l'affaire. Puisqu'il vient, puisqu'il porte de son plus grand prophète sur la victime même. Il est donc culminant par son point d'origine et par son point d'arrivée. *Bernard-Lazare, né à Nîmes le 14 juin 1865 ; mort à Paris le premier septembre 1903*. Il avait donc trente-huit ans. Parce qu'un homme porte lorgnon, parce qu'il porte un binocle transverse barrant un pli du nez devant les deux gros yeux, le moderne le croit moderne, le moderne ne sait pas voir, ne voit pas, ne sait pas reconnaître l'antiquité du regard prophète. C'était le temps où quand il rencontrait Maurice Montégut[3] il disait. L'autre avait mal à l'estomac, comme tout le monde, comme tout pauvre mercenaire intellectuel. Et lui aussi il croyait avoir mal à l'estomac comme tout le monde. Il disait à Montégut : *Hein, Montégut,* en riant, car il était profondément gai, intérieurement gai : *Eh bien, Monté-*

gut, hein ça va bien avant le déjeuner, quand on n'a rien dans l'estomac. On est léger. On travaille. Mais après. Il ne faudrait jamais manger. Dreyfus venait de revenir. Dreyfus était rentré et presque instantanément, aux premières démarches, aux premiers pourparlers, au premier contact tout le monde avait eu brusquement l'impression qu'il y avait une paille, que ce n'était pas cela, qu'il était comme il était, et non point comme nous l'avions rêvé. Quelques-uns déjà se plaignaient. Quelques-uns, sourdement, bientôt publiquement l'accusaient. Sourdement, publiquement Bernard-Lazare le défendait. Âprement, obstinément. Tenacement. Avec cet admirable aveuglement volontaire de ceux qui aiment vraiment, avec cet acharnement obstiné invincible avec lequel l'amour défend un être qui a tort, évidemment tort, publiquement tort. — *Je ne sais pas ce qu'ils veulent,* disait-il, riant mais ne riant pas, riant dessus mais dedans ne riant pas, *je ne sais pas ce qu'ils demandent. Je ne sais pas ce qu'ils* lui *veulent. Parce qu'il a été condamné injustement,* on lui demande tout, *il faudrait qu'il ait toutes les vertus.* **Il est innocent, c'est déjà beaucoup.**

Non seulement nous fûmes des héros, mais l'affaire Dreyfus au fond ne peut s'expliquer que par ce besoin d'héroïsme qui saisit périodiquement ce peuple, cette race, par un besoin d'héroïsme qui alors nous saisit nous toute une génération. Il en est de ces grands mouvements, de ces grandes épreuves de tout un peuple comme de ces autres grandes épreuves les guerres. Ou plutôt il n'y a pour les peuples qu'une sorte de grandes épreuves temporelles, qui sont les guerres, et ces grandes épreuves-ci sont elles-mêmes des guerres. Dans toutes ces grandes épreuves, dans toutes ces grandes histoires c'est beaucoup plutôt la force intérieure, la violence d'éruption qui fait la matière, historique, que ce n'est la matière qui fait et qui impose l'épreuve. Quand une grande guerre éclate, une grande révolution, cette sorte de guerre, c'est qu'un grand peuple, une grande race a besoin de sortir; qu'elle en a assez; notamment qu'elle en a assez de la paix. C'est toujours qu'une grande masse éprouve un violent besoin, un grand, un profond besoin, un besoin mystérieux d'un grand mouvement. Si le peuple, si la race, si la masse française eût eu envie d'une grande guerre il y a quarante ans, cette misérable, cette malheureuse guerre elle-même de 1870, si mal commencée, si mal engagée qu'elle fût, fût devenue une grande guerre, comme les autres, et en mars 1871 [1] elle n'eût fait que commencer. Une grande histoire, je dis une grande histoire militaire comme ces guerres de la Révolution et de l'Empire ne s'explique aucunement que par ceci : un saisissement de besoin, un très profond besoin de gloire, de guerre, d'histoire qui à un moment donné saisit tout un peuple, toute une race, et lui fait faire une explosion, une éruption. Un mystérieux besoin d'une inscription. Historique. Un mystérieux besoin d'une sorte de fécondité historique. Un mystérieux besoin d'inscrire une grande histoire dans l'histoire éternelle. Toute autre explication est vaine, raisonnable, rationnelle, inféconde, irréelle. De même notre affaire Dreyfus ne peut s'expliquer que par un besoin, le même, par un besoin d'héroïsme qui saisit toute une génération, la nôtre, par un besoin de guerre, de guerre *militaire,* et de gloire militaire, par un besoin de sacrifice et jusque

de martyre, peut-être (sans doute), par un besoin de
sainteté. Ce que nos adversaires n'ont pu voir que en
face, de l'autre côté, de face, ce qu'ils n'ont pu
recevoir que en creux, ce que nos chefs mêmes ont
toujours ignoré, c'est à quel point nous marchâmes
comme une armée, militaire. Comment tant d'espérance, tant d'entreprise a été brisée sans obtenir, sans
effectuer une inscription historique, c'est précisément
ce que j'ai essayé non pas seulement d'expliquer, mais
de représenter *à nos amis* et *à nos abonnés* dans un cahier
de l'année dernière sensiblement à la même date [1].
Que si nous avons été, une fois de plus, une armée de
lions conduite par des ânes, c'est alors que nous
sommes demeurés, très exactement, dans la plus pure
tradition française.

Nous avons été grands. Nous avons été très grands.
Aujourd'hui ceux dont je parle, nous sommes des gens
qui gagnons pauvrement, misérablement, miséreuse-
ment notre vie. Mais ce que je ne vois pas, ce soit que
les Juifs pauvres, ici encore, se séparent de nous, qu'ils
gagnent leur vie en un tour de main, qu'ils n'aient
point de mal, qu'ils aient moins de mal que nous à
gagner leur vie. Peut-être au contraire, car s'ils se
soutiennent un peu entre eux, moins qu'on ne le croit,
moins qu'on ne le dit, et quelquefois ils se combattent,
et se trahissent, en revanche ils se heurtent à un
antisémitisme aujourd'hui revenu, aujourd'hui crois-
sant. Ce que je vois, c'est que juifs et chrétiens
ensemble, juifs pauvres et chrétiens pauvres, nous
gagnons notre vie comme nous pouvons, générale-

ment mal, dans cette chienne de vie, dans cette chienne, dans cette gueuse de société moderne.

Mais dans cette misère même, et à cause de cette misère même, nous voulons avoir été grands, nous voulons avoir été très grands. Justement parce que nous n'aurons jamais une inscription historique. Si nous avions comme tant d'autres une inscription historique, si nous avions comme quelques-uns une grande inscription historique, si seulement nous avions une inscription historique assez mesurée à notre effort, à notre intention, à ce que nous fûmes en réalité, alors nous saurions la payer le prix, alors nous aurions mauvaise grâce à insister sur la considération qui nous est due. Nous sommes si attachés, nous mettons un tel prix à l'enregistrement historique dans la mémoire temporelle de l'humanité que la considération de l'histoire nous dispenserait de toute autre considération. Et nous y gagnerions encore. Nous croirions encore y gagner. Mais justement parce que nous sommes pauvres, pauvres de biens et pauvres d'histoire, justement parce que nous avons sur nous le mépris et la méconnaissance des riches, et de cette grande riche d'histoire, il faut qu'il soit bien entendu pour nous et entre nous que nous savons que nous fûmes très grands. Nous pouvons ne pas le dire aux autres, nous savons que les autres, s'ils veulent, n'ont pas à s'occuper de nous, nous pouvons ne pas le dire à l'histoire, nous savons que l'histoire, si elle veut, n'a pas à s'occuper de nous. Mais si nous ne le disons pas entre nous, et dans le secret de nos propos, c'est parce qu'il est bien entendu que nous le savons. Et surtout nous n'avons pas à dire le contraire et aux autres et à l'histoire.

Nous voulons bien avoir été bernés, mais nous voulons avoir été grands.

Voilà, *cher Halévy, à quel point nous en sommes* ; voilà, mon cher Halévy, ce que je nomme un examen de conscience. Voilà ce que je nomme exprimer des regrets, faire des (mes) excuses. Voilà ce que je nomme une amende honorable, faire amende honorable. M'infliger un désaveu. C'est ce que je nomme être timoré. C'est ma manière d'être timoré. C'est comme ça que je porte la chemise longue, et la corde au cou, la corde de chanvre. C'est comme ça que je tiens mon cierge. On parle toujours comme si dans une société d'ordre nous étions venus introduire un désordre. Arbitrairement. Gratuitement. Mais il faut tout de même voir qu'il y a des ordres apparents qui recouvrent, qui sont les pires désordres [1]. Nous retrouvons ici ce que nous avons dit de l'égoïsme des riches dans le monde moderne, de la classe riche, de l'égoïsme bourgeois. Cet égoïsme porte sur leur entendement même. Sur leur vue. Même sur leur vue politique du monde politique. Il y avait un ordre sous Méline [2]. C'était un ordre pourri, un ordre mou, un ordre apparent, un ordre purement bourgeois. Notre collaborateur Halévy l'a très bien marqué, c'était un ordre comme sous Louis-Philippe, comme sous Guizot, comme dans les huit, dix, douze dernières années de Louis-Philippe. Un ordre de surface (comme aujourd'hui d'ailleurs), un ordre gangrené, mortifère, mort, une chair morte (comme aujourd'hui). De toute façon une crise venait, comme elle vient aujourd'hui.

Un ordre mortel pour la fécondité, pour les intérêts

profonds, pour les intérêts durables de la race et du
peuple, de la patrie.

En réalité la véritable situation des gens que nous
avions devant nous était pendant longtemps non pas
de dire et de croire Dreyfus coupable, mais de croire et
dire qu'innocent ou coupable on ne troublait pas, on
ne bouleversait pas, on ne *compromettait* pas, on ne
risquait pas pour un homme, pour un seul homme, la
vie et le salut d'un peuple, l'énorme salut de tout un
peuple. On sous-entendait : le salut *temporel*. Et précisément notre mystique chrétienne culminait si parfaitement, si exactement avec notre mystique française,
avec notre mystique patriotique dans notre mystique
dreyfusiste que ce qu'il faut bien voir, et ce que je
dirai, ce que je mettrai dans mes confessions, *c'est que
nous ne nous placions pas moins qu'au point de vue* **du salut
éternel de la France.** Que disions-nous en effet ?
Tout était contre nous, la sagesse et la loi, j'entends la
sagesse humaine, la loi humaine. Ce que nous faisions
était de l'ordre de la folie ou de l'ordre de la sainteté,
qui ont tant de ressemblances, tant de secrets accords,
pour la sagesse humaine, pour un regard humain.
Nous allions, nous étions contre la sagesse, contre la
loi. Contre la sagesse humaine, contre la loi humaine.
Voici ce que je veux dire. Qu'est-ce que nous disions
en effet. Les autres disaient : Un peuple, tout un
peuple est un énorme assemblage des intérêts, des
droits les plus légitimes. Les plus sacrés. Des milliers,
des millions de vies en dépendent, dans le présent,
dans le passé (dans le futur), des milliers, des millions,
des centaines de millions de vies, le constituent, dans

le présent, dans le passé (dans le futur) (des millions de mémoires), et par le jeu de l'histoire, par le dépôt de l'histoire la garde d'intérêts incalculables. De droits légitimes, sacrés, incalculables. Tout un peuple d'hommes, tout un peuple de familles ; tout un peuple de droits, tout un peuple d'intérêts, légitimes ; tout un peuple de vies ; toute une race ; tout un peuple de mémoires ; toute l'histoire, toute la montée, toute la poussée, tout le passé, tout le futur, toute la promesse d'un peuple et d'une race ; tout ce qui est inestimable, incalculable, d'un prix infini, parce que ça ne se fait qu'une fois, parce que ça ne s'obtient qu'une fois, parce que ça ne se recommencera jamais ; parce que c'est une réussite, unique ; un peuple, et notamment, nommément ce peuple-ci, qui est d'un prix unique ; ce vieux peuple ; un peuple n'a pas le droit, et le premier devoir, le devoir étroit d'un peuple est de ne pas exposer tout cela, de ne pas s'exposer pour un homme, quel qu'il soit, quelque légitimes que soient ses intérêts ou ses droits. Quelque sacrés même. Un peuple n'a jamais le droit. On ne perd point une cité, un cité ne se perd point pour un (seul) citoyen. C'était le langage même et du véritable civisme et de la sagesse, c'était la sagesse même, la sagesse antique. C'était le langage de la raison. A ce point de vue il était évident que Dreyfus devait se dévouer pour la France ; non pas seulement pour le repos de la France mais pour le salut même de la France, qu'il exposait. Et s'il ne voulait pas se dévouer lui-même, dans le besoin on devait le dévouer. Et nous que disions-nous. Nous disions une seule injustice, un seul crime, une seule illégalité, surtout si elle est officiellement enregistrée, confirmée, une seule injure à l'humanité, une seule injure à la justice, et au droit surtout si elle est universellement, légalement, nationalement, commodément acceptée, un seul crime rompt et suffit à rompre tout le pacte social, tout le contrat social, une seule forfaiture, un seul déshonneur suffit à perdre, d'honneur, à déshonorer tout un peuple. C'est un point de gangrène, qui corrompt tout le corps. Ce que nous défendons, ce n'est pas seulement notre honneur. Ce n'est pas seulement l'honneur de tout notre peuple, dans le présent, c'est l'honneur historique de notre peuple, tout l'honneur historique de toute notre race, l'honneur de nos aïeux, l'honneur de nos enfants. Et plus nous avons de passé, plus nous avons de mémoire (plus ainsi, comme vous le dites, nous avons de responsabilité) plus ainsi aussi ici nous devons la défendre ainsi. Plus nous avons de passé derrière nous, plus (justement) il nous faut le défendre ainsi, le garder pur. *Je rendrai mon sang pur comme je l'ai reçu* [1]. C'était la règle et l'honneur et la poussée cornélienne, la vieille poussée cornélienne. C'était la règle et l'honneur et la poussée chrétienne. Une seule tache entache toute une famille. Elle entache aussi tout un peuple. Un seul point marque l'honneur de toute une famille. Un seul point marque aussi l'honneur de tout un peuple. Un peuple ne peut pas rester sur une injure, subie, exercée, sur un crime, aussi solennellement, aussi définitivement endossé. L'honneur d'un peuple est d'un seul tenant.

Qu'est-ce à dire, à moins de ne pas savoir un mot de français, sinon que nos adversaires parlaient le langage de la raison d'État, qui n'est pas seulement le

langage de la raison politique et parlementaire, du
méprisable intérêt politique et parlementaire, mais
beaucoup plus exactement, beaucoup plus haut qui
est le langage, le très respectable langage de la
continuité, de la continuation temporelle du peuple et
de la race, *du salut temporel du peuple et de la race*. Ils
n'allaient pas à moins. Et nous par un mouvement
chrétien profond, par une poussée très profonde
révolutionnaire et ensemble traditionnelle de christianisme, suivant en ceci une tradition chrétienne des
plus profondes, des plus vivaces, des plus dans la
ligne, dans l'axe et au cœur du christianisme, nous
nous n'allions pas à moins qu'à nous élever je ne dis
pas (jusqu')à la conception mais à la passion, mais au
souci d'un salut éternel, du salut éternel de ce peuple,
nous n'atteignions pas à moins qu'à vivre dans un
souci constant, dans une préoccupation, dans une
angoisse mortelle, éternelle, dans une anxiété
constante du salut éternel de notre peuple, du salut
éternel de notre race. Tout au fond nous étions les
hommes du salut éternel et nos adversaires étaient les
hommes du salut temporel. Voilà la vraie, la réelle
division de l'affaire Dreyfus. Tout au fond nous ne
voulions pas que la France fût constituée en état de
péché mortel. Il n'y a que la doctrine chrétienne au
monde, dans le monde moderne, dans aucun monde,
qui mette à ce point, aussi délibérément, aussi totalement, aussi absolument la mort temporelle comme
rien, comme une insignifiance, comme un zéro au prix
de la mort éternelle, et le risque de la mort temporelle
comme rien au prix du péché mortel, au prix du
risque de la mort éternelle. Tout au fond nous ne
voulions pas que par un seul péché, mortel, complai-

samment accepté, complaisamment endossé, complaisamment acquis pour ainsi dire notre France fût non
pas seulement déshonorée devant le monde et devant
l'histoire : qu'elle fût proprement constituée en état de
péché mortel. Un jour, au point le plus douloureux de
cette crise, un ami vint me voir, qui fortuitement
passait par Paris. Un ami qui était chrétien. — Je ne
connais pas cette affaire, me dit-il. Je vis dans le fond
de ma province. J'ai assez de mal à gagner ma vie. Je
ne connais rien de cette affaire. Je ne soupçonnais pas
l'état où je trouve Paris. Mais enfin on ne peut pas
sacrifier tout un peuple pour un homme. Je n'eus rien
à lui répondre que de prendre un livre dans mon
armoire, un petit livre cartonné, une petite édition
Hachette [1] — 27. lui dis-je. « *Or vous demant-je, fist-il,*
lequel vous ameriés miex, ou que vous fussiés mesiaus (mesiaus
c'est lépreux), *ou que vous eussiés fait un pechié mortel ?* »
Et je, qui onques ne li menti, li respondi que je en ameroie miex
avoir fait trente que estre mesiaus. Et quant li frere s'en furent
parti (c'étaient deux frères qu'il avait appelés), *il*
m'appela tout seul, et me fist seoir à ses piez et me dist :
« *Comment me deistes-vous hier ce ?* » *Et je li diz que encore li*
disoie-je. Et il me dist : « *Vous deistes comme hastis musarz* [2] ;
car vous devez savoir que nulle si laide mezelerie n'est comme
d'estre en pechié mortel, pour ce que l'ame qui est en pechié
mortel est semblable au dyable : par quoy nulle si laide
meselerie ne puet estre. 28. — « *Et bien est voirs que quant li*
hom meurt, il est gueris de la meselerie dou cors ; mais quant li
hom qui a fait le pechié mortel meurt, il ne sait pas ne n'est
certeins que il ait eu en sa vie tel repentance que Diex li ait
pardonnei : par quoy grant poour doit avoir que celle mezelerie
li dure tant comme Diex yert en paradis. Si vous pri, fist-il,
tant comme je puis, que vous metés votre cuer à ce, pour l'amour

de Dieu et de moy, que vous amissiez miex que touz meschiez
avenist au cors, de mezelerie et de toute maladie, que ce que li
pechiés mortex venist à l'ame de vous. » On voit que si pour
une présentation, dans une présentation récente [1] je
me référais à ce grand chroniqueur ; à ce grand
chroniqueur d'un autre grand saint ; et d'un autre
grand saint français, j'avais pour le faire de multiples
autorités de raison.

Mais tel est le jeu des partis. Les partis politiques,
les partis parlementaires, tous les partis politiques ne
peuvent tenir aucun propos que dans le langage
politique, parlementaire, ils ne peuvent engager,
soutenir aucune action que sur le terrain, sur le plan
politique, parlementaire. Et surtout, et en outre, et
naturellement ils veulent que nous en fassions autant.
Que nous soyons constamment avec eux, parmi eux.
De tout ce que nous faisons, de tout ce qui fait la vie et
la force d'un peuple, de nos actes et de nos œuvres, de
nos opérations et de nos conduites, de nos âmes et de
nos vies ils effectuent incessamment, automatiquement, presque innocemment une traduction en langage politique, parlementaire, une réduction, un
rabattement, une projection, un report sur le plan
politique, parlementaire. Ainsi ils n'y entendent, ils
n'y comprennent rien, et ils empêchent les autres d'y
rien comprendre. Ils nous déforment, ils nous dénaturent incessamment et en eux-mêmes dans leur propre
imagination et auprès de ceux qui les suivent, de ceux
qui en sont, dans les imaginations de ceux qui les
suivent. Tout ce que nous disons, tout ce que nous
faisons, ils le traduisent, ils le trahissent. *Traducunt.*
Tradunt [2]. On ne sait jamais s'ils vous font plus de tort,

s'ils vous dénaturent plus quand ils vous combattent
ou quand ils vous soutiennent, quand ils vous combattent ou quand ils vous adoptent, car quand ils vous
combattent ils vous combattent en langage politique
sur le plan politique et quand ils vous soutiennent,
c'est peut-être pire, car ils vous soutiennent, ils vous
adoptent en langage politique sur le plan politique. Et
dans ces tiraillements contraires ils ont également et
contrairement tort, ils sont également et contrairement insuffisants. Ils sont également et contrairement, des dénaturants. Ils ne présentent, ils ne se
représentent, ils ne conçoivent également et contrairement qu'une vie diminuée, une vie dénaturée. Un
fantôme, un squelette, un plan, une projection de vie.
Quand ils sont contre vous, ils vous combattent et
vous feraient un tort mortel. Quand ils sont pour
vous, et qu'ils croient que vous êtes pour eux, ils vous
accaparent et vous font certainement un tort mortel.
Ils veulent alors vous endosser, et qu'on les endosse.
Ils vous protègent. Quand ils vous combattent, ils
combattent vos mystiques par des bassesses politiques, par de basses politiques. Quand ils vous soutiennent ils traduisent, ce qui est infiniment pire, ils
traduisent vos mystiques par des bassesses politiques,
par de basses politiques. Et ce que nous avons fait
pour nos mystiques, l'ayant interprété pour leurs
politiques, pour les politiques correspondantes. pour
les politiques issues, c'est là-dessus précisément qu'ils
se fondent, c'est là-dessus qu'ils arguënt pour nous
lier à leurs politiques, à ces politiques, pour nous
interdire les autres mystiques, transférant ainsi, transférant arbitrairement dans le monde des mystiques

des oppositions, des contrariétés qui n'existent, qui ne se produisent, qui ne jouent que sur le plan politique.

C'est ainsi que les partis vous récompensent de ce que vous avez fait pour eux dans les moments où ils étaient en danger ; je veux dire de ce que vous avez fait pour les mystiques dont ils sont issus, pour les mystiques dont ils vivent, pour les mystiques qu'ils exploitent, qu'ils parasitent. C'est de cela précisément qu'ils prennent barre, qu'ils veulent prendre barre sur vous, c'est partant de cela qu'ils veulent vous lier à leurs politiques, vous interdire les autres mystiques.

Parce que depuis la dégradation de la mystique dreyfusiste en politique dreyfusiste, remontant tous les courants de toutes les puissances, remontant des épaules toutes les puissances de tyrannie, toutes les démagogies de tous nos amis (politiques), nous avons risqué, nous avons éprouvé quinze ans de misère pour la défense des libertés privées, des libertés profondes, des libertés chrétiennes, pour la défense des consciences chrétiennes, pour nous récompenser les politiques, les politiciens réactionnaires nous interdi-saient volontiers d'être républicains. Et parce que nous avons mis non pas comme ces ouvriers des semaines et des mois mais quinze années de misère au service de la République, pour nous récompenser les politiques, les politiciens républicains nous interdi-raient volontiers d'être chrétiens. Ainsi la République serait le régime de la liberté de conscience pour tout le monde, excepté précisément pour nous, précisément pour nous récompenser de ce que nous l'avons quinze ans défendue, de ce que nous la défendons, de ce que

nous la défendrons encore. Pour nous récompenser
d'avoir mis quinze ans de misère au service de la
République, d'avoir défendu, d'avoir sauvé un régime
qui est le régime de la liberté de conscience, on
accorderait la liberté de conscience à tout le monde,
excepté seulement à nous. Nous nous passerons de la
permission de ces messieurs. Nous ne vivons pas, nous
ne nous mouvons pas sur le même plan qu'eux. Leurs
débats ne sont pas les nôtres. Les douloureux débats
que nous avons, que nous soutenons parfois n'ont rien
de commun avec leurs faciles, avec leurs superficielles
polémiques.

La République serait le régime de la liberté de
conscience pour tout le monde, excepté précisément
pour les républicains.

Nous demanderons à ces messieurs la permission de
nous passer de leur permission. Nos cahiers sont
devenus, non point par le hasard, mais ils se sont
constitués par une lente élaboration, par de puis-
santes, par de secrètes affinités, par une sorte de
longue évaporation de la politique, comme une
compagnie parfaitement libre d'hommes qui tous
croient à quelque chose, à commencer par la typographie, qui est un des plus beaux art et métier. Malgré
les partis, malgré les (hommes) politiques, malgré les
politiciens contraires, (contraires à nous, contraires
entre eux), c'est cela que nous resterons.

Voilà, mon cher Variot, quelques-uns des propos que j'eusse tenus aux cahiers le jeudi, si on y parlait moins haut, et si on m'y laissait quelquefois la parole[1]. Dans ces cahiers de M. Milliet vous trouverez ce que c'était que cette mystique républicaine. Et vous monsieur qui me demandez qu'il faudrait bien définir un peu par voie de raison démonstrative, par voie de raisonnement de raison ratiocinante ce que c'est que mystique, et ce que c'est que politique, *quid sit mysticum, et quid politicum,* la mystique républicaine, c'était quand on mourait pour la République, la politique républicaine, c'est à présent qu'on en vit. Vous comprenez, n'est-ce pas.

Les papiers de M. Milliet que nous publierons donneront immédiatement l'impression d'avoir eux-mêmes été choisis d'un monceau énorme de papiers. On ne peut naturellement tout donner. A partir du moment où M. Milliet m'apporta les premiers paquets de sa copie, un grand débat s'éleva entre nous. Il voulait toujours, par discrétion, en supprimer. Mais j'ai toujours tout gardé, parce que c'était le meilleur. On en avait assez supprimé pour passer des textes à la copie, pour constituer la copie elle-même. — Cette lettre est trop intime, disait-il. — C'est précisément parce qu'elle est intime que je la garde. Il avait marqué au crayon les passages qu'il pensait que l'on pouvait supprimer. J'achetai une gomme exprès pour effacer son crayon. Il voulait s'effacer. Je lui dis : Paraissez au contraire. Un homme qui ne se propose plus que de se rappeler exactement, fidèlement, réellement sa vie et de la représenter est, devient lui-

même le meilleur des papiers, le meilleur des monu-
ments, le meilleur des témoins ; le meilleur des textes ;
il apporte infiniment plus que le meilleur des papiers ;
il est infiniment plus que le meilleur des papiers ; il
apporte, à infiniment près, le meilleur des témoignages.

Vous remarquerez, Variot, vous entendrez le ton de
ces *mémoires*. C'est le ton même du temps. Je ne serais
pas surpris qu'un imbécile, et qui manquerait du sens
historique trouvât ce ton un peu ridicule. Il est passé.
Ces hommes, qui avaient ce ton, ont fait de grandes
choses. Et nous ?

Le civisme aussi paraît aujourd'hui ridicule. Civique est un adjectif aujourd'hui qui se porte très mal. Il
sonne en *ique*. *Civique* a l'air de rimer avec *bourrique* et
avec *atavique*. Et même avec *ataxique*. Que des vieil-
lards, que des malades, que des mourants se fissent
(trans)porter aux urnes, évidemment ce n'est pas les
cuirassiers de Morsbronn [1]. Pourtant tous ceux qui
ont vu Coppée se faire porter mourant à l'Académie
pour assurer l'élection de M. Richepin ont trouvé que
c'était très grand [2].

La seule valeur, la seule force du royalisme, mon
cher Variot, la seule force d'une monarchie traditionnelle, c'est que le roi est plus ou moins aimé. La seule
force de la République, c'est que la République est
plus ou moins aimée. La seule force, la seule valeur, la
seule dignité de tout, c'est d'être aimé. Que tant
d'hommes aient tant vécu et tant souffert pour la

République, qu'ils aient tant cru en elle, qu'ils soient
tant morts pour elle, que pour elle ils aient supporté
tant d'épreuves, souvent extrêmes, voilà ce qui
compte, voilà ce qui m'intéresse, voilà ce qui existe.
Voilà ce qui fonde, voilà ce qui fait la légitimité d'un
régime. Quand je trouve dans l'*Action française* tant de
dérisions et tant de sarcasmes, souvent tant d'injures,
j'en suis peiné, car il s'agit d'hommes qui veulent
restaurer, restituer les plus anciennes dignités de
notre race et on ne fonde, on ne refonde aucune
culture sur la dérision et la dérision et le sarcasme et
l'injure sont des barbaries. Ils sont même des barba-
rismes. On ne fonde, on ne refonde, on ne restaure, on
ne restitue rien sur la dérision. Des calembours ne font
pas une restitution de culture. J'avoue que je n'arrive
point à comprendre tout ce que l'on met, tout ce qu'il
y a évidemment d'esprit dans cette graphie des
Respubliquains que l'on nous répète à satiété. Cela me
paraît un peu du même ordre que les sots de l'autre
côté qui écrivent toujours *le roy*. Avec un *y*. Cet *s* et ce
qu me paraissent du même alphabet que cet *y*. J'ai
peur qu'il ne soit presque également sot de se moquer
de l'un et de l'autre. Le roi a pour lui toute la majesté
de la tradition française. La République a pour elle
toute la grandeur de la tradition républicaine. Si on
met cet *s* à *Respubliquains* on ne fait rien, on ne peut
rien faire que de lui conférer un peu de la majesté
romaine. Je suis plongé en ce moment-ci, pour des
raisons particulières, dans le *de Viris*[1]. J'avoue que
respublica y est un mot d'une grandeur extraordinaire.
D'une amplitude, d'une voûte romaine. Quant au
changement de *c* en *qu*, au féminin de *public* en *publique*,
il ne me paraît pas plus déshonorant que le féminin de

Turc en *Turque*, et de *Grec* en *Grecque*, et de *sec* en *sèche*
comme la grammaire (française) nous l'enseigne. On
a le féminin qu'on peut. Quand je trouve dans l'*Action
française*, dans Maurras des raisonnements, des logi-
ques d'une rigueur implacable, des explications
impeccables, invincibles comme quoi la royauté vaut
mieux que la république, et la monarchie que la
république, et surtout le royalisme mieux que le
républicanisme et le monarchisme mieux que le
républicanisme, j'avoue que si je voulais parler grossièrement je dirais que ça ne prend pas. On pense ce
que je veux dire. Ça ne prend pas comme un mordant
prend ou ne prend pas sur un vernis. Ça n'entre pas.
Des explications, toute notre éducation, toute notre
formation intellectuelle, universitaire, scolaire nous a
tellement appris à en donner, à en faire, des explications et des explications, que nous en sommes saturés.
Au besoin nous ferions les siennes. Nous allons au-
devant des siennes, et c'est précisément ce qui les
émousse pour nous. Nous sortons d'en prendre. Nous
savons y faire. Dans le besoin nous les ferions. Mais
qu'au courant de la plume, et peut-être, sans doute
sans qu'il y ait pensé dans un article de Maurras je
trouve, comme il arrive, non point comme un argument, présentée comme un argument, mais comme
oubliée au contraire cette simple phrase : *Nous serions
prêts à mourir pour le roi, pour le rétablissement de notre roi,*
oh alors on me dit quelque chose, alors on commence
à causer. Sachant, d'un tel homme, que c'est vrai
comme il le dit, alors j'écoute, alors j'entends, alors je
m'arrête, alors je suis saisi, alors on me dit quelque
chose. Et l'autre jour aux cahiers, cet autre jeudi,
quand on eut discuté bien abondamment, quand on

eut commis bien abondamment ce péché de l'explication, quand tout à coup Michel Arnauld[1], un peu
comme exaspéré, un peu comme à bout, de cette voix
grave et sereine, douce et profonde, blonde, légèrement voilée, sérieuse, soucieuse comme tout le monde,
à peine railleuse et prête au combat que nous lui
connaissons, que nous aimons en lui depuis dix-huit
ans, interrompit, conclut presque brusquement : *Tout
cela c'est très bien parce qu'ils ne sont qu'une menace imprécise
et théorique. Mais le jour où ils deviendraient une menace réelle
ils verraient ce que nous sommes encore capables de faire pour la
République,* tout le monde comprit qu'enfin on venait
de dire quelque chose.

CHRONOLOGIE

1873. *7 janvier :* Naissance de Charles Pierre Péguy, à Orléans, 50, rue du faubourg Bourgogne. Fils unique de Désiré Péguy, menuisier, d'ascendance vigneronne, né à Saint-Jean-de-Braye le 21 février 1846. Celui-ci épouse à Orléans le 8 janvier 1872 Cécile Quéré, née à Moulins le 22 novembre 1846, fille naturelle d'Étiennette Quéré, originaire de Gennetines, Allier. Péguy a dix mois lorsque son père meurt, le 18 novembre 1873. Sa mère apprend le métier de rempailleuse de chaises.

1879. *Octobre :* Entrée à l'école primaire annexée à l'École normale d'instituteurs du Loiret, 72, rue du faubourg Bourgogne. Scolarité remarquable.

1884. *Juillet :* Obtention du certificat d'études primaires.

Octobre : Entrée à l'École primaire supérieure, à l'époque École professionnelle, Cloître Sainte-Croix.

1885. *Pâques :* Entrée en 6e au lycée d'Orléans, grâce à une bourse municipale de demi-pensionnaire obtenue par M. Naudy, directeur de l'École normale du Loiret.

25 juin : première communion, après avoir suivi le catéchisme à l'église Saint-Aignan.

1885-1891 : De la sixième à la philosophie, études régulières et brillantes. Péguy suit les cours d'instruction religieuse jusqu'à la première.

1891. *21 juillet :* Obtention du baccalauréat ès lettres.

Octobre : Entrée au lycée Lakanal, à Sceaux, en première vétérans, comme boursier d'État.

1892. *Juillet :* Échec à l'École normale supérieure.

Septembre : Devançant l'appel, Péguy s'engage au 131ᵉ régiment d'infanterie, à Orléans, et bénéficie de la loi dite du « volontariat d'un an ».

1893. *Juillet :* Second échec à l'École normale supérieure.

Octobre : Avec une bourse du conseil d'administration, Péguy entre comme interne au collège Sainte-Barbe, à Paris, d'où il peut suivre les cours de rhétorique supérieure au lycée Louis-le-Grand. Il noue une profonde amitié avec Marcel Baudouin.

1894. *Août :* Admission à l'École normale supérieure avec le numéro 6. Voyage à Orange pour assister à la représentation d'*Antigone* et d'*Œdipe-Roi* de Sophocle.

Novembre : Obtention de la licence ès lettres, mention philosophie. Première année d'École normale supérieure.

1895. *Mai :* Adhésion à un parti socialiste.

Fin octobre : Voyage à Domrémy et à Vaucouleurs.

Novembre : Péguy se fait mettre en congé pour l'année scolaire. Il retourne à Orléans où il apprend la typographie, fonde un groupe socialiste et commence à rédiger la première *Jeanne d'Arc*.

1896. *Juin :* Visite de Marcel Baudouin à Orléans et conception de *Marcel, premier dialogue de la cité harmonieuse*.

25 juillet : Mort de Marcel Baudouin.

Novembre : Retour à l'École normale supérieure pour une seconde année d'études.

1897. *Février :* Publication dans la *Revue socialiste* d'un premier article signé C.P. : « Un économiste socialiste, M. Léon Walras. » Six autres articles paraîtront dans la même revue sous les pseudonymes de Pierre Deloire et Jacques Deloire, entre autres un manifeste « De la cité socialiste » en août.

    28 octobre : Mariage avec Charlotte Françoise Baudouin, née en 1879, sœur de l'ami disparu. Installation 7, rue de l'Estrapade (5ᵉ).

    Novembre : Démissionnaire de l'École normale supérieure, Péguy obtient une bourse d'agrégation et la permission de suivre, comme auditeur libre, les cours de Georges Lyon, et à partir de février 1898 ceux de Bergson.

    Décembre : Publication de *Jeanne d'Arc*, drame en trois pièces et vingt-quatre actes, sous la signature de Marcel et Pierre Baudouin. Cette trilogie retrace la vie entière de Jeanne : l'enfance, les batailles et le procès.

1898. *Février :* Péguy participe à la campagne pour Dreyfus en rendant visite à Zola et à Jaurès et en signant des pétitions pour la révision dans l'*Aurore* et la *Petite République*.

    Mai : Péguy fonde une librairie socialiste sous le nom de Librairie Georges Bellais, 17, rue Cujas (5ᵉ). Il y engage la dot de sa femme (40 000 francs-or).

    Juin : Publication à la Librairie Georges Bellais de *Marcel, premier dialogue de la cité harmonieuse*, sous la signature de Pierre Baudouin. Péguy y expose sa conception de la cité utopique dont il prépare l'avènement.

    Août : Échec à l'agrégation de philosophie.

    10 septembre : Naissance de Marcel Péguy, premier enfant de l'écrivain.

    Novembre : Péguy entreprend la rédaction de *Pierre, commencement d'une vie bourgeoise*, autobiographie qu'il signe Pierre Baudouin et laisse inachevée. Elle sera publiée en 1931 par son fils Marcel Péguy.

    15 novembre 1898-15 janvier 1899 : Publication dans la *Revue blanche* d'une série de cinq articles qui, sous le pseudonyme de Jacques Laubier, militent pour Dreyfus. L'un d'eux oppose à la Ligue de la Patrie Française le patriotisme de l'Internationale socialiste.

1899. *1ᵉʳ février-15 novembre :* Péguy signe de son nom onze articles dans la *Revue blanche,* où il fustige la lenteur des socialistes à prendre parti pour Dreyfus et, dans ce combat, soutient Jaurès contre Guesde.

Juillet : Installation à Saint-Clair, près d'Orsay.

Août : Par suite de difficultés financières, la Librairie Georges Bellais se transforme en Société nouvelle de librairie et d'édition. Lucien Herr et Léon Blum font partie du conseil d'administration. Péguy n'est plus que « délégué » à l'édition.

Décembre : Un congrès des organisations socialistes ayant voté l'instauration d'un contrôle de la presse socialiste, Péguy décide de publier en toute liberté des cahiers de documentation et de réflexion. Il rompt avec Lucien Herr qui le traite d'anarchiste.

1900. *5 janvier :* Premier numéro des *Cahiers de la Quinzaine,* dont l'adresse provisoire est 19, rue des Fossés-Saint-Jacques, chez les Tharaud. En guise de manifeste, la *Lettre du provincial* donne une seule consigne : « dire la vérité ».

Février-avril : Dans *De la grippe, Encore de la grippe* et *Toujours de la grippe,* Péguy ridiculise la démagogie socialiste et rejette le dogme catholique de l'enfer (Cahier I-4, I-6, I-7).

Novembre : Les *Cahiers* s'installent 16, rue de la Sorbonne, dans l'immeuble de l'École des hautes études sociales. Péguy prend André Bourgeois comme administrateur.

29 novembre : Premier cahier de la deuxième série, chaque série couvrant une année scolaire et non une année civile.

1901. *2 mars :* Dans *Casse-cou,* Péguy met en garde Jaurès contre le danger de lier le socialisme à un système philosophique (Cahier II-7).

15 juillet : La famille Péguy déménage à Orsay, rue des Sablons.

7 septembre : Naissance de Germaine Péguy, seconde enfant de l'écrivain.

Octobre : Installation définitive des *Cahiers* 8, rue de la Sorbonne.

5 décembre : Dans *De la raison,* Péguy se dresse contre toute métaphysique d'État et formule un bon usage de la raison (Cahier III-4).

1902. *5 avril : Personnalités* plaide pour la nécessité d'incarner les idées dans des hommes (Cahier III-12).

4 novembre : A propos d'un roman d'A. Lavergne sur les instituteurs, *De Jean Coste* oppose misère et pauvreté (Cahier IV-3).

4 décembre : Les récentes œuvres de Zola exprime le regret que, dans ses derniers romans, l'auteur de *J'accuse* célèbre plus la conquête bourgeoise que l'évangile socialiste (Cahier IV-5).

1903. *12 mai : Débats parlementaires* offre une critique du parlementarisme (Cahier IV-18).

16 juin : Reprise politique parlementaire poursuit l'analyse de la décomposition du dreyfusisme (Cahier IV-20).

25 juin : Naissance de Pierre Péguy, troisième enfant de l'écrivain.

1904. *Janvier-février :* Dans trois conférences sur l'*Anarchisme politique,* Péguy distingue « l'autorité de commandement » de « l'autorité de compétence » (publié en 1969 dans les *Œuvres posthumes* éditées par Jacques Viard).

1er mars : L'*Avertissement au cahier Mangasarian* établit qu'une révolution est une plus pleine tradition (Cahier V-11).

30 octobre : Zangwill entame une longue critique des méthodes historiques positivistes (Cahier VI-3).

8 novembre : Un essai de monopole décrit ce que pourrait être un totalitarisme de gauche (Cahier VI-4).

1905. *29 janvier : La délation aux Droits de l'Homme* flétrit le combisme (Cahier VI-9).

Juillet-septembre : La menace allemande inspire à Péguy *Notre patrie* (Cahier VII-3) et *Par ce demi-clair matin* (publié en 1952). Il écrit également l'*Esprit de système* où il s'en prend au terrorisme idéologique (publié en 1953).

12 décembre : *Les suppliants parallèles* montre l'actualité de la tragédie grecque et invite à ne pas confondre révolte et révolution (Cahier VII-7).

26 décembre : *Louis de Gonzague* exhorte à une vigilance tranquille devant l'éventualité d'une guerre (Cahier VII-8).

1906. *Juillet-septembre :* Continuant les analyses entreprises en 1904 dans *Zangwill,* Péguy écrit *De la situation faite à l'histoire et à la sociologie dans les temps modernes* (Cahier VIII-3), *De la situation faite au parti intellectuel dans le monde moderne* (VIII-5), *Cahiers de la Quinzaine* (VIII-II) et *Brunetière* (publié en 1953), où il approfondit sa critique des héritiers de Taine et de Renan.

1907. *Mars :* Péguy confie à Jacques Maritain son nouveau cheminement vers la foi chrétienne.

Juillet-septembre : Poursuivant les investigations de 1904 et 1906, *De la situation faite au parti intellectuel devant les accidents de la gloire temporelle* s'achève sur un poème en prose à la gloire de Paris, de la Beauce et du Val de Loire (Cahier IX-I).

Décembre : *Un poète l'a dit* ajoute de nouveaux arguments à la critique de la métaphysique moderne (publié en 1953).

1908. *Janvier :* Installation de la famille Péguy à Lozère, dans la Maison des Pins.

Printemps-Été : *Deuxième élégie XXX* oppose le savant au philosophe, le classique au romantique et célèbre l'Île-de-France (publié en 1955).

10 septembre : Atteint d'une grave maladie et au comble de la détresse, Péguy avoue à Joseph Lotte sa nouvelle adhésion au catholicisme.

Octobre-décembre : Commencement de la *Thèse,* réflexion sur la philosophie des sciences, où l'auteur préfère aux trois états d'Auguste Comte sa propre théorie de l'âge empirique, l'âge scientifique et l'âge de la compétence (publié en 1955).

Décembre : Jacques Maritain tente en vain de faire accepter à Péguy un directeur de conscience.

1909. *16 juin :* Dépôt en Sorbonne du titre exact de la thèse : *De la situation faite à l'histoire dans la philosophie générale du monde moderne.* Ce travail ne sera jamais achevé ni soutenu.

20 juin : Tragique bilan de dix ans de gestion des *Cahiers, A nos amis, à nos abonnés* (Cahier X-13) se poursuit avec *Nous sommes des vaincus* (publié en 1953).

Juillet : Maladroite intervention de Maritain pour persuader Madame Péguy de faire baptiser ses enfants.

Juillet-août : Péguy commence les dialogues de l'histoire dont la rédaction se continuera jusqu'en 1913 et qui ne paraîtront qu'après sa mort. Le *Dialogue de l'histoire et de l'âme charnelle* est un pamphlet contre la « faute de mystique » des chrétiens qui ont oublié le temporel (publié en 1955 sous le titre de *Véronique*). Le *Dialogue de l'histoire et de l'âme païenne* associe à une nouvelle critique des méthodes historiques une méditation sur le vieillissement et la mort (publié en 1917 sous le titre de *Clio*).

1910. *16 janvier :* Le *Mystère de la charité de Jeanne d'Arc* reprend et amplifie l'interrogation sur l'enfer de la première *Jeanne d'Arc* et suggère une issue dans la contemplation de la passion du Christ, séquence écrite en vers libres (Cahier XI-6).

12 juillet : *Notre jeunesse* dresse un bilan de l'affaire Dreyfus et, à travers le portrait de Bernard-Lazare, montre la dégradation de la mystique en politique (Cahier XI-12).

30 juillet : Mariage de Blanche Raphaël, habituée des *Cahiers,* pour laquelle Péguy éprouve une passion douloureusement surmontée.

23 octobre : *Victor-Marie comte Hugo* évoque les ancêtres vignerons de Péguy, renouvelle le parallèle Corneille-Racine et voit dans Hugo un prophète païen de Jésus (Cahier XII-1).

1911. *Avril :* Péguy publie chez Grasset ses *Œuvres choisies 1900-1910.*

8 juin : L'Académie Française lui décerne le Prix Estrade-Delcros (8 000 F), à défaut du Grand Prix de Littérature (10 000 F) qui n'est pas attribué.

24 septembre : Un nouveau théologien M. Fernand Laudet foudroie les catholiques bien-pensants en célébrant la vie cachée de Jésus (Cahier XIII-2).

22 octobre : Écrit en vers libres, le *Porche du mystère de la deuxième vertu* introduit à la contemplation de la « petite fille espérance » (Cahier XIII-4).

Octobre-décembre : Rédaction de la *Ballade de la peine,* première partie de la *Ballade du cœur,* poème en quatrains réguliers où Péguy rumine son amour malheureux pour Blanche Raphaël (publié en 1941, éd. complète en 1975).

1912. *24 mars : Le Mystère des Saints Innocents* revient au vers libre et approfondit la contemplation de l'enfance (Cahier XIII-12).

Avril : Rédaction de la *Ballade de la grâce,* seconde partie de la *Ballade du cœur,* où la parabole de l'enfant prodigue purifie l'homme égaré par les passions (publié en 1941, éd. complète en 1975).

14-17 juin : Premier pèlerinage à Chartres, avec à l'aller Alain-Fournier jusqu'à Dourdan.

10 novembre : Péguy publie dans la revue *Le Correspondant* quatre *sonnets* et les *Sept contre Thèbes,* écrits en alexandrins.

25 novembre : Publication dans l'hebdomadaire *l'Opinion* de *Châteaux de Loire.*

1er décembre : La Tapisserie de sainte Geneviève et de Jeanne d'Arc propose un ensemble de pièces qui, partant du sonnet, culminent en un poème de neuf cents alexandrins sur les « armes de Jésus » et les « armes de Satan » (Cahier XIV-5).

1913. *16 février : L'Argent* évoque l'enfance de Péguy, les « hussards noirs » qui lui enseignaient la République, les ouvriers qui aimaient « l'ouvrage bien faite » (Cahier XIV-6).

10 mars : Publication dans *La Grande Revue* des *Sept contre Paris*

22 avril : L'Argent suite exalte la défense nationale au nom des Droits de l'Homme et fustige le pacifisme de Lavisse et de Jaurès, en même temps qu'il ridiculise Lanson (Cahier XIV-9).

11 mai : Toujours en alexandrins, *La Tapisserie de Notre Dame* réunit la *Présentation de la Beauce à Notre Dame de Chartres* et les *Prières dans la cathédrale de Chartres* (Cahier XIV-10).

25-28 juillet : Second pèlerinage à Chartres.

Août : Installation de la famille Péguy à Bourg-la-Reine, 7, rue André-Theuriet.

16 août : Publication dans *Le Figaro* de *Sainte Geneviève patronne de Paris.*

28 décembre : En huit mille alexandrins, *Ève* offre une somme théologique et mystique du christianisme de Péguy, épopée de l'innocence perdue et de l'incarnation du Fils de Dieu dans l'histoire humaine (Cahier XV-4).

1914. *20 janvier :* Sous le pseudonyme de Durel, Péguy donne un commentaire d'*Ève* dans le *Bulletin des professeurs catholiques de l'Université* que dirige Joseph Lotte.

Mars : Parution chez Ollendorff de *Morceaux choisis des œuvres poétiques 1912-1913.*

26 avril : La *Note sur M. Bergson et la philosophie bergsonienne* fait l'apologie des « méthodes souples » contre les « méthodes raides » (Cahier XV-8).

Mai-juillet : Poursuivant la défense de Bergson, la *Note conjointe sur M. Descartes et la philosophie cartésienne* dénonce la sottise des néo-thomistes qui font mettre à l'Index leur meilleur allié dans la lutte de l'Évangile contre le livret de Caisse d'Épargne (laissé inachevé et publié en 1924).

12 juillet : Deux cent vingt-neuvième et dernier *Cahier de la Quinzaine.*

2 août : Péguy est mobilisé comme lieutenant de réserve.

11-28 août : Campagne de Lorraine avec le 276e régiment d'infanterie, 19e compagnie.

15 août : Péguy entend la messe de l'Assomption dans la paroisse de Loupmont.

29 août-4 septembre : Retraite à pied vers Paris.

5 septembre : Péguy est tué à la tête de sa section, près de Villeroy, le premier jour de la bataille de la Marne.

1915. *4 février :* Naissance de Charles-Pierre Péguy, fils posthume.

RÉCEPTION
DE « NOTRE JEUNESSE »

Nous avons regroupé ici quelques lettres reçues par Péguy ou des tiers, au moment de la parution de Notre jeunesse. *Classées en « pour » et « contre », elles montrent quels étaient les amis et les adversaires de l'auteur et comment se perpétuaient, dix ans après l'événement, les clivages de l'affaire Dreyfus.*

POUR

C'est très beau, mon cher Péguy. Voilà un Cahier qui survivra au temps. Courage ! On se souviendra de nous, plus tard. Que notre petite armée reste unie. C'est du bon travail pour la France.

> *Romain Rolland* (Lettre à Péguy, 12 juillet 1910,
> dans *Pour l'honneur de l'esprit*,
> Correspondance Péguy-Rolland,
> Albin Michel, 1973, p. 291.)

Il faut que je vous dise combien *Notre jeunesse* m'a ému, et enthousiasmé, par toutes les beautés, tout le courage, toute la clairvoyance, tout l'immense talent que vous y avez mis. Je n'ai jamais rien lu qui soit, comme le vôtre, le livre qui réconforte, qui éclaire et qui rassure. Qui rassure : parce qu'éclairée par vous, notre route devient facile, si nous voulons vous suivre ; et aussi parce que vous cherchez dans le passé autre chose qu'une source de découragement et des conseils de paresse.

> *Claude Casimir-Perier*
> (Lettre a Péguy, 18 juillet 1910, dans *FACP*
> n° 187, 20 mai 1973, p. 20.)

Notre jeunesse est un livre sublime. Voilà. Les cinquante pages sur Lazare, les prophètes juifs, la psychologie des juifs, le métro, la tente, la vie nomade, etc., sont naturellement le chef-d'œuvre ; et, dans tout le reste, mille choses profondes et admirables, et tant de verve de terroir et de grasse satire ! C'est vraiment un morceau de première beauté, et, je le crois, un livre historique. Certainement, ce qu'a fait sortir de plus beau cette étonnante affaire.

> *Louis Gillet*
> (Lettre à Péguy, 18 juillet 1910, dans *FACP*
> n° 190, 1ᵉʳ octobre 1973, p. 31.)

Très important et à plus d'un endroit admirable.

> *André Gide*
> (Lettre à Jean Schlumberger, fin juillet 1910,
> dans A. Anglès, *André Gide et le premier groupe de la NRF*,
> tome I, Gallimard, 1978, p. 289.)

Trouvez d'abord ici mon remerciement personnel. J'ai l'immodestie de dire que ce que vous avez écrit de moi est juste et vrai. Je ne pensais pas qu'il se trouverait quelqu'un pour l'écrire. Vous avez été là. Merci. Cependant je ne sais pas ce que c'est que « le parti politique juif » (...) Le portrait que vous tracez de Bernard-Lazare est très beau, parce que toujours — à mon sens — exact, d'une pénétration profonde. Nous avons été pourtant quelques républicains à lui rendre justice, Ranc, mon frère Salomon et moi — et d'autres encore.

> *Joseph Reinach*
> (Lettre à Péguy, 18 août 1910, dans *OEPC*,
> tome III, 1992, p. 1523-1524.)

Laissez-moi vous dire que jamais, je crois, je n'ai lu de vous rien d'aussi net et tout ensemble d'aussi compréhensif. Vous avez atteint de votre coutre le roc d'une grande loi et toute la terre encore chaude de notre jeunesse en est profondément remuée. De l'Affaire et de Bernard-Lazare vous écrivez des pages qui fixeront la physionomie de l'une et de l'autre dans cette histoire que vos cahiers contribuent à édifier mieux que tous les « fichiers » des séminaires à l'allemande (...)

Par ailleurs, je ne puis vous taire ma joie de vous voir revenir, *revenir* selon les apparences car pour la substance j'estime à présent que vous ne vous étiez point en-allé — cette reconnaissance est une amende honorable — à ce qui m'avait toujours paru devoir constituer la raison d'être des *Cahiers* et l'appel propre de votre vocation, j'entends l'expression de la mystique d'hier et la préfiguration de la mystique de demain, celle de l'instant étant, comme chacun sait, vivable mais exprimable nullement. Cette mystique réunissait celle de deux traditions, la française et la révolutionnaire où vous savez voir celle de l'ordre nouvellement révolu et de ses développements mystérieux.

J'avoue que ni mon milieu, ni mon éducation, ni Taine qui, dans sa formule de l'ancienne France, oublia un petit exposant, celui des cathédrales, ne m'inclinaient à y adjoindre la mystique de la tradition chrétienne. Et je ne suis pas le seul. L'aspect politique du problème a absorbé l'effort de ma génération. Faut-il le regretter ? Pour ma part, je ne le pense pas. Les gains spirituels de la séparation sont indiscutables : un éclaircissement de la politique française ; un accroissement des sincérités, de la sincérité chrétienne, de la sincérité anti-catholique, même anti-chrétienne et l'étiage de la sincérité sera toujours celui de la vertu ; un affrontement des deux mystiques (je vous dois de pouvoir préciser cette vue) et par conséquent leur mutuel renforcement.

Mais il faudrait, n'est-ce pas, que cette double croissance pût se continuer non pas parallèle, comme c'est le cas depuis la Renaissance, en s'affrontant, mais bien plutôt en confluant, par le concours des sèves et des poussées (...) Mon anticléricalisme n'y répugne point. Nul anticléricalisme n'y devrait répugner (...) Je considère comme nécessaire impérieusement de sauver la vertu, faite d'essor et de discipline, que l'Église représente pour tant d'âmes nobles. Faire rentrer cette mystique chrétienne dans la nouvelle tradition de la nouvelle culture française, voilà ce qui m'a, depuis quinze ans, paru l'opération éminente à tenter (...) Vous, votre socialisme à antennes délicates, qui s'est abstenu de l'action politique jusqu'à en être exaspérant, vous permet de mettre les deux mains à cette tâche, et l'épaule, voire le cœur et tout l'homme. Votre *Jeunesse* le dit, avec une gravité et une émotion qui ne peuvent se dédire.

Charles-Marie Garnier
(Lettre à Péguy, 22 août 1910,
dans *FACP* n° 83, avril 1961, p. 5-7.)

Notre jeunesse m'est arrivé pendant une absence. On l'avait si bien mis de côté que ce n'est qu'hier matin que par hasard, je l'ai aperçu. Je l'ai dévoré dans mon après-midi en roulant en wagon. Il y a dans vos 220 pages plus de pensée et de substance que dans toute une bibliothèque (...)
   Votre passage sur Bernard-Lazare et la Cour de Cassation est une petite merveille. J'ai été bien content aussi de ce que vous dites de Joseph Reinach. C'est juste et il fallait que ce fût dit. Par contre, je vous trouve injuste pour Dreyfus. Non seulement, selon le mot si comique et si profond de Bernard-Lazare, c'est déjà beaucoup qu'il soit innocent, mais c'est tout ce que nous avons le droit de lui demander. Exiger de lui par surcroît les vertus de l'héroïsme d'un fondateur de religion, ça c'est du romantisme. Plus il est qui il est, plus l'affaire prend de caractère, de sens et de grandeur.

Alexandre Millerand
(Lettre à Péguy, 16 septembre 1910,
dans *FACP* n° 179, 15 juillet 1972, p. 25-26.)

Souvent, ces mois derniers, perdu dans d'innombrables subtilités, j'ai repris vos livres ou plutôt vos chroniques ou plutôt vos discours. Et c'étaient comme de rudes gorgées d'enthousiasme.
   Dans un court portrait que je traçais de vous dernièrement et qui paraîtra sans doute, je vous montre ivre d'idées, ivre d'intelligence comme Rabelais était ivre de mots.
   Mais ce que j'aime en vous surtout, c'est que vous n'êtes pas seulement un professeur, qui se grise à expliquer les choses, mais

vous les montrez, vous les faites voir, et pour cela vous devenez
poète et visionnaire (...)

Pour ceux qui ont vingt ou vingt-cinq ans, l'affaire Dreyfus est
comme pour moi, sans doute, ce numéro du journal *L'Aurore* où la
lettre « J'accuse » était publiée et qu'on avait envoyé à tous les
instituteurs de France. Mes parents avaient à peine voulu la lire
tant elle les inquiétait. J'en avais couvert un de mes cahiers et
longtemps je l'ai gardée sous les yeux, sans la comprendre.

Mais maintenant je comprends. Je vois. Tout le passage où vous
montrez Dreyfus héros antipathique m'a paru extraordinairement
tragique. Je me rappelle qu'autrefois j'entendais dire par les
antidreyfusards : « Même ses partisans ne l'aiment pas. » Je vois, je
sais en lisant votre livre combien vous autres, ses partisans, vous
avez dû souffrir de cela.

Alain-Fournier
(Lettre à Péguy, 28 septembre 1910,
dans *Correspondance Péguy-Alain-Fournier*,
Fayard, 1990, p. 51-54.)

Si je n'avais été très fatigué et mal disposé pendant toutes ces
vacances, je vous aurais écrit pour vous féliciter de votre cahier sur
« la mystique et la politique ». Certains de vos jugements sont peut-
être un peu sévères ; mais vous n'avez rien écrit de meilleur que ce
cahier, ni de plus émouvant.

Henri Bergson
(Lettre à Péguy, 2 décembre 1910,
dans *FACP* n° 155, janvier 1970, p. 32.)

Votre philosophie du dreyfusisme, cette distinction entre la
mystique et la politique, mais cela va loin, très loin. Au fond il faut
le dire tout bas, mais enfin on peut le dire — au fond c'est toute
l'histoire de l'Église. Il y a là de quoi méditer éternellement et vous
avez une certaine façon d'imposer la méditation qui est souverainement bienfaisante.

Henri Bremond
(Lettre à Péguy, 2 décembre 1910,
dans *FACP* n° 171, 10 juillet 1971, p. 4.)

Vous devinez quelles ont été mes pensées en vous lisant. On aime dans un livre à se retrouver et à rencontrer, discernées et discriminées, les idées qui sont confuses en nous. Or, vous savez que, à votre suite et sous votre influence surtout, j'ai suivi la même évolution que vous devant les grands événements de notre temps et que, humblement, j'ai effectué, moi aussi, toutes vos étapes. Vous montrez d'ailleurs que ce n'est pas nous qui avons évolué devant les événements, mais plutôt les événements devant nous.

Nous, nous avons été les *mystiques* et nous nous reconnaissons dans votre chronique. Mais les *politiques* ne pourraient-ils pas s'y reconnaître aussi ? (...)

Si je lis d'abord *Notre jeunesse*, puis le *Mystère de la charité*, j'éprouve un peu comme si je lis d'abord dans Pascal le fragment I, article X (dans l'édition Havet), sur la règle des partis, puis après, « Joie, joie, pleurs de joie » ou « Je pensais à toi dans mon agonie ». Même plaisir et différencié de même façon.

Ernest Psichari
(Lettre à Péguy, début 1911,
dans *Lettres du Centurion,* Conard, 1933, p. 123-125.)

CONTRE

J'ai vu hier Barrès. Il n'a pas reçu le Cahier *(Notre jeunesse)*. Comment cela se fait-il ? Tu ferais bien de lui en renvoyer un. Il a trouvé l'autre jour (Paul) Bourget le lisant : mélange d'admiration et de haussements d'épaule pour le « sentimental ».

Charles Lucas de Pesloüan
(Lettre à Péguy, 16 juillet 1910,
dans *ACP* n° 45, janvier-mars 1989, p. 26.)

Je suis effrayé de voir à quel point Péguy sacrifie la réalité (qui ne semble nullement l'intéresser) aux convenances de développements oratoires. C'est ainsi qu'il place quelques belles phrases sur Hervé. Il lui a prêté quantité d'idées que celui-ci n'a jamais soupçonnées.

Ce défaut qu'ont tant de gens de lettres est également très marqué dans ce qu'il dit de Bernard-Lazare; en voulant en faire un Darmesteter, il l'a rendu méconnaissable; il n'y avait aucune analogie entre ces deux hommes. Bernard-Lazare avait l'imagination très peu active. Il n'a excellé que dans les analyses brèves; aucun grand travail ne put être mené à bien et fini par lui, tandis que Darmesteter était un homme de grande envergure scientifique. La vérité eût été moins oratoire peut-être, mais plus poignante (...)

Ce qui est dangereux pour Péguy, c'est qu'il met ce cahier chez les Ollendorff; les lecteurs se demanderont ce que veulent dire toutes ces allocutions décousues et si manifestement dédaigneuses de la réalité. Il pourrait arriver que ce volume détruisît toute la réputation que Péguy s'était acquise jusqu'ici. Il est bien plus facile de faire le plongeon que de se hisser sur le rocher de l'Acropole (...)

Je crois que Péguy a été fort mal inspiré quand il a voulu aborder la psychologie des dreyfusistes; qu'est-ce que c'est que cette grandeur qu'il s'attribue, tout en disant qu'il a été *berné*? Il est difficile d'accorder ces deux choses; il a appartenu à la catégorie des gens qui se sont jetés dans l'Affaire par légèreté d'esprit, désir de vivre des aventures, esprit de chimères; vous avez appartenu à la catégorie (peu nombreuse) des gens qui ont bien accompli un devoir douloureux; vous avez le beau lot. L'homme moral a toujours des retours pleins de tristesse sur lui-même. L'homme léger demeure content de lui-même et accuse Pierre, Paul, Jean de ses déconvenues. Je crois que Péguy n'a point pénétré ce qu'il y a de noble dans votre « cahier ».

Georges Sorel
(Lettre à Daniel Halévy, 22 juillet 1910,
dans *ACP* n° 12, octobre-décembre 1980, p. 208-209.)

Je suis à la lecture de *Notre jeunesse*. Vous y avez heureusement parlé du camp de Cercottes, et vous y avez merveilleusement dit que les tentes sous lesquelles nous avons dormi étaient, au lendemain de notre installation, nos maisons; tandis que les plus solides maisons de France, en pierre de taille, en granit même, ne sont jamais que des tentes pour les gens d'Israël — comme par exemple pour Bernard-Lazare.

Puisque vous savez cela, comment pouvez-vous donner les preuves d'une absolue « inaptitude à concevoir la question juive »,

comme vous le faites à partir de la page 178? Vous dites que
« parmi les protagonistes de nos hontes nationales il n'y a aucun
juif ». Et le suicidé de Vivilliers, le « baron » Jacques de Reinach?
Et Cornélius Herz? Et Arton? Et Dreyfus enfin, trois fois traître,
traître à la patrie française, traître à la « mystique » dreyfusiste,
traître à la « politique » dreyfusiste?

Mais la question n'est pas là : il ne s'agit pas de savoir si les Juifs
ont plus ou moins de qualités morales que les Français, s'ils sont
plus ou moins habiles, s'ils sont plus ou moins industrieux, s'ils sont
méprisables ou non, s'ils sont riches ou pauvres. Il s'agit de savoir
si, oui ou non, ils font partie de la communauté française, ou bien
s'ils appartiennent seulement à la communauté juive, à la nation
juive, qui est répandue dans tout l'univers civilisé (...)

Ils ne peuvent pas être Français, parce que, vous l'avez dit,
partout, dans nos maisons de pierre, ils sont sous la tente; ils sont
en voyage. Voilà pourquoi nous sommes antisémites — lorsque les
nomades tiennent l'État dans notre pays.

Georges Valois
(Lettre à Péguy, 27 juillet 1910,
dans Éric Cahm, *Péguy et le nationalisme français*,
Cahiers de l'Amitié Péguy, 1972, p. 100-101.)

Je veux vous écrire sans tarder pour vous remercier de votre beau
livre *Notre jeunesse* que je viens de lire tout d'un trait. Gide m'avait
envoyé votre *Charité de Jeanne d'Arc* et j'avais été étonné de trouver
un cœur si profondément et si délicatement chrétien chez un
homme que je considérais (sans le connaître d'ailleurs) comme
l'incarnation du dreyfusisme. Vos livres sont comme un torrent
impétueux dont il faut chercher la flèche au milieu de l'ouvrage
tandis que le début et la fin sont des espèces de contrecourants.
Toute cette partie du livre si belle, si éloquente, où vous parlez des
Juifs et de Bernard-Lazare a arraché de force mon admiration, bien
que je sois fort peu sympathique aux thèses et aux gens que vous
soutenez. Quel dommage de trouver un vrai Français, un soldat de
saint Louis (je pense à vos admirables pages sur le péché mortel)
combattant avec des gens qui ne sont pas de sa race contre la
sienne, avec des gens tout primitifs et imbus de la malédiction de

Dieu! Voulez-vous me permettre de m'expliquer à ce sujet en toute franchise? Un esprit vigoureux comme le vôtre préfère certainement la contradiction, la *réaction,* dont l'intensité est la mesure même de l'impression subie, à de fades louanges.

Tout d'abord y a-t-il forcément discontinuité et contradiction entre la *mystique* et la *politique,* et l'un n'est-il pas lié à l'autre comme l'acte à la puissance? Le combisme est lié au dreyfusisme comme les massacres de septembre aux principes de 89. Cela a la force d'un fait. C'est un bloc. C'est un seul individu organique qu'il est impossible de dissocier. Quant à la politique cléricale, à quel moment l'Église a-t-elle eu le dessus dans le gouvernement depuis cinq ou six siècles? La politique de l'Église, c'est l'héroïque et admirable Pie X qui la représente aujourd'hui, elle n'a rien à craindre d'aucune critique (...)

Vous m'étonnez profondément quand vous dites que le mouvement dreyfusiste fut un mouvement chrétien. Il n'y a rien de si opposé à l'esprit chrétien que la préférence du sens propre. Cela est protestant, c'est-à-dire abominable à tout cœur catholique. Il y a eu au XVIe siècle une affaire Dreyfus, c'est l'affaire Savonarole. Là le révolté était une sorte de saint, et le pape était un infâme. Et cependant aucun homme vraiment catholique ne jugera que Savonarole n'ait été justement condamné et exécuté. Si l'Évangile nous donne une forte leçon, c'est le devoir d'obéir aux maîtres même fâcheux, de ne pas juger de peur d'être jugés nous-mêmes — là où la question de foi n'est pas engagée.

Enfin je comprends difficilement que vous niiez l'action de la juiverie dans cette affaire. J'ai vécu dans tous les pays du monde et partout j'ai vu les journaux et l'opinion entre les mains des Juifs. J'étais à Jérusalem en décembre 1899 et j'ai vu au moment de la seconde condamnation (de Dreyfus) la rage de ces punaises à face humaine qui vivent en Palestine par centaines de mille des razzias que leurs congénères opèrent sur la chrétienté (...)

Le dreyfusisme me semble très certainement avoir été l'œuvre de ce qu'on appelle les intellectuels, de ceux qui sont en Chine les lettrés et dont on retrouve la main dans tous les troubles, de ceux que j'appellerai les « inadaptés ». Un homme qui a une tâche, un devoir précis, a le cœur satisfait, il est trop intéressé par son devoir immédiat pour lire les journaux, pour s'occuper de ce qui ne le regarde pas. Il sait que Dieu ne le jugera pas pour des choses dans lesquelles il n'a pas compétence ni élection et s'en remet aux gens qui ont autorité : à eux seuls est le devoir parce qu'à eux seuls la responsabilité.

Je vous demande pardon de m'être ainsi échauffé, mais vos livres me donnent une haute opinion de vous, je vous aime beaucoup, et je voudrais mieux savoir votre position actuelle. Car si vous êtes chrétien, vous êtes ami de l'ordre; si vous aimez l'ordre, vous reconnaissez l'autorité : et quelle autorité y a-t-il, si vous la jugez comme ayant vous-même autorité sur elle?

Paul Claudel
(Lettre à Péguy, 10 août 1910,
dans Henri de Lubac et Jean Bastaire, *Claudel et Péguy*,
Aubier, 1974, p. 131-133.)

Je me fais lire en ce moment *Notre jeunesse*, de Péguy. Je ne peux pas tout comprendre, pour deux raisons : 1) je ne suis pas au courant des faits auxquels il fait allusion; 2) l'emploi du mot mystique, en des sens très divers, me gêne un peu.

Mais il y a une chose que je crois avoir bien comprise et elle m'a affligé à cause de la haute estime que j'ai de l'intelligence et du caractère de M. Péguy. Il accuse nettement l'Église de détourner l'attention vers le modernisme intellectuel pour cacher le modernisme de la charité et se dispenser ainsi de faire les frais de la révolution industrielle nécessaire. De plus l'Église, dans cette affaire, serait d'accord avec les radicaux (...) Je m'étonne que M. Péguy n'ait pas vu que l'Église n'a pas à créer directement des formes politiques et des états sociaux, mais qu'elle a été chargée de sanctifier et de sauver les âmes dans tous les états politiques et conditions sociales (...)

Ce qu'il eût été bon de faire ressortir, c'est : 1) dans l'état de désordre où s'agite la société moderne, l'Église a trouvé toujours, sinon un remède suffisant, du moins un palliatif considérable à opposer au mal. Elle n'a pas été moins féconde que par le passé en institutions en faveur des pauvres; 2) l'encyclique *Rerum novarum*, de Léon XIII, la dégage nettement de tout accord avec le bourgeoisisme.

Je prie M. Péguy de prendre ces réflexions en bonne part comme venant d'un homme qui l'aime sans le connaître et l'aime beaucoup, ce qu'il lui témoigne en priant pour lui, afin qu'il remplisse entièrement la noble mission que Dieu lui a confiée.

Je le remercie de m'avoir fait penser aux malheurs des Juifs de Russie et d'ailleurs. Trop occupé des souffrances de tant de religieux et de religieuses victimes du *combisme,* je ne pensais guère aux Juifs. Ils sont pourtant, eux aussi, notre prochain. Je m'en souviendrai désormais un peu plus.

Père Exupère, capucin
(Lettre à Joseph Lotte, 26 mai 1914,
dans *FACP* n° 45, mai 1955, p. 8-9.)

BIBLIOGRAPHIE

Pour une bibliographie quasi exhaustive, il faut se reporter à Pia Vergine, *Studi su Charles Péguy, Bibliografia critica ed analitica (1893-1978)*, Lecce, Milella, 1982, 2 vol., 1110 p. Jean Bastaire a donné une bibliographie plus restreinte, rassemblant et amplifiant les bibliographies antérieures, dans le Cahier de l'Herne consacré à Péguy en 1977.

ŒUVRES DE PÉGUY

1) *Cahiers de la Quinzaine*

Toutes les œuvres de Péguy publiées de son vivant, sauf quelques poèmes, ont paru dans les *Cahiers de la Quinzaine*. Sont disponibles en librairie la série des pré-cahiers (1897-1899) et les trois premières séries (1900-1902), regroupées en onze volumes et reproduites par Slatkine Reprints, diffusion Champion.

2) *Œuvres complètes*

Publiées de 1916 à 1955 chez Gallimard, la collection dite des *Œuvres complètes,* comportant vingt volumes in-octavo, a rendu de grands services, mais se trouve déficiente pour bon nombre de pages en prose et en vers et pour son classement des textes.

La Bibliothèque de la Pléiade, toujours chez Gallimard, a progressivement pallié ces lacunes. Elle offre à présent les *Œuvres poétiques complètes* en un volume (1975) et, sous la responsabilité de Robert Burac, les *Œuvres en prose complètes* en trois volumes (1987, 1988 et 1992).

3) *Éditions courantes*

Dans la collection blanche, vingt-trois volumes ont paru chez Gallimard, offrant l'essentiel des œuvres en prose et en vers.

En édition de poche, toujours chez Gallimard, la collection « Poésie » reproduit *Les Tapisseries* (1972) et *Le Porche du mystère de la deuxième vertu* (1986), la collection « Folio » *Notre jeunesse* et *De la raison* (1993), ainsi que *Péguy tel qu'on l'ignore*, anthologie de Jean Bastaire (1993).

Deux volumes édités par les Cahiers de l'Amitié Charles Péguy, diffusion Centre Charles Péguy, 11, rue du Tabour, 45000 Orléans, donnent les *Notes politiques et sociales* présentées par André Boisserie (1957) et les *Œuvres posthumes de Charles Péguy*, fragments présentés par Jacques Viard (1969).

4) *Éditions critiques*

Il n'en existe que trois :
- *Le Mystère de la charité de Jeanne d'Arc*, avec deux actes inédits, éd. critique établie par Albert Béguin, Club du Meilleur Livre, 1956.
- *La ballade du cœur*, éd. critique établie par Julie Sabiani, Klincksieck, 1973.
- *De Jean Coste*, éd. critique établie par Anne Roche, Klincksieck, 1975.

5) *Correspondance*

La source principale est constituée par les *Feuillets de l'Amitié Charles Péguy* (1948-1977) et par le bulletin *L'Amitié Charles Péguy* qui, depuis 1978, leur fait suite (chez F. Gerbod, 12, rue Notre-Dame-des-Champs, 75006 Paris). On y trouve plus de trois mille lettres de Péguy ou adressées à Péguy.

On y ajoutera les volumes suivants :
- *Le Péguy que j'ai connu*, par Maurice Reclus, Hachette, 1951 (lettres à Geneviève Favre).
- *Lettres et entretiens*, présentés par Marcel Péguy, Éd. de Paris, 1954 (lettres à Louis Baillet et à Joseph Lotte).
- *Pour l'honneur de l'esprit*, introduction et notes par Auguste Martin, Albin Michel, 1973 (lettres à Romain Rolland).
- *Claudel et Péguy*, par Henri de Lubac et Jean Bastaire, Aubier, 1974.
- *Correspondance de Charles Péguy et Louis Boitier*, présentation et

commentaire de Jacques Birnberg, Cahiers de l'Amitié Péguy, 1976.
- *Correspondance de Charles Péguy et Pierre Marcel*, présentation et notes par Julie Sabiani, Cahiers de l'Amitié Péguy, 1980.
- *Correspondance de Charles Péguy et Alain-Fournier*, présentation et notes par Yves Rey-Herme, Fayard (nouvelle édition, 1990).

6) *Enregistrements sonores*
- *Charles Péguy*, choix de textes par Pierre Sipriot, lus par Madeleine Renaud, Claude Nollier, Alain Cuny, Piere Vaneck, Édition Lucien Adès, 1973 (disque du centenaire).
- *Dit Dieu*, textes de Charles Péguy choisis par Robert Marcy, lus par Denise Bosc et Robert Marcy, Édition AUDIVIS, 1983, AV 5371 (cassette donnant des extraits du *Porche* et des *Saints Innocents*).

ÉTUDES SUR PÉGUY

Elles sont fort nombreuses. Nous nous contenterons d'indiquer les principaux titres parus depuis une trentaine d'années, avec un rappel d'essais plus anciens.

1) *Ouvrages d'initiation*
- *Péguy*, par Bernard Guyon, Hatier, coll. « Connaissance des Lettres », 1960, nouvelle édition revue 1973.
- *Péguy*, par Yves Rey-Herme, Bordas, coll. « Présence littéraire », 1973.
- *Péguy*, par Simone Fraisse, Seuil, coll. « Écrivains de toujours », 1979.

2) *Principales études*
- *Saint-John Perse et quelques devanciers, études sur le poème en prose,* par Monique Parent, Klincksieck, 1960 (étude sur la phrase poétique de Péguy dans le *Porche*).
- *La gloire et la croix,* tome II : *Styles,* par Hans Urs von Balthasar, 1962, traduction R. Givord et Hélène Bourboulon, Aubier 1972.
- *Introduction aux « Mystères » de Péguy,* par Jean Onimus, Cahiers de l'Amitié Péguy, 1962.
- *La religion de Péguy,* par Pie Duployé, Klincksieck, 1965.

- *L'univers féminin dans l'œuvre de Péguy*, par Robert Vigneault, Desclée de Brouwer, 1967.
- *Péguy entre Jaurès, Bergson et l'Église*, par André Robinet, Seghers, 1968 (réimprimé sous le titre *Métaphysique et politique selon Péguy*).
- *Philosophie de l'art littéraire et socialisme selon Péguy*, par Jacques Viard, Klincksieck, 1969.
- *Péguy et Israël*, par Lazare Prajs, Nizet, 1970.
- *Péguy et le nationalisme français*, par Éric Cahm, Cahiers de l'Amitié Péguy, 1972.
- *Péguy soldai ae ta vérité*, suivi de *Péguy aujourd'hui*, par Roger Secrétain, Perrin, 1972.
- *Proust et Péguy, des affinités méconnues*, par Jacques Viard, University of London, The Athlone Press, 1972.
- *Péguy et le monde antique*, par Simone Fraisse, Colin, 1973.
- *Les critiques de notre temps et Péguy*, par Simone Fraisse, Garnier, 1973.
- *Charles Péguy*, par Marie-Clotilde Hubert, Bibliothèque nationale, 1974 (catalogue de l'exposition du centenaire).
- *Claudel et Péguy*, par Henri de Lubac et Jean Bastaire, Aubier, 1974.
- *Péguy devant Dieu*, par Bernard Guyon, Desclée de Brouwer, 1974.
- *Péguy et l'Allemagne*, par Raymond Winling, Université de Lille III et Champion, 1975.
- *Péguy et Renan*, par Raymond Winling, Université de Lille III et Champion, 1975.
- *Péguy l'insurgé*, par Jean Bastaire, Payot, 1975.
- *Péguy et le Moyen Âge*, par Simone Fraisse, Champion, 1978.
- *Ipotesi e proposte esistenziali. Introduzione a Péguy*, par Angelo Prontera, Lecce, Milella, 1980.
- *Écriture et histoire dans l'œuvre de Péguy*, par Françoise Gerbod, Université de Lille III et Champion, 1981.
- *Charles Péguy*, par Henri Guillemin, Seuil, 1981.
- *Péguy entre l'ordre et la révolution*, par Géraldi Leroy, Presses de la Fondation Nationale des Sciences Politiques, 1981.
- *Péguy en son temps*, par Géraldi Leroy et Julie Sabiani, Orléans, Centre Charles Péguy, 1982.
- *Péguy et ses Cahiers de la Quinzaine*, par Frantisek Laichter, Maison des Sciences de l'Homme, 1985.
- *Catalogue des manuscrits de Charles Péguy*, par Julie Sabiani, Orléans, Centre Charles Péguy, 1987.

- *Colère de Péguy*, par Jean-Michel Rey, Hachette, 1987.
- *Péguy e la cultura del popolo*, par Jean Bastaire, Lecce, Milella, 1987.
- *Éros de Péguy*, par Roger Dadoun, Presses Universitaires de France, 1988.
- *Péguy et la terre*, par Simone Fraisse, Éd. Le Sang de la Terre, 1988.
- *La Filosofia come metodo. Libertà e pluralità in Péguy*, par Angelo Prontera, Lecce, Milella, 1988.
- *Charles Péguy, l'espérance d'un salut universel*, par Thierry Dejond, Éd. Culture et Vérité, Diffusion Brépols, 1989.
- *Donna, amore e rivoluzione. Femminismo e socialismo da G. Sand a Péguy*, par Julie Sabiani, Lecce, Milella, 1991.
- *Péguy, filosofia e politica*, par Angelo Prontera, Lecce, Milella, 1991.
- *Péguy l'inchrétien*, par Jean Bastaire, Desclée, 1991.
- *Le mécontemporain*, par Alain Finkielkraut, Gallimard, 1992.
- *Charles Péguy, biographie*, par Robert Burac, Laffont, 1993.
- *Péguy, biographie*, par Marc Tardieu, François Bourin, 1993.

3) *Numéros spéciaux et volumes collectifs*
- *Péguy reconnu*, n° spécial de la revue *Esprit*, août-septembre 1964.
- *Actes du colloque international d'Orléans 1964*, Cahiers de l'Amitié Péguy, 1966.
- *L'esprit républicain*, colloque d'Orléans 1970, Klincksieck, 1972.
- *Littérature et société*, mélanges offerts à Bernard Guyon, Desclée de Brouwer, 1973.
- *Péguy*, n° spécial de la *Revue d'Histoire Littéraire de la France*, mars-juin 1973.
- *Charles Péguy et la critique littéraire*, n° spécial de *l'Australian Journal of French Studies*, 1973, vol. X, n° 1.
- *Rencontres avec Péguy*, colloque de Nice 1973, Desclée de Brouwer, 1975.
- *Péguy mis à jour*, colloque de Montréal 1973, Québec, Presses de l'Université Laval, 1976.
- *Péguy*, Cahier de l'Herne, 1977.
- *Péguy écrivain*, colloque d'Orléans 1973, Klincksieck, 1978.
- *Péguy vivant*, colloque international de Lecce 1977, Lecce, Milella, 1978.
- *Charles Péguy chez les protestants*, n° spécial de la revue *Foi et Vie*, mars 1982.

- *Péguy et l'espérance,* n° spécial de la revue *Vives flammes,* Venasque, Éd. du Carmel, 1982, n° 137.
- *Péguy homme du dialogue,* colloque en Sorbonne 1983, Cahiers de l'Amitié Péguy, 1986.
- *La réception de Charles Péguy en France et à l'étranger,* colloque d'Orléans 1988, Orléans, Centre Charles Péguy, 1991.
- *Charles Péguy, poeta, educatore, teologo,* colloque 1989, Verona, Éd. Il Segno, 1991.

4) *Revue des Lettres Modernes, série « Charles Péguy »*
Sous la direction de Simone Fraisse, la *Revue des Lettres Modernes,* éditée par M.-J. Minard, publie une série de numéros sur Péguy dont chacun est consacré à un thème :
- *Polémique et théologie. Le « Laudet »* (1980).
- *Les « Cahiers de la Quinzaine »* (1983).
- *Péguy romantique malgré lui* (1985).
- *Les Dialogues de l'histoire* (1988).
- *L'écrivain* (1990).
- *« Victor-Marie comte Hugo »* (1993).

5) *Essais plus anciens*
- *Avec Charles Péguy, de la Lorraine à la Marne,* par Victor Boudon, Hachette, 1916 (édition revue et augmentée sous le titre *Mon lieutenant Charles Péguy,* Albin Michel, 1964).
- *Notre cher Péguy,* par Jérôme et Jean Tharaud, Plon, 2 vol., 1926.
- *Pour les fidèles de Péguy,* par Jérôme et Jean Tharaud, L'Artisan du Livre, « Cahiers de la Quinzaine », nouvelle série, XVIII-12, 1927 (édition augmentée, Saint-Étienne, Éd. Dumas, 1949).
- *La pensée de Charles Péguy,* par Emmanuel Mounier, Marcel Péguy et Georges Izard, Plon, coll. « Le roseau d'or », 1931.
- *Péguy et les Cahiers de la Quinzaine,* par Daniel Halévy, Grasset, 1941 (réimprimé en livre de poche, coll. « Pluriel », 1979, préface de Robert Debré, introduction et notes d'Éric Cahm).
- *Le destin de Charles Péguy,* par Marcel Péguy, Perrin, 1941.
- *La prière de Péguy,* par Albert Béguin, Neuchâtel, Éd. de la Baconnière, « Cahiers du Rhône », Bleu III, 1942.
- *Jeunesse de Péguy,* par A. Mabille de Poncheville, Éd. Alsatia, 1943.
- *Connaissance de Péguy,* par Jean Delaporte, Plon, 2 vol., 1944 (refondu sous le titre *Péguy dans son temps et dans le nôtre,* coll. 10/18, 1967).

– *Péguy,* par Romain Rolland, Albin Michel, 2 vol., 1944 (réédité avec une préface d'Hubert Juin et une postface d'Henri Guillemin, Édito-Service, Suisse, 1972).
– *Le prophète Péguy,* par André Rousseaux, Albin Michel, 2 vol., 1946.
– *La poétique de Péguy,* par Albert Chabanon, Robert Laffont, 1947.
– *L'art de Péguy,* par Bernard Guyon, Cahiers de l'Amitié Péguy, 1948.
– *L'Ève de Péguy,* par Albert Béguin, Cahiers de l'Amitié Péguy, 1948 (réimprimé au Seuil, 1955).
– *Les grandes amitiés,* par Raïssa Maritain, Desclée de Brouwer, 1949.
– *Vie et mort de Péguy,* par René Johannet, Flammarion, 1950.
– *Le Péguy que j'ai connu,* par Maurice Reclus, Hachette, 1951.
– *Incarnation, essai sur la pensée de Péguy,* par Jean Onimus, Cahiers de l'Amitié Péguy, 1952.
– *Péguy socialiste,* par Félicien Challaye, Amiot-Dumont, 1954.
– *Le vocabulaire, la syntaxe et le style des poèmes réguliers de Péguy,* par Joseph Barbier, Berger-Levrault, 1957.
– *Péguy et le mystère de l'histoire,* par Jean Onimus, Cahiers de l'Amitié Péguy, 1958.
– *Expériences de ma vie : Péguy,* par Jules Isaac, Calmann-Lévy, 1959.

6) *Documentation générale*

Depuis 1946 existe une association *L'Amitié Charles Péguy,* fondée par Auguste Martin. Elle a publié un bulletin, les *Feuillets* (216 numéros de 1948 à 1977). En 1978, les *Feuillets* ont fait place à une revue trimestrielle, *L'Amitié Charles Péguy,* où l'on trouve des inédits, des témoignages, des études critiques, des comptes rendus de livres, une bibliographie annuelle et toutes les informations sur l'actualité péguyste (chez Françoise Gerbod, 12, rue Notre-Dame-des-Champs, 75006 Paris).

A Orléans, un Centre Charles Péguy a été ouvert en 1960 par la Municipalité. A la fois musée et bibliothèque, il possède presque tous les manuscrits de Péguy et toutes les archives des *Cahiers de la Quinzaine.* A ses huit mille volumes s'ajoutent une iconographie, des périodiques et des microfilms. Ses salles de travail sont ouvertes du lundi au vendredi (11, rue du Tabour, 45000 Orléans, tél. 38-53-20-23).

NOTES

De la raison

Page 65.

1. *De la raison* est placé en « avertissement » à un volume de Jean Jaurès, *Études socialistes* (CQ, III-4, 5 décembre 1901).

Page 66.

1. « La discipline fait la force principale des armées » : formule classique du livret d'instruction militaire.

Page 67.

1. Le culte de la déesse Raison fut instauré par les hébertistes, notamment Chaumette, durant la Révolution française. Le 10 novembre 1793, la Commune de Paris organisa une cérémonie à Notre-Dame où la déesse Raison fut incarnée par une actrice, Mlle Aubry. Robespierre désavoua cette entreprise contraire à sa conception du culte de l'Être Suprême.

2. « La prière de Renan sur l'Acropole » parut dans la *Revue des Deux Mondes* le 1er décembre 1876. Elle s'inspire de deux séjours que Renan fit en Grèce en mars et mai 1865. Péguy l'a reproduite dans le cahier *Le monument de Renan* (CQ, V-3, 10 novembre 1903).

Page 70.

1. Renan exprime ce rêve dans un ouvrage juvénile, *L'Avenir de la science* (1848-1849), et dans un recueil plus mûr, *Dialogues et fragments philosophiques* (1876). Péguy cite des extraits de ces deux ouvrages dans *Zangwill* (CQ, VI-3, 25 octobre 1904).

2. Un des premiers textes publiés par Péguy, *Marcel premier*

dialogue de la cité harmonieuse (Librairie Georges Bellais, juin 1898), développe cette conception.

Page 74.

1. Péguy fait écho à la première phrase de l'évangile selon saint Jean : « Au commencement était le Verbe. »

Page 76.

1. Péguy vise un article d'Urbain Gohier paru dans *L'Aurore* du 28 octobre 1901. Intitulé « Jaurès et Dieu », l'article attaquait la thèse de Jaurès, *De la réalité du monde sensible*, publiée en 1891 chez Félix Alcan.

Page 77.

1. Henri marquis de Rochefort-Luçay, dit Henri Rochefort (1831-1913), fut un homme politique et surtout un virulent pamphlétaire. Il fut successivement contre le Second Empire, pour la Commune, pour le général Boulanger, contre le dreyfusisme et pour le nationalisme intégral.

Page 84.

1. Jaurès commence de publier en 1901 une *Histoire socialiste de la Révolution française* que Péguy critique dans *Casse-cou* (CQ, II-7, 2 mars 1901) : « L'histoire n'est pas socialiste. Elle est historique. » (OEPC, I, 1987, p. 713).

Page 87.

1. Dans la même série où fut publié *De la raison*, Péguy a consacré plusieurs cahiers aux Universités Populaires : Charles Guieysse, *Les Universités Populaires et le mouvement ouvrier* (CQ, III-2, 17 octobre 1901), *Les Universités Populaires. Paris et banlieue* (CQ, III-10, 27 février 1902), *Les Universités Populaires. Départements* (CQ, III-20, 22 juillet 1902). Il devait revenir plus tard sur ce problème dans ses *Notes pour une thèse* (OEPC, II, 1988, p. 1146-1161).

Notre jeunesse

Page 95.

1. *Mes cahiers rouges*, de Maxime Vuillaume, regroupent en dix cahiers les souvenirs de l'auteur sur la Commune de 1871. Leur parution s'échelonne du 4 février 1908 au 9 juin 1914. Les cahiers 1, 2, 3, 4, 5 et 7 ont été repris, avec variantes et suppressions, dans un volume publié par Ollendorff en 1909 et réédité par Albin Michel en 1971.

Page 98.

1. *Panem quotidianum :* quatrième demande de la prière chrétienne « Pater noster » (« Panem quotidianum da nobis hodie »).

Page 114.

1. Jean Variot (1881-1962), journaliste et écrivain d'*Action française*. Avec Georges Sorel, il fonde en 1911 le périodique *l'Indépendance*. En 1935, il publie chez Gallimard les *Propos de Georges Sorel*. Sous l'Occupation, il s'active à Paris dans les milieux collaborationnistes où il présente Péguy comme un grand poète et un mauvais politique.

Page 118.

1. Date de la première des grandes lois laïques de la réforme scolaire instaurée par Jules Ferry.

Page 124.

1. Allusion au célèbre poème de Victor Hugo, *l'Expiation*, publié en 1853 dans *Les Châtiments*.

Page 141.

1. *De la situation faite à l'histoire et à la sociologie dans la philosophie générale du monde moderne.* Cette indication rappelle un ouvrage publié par Péguy aux *Cahiers* le 4 novembre 1906 sous le titre *De la situation faite à l'histoire et à la sociologie dans les temps modernes* (CQ, VIII-3) et la thèse que Péguy avait en projet en 1908-1909 et dont il a laissé les notes préparatoires sous le titre *De la situation faite à l'histoire dans la philosophie générale du monde moderne* (OEPC, II, 1988, p. 1053-1267).

Page 143.

1. Le jeudi était le jour où amis et sympathisants des *Cahiers* se retrouvaient à la revue, 8, rue de la Sorbonne, pour discuter de l'actualité. On y entendait souvent le philosophe Georges Sorel. Le jeudi, jour de congé scolaire, était propice à la présence d'enseignants.

2. *C'est le niveau des vies.* Expression empruntée à la conclusion d'*Apologie pour notre passé*, l'ouvrage de Daniel Halévy que Péguy réfute.

Page 145.

1. Titre d'un célèbre ouvrage de la Comtesse de Ségur, paru en 1859-1860 dans la *Semaine des enfants* et en 1860 dans un volume de la Bibliothèque Rose, chez Hachette.

Page 154.

1. Barrès écrit par exemple, dans son article sur le *Mystère de la charité de Jeanne d'Arc* publié le 28 février 1910 dans *l'Écho de Paris* : « Nous avons vu dans le dreyfusisme la stérilité des élans religieux les plus sincères, quand ils ne sont dominés par aucune discipline traditionnelle : leur force ne vaut que pour détruire et bientôt se disperser en fumée. »

Page 155.

1. Jules Isaac (1877-1963), historien, compagnon de Péguy dès leurs années d'études et fidèle dreyfusiste à ses côtés. Il lui a consacré un important volume de souvenirs, *Expériences de ma vie. Péguy* (1959).

Page 159

1. Régiment où le jeune Péguy s'est engagé par devancement d'appel en novembre 1892, à Orléans, pour accomplir son année de service militaire.

Page 162.

1. Bernard-Lazare (1865-1903), de son vrai nom Lazare Bernard, critique littéraire, écrivain et journaliste de tendance anarchiste. Un des tout premiers, il prit la défense de Dreyfus avec *Une erreur judiciaire, la vérité sur l'affaire Dreyfus* (1896). Il fut un des principaux soutiens des *Cahiers de la Quinzaine* de Péguy, où il publia plusieurs textes contre l'antisémitisme en Europe. Cf. « L'amitié de Péguy et de Bernard-Lazare », par Nelly Wilson (ACP, n° 13, janvier-mars 1981), *Correspondance Péguy-Bernard-Lazare*, présentée par Nelly Wilson (ACP, n° 14, avril-juin 1981), *Bernard-Lazare*, par Nelly Wilson (Albin Michel, 1985), et *Bernard-Lazare, de l'anarchiste au prophète,* par Jean-Denis Bredin (Éd. de Fallois, 1992).

2. James Darmesteter (1849-1894), professeur au Collège de France, spécialiste des langues et des religions de la Perse ancienne, auteur d'un ouvrage sur les *Prophètes d'Israël* (1892).

3. Ce texte, commencé en septembre 1903 au lendemain de la mort de Bernard-Lazare, est resté inachevé. On peut le lire dans OEPC, I, 1987, p. 1207-1245.

Page 166.

1. « Un Juif », par Édouard Drumont (*La Libre Parole*, 5 septembre 1903) : « Nous ne pouvons souhaiter qu'une chose, c'est que les chrétiens se fassent de la grandeur et des devoirs du nom de chrétien l'idée que Bernard-Lazare se faisait de la grandeur et des

devoirs du nom de Juif. » Édouard Drumont (1844-1917), auteur
d'un pamphlet monumental, *La France juive* (1886), anima pendant
de longues années *La Libre Parole,* journal nationaliste et antisémite.

Page 167.

1. *Génération et corruption.* Titre d'un ouvrage d'Aristote.

2. Baudelaire, *Les Fleurs du Mal,* « Le cygne ».

3. Salomon Reinach (1858-1931), archéologue et philologue,
dreyfusard de la première heure, cofondateur de la Ligue des droits
de l'homme.

Page 168.

1. Extrait du compte rendu sténographique du *Procès Zola*
(Stock, 1898, tome I, p. 33 et 34).

2. Ludovic Halévy (1834-1908), romancier et auteur, avec Henri
Meilhac, de livrets d'opérettes célèbres. C'était le père de Daniel
Halévy.

3. Fernand Labori (1860-1917), un des avocats de Dreyfus et de
Zola.

Page 170.

1. Georges Sorel (1847-1922), polytechnicien, ingénieur des
ponts et chaussées et philosophe politique. Entre 1901 et 1912, il a
collaboré à plusieurs *Cahiers de la Quinzaine* et animé les réunions du
jeudi à la boutique des *Cahiers.* Maître à penser du syndicalisme
révolutionnaire, il a influencé des hommes aussi différents que
Lénine et Mussolini. Il est l'auteur de nombreux articles rassemblés
en volume : *L'avenir socialiste des syndicats* (1898), *Les réflexions sur la
violence* (1908), *La révolution dreyfusienne* (1909), *Matériaux d'une théorie
du prolétariat* (1919).

Page 172.

1. Allusion aux pourparlers qui aboutirent à la création du
quotidien *L'Humanité,* en avril 1904, sous la direction de Jaurès.

Page 173.

1. Louis Louis-Dreyfus (1867-1940), banquier, armateur, action-
naire de *L'Humanité,* député socialiste de la Lozère (1905-1910).

Page 175.

1. Bernard-Lazare a publié dans les *Cahiers de la Quinzaine* un
volume sur *l'Oppression des Juifs dans l'Europe Centrale. Les Juifs en
Roumanie* (CQ, III-8, 13 février 1902)

Page 176.

1. Leconte de Lisle, *Poèmes antiques*, « Dies irae ».

2. *La foire sur la place* et *Dans la maison* sont les titres de deux épisodes de *Jean-Christophe*, la fresque de Romain Rolland publiée aux *Cahiers* (CQ, IX-13 et 14, 22 et 29 mars 1908, CQ, X-9 et 10, 21 et 28 février 1909).

Page 180.

1. Jean Deck, pseudonyme de Jean Poirot (1873-1924). Il publie aux *Cahiers* le 16 août 1902 *Pour la Finlande, mémoire et documents* (CQ, III-21). Le cahier se termine par un texte de Bernard-Lazare, *La loi et les congrégations*.

Page 182.

1. Georges Picquart (1854-1914). Officier au service des renseignements de l'armée, il acquiert la conviction de l'innocence de Dreyfus et se voit pour cela déplacé. Nommé général après la révision du procès Dreyfus en 1906, il devient la même année ministre de la Guerre dans le cabinet Clemenceau. Peu avant, il a publié aux *Cahiers* un volume, *De la situation faite à la défense militaire de la France* (CQ, VII-13, 11 mars 1906).

Page 188.

1. La Cour de Cassation s'était appuyée sur le paragraphe final de l'article 445 du Code d'instruction criminelle, parce que rien ne subsistait de l'accusation portée contre Dreyfus, pour annuler, le 12 juillet 1906, le jugement du conseil de guerre de Rennes, formulé en août 1899. L'annulation avait été prononcée sans renvoi devant un nouveau conseil de guerre. Les nationalistes avaient crié à la violation du droit. Bernard-Lazare pensait comme eux.

Page 191.

1. L'enterrement de Bernard-Lazare eut lieu le 4 septembre 1903. Péguy y assistait avec André Bourgeois, l'administrateur des *Cahiers*, pour bien marquer le rôle unique qu'avait joué le défunt comme inspirateur de la publication.

Page 192.

1. De deux cents à quatre cents personnes, selon les estimations de la police qui surveillait le parcours.

Page 195.

1. Un cancer à l'intestin. Bernard-Lazare avait un frère cadet, Armand, qui était chirurgien.

2. *Morientium ac mortuorum :* « Des mourants et des morts. »

Page 197.

1. Victor Hugo, *La légende des siècles*, « La conscience ».

2. Edmond-Maurice Lévy (1878-1971), ami de Péguy, bibliothécaire à la Sorbonne.

3. Cercottes, camp militaire près d'Orléans, où Péguy accomplit une partie de ses périodes d'entraînement comme officier de réserve.

4. *Nombres,* XXIV, 5. C'est la première phrase de la prière quotidienne des Juifs.

5. Claude Casimir-Perier (1880-1915), fils d'un président de la République, ami de Péguy. Lieutenant de réserve comme lui au 276ᵉ régiment d'infanterie, il a effectué au mois de mai 1909, avec le gérant des *Cahiers*, une période militaire au camp de Cercottes.

Page 198.

1. A la suite d'une première crise dans sa maladie, début 1903, Bernard-Lazare était parti se reposer à Grasse, Nice, Marseille, Avignon et Nîmes.

Page 199.

1. Romain Rolland, *Vie de Beethoven* (CQ, IV-10, 27 janvier 1903).

Page 204.

1. Dans sa trilogie dramatique de 1897, *Jeanne d'Arc,* Péguy avait fait dire à Raoul de Gaucourt, au sujet de Jeanne : « C'est une femme qui ne prend son parti de rien » (*Les batailles,* 2ᵉ partie, acte I, *Œuvres poétiques complètes,* Pléiade, 1957, p. 157).

Page 207.

1. Péguy reproche à Dreyfus et à sa famille d'avoir confié à Jaurès la reprise de l'Affaire. Il avait traité de cette circonstance dans *Reprise politique parlementaire* (CQ, IV-20, 16 juin 1903).

Page 208.

1. Gustave Hervé (1871-1944), professeur d'histoire révoqué pour son antimilitarisme, fondateur du journal *La Guerre sociale*, auteur en 1905 de *Leur Patrie.* Au début de la guerre de 1914, il se rallie à l'Union sacrée et intitule son journal *La Victoire.* En 1927, il fonde le parti socialiste français, inspiré du fascisme. Sous l'Occupation, on le retrouve dans les milieux de la collaboration pétainiste.

Page 209.

1. Bernard-Lazare, *La loi et les congrégations* (CQ, III-21, 16 août 1902).

Page 215.

1. Titre de trois cahiers publiés par Edmond Bernus (1871-1954), *Polonais et Prussiens, de la résistance du peuple polonais aux exactions de la germanisation prussienne* (CQ, VIII-10, 12, 14, 20 janvier, 17 février et 17 mars 1907).

2. C'est-à-dire *La loi et les congrégations* (CQ, III-21) dans *Notre jeunesse* (XI-12).

Page 217.

1. Sans doute Pierre Quillard (1864-1912), poète et publiciste, dreyfusiste, auteur d'un cahier *Pour l'Arménie* (CQ, III-19, 24 juin 1902).

Page 220.

1. « La morale des producteurs » est le titre du dernier chapitre des *Réflexions sur la violence,* de Georges Sorel, dont une deuxième édition venait de paraître. En 1909, dans *A nos amis à nos abonnés,* Péguy avait déjà rendu hommage à « notre maître M. Sorel » et à son ouvrage sur *L'avenir socialiste des syndicats* paru en 1898 (OEPC, tome II, 1988, p. 1304).

Page 226.

1. Péguy pense à certaines réactions hostiles qui lui sont venues de catholiques comme Jacques Maritain, converti de fraîche date, ou Georges Dumesnil, directeur de *l'Amitié de France,* au moment de la parution du *Mystère de la charité de Jeanne d'Arc,* six mois plus tôt.

Page 235.

1. Sur Gustave Hervé, cf. note plus haut. Déjà condamné à la prison en 1906 et 1907, ce socialiste antimilitariste vient encore de l'être — à quatre ans — le 23 février 1910 pour avoir tenté d'arracher Liabeuf, meurtrier d'un agent de police, à l'échafaud.

Page 238.

1. *Tout a changé de face, depuis que sur ces bords.* Vers emprunté à Racine, dans *Phèdre* (acte I, sc. I, v. 34-35).

Page 244.

1. *Hinterland :* arrière-pays, zone d'influence.

Page 246.

1. Léon Gérault-Richard (1860-1911), rédacteur en chef de *La Petite République*, journal de Jaurès, de 1897 à 1905. A la fondation de la SFIO, en 1905, il s'éloigne du nouveau parti socialiste, en particulier à cause de l'antipatriotisme de Gustave Hervé Devenu directeur de *Paris-Journal* en 1908, et réélu député de la Guadeloupe en 1910, il vient d'être grossièrement attaqué à la première page de *L'Humanité* par André Morizet, dans quatre articles intitulés « Un roman colonial » (3, 5, 6 et 11 juin 1910).

Page 249.

1. Gustave Hervé était né en Bretagne. Agrégé d'histoire en 1897 et nommé professeur au lycée de Sens en 1899, il avait été révoqué en décembre 1901 à cause d'une série d'articles antimilitaristes qu'il avait donnés au *Travailleur socialiste de l'Yonne* et au *Pioupiou de l'Yonne*. Péguy s'était fait l'écho de l'affaire dans plusieurs cahiers où il avait reproduit intégralement les articles d'Hervé sous le titre général *Mémoires et dossiers pour les libertés du personnel enseignant en France. Attentats dans l'Yonne* (CQ, II-15, III-1, III-5, III-7, 23 juillet 1901 à 16 janvier 1902).

Page 254.

1. *Obumbration*. Mot de l'ancienne langue dérivé de *obumbrer* : couvrir d'une ombre.

Page 256.

1. *De la situation faite à l'histoire dans la philosophie générale du monde moderne*. Cf. note plus haut.

Page 262.

1. Dans les premières pages de *Juifs* (CQ, III-5, 19 décembre 1901), Georges Delahache a évoqué les graves conséquences suscitées par l'affaire Dreyfus dans l'existence quotidienne des Juifs.

Page 270.

1. Bernard-Lazare écrivait déjà, en 1896, dans *Contre l'antisémitisme* (Stock) : « Écoutez-moi Drumont, vous ne connaissez pas les Juifs, ou du moins vous ne les connaissez pas tous » (p. 12). Et encore : « Si M. Drumont connaissait les questions dont il veut parler, il saurait que, s'il y a huit millions de Juifs dans le monde, les sept huitièmes sont des prolétaires ou des pauvres. »

Page 273.

1. Né en 1880, Pierre Duchesne-Fournet, ancien élève de l'École Normale Supérieure (1901), était directeur d'une usine de maté-

riaux de construction. En 1905, Péguy avait dû commencer à lui rembourser une somme de 15 000 francs-or.

2. Sans doute Georges Valois (1878-1945), militant d'*Action Française*, qui vient de consacrer à Péguy un long article dans le journal de Maurras : « Après une conversation avec M. Charles Péguy » (19 juin 1910, reproduit dans Éric Cahm, *Péguy et le nationalisme français*, Cahiers de l'Amitié Charles Péguy, 1972, p. 181-185). A la suite de *Notre jeunesse*, Georges Valois écrira à Péguy une lettre où il lui reproche son plaidoyer en faveur des Juifs : « Ils ne peuvent pas être Français, parce que, vous l'avez dit, partout, dans nos maisons de pierre, ils sont sous la tente ; ils sont en voyage. Voilà pourquoi nous sommes antisémites — lorsque les nomades tiennent l'État dans notre pays » (Éric Cahm, op. cit., p. 101).

Page 275.

1. Des traductions françaises de deux ouvrages du Danois Jörgen Peter Müller avaient paru en 1909 : *Mon système, quinze minutes de travail par jour pour la santé* (5ᵉ éd., la première datant de 1905) et *Le livre du plein air*.

2. Charles-Lucas de Peslöuan (1878-1952), polytechnicien, ami intime de Péguy qu'il connut au Collège Sainte-Barbe. Cf. *Correspondance Péguy-Peslöuan*, présentée et annotée par Françoise Gerbod (*Amitié Charles Péguy*, n° 45 et 46, janvier-mars et avril-juin 1989, et n° 49 et 50, janvier-mars et avril-juin 1990).

Page 276.

1. Sarah Bernhard s'était engagée à monter une adaptation du *Faust* de Goethe par Henry Bataille, mais ne l'avait finalement pas jouée. Le dramaturge la fit condamner à un dédit de 20 000 francs-or. Des saisies furent opérées en l'absence de la comédienne à son domicile et à son théâtre, les 31 mai, 1ᵉʳ et 2 juin 1910.

Page 277.

1. Joseph Reinach (1856-1921), avocat et homme politique français, soutint avec passion la cause de Dreyfus. En 1898, il dénonça dans *Le Siècle* le faux fabriqué par le colonel Henry, ce qui lui valut d'être rayé du cadre des officiers de réserve. Il écrivit une *Histoire de l'affaire Dreyfus* en sept volumes (1901-1911).

2. *La délation aux Droits de l'homme* est le titre d'un cahier publié par Péguy le 24 janvier 1905 (CQ, VI-9).

3. Sur Georges Sorel, cf. note plus haut.

Page 278.

1. Gabriel Monod (1844-1922), historien, spécialiste de Michelet, a été le professeur de Péguy à l'École Normale Supérieure.

Page 280.

1. Péguy eut en effet un petit différend avec Gabriel Monod, dont il avait publié sans autorisation une lettre à Célestin Bouglé sur la délation à la Ligue des Droits de l'homme (CQ, VI-10, 7 février 1905, et VII-10, 28 janvier 1906 ; OEPC, tome I, 1987, p. 1864, et tome II, 1988, p. 418-436).

Page 281.

1. *Antoinette* est le titre d'un épisode du roman-fleuve de Romain Rolland, *Jean-Christophe* (CQ, IX-15, 5 avril 1908).

Page 282.

1. *Invitus invitam adeptus gloriam :* « malgré lui et malgré elle il acquit la gloire ».

Page 285

1. *Notre maître Napoléon.* Autant qu'à Victor Hugo, clin d'œil à un collaborateur des *Cahiers,* André Suarès, qui devait y publier un essai, *De Napoléon* (CQ, XIV-1, 28 juillet 1912).

2. Alfred Dreyfus se désabonna aux *Cahiers* en octobre 1910, après la parution de *Notre jeunesse.*

3. Maurice Montégut (1855-1911), poète, auteur dramatique et romancier juif.

Page 287.

1. Mars 1871 marque le commencement de la Commune de Paris, qui refusait la capitulation devant l'Allemagne.

Page 288.

1. *A nos amis à nos abonnés* (CQ, X-13, 20 juin 1909).

Page 290.

1. « Il y a des ordres apparents qui recouvrent, qui sont les pires désordres ». Disciple de Péguy, Emmanuel Mounier reprendra cette idée, lorsqu'il fondera en 1932 la revue *Esprit* pour « rompre avec le désordre établi ».

2. Jules Méline (1838-1925), homme politique français, chef du gouvernement au temps de l'affaire Dreyfus. Hostile à la révision du procès, il se retira après les élections de 1898.

Page 293.

1. *Je rendrai mon sang pur comme je l'ai reçu.* Vers de Corneille dans *Le Cid,* acte I, sc. VI, v. 344.

Page 295.

1. Joinville, *Histoire de saint Louis,* édition Natalis de Wailly, Hachette, collection des « Classiques français », 1881, nombreuses réimpressions.

2. *Hastis musarz :* « hâtif étourdi ».

Page 296

1. Le prière d'insérer de l'édition Plon-et-Nourrit du *Mystère de la charité de Jeanne d'Arc.*

2. *Traducunt :* « ils font passer, ils traduisent ». *Tradunt :* « ils font passer, ils livrent ». Même idée dans la formule italienne *traduttore, traditore :* « traducteur, traître ».

Page 300.

1. C'est sans doute Georges Sorel qui est visé, lui qui accaparait la conversation chaque jeudi aux *Cahiers.*

Page 301.

1. Épisode de la guerre de 1870 : la fameuse charge des cuirassiers de Reichshoffen.

2. Jean Richepin (1849-1926) avait été élu à l'Académie Française le 5 mars 1908. François Coppée (1842-1908) était mort d'un cancer le 23 mai suivant.

Page 302.

1. Péguy enseignait le latin à son fils aîné Marcel et traduisait avec lui le *De viris illustribus urbis romae a Romulo ad Augustum* de l'abbé Lhomond.

Page 304.

1. Michel Arnauld, de son vrai nom Marcel Drouin (1871-1943), ancien normalien, professeur, beau-frère de Gide. Péguy l'a connu durant ses études, en 1892, et s'est retrouvé avec lui dans les rangs dreyfusistes. En novembre 1909, Michel Arnauld publia sur Péguy une étude importante dans la *Nouvelle revue française.* La même revue donna de lui, en septembre 1910, un compte rendu intéressant de *Notre jeunesse.*

*

L'établissement de ces notes a largement bénéficié du travail accompli par Robert Burac dans son édition de la Pléiade. Qu'il en soit remercié.

ŒUVRES DE CHARLES PÉGUY

Aux Éditions Gallimard

Essais

NOTRE PATRIE.

CLIO.

L'ARGENT *suivi de* L'ARGENT (SUITE).

NOTRE JEUNESSE (*Idées*, n° 176).

VICTOR-MARIE, COMTE HUGO.

NOTE CONJOINTE.

UN NOUVEAU THÉOLOGIEN. MONSIEUR LAUDET.

DE JEAN COSTE.

SITUATIONS.

LA RÉPUBLIQUE... NOTRE ROYAUME DE FRANCE.

PÉGUY ET LES *CAHIERS*.

PAR CE DEMI-CLAIR MATIN.

L'ESPRIT DE SYSTÈME.

UN POÈTE L'A DIT...

DEUXIÈME ÉLÉGIE XXX.

LA THÈSE.

VÉRONIQUE. *Dialogue de l'histoire et de l'âme charnelle.*

MARCEL. *Premier dialogue de la cité harmonieuse.*

PÉGUY TEL QU'ON L'IGNORE (*Idées*, n° 291).

Poésie

LE MYSTÈRE DE LA CHARITÉ DE JEANNE D'ARC.

MORCEAUX CHOISIS. *Poésie.*

LE MYSTÈRE DES SAINTS INNOCENTS.

LE PORCHE DU MYSTÈRE DE LA DEUXIÈME VERTU (*Poésie / Gallimard*).

ÈVE. *Les Tapisseries.*

LES TAPISSERIES *précédé de* SONNETS, *des* SEPT CONTRE THÈBES *et de* CHÂTEAUX DE LOIRE. Nouvelle édition revue et augmentée en 1962 *(Poésie / Gallimard)*.

CINQ PRIÈRES DANS LA CATHÉDRALE DE CHARTRES.

SAINTE GENEVIÈVE.

JEANNE D'ARC. *Cinq poèmes.*

ÈVE PREMIÈRE MORTELLE. *Stances.*

Théâtre

JEANNE D'ARC. *Drame en trois actes.*

Varia

LE CHOIX DE PÉGUY. *Œuvres choisies 1900-1910.*

Bibliothèque de la Pléiade

ŒUVRES POÉTIQUES COMPLÈTES.

ŒUVRES EN PROSE COMPLÈTES. *Nouvelle édition.*

    Tome I. Période antérieure aux *Cahiers* (1897-1899) — Période des six premières séries des *Cahiers* (Janvier 1900 – Mai 1905).

    Tome II. Période de la septième à la dixième série des *Cahiers* (Juin 1905 – Juin 1909).

    Tome III. Période de la onzième à la quinzième et dernière série des *Cahiers* (Octobre 1909 – Juillet 1914).

ŒUVRES POÉTIQUES ET DRAMATIQUES.

DANS LA COLLECTION FOLIO / ESSAIS

Composition CPI Bussière
Impression Novoprint
à Barcelone, le 15 mars 2020
Dépôt légal : mars 2020
1er dépôt légal dans la coleccion : septembre 1993

ISBN 978-2-07-032786-7./Imprimé en Espagne.

365473